Library of
Davidson College

Death and Property in Siena, 1205–1800

The Johns Hopkins University Studies in Historical
and Political Science
106th Series (1988)

1. *Pastoral Economics in the Kingdom of Naples*
   by John A. Marino

2. *Death and Property in Siena, 1205–1800: Strategies for the Afterlife*
   by Samuel K. Cohn, Jr.

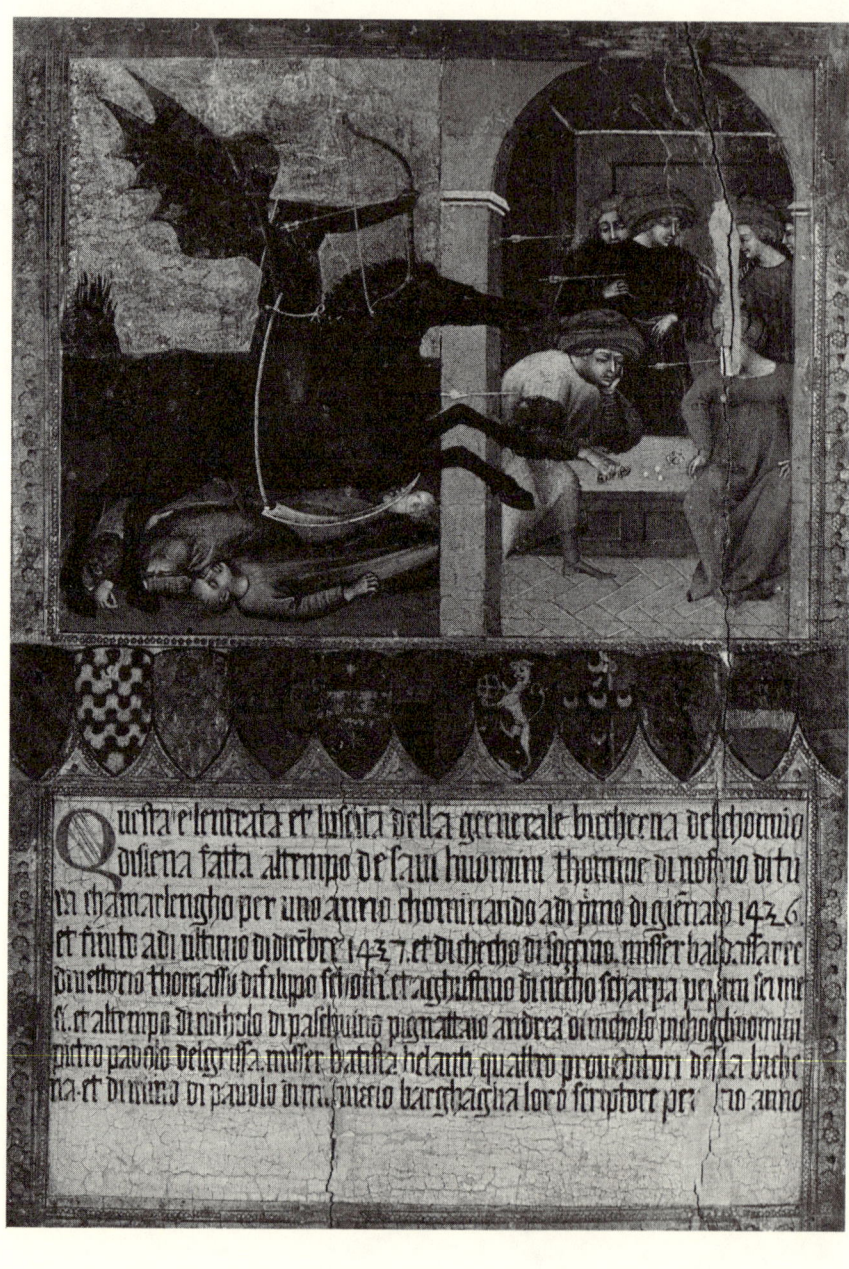

Questa e lentrata et luscita della generale biccherna delchomuno
disiena fatta altempo de savi huomini thomme di nostro dituu
ra chamarlengho per uno anno chomiuciando adi pmo di gienato 1436
et finito adi ultimo di dicebre 1437. et dicecho di sogno. misser baldassarre
di ettorio thomasso di filipo scholti. et aghustino di checho scharpa pe pmi sei me
si. et altempo di nicholo di paschuino pignattaio andrea di nicholo iuchoghuomini
pietro pavolo del grissa. misser batista belanti quattro provveditori della bicche
na. et di mino di pavolo iumuieio barchaglia loro scriptore pl. dto anno

Death and Property in Siena, 1205–1800
Strategies for the Afterlife

Samuel K. Cohn, Jr.

The Johns Hopkins University Press
Baltimore and London

This book has been brought to publication with the generous
assistance of the Andrew W. Mellon Foundation.

© 1988 The Johns Hopkins University Press
All rights reserved
Printed in the United States of America

The Johns Hopkins University Press
701 West 40th Street, Baltimore, Maryland 21211
The Johns Hopkins Press Ltd., London

The paper used in this publication meets the minimum
requirements of American National Standard for
Information Sciences—Permanence of Paper for Printed
Library Materials, ANSI Z39.48-1984.

Library of Congress Cataloging-in-Publication Data

Cohn, Samuel Kline.
  Death and property in Siena, 1205–1800 : strategies for
the Afterlife / Samuel K. Cohn, Jr.
     p.   cm. — (The Johns Hopkins University studies
in historical and political science ; 106th ser., 2)
  Bibliography: p.
  Includes index.
  ISBN 0-8018-3594-1 (alk. paper)
  1. Siena (Italy)—Religious life and customs. 2. Siena
(Italy)—Social life and customs. 3. Charitable bequests—
Italy—Siena. 4. Death—Religious aspects—Catholic
Church. 5. Catholic Church—Italy—Siena.   I.
Title.   II. Series.
BX1548.S5C64 1988
306'.32'094558—dc19   87-35249

Frontispiece: Tavoletta of Giovanni di Paolo.
Kunstgewerbemuseum, Staatliche Museen Preussischer
Kulturbesitz, West Berlin, inventory number K9224.

For Gruppo Sportivo Beccali

༄ Contents

List of Tables and Illustrations   xiii
Acknowledgments   xv
A Note to the Reader   xvii

1. Introduction   1
   A Note on the Historiography   2
   Siena: The Scene   5

PART I. FROM MENDICANCY TO HUMANISM

2. Pious Choices   15
   Hospitals   17
   Confraternities   24
   The Poor   25
   Dowry Funds   28
   Parishes and Monasteries   32

3. The Structure of Pious Giving   37
   The Values of Pious Gifts   45
   Styles in Pious Giving   50

4. Souls and Bodies: The Subsoil of Humanism   58
   Formulas   58
   Bodies   60
   Masses   62
   Time   65
   Property   68

5. High Culture   72
   Colombini and Catherine   72
   Flagellants and Beati   78
   Bernardino   83
   Enea Silvio Piccolomini   85
   Petrarch   87

PART II. THE HIGH RENAISSANCE

6. The Great Age of Selfishness 97
Calculations of Piety 98
Miscellaneous Gifts 100
Chapels 102
Burials 113
Pious Choices: The Bulk of Giving 115
The Arithmetic of Piety 119
The Economic Straits of Those Who Gave 121
Social Class 125
A Recalculation of Piety 127

7. Property 128
A Charity of Familiarity 129
Illegitimate Heirs 130
Adoption 132
Disinheritance 135
Conditional Gifts 139

8. Universal Heirs 146
Family and Lineage—the Male Line 151
Conclusion 155

PART III. COUNTER-REFORMATION PIETY AND THE STATE

9. The Counter-Reformation 161
The Pattern of Piety 162
The Grip of Purgatory 166
Mary 169
Time 171
The Cult of the Saints 171
Objects and Icons 175
Preambles 176
Funerals 179
Conclusion 183

10. The Differentiated Consequences of Trent 185
The Papal Visitations 186
The Nobility 188
Piety in the Countryside 194
The Urbanites: Artisans and Petty Merchants 196
Counter-Reformation Women 198

11. Late Counter-Reformation Piety 210
Pious Choices 211
Piety into Coin 219

The Bifurcation of Piety   222
Funerals   225

12. Enlightened Despotism   231
    Mortmain   233
    Fidecommission   243

13. Conclusion   247

    Appendix: Selecting the Samples, 1205–1800   251
    Comparison of the Two Archival Sources   252

    Notes   259
    Bibliography   313
    Index   327

Tables and Illustrations

TABLES

- 2.1. Pious Bequests and Masses, 1205–1500   18
- 2.2. Values of Gifts to Hospitals, 1205–1500   23
- 2.3. Monasteries, 1205–1500   34
- 3.1. Pious Bequests from the *Diplomatico*   41
- 3.2. Nonpious Bequests and the Ratios of Bequests, 1205–1500   43
- 3.3. Class and Geography, 1205–1500   44
- 3.4. Value of Pious Bequests, 1205–1500   47
- 4.1. Value of Masses, 1276–1500   62
- 6.1. Value of Pious Bequests, 1401–1800   98
- 6.2. Miscellaneous Pious Bequests, 1205–1800   101
- 6.3. Percentage of All Miscellaneous Pious Bequests, 1205–1800   104
- 6.4. Pious Choices, 1501–1800   116
- 6.5. Percentages of All Pious Choices, 1501–1800   117
- 6.6. Gifts to the Parish, 1451–1800   119
- 6.7. Gifts to Hospitals, 1401–1800   120
- 6.8. Gifts to the Poor, 1401–1800   120
- 6.9. Value of Nonpious Bequests, 1401–1800   121
- 6.10. Dowry Prices for Wives   126
- 7.1. The Frequency of the *Non-Petere* Clause   135
- 8.1. Contingent Heirs, 1205–1800   147
- 9.1. Masses, 1501–1800   167
- 10.1. Pious Bequests of the Nobility   189
- 10.2. Nonpious Bequests of the Nobility   190
- 10.3. Pious Bequests from the Country   194
- 10.4. Nonpious Bequests from the Country   195

10.5. Pious Bequests of Urbanites   197
10.6. Nonpious Bequests of Urbanites   198
10.7. Piety by Gender, 1451–1800   200
11.1. Gifts to Servants, 1401–1800   217
12.1. Pious Gifts by Decade, 1701–1770   233

FIGURES

1. Detail from Guido da Siena's Beatus Gallerani *Sfama i poveri* (Courtesy Photo Grassi)   26
2. Detail from Lorenzo Vecchietta's *Last Judgment—The Bad Death*, painted between 1444 and 1471 in the old sacristy, Santa Maria della Scala (Courtesy Photo Grassi)   52
3. Detail from Lorenzo Vecchietta's *Last Judgment—The Good Death*, painted between 1444 and 1471 in the old sacristy, Santa Maria della Scala (Courtesy Photo Grassi)   64
4. Sano di Pietro's *San Bernardino Preaching in the Piazza del Campo (Siena)*, circa 1444, in the cathedral of Siena, Sala del Capitolo (Courtesy Photo Grassi)   84
5. Pinturicchio, fresco of Alberto Arringhieri, in the Arringhieri chapel of San Giovanni, the cathedral of Siena, 1502 (Courtesy Photo Grassi)   156
6. Giuseppe Nicola Nasini, *Immaculate Conception*, in the sacristy of Sant'Andrea (Siena) circa 1730 (Courtesy of the Kunsthistorische Institut, Florence)   223
7. The 1205 testament of Arrichenus (Courtesy of the Archivio di Stato, Siena)   254

GRAPHS

2.1. Composition of Pious Bequests, 1205–1500   20
3.1. Value of Bequests, 1205–1500   42
6.1. Value of Bequests, 1501–1800   99
6.2. Composition of Pious Bequests, 1501–1800   118

MAP

1. Place Names of Testators from the Territory of Siena   6

Acknowledgments

This book began in a bar in San Domenico, outside of Florence, in October 1982. Anthony Pagden, then professor of History at the European University (Badia Fiesolana), after some arm-twisting, convinced me to drop momentarily my research on the land market in late medieval Siena to participate in a conference on comparative religious thought in the early modern period. Impressions garnered from a cursory glance through eighteenth-century testaments became the original kernel of the present book. The testaments told stories not only in aggregate statistical terms, as the land conveyances had promised, but also in and of themselves, which provided more solace in the day-to-day endeavors of archival reading than the madding marathon of amassing thousands of standardized land conveyances. After the conference, in part because of the audience's questions and apparent enthusiasm, I pushed aside the land market and read more testaments. Impressions from one period had to be judged in the context of previous periods. In Marc Bloch's felicitous phrase, I found myself unwittingly "turning the movie camera's film backwards"; the Enlightenment led to the Counter-Reformation to the Renaissance to the mendicant spirituality of the Trecento to the hazy and fragmented evidence of Siena's earliest testaments redacted at the outset of her halcyon days of commercial and political success.

All along, public lectures have spurred and guided work on this project—at the Michigan Villa, Florence (1983); the Facoltà di Lettere e Filosofia of the University of Siena (1983); Simon Shama's postdoctoral seminar, Harvard (1983); the New England Historical Association (1983); the Center for the Humanities, Wesleyan University (1984); Dante della Terza's postdoctoral seminar in Romance Languages, Harvard (1984); the New England Renaissance Conference, Wellesley, Massachusetts (1984); Niccolai Rubinstein's seminar at the Historical Institute, London (1984); Peter Burke's and Bob Scribner's seminar, Emmanuel College, Cambridge University (1985); the Academy for Arts and Sciences, Cambridge, Massachusetts (1985); the American Historical Convention (1985); the 350th anniversary of Harvard University (1986); the Center for European Studies, Harvard (1986); the Getty Center for the Humanities in Santa Monica (1987); and the New England Renaissance Conference, New London, Connecticut (1987). I wish to thank my hosts for these opportunities and the various audiences for their support and provocative questions.

This book would still be miles from completion without the programming and computer assistance offered by members of Brandeis University: Scott Magoon and Machiko Hollifield in Computer Sciences, and William Crown of the Heller School. In addition, Francis Short went beyond the call of duty and the meager sums of a work-study grant in entering into the computer the majority of records on which this study is based. And as always Ina Malaguti has offered indispensable assistance on this side of the Atlantic.

Financial assistance to pursue research in London and Siena came from a National Endowment for the Humanities Fellowship during the academic year 1982–83, and two Mazar Summer Fellowships in 1984 and 1986. I wish to thank Gregory Shesko of Brandeis University for additional funding and his general support of my work.

The manuscript benefited immensely from critical readings of earlier drafts by my colleagues, teachers, and friends: Eugene Black, Rudolph Binion, Alice Cooper, Oscar Di Simplicio, David Herlihy, Christine Heyrman, Alice Kelikian, Robert Proctor, Morton Keller, Donna Vinson, and Stephen White. As in the past, David Herlihy's sharp eye caught numerous and embarrassing errors. Alice Cooper kindly let me know when I was best off consigning sections to the waste basket. Rudolph Binion's reading went far beyond any conceivable duty of academic collegiality. Although I cursed him, his red ink forced me to rethink or reargue major portions of this book. He will no doubt still remain dissatisfied with my solutions, but I hope we will continue to argue. The same should be said for my anonymous reader at the Johns Hopkins University Press. His sensitive and prodigiously informed critique helped me to produce a more sophisticated book in terms of my statistics and my attention to debates current in the historiography.

In the course of research, I received hospitality and assistance from numerous sources. Gino Corti was always willing to interrupt his work in the Sienese archives to decipher a paleographical problem. The staffs at the Warburg Library, the Historical Institute of the University of London and, most especially, the archivists at the Archivio di Stato in Siena—Nello Barbieri, Carla Zirilli, Maria Assunta Ceppari, and Sonia Fineschi—provided ideal working conditions and informed assistance. Even more than a model for efficiency and documentary expertise, the Archivio di Stato in Siena under direttrice Fineschi's guidance is becoming a research institute. I leave work in Siena with profound regrets.

Perseverance particularly through the damp winter months (infamous among those foreign *studiosi* who have chosen to remain in Siena) would have been impossible without the friendship and support of Giorgio Giorgi, Sandro Berini, Carlo Liberati, Luca Liserani, Sarah Ingle, Oscar Di Simplicio, Mario Ascheri, Nicholas Adams, Simon Pepper, Pietro Barraqueddu, Lorenzo Epstein, and my running team, Gruppo Sportivo Beccali, to whom this book is dedicated.

A Note to the Reader

NAMES

In this text, names and citations for archival sources have been rendered according to the orthography found in the original, including the use of accents.

DATES

Before 1750 the Sienese calendar began each year on 25 March. In the text dates have been rendered according to the Gregorian calendar. In the notes to the text, dates appear as given in the documents.

Death and Property in Siena, 1205–1800

1 Introduction

> *Thanks to Vovelle, religious sociology—the sociology of death and of earthly existence—has, in the history of the ancien régime, gone beyond the stage of counting heads—whether of those who take the sacraments or of those who attend mass. It is leading to a truly serial, mass-scale history of religious attitudes.*
> —Emmanuel Le Roy Ladurie

This book sets forth an intellectual history of local notables, merchants, shopkeepers, artisans, and peasants, a population that runs the gamut of social classes but lies beneath the horizons of those groups normally figured in the history of ideas—saints, humanists, and *philosophes*. It does not provide the usual or expected history of ideas based on the explication and exegesis of literary or philosophical texts. Rather, the ideological trends and transformations take the form of a statistical essay. The persons soon to introduce the story appear for us through their last wills and testaments redacted in 90 percent of the cases not by themselves alone but with the assistance of outsiders, usually the notary and sometimes the local cleric.[1]

These choices both individual and collective are not to be taken lightly. They involved far more than the casual response given to the interpreter for an anthropological study or the filled-in blank on the sociologist's questionnaire. Rather, they embraced lifelong, often multigenerational, accumulations and attachments to property and revealed commitments to friends and family. They touched concerns no less important than the uncertainties of eternity. Beyond the bare bones of statistical aggregations, the testaments afford glimpses of family life, of individual beliefs and actions about property and about the soul. Each chapter will mesh two pictures of human reality, one taken from the collective patterns reflected by statistical series, the other from individual experiences narrated through particular testaments.

The testators in our samples are extraordinarily diverse. They span most of the spectrums that historians and social scientists usually devise for the study of societies: men/women, city/rural, lower/middle/upper socioeconomic strata (nobles, merchants, shopkeepers, artisans), and clerics/laity.[2] But they tend to be alike in that few left any scraps of literary evidence behind other than their wills. To my knowledge only one individual, whose bequests figure in our tables, was so important as to have been immortalized in a dictionary of illustrious men.[3]

With the notary and on occasion the local cleric at their side, the testators worked out their fears and hopes for the "other side of death" largely but not entirely within the formulaic patterns set by the will. For the most part their responses need to be read collectively using sampling techniques and inferential statistics. But wills, unlike most other contracts found in the notaries' protocols, permit a reading beyond aggregations of data in tabular form. By the Quattrocento, numerous documents broke from the standardized notaries' forms and can be read individually. On occasion, the testators were explicit. They ordered their posterity to preserve their testaments, demanding yearly recitations to assembled kin of the dead man's commands and admonitions.[4] Even peasants used the will as a final conduit for expressing gratitude to spouses and advice to children. The testament thus offers the historian a rare moment, if only with short phrases, for listening to those who have had no intellectual history by the traditional standards.

A Note on the Historiography

Methodologically, the historian of testaments must begin by paying homage to the now classical work of Michel Vovelle, *Piété baroque et déchristianisation en Provence au XVIIIe siècle*. Through the quantitative evaluation of testaments, Vovelle directed the historian's scrutiny into altogether new territories of thought and action, heretofore surveyed almost exclusively through the filter of printed narrative. Instead of speculating from the high ground of literary criticism and reading the cultural "underworld" out of the texts of literati, Vovelle created new subcultural "texts" from the analysis of thousands of last wills and testaments. The "texts" took the form of tables and graphs—the aggregations of thousands of individual decisions. They penetrated the households of notables, merchants, artisans, and peasants in seventeenth- and eighteenth-century Provence, detecting trends that lay beneath the printed Baroque, Jansenist, and Enlightenment cultures.

Vovelle's innovative study of mentality sets out clearly the theme central to the historiography of the French school formed around the journal *Les Annales*: the dominance of glacially slow movements in history over surface events (*"histoire événementielle"*) such as laws or political decisions.[5] Vovelle's originality rests on his transport of the principles and techniques developed by structural studies of the regional history to the realm of thought and culture. Through aggregating large numbers of testaments from the region of Provence he mapped the slow-moving, glacial flow of changes in custom and piety imperceptible to contemporaries.[6]

To recapitulate with broad strokes, Vovelle's story unfolds as follows. The "de-Christianization" policy initiated by Robespierre in the year II of the

French Revolution did not strike the population of Provence abruptly or blindly as political and cultural historians had once assumed. Instead, the decline of Counter-Reform piety and secularization of large geographical areas and across various social classes began fully forty to fifty years before the French Revolution. Vovelle detects these transformations in religious sentiment by graphing changes in the patterns of charity, burial customs, the role of religious confraternities, and notarial formulas beseeching spiritual intercession. But his key statistic regards the percentage of those requesting masses for the health of their souls. By 1750 large sections of the population of Provence were drifting away from the old "baroque" forms of piety—ornate burials and funeral processions with numerous mourners, reliance on lay confraternities, and bequests for thousands of masses and offices for the dead. To explain this structural transformation in mentality which swept Provence before the direct and visible intervention of legislation and force in the year II, Vovelle invokes the Enlightenment: its ideas caused the mid-century transformations in belief and piety.

The exhaustive investigation of 8,244 notarial testaments by Pierre Chaunu and his *équipe* of more than fifty students hammered out for Paris the same broad interpretive framework in religious piety and consciousness.[7] For the capital, these structural changes occurred forty to fifty years earlier than in Provence. Again, the explanation proffered is the Enlightenment. Despite the discrepancies in chronology, Chaunu's findings corroborate Vovelle's earlier conclusions. One would expect the change to occur first in the capital of the Enlightenment before penetrating the provinces.

More recently, Jacques Chiffoleau has employed the methods of Vovelle and Chaunu to investigate changes in mentality for Avignon during the late Middle Ages.[8] Like Vovelle and Chaunu, Chiffoleau sees the dominance of slow-moving structural change over the event. Vovelle and Chaunu had traced the "de-Christianization" of Paris and Provence during the Enlightenment; Chiffoleau considers the opposite process—the Christianization of the late Middle Ages. Curiously, behind these two contrary developments each of the authors charts a similar line of progress, toward modernization and individualism. Chiffoleau, however, explains these broad transformations in religious sensibility, not with ideas (as Vovelle did), but rather by concomitant shifts in social structure. To recapitulate briefly: the changes in religiosity of the late fourteenth and fifteenth centuries did not spring from the psychological trauma provoked by that catastrophic event, the Black Death of 1348, or by subsequent waves of plague. Rather, the plagues only intensified developments already on the social horizons. The rise of commerce and urbanization during the twelfth and thirteenth centuries stimulated social and geographical mobility, which undermined the old forms of village sociability, solidarity, and family lineage, "coupant les citadins de leurs racines."[9] In these conditions, citizens of Avignon, well before the onslaught of the Black Death, faced death far away from kin, their birth places, and family burial grounds. These changes, Chiffoleau argues, induced new forms of expenditure and ritual at death: "the flamboyant funeral," "the outburst of devotion" (from masses for the soul to charitable bequests to the poor), inaugurating what Philippe Ariès has called "death as one's own death."[10]

In the absence of kin, urban testators of Avignon could not assume that relatives would bear the responsibilities of their last rites. These testators thus had to look to others for support and comfort in their transition to the other world. Through pious gifts, their testaments recruited large numbers from the poor and the clergy along with members of their new surrogate families—the religious confraternities—to fill the ranks of new grandiose funeral processions. Testators further relied on increasing numbers of masses for the health of their souls. Thus the loss of kin and of ties of lineage, the dissolution of the feudal links with the old Benedictine monasteries, and the abandonment of ancestral burial grounds gave rise to new forms of piety and religious devotion, which were themselves new forms of self-expression illustrative of a progressive liberation of the individual during the late Middle Ages and the Renaissance.

It would be incorrect to claim that Michel Vovelle along with other French historians—Lebrun, Ariès, Chaunu, Lorcin, Chiffoleau, Croix—discovered the testament as a source for social history.[11] This document has long undergone the scrutiny of juridical historians, and social and economic historians have used testaments to map out inheritance systems and property relations over vast expanses of Western Europe.[12] While Vovelle and others were quantifying masses and religious formulas, other new social historians, principally in England, were deciphering changes in "the bundle of rights" during the early modern period—the transfer of land from one generation to the next. Armed with theories and methods drawn from anthropology, they have plotted the strategies of succession responsible for the nobility's social and economic resilience through the modern period and have uncovered the "logic" for the demise of the English yeomanry.[13]

Thus within the ambit of social history for late medieval and early modern Europe, the systematic use of testaments now forms two separate and, at present, unrelated literatures. One (which we will label the French school) concentrates on broad transformations in mentality and religious sensibility and says almost nothing about property and inheritance.[14] The other (deriving largely from English historians) traces inheritance patterns while almost completely ignoring the religious character of the will or its value as a source for the intellectual history of those beneath the levels of "official" culture.[15] As I read them, a dual quality and purpose pervades nearly all the testaments from the early thirteenth century through the Enlightenment. Both individually and collectively, they bear witness at once to belief and to property relations. This dual perspective underlies a theme running through this book. Two strategies for the afterlife competed over the long duration: one placed faith in property and family name; the other looked to matters of the soul. Testators from the earliest days of mendicant piety through the Enlightenment had to juggle these competing claims: family versus the church. The two literatures—one on mentalities, the other on inheritance—have, in contrast, each seen only one-half of the will, either its pious bequests or its dispersions to kin and the bloodlines of succession.

Siena: The Scene

Before the arrival of the Black Death, Siena had been one of the largest cities in Europe; larger than Paris and London, its urban population numbered 52,000 and commanded territorially a vast city-state—295 communities (circa 1346) extending from the hills of the Chianti, at times as far to the northeast as Monte San Savino, south through the mountains of Amiata and west to the seaports south of Grosseto.[16] (See map.) Siena's political development in the early communal stage resembled other northern city-states. From the constitutional incorporation of the *popolani* (the non-noble merchant elites) in 1147 to the coming to power of the merchant government of the Nine in 1287, the struggles between merchants and the old aristocratic families yielded to the blending of these classes with the gradual dominance of the latter.[17] Many historians have seen this period of social amalgamation with the government of Twenty-Four as the halycon years of Sienese history, a pinnacle crowned by Siena's victory over the Florentines at Montaperti in 1260. With the changing fortunes of the international party of the Ghibellines (those originally allied to the Holy Roman Emperor), Siena's crushing defeat at the hands of the Guelfs (those allied originally to the pope) at Colle (1269), and the fall of the government of Twenty-Four, Siena embarked on what many historians have chronicled as its long and progressive decadence, morally, politically, and economically.[18] Others have extended Siena's prominence through the period of peace and stability inaugurated by the "merchant" government of the Nine (1287–1355),[19] "which experienced a longevity surpassed among the Italian Republics only by the Venetian oligarchy."[20] The fall of the Nine then opened a new and longer period of factionalism. Governments fell in short succession, creating the rule of new amalgams of social and political forces: factions called the Twelve, the Riformatori, and the Popolo Minuto.[21] In 1368 no less than four governments rose and fell from power. These political factions, called *monti*, together with the old patrician elites, the *monte* of the *gentilhuomini*, who were allowed formally to share power through the prompting of Pope Pius II (Enea Silvio Piccolomini) in 1459, determined membership in the ruling council, the Concistoro, and became the criterion for noble status by the early Cinquecento.[22] Only "the tyranny" of Siena's Machiavellian Pandolfo Petrucci (1487–1512) punctuated the internecine struggles with some semblance of stability.[23] As a result, the post–Black Death history of Siena differed from the northern Italian model, in which power inexorably gravitated toward the rule of the prince, whether as despotic *signoria* or as Medici under republican forms. Siena, by contrast, continued in the more medieval and more democratic tradition of the broadly based oligarchy until her loss of independence in 1555 and subsequent incorporation

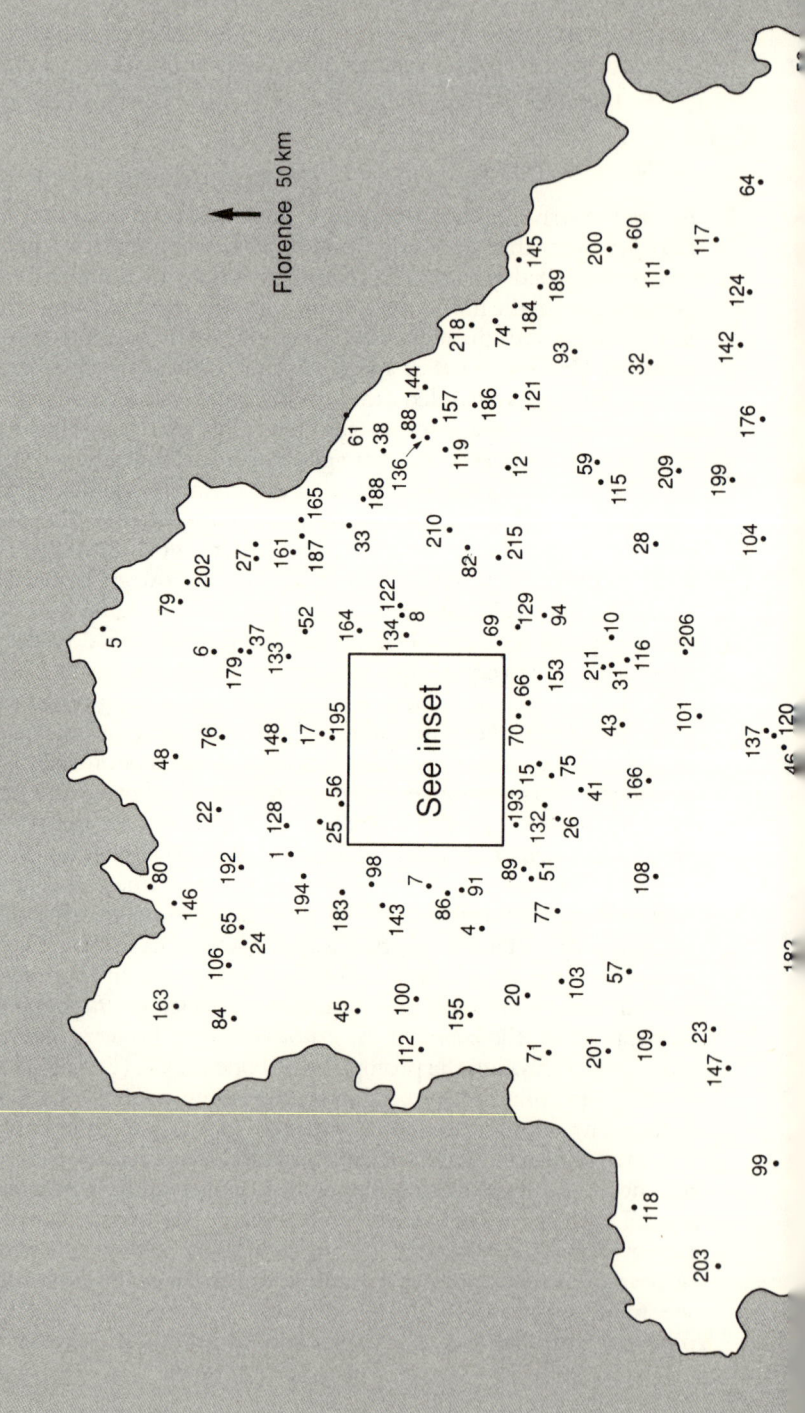

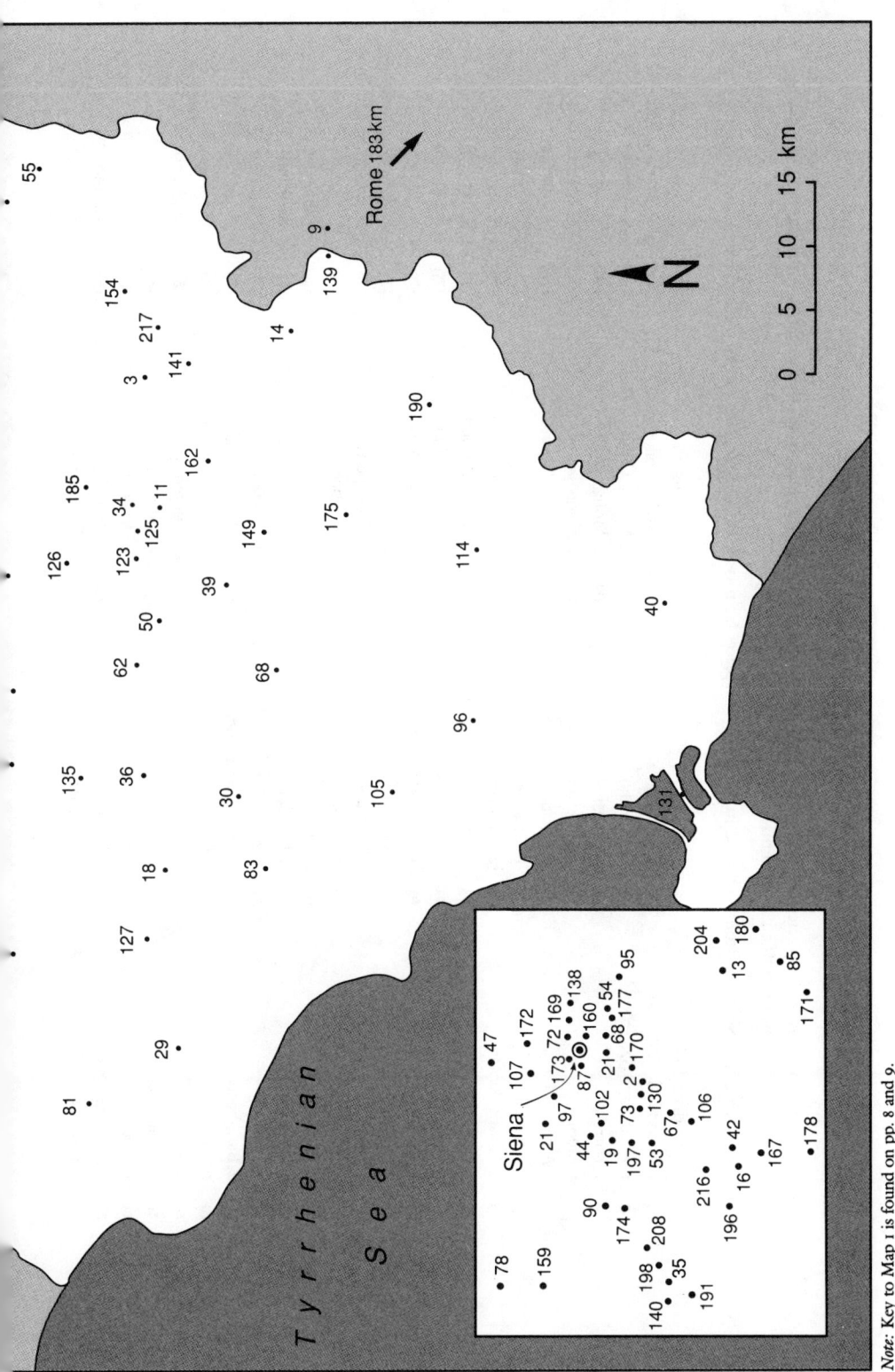

Note: Key to Map 1 is found on pp. 8 and 9.

Place Names of Testators

KEY: The first number is the map reference; the second, the number of appearances of a place name whether a testator at the time of redaction resided in that place or was identified as from that place.

Beyond the territory of Siena, testators originated from 121 different places from as far as Seville to places in the Chianti mountains bordering the territory of Siena.

1 3 Abbadia a Isola	55 2 Cetona	110 1 Montantico	166 2 S. Lorenzo a Merse
2 1 Abbadia S. Abundio	56 2 Chiocciola	111 5 Monte Follonico	167 4 S. Maria a Pilli
3 1 Abbadia S. Salvatore	57 1 Chiusdino	112 2 Monte Guido	168 1 S. Maffei
4 1 Torre	58 5 Chiusi	113 2 Montemassi	169 3 S. Mamiliano
5 1 Albola	59 4 Chiusure	114 1 Montemerano	170 1 S. Margherita
6 1 Ama	60 1 Ciliano	115 1 Monte Oliveto	171 1 S. Martino
7 5 Ancaiano	61 1 Ciggiano	116 1 Monteorgiali	172 1 S. Miniato
8 2 Ansano Dofano	62 2 Cinigiano	117 3 Montepulciano	173 3 S. Petronilla
9 2 Aquapendente	63 1 Civitella Marittima	118 5 Monte Rotondo	174 1 S. Pio
10 1 Arbia	64 2 Chianciano	119 1 Monte S. Maria	175 1 Samprugnano
11 2 Arcidosso	65 3 Colle Val d'Elsa	120 2 Monte Acuto	176 6 S. Quirico
12 36 Asciano	66 1 Corsano	121 1 Montalceto	177 3 S. Regina (Reina)
13 1 Borgo Vecchio	67 3 Costalpino	122 2 Montaperti	178 3 S. Salvatore a Pilli
14 1 Bafalaie	68 3 Cotone	123 1 Monticello	179 1 S. Sano
15 2 Bagnaia	69 5 Cuna	124 8 Monticchiello	180 1 Salteano
16 3 Barontoli	70 1 Le stine	125 1 Montelatrone	181 5 Sarteano
17 2 Basciano	71 7 Elci	126 2 Montenero	182 1 Sassoforte
18 2 Batignano	72 8 extra porta (Siena)	127 1 Montepescali	183 2 Scorgiano
19 1 Belcaro	73 1 Costalfabri	128 1 Monteriggioni	184 1 Scrofiano
20 3 Beforte	74 1 Farnetella	129 1 Monterone	185 5 Seggiano
21 1 Belriguardo	75 1 Filetta	130 8 Munistero	186 5 Serre
22 1 Bibbiano	76 1 Fonterutoli	131 1 Orbetello	187 2 Sesta
23 1 Boccheggiano	77 1 Frosini	132 1 Orgia	188 1 Sestano
24 1 Boscona	78 1 Fungaria	133 2 Pieveasciata	189 2 Sinalonga

8

25	1 Bracciano	79	1 Gaiole	134	3 Presciano	190	1 Sovana
26	2 Brenna	80	1 Gavignano	135	2 Paganico	191	2 Sovicille
27	1 Brolio	81	1 Gavorrano	136	1 Palazetta	192	1 Staggia
28	1 Buonconvento	82	1 Grania	137	1 Pari	193	3 Stigliano
29	1 Buriano	83	12 Grosseto	138	1 Pecorile	194	2 Strove
30	1 Ischia (Istia)	84	1 Guincaia	139	1 Proceno	195	1 Tabiano
31	1 Murlo	85	3 Isola Cuna	140	1 Petriccio	196	1 Tegoia
32	3 Castel Muzio	86	1 Molli	141	4 Piancastagna	197	2 Terrensano
33	8 Castelnuovo Berardenga	87	1 Laterina	142	9 Pienza (Corsignano)	198	2 Toiano
		88	1 Laticastello	143	1 Pietralata	199	1 Torrenieri
34	4 Castel del Piano	89	1 le Palaze	144	2 Poggio S. Cecilia	200	5 Torrita
35	1 Castro Pieve	90	2 Leccceto	145	1 Poggiolo	201	1 Travale
36	4 Campagnatico	91	1 Linari	146	3 Poggibonsi	202	1 Trebbio
37	1 Campi	92	1 Litiano	147	2 Prata	203	1 Tricasi
38	1 Campilia	93	1 Lorocciano	148	1 Quercegrossa	204	1 Usinina
39	1 Cana	94	2 Lucignano	149	1 Roccalbegna	205	1 Villa Monte Giuchi
40	1 Capalbio	95	6 Maggiano	150	1 Roccastrada	206	1 Pompane
41	2 Capraia	96	1 Magliano	151	3 Roccatederighi	207	2 Vagliagli
42	2 Carpineto (Villa)	97	2 Marciano	152	3 Roca Tintintani	208	2 Valli
43	3 Casciano	98	4 Marmoraia	153	1 Radi	209	1 Vergelle
44	1 Casciano (Masse)	99	5 Massa Marittima	154	1 Radicofani	210	1 Vescona
45	7 Casole	100	1 Mensano	155	12 Radicondoli	211	8 Vescovado
46	1 Casale Pari	101	2 Montepescini	157	4 Rapolano	213	2 Vico d'Arbia
47	1 Castagna	102	1 Montalbuccio	158	3 S. Angelo in Colle	214	5 Vignano
48	2 Castellina	103	1 Montalcinello	159	4 S. Columba	215	1 Villa Nuova
49	2 Castiglion D'Orcia	104	10 Montalcino	160	5 S. Eugenio	216	5 Viteccio
50	1 Castiglioncello Bandini	105	2 Montiano	161	3 S. Felice	217	1 Voltolina
51	2 Causa	106	1 Montecchio	162	2 S. Fiora	218	2 Rigomagno
52	3 Cerreto	107	2 Monte Celso	163	7 S. Gimignano		
53	1 Certano	108	4 Monticiano	164	1 S. Giovanni a Vena		
54	1 Certosa	109	1 Montieri	165	2 S. Gusmé		

into the Medicean Grand Duchy of Tuscany.[24] For most historians since Malavolti, Siena's history then ended.[25]

Unfortunately, the economic history of Siena has not yet received the attention that her artistic and political past has.[26] According to Chiaudano, the Sienese were "the pioneers" of European expansion. They were the first bankers of the papacy, having won from Clement IV the right to collect tithes from the Holy Land.[27] For the periods beyond these auspicious beginnings, the researcher must depend on Mengozzi's multivolume history (*Il monte dei Paschi*). With few exceptions, the late-nineteenth-century liberal saw the economy of Siena in step with her "moral" and political "decadence," losing economic hegemony to the Florentines before the fall of the Nine and then declining unremittingly until Grand Duke Pietro Leopoldo's implementation of laissez-faire grain policies in 1767 (which the Sienese physiocrat Sallustio Bandini had formulated in the 1730s).[28] Recently, historians have seen more dynamism to her Renaissance economy.[29] In addition, the demographic trends and price-series analyses do not map out such a simple sketch for the early modern period.[30] Although Siena did not regain her preplague population until the twentieth century, demographic and price fluctuations show an economy that followed closely the societal trends of large swaths of Western Europe: a "phase A" of an expanding economy from the late Quattrocento to the 1590s followed by "phase B" of demographic, agricultural, and industrial crisis, which did not begin to lift until the second half of the eighteenth century.[31] Even the devastating struggle to retain her independence (1552–55), when the allied forces from Spain, Germany, and Florence ravaged the countryside and sent population levels beneath the lowest depths incurred through the Black Death, did not fundamentally alter these long economic cycles.[32]

Finally, the history of religion and art has dominated the picture of Siena's cultural past. The romanticization of Siena's mystics (principally, Colombini, Catherine, and Bernardino)[33] and the veneration of Siena's artistic masters, Duccio and Simone Martini, have argued for a distinctive Sienese civilization—one which, in contrast to Florence, was more lyrical and spiritual, which after the Black Death refused to enter the Renaissance but instead retreated to its late medieval sensibilities. Just how distinctive was this civilization? Although a forceful answer to this question must await comparative studies of other city-states (and not only of Florence), our sense from the outset is akin to our view of her economy: we are here examining forces that were not wholly peculiar to Siena and her territory.[34] Regardless of the final answer to this question, the testaments of ordinary citizens and villagers make it possible to examine the questions of Sienese culture over a grander canvas socially, temporally, and geographically than heretofore has been the case from the conventional studies of the great mystics and masters.

Though this intellectual history of peasants, artisans, and notables and its methods may not be traditional, my theme is as old as Thucydides. It is chronology. I am interested in finding the cleavages, the times when one stamp of piety or of property transaction broke down and another took its place. This analysis of 600 years will not propose a general theory of piety nor will it chant hackneyed themes such as "ideas emanated from the city to the countryside," or "from the masses to the elites," or vice versa. Instances of each of these directions in the flow of ideas can be isolated at different historical junctures over the course of this examination. No single line of argument, no simplistic correspondence between abstract actors such as substructure and superstructure, will explain significantly or consistently the changes over the long duration of Siena's history. Instead, the historical episodes themselves established their own peculiar constraints and rules for interaction.

To avoid a toothless, relativistic approach, let us, however, hazard one proposition at the outset. The strategies for the afterlife for late medieval and early modern Siena cut against the grain of the lessons taught by *Les Annales*. Instead of the predominance of long-term, slow-moving social change—where the term "crisis" has been "fast disappearing" and has been found "unsuitable"—the four central transformations revealed by the patterns of piety took form rapidly.[35] Moreover, at least three of them turned on events, which can be dated with "specificity": the summer plague of 1363; the diffusion of the Canons and Decrees of the Council of Trent through the papal visitations of 1575–76; and the laws of the enlightened Lorrainian Grand Duke of Tuscany, Francesco Stefano, first promulgated in 1747 and 1751.[36] These "crisis" points then gave rise to "structural transformations," prefixing long periods of apparent stasis in the patterns of piety. Yet they did not evolve along constant, steady lines with imperceptible momentum, like the silting-up of the Arno. We refute Philippe Ariès's contention that before the twentieth century "these periods of immobility span several generations and thus exceed the capacity of the collective memory."[37] The cleavages found for Siena over 600 years may have been few, but when they occurred their effects were rapid and decisive. Contrary to the drift of French historiography, studies of ideas and mentalities need to reaffirm the terms "revolution" and "crisis."

I

From Mendicancy to Humanism

❧ 2   Pious Choices

Do you know what the moth of the spirit is? It is avarice. All day you shake and hang up your clothes, while that beggar is shivering with cold. Could you but hear, you would hear his shivering cry, "Vengeance, vengeance!" . . . And you see the beggar dying of cold and care not! You do not hear his cries! Do you know why? Because you are not cold, because your stomach is filled with good food and good wine, because you have enough clothes and often a fire. . . . And how many shifts have you sent to those poor prisoners? . . . I hear that you have two vests, two pairs of drawers and a pair of broken shoes. I think that at the last you will die in all your fine things, and the Devil will bear you away.
—San Bernardino, *Le prediche volgari*

Le Roy Ladurie compared Vovelle's analysis of testaments for religious change in *ancien régime* Provence to contemporary opinion polls.[1] Certainly, the testament was not the only time when the devout gave to pious causes. They gave as members of their parishes, guilds, and confraternities and as citizens.[2] Moreover, the testaments themselves do not represent a single moment—that is, when the pious lay on the deathbed. As we march through time, greater proportions of the Sienese drew up their testaments when in good health, from 20 percent before the Black Death to 33 percent in 1349–1500 to 44 percent after 1500. We even know of minors making wills, young boys about to join monastic orders or preparing to fight the Turks, and girls as young as twelve. It is curious that before 1500 those in good health gave more to pious causes than those lying on their deathbeds, even after the financial well-being of the testator has been factored out. But for the next three centuries, piety changed; those facing imminent death gave to the church more generously.[3] I cannot explain the change.

Nor was the testament the only contractual gift of the pious. On occasion, the notaries recorded *donationes inter vivos*. As with wills, the *gabelle* offices regularly taxed these contracts and entered them into their ledgers now extant in the state archives, but their presence was extraordinarily rare.[4] Along with Kathryn Norberg, we can conclude that although "wills may not be the 'whole story' [of charity] . . . they are certainly a very important part of it."[5] Richard Trexler has argued with greater precision: "But the church lived not by *decime* or by offerings at Easter, certainly not by everyday alms; the church lived first of all off its landed investment, and it ever reinvigorated this investment through testamentary charity."[6]

Yet our study will not probe changes in charity so much as changes in the ideas and attitudes of individual peasants, shopkeepers, and notables. And in this respect the researcher of the testamentary "opinion polls" can go beyond Vovelle's or Chaunu's quantification of masses and changes in notarial formulas. These scholars counted only a small part of the variable information. In addition to ignoring completely the lists of nonpious legacies, they gave only scant notice to those pious bequests without requests for masses as well as to the choices of beneficiaries—hospitals, lay confraternities, parish churches, chapels, monasteries, and nunneries.

On the other hand, historians of the late Middle Ages and the early Renaissance in Tuscany *have* considered changes in the dominance of different religious institutions, such as the decline of the old Benedictine orders in Pistoia and the rise in the wealth of new hospitals. These historians, however, have argued from a different documentary base. Their point of departure has not been the individual or his or her itemized pious choices but rather the pious institution—shifts in devotion interpreted through tax records or illustrations gleaned from the contributions by prominent and wealthy donors.[7] The changes observed through these sources reveal shifts in the dominance of certain religious institutions over time. Yet such shifts at the institutional level might not signal changes in collective attitudes, especially if the collective group happened to be ordinary shopkeepers, artisans, and villagers. A single decision by a Medici or a Piccolomini might dwarf into insignificance thousands of individual pious decisions by hundreds of artisans and peasants. A change of mind or heart for Francesco Datini (the fabulously wealthy merchant of Prato) may or may not have resonated through the neighborhoods and villages of Tuscany. Through the "public opinion polls" recreated in the statistical analysis of testaments, the historian can penetrate below the grandiose donations of a few pious magnates and merchants or changes seen from the institutional perspective. With finer tuning, these documents allow the historian to hear the voices of hundreds of ordinary villagers and shopkeepers graced only by patronymics and unknown to the city chronicles.

Historians of Florence and Pistoia have seen a fundamental shift in piety occurring around the beginning of the fifteenth century.[8] Renaissance piety fanned out in two directions: toward social responsibility and public charity aimed at alleviating pain and suffering of the poor and sick; and toward a taste for "ceremonial magnificence" expressed in lavish ecclesiastical building programs.[9] Both directions diverged from the earlier inward spirituality of penance and asceticism. Hospitals, lay confraternities, and the *operai* (building organizations) of churches and cathedrals benefited from the new moral tone of this

"Civic Christianity"; the parishes and the old Benedictine orders were the losers.

By quantifying testamentary bequests from Siena and its territory, these conclusions can be tested for the southern half of Tuscany. At the same time, our documentary base extends the social area of analysis, for testaments redacted by humble artisans or by peasants or rural residents who owned only a few strips of arable land were not uncommon from the last decades of the thirteenth century on. If any group other than the *miserabili* is underrepresented in these records, it is, oddly enough, the patrician merchant class—that group whose piety thus far has been the focus of Renaissance histories to the near exclusion of other groups.

Hospitals

The evidence amassed from numerous pious bequests in southern Tuscany from 1205 to 1500 (see Table 2.1, Graph 2.1) does not clearly corroborate the trends concluded for the north. First, the proportion of contributions that went to hospitals remained relatively constant from the earliest documents through the period of the Black Death, fluctuating from 13 percent in the first period of analysis (1205–50) to 16 percent to 12 percent to 14 percent during the next seventy-five years. Then, in the year of the Black Death (for which the testaments provide 366 pious bequests for the horrific summer months alone) the proportion of contributions to hospitals dipped in the opposite direction from what the Florentinists have argued. It declined from 15 percent of all pious bequests in 1326–47 to 9 percent in 1348.[10] Nor was 1348 an aberration. In the years immediately following the plague until its recurrence in 1363, the rate slid to less than 9 percent.

Only when the plague returned in 1363 did these statistics register a significant jolt forward, nearly doubling to 17 percent—its highest point through the long duration of this study.[11] This spurt in enthusiasm for the hospital was, however, short-lived. For the next eleven years, the proportion of gifts to hospitals declined, and, for the whole of the fifteenth century, its high point never returned to the levels approximating those during the outbreak of plague in 1363 but instead fluctuated between 7 and 12 percent. At the end of the century of humanism, the proportion of gifts flowing to these institutions of social charity was less than that found in the earliest documents, before the epoch of the new Christian social consciousness. Thus the actual choices of the integral population with a minimum of disposable property fail to corroborate the picture of religious change for the north seen from the foundations of new hospitals and the significant donations of merchant princes.

The property values of a single hospital or even the general share of property going to hospitals possibly might have increased from the Black Death to the end of the fifteenth century. Stephan Epstein has carefully traced the economic fortunes of the principal hospital of Siena, Santa Maria della Scala.[12] From a

Table 2.1. Pious Bequests and Masses, 1205–1500

Period	Testators	Frequency	Parish	Monastery	Hospital	Confrater.	Poor	Dowries	Servants	Misc.
1205–1250 % total	12	71 5.92	17 23.94%	22 30.99%	9 12.68%	0 0.00%	9 12.68%	0 0.00%	0 0.00%	14 19.72%
1251–75	23	199 8.65	45 22.61%	68 34.17%	32 16.08%	0 0.00%	16 8.04%	0 0.00%	3 1.51%	35 17.59%
1276–1300	44	398 9.05	58 14.57%	161 40.45%	47 11.81%	2 0.50%	50 12.56%	0 0.00%	3 0.75%	77 19.35%
1301–25	50	614 12.28	92 14.98%	270 43.97%	85 13.84%	13 2.12%	67 10.91%	1 0.16%	5 0.81%	81 13.19%
1326–47	67	628 9.37	91 14.49%	275 43.79%	95 15.13%	20 3.18%	55 8.76%	1 0.16%	9 1.43%	82 13.06%
1348	55	366 6.65	105 28.69%	121 33.06%	34 9.29%	12 3.28%	49 13.39%	2 0.55%	5 1.37%	38 10.38%
1349–62	40	251 6.28	26 10.36%	140 55.78%	22 8.76%	11 4.38%	25 9.96%	1 0.40%	8 3.19%	18 7.17%

Table 2.1. (continued)

Period	Testators	Frequency	Parish	Monastery	Hospital	Confrater.	Poor	Dowries	Servants	Misc.
1363	24	77 3.21	13 16.88%	30 38.96%	13 16.88%	5 6.49%	6 7.79%	0 0.00%	4 5.19%	6 7.79%
1364–75	25	104 4.16	21 20.19%	45 43.27%	9 8.65%	2 1.92%	9 8.65%	2 1.92%	4 3.85%	12 11.54%
1376–1400	61	184 3.02	27 14.67%	56 30.43%	22 11.96%	19 10.33%	23 12.50%	11 5.98%	1 0.54%	25 13.59%
1400–25	45	196 4.36	51 26.02%	49 25.00%	15 7.65%	5 2.55%	14 7.14%	18 9.18%	5 2.55%	39 19.90%
1426–50	56	141 2.52	32 22.70%	36 25.53%	14 9.93%	9 6.38%	10 7.09%	12 8.51%	4 2.84%	24 17.02%
1451–75	59	129 2.19	43 33.33%	25 19.38%	7 5.43%	10 7.75%	4 3.10%	7 5.43%	7 5.43%	26 20.16%
1476–1500	99	176 1.78	37 21.02%	32 18.18%	19 10.80%	4 2.27%	4 2.27%	13 7.39%	9 5.11%	58 32.95%
Total	660	3405	615 18.06%	1305 38.33%	416 12.22%	102 3.00%	337 9.90%	61 1.79%	60 1.76%	509 14.95%

20   From Mendicancy to Humanism

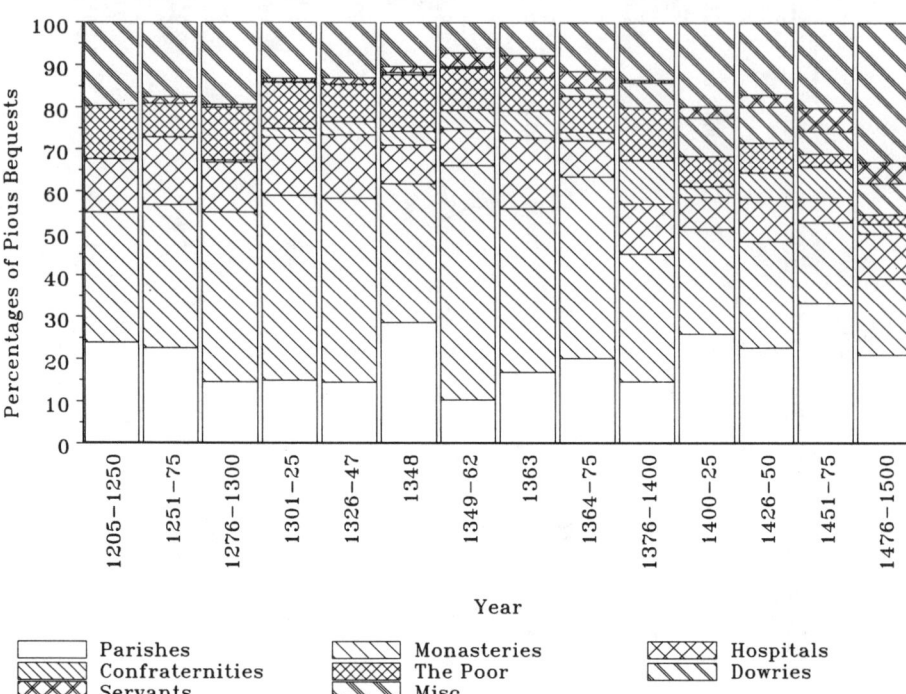

Graph 2.1. Composition of Pious Bequests, 1205–1500

microscopic view of one of the hospital's estates, the Grancia di Serre di Rapolano, the patterns of economic expansion appear consistent with those found for the north of Tuscany. The hospital expanded rapidly in the opening years of the Trecento; then after a period of decline, it began acquiring properties in the 1320s. Its expansion came to a halt with the mid-century plagues, and its holdings declined with the economic dislocations of the 1370s. In the last fifteen years of the century, however, the pendulum swung in the opposite direction as the hospital entered a period of aggressive expansion, finishing the Trecento with double its holdings of a hundred years before.

In contrast to the fortunes of this hospital, however, Siena's second hospital, the Misericordia, lost its autonomy and fell under the strict control of the government of the Twelve in 1363; in 1371, the commune again was forced to assume the debts of this house. Finally, at the turn of the century the "Domus," forced into bankruptcy, became in 1404 the Casa di Sapienza, the new seat of the University of Siena.[13] The testaments suggest, moreover, that the economic experience of Santa Maria della Scala was not typical. By the Quattrocento, it had achieved a near monopoly at the expense of the smaller hospitals attached to monasteries and associated with confraternities, which all but disappear from our records.

Earlier, the testators made bequests to a wide range of different hospitals. Within the city, the hospitals of the Donne Agnese, Sant'Onofrio, and the Misericordia garnered numerous individual gifts. They occur almost as frequently as for Siena's principal hospital, Santa Maria della Scala. In addition, just beyond the city walls, a rich fabric of charitable organizations dotted the religious landscape. The lepers' hospital of San Lazzaro appeared regularly as the beneficiary of piety. At least one other hospital, called the *leprosis de abbatia al fangho*, the "lepers of the Abbey of Mud," housed lepers.[14] The testaments cite other hospitals attached to monasteries scattered through the city and suburbs and mention a host of now unknown, small and possibly, in many cases, short-lived institutions.[15] Several were connected with neighborhood churches, others with prominent Sienese families.[16] Finally, numerous hospitals in the surrounding countryside attracted pious gifts.[17]

By the second half of the fourteenth century the majority of these institutions vanished altogether from the testamentary legacies. The hospitals of the Donne Agnese, Sant'Onofrio, and the Misericordia recur, but without regularity. Santa Maria della Scala had become the hospital that dominated the thoughts of the testators from the city and the territory as they lay on their deathbeds. From the earliest documents to 1347, this hospital was the recipient of less than one-third of the bequests to hospitals (31.3 percent); from the Black Death of 1348 to the end of the century, its share increased to nearly one-half (47.5 percent); and for the Quattrocento, it culled more than two-thirds of the gifts to hospitals.[18]

This change in the map of hospitals might have prejudiced our earlier conclusions on the decline of hospitals as the recipients of charitable gifts in the age of humanism. Because of the wide spectrum of choices before the Black Death, a single testator might have given (as indeed many did) five or more gifts to various hospitals attached to monasteries and parishes, some possibly of dubious and short-lived existence. Later, testators interested in the welfare of the sick and poor may have donated as much or more of their fortunes. Unlike their ancestors, however, they may not have chosen to scatter their resources over a number of tiny institutions; instead, they may have simply left a single bequest to Santa Maria della Scala. The statistics on individual choices of piety would then have registered as a decisive decline what may in fact have been the continuity in hospital charity.

As is discussed in the Appendix, a quantification of the monetized sums of gifts involves problems. Even before confronting the questions of estimating the "real" values of currency over time, other considerations hamper this analysis. For example, not all the gifts were monetary bequests or estimated in currency by the notary.[19] Often, sizable grants of land or the nomination of a religious institution as the universal heir were not evaluated in coin. Here the bias would in fact undervalue the gifts from the preplague period. The samples include the foundation charters for four hospitals. All of them come from a single donor at the end of the thirteenth century, and none are given in monetary terms.

The benefactor, who initiated truly the most important contribution to hospitals found throughout the entire series of our documentation, came not from the burgeoning merchant elites of the Duecento but was instead a pious aristocrat. *Nobilis et sapiens Vir miles dominus* Blasius quondam domini Tolomei de Tolomeis on 22 January 1299 granted his entire estate, both real and movable properties, for founding and constructing four hospitals. These new houses were to provide care for "the poor, the sick, pilgrims, and the indigent (*pro refugio et substentione pauperum infirmorum et peregrinorum miserablilium personarum*)." They were to be built in places where such foundations did not exist but where the services were needed (*in eo loco ubi fuerit maior commoditas*). The knight entrusted his property to four different ecclesiastical corporations to build and govern these new hospitals—the hospital of Santa Maria della Scala and the three principal mendicant orders of Siena, the Augustinians, the Dominicans, and the minor friars. These houses received equal proportions of the patrimony and similar obligations. The knight, for instance, required Santa Maria della Scala to build a hospital for "refugees" in an area where it had no foundations. He gave them one year following his death to build it, and they were to govern it in perpetuity.

In addition, dominus Blasius left each of these religious corporations annuities of 50 lire for the perpetual celebration of masses for his soul and the souls of his ancestors. With 30 lire a year each house was to provide twenty-five gowns for the poor and the indigent. If these houses failed to provide the stipulated services or to build suitable hospitals within a year of his death, then the bequests would fall to the monastery south of Siena, San Galgano, which would assume the same conditions and responsibilities just stipulated.[20] In short, the only monetized values, 30 and 50 lire, though large for the ordinary testator, seriously understate the magnitude of this nobleman's extraordinary gift—a substantial proportion of the estates of the Tolomei, one of the oldest and wealthiest of the noble Sienese lineages. Unfortunately, in this instance, as in most testaments throughout this study, the *omnia mobilia et omnia immobilia* cannot be valorized or in any way quantified.

Did the Sienese in fact give more (in terms of value) to hospitals, even while making fewer individual bequests to them? Although the data cannot provide the precision of modern economic sources, such as annual growth rates of bequests to hospitals, they nonetheless can indicate long-term shifts and might control against our earlier perceptions. These indices—the values of hospital bequests as a proportion of total pious spending—similar to our earlier findings do not chart a single and dramatic shift in charity from the earliest documents through the Renaissance (see Table 2.2). These contributions measured in coin rose through the first half of the fourteenth century; then, in the year of the Black Death their share fell. And in the years before the next strike of pestilence (1363), their share declined even further. However, in 1363 and further in 1364–75, these sums began to mount, until they reached in the last twenty-five years of the

Table 2.2. Values of Gifts to Hospitals, 1205–1500

Period	Testators	Bequests	% Monetized	Average Value per Gift	Average Value in Florins per Testator	% of Pious Gifts
1205–1250	12	9	55.56	3.60	2.70	4.15
1251–75	23	32	68.75	6.38	8.87	11.01
1276–1300	44	47	91.49	3.76	4.01	2.25
1301–25	50	85	88.24	2.50	4.25	10.47
1326–47	67	95	75.79	67.91	96.29	72.26
1348	55	34	70.59	23.02	14.23	25.91
1349–62	40	22	81.82	6.35	3.49	7.70
1363	24	13	84.62	10.26	5.56	12.74
1364–75	25	9	33.33	34.67	12.48	30.52
1376–1400	61	22	31.82	324.91	117.18	91.46
1401–25	45	15	73.33	71.09	23.70	22.26
1426–50	56	14	14.29	32.50	8.13	18.10
1451–75	59	7	14.29	5.00	0.59	2.79
1476–1500	99	19	42.11	18.90	3.63	7.22

century a staggering 91 percent of gifts evaluated in coin. Should we now conclude that the original observations from the simpler statistics on the frequencies of pious choices were misleading? The broad shifts in charity may have taken longer to reach Siena, but did Siena not follow the essential lines found for Florence and Pistoia?

Such a conclusion would be unwarranted. Closer scrutiny discloses the problems of our limited series of widely fluctuating values. The last quarter of the Trecento saw few bequests of coin or of clothing, bedding, or land indicated in monetary terms. Of twenty-two gifts only seven could be computed. Again, the figures in this case were heavily skewed by a single gift, which the notary happened to calculate in florins. Johannes Cionis de Salimbenis on 23 July 1383 bequeathed to the hospital of Santa Maria della Scala an entire inheritance from his relative Adovardo, which the notary valued at 2,000 florins.[21] This sum (one of the largest found in the entire series of documents, despite the rampant inflation of the "long sixteenth century") overshadowed the meager sums found in the remainder of the series. It accounts for the extraordinary percentage of money donated to hospitals for this period. But did our earlier estimates nonetheless understate the donations to hospitals? Did the return of the plague in 1363 initiate a shift toward "Civic Christianity," a this-worldly morality in the age of humanism?

It did not. At the beginning of the fifteenth century Sienese charity slipped from the expected path marked by Florentine historians. The sums to hospitals began to fall relative to other bequests; the decline was secular and continued through the second half of the Quattrocento, when the hospitals' share (principally to Santa Maria della Scala) fell to the lowest point thus far observed.

Confraternities

Hospitals were not the only religious corporations of the late Middle Ages that sought to alleviate pain and suffering in the temporal sphere. Historians have seen the popularity in lay religious confraternities as another benchmark of change in the direction of "Civic Christianity."[22] These brotherhoods, concerned with the social dilemmas of nascent urbanization, organized new charities with goals as diverse as assuaging the psychological trauma of prisoners facing execution and the material needs of impoverished girls who wished to find husbands.[23] They also introduced new forms of devotional life. Instead of receiving religion passively from monks and priests, lay brothers from magnates to humble artisans engaged actively in devotion through singing the Lord's praises (the *laudesi*), or through collective flagellation, the *disciplinati*.[24]

Do shifts in piety here corroborate the changes found for the north? The proportion of bequests to these religious organizations did increase over the first 300 years of our records. Indeed, these lay societies do not even appear until 18 July 1300, when Filippus filius quondam (henceforth f. q.) Orlandi del Mesticcius of Siena, then living in the village of San Quirico Osenna, bequeathed 20 soldi to the *fraternitati* of Abbadia Nove attached to the monastery and Sienese parish of the same name.[25] He followed this gift with another of 10 soldi to the *fraternitati* associated with the church of San Domenico.[26] In the records before 1325, two legacies went to the confraternity of San Domenico, also called "de Comporeggio," two to the Beate Marie Virginis, two to a society associated with the minor friars of Siena, one to a confraternity attached to the *pieve* of Santa Maria in the village of Casole, and one to a society in the rural town of Torrita.[27] These early testaments witness the foundation of a new house for a confraternity, which restructured that lay society's charitable functions. On 5 June 1313, ser Silvius f. q. Allegretti (probably a rural notary) identified as from the *contado* or countryside of Florence gave his house in the village of Rencina (located in the Chianti, near the border of the Sienese territory) "in reverence for the omnipotent Lord, the grace of the Virgin Mary, and all the saints" to the *sotietas* of the blessed Virgin Mary of Rencina. The testator required this confraternity to house the "poor of Christ" and to provide for their needs (*ad Ghubernationem ad usum et commodum . . . in servitium pauperum christi.*) He, moreover, bequeathed the "fruits and labor" from several pieces of land for the praise and reverence (*ad laudem et reverentiam*) of God, the Virgin, and the saints and to finance the gathering each year of twelve priests to celebrate masses for the health of his soul and the remission of his sins as well as for the souls of all the deceased brothers of the confraternity (*omnium defunctorum societatis*).[28]

The proportion of gifts to lay religious societies gradually increased from a slender 2.1 percent for 1301–25 to 3.2 percent in 1326–47 to 3.3 percent in the year of the Black Death, to 4.4 percent in the interval between the plagues, to 6.5 percent in the year of the second strike of pestilence, 1363. (See Table 2.1.) Then, after a momentary fall, their proportion climbed to its high point of the first 300 years of this study: 8.2 for the last twenty-five years of the Trecento.

Seen from the early Quattrocento, however, these last years of the Trecento were only an auspicious moment. For the first twenty-five years of the fourteenth century, the rate declined to 2.6 percent, then bounced back up to 6.4 percent, then to 7.8 percent, before finally falling at the end of the century to what it had been at the beginning of the Trecento, a meager 2.3 percent of all pious gifts. For Siena and her territory, religious confraternities, while making a presence on the religious landscape during the Trecento, failed to channel sacramental rites or charitable responsibilities away from the older corporative entities, the parish church and the monastery. Nor does the Black Death emerge as the critical divide; the Quattrocento again was a century of retreat rather than the initiator of new forms of charity and devotion.

The Poor

Do contributions to "the poor" indicate a shift in the direction of piety? First, we need to define, as clearly as the records allow, what was meant by the poor. A large literature now cautions against approaching late medieval records with modern eyes on questions of poverty.[29] The poor, this literature insists, was a relative term, not to be confused with absolute indigence. The term connoted the extent one had fallen from one's station in life. The testaments do not contribute much toward a sociological typology of the legatees of pennies, bread, grain, and gowns. In rare instances, such as in the testament of Vannius f. q. Gherradi from the village of Montechiello, the notary listed the poor individually by name. For the health of this testator's soul and the remission of his sins, gowns were doled out to eighteen *pauperibus* listed by name; all but one was a woman. Most were given only a first name; two were identified by patronymics, one by a matronymic, and a fourth by her daughter, Margherita mater Brunelle. Nine were widows.[30]

Such flimsy identification makes it impossible to link these individuals to contemporary tax records, the *estimi* or the *Tavole delle possessioni* (1317–18), even if they had possessed enough taxable wealth for enumeration.[31] It is no accident, however, that when identified by name, the poor, quite unlike other recipients of testamentary gifts, were seldom dignified with more than a first name and none possessed a family name. Their marginal status is further suggested by the fact that none (unlike relatives and friends regularly listed as beneficiaries) appear with fixed occupations or residences.

For the less disadvantaged—those who had fallen from higher social stations—testators and notaries reserved a special nomenclature, the "shamefaced poor"(*poveri vergognosi*).[32] But, this relativist sense of property rarely appeared.

Figure 1. Detail from Guido da Siena's Beatus Gallerani *Sfama i poveri*.

Before 1500, only two gifts, out of literally thousands to the "poor of Christ," went to the "shamefaced poor."[33] To identify "the poor," notaries in the testaments before the Black Death of 1348 instead usually labeled them the *pauperes cristi*. Whether these "poor of Christ" were always the lay poor is difficult to know.[34] In his testament founding the four hospitals, Blasius Tolomei placed these "poor of Christ" side by side with pilgrims, who may have been laypeople or clerics. In many other instances, the "poor of Christ" are lumped together with general and vague allocations of gifts "to holy places" (*locii pii*). Could these "poor of Christ" have been members of the mendicant orders, or wandering monks and hermits? Perhaps. But bequests to the *pauperes cristi* normally occur in long itemized lists after the testator had already enumerated different sums of money to the religious whether hermits or mendicants.

Often the notaries amplified the bequests to the "poor of Christ" with phrases such as the ones found in the Tolomei hospital foundations cited previously: in one place, "subventions for the poor, the sick, wanderers, and the impoverished;" in another, to "the poor and indigent." It is difficult to know whether these categories were included to modify one another or to distinguish subgroups within "the poor." Were the "sick" considered, for instance, as separate from the "poor"? Did the notaries think of the "poor" as different from the indigent or from the *miserabile*? The juxtapositions of adjectives as well as the nature and value of gifts bestowed on the "poor" suggests, however, that "the poor" of the Trecento were not so far removed from our notions of the poor today—that is, those who truly need food, clothing, and shelter. Except for foundations such as the rural notary's gift to his confraternity, these gifts were always of negligible value: small quantities of grain, handouts of bread, the distribution of pennies (denarii) never exceeding a soldus (one shilling) or two. Otherwise, the most substantial gift was the gown (*tunica*) valued between 20 and 40 soldi. Such bequests were not the stuff to have shorn up the honor or the subsistence of a nobleman or even a shopkeeper-artisan who had fallen on hard times. Instead, the distribution of these paltry gratuities arose and reached their apex during a period of overpopulation, chronic underemployment, famine, and, later, plague.[35]

From the earliest documents until the cataclysmic mortality of 1348, the percentage of Sienese pious bequests to "the poor" fluctuated between about 8 and to just under 13 percent, reaching its zenith for the entire 600 years of this study, 13.4 percent, in the year of the Black Death.[36] The catastrophic mortality, however, jolted consciousness only briefly. Legacies to the poor gradually declined to just under 10 percent of pious bequests in the period immediately following, and to 7.8 percent when the plague returned in 1363.[37] After the second plague, in a period of continued economic and social dislocation characterized by wide fluctuations in the prices of grain, gifts to the poor mounted to 8.7 percent and then further to 12.5 percent during the final quarter of the century. The early Renaissance, however, marked once again the reversal of trends. From 1401 to the end of the century, this outlet for piety declined steadily—to 7.1, then 3.1, then 2.3 percent. Not even this form of socially minded piety signaled a transformation in the charitable sensibility of the Sienese during the age of humanism.

Dowry Funds

A comparison of dowry bequests to poor girls with other gifts to the poor charts one of the few decisive and long-ranging transformations for the late Trecento and Quattrocento. Dowry funds administered by the executors, parish priests, monasteries, religious confraternities, or spouses took more planning than the indiscriminate allotments to the poor; testators usually allowed their executors one year to make their selections and to distribute the dowries. For the first 70 years, dowry gifts were completely absent from these records and remained rare until 1376–1400: earlier, testators had established only seven funds to dower poor girls. The first appears in the 1318 testament of Nicholaus olim Vannuccij from the *contado* town of Torrita, southeast of Siena.[38] The next does not occur for another 18 years (1346). Two appear in 1348—a negligible portion of the 366 pious gifts bequeathed during these summer months.[39] But, in the final years of the Trecento, charitable patterns changed. For 1376–1400 alone, testators channeled more pious funds than they had during the past 170 years to poor girls to initiate marital life. These years were not just an aberration or a false start like other propitious moments of the late Trecento. In the first 25 years of the Quattrocento, dowry funds increased in relation to other pious bequests from 6.8 to 11.6 percent, and fluctuated roughly around this proportion for the remainder of the century until the last quarter of the century when it reached its apex—11.9 percent of pious gifts.[40]

When the two forms of social charity (alms and dowries) are coupled, their aggregation charts another trend that outstrips the twenty-five- or fifty-year period. In 1363 the total number of gifts to the poor, both as dowries and as handouts to *pauperes cristi,* stagnated. Immediately following the plague, 1364–75, the combined number mounted to 12.5 percent of all gifts. Then generosity to the poor nearly doubled, reaching 21.1 percent of all pious gifts by the final quarter of the Trecento. Unlike contributions to hospitals and confraternities which declined or waffled in the succeeding periods of the early Renaissance, these charities remained at a high level for the next fifty years (18.8 percent and 18.3 percent), declining only by the latter half of the century.

When the two forms of poor-relief are compared a transformation of even longer duration emerges. By the beginning of the Quattrocento, the dowry fund became the principal form of social charity, eclipsing all other donations to the poor. Not until the late seventeenth century did the indiscriminate gifts to "the poor of Christ" overtake dowry funds, and then only momentarily. In effect, this trend was never reversed over the long spectrum of this documentation. During the Quattrocento, moreover, the gap separating these two forms of social charity widened. At the beginning of the century, dowry funds comprised just over half of these charities; by the end of the century, they comprised three-quarters of them.

Do these shifts in poor-relief then point in the direction of a Quattrocento "Civic Christianity"? Both bread-lines and dowries addressed social problems of the present temporal world. Prima facie, neither was more or less ascetical or penitential than the other. Both addressed the urban and commercial problems of poverty, swings in the "grand agricultural cycle," famines, and plagues. Yet the dowry fund did constitute a more foresighted approach to the problem of poverty than the makeshift, "one-shot" grant of bread, pennies, or clothing. The latter type dispersed small gratuities to many individuals. Solace for the soul may have been as important to the donor as any belief that it might actually help to change matters in the temporal shere or systematically alleviate suffering beyond the morrow.

On the other hand, forces beyond mentalities may have been behind this shift in poor-relief. The demographic crisis of the late Trecento must have been crucial. Although testamentary data from other city-states from 1348 through the Quattrocento have not yet been assembled, evidence from institutions such as the confraternity and granary of Orsanmichele in Florence indicates that the shift from small and indiscriminate gifts to the poor to the dowry fund was not peculiar to Siena. In 1352, the brothers of Orsanmichele changed their form of allotments to the poor from handouts of grain or bread to dowries for young girls.[41]

The logic underlying this decision and the sentiments of individual testators in the city and countryside of Siena may have been twofold. For one thing, they may simply have been fewer *pauperes cristi* around, with their hands outstretched, waiting for the funerals of the better-heeled to receive cheap cloaks, small sums of pennies, and bread. Perhaps the chroniclers were right. The wake of the plague and decline in population created gross labor shortages and as a consequence almost instant new wealth for some groups. Certainly, after the first twenty to thirty years of social and economic dislocation, conditions for the poor did improve.[42] Changes in land distribution, wages, and the caloric intake of peasants, created a "Malthusian Renaissance" across wide stretches of Western Europe.[43] The havoc struck by the plagues completely altered the economics of Europe from chronic unemployment and underemployment to labor scarcity. Thus, after the dislocations of the third quarter of the Trecento, moral anxieties would have changed from frustrations over being unable to feed the starving to being unable to repopulate deserted neighborhoods and villages.[44]

A comparison of the attitudes toward marriage presented by Siena's two most notable religious figures of the late Middle Ages, Saint Catherine and San Bernardino, confirms conclusions drawn from demography and economics. In a letter from 1375, Catherine responded to a Sienese notary, ser Cristofano Giudini, troubled over which of two brides to marry. Instead of addressing directly the source of his anguish—to wed the maiden or the widow—Catherine emphasized the higher ideal of celibacy above the pedestrian choice of one bride over the other: "I am sorry that you are hanging back from entering into this holy state [the monastic life]. It seems to me that you ought to have more conscience about not leaving her [the widow whom he was considering marrying] than about leaving her." In a letter to the nuns of San Gaggio, Catherine extolled the virtues of celibacy: "As your bodies are physically enclosed, so let your desires and affections be kept under lock and key, turned away from the pride and pleasures of the world to follow Christ Jesus, your loving bridegroom."[45] Like so many of the saints and *beati* of the late thirteenth and fourteenth centuries—the marriage of Siena's *beatus* Francis to the Virgin Mary, or *beatus* Giovanni Colombini's abandonment of wife and family to pursue the love of Christ—Catherine went to extremes of self-mortification to uphold her vows of marriage to Jesus against all claims of family and suitors.[46] She preached the higher order of mystical and ethereal marriage for other women as well: "Jesus Christ, your loving Bridegroom."[47]

While Catherine learned to feast her soul on the drudgery of domestic toil and, according to her first hagiographer, Raymond of Capua, was transfixed by the horror of her beloved father's impending death, her letters do not conjure up cuddly feelings of earthly affection for children and lasting loyalty and attachment to family.[48] To the same notary, ser Cristofano, she invoked the words of Jesus in Matthew 10:37, "Whoever does not abandon mother and father and sisters and brothers and himself is not worthy of me" (81). In a letter of 1375 to Berenquino, abbot of San Pietro, Lérat, she preached, "There are two things in particular defying the bride of Christ. . . . One is too much attachment to and concern about one's own relatives, a thing that especially needs to be mortified once and for all" (86). To monna Giovanna, a married friend, she pleaded, "I want you to strip off all earthly love you may have for yourself, your children or any created thing outside God" (132).

In contrast, San Bernardino preached in Siena's Piazza del Campo (1427) the virtues of married life and the importance of procreation at the very moment when dowry funds first outstripped legacies to the "poor of Christ." In the early Quattrocento, he delivered five sermons on guides to married life.[49] In these, he elevated marriage from a perhaps necessary but secondary mode of existence to the dignity of "a worthy profession." He lectured to his predominantly feminine audience:[50] "And I say the same of any profession or trade. . . . The girl who is to be married has chosen her trade and must learn how to perform it honestly and purely. If she does not, she is sinning" (54). He further advised the young men in his audiences on how best to choose a wife: "If she is full of charity, faith, humility, rectitude, and patience and besides all this, is capable of bearing you children—how great should be your mutual friendship" (58). Instead of striving to convince Tuscan mothers (as Catherine did for her married friend) to suppress motherly attachment to children, San Bernardino instructed the women in his audiences on the mundane level of the day-to-day matters of rearing children: "You must become half a man; keep your children under the heel of your clogs. . . . Teach them, when they are of the right age, with slaps and floggings" (70). Before admonishments to take communion, attend church, or even listen to his own sermons, he harangued his women listeners first to attend to the matters of the household: "Have you a sick man at home?—'Yes!'—Do not leave him to come to the sermon! Have you children?—'Yes!'—Do not leave them. . . . First take heed to the things that are needful at home, and then come to the sermon" (46).

For instructing his women listeners, Bernardino staged his imaginary character Madonna Discrezione: "She will teach you how much and when and how, and if you follow her advice, you will never sin" (54). The answer to the question of "how much," moreover, was not the old ascetic, otherworldly, and antisexual one of the previous generation. San Bernardino, preaching in a period of population decline and fertility stagnation, was obsessed with problems of sex and procreation in a way that contrasted sharply with his mendicant forebears. He railed against the young for reading Ovid and made bonfires of women's wigs and cosmetics. These stimulants of sexual license, however, outraged him not because they treatened the ascetic life, but because they might divert men away from a procreative, family life or indeed from sexual interest in women altogether. One of Bernardino's most impassioned crusades was directed against sodomites. Again, his righteous moralism may have hidden a functional, demographic concern:

> Go to the Ponte Vecchio, there by the Arno, and put your ear to the ground and listen: you will hear a great lament. Go to the privies, the stables, the gardens, both in the country and in Florence itself; go to the barbers' and apothecaries' shops and the doctors' houses. . . . Listen, and you will hear voices rising to heaven, crying, "Vengeance! Vengeance! O God!" . . . What are these cries? They are the voices of the innocent babies thrown into your Arno and your privies or buried alive in your gardens and your stables, to avoid the world's shame, and sometimes without baptism; the cries of babies killed in their mother's bellies by the drugs of the barbers, apothecaries and doctors. . . . The cries of souls who might have been born, but were not on account of the cursed vice of sodomy. (198)

This sermon's populationist plea was clear. Because of sodomy and contraception, Bernardino claimed, the Florentines were only half as many as they had been fifteen years before—and if they continued "in this fashion," in another fifteen years they would be half as many again (198). Clearly, the dramatic reversal in demographic conditions must have influenced these changes in the attitudes of saints as well as those demarcated by our statistics on mundane giving.

The demographic undercurrent following the Trecento plagues and the ensuing years of economic and social dislocation cannot alone explain, however, the predominance of the dowry fund well into the seventeenth century. By the beginning of the sixteenth century, the "Malthusian Renaissance" had ended and the Four Horsemen of the Apocalypse had returned on the social horizons of Europe. Yet the old forms of social charity prevalent before the Quattrocento did not revive. As we will see, matters other than demography and attitudes toward population may have been at the root of these shifts in giving.

Parishes and Monasteries

The two great medieval corporations of the central Middle Ages, parish churches and monasteries, consistently reaped the largest harvests of bequests from our earliest documents until the beginning of the sixteenth century. By comparison with contributions to hospitals, lay confraternities, poor-relief, and dowry funds, historians regard bequests to these institutions, several founded before the year 1000, as a more traditional, medieval form of piety—one that belonged to the old sodalities of a corporatist society. For Florence, historians have considered these ancient corporations to be the losers when devotion shifted to the new forms of social charity and lay piety in the period of Christian humanism.[51]

Before considering the overall importance of these two pillars of the traditional church, let us look at them in relation to one another. In the first seventy years of the testaments, gifts to monasteries and nunneries were slightly more numerous than bequests to parishes. From the last quarter of the Duecento through the plagues and economic dislocation, the cloistered institutions widened their lead over the neighborhood churches still further. By the last quarter of the Trecento, however, and more decisively during the early Quattrocento, this secular trend reversed. From nearly equal frequencies during the first half of the century, the share of bequests flowing into the coffers of neighborhood churches then eclipsed the ancient dominance of the enclosed orders.[52] In 1451–76, parishes captured a third of all pious legacies, while monasteries fell to 19 percent.[53]

Were neighborhoods becoming more important focal units for liturgy and piety during the Quattrocento? Do these patterns reflect sociological underpinnings similar to those found for Quattrocento Florence?[54] After the defeat of the Ciompi revolution (the artisan/workers' revolt of 1378), the ousting of the government of the minor guilds (*arti minori*), and the steady centralization of executive power during the rule of the Medici, the laboring classes of fifteenth-century Florence retreated into narrower networks of association, centered largely around their parish communities. If similar centrifugal forces were at play in Quattrocento Siena, then one might expect a heightened sense of identity with the parish and a closer rapport with the parish priest, at least within the communities of laborers, artisans, and local shopkeepers. This hypothesis, however, will have to await more careful study of other documentary funds in the State Archives of Siena.[55]

Were there internal changes within various monastic orders in the territory of Siena over this period which might contribute to an understanding of this shift in piety? First, my broad category of monasteries covers various types of pious giving: bequests to individual monks and nuns, gifts to nunneries as opposed to friaries, and bequests to the relatively new orders of mendicants—the Carmelites, the Augustinian hermits, the Servites, the Dominicans, and the minor friars, who in the early fifteenth century split into the Observants of La Capriola and the Conventuals who remained at Ovile. The five mendicant orders—all creations of the early Duecento—constituted throughout this period the major monastic beneficiaries of the Sienese testators (see table 2.3).[56] Against the backdrop of previous accounts of the rise and spread of mendicant houses through Italy, the statistics in Table 2.3 might strike the historian of monastic culture as odd.[57] These orders failed to dominate the souls of the Sienese as they lay on their deathbeds during the first seventy years of our sample—the period of the great rise of mendicant houses not only through central and northern Italy, but through Western Europe. Instead, contributions to these houses increased through the Trecento, reaching their pinnacle in absolute numbers in the period before the Black Death. But in relation to gifts to monasteries, gifts to the mendicants soared during the Quattrocento, their share more than doubling from 30 percent of all monastic gifts during the first seventy years of these documents to 73 percent for the fifteenth century. Despite the general decline in monasteries as beneficiaries, the share of pious gifts cornered by the mendicants over this period increased from 10 to 16 percent.

These statistics for hospitals and monasteries show a consolidation and rationalization of ecclesiastical functions and services. The Black Death, however, did not initiate the process for Siena. For both institutions, the thicket of numerous and virtually unknown small houses became cleared and simplified in the 1320s well before the onslaught of pestilence and demographic crisis.[58] During the last years of the Duecento and the early Trecento, testators regularly paid homage to a plethora of nunneries and monasteries. In the city and surrounding suburbs of Siena, at least twenty-seven different monastic houses appeared in these samples during the Duecento and early Trecento. Beyond the five mendicant orders, the male houses included (1) monasteries that also served as parish churches—San Martino, the Abbadia de Arco, the Abbadia de Nove, San Donato, and San Vigilio; (2) monasteries of second rank but nonetheless of modest proportions—Santo Spirito, Santa Croce, and the Humiliati; these houses of course never disappeared; (3) several others that vanished at least from the testamentary samples—the hermits of Sant'Agata (which became a part of Sant'Agostino, the Templars, the fratres de Sacco, the fratres seu bachucchii, the fratres de Arminio, the Mantellini or male tertiary groups, the Fraticelli near the Porta Uliveria; and (4) other monasteries beyond the city walls in the adjacent suburbs of the Masse—Sant'Eugenio, the charterhouse of Pontigiano, the charterhouse of Maggiano, the order of Saint John the Baptist, Santa Maria della Rosa beyond the Porta Laterina, the hermitage of San Leonardo Silva Laccas, the Augustinian house of Lecceto, and the chapter house of Monte Oliveto near the city. This fourth group continued to reap legacies throughout our documents; their pull over the pious, however, diminished after the 1320s.

The nunneries of the city and surrounding rural suburbs fared even worse

Table 2.3. Monasteries, 1205–1500

Period	Total Bequests	Total to Monasteries	Dominicans	Franciscans	Servites	Augustinians/ Nunneries	Individual		Country	Franciscans Mendicant	Other orders
							Monks	Nuns			
1205–75	270	90	8	9	6	27	6	2	2	23	82
1276–1347	1640	706	41	40	88	196	122	22	33	169	562
1348–1400	982	392	31	27	57	12	57	11	32	115	324
1401–1500	642	142	11	41	30	0	11	8	8	82	123
Percentage of Bequests to Monasteries											
1205–75			8.89%	10.00%	6.67%	30.00%	6.67%	2.22%		28.05%	
1276–1347			5.81%	5.67%	12.46%	27.76%	17.28%	3.12%		30.07%	
1348–1400			7.91%	6.89%	14.54%	3.06%	14.54%	2.81%		35.49%	
1401–1500			7.75%	28.87%	21.13%	0.00%	7.75%	5.63%		66.67%	
Monasteries as a Proportion of All Pious Bequests											
1205–75			2.96%	3.33%	2.22%	10.00%	2.22%	0.74%	0.74%	8.52%	
1276–1347			2.50%	2.44%	5.37%	11.95%	7.44%	1.34%	2.01%	10.30%	
1348–1400			3.16%	2.75%	5.80%	1.22%	5.80%	1.12%	3.26%	11.71%	
1401–1500			1.71%	6.39%	4.67%	0.00%	1.71%	1.25%	1.25%	12.77%	

than the male orders. In the early Trecento, testators left legacies to at least twenty separate nunneries spread through the city and suburbs. They included the sister house of the Franciscans, Santa Clare, Santa Barnaba called the *fratellate,* San Prospero (*infra Castellacciam*), the sisters of Sperandio, Santa Petronilla, Sant'Abundi, Santa Caterina, Santa Marta, the sisters of Vico Alto, San Lorenzo, San Benedetto, the sisters of Melianda near the Porta Uliveria, the house of San Gregorio in the neighboring village of Lapi, Santa Mamilliana, Omnisanti, Santa Lucia, Santa Maria Novella near the Porta Camillia, Santa Margherita in Siena, Santa Margherita in the Masse village of San Maffeo, and the *donne* (women) of Santa Maria Maddalena. Although most of these houses, curiously, did not actually disappear as functioning institutions, all but one vanished as beneficiaries of pious largess, the Franciscan sisters of Santa Clara being mentioned only once in the Quattrocento.[59] The remarkable collapse of these nunneries underscores once again a transformation in the Sienese view of women, celibacy, and marriage. Although the rise of that other form of bequest to women—the dowry—came after the decline of testamentary sponsorship of nunneries, the change in demographic and social conditions wrought by a half-century of plague and drastic population decline must have stimulated the zeal to "secularize" women and to exalt as never before their roles as mothers and wives.

Yet, despite the shift in importance from the monastery to the parish during the Quattrocento, the long-term picture of these two religious corporations shows remarkable stability once they are considered together. Until the last quarter of the fifteenth century they consistently garnered about one-half of all pious contributions. Thus once again Siena and its territory, at least viewed from the perspective of testamentary legacies, does not clearly corroborate the transformations found for Florence and Pistoia. In the south, the two pillars of medieval corporative religious life held their own. The newer forms of religious devotion and social charity, particularly hospitals and lay confraternities, experienced only short-term fluctuations upward. If Siena entered the world of "Civic Christianity" during the later years of the Trecento, it did so only briefly. The early Renaissance reversed most of those nascent movements in charity.

How do we assemble these patterns of piety? First, our methods have been different from those studies on "popular piety" for the north of Tuscany. Whereas Herlihy, Brucker, and Becker have regarded the transformations of the early Renaissance largely from the standpoint of the remarkable gifts and foundations of the *ottimati* (the most wealthy of the patriciate) or through the lens of tax records and changes in the concentrations of ecclesiastical wealth, our study has viewed the problem from the other side of the lens—through the cross-section of that population which left last wills. Although the last decisions of *miserabili* hardly appear in these records, the pious demands of small merchants, shopkeepers, artisans, and even peasants (*laboratores terrarum*) dominate our samples.

Perhaps the religious ideas and cultural ideals of the Florentine north and the

Sienese south differed. The picture drawn by our statistics may indeed conform with the one that art historians and writers of general histories have had for years. According to Ferdinand Shevill (1909):

> The fifteenth century broke over Siena and produced, at least as far as painting is concerned, no art specifically of the Renaissance. To be sure, this century witnessed the labors of a most fascinating group of artists, who signify a second blossoming of the Sienese genius; but the striking fact remains that they hardly deign to take notice of the new movement of civilization, and . . . exhibit a devoted loyalty to the medieval traditions of their home.[60]

The art historian George H. Edgell (1932) recapitulated this judgment without variation, and John Pope-Hennessy carried the same message through the 1940s.[61] Thus the sentiments voiced by the chorus of aggregated pious bequests from ordinary neighbors and villagers may have been the cultural underside of what the art historians and general historians have already told us: after a glorious communal past, Siena became the backwater of Tuscany. She reacted against the Renaissance as it developed in Florence, and denied the fifteenth century. In the next chapter, we will go beyond the simple matter of pious choices to investigate structural changes in the character of gift giving and piety over the period stretching from the rise of mendicancy through Renaissance humanism. When the pious votes are counted by other means, we will see that our statistics invalidate what has now become textbook knowledge.

~~3   The Structure of Pious Giving

Now I come to the disposal of those things which men call goods, although frequently they are rather impediments to the soul.
—Petrarch's last will and testament

Jacques Chiffoleau's *La comptabilité de l'au-delà*, the most rigorous and exhaustive study of late medieval testaments to date, emphasizes the slow, long development of "Christianization" in Avignon. According to Chiffoleau the social forces of "urbanization" and the consequential changes in migration and family structure of the early thirteenth century stimulated new forms of piety and notions about the afterlife. The Black Death in 1348 was not a sharp turning point in the history of these mentalities, as students of fifteenth-century culture have stressed since Huizinga.[1] Instead, the plague and the recurrence of pestilence only accelerated processes well under way by the early fourteenth century—the breakdown of the old familial and feudal sodalities, the "individuation" of the testator, the staging of elaborate funerals assisted by the surrogate families of the religious lay confraternities and crowds of the tunic-clad poor. The slow, barely perceptible forces of early commercialization and urbanization had ushered in these new psychological forces, expressed in new types of funeral processions and new forms of devotion.

Closer to Siena, historians of Florence have seen the plague of 1348 as the pivot of societal change: "In the wake of the Black Death private benefactions and testamentary gifts increased astronomically, and for the following two decades the government acted to guard the swollen patrimonies of the confraternities and pious foundations." According to Marvin Becker, confidence in the state as an executor of pious benefactions and the general increase of civil encroachment on former communal and corporatist institutions such as the guild and the *consorterie* shaped a new lay piety. Despite the different origins of change, Becker's Florence dovetails closely with Chiffoleau's Avignon: "Indeed," Becker observes, "as the individual's isolation increased and he lost guild and *consorterie* support, he might be aided by the many charitable institutions founded between the mid-fourteenth and mid-fifteenth centuries."[2] A cursory glance through the Sienese wills strikes a similar impression.[3] The number of pious bequests did increase "astronomically." But was this increase simply a quantitative matter resulting from the fact that so many people died in the three summer months of 1348 who collectively emptied massive properties into the hands of ecclesiastical institutions? Did the ensuing institutional transformations result simply from pragmatic state action? Or was there correspondingly a change in mentality of individuals shaken by the demographic devastations of that year? These questions at present remain uninvestigated in the Florentine historiography.[4]

Other authors north of the Alps, from Johan Huizinga to Jean Delumeau, have placed the plague at the heart of profound and enduring religious and psychological change. But for these historians, relying almost exclusively on literary and artistic sources, the psychological consequences of the plague conflict sharply with the picture drawn by Renaissance historians. Instead of initiating or accelerating the growth of new, socially responsible hospitals and charitable confraternities, the plagues were the sociodemographic context of the "waning of the middle ages," the atrophy of culture into more totemistic and primitive forms of art, communication, and belief.[5] The Black Death and the high levels of mortality sustained through the fifteenth century, far from being at the gateway of a Renaissance grounded in the "this-worldly" philosophy of the "dignity of Man," colored a century in the dark hues of pessimism and gloom. For these historians, there was no Renaissance; Petrarch, Leonardo Bruni, and a handful of other humanists only skirted a sea of despair. While Huizinga concentrated on French and even northern French materials, Delumeau has carried his research and generalizations to characterize all of Europe, edging even into the Spanish dominion. And William McNeil expands still further this relationship between plagues (or disease in general) and the transformation from secular, this-worldly philosophies to pessimistic, transcendental, other-worldly religions beyond the Black Death and Western Europe to world history at large.[6]

What can our statistics tell us about the effects of the plague years on the psychologies of individual testators in Siena? From the perspective of the shopkeeper and the better-off peasant, was there a Renaissance? In Table 2.1, concerning pious choices, the second column ("Frequency") shows the number of bequests per testator. This statistic forms a decisive long-term change—more profound than any of the changes regarding the allocation of alms to specific beneficiaries. The number of bequests per testator climbed steadily from the earliest documents of the thirteenth century through the first quarter of the Trecento. At this high point, the Sienese left on average more than twelve *legati* to pious causes or ecclesiastical institutions, either as outright gifts or for masses for the soul. In these years numerous testators left extraordinary numbers of bequests to a multitude of causes in the city and territory of Siena. And few of these big donors bore family names of the old feudal or of new mercantile lineages. In 1271 Iacobo, identified only as the son of Campagno, together with his wife Contessa, left sums of money to thirty-one separate pious causes or institutions.[7] In 1290 Ugolinus olim Bonaventura from the parish of San Vincentio left thirty-eight pious gifts. Tuccius olim Bonguidi de Marziis in 1297 left gifts to forty institutions. Salvinus olim Ruffoldi of Montaperti, in 1298, left forty gifts to pious causes.[8]

By the turn of the century the frequency of testators who granted more than twenty-five separately itemized pious gifts increased. In 1301, the pious legacies of domina Flora olim Bramanzone, the widow of Bartolommeo Iludini Vincentis, numbered sixty. In 1312 her in-law Minus olim Iludini Vincentis spread his pious wealth to forty-five institutions and individuals. One Ventura olim Johannis from the parish of Sant'Andrea in 1314 gave to thirty-five charitable causes. In 1317 Guidergha, the widow of Cione domini Bernardini of the magnate Malavolti family, gave twenty-seven times to pious causes. The following year the friar Manfredus olim Albizzi, a citizen of Siena and an oblate of the hospital of Santa Maria della Scala, disposed of twenty-eight separate pious legacies. Iacobo Guglielmi, a citizen of Siena in 1323, made fifty-eight gifts to charitable causes. In 1325, a woman from an artisan family and the wife of a tanner left pious bequests to forty-six different causes.[9]

In the twenty-one years preceding the Black Death of 1348 the high level of the early Trecento tapered off and declined by nearly a quarter. Although statistically insignificant, the decline might be explained in part by papal action (going back to the Bull of Boniface VIII, *Super Cathedram*) and the bishops to redress their declining revenues over the past century from competition of a multiplicity of new pious causes, principally the mendicant orders. But the bishops encouraged testators to fragment their patrimonies in other ways (which we will examine shortly)—vague bequests to the numerous *pauperes cristi* or to indistinct "pious places" from which seculars could control one-third of the revenues.[10] Second, the decline might be explained partially by the democratization of will writing and partially by the disappearance, at least from our records, of the numerous nunneries, hermitages, and small hospitals witnessed in the previous chapter. Nonetheless, individuals, again largely undistinguished by prominent family names, continued to spread large numbers of gifts across the charitable landscape of Siena. Third, could the famines which spread through central and northern Italy in 1328–30 have forged a change in mentalities? Our statistics suggest strongly that this was not the case. First, the famines occurred after the mean numbers of bequests per testator had begun to decline; second, these years wrought no significant changes in our statistics. Moreover, the old style of fragmenting patrimonies into numerous but small charitable gifts persisted. In 1326 Sozzio olim Orlandi, a mere cobbler from the parish of San Martino, left twenty-six separate legacies to pious institutions. A decade later Guccio olim Gerii de Montanini left forty-five. In the summer months of disease in 1340, a citizen from the parish of San Egidio bequeathed forty-nine, and four years later an innkeeper of the parish of San Vencentis left twenty-eight pious bequests.[11]

Then, surprisingly, in the year of colossal rates of mortality, 1348, the number of masses and pious bequests declined again, by almost the same percentage as the previous period of analysis (29 percent). Thus, although the sheer facts of this massive mortality may have created an "astronomic" rise in the flow of properties to ecclesiastical coffers, its psychological impact, from the perspective of the individual testator, did not change, at least in the direction suggested by the aggregate outpouring of generosity. Instead, those assailed by pestilence in their last throes gave actually fewer gifts to the church and to the poor *pro salute anime* than in the previous generation. In the years immediately following 1348, moreover, the level of individual giving did not change until the plague's recurrence, in 1363.[12]

The second strike of bubonic plague in Siena did not hold a significant place in the memory of Siena or Italy which can in any way be compared to the manifestations of disease in 1340 or, especially, the catastrophic devastations of 1348.[13] In Siena it is even less well remembered than subsequent plagues, such as the one of 1400 imprinted forcefully on the Sienese past by the gallant deeds of one of Siena's most notable saints, San Bernardino. In that year of the papal jubilee, the swarm of pilgrims passing Siena en route to Rome spread in their trail the infection which raged through the summer months. In the first weeks of the plague the doctors of Siena's principal hospital died along with a number of the priests. "The dying lay untended, the dead unburied." San Bernardino with twelve of his friends heeded the prior's appeal for assistance and stayed constantly in the hospital's service, never setting foot outside the wards until the early winter quelled this source of staggering mortality. Yet this plague (which Iris Origo claimed was "almost as severe as the first outbreak half a century before" hardly registers in our collection of testaments.[14] Ten testaments are found for the preplague pestilence of 1340, twenty-four for 1363, and fifty-five for 1348, whereas the plague that was the occasion of San Bernardino's heroism registers in our samples only one deathbed victim.[15]

The plague of 1363 did arouse the laconic remarks of the chroniclers but did not have the devastating consequences of several other plagues that swept through Italy in the late Trecento.[16] In the words of the chronicler Donato di Neri: "The disease occurred in Siena and almost everywhere in Italy. . . . Many of the commune's employees died of the disease at this time . . . many children and the young died; few remain in Siena and, in the wards of the city, of those accounted for, 900 died."[17] The victims of the plague of 1363 were similar to those of the earlier plague of 1361, which struck parts of England and areas such as Milan but had spared Siena as well as other city-states in Tuscany.[18] Both were plagues of the young—adolescents born after 1348 who had not been exposed to the earlier outbreak of bubonic pestilence. Yet the chroniclers, who usually were wont to overdramatize and overestimate the ravages of the disease, reported that 900 had died in Siena. Certainly, this was no negligible number, but by any yardstick it was incomparable to the devastation wrought fifteen years earlier.

And yet the statistics compiled from the masses and pious bequests of 1363 disclose a significance for these months of plague which bypassed contemporary chroniclers and has eluded historians ever since. The year 1363 marked a distinct break in the pattern of pious giving. Suddenly, for the summer months of this year, the number of gifts per testator collapsed in half from 6.3 per testator to 3.2.[19] More important, the change was unlike the bulk of short-term shifts in pious choices; 1363, here, was the watershed. The per capita number of pious gifts never again rebounded to pre-1363 levels. In the following twelve years the number of gifts increased slightly to 4.2 per capita, then fell back to 3 gifts during the last quarter of the century. After another jump upward to 4.4 in the first quarter of the Quattrocento, the downward trend resumed, arriving at less than 2 pious bequests per testator by the end of the century.

The decline in the summer months of 1363 was the most drastic for any period; it doubled the fall prompted by the plague of 1348. But should we conclude that 1363 marked a dramatic change in the structure of pious giving? Could the decline have resulted from a change in the documentation—the gradual shift in importance of documents from the wealthier collections of the *Diplomatico* to the *Notarile*? If the records of the *Diplomatico* (whose archives contain the greater number of testaments for the first part of this study) are considered alone, the radical change wrought by the summer months of 1363 appear in even bolder relief (see Table 3.1, Graph 3.1). Similar to the combined data, testators in 1301–25 donated the greatest number of pious gifts (13.11). Thereafter, however, the decline is not as steep. In 1326–47 the rates returned to what they had been in the last decades of the Duecento. In 1348 the per capita averages fell by less than 17 percent and remained constant until the return of pestilence. Then, in 1363, the number of gifts per testator collapsed from 7.44 gifts to 2.93–a fall of 61 percent from the previous period. For the remainder of the century the trend traced by the *Diplomatico* bequests followed closely those of the combined data.

Could other variables better account for the shift? We suggested earlier that changes in the social composition of testament writers may have contributed to

Table 3.1. Pious Bequests from the *Diplomatico*

Period	Testators	Frequency	Per Capita
1205–50	8	51	6.38
1251–75	17	161	9.47
1276–1300	43	398	9.26
1301–25	45	590	13.11
1326–47	65	606	9.32
1348	39	303	7.77
1349–62	27	201	7.44
1363	14	41	2.93
1364–75	24	95	3.96
1376–1400	35	118	3.37

Graph 3.1. Value of Bequests, 1205–1500

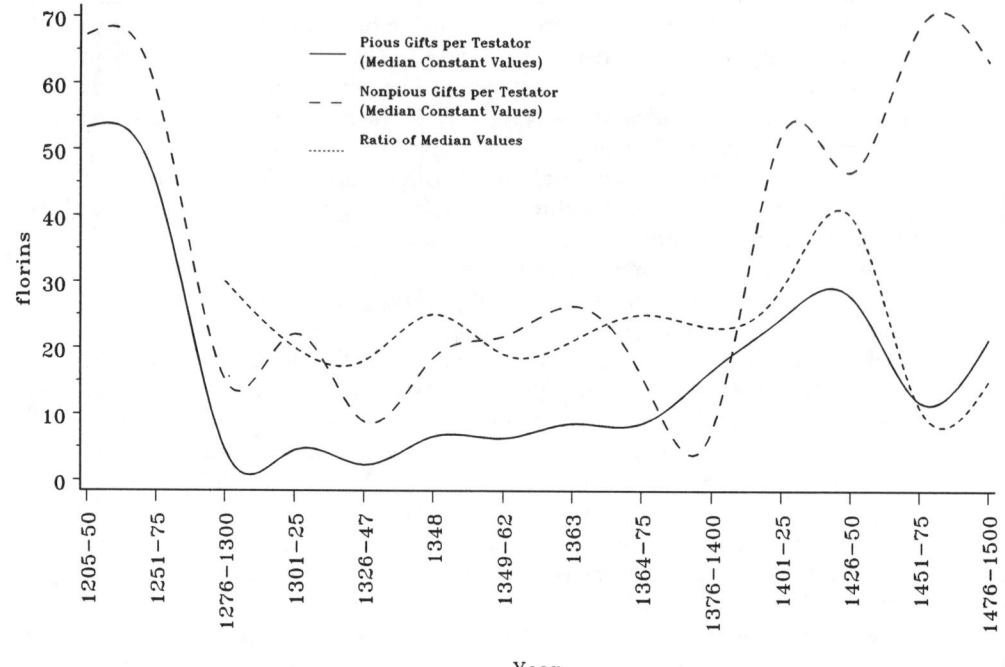

the decline in pious gifts after 1325. One way to tackle the problem might be to examine the ratio of pious to nonpious gifts. If nonpious gifts fell off correspondingly in 1363 through the end of the Quattrocento, then the wherewithal of the testators instead of their piety may have been at the crux of change in pious giving. Yet, by these statistics, 1363 as the critical divide emerges again in even bolder relief (see Table 3.2). From the mid-Duecento through the interval between the two outbreaks of pestilence, testators consistently gave three pious gifts for every two to neighbors and kin. Then in 1363 the ratios reversed themselves: two pious gifts were granted for every three to nonreligious causes. This pattern persisted through the Quattrocento when the ratios fell even further, when nonpious doubled pious ones. These statistics, moreover, do not portray 1348 as the initiator of a gradual decline in pious giving; instead relative piety for these summer months reached its pinnacle: pious donations nearly doubled the nonpious ones. But perhaps the demographic crisis itself may explain the nonpious side of the ratio. Because of the plague's onslaught, simply fewer friends and kin were around to benefit from a testator's largess. In 1348, Francesco Petrarch lamented: "Consider that I am bewailing not something inconsequential, but the 1348th year of the sixth age, which not only deprived us of our

Table 3.2. Nonpious Bequests and the Ratios of Bequests, 1205–1500

Period	Testators	Number of Nonpious Bequests	Number per Testator	Ratio of Pious to Nonpious	% Monetized	Average per Testator	Median Testator	Average in Constant	Median in Constant	Ratio of Pious to Nonpious (Averages)	Ratio Median Values
1205–50	12	104	8.67	68.27	52.88	1499.16	67.17	1499.16	67.17	0.04	0.79
1251–75	23	118	5.13	168.64	45.76	165.66	58.69	165.66	58.69	0.49	0.76
1276–1300	44	311	7.07	127.97	58.52	386.63	15.06	386.63	15.06	0.46	0.30
1301–25	50	361	7.22	170.08	51.52	292.92	22.02	292.92	22.02	0.14	0.20
1326–47	67	446	6.66	140.81	45.74	193.64	12.38	137.34	8.78	0.69	0.18
1348	55	192	3.49	190.63	58.33	307.62	25.97	218.17	18.42	0.18	0.25
1349–62	40	170	4.25	147.65	45.88	303.41	32.94	199.61	21.67	0.15	0.19
1363	24	123	5.13	62.60	57.72	156.67	39.92	103.07	26.27	0.28	0.21
1364–75	25	155	6.20	67.10	41.94	425.13	33.73	199.59	15.83	0.10	0.25
1376–1400	61	276	4.52	66.67	34.06	408.07	15.38	192.49	7.26	0.31	1.08
1401–25	45	215	4.78	91.16	38.14	1077.53	86.00	657.03	52.44	0.10	0.29
1426–50	56	249	4.45	56.63	36.55	703.02	68.92	475.02	46.57	0.06	0.40
1451–75	59	240	4.07	53.75	32.50	690.79	108.49	437.21	68.66	0.03	0.11
1476–1500	99	324	3.27	54.32	43.21	697.25	141.81	311.27	63.31	0.07	0.15

Table 3.3. Class and Geography, 1205–1500

Period	Testament	Bequests	Ratio	Period	Testament	Bequests	Ratio
I. The Countryside				III. The Patriciate			
1205–1300	23	148	6.43	1205–1300	10	106	10.60
1301–47	42	344	8.19	1301–47	17	180	10.59
1348	32	232	7.25	1348	5	23	4.60
1349–62	13	49	3.77	1349–62	6	46	7.67
1363	4	8	2.00	1363	3	7	2.33
1364–1400	21	55	2.62	1364–1400	13	43	3.31
1401–1450	25	88	3.52	1401–1450	19	79	4.16
1451–1500	53	83	1.57	1451–1500	32	63	1.97
II. Artisans and Shopkeepers				IV. The Residual			
1205–1300	5	44	8.80	1205–1300	41	370	9.02
1301–47	18	203	11.28	1301–47	40	515	12.88
1348	7	57	8.14	1348	11	54	4.91
1349–62	6	45	7.50	1349–62	15	111	7.40
1363	8	31	3.88	1363	9	31	3.44
1364–1400	26	76	2.92	1364–1400	26	114	4.38
1401–1450	32	77	2.41	1401–1450	25	93	3.72
1451–1500	54	90	1.67	1451–1500	19	69	3.63

friends but the entire world of actual nations." He continued, "We used to be a crowd, now we are almost alone. We must seek new friendship. But where or for what reason when the human species is almost extinct and the end, as I hope, is near? . . . See to what a small number we have been reduced from so large a group of comrades."[20] But just as Petrarch rapidly found new recipients for his prodigious epistolary production, so our statistics on nonpious giving record the remarkable speed by which the Sienese reestablished and restructured new social networks in the years immediately after the plague.

Not only relative largess, but the interaction of other variables—wealth, sex, occupation, residence (city or country), and health (of "sound" body or on deathbed) may have greatly influenced the number of pious gifts per testator. To control for these possible changes in the composition of our samples, we have subjected the data to regression analyses to measure the weight of these "independent variables" on the "dependent variable"—the mean number of pious bequests. When the data are treated without chronological distinctions, only wealth emerges as a significant variable.[21] Entering the historical dimension—

the periods before 1348, 1348, the interval between the plagues, 1363, and the period afterward—immensely improves our model.[22] Here, wealth once again correlates positively and significantly with changes in the number of pious gifts.[23] All the other significant variables concern time: the period before the plague,[24] the period after the plague[25] and the year 1363 (despite the small sample size).[26] The year 1348, on the other hand, was highly insignificant.[27] Once changes in residence, status, health, and wealth have been controlled, the change for this year barely registers any influence for the overall model.[28]

The first plague victims of the summer months in 1348 continued to redact their wills in the style of their fathers and grandfathers. The second onslaught of pestilence etched lasting and decisive marks on the Sienese psyche. The victims of the holocaust of 1348 continued to divide their pious bequests over a vast landscape of religious institutions, despite the fact that the large array of hospitals and nunneries had disappeared (if not in actual fact, at least from these records) by the 1330s. Testaments containing twenty-five pious bequests or more continued to fill the notarial protocols. During the traumatic summer months of 1348, for instance, Picardinus Francischi domini Pice from Fabriano (in the Marche) but living in Siena bequeathed twenty-nine pious legacies, and Landus olim Baldi from the village of Pietrallata gave to thirty-one separate pious institutions.[29] During the summer months of 1363, on the other hand, and continuing through the end of our documentation, this pattern of piety vanishes from the Sienese records. Afterward, not a single testament conveyed more than twenty-five separately itemized pious gifts. The psychological impact of 1363, moreover, was democratic. As best we can envision from the limited distinctions notaries employed to identify their clientele, the changes of 1363 did not "trickle down" through social classes or across geography from city to countryside. Rather, as for the massive rates of mortality for the late Trecento, it was a change for the population as a whole (see Table 3.3).

The Values of Pious Gifts

Was the reduction in the number of gifts a sign of a new secularism or selfishness in Sienese society? From the arguments of the art historians of Siena and Florence, principally Millard Meiss, we should expect that it was a sign of the opposite, not only immediately after the plague of 1348, but for the entire Trecento. The trauma of plague and economic depression stifled developments in artistic perspective and caused painters and their patrons to turn their backs on the proto-humanism prevalent in the early Trecento. The Renaissance of Giotto, Duccio, and Simone Martini was buried along with thousands of nameless corpses. Artists in the period starting even before the plague of 1340 reacted against artistic influences of the earlier part of the century and returned to the hierarchic, frontal arrangements of figures found in the more primitive and didactic painting of the previous century.[30] Even if Meiss's insights are accurate, should the reactions of late Trecento painters be generalized to embrace the broad swath of the Sienese population represented by those who redacted wills?

The contemporary chroniclers would have counted these didactic artists and their pious patrons among the minority. In Florence, Matteo Villani concluded that the plague had instead loosened the bonds of common morality and religious observance for those lucky enough to have survived. According to Villani, their memories were short; even before all the bodies had been buried, they had lost sight of the scourge of God and felt liberated from the pains and obligations of contrition.[31] The chronicler of Siena, Agnolo di Tura del Grasso, made similar observations: "Once the plague was over, all who escaped devoted themselves to pleasure: friars, priests, nuns and monks, women, all of them; and they made no bones about spending and gambling; everyone took himself for rich . . . and nobody had patience for anything." For the entry of 1349, Agnolo continued: "After the great plague of the year before, everyone lived according to his fancy; and everybody aimed to enjoy eating, drinking, hunting, hawking and gambling; and all the money went into the hands of the *gente nuova*."[32] Should we believe the art historians or the chroniclers? Perhaps both were right. As the chroniclers suggest, two reactions prevailed—some returned to the stricter, more hieratic and moral values of the thirteenth century; others began to question the efficacy of ecclesiastical dictates and became liberated from guilt and social responsibility. Was it the second reaction that actually cut the major mold?

In brief, our statistics do not corroborate the chroniclers' stress on the second reaction. When the pestilence raged once again in the city and territory in 1363 the numbers of pious bequests fell precipitously. The decline, however, does not point to a new selfishness, this-worldliness, or a failure in social responsibility on the part of the survivors of the first plague. Instead, the value of individual bequests nearly doubled from 7.23 florins on average during the interplague years 1349–62 to 13.60 florins in 1363. If the medians are considered—here, a more exacting statistic, because of the extraordinary variance created by a few large bequests—the jolt of 1363 was even more dramatic. The size of bequests trebled (see Table 3.4). As a result, while the number of gifts per testator slid, the total value of pious gifts per testator increased during the summer months of plague from 6.28 to 8.50 florins.

Nor was 1363 an aberration. Instead of a decline in the flow of property into church coffers (as the diminution in the number of gifts after 1363 may have suggested), Sienese testators became more zealous in charity and religious devotion. The median values of individual gifts more than doubled again during the last quarter of the fourteenth century. With the exception of 1451–75, Sienese generosity (at least in nominal sums) continued its upward trajectory through the Quattrocento. Pious bequests per testator rose from 6.52 florins in 1348, to more than two-and-a-half times that value during the last quarter of the century and well over four times that Black Death value by the middle of the Quattrocento, reaching the pinnacle of pious giving (27.8 florins) in nominal terms.

Table 3.4. Value of Pious Bequests, 1205–1500

Period	Testators	Pious Bequests	% Monetized	Average Value per Testator	Median Value per Testator	Constant Florins	Average in Constant Florins	Median in Constant Florins
1205–50	12	71	80.28	65.01	53.25	1.00	65.01	53.25
1251–75	23	199	88.44	80.59	44.73	1.00	80.59	44.73
1276–1300	44	398	86.43	178.02	4.52	1.00	178.02	4.52
1301–25	50	614	86.32	40.61	4.42	1.00	40.61	4.42
1326–47	67	628	82.17	133.29	2.25	1.41	94.53	1.60
1348	55	366	76.50	54.90	6.52	1.41	38.94	4.63
1349–62	40	251	86.45	45.37	6.28	1.52	29.85	4.13
1363	24	77	83.12	43.63	8.50	1.52	28.71	5.59
1364–75	25	104	75.96	40.89	8.53	2.13	19.20	4.00
1376–1400	61	184	55.98	128.14	16.59	2.12	60.44	7.83
1401–25	45	196	70.41	106.45	24.52	1.64	64.91	14.95
1426–50	56	141	54.61	44.89	27.80	1.48	30.33	18.78
1451–75	59	129	48.84	21.25	11.87	1.58	13.45	7.51
1476–1500	99	176	49.43	50.35	21.33	2.24	22.48	9.52
Total	660	3534	77.28	1173.76	329.57			

To what extent did this trend depend on inflation? Here the Sienese data again present problems. For Siena, unlike Florence, prices-series, even for grain, are not available until the end of the sixteenth century. On the other hand, the grain prices compiled by de la Roncière and Goldthwaite bear a close correspondence to the fragmentary evidence that Stephan Epstein has assembled from the hospital records of Santa Maria della Scala.[33] Moreover, when comparable price-series become available for Siena at the beginning of the sixteenth century—the grain prices compiled by Giuseppe Parenti from the Markets of the Piazza del Campo—a remarkable correspondence appears between the Florentine and the Sienese prices, despite slight differences in coinage and grain measurements.[34] Although we cannot presume that earlier prices always bore such a close resemblance, we do know that markets in grain had assumed a regional character by the early fourteenth century. High prices and famine in one area of Tuscany coincided immediately with regionally high prices and regional grain shortages throughout Tuscany, even spilling into Umbria and probably beyond.[35] At any rate, the prices from Florence are the best indices we have until the mid-sixteenth century when the commune began to compile meticulously the daily prices in the Piazza del Campo. The ebb and flow of prices from neighboring Florence will at the very least serve as a benchmark for assessing rough changes in the real values of testamentary wealth.

Our problems, however, do not end with the estimation of constant values over time. First, for the period preceding 1309 grain prices are wholly absent for

Florence as well as for Siena. There are no estimates for the plague period 1335–59; nor do they exist for the critical year 1363. Second and perhaps more important, grain and bread prices might not be the most suitable indices for estimating changes in the monetary values of patrimonies. Instead of the short-term fluctuations of bread, the longer trends of the housing market or of dowries would more precisely approximate changes in the monetary value of a person's lifetime or even generational wealth. The use of these indices must await future work in the little rewarded field of price-series analysis. Meanwhile, to assess changes in the generosity of the Sienese testament writers, we rely on the one index available and used universally at this point for the analysis of preindustrial price series: the cost of grain.

To standardize the pious contributions of the Sienese in constant florins an index of 1.00 florins will be set for the earliest evidence on grain prices, 1309–25. Once the series of pious legacies has been adjusted, few surprises arise; roughly the same trend emerges as with the nominal values. These recalculations dampen slightly the increases of the last years of the Trecento; on the other hand, the increases in pious spending of the mid-Quattrocento are accentuated. After the economic and social dislocations in the wake of the Black Death, productivity in agriculture may have begun to increase as early as 1375, demand slackened (especially for grain), and the real value of money increased. This secular deflationary trend began to reverse only by the 1470s.

The upward movement of the values of pious bequests, however, might not have been connected to changes in piety or changes in the value of money. Although those chroniclers who harangued their fellow citizens for profligacy may have been wrong in assessing the absence of piety, they might not have been far from the mark in judging the economic resources now available to new classes of artisans and peasants. Those who survived inherited property earlier and more of it than their compatriots had before the plagues. Those who remained alive had fewer competitors with claims to the succession of property. In addition, peasants could buy land more cheaply, and those who worked for wages found their services in greater demand. Thus testators during the late Trecento and the first half of the Quattrocento—especially the *gente nuova* (newly rich), who formed, after all, the backbone of our samples—were relatively better off, relieved from the population pressures that had burdened the previous generation. Their generosity relative to their wealth thus may not have changed.

Did rises in piety simply correlate positively with prosperity? The last quarter of the fourteenth and the first quarter of the fifteenth century witnessed the most dramatic increases over this 300-year period; in constant florins the median value of pious bequests nearly doubled from 7.83 to 14.95. Yet from the chroniclers' descriptions, these 50 years do not present a consistent picture of either prosperity or poverty. The 1370s and 1380s were by these accounts days of plenty: "1372—In this year was the best grape harvest and the most abundant supply of wine generally that the world had ever known. . . . 1386— . . . a massive wine harvest and an abundance of wine generally throughout the entire world, the likes of which had never been remembered, and the same for grain and other things; there was plenty of bread, wine, oil and fruit and fire wood; and in everything there abounded love, faith, charity and courtesy."[36]

On the other hand, the period ushered in by 1400 was without rosy claims of prosperity, charity, and abundance. Instead, 1411 was a famine year: grain soared to 4 lire per staio. In 1413 too much rain fell, bringing crop failures; high grain and wine prices ensued. A heat wave in 1414 led to excessive desiccation (grandi caldi e molto asciuttore). As a consequence, quartan and other fevers weakened and endangered the population: "The young and the old died." The year 1417 saw the return of the plague. And 1419 was a year of heavy rains, which meant four successive bad harvests; in addition, the plague struck again. In 1420, "the harvest was even sadder than in the past years," and was made still more miserable by the return of the plague. According to Donato di Neri, in that year "more died than ever before." Finally, 1421 was again a year of famine.[37] Yet charity in Siena by our statistics continued to soar.

The shift to years of plenty in the mid-Quattrocento again cannot explain fluctuations in pious expenditure. As in many areas of Western Europe, these years were the golden age for artisans, shopkeepers, and peasants.[38] For central Italy, unlike the north of France, moreover, it was a period of relative peace. Between the famines (carestie) of 1421 and 1471, the chroniclers of Siena do not mention a single year of famine or of plague, nor do they make any reports of ravagingly high grain prices and scarcity.[39] Yet, despite the disappearance of these most outward and demanding conditions for charity and piety, pious bequests continued to climb.

But should secularization be ruled out altogether? After all, the Florentine historians have stressed the role of the state after the Black Death as "the regulator and benefactor" of philanthrophic institutions.[40] Parallels, indeed, emerge for Siena, particularly in regard to those institutions that the Florentinists have stressed as the leading edge of "Civic Christianity." But the commune's encroachment on these institutions does not correspond with the chronology outlined by our statistics on the structure of pious bequests. Neither 1348 nor 1363 were crucial dates in these developments between church and state. First, the government of the Nine in the early decades of the Trecento had already assumed an active role in the administration of Siena's largest philanthropic corporation, the hospital of Santa Maria della Scala, as well as with other smaller hospitals.[41] The next decisive changes occurred well after the plague. In 1374, the "omnipotent state" declared the hospital to be "its hospital," wresting the right to elect its rectors from the canons and friars of the hospital.[42] Similarly, toward the end of the century the commune rescued Siena's second hospital, the Misericordia, from bankruptcy and in so doing assumed the administrative prerogatives of the hospital.[43]

Styles in Pious Giving
Hermits

A closer look at changes in the character of pious bequests, beneath the arithmetic of frequencies, means, and medians, further corroborates the changes thus far outlined by the structure of bequests. The year 1363 saw the sudden erosion of a style of pious giving that had prevailed for at least one hundred years. Of these, one of the most significant was the scattering of tiny sums of money to all the hermits (*hermiti/e, romiti/e*) living within the city or within a mile radius of Siena (see chapter 6). On occasion, testators identified these communities of unhoused and unorganized hermits geographically. In a testament of 1296, 2 soldi were given to each hermit who stayed around the Porta Scoppie and around the Calcinaria (the limestone works) near the house of the sons of Ciampoli.[44] In a testament of 1325, 2 soldi each were distributed to those hermits living (*moranti*) in the *celle* of friar Geri as far as the piazza of the Castro Montone, to those who live around the nunnery of Santa Petronille as far as the hospital of Santa Croce, and to those living in the Piazza Laterina and in the street leading to the monastery of Santa Caterina.[45] In some cases, the organizational life of these hermits appears to have been more formalized. For instance, a testament in 1318 gave small donations specially to sisters Francesca and Andrea "at the hermitage (*apud eorum heremitorium*) beyond the gate," and another donation of 12 pennies to each of fifteen hermits at the hermitage beyond the gate of Castro Montone to be distributed by the friar Manfredi q. Albizi civis Senensis, "an oblate of the hospital" of Santa Maria della Scala.[46] Finally, a villager from Corsignano (later, the showpiece of Renaissance urban planning, Pienza) gave in 1321 the only substantial gift to a hermit—two gowns worth 100 soldi, to be renewed each year as long as this hermit stayed (*si steterit et moram contrasserit*) in the *romitorio* in the curia of Corsignano at a place called Pietracovecia.[47]

But these were the exceptions. In the remaining fifty-eight donations to hermits, the gifts were indiscriminate; no one chose among them; none were individuated; nor was the geography clarified beyond the phrase "to all those *hermiti* and *romite* living in the city or within one mile of Siena." Almost all these gifts were cash sums, and for the most part of extraordinarily low values. The mode was 12 pennies; the largest handout, 30 soldi.[48] Though fifty times the value of the usual donation to hermits, this grant in 1301 would not have sufficed even to buy that common article of cheap clothing extended to the poor, the *tunica*.[49]

At least one document provides information for estimating to what extent these small sums were spread over the population of hermits. In 1348, the widow of a notary from the parish of San Giovanni made the standard gift of 12 denarii to each hermit in the city and within a mile of Siena. She then instructed her *fideicommissarii* to distribute 25 lire to cover the donation.[50] Hence, her executors would have had to hand out these pocketfuls of pennies to 500 individual hermits. The scattering and fragmentation of the patrimonies in tiny parcels was thus even more exaggerated than our means and medians of the numbers of "itemized" bequests previously suggested.

During the plague of 1348 and the interplague years, these gifts remained a prevalent form of legacy for the pious of Siena and its territory. Beginning in 1363, they disappear almost altogether. In 1376, the *prudens domina* and widow from the parish of Mansonis Templi granted each *hermite recluse pro presentia in cellis* within a mile of Siena 5 soldi.[51] After this date, the only other such bequest occurs in a testament redacted by a testator from a foreign city-state. How the testament of domina Alessandra f. q. Luce Raymicij from Todi (Umbria), the widow of Paulo from the same city, found its way into the Sienese *Diplomatico* is a mystery; it makes not a single donation to any person or institution within the territory of Siena. Other donations listed in this testament (as we will see later) have the imprint of a prior age. She fragmented her holdings to many more individuals than the mere counting of itemized gifts would indicate: one was bequeathed to an unspecified number of nameless prisoners jailed in a place next to the monastery of Santa Margherita in Todi; another, brought on by guilt and inspired by mendicant preaching, compensated an unspecified number of nameless individuals who earlier had been damaged "because of the uncertain gains obtained through sin."[52]

Prisoners

San Bernardino's sermons of the opening decades of the fifteenth century exhorting the Sienese to pity and assist poor prisoners must have fallen on deaf ears at least as far as testamentary largess is concerned.[53] Gifts to prisoners had been common before the plagues, but the Sienese granted only two bequests to prisoners found in "the deplorable conditions of Sienese jails" during the whole of the fifteenth century.[54] And in one of these cases the testator, although a citizen of Siena, came from Perugia. In 1363 and its aftermath, grants to poor or indebted prisoners vanished almost entirely from the testaments. Not until the Counter-Reformation did alms to poor prisoners become once again popular among the pious in Siena.

Usury and Ill-gotten Gains

As far as the testamentary evidence is concerned, Bernardino's harangues against ill-gotten gains, cupidity, and unfair profit likewise appear to have been ineffective.[55] Curiously, the period of Sienese commercial efflorescence, the Duecento and early Trecento, moved successful merchants nearing death to turn sharply against the very practices which in fact enabled them to bestow largess on numerous monasteries, parish churches, and other pious causes.[56] During the period of commercial expansion, numbers of Sienese shopkeepers and merchants, because of their remorse over patrimonies accumulated through uncertain and evil means (*incertis et male abblatis*) "instituted" the "poor of Christ" or an ecclesiastical institution as the universal heirs to their estates.[57]

Figure 2. Detail from Lorenzo Vecchietta's *Last Judgment—The Bad Death*, painted between 1444 and 1471 in the old sacristy, Santa Maria della Scala

Guilt over usury, gambling, and profiteering did not afflict only those on the middling rungs of commercial activity during these halcyon years of urban growth.[58] Such pangs on occasion also struck the nobility. The knight dominus Blasius de Tolomeis (the founder of the four hospitals described in chapter 2) ordered in the last "item" of his 1299 testament the restitution of losses to all from whom he had gained usurious profits.[59] One of his kinsmen, a Baldus q. Ildibrandini de Tolomeis, began his testament of 1285 by providing a large fund, 600 lire, to restitute all usurious transactions (*restituantur omnes et singulas usuras quas habui et extorsi*) found in his account book. For the most part, however, these were the stipulations and bequests of hard-headed shopkeepers.[60] Among those identified by profession, four were notaries, two carpenters, two butchers, a grocer, a *maestro,* a blacksmith, and a silk manufacturer.

Guilt over usury and compensation to such injured individuals go back to the earliest testaments. In 1242 Silimanus q. Alberti, a baker, had his heirs return sums of money ranging from 2 soldi to 7 lire, 10 soldi to nine clients indebted to him. The baker preceded these pious legacies with the phrase "ab eo accepi usuarum pravitate," "pro utilitate usuarum," "quos eis debeo pro usuaris," and "quos ab ea accepi ultra sortem pro usuaris."[61] Often, as with the *miles* Blaxius, the beneficiaries of the "ill-gotten sums" remained anonymous both in name and in number. The testator only instructed his executors to dole out sums to those who claimed damages from the moral crimes of profit and commercial life. Again, the fragmentation of their patrimonies and charities was more extreme than a mere counting of the number of itemized bequests would indicate. In the majority of cases (86 of 165 bequests), testators, experiencing qualms about worldly success, in fact, made no attempt to identify, track down, and compensate the injured parties; instead, these pious merchants and shopkeepers, after admitting their guilt, assuaged their consciences spotted by avarice and the normal affairs of late medieval urban life through donations to pious institutions, most often to the nondescript "poor of Christ" or to the poor housed in particular hospitals.[62]

Of those bequests prompted by guilt over commercial activities, the majority (112 bequests) are found in the years 1276–1362, a period that led from political and economic hegemony in southern Tuscany to commercial decline and political disorder.[63] These were years marked by population pressure, waves of famine in the countryside, and the loss of hegemony in international banking and long-distance trade.[64] We might then hypothesize that economic decline induced Senesi to listen more intently to the sermons of mendicant preachers, to question their transient gains, and to look more seriously at matters governing the soul.

Yet the economic determinants of these emotional tensions and decisions can be stretched only so far. First, these negations of lifelong commercial activity reached back to the earliest documents, redacted during the heyday of Siena's economic expansion. They then began to mount in importance and to peak in number during the last quarter of the Duecento, before the tremors of international bankruptcies and before the famines of the early Trecento.[65] Finally, the most disastrous period, at least for merchants and shopkeepers, occurred after the Black Death continuing into the Quattrocento, when Siena fell subject to the regional economic dominance of Florence. But these years of peril, both absolutely and relative to her neighbors, saw the near disappearance of expressions of guilt for sins over commercial success.[66] From the plague of 1363 to the end of the fifteenth century, only fourteen bequests (8.5 percent) restituted sums to individuals for ill-gotten gains or left property to pious beneficiaries to compensate for usury. And, remarkably, testators of foreign city-states redacted more than half of these bequests after 1363.[67] Instead of bearing a close correlation to either economic success or failure, the rise and fall of these clauses fits the more general pattern in the structure and styles of giving. Once again, the plague of 1363 was the watershed.

Pious Places

Prior to 1363 the Sienese made other bequests that understated the fragmentation of the sheer number of itemized charitable gifts. On occasion they gave substantial amounts of money and property, not to specific institutions but rather to all the churches or monasteries within a certain area, such as the city of Siena or even its entire territory. Such a scattering of last resources was counted as a single gift to a single pious entity. Often, the language was even more vague, testators simply stating that their gifts were to go to pious places, *piis locis*. In 1247, Frater ser Aldobrandinus left 200 lire (then equivalent to 200 florins) to *pauperibus et piis locis:* his brother and nephews were to "arbitrate" the distribution of this sizable donation.[68] In 1285 Baldus q. Ildibrandini de Tolomeis for the crimes of usury left 500 lire to be handed out to "paupers, to the religious and religious places, and to the destitute (*pauperibus et religiosis et locis religiosis et miserabilibus personis*)."[69] These singularly itemized gifts were not substantial presents to a particular place or a single institution as our statistics previously assumed. They were not the gifts that future heirs or citizens could possibly connect with the personal contribution of a Frater Aldobrandinus or a Tolomei. Rather, similar to the handouts to the poor, testators on their deathbeds instructed their executors to spread these large sums thinly, over a vast range of undefined pious parties. Unlike the foundation of a hospital or sums for perpetual masses, the vagueness of these gifts suggests that the benefactors were not obsessed with leaving their earthly memory to be imprinted in the minds of the recipients of their pious largess. After 1363, these gifts to unspecified pious places did not vanish from the records altogether, but did decline to less than one-third of what they had been before 1363.[70]

Social Charity

To return to the larger patterns of pious choice (Table 2.1): one of the few changes observed over the long run was the transformation of social charity from handouts to the foundation of dowry funds. The preceding chapter explained this shift demographically. The population slump, wrought by the plague's carnage, provoked a change in attitude among the clergy, the government, and testators toward marriage and procreation. If not in practice, then at least in ideology, the Sienese became pro-populationists in the face of demographic disaster. Now, in the context of the changes in the structure and *style* of giving, this fundamental shift in charity assumes a new significance. Although the demographic context is not to be denied, this change, once again, reflects not only a change in the beneficiaries but also a change in the style and structure of giving. Handouts distributed indiscriminately to the poor, often parceling out large bequests into negligible sums of money, again understate the fragmentation and splintering of gifts registered in our earlier tables. On occasion, the pious specified the maximum that could go to any individual pauper. The sums were tiny. A Mita olim Michelis, wife of Ture Gratie from the parish of Sancti

Quirici Castri Veteris (Siena) donated money in 1322 to "paupers, widows, orphans, the downcast, and other indigent persons and places (*pauperibus viduis orphanis contrattis prohiectis et aliis miserabilibus*)." She stipulated that none should receive more than 2 soldi apiece.[71] Puccius Johannis from Siena (but then living in Urbino) instructed his executors in his testament of 1346 to give for a period of five years 4 pennies a year to each of fifty paupers. In another bequest he allotted to the monks of Santo Spirito 100 lire to be distributed to the poor in sums no greater than 12 pennies. Thus the grant was for fistfuls of denarii to at least 2,000 individuals.[72] Many other testaments of the late Duecento and early Trecento doled out grain and loaves of bread to the poor. As a single itemized gift these could be substantial. On an individual basis, however, they amounted in value to even less than the small handouts of pennies. In one instance, even funeral wax was the commodity of piety. Ruccius olim Ciatti from the village of Casole donated 6 pounds of wax (*bona cerea seu dupplerea de cera bona pulcra et decentia*) to be burnt at the funerals of paupers for as long as his widow lived.[73] How do we begin to estimate the number of beneficiaries of this act of piety?

On the other hand, gifts to poor girls enabling them to marry appeared infrequently in the numerous itemized lists of pious gifts before the Black Death and began to mount in frequency only in the last quarter of the Trecento. In monetary value, the foundation of a dowry may not have amounted to more than the total of those sums previously bequeathed to the *pauperes cristi*. The distribution of these sums, however, differed markedly from the handouts of bread, grain, pennies, clothing, or wax that would go into smoke after the beneficiary had passed away. Instead of dispersing them to hundreds or even thousands of the poor, dowry funds specified a small number of girls, generally to two or three *puellae pauperae*. For the individual legatee, on the other hand, these gifts were substantial; even those funds set up by rich peasants and artisans far outstripped the largest prize a pauper could have expected from a nobleman (usually the *tunica* valued at 30 soldi). For instance, in 1390, Guido olim ser Giorgij Johannis donated for the spiritual health of his predecessors 100 florins in order "to marry four virgins, who were pauper girls." Each girl would receive 25 florins, a dowry which would not have been far beneath the reach of even the self-employed artisan during the late Trecento.[74] Even when doled out by peasants and artisans, the sums rarely dipped below 10 lire; often they came to 10 florins or more—which by 1400 amounted to 800 times more than the usual dole of 12 pennies to the poor of Christ.

In addition to the values of these gifts from the recipient's view, the dowry as a spiritual investment differed from the handouts to crowds of paupers in other respects. It was not a makeshift, one-shot gesture; rather it went to support an ongoing institution, the family. Second, as in the case of Guido's largess of 1390, expectations did not end with the payment of the legacy: each of the lucky girls were required to have five masses said for their souls (*quod pro earum animabus dici fiant .V. misse*). The process of selection, moreover, demanded more from the executors of the estate, the spouse, or the holy ones entrusted with distributing these dowries. Not only did the beneficiaries have to be virgins and *puelle paupere,* testators by the Quattrocento required those selected to be of *buon costumi* (suitable morality); occasionally even the moral character of the girls' parents mattered. By the early modern period, selection became increasingly more intricate. By the end of the seventeenth century, dowry allocations on occasion had the characteristics of a grant application today. A testament of 1690 highlights the difference between the single-line, indiscriminate dole to the nameless poor as opposed to the duties inherent in the selection of dowry legacies. The "patrician of Siena," Bernardino dell'Illustrissimus gia Signore Giulio, a *cavaliere* of the Sacred Order of Santo Stefano, of the Bandinelli family, made the *legato pio* for the love of God and charity of 1,000 scudi (worth 7 lire) to his confraternity of *disciplinati,* the Blessed Virgin Mary under the arches of the hospital of Santa Maria della Scala. From the fruits of this sum, he required the confraternity every year to grant dowries of 8 florins apiece to four girls between the ages of eighteen and twenty-five who lived in the rural district (*corte*) of Contignano and who were of *buona vita, fama e costumi*. Further, "to liberate this confraternity from the tasks of judging the qualities and prerequisites of these girls," he required "those girls who wished to enter the competition (*lo scrutinio*) to submit a note to the parish priest of Contignano at least one month in advance of the selection." From this information, the priest would give the confraternity in Siena "a written page specifying the name of each girl, her father, her surname and her address." He would, in addition, indicate "her precise age," the "quality of her life, her habits, her skills, the extent of her poverty, the number of persons and the quality of her family, and the true state of the household of each candidate (*e lo stato vero della Casa di ciasc'una Pretendente*)." The *Signori confratelli* would thus be "sincerely informed" and each year would be able to elect "with prudence and piety" the four girls "most worthy and deserving of the dotal charity." The election would take place on the Sunday immediately following the festival of San Bernardino of Siena.[75]

Thus the handouts in the long lists of single-line, itemized gifts, which prevailed from the late Duecento through the period of plagues, were strikingly simple in comparison to the bequests from the early Renaissance through the Enlightenment. Before 1363, testators normally parceled out their patrimonies in a myriad of small portions destined for many ecclesiastical corporations and pious causes. Testators most often expected or at least required nothing of their beneficiaries. Aggregately, and again in comparison with the later documents, these testaments leave a scent of death particular to late medieval Siena. Those hard-headed, commercially minded merchants, shopkeepers, and artisans who carried Siena to its commercial apogee, assumed that once interred, usually in unindividuated ditches beneath the *pavimenti* of monasteries, hospitals, or cathedrals, or in the yards of parish churches, matters of the temporal world were both beyond their control and irrelevant to the higher concerns of spiritual eternity. In 1363, the testators of Siena began to think otherwise. Whether with gifts to the poor or by contributions to ecclesiastical institutions, they sought to mold the earthly remains of their patrimonies into few but sizable gifts. The changes in statistics, along with transformations in the styles of giving, chart the shift to another psychology—one where earthly memory of the individual mattered. These sources show that the old Burckhardtian notion of Renaissance individualism may not have been the preserve solely of the rich, the mighty, and the influential of high culture.

4 Souls and Bodies
The Subsoil of Humanism

> *I say 'many' rather than giving you any number, because when the soul is grounded in charity . . . her desire must reach to the infinite.*
> —Catherine of Siena

To further investigate the psychological transformations of the late Trecento, we need now to consider those aspects of the will which form the center of analyses in recent French historiography on last testaments: religious formulas and requests for masses.[1] Since Michel Vovelle's magisterial work, the quantification of masses has become the key statistic for assessing changes in religiosity, the appearance and decline of "Christianity." But this spiritual side of masses governing the soul's journey through the geography of purgatory, heaven, and possibly hell, comprised only half the story. Historians of mentality have overlooked the implications of requests for masses for the terrestrial sphere.[2] The mere absence of masses in pious testaments should not (as the French historiography too readily assumes) be indicative of any lack of "Christianization."[3] The long lists of pious bequests to numerous churches, monasteries, and the "poor of Christ" from the late Duecento and early Trecento portray a piety certainly different from the forms and notions of spirituality that emerge after the plague of 1363. Yet, despite the simplicity of the preambles found in the earlier testaments and the scant attention paid to masses, it would be absurd to conclude that the testators of this earlier mendicant period were any less "Christian" than those of the early Renaissance. Instead, "Christianity," examined from the world of well-to-do peasants, shopkeepers, and petty merchants, changed from late Duecento through the Quattrocento.

Formulas

Testators of the commercial milieu in late medieval Siena did not lack altogether a sense of the intermingling of the temporal and spiritual spheres. They thought that the earthly acts to be performed after their deaths by pious institutions, their *fideicommissarii*, and universal heirs would prove beneficial to their souls in the next. Although the word "purgatory" does not enter these documents until the late sixteenth century, these late Duecento and Trecento men and women nonetheless had a notion of purgatory.[4] Not only did they occasionally request masses to be sung for their souls: the very language that prefaced a large number of their pious acts—*pro remissione suorum peccatorum, pro salute anime*—implied the existence of purgatory. From the earliest documents to 1363, however, these formulas prefaced less than 21 percent of all pious bequests. Afterward, their frequencies more than doubled to 42.4 percent.[5]

In addition, the testamentary preambles changed over time. The earliest testators introduced their lists of itemized bequests laconically. After the date of redaction, the identification of the testator, whether or not the testator lay on his or her deathbed—*sanus per gratiam dei tamen mente et intellectu et corpore* or *licet corpore languens*—the notary of these testaments often embarked immediately onto the matter-of-fact conveyances of property. For instance, the earliest testament found in the *Notarile* began simply, "In nomine Domini amen. Ego Crescebene Garardi de Artio nuncupativum facio testamentum in primis reliquo. . . ."[6] The early documents of the Duecento could be even more direct. The testament of the priest Guido f. q. Bernardi from the village of Villa Nova and rector of the parish of San Giovanni in the *Masse* village of Sant'Eugenio began: "volens fare testamentum. . . ."[7] In others, the rationale for "making the testament" was far removed from matters of the soul and instead lodged firmly in hard-headed considerations of the legal problems of inheritance and property transmission: "volens futuros casus prevenire quia intestatus decedere noluit per nuncupatum testamentum facere ordinavit."[8] In many other instances, the notary simply wrote "volens" or "volo disponere bona mea." As we move into the Trecento, the notaries lengthened these preambles by including clichés such as, "Cum nichil sit certius morte et nil hora mortis reperiatur incertius, idcirco. . . ."[9] Domina Nutina f. Martini, the wife of Vannini ser Palmeri of the parish of San Martino, began with this standard phrase and then continued with another: "ego . . . infirmo corpore, sana tamen mente et intellectu, volens evitare mortis eventum, ne moriar intestata, et facere testamentum et bona et de bonis meis disponere in hunc modum. . . ."[10] Another popular formula of the early fourteenth century ran: "Quoniam hominem cinerea compositione formatum operam mortis subiacere imperio et extreme calamnitatis laborare iacturam . . . timens mortis eventum et volens anime sue providere salute. . . ."[11] These phrases, however, became more common only by the last quarter of the Trecento.

In the preplague testaments, considerations of the soul were not altogether missing from the preambles. As early as 1252, the notary ser Ugolino di Gionta prefaced a testament that adumbrated testament writing in Siena from the Quattrocento through the late eighteenth century: "*In primis quidem pro anima mea, quia dignior esse corpore. . . .*"[12] Then followed his first legacy, 20 soldi to the parish church of San Quirico, which most likely constituted his burial expenses. Later, notaries together with their clients would elaborate on this soul-body split as preambles assumed more space and greater importance. By the late Trecento, after declaring that the soul was the "nobler part," testators invoked the spiritual intercession of the "omnipotent God, the ever Virgin Mary, and the entire celestial court of Saints . . . once the soul had migrated from the present world."[13] By the Quattrocento, testators on occasion specified "particular advocates" and "protectors" beyond their "humble" and "devout" "commendations" to God. The earliest example of an appeal to specific patron saints comes in a testament of 1311 redacted by a master carpenter, Guidarellus f. q. Accursii from the parish of San Egidio. He "commended" his soul to the angelic (*seraffiniis*) apostles Paul and Peter, to the beatific Giles and to the Blessed Dominick.[14] Before the fifteenth century, however, only one other special appeal to a particular saint appears. In the year of the Black Death, a widow from San Gimignano "humbly and devoutly" bequeathed and commended her soul to the omnipotent God, the Blessed and Glorious Virgin Mary and to the *Beato* Francesco. She then elected her grave in the "place" of Franciscan friars at San Gimignano and instructed her heirs to dress her in the habit of the lay sisters (*mantelattarum*) of the friars.[15] The number of these special invocations increased in the Quattrocento, although Siena's own received scant notice in this century: only one invocation for San Bernardino and none at all for Catherine.[16] Instead, lay testators of the Quattrocento looked to the saints of their parish church—to Sant'Andrea in the case of a man who resided in the parish of that saint in Monte Massi, to San Leonardo in the case of a woman from Montichielli.[17] And those settling their obligations over property and to kin before taking monastic vows invoked the intercession of the founding saints of their monasteries.[18] These special appeals to individual protectors did not, however, become common until after the beginning of the Counter-Reformation in Siena. By the seventeenth century, the pious singled out as many as twelve individual saints to intercede for their safe passage to the next world. These testators expressed with far more formulaic elaboration their desires as "faithful and orthodox Christians" to enter the "loving lap of the everlasting paradise." Nonetheless, subtle but distinct changes structured the late medieval and Renaissance testaments. Before 1363 even the mention of the soul in preambles was rare. The notaries introduced testaments with concerns over the soul in only 13 percent of the testaments. Later, when the soul-body split became standard, the soul as the *noblior pars* introduced 65 percent of the testaments from 1363 through 1500 and 84 percent by the beginning of the Quattrocento.

Bodies

The soul-body split reflects the interdependency between the terrestrial and spiritual realms during the early Renaissance. At the very moment when the soul became the first and most noble consideration, testators also began to pay more attention to their bodies. Before 1363, they selected graves in only 70 percent of all testaments; afterward (until the end of the Quattrocento), they "elected" their precise place of burial in 83 percent of the documents. (For both periods, usually the choice was either their parish church or the local monastery.)[19]

Explicit instructions concerning funerals and how the body was to be dressed are almost completely absent from the preplague wills.[20] The widow from San Gimignano who died in 1348 (mentioned earlier) was the only testator before 1363 to give specific instructions on how her body should be presented for the funeral and burial.

After the recurrence of the plague, specific orders regarding the dressing of the body and its appearance become more frequent. In 1396, a Filippo q. Ganij domini Gabrielli of the Piccolomini family "desired to be dressed in a habit of damphanium. In 1410 a domina Beccuccia from the Malavolti family asked to be dressed in the habit of San Domenico. In 1446 domina Magia of the Tolomei family was to be dressed as a lay sister of the order of Saint Francis. In 1473, a widow of a butcher from the parish of San Donato wished to be cloaked in the habit of the sisters of Saint Francis. And in 1488 a certain Sanus Mathei ordered that he be dressed in the clothes (*pannis*) of the Servites.[21]

Not until the Quattrocento did testators try to regulate the mourning of their kin. In 1426 the *sapiens vir* Matheus q. Bartholomei Bertini dictus Matheo Canelle commanded his wife to wear only blue clothes and nothing else after his death; otherwise, he threatened her with disinheritance. In 1457, Marco di Matteo di Marco, a linen manufacturer, ordered that none of his heirs should wear the color brown. By the fifteenth century testators not only specified more frequently their places of burial, but they began to take pains to individuate and to memorialize their corporeal remains.[22] Through inscribed stones and written messages they sought to demarcate in their wills precisely the place within sacred buildings where their bodies were to lie. The earliest examples date only from the later part of the Quattrocento. In 1484, dominus Nicholao Magistrello stipulated: that if no tombstone (*lapis*) was properly placed above his sepulcher during his lifetime, then his heirs ought to make a new one on which was to be written: "Dno Nicholao Magistrello causidico Senensis cive. posteris dedicatum est hoc sepulcrum" (For Lord Nicholas Magistrello, citizen of Siena, whose tomb is dedicated to posterity).[23] In 1486, the *civis Senensis* Matheus Ser Iacobi de Paccinellis desired to be buried in the church of Santa Maria della Grotta with a tombstone (*lapide*) bearing his family coat of arms. In 1499, domina Marna olim Antonii Nicholaii de Nobilibus from the rural suburb of Monasterio, widow of the knight and doctor of law dominus Iacobus Pietri de Tolomeis, specified that "she should be buried under the tombstone (*sub lapide*) of the bishop Siracusanus, the deceased son of the testator, in the place presently called the 'lapis' in the church of Saint Francis and not in the place where the monks (*dictorum clamidatorum*) of this order lie.[24]

Tombstones were not the only means of individuating the corporeal remains of testators. Altars and family chapels, as any tourist to Tuscany knows, date back before the period of the Black Death. Art historians, however, rarely evaluate artistic production quantitatively. We will show in chapter 6 that the appearance and commissioning of chapels to house the testator's bones and those of his or her lineage increased significantly during the late fifteenth century, penetrating for the first time classes beneath the nobility and the merchant elites. These changes, we will argue, were indeed related to changes in the strategies for the afterlife.

Masses

To return to the question of masses for the soul: until 1276, specific instructions to individuals or religious corporations to sing masses are almost completely missing from the testaments. Out of 270 pious bequests only 1 required masses. Ventura olim Dietaiuti from the village of Serre (di Rapolano) gave in 1269 a piece of land with a hut to his parish priest, Jacob. The rural testator stipulated "for the health of his soul" that the priest ought to give annually 100 soldi (presumably for pious causes). Of this sum, 20 were to go to the altar of San Lorenzo—5 for masses, 5 for burial expenses, 5 for candles, and 5 for the altar of San Angelo in the curia of Serre.[25]

During the last quarter of the Duecento, masses became more usual: 11.8 percent (47 of 398) pious bequests went for masses for testators' souls. (See Table 4.1.) The proportion remained roughly the same over the next twenty-five years (11.6 percent, 50 of 614). Then, in the years preceding the Black Death, 1326–47, the numbers peaked to 16.9 percent of all pious acts (67 of 628). After falling during the summer months of 1348 to 11.7 percent (55 of 366), they rebounded to 16.7 percent for the interplague years (42 of 251). When pestilence struck again in 1363 this rate plummeted to its lowest point since the late thir-

Table 4.1. Value of Masses, 1276–1500

Period	Bequests with Testators	Masses	Average Value of Bequests with Masses	% of the Value of Masses/ All Pious Bequests
1276–1300	44	47	3.69	2.21
1301–25	50	71	1.15	4.02
1326–47	67	106	1.59	1.89
1348	55	43	1.77	2.52
1349–62	40	42	2.44	5.65
1363	24	4	4.90	1.87
1364–75	25	16	2.10	3.29
1376–1400	61	23	2.80	0.82
1401–25	45	26	3.13	1.70
1426–50	56	21	12.60	10.52
1451–75	59	30	12.50	29.91
1476–1500	99	67	13.10	17.61

teenth century (5.2 percent, 4 of 77). The sharp downturn, however, was only momentary. For the remainder of the Trecento and the first half of the Quattrocento, the percentage returned to the higher levels of the Trecento, though not surpassing the 1326–47 peak.[26] In the second half of the Quattrocento a lasting change, however, did occur. For 1451–75 the rate almost doubled: testators demanded masses for their souls in nearly a quarter of their pious bequests (23.3 percent, 30 of 129). In 1476–1500 the rate climbed still higher, to 38.1 percent (67 of 176), approximately double the peaks set before preplague rates.[27]

The monetary sums that testators spent on masses traces a similar trend. These figures, however, show a more considerable gulf between the simple and direct expenditures on piety in the late Duecento and early Trecento, on the one hand, and those gifts which demanded a spiritual return during the second half of the Quattrocento (see Table 4.1). Before the Black Death the amount spent on masses as a percentage of all pious expenditures was low; it ranged from 2 percent to 4 percent. In the interval immediately following the Black Death of 1348, this proportion peaked to 5.7 percent. In 1363, similar to the crude numbers of itemized masses, the percentage costs sank to the lowest level since the Duecento. It remained below the levels of the first half of the Trecento until 1426–50. Then, twenty-five years before the significant shift registered by the number of itemized masses, the amount contributed to the celebration of masses (10.5 percent of all pious expenditures) more than doubled that of any period before the Black Death, and in the next quarter nearly one-third (29.9 percent) of pious spending demanded masses in return. Unlike other transformations in the structure and style of pious giving, 1363 failed to mark the critical moment of change for masses. In fact, for that year, the demand for masses reversed itself, falling back to the levels of the Duecento. Here, changes in the different parts of the testaments do not neatly mesh. While the notaries and their clients turned increasingly to the soul in the prefaces, the testators, at least momentarily, requested fewer masses to help ensure the future health of their souls.

Certainly no holistic change in consciousness occurred with the year 1363. Stitches in the new fabric of piety became interlaced later. By the second half of the Quattrocento, testators normally demanded something in return for their piety as they attached conditions to their good wishes. These early Renaissance testators were more confident than their ancestors had been in acts and institutions grounded in the temporal world for later assistance "on the other side of death." Previously, the simple and direct legacies with no conditions and no masses suggest that testators firmly believed what Petrarch preached before the second occurrence of plague in Milan (1361): to prepare for death the best that could be done was to strip away the "mortal garment and the fetters of this gloomy dwelling."[28]

The frequencies observed here, however, might understate the changes of the early Quattrocento. Before the late Trecento, testators occasionally accompanied their long lists of pious bequests with requests for masses. Their instruc-

Figure 3. Detail from Lorenzo Vecchietta's *Last Judgment—The Good Death*, painted between 1444 and 1471 in the old sacristy, Santa Maria della Scala

tions, however, were vague, without any attention to the kinds of masses, the number, and when and by whom they were to be performed. Following the perfunctory itemization of the property and the beneficiary, these testators simply added *pro missis et officiis*. For instance, in the 1313 testament of ser Silvius q. Allegretti from the *contado* of Florence, this phraseology followed the itemization of twenty separate pious bequests. In none did the notary specify the number of masses, the time period, the days on which they should be performed, or by what date they should have been executed. The inclusion of requests for masses, moreover, does not seem to have affected in the least the size of the donation. Whether the notary included the phrase *pro missis* or not, the bequests in Silvius's will distributed sums that were of small values: 10 soldi to the *plebis* San Leonino in the village of Rencine for masses and offices; 5 to the church of San Lorenzo in the village of Treude for masses and offices; and 5 to the priest of that church for masses and offices.[29] These were among the smallest donations found in this testament. The rural notary conveyed the same sums to churches, priests, hospitals, and other religious institutions without including the phrase *pro missis et officiis*. Of course, one might speculate that testators and notaries of the late Duecento and early Trecento who did not explicitly request masses simply could assume that their beneficiaries would say them just the same. Even if this were the case, our point would be the same: testators of the late Duecento and early Trecento sought to spread their sums over as many pious beneficiaries as possible. They did not pause to orchestrate precise instructions to their beneficiaries or to heap conditions on them. Their laconic requests suggest that once they had passed from the earthly realm, attempts to determine the futures of their souls through elaborate legal and temporal mechanisms would have been senseless. An almost unbridgeable gulf stretched between "this gloomy dwelling" and the next life, the higher spiritual existence of the soul.

By the late Trecento, the two realms of existence began to come closer together. Before the plague of 1363, less than 11 percent (34 of 310) of those bequests requiring masses specified the number of masses to be sung. These numbers ranged from 1 mass or office (the modal number, in fact) to 1,000.[30] From 1363 to 1500, testators specified the precise number in nearly half of their bequests for masses (86 of 183). Again, the specification of a single mass was the mode; the 30-mass office did not become the standard until after the Council of Trent. But the bonds between the spiritual and temporal had tightened. Testators of the Quattrocento were not content (as their preplague ancestors had been) to disperse their patrimonies to a myriad of ecclesiastical corporations and pious causes with nothing in return. As with their preoccupations with their corporeal remains, death did not terminate these testators' concern with the earthly realm. Increasingly, they tried to manipulate temporal affairs from the grave.

Time

Testators after 1363 became more rigorous in stipulating when their masses should occur (every day, week, month, or year or its duration, from a year to in perpetuity). Before 1363, they made such specifications in only 9 percent of the wills (29 of 310); later the rate rose two-and-a-half times to 23 percent (42 of 183).[31] A more precise and finite sense of time, moreover, structured the beneficiaries' obligations during the late fourteenth and fifteenth centuries. Before 1363, testators in only three instances (or less than 1 percent of all requested masses) specified the time or duration during which their heirs, spouses, or beneficiaries were to celebrate the commemorative masses. In 1305 a testator from Casole ordered the executors to have masses sung on the seventh and thirtieth days after his burial and on the anniversary of his death. In 1325 a villager from Radicondoli required a similar formulaic timing for the benefit of his soul: the day of burial and the seventh and thirtieth days after his death. In a testament of 1334, the formulaic timing reappears. Before 1363, the testaments rarely ventured into the future between the day of burial and perpetuity (masses to be sung *in perpetuum*). And in the three cases when they did, liturgical formulas ruled these forays. Instead, artisans and merchants of the early Trecento, for whom daily calculations of commerce filled their working lives, found, like Saint Catherine, "number" (see epigraph) to be absurd when confronting the mysterious and infinite void of the afterlife.

After 1363, the frequency of these specifications of precise time after death increased to 20 percent of all masses (a 2,000 percent increase over the pre-1363 period). Furthermore, none of these stipulations for specific and finite time periods were set by the formula—the seventh, the thirtieth, and the anniversary day of the testator's death. Instead, these requests varied without formulaic routine from eight days following the burial to twenty years.[32] In each of these cases, the testator bequeathed a specific amount of money or property for a specific number of masses to be said on a certain day of the year, often his or her death day, for the spiritual health of his or her soul. For instance, in 1383, a man from the curia of Poggibonsi, Muccius olim Ghuccij Mucij, donated the income from a piece of wooded plough land to his parish church of Saint Peter for a period of ten years. Although the parish priest of Saint Peter's was allowed to use the land as he saw fit, Muccius's universal heirs (his son and those sons to be born) were to scrutinize the priest's obligations. They were to see that the church performed the ten offices for their father's soul and the souls of their ancestors during these ten years.[33] Of those masses stipulated over finite periods most were ordered to be sung annually. In one case, however, a testator donated 4 soldi per mass to be said every month over a ten-year period.[34]

Stipulations for masses are not the only juncture where the Sienese in the years following the plague of 1363 show a new preoccupation with specific timing after their departure from the temporal sphere. Before 1363 testators regularly donated the usufructus of property, especially in bequests husbands made to their wives. Upon the death of the beneficiary, the property then would revert to another party, usually a pious institution or the universal heirs. Yet before the second coming of pestilence not a single testator specified precisely the period of time the first beneficiary was to enjoy the fruits of the property or to obey certain conditions in temporal "space." At least by the middle of the Quattrocento, a new sense of temporality after death had emerged in the minds of testators ranging from noblemen to the widows of tanners.

In 1444 a member of the Salimbene family, for the souls of his father, his mother, and his ancestors (*di miei morti*), gave the minor friars 3 staii of grain a year "for the space of eight years (*per lo spazio di viii anni*)."[35] A testator from the village of Batignano, in 1449, ordered his heirs to dole out annually to a neighbor for four years 8 florins "in grain, wine, linen, or other things" computed according to "a just price in the opinion of his heir."[36] In 1453, Caterina, the widow of a tanner from the parish of San Martino, gave to the cloth dealer Simone di Piero di Mano di Paulo the use of her house in San Martino "for the space of four years" beginning with the day of her death. At the end of this period her heirs were then ordered to sell the house to Simone for 95 florins. The testator gave Simone at that future date the option of buying either the entire house or, if he wished, only half of it; in the latter case, the other half was to be given to Contessa f. q. domini Conti Costantinis, but only after she had married and the period of Simone's usufruct had expired. Should she die without marrying, then Simone along with another of the testator's heirs, her daughter donna Gaccia, were to sell this other half of the house and to distribute the money "as they best saw fit" for "the love of God" and the health of Caterina's soul. Of these potential sums, 5 florins were to be spent on an office celebrated in the church of San Domenico for the testator's soul.[37]

By the fifteenth century wills became more complex as testators tried to determine the flow of their properties and the course of future temporal events after their deaths. With complex contingency plans, they sought to dictate events in that previously uncharted geography of time between the day of death and earthly perpetuity. By the latter half of the Quattrocento instructions passed increasingly from the ultimate purposes of the soul to the temporal, material affairs of heirs and of property. In 1470 a notary, ser Laurentius olim Juste, insisted that his sons remain together in a clothing business ("teneantur in comunionem et societatem artis pannilini") for twenty-five years starting on the day of his death. Giovanni di Antonio del Bianco called Giovanni Ruggina from the Chianti town of Castelnuovo Berardenga, commanded his sons and heirs in 1478 to give 40 lire to another son, three-year-old Pasquino, not designated as a universal heir: they were to pay a first installment of 20 lire one year after the death of their father and the other half in the following year. In 1479, Petrus Johannis Galduccii de Bonis gave the couple Cristofanus Johannis Mei and donna Pia from Grosseto a house in the parish of San Cristofano (Siena) on condition that "four years in the future" they ought to dower four nubile girls at 10 florins apiece. In three years' time, moreover, they were to spend 10 florins to buy an altar cloth (*dananzale*) to be placed on the altar of the confraternity San Ansano housed in the parish church of San Vigilio. Finally, in 1484, domina Bartholomea f. olim Laurentij of the Renaldini family, the widow of a spice merchant and later the widow of a saddle maker, designated her grandson Bartholommeus as her universal heir, requiring him, however, "to raise, govern and feed" his brother Lodovico in his own household until Lodovico became twenty years old.[38]

The French historian Jean Delumeau has recently argued: "Since the fourteenth century, plagues, famines, revolts, the advance of the Turks added their traumatic effects to a Christian culture which felt itself under siege.[39] Largely from the texts of Italian preachers (Angelo da Foligno, Bernardino da Feltre, Bernardino of Siena, Antoninus of Florence, and Fra Girolamo Savonarola) and from proclamations of church councils (such as the Fifth Lateran held in Florence in the mid-fifteenth century), Delumeau maintains that the optimism of the Renaissance cut a thin veneer indeed. More fundamental to the age was a deepening sense of pessimism and of the "fragility" of the world.[40] Prophecies of doom and despair, the coming of the Apocalypse and of the Antichrist, multiplied throughout the Italian peninsula.[41] The Augustinian theme of the "vieillesse du monde . . . connut un regain d'actualité entre le XVe et le XVIIe siècle." "Le sentiment de la fin du monde était alors dans l'esprit de tous."[42]

The testaments of unillustrious noblemen, artisans, and ordinary villagers, however, saw the future differently. Before 1363 scarcely any of these testators plotted specific rituals or calculated changes in property relations at specific moments in the future once they had passed to "the other side of death." Other than the rare formulaic command to celebrate masses at their burial and on the seventh, the thirtieth, and the anniversary days of their death, testators of the Duecento and the first half of the Trecento refrained from venturing into finite, temporal "space" after death. Whereas, after 1363 and increasingly during the Quattrocento, testators invested far more of the notary's time in attempting to manipulate future temporalities once they had passed to the *noblior* existence. Far from a sense of heightened despair and the belief in the imminent destruction of the world, these testaments assumed a certain confidence in the continuation of time in the everyday affairs of their churches and their families. Increasingly, they punctuated the future, whether for spiritual or secular obligations, with precise instructions to be followed at precise moments of time— within eight years, for "a space" of six years, or when a nephew reached his twentieth birthday.

Property

Masses and pious bequests are not the only sources to attest the growing consciousness and concern with temporal matters by those on their deathbeds. As has been shown, the earliest testaments through the Trecento instructed the executors of the estate to sell off significant portions of patrimonies to finance the distribution of numerous small monetary gifts, both pious and nonpious, to multifarious beneficiaries. Testators gave regularly and formulaically to their executors or heirs "full license and authority to sell and alienate" all the properties of the estate, both movables and nonmovables. Before 1363 only three testators restricted the heirs' use over the residual properties of the estate. The earliest comes in 1285: Romeus q. Gherardi from the parish of San Donato designated his nephew Riccius Boncompagni as his heir under the conditions that he "could not sell, give or alienate any right or in any way the immovables" of the estate. If his heir "sold, mortgaged (*pignorationem faceret*), donated, or alienated" these properties, his claims as universal heir would no longer be valid. The testator added further a second condition that domina Tommasa, the wife of Riccius, "had no rights to acquire or possess any of these properties."[43] In 1290 Ugolinus olim Bonaventura from the parish of San Vincenti ordered that his heirs "could in no way sell or alienate" a farm (*podere*) with a house, vineyards, and other possessions located in the village of Sciano; these real properties should always remain in the same place. Finally, a man from the Montagnola village of Strove in a codicil of 1300 forbade his daughter and grandchildren from alienating, renting, or exchanging the residual properties of the will without the permission of a Biago di Corso di Mazzocchio.[44]

Then, from 1300, despite the steady increase in the survival of wills as well as an increase in the representation in our samples of testators from the old, noble lineages of Siena, not a single instance of a property restriction placed on heirs occurs again until 1373. This complete absence of property restrictions was concomitant with the rise in the number of bequests per testator and the fragmentation of estates into a multitude of tiny gifts. Indeed, we might speculate that these examples of clauses restricting the future alienation of the estate derived from the premendicant feudal past and by the time of the outset of these documents had already become archaic.[45] In the second half of the fourteenth century and continuing through the fifteenth, however, a reversal ensued: testamentary clauses aimed at controlling the fate of terrestrial gains surfaced once again. In 1373 the merchant-citizen (*mercator civis Senis*) Tennduccius q. Luce prohibited his sons from alienating the real properties of his estate. In 1390 the notary ser Sozzus of San Pietro d'Ovile prevented his son Nicholaus from alienating the properties of his estate without the permission of his *fideicommissari*. In 1426 the pork-butcher Corsinus olim Ambrosij prohibited on pain of disinheritance his daughter, the wife of a wool shearer, and his grandson from alienating or leasing out any of the residual properties of the estate so long as the testator's son was alive. If they disobeyed, the inheritance would pass to his confraternity, the *disciplinati* of San Niccoló and San Luca.[46]

In a testament of 1446, contingencies over the future flow of real property became more complex. The "vir providens" Antonius from the town of Montalcino named Santa Maria della Scala as his heir, provided that the hospital's friars, Francesco, Marianus, and Felice, might not touch ("maneggiare, alienare neque dispensare") any of his goods. He also prohibited the hospital (for reasons left unexplained) from alienating any of his properties involved in a legal suit against a certain Lodovico.[47] Cecchius f. q. Pietri Guccii left his brother Marianus as his heir in 1467 on condition that he not alienate or sell any *bona immobilia*, or else the estate would pass to two men who do not appear as his kinsmen: Niccolai Cionis and Leonardus Andree Tolomeis. The testator stipulated further that "if his brother should manage his business affairs poorly or not behave himself (*male se gerat in negociis et non bene se gubernet*)," then one Marianus Mei and the just-mentioned Leonardus should assume the "care and management" of the testator's farm together with its rural cottages and dovecotes; they would then dole out 30 staii or grain, 12 staii of wine, and a half-staio of oil annually to Marianus, plus 12 staii of grain and a half-staio of oil to Marianus's servant Catherina. Should Leonardus decline to assume these responsibilities, then Catherina should take his place as heir.[48] In 1478 Pierfrancischus olim Filippi Pieri de Ubertinis made Manus Johannis Bactiste of the Piccolomini family his heir on condition that he not sell or alienate any of the landed properties after the dowry and bride's gift of the testator's widow had been paid back.[49] In the following year, Pietrus Johannis Galduccii de Bonis left the brothers and monastery of Saint Benedict of the order of Monte Oliveto, located in the Masse of Siena just beyond the Porta Tufi, as the heirs to his estate, with the proviso that these friars and the monastery never alienate or sell his possessions in the suburban village of San Maffei. To protect the future of his patrimony from possible lawsuits or indebtedness on the part of the monks, the pious testator declared that these landed properties "should remain free and exempt from all other burdens" which might later fall on the inheritance. On the other hand, the monks might dispose freely (*ad libertum*) of the movable properties. For these gifts, the testator, however, required something in return, this time during his own lifetime: "the use of a prayer book and a monk's cowl (*usum unum breviarium et unum monachinum*)."[50] Finally, in 1482 a testator from the village of Santa Colomba on the slopes of the Montagnola imposed on his daughter and granddaughter conditions similar to *rétrait lignager*: to alienate the testator's house they had to obtain the consent of three of the testator's nearest blood relatives. If they violated this condition, the inheritance would descend to these nearest kinsmen.[51]

During the sixteenth century, as we will see shortly, the frequency of these clauses preventing heirs from alienating properties exploded in number. And their complexities took on new dimensions. But the examples from the late Trecento and Quattrocento evince the beginnings of a new outlook whereby testators sought to direct and control future temporal events—the behavior of heirs, the fates of their real properties—from the grave through the legal instrument of the testament. These examples contrast starkly with the complete absence of conditions and restrictions placed on the transmission of landed property even by the patriciate from the beginning of the fourteenth century until 1373. These Sienese instead did the opposite; they not only gave their executors "complete license and authority" to alienate and sell off estates as they saw fit, the principal obligation of the *fideicommissarius* was to liquidate estates to convert landed property and personal possessions into money to facilitate the parceling out of a myriad of tiny gifts to various pious causes as well as to relatives and friends. These pragmatic merchants, shopkeepers, artisans, and peasants from the glorious days following Montaperti were not obsessed with preserving the inalienable status of a piece of landed property, an estate, or an entire inheritance. Their preparations for the migration of their souls demanded just the opposite, the fragmentation and obliteration of these lifelong accumulations and material attachments.

As with the literary and artistic subjects from Alberto Tenenti's *Il Senso della morte*, ordinary citizens and villagers of Siena suddenly "reached out to affirm irrevocably their love of life and the essential value of terrestrial existence."[52] Previously, the principal task of a testator's executors had been to sell off the estate's properties and to convert these tangible goods with lifelong, even generational remembrances, into the abstractions of fungible money to be then sprinkled, often indiscriminately, across a wide range of pious and nonpious recipients. (In the late Duecento and early Trecento 86 percent of pious bequests were gifts in coin; by the last quarter of the Trecento the percentage had fallen to nearly half of all pious gifts.) The plague of 1363 separated two distinct strategies for the afterlife congruent with two conceptions of the self. What relation do these data from the last moments of ordinary lives bear to the loftier notions usually associated with the Renaissance? The next chapter will leave the wills to visit the literary remains of high culture.

❧ 5   High Culture

> *In hungry desire for my honor and the salvation of souls let her attend to those interior virtues which give proof that her will is dead and her sensuality is continually being slain by the affection of love for virtue.*
> —Catherine of Siena

Literary documents—letters, *exempla*, saints' lives, and humanist texts—might provide a key to interpret further changes in the intellectual makeup of ordinary citizens and villagers. In jumping to this loftier realm in the history of ideas, let us be explicit from the outset. The texts of Giovanni Colombini, Saint Catherine, Petrarch, and Pope Pius II will *not* be used to corroborate our statistical and qualitative findings. These must stand or fall by their own statistical tests, their power of example, and their fit into overarching arguments. There is no reason to presume that the materials drawn from literary culture should faithfully "reflect" general culture. Instead, these texts might supply a mental framework to probe further the mysteries still embedded in the laconic texts of last wills, as well as in our tabular reductions of them. What motivated artisans, shopkeepers, and petty merchants in the very period of Siena's commercial apogee to terminate their lives of commercial accumulation, to repent for "ill-gotten gains," and to fragment their earthly holdings, scattering them to numerous pious causes?

Colombini and Catherine

On a less saintly plane, ordinary citizens of Siena followed in their final decisions over property the models of Saint Francis or, closer to home in time and place, the Blessed Saint Francis of Siena (1266–1310) and, later, Blessed Giovanni Colombini (1305–67). Colombini, like Francis, came from a well-to-do merchant family. But, unlike Francis, he waited until he was fifty-one, after a successful career in international commerce, before turning his back on family and all worldly possessions to sing the praises of Jesus, *andando impazzendo per Cristo*. Just after the fall of the government of the Nine (of which he had been a member) and the death of his son, Giovanni convinced his rich and respectable friend, Francesco Vincenti, to follow his "example of humility, self-mortification, self-contempt." "Bare-headed, dressed in patches" they begged for "stale crusts of bread," performed the most menial jobs without compensation, and "took sneers and derision with joy.[1] Others followed their example, forming a small *brigata* of *poverelli* called the Jesuati who traveled through the countryside, camping along roadsides between Monte San Savino and Viterbo. Like their Franciscan prototypes of the previous century, the Jesuati preached the life of poverty, strenuously repudiating self-interest and worldly love of property and family.[2]

Colombini's thoughts and preaching have been preserved in a collection of letters which he wrote to the abbess and nuns of Santa Bunda, located just beyond the city walls of Siena. His words give texture to what successful merchants, shopkeepers, artisans and peasants etched collectively in their wills, if not during their lives of quotidian commerce, then at the very last moment, while they contemplated their futures in the afterlife. Colombini's rhetoric was raw and ecstatic:

> Well, the soul hates the self for the love of its sweet Jesus, and will thus desire to suffer forever pain for its love . . . and will go on searching for everything it believes might please its sweet groom.[3]

> In giving Christ to the soul you must refute and despise temporal things. And you must even despise your own relatives. And you should love more a soul in love with God, a mere stranger, than a thousand fashionable relatives, none of whom would be worth as much as that friend in Christ. (59)

> Give yourselves and find Christ above all things, and scorn what everybody loves—the world. (104)

> Despise temporal things, leaving the world to its followers, since we seek the high and mighty concerns of the heavens and all virtue. (116)

> . . . always speak of Christ and never of this world . . . drowning in charity, so that the soul becomes one with its delectable groom. (160–61)

> Most sweet servants of Jesus Christ, how can we not see that nothing could be so delectable as Christ crucified, such that anything else is disgusting, bitter, fetid, and full of stench. (164)

Nor was charity or the rehabilitation of society the principal objective of this holy man's renunciations:

> Strip yourselves of these vile delights and titles . . . if you want to possess God in your souls, give away those things to those who might need them, and what is better, if you should not be able [to find such people], just throw them away, and only want and desire God. (3–4)

Instead, Colombini, as well as many other "blessed ones" of the early Trecento, damned the temporal sphere as being beyond reform and beneath salvation.[4]

Saint Catherine of Siena, with a more graceful and poetic verve, stressed the same—renunciation of self, family, and worldly concerns.[5] Worldly goods encumbered the Christian's mission for oneness with God. According to Catherine those accouterments of temporal life were not even ours in the first place, but were merely "given on loan" for which mortals enjoyed only the *usufructus*. Catherine's mysticism revolved around her concept of self-knowledge, which was in fact the opposite of what it might imply to modern (or even Renaissance) ears. One of her earliest letters (1373 or 1374) addressed her eldest brother: "Then we have his [Christ's] cry of joy: 'Consumatum est' which may sound like a cry of anguish, but was in fact one of joy from the incarnate Word, God's son, utterly consumed in the fire of divine Charity."[6] She continued:

> . . . the generosity which tore open his body so that he might bathe and baptize us in his Blood . . . swallows up every injury . . . and we receive the fullness of grace, which leads us along the right way; it cannot but want to destroy and drown entirely its own perverse sense-appetite—always a rebel against the soul itself and its Creator—and, forgetful of self, be on fire with love for the honor of God and the salvation of souls. Like a man in love, it will have no time for thought of self, but will be totally absorbed in the object of its love. (63)

A letter to Fra Bartolommeo Dominici (1375) begins:

> I, Catherine, servant and slave of the servants of Jesus Christ, write to strengthen you in the precious blood of the son of God, desiring to see you wholly consumed in the fire of his charity, for I know that this burns up all thought of self. And this I want for you. By means of this burning charity, I invite you to enter into a calm deep sea. (67–68)

She waxed further on self-annihilation to her confessor and later hagiographer, Raymond of Capua: "My soul longs to see your hearts and affections so grafted into the incarnate Word, sweet Jesus, that no devil or creature can ever part you from him. . . . The soul then becomes one with its neighbors too, and the more wood of self-knowledge it puts on the fire, the hotter burns its love for Christ and its neighbor" (114).

Catherine's writings are replete with scorn for earthly pleasures and honors: "O inestimable and sweetest Charity, which is your way, the one you choose with so much love? Not, I see, the way of honour, luxury and human glory; nor of self-love, for charity seeks not self but God's honour and the salvation of creatures."[7] In a letter to Pope Gregory XI (1376) she preached the mendicant virtues of poverty and the contempt for worldly matters:

> Alas, what a spectacle! To see the very men who should be mirrors of voluntary poverty, humble lambs distributing the church's wealth to the poor, more involved in

the empty pleasures, pomp and power of the world than if they belonged to it a thousand times over. (107)

In this way you will come, and then you will see the holy Church reformed through the appointment of good pastors; you will restore to her the colour of glowing charity she has lost—so much blood has been sucked out of her by wicked gluttons that she has gone pale all over. (109)

In 1376, she attacked the military tribunal of Florence, the Otto di Guerre, which was then engaged in war against the church: "You seem to me to be losing every other good thing along with your conscience; to care only about sensual transitory things which come and go like the wind, while we fail to see that we are mortal and must die, we know not when!" (126).

From denial of self to the transitory character of earthly matters, Catherine, like Colombini, railed against affections for family as yet another form of self-love. Trying to dissuade the notary ser Cristofano from marrying (in a letter cited earlier), Catherine went from a rebuke of matrimony to a wholesale condemnation of familial ties with the words of Matthew 10:37. "Whoever does not abandon mother and father and sisters and brothers and himself is not worthy of me" (81). In an early reformist letter to the papal nuncio in Italy (1375), Catherine attacked Pope Gregory XI: "There are two things in particular defying the bride of Christ. . . . One is too much attachment to and concern about one's own relatives, a thing that especially needs to be mortified once and for all" (86). A year later she expressed the inextricable tangle of self-love, loyalty to blood relations, and concerns for earthly pomp and pleasure in a letter to the pope: "I desire to see you a real man, fearless and making no concessions to self-love, whether for yourself or for any of your blood relations. Justice you can mete out; peace you can have, if you disentangle it from perverse pomp and worldly luxury and retain only God's honour" (123).

Catherine's scorn for familial relations was not confined to the worldly and familial affections of clerics. In 1376, she advised one of her followers, monna Giovanna of Siena,

I want you to strip off all earthly love you may have for yourself, your children, or any created thing outside God. . . . No one can serve both God and the world as they are incompatible. The world seeks honour, status, wealth, good positions for their children, noble birth, sensual pleasure and delight—all of which are grounded in perverse pride. God, however, seeks and wants quite the opposite. He wants voluntary poverty, humility of heart, contempt of self and of all worldly pleasure and delight. (132)

Catherine went on to attack maternal attachment:

In other words, you must not love them because of any useful purpose they may serve, or as if they belonged to you, but only as something on loan—for everything we have been given in this life has been given to us on loan for our use, and is left with us only for as long as it shall please the divine Goodness who gave it to us. So you must use all things as though dispensing them on the behalf of Christ crucified: whether it be material wealth—in so far as you have a say in its distribution to the poor who stand in the place of God—or the care of your own children, whom you must always feed and bring up in the fear of God, preferring that they should die rather than offend their Creator. (133)

Throughout Catherine's letters the terminology of family relations resounded incessantly—"the bride of Christ," "the wedding feast of eternal life," "daughter in Christ Jesus," "dearest mother in Christ."[8] Catherine constituted and juxtaposed her own spiritual "family" of followers as a new and holy surrogate family in opposition to biological ones and blood affections. In ending her letter to monna Giovanna, the Sienese saint highlighted the two competing notions of family by placing her own claims of spiritual progeny over Giovanna's motherhood: "Please convey my greetings to Corrado and bless the rest of the family for me, especially my new seedling who has just been planted out again in the garden of the holy Church" (135). That "new seedling" happened to be Giovanna's son Stefano.[9]

Catherine's younger contemporary, Fra Filippo degli Agazzari, had no sympathy for the *grande usurario* who was willing to risk hell for himself so that his children would not starve. The religious wise man of Agazzari's moral *exemplum* damned the usuror, not just because of his commercial practices but even more because of *tanto amore* for his children:

And the foolish and bestial love which you have for your children will always come back to haunt and torment you, and their evil lives, which you have made possible, will multiply your penalties in hell by their penalties in hell, where together one against the other you will have so much hate and iniquity for one another that like rabid dogs you will forever gnaw and devour one another.[10]

Now to translate the literary scraps back to the mundane existence of commercial life and testamentary statistics: Mendicant culture, most eloquently expressed in the mysticism of the late Trecento tertiary, Catherine, had effectively penetrated Sienese society from the late thirteenth century through the first sixty years of the fourteenth century. In preparation for death and salvation, testators in Siena earnestly believed (if not during their lives, at least when the hour of death was upon them) that their worldly goods were no longer advantageous but an encumbrance to entering the "calm deep sea." Unlike the earlier feudal wills and those redacted after the second coming of pestilence, the Sienese of the late Duecento and early Trecento strove in their testaments to accomplish what former merchant *beati* such as Giovanni Colombini, Francis of Siena, and Gioacchino of Siena (1258–1306) had done during their lifetimes: "to strip" themselves of "vile delights and honors." From the late Duecento through the first two-thirds of the Trecento, the Sienese liquidated their worldly remains and changed them into thousands of bequests that left few strings attached and put little hope in the transitory world of everyday temporality.

From peasants to merchant-magnates, the testators internalized notions of charity preached by Colombini, Catherine, and several generations of mendicant preachers who unfortunately have left us no published works.[11] Their minute sums scattered over a wide array of holy institutions testify to Catherine's dictum: "charity seeks not self but God's honour." This pattern of giving negated any cult of remembrance and witnessed the very opposite. The Sienese sought to break what Catherine called the "earthly cell" to obtain "self-knowledge," that is, the annihilation of all thought of self. Their numerous vague and indiscriminate allocations to the *pauperes cristi* or simply to *locii pii* may not have been inspired so much by the suffering or needs of the poor or by any attempt at lasting rehabilitation as by the spiritual demands to cast off their worldly skins; in Colombini's words, "just to throw them away." The testators from the mundane world of shops and drawing rooms strove after Catherine's notion of charity and not our own. It was not a charity for improvement "but," to repeat Catherine's words, "for God's honour and the salvation of creatures."

Moreover, the sentiments of these saints toward family—in Colombini's words, to "despise your own relatives"—may strike us today as cold. Another blessed one from southern Tuscany, Agnes of Montepulciano, after nine years abandoned her children to join the Franciscan tertiaries in Cortona and expressed no emotions when told that her son had drowned himself in a well at Arezzo.[12] But not all contemporaries were so accepting of the "Puritanism" espoused by these blessed ones and mendicant preachers. The poet of Siena and contemporary of Dante, Cecco Angiolieri, railed against the hypocrisy and self-righteousness of his parents who rigidly observed fasts, sang psalms, and recited offices, but who had little regard for the well-being of their son. Cecco gives us the side of family relations not exposed by Catherine's obliging monna Giovanna. He longed for the day when his father died, and afterward squabbled continually with his mother over the rights of inheritance. To them, he has left us his embittered response:

> if I were death I would go to my father;
> if I were life I would flee from him;
> Similarly I would do for my mother.[13]

The use of these literary sources to ferret out meaning from our statistical series, nonetheless, might be faulted on two counts. First, the asceticism of Giovanni Colombini and Catherine was nothing new, not only to the era of mendicant culture of the late Duecento and early Trecento but even in the wider context of Christian thought.[14] It was well formulated in the Bible and by the church fathers. Moreover, the ascetic ideal and the distrust for the transitory character of the temporal existence persisted in Christian theologies through the modern period. Second, the critical reader may have noticed that Colombini preached at the very end of that period, which through the aggregation of last wills we have earmarked as the period of mendicant culture. More damaging,

Catherine's letters all date from the 1370s, slightly after the critical moment in our analysis, the recurrence of pestilence in 1363. Both considerations require a closer look at the chronologies of religious movements and changes in religious thought.

Flagellants and *Beati*

In considering cultural and religious ideals, the historian must distinguish between the background continuity of certain ideologies and when they take new shape or come more prominently to the foreground. Mendicant culture came to the foreground in the religious and cultural life of the late thirteenth century. Its ecstatic joy in embracing penitence and asceticism—its enraptured denial of self, family, and worldly cares—differed from the more sober and aristocratic religious ideals of the early commune. Yet, these mendicant ideals found their most eloquent expressions in Siena at the very time when another pattern of religion and cultural was forming.

To begin, let us glance at the earlier limits of this intellectual chronology. The mendicant preachers from the time of Saint Francis to the spread through Europe of numerous itinerate Franciscan, Dominican, Augustinian, and Servite preachers in the thirteenth and fourteenth centuries may not have invented anything new doctrinally but their emphasis on voluntary poverty, the rapture over self-denial, and the much heavier psychological burden they placed on individual penitence distinguished their piety from the mechanistic rules of the older Benedictine orders. The new mendicant houses spread rapidly during the later half of the thirteenth century.[15] However, by our statistics on pious choices, they did not take hold of the Sienese populace, dominating their pious votes until the last decades of the Duecento. Correspondingly, the earliest penitent and disciplinary movements, the *compagnia dei battuti,* which marched through central and northern Italy singing the praises of Christ and flagellating themselves, go back to the 1260s. Such popular movements for self-renunciation did not, however, become numerically important until the last years of the Duecento, flourishing in the early part of the Trecento.[16]

Contemporary Sienese chroniclers corroborate our statistics.[17] In their year-to-year notices, the first half of the Trecento as opposed to the earlier days of Saint Francis or the later days of Saint Catherine emerges as the height of mendicant preaching in the Campo of Siena and popular arousal over it.[18] Beginning only with the first decade of the Trecento and slowing well before the suffering of Catherine, numbers of itinerant preachers and heretics caught the attention of those chroniclers who wrote from the street level. The parade begins in 1310. Agnolo di Tura del Grasso reported that the Senesi gathered to celebrate their Blessed Austino Novello, who died that October:

> The "third" (*terzo*) of the city called La Città, began anew to celebrate grand festivities in praise of this blessed one. Nine *contrade* of this third engaged in festive competi-

tion: made costumes and played new games and ran a *palio;* for the event many people gathered in Siena.¹⁹

For the same year the chronicler described the itinerary of the hermit friar Cristofano and his band of pious flagellants:

> A hermit (*romito*) named frate Cristofano appeared in Piedmont and came through Lombardy, then down the "riviera" to Genoa, then through Tuscany and then through almost all the rest of Italy. Many "gente minuta" followed him, men and women and children beyond number. They left their occupations and with crosses in hand went from place to place beating themselves and preaching for peace and screaming "Mercy." They brought peace to many places, and in so doing converted many to the penitentiary life. (308)

In 1320, the government of the Nine proceeded with the trial of a heretic called Baroccino. With the counsel of the bishop of Siena he was condemned to death by fire. He refused "to correct his errors" and never confessed. He was burnt in the *contrada* of Valdimontone on the sixteenth of November. So that others who "held this heresy would reform and return to the right faith," the chronicler tells us that "every day the masters of theology preached in such a way as to benefit the salvation of the faith and the souls of the many (390). In the next year, a newly elected cardinal came to Siena. Preaching on the pope's behalf, he promised "plenary indulgences" to all "who desired to take up the cross against the Turks." According to the chronicler, he "collected great sums of money" and "gathered many people" who desired to take part in this crusade. In 1335, the chronicler described the success of a friar from the preaching order of San Domenico, "known for his prodigious scholarship and sermons."

> Many followed this one, named friar Venturino. He preached for peace in the city of Bergamo and resolved numerous conflicts . . . and granted pardon to men and women. . . . He then came to Siena and gathered many who followed him on to Rome. (514)

In 1338, he reported the death of Messer Giovanni di Tese de' Tolomei, rector of the hospital of Santa Maria della Scala for the past twenty years. He was praised for his "good life and fame both for his services to the hospital and for other works." Messer Giovanni had donated his vast ancestral holdings in the curia of Rapolano to the needs of the poor (552). In an entry for the same year, the chronicler interrupted his narration of political events and description of the "happiness and prosperity" of the Senesi to mention a *Beato* Niccolò Tini, citizen of Siena, who recently had been made a brother of San Salvatore a Selva del Lago, the Augustinian hermitage located several kilometers from the city walls: "He began to preach and pronounce the wrath (*fragello*) of God, that the people ought to live in the fear of God; year after year he continued to preach the fear of God" (523). In the 1340s, Agnolo di Tura, again interrupting the annual flow of political and other events, paused to recall the number of blessed ones who recently had flourished in Siena: one, named Mea whose body was placed in the church of the Servites; the Blessed Tommaso de' Fonti, who the chronicler claimed was the spiritual father of Saint Catherine; a Pietro de' Petroni; Pettinaio; and Manfredi di Santo Austino (523).

As with Florence, the parade of religious characters in Siena begins to thin out in the later years of the Trecento. The glorious, exuberant years both for *beati* and heretics had cooled down by the latter half of the century.[20] Other signs of change, moreover, began to color the reports of contemporary chroniclers during the last decades of the Trecento. An increasing number of festivals, enlivened by the lavish robes of a new "pseudonobility," fill the yearly entries in these chronicles.[21] Earlier public events, such as the *armegiarie,* unlike in Florence, had been almost completely absent.[22] These secular rituals differed sharply from the outbursts of penitence and the cries of the imminent end of the world characteristic of the *disciplinati* movements.[23] They contrast, moreover, with the solemn barefoot (*scalzi*) marches of the religious and the citizenry after natural calamities, such as after the earthquake of 1320, when the chroniclers tell us the city rose up in supplication begging for the Lord's *misericordia*.[24]

The festivals chronicled for the late Trecento and Quattrocento paid scant notice to religious matters. Gaity (*Alegreza*) as opposed to solemnity (*solemnità*) characterized these public rituals. The chronicle of Paolo di Tommaso Montauri opens with one of these new secular rituals: "And in Siena the grandest festivities, merriment, and bonfires raged throughout the entire city with great mirth and dancing and such lasted for months for the city—a great festivity for all good citizens. This was the year 1381."[25] In the following year, the chronicler reported "grandi procisioni."[26] Against the religious frenzy and self-condemnation of the solemn preplague processions, he focused on the rich ornamentation of these religious celebrations. In 1385, after the new political coalitions had hounded the Riformatori from their brief tenure in power and new consitutional reforms had been instituted, the Sienese celebrated a festival with dances and jousts and the competitions between bands of noble youth called *armegiarie*. In the next year, the chronicler reported gleefully more of the same: "grand feasts, gaity, bonfires, gifts, and uniforms, prepared magnanimously for dancing, tournaments, and armed competition."[27] These festivals, jousts, and games, and the *brigate* of 1390, brought "priests, friars, and nuns throughout the city and the *contado*" into the city "to partake of the dinners" to dance and "to burn wax and give sweets with holy wine" and "to light bonfires."[28] These religious participants had traveled far from the other-worldly reproaches of Colombini, Catherine, and Agazzari.

The lives of Sienese saints support the impressions given by the chroniclers. As in Florence, blessed ones spiraled in number during the last decades of the thirteenth century through the 1340s.[29] Their claims for sanctity rested on stories of the severity of their asceticism, on heroic degrees of self-afflicted acts of penitence, which in some cases (for example Saint Catherine) led to death and thereby to a new form of self-imposed martyrdom. In broad outline, the lives of holy ones such as the late thirteenth-century Blessed Francesco of Siena (not the saint) resembled that of Saint Catherine. He too refrained from marriage and the responsibilities of family through a mystical marriage—in his case, to the Virgin Mary. He, too, sought a life of voluntary poverty and performed superhuman feats of charity and self-denial. He abandoned food to escape the corpulence of this world (even while surviving through it) and dedicated "every act" to the service of his *Signora*. Catherine, moreover, modeled her devotion after the life of Agnese of Montepulciano (1274–1317). She found in Agnese "the doctrine and example of true humility." Agnese also was dominated by an intense devotion to Christ and may have had oral fixations similar to Catherine's. Her hagiographer, Raymond of Capua (the same as Catherine's) described Agnese as "the great eater and sapper of souls."[30]

Numerous other *beati* and *beate* crowd the spiritual landscape of Siena from the middle of the thirteenth through the mid-fourteenth century.[31] Their merits for beatitude rested on the virtues of asceticism. The widow Aldobrandesca of Siena (1245–1309) was known for her penitential life of solitude and service to the pilgrims, the poor, and the sick. Ambrogio of Massa Marittima became a minor friar in 1225 and dedicated the remainder of his life (died 1240) to penitence and charitable works. Andrea Gallerani (died 1251), who founded the hospital of the Misericordia, dedicated his life completely to the sick and the poor. He was known for his charitable works, abnegation, and life of poverty. Ambrogio Sansedoni (1220–1268?) was dedicated to the love of the poor and to study. Bandinus Balzettis (died 1270), prior of the hermitage of San Leonardo, observed strict vows of silence. Pietro Pettinaio, the humble comb maker and first Franciscan tertiary (died 1289), "showed great charity to the poor," incessantly visited the patients at Santa Maria della Scala, and "like another Saint Francis" kissed the sores of the sick. Pietro had a special devotion to the Virgin, fasting in her honor and commending himself to her "day and night." Bartolommea of Siena, a tertiary of Santa Maria Carmine, took vows of chastity and enjoyed fasting and the mortification of her body at the lavish banquets of the aristocracy. She spent long periods in silence, transfixed in prayer. Francesco Lippi of Siena (died 1291) lived the last five years of his life in solitary confinement, *facendo grandi penitenze*. Iacobus vulgò Muratus (died 1294) likewise sought out bodily punishment. He mutilated his left hand and cut off his right foot. The widow Bonizella of Siena (died 1300) was "celebrated for heroic charity" to the poor and infirm. Gioacchino of Siena (1258–1306) possessed a special devotion toward the Mother of God. One night while staying at an inn, he encountered an epileptic. Wishing to share totally in the disease, he prayed for the illness to be transferred to himself. He was distinguished above all by his charity, obedience, and contemplation. Later he was "blessed" with the ulcerous sores "stolen" from another sick man. Agostino Novello (died 1310), a hermit of San Leonardo al Lago, followed the life of poverty and hardship (*vita povera e vile*), living the last nine years of his life in solitude. *Beata* Caterina of Siena (died 1342, not the saint), a follower of the blessed Francis of Siena, led the penitent life, whipping herself frequently, wandering barefoot and abstaining from food on the days before communion. The hermit Bernardus Ptolomaeus (1272–1348) lived the life of prayer and austerity. During the plague of 1348 he left the life of solitude to assist the afflicted and became "a victim of charity." Pietro Petrini of Siena (1311–61) slept on the ground and on doormats for pentinence and mortification and gave assistance to the lepers at San Lazzaro. In 1328 he stripped himself of all his worldly possessions and entered the Certosa in Maggiano (in the suburbs of Siena). Against the encouragement of his superiors, he refused out of "pure humility" to ascend the hierarchy of the order or to become a priest. Instead, he cut off a finger on his left hand and dedicated himself to solitude and divine contemplation. Giovanni Chigi (1300–1363) was recognized for his life of prayer and penitence.

In addition, other *beati* and *beate*, for whom little information survives, filled the ranks of the pious in Siena during the late Duecento and early Trecento: Agnela Ptolemaea (died 1310), Umberto Accarigi (died 1348), Bonaventura Ptolomaeo (died 1348), Bonaguida Lucarus (born in 1260).

Catherine gave eloquent expression to religious sentiments that had flourished since the late Duecento and which in terms of our statistics on giving and the quantification of *beati* had already reached their apex of popularity by the early days of her childhood. Even in Catherine's life and work a shift of religiosity can be noted. In the 1370s her intense and introspective mysticism opened out to encompass a zealous engagement in international political issues—Florence's war against the papacy, the threat of the Turks, the Babylonian captivity, and the return of the papacy to Rome in 1377. Catherine, moreover, spurred the reform movement of the 1380s and 1390s, under the leadership of her confessor and hagiographer Raymond of Capua. Unlike such figures as Giovanni Colombini or other "mystics" and mendicant preachers of the early and mid-Trecento, the late Trecento followers of Catherine led a politically astute movement for church reform. Men such as Catherine's Florentine follower Giovanni Dominici were not politically marginal. They did not concentrate their energies on singing the praises of Christ in small itinerant bands across abandoned fields on the countryside. Instead, they were engaged in the day-to-day legal battles of the church and its politics.

The blessed ones of the late Trecento and early Quattrocento were few indeed. For those who did gain recognition, however, the stamp of sanctity differed markedly from what it had been during the hundred years preceding the pestilence of 1363.[32] First, the majority of the *beati* in the generation after Catherine and Colombini achieved their "blessedness" simply by their former association and membership in the *brigate* of these two pious figures.[33] Others of the early Quattrocento received recognition not for lives of extreme austerity and the pains of self-mortification, but for their administrative skills and their rise to bureaucratic leadership in their respective religious orders. Unlike the *beatus* Pietro Petrini, who refused office and promotion in the monastic life, Antonio da Montecchio (Siena), who became prior of the hermits of Lecceto, was recognized for his "prudent rule." Antonio Bettini, born in Siena at the end of the fourteenth century, became the bishop of Foligno and won fame as an expert on law at the Council of Mantua in 1459. Finally, Stefano Agazzari of Siena instituted a new congregation of regular canons and became its first superior general. In addition, he was praised for his scholarship in science and letters.[34]

Bernardino

To gain a deeper sense of the magnitude of change from the mendicant culture of the late thirteenth and fourteenth centuries, we must turn to the next internationally renowned figure in the religious history of Siena, San Bernardino. For the period after 1363, our statistics on "pious choices" show that the mendicants' presence in Siena certainly did not disappear; instead, they dominated the flow of charitable bequests to a greater degree than ever before. Yet a change had occurred. Although Pope John XXII had in 1317 outlawed the radical groups who interpreted the ideas of Saint Francis most strictly—the Spirituals and the Fraticelli—they continued to flourish in Tuscany and Umbria through the period of the early plagues. Their conflicts with the dominant and officially recognized minor friars—the more lax Conventuals—in fact raged with greater intensity through the 1360s and early 1370s. Then, in 1373, Pope Gregory XI recognized another splinter group—the Observants—who successfully eased the tensions between the warring factions. By the beginning of the Quattrocento, this new group had managed to incorporate and control the old radical ascetics of the previous century.[35] Beyond the Franciscans, mendicancy in general smacked of a different religious character in the Quattrocento, perhaps in part as a result of its financial success in attracting greater wealth from the patrimonies of dying testators in the late fourteenth through the fifteenth centuries.

A comparison of the sermons of San Bernardino and the letters of Colombini and Catherine illustrates the direction of change. San Bernardino in fact did not drift with the major flow of fifteenth-century Franciscan thought and discipline—in the direction of laxity, as with the politically more powerful Conventuals. Rather, he was an early member of the stricter splinter group, the Observants, who had recently established a new Franciscan house at La Capriola, just beyond the city walls of Siena. Although more moderate than their radical predecessors, the Observants upheld the appearances of the ascetic life and placed restrictions in the order's accumulation of earthly possessions and ownership.

Indeed, San Bernardino's sermons vehemently scorned luxurious practices and excesses, from cosmetics to gluttony; his message, however, was a world apart from that of the religious luminaries of the previous generation. Bernardino, unlike Catherine, "did not cast a hasty glance over the real world and then leap at once into the transcendental."[36] Nor did he labor over spiritual rewards

Figure 4. Sano di Pietro's *San Bernardino Preaching in the Piazza del Campo (Siena)*, circa 1444, in the cathedral of Siena, Sala del Capitolo

and punishments. Instead, he held out to his public in the Piazza del Campo the carrot of secular rewards gained through the moral life "on this side of death."[37] Bernardino's sermons were guidebooks directed specifically to mundane daily existence.[38] "Almost always, he dwelt upon what he called the 'temporal' or 'corporeal' repercussions of human behavior."[39] As we have already seen, his lessons to the populace of Siena on marriage, sex, and familial interaction were moral codes of conduct and not pleas for the mystical loss of self to distance oneself from "the bestiality of earthly pride," that is, attachment to family; rather they were intended to correct behavior, to reform such temporalities as familial relations and sexual practices for the here and now.[40] Catherine might have done housework for her family and even learned to find joy in it. She did so, however, not for moral commitment to family but as a form of penitence and self-humiliation.[41]

Catherine, the tertiary of San Domenico, daughter of a Sienese dyer and perhaps illiterate, achieved the most eloquent expression of the mendicant posture in the history of Sienese culture and religiosity. Yet she was in the literal sense a reactionary, struggling against the very grain of cultural change. The drift in the style, structure, and character of pious bequests testifies to the divergence in popular or general consciousness and the articulation of high religious culture in the disruptive decades of the late Trecento. The divergence was not, however, what Boccaccio and the contemporary chroniclers Matteo Villani and Agnolo di Tura reported. The patterns of piety cast by the aggregation of the testaments do not reveal a population that had turned its back on charity and the needs of the ecclesiastical corporations, but one that had changed its outlook on earthly remembrance and on the efficacy of earthly deeds for salvation. The recurrence of plague set in motion the transition from the mendicant annihilation of self—breaking "the earthly cell"—to a cult of earthly memory.

Enea Silvio Piccolomini

This new model of self and salvation becomes fully blown in the literate religious culture only with the mid-Quattrocento. The most significant work of Siena's next and perhaps foremost religious and philosophical luminary, Enea Silvio Piccolomini, archibishop of Siena, cardinal, and in 1458 Pope Pius II, was the thirteen-volume autobiography *I commentari*. It describes his travels, international appointments, diplomatic skills and negotiations, his rise to fame, and his judicious, heroic acts, which he chose to enshrine for posterity with an aim of self-promotion that rivals Benevenuto Cellini's. Here, less than a century after Catherine's death, elite religious culture had deviated to the furthest extreme from her philosophy of "self-knowledge." The *Commentaries* as much as the chapel statuary of a Filippo Strozzi, a Cosimo de' Medici, or, later, Boniface VIII, is a monument for the glorification of earthly achievement.[42] In the preface to these volumes, Piccolomini was straightforward about his reasons for self-glorification:

> If the soul dies with the body, as Epicurus wrongly supposed, fame can advantage it nothing. If . . . the soul lives on after it is released from this corporeal frame, as the Christians and the noblest philosophers tell us, it either suffers a wretched lot or joins the company of happy spirits. Now in wretchedness is no pleasure ever from renown and the perfect felicity of the blest is neither increased by the praise of mortals nor lessened by their blame. Why then do we so strive for the glory of a fair name? Do souls in Purgatory perhaps taste some sweetness from the reputation they left on earth? But let the argumentative think what they please about the dead, provided they do not deny that while men live they take pleasure, which they hope will continue after death. It is this which sustains the most brilliant intellectuals and even more than the hope of a celestial life, which once begun shall never end, cheers and refreshes the heart of man. This is especially true of the Popes of Rome, whom almost all men abuse while he lives among them but praise when he is dead. . . . Men said of Christ, our Saviour, while He lived, that He had an evil Spirit, but when He hung upon the cross, they acknowledged Him to be the Son of God. The . . . treacherous tongue that has not spared so many of Christ's vicars or Christ Himself will not spare Pope Pius II. He is accused and censured while he lives among us. When he is dead, he will be praised: and men will desire him when they can no longer have him. After his death Envy will be still and when those passions which warp the judgment are no more, true report will rise again and number Pius among the illustrious popes.[43]

Thus, Eneas Silvio Piccolomini went so far as to equate his worth and fate with that of Christ. Catherine may not have rested well in her grave had she learned that this man, in 1461, was responsible for her canonization. With a degree of pomp probably unknown to the Sienese of the Trecento, the city on 16 August orchestrated "a noble festival which paraded through all the streets and *piazze* of Siena and constructed a scene of heaven in the chapel of the Campo with many floats (*trionfi*). In the house where Catherine was born a beautiful chapel was constructed most honorably from offerings given by the *Signoria* and from all the guilds."[44]

Here, the pride and conceit of the humanist certainly outstripped the self-image of the ordinary peasant or artisan. Nonetheless, the aggregation of their pious bequests attests to a broadly based cultural change that realigned notions of the self, remembrance, and the importance of posterity on earth. The new vision of salvation grounded in "this-worldly" remembrance was not peculiar to the higher echelons of scholars and civic humanists. Indeed, the psychological transformations recorded by the seismograph of the last wills may have even anticipated the articulation of these urges through various media in high culture. Unfortunately, I do not know of any religious figures or intellectuals in Siena who traversed the troubled terrain of the plagues from the mendicant past before the Black Death of 1348 into the period following the return of pestilence in 1363 and left day-to-day accounts of their emotional reactions.

Petrarch

If we permit ourselves to peer over the walls of Siena, the intellectual, religious, and psychological development of at least one humanist covers quite strategically the crucial years of psychological and cultural transformation. The letters of Francesco Petrarch provide an opportunity for speculating on the flesh and substance of ideas, which otherwise remain opaque through the laconic lenses of testaments.[45] According to a recent biographer, "Petrarch cultivated self-disclosure to an extraordinary degree, more indeed than any previous human being of whom we have record."[46] From 1342 to his death in 1374, he drafted more than 600 letters which fill thirty-five books. Some of these letters were little more than single-page greetings; others were treatises of more than 10,000 words on aesthetics and moral philosophy. Although Petrarch revised these epistolary works and on occasion rearranged their chronological sequence, they form a diary of Petrarch's emotions from 1325 until his death in 1373.[47] Even though he may reflect another intellectual stratum and another place, his development spans the period critical to our analysis. Before 1348 Petrarch resided principally in Avignon and Vaucluse; in the year of the Black Death, 1348, he returned to Italy (Parma), and when the pestilence recurred (for the north in 1361 as opposed to 1363 for most of Tuscany), he resided in Milan.

Throughout these letters, one theme persists—an obsession with death. Petrarch wrote numerous letters of consolation to friends and men in important positions who had lost loved ones. Until rumors of a second wave of pestilence reached the gates of Milan (1361), his sentiments carved out a single pattern. In one of his earliest letters, "shocked by the bitter report of the premature death," he consoled his friend the bishop of Cavaillon (the diocese of Vaucluse):

> It is human at the death of one's dear ones to shed tears as evidence of one's devotions; it is manly to place a limit upon them and to control them after they have flowed for some time.
>
> If you consider the destiny and variability of human affairs, not only will you not mourn, but perhaps you may even rejoice that he is dead.
>
> . . . who could enumerate the anxieties and distresses of this world, the afflictions, the tribulations and all the insults of fortune; who could enumerate the dangers of the soul and body and the throng of diseases that vie for both?
>
> We are wrong, oh kindest sire, and we err too vulgarly when we say that in dying we are snatched from an agreeable life. . . . we avoid countless evils through death.
>
> . . . the departure of good people should be accompanied by joy because, mercifully snatching them from this valley of afflictions, God has transferred them to more joyful things.
>
> This world was never his nor our homeland, we are but pilgrims here where we awaited him with useless prayers as he hastened to higher goals. This is a place of exile; he has set forth for his homeland.[48]

On the subject of exile (to console his friend Severo Apennincola), Petrarch's thoughts turned immediately to mortality: "Similarly in death, which is very similar to exile, it is not so much the harshness of the thing itself as the anxiety and distortion of opinion that is painful. When these are removed you will see many men dying not only bravely but even joyfully and happily." In an early letter to Giovanni Colonna, Petrarch juxtaposed his diatribe against earthly existence with the joys of death: "I have set out on this road, the journey of our life leading to death. . . . In short, one must suffer many things until that day awaited by the devout and feared by the wicked when this mortal garment and the fetters of this gloomy dwelling are cast off from those minds striving for heaven." And in a later letter, pessimism about life finds solace with an optimism about death: "What is there of real consequence between the day of birth and death? Basically a great deal. Our birth envelopes us in the labors of human life, death sets us free." In the same book, Petrarch concluded that "the entire life of learned men is nothing more than a preparation for death." To console Robert, king of Sicily, over the loss of his granddaughter sometime before 1343, he stressed the same themes of the dread of mortal affairs, his long-awaited desire for death, and the true role of mourning. He said the girl was to be envied rather than pitied, "for what greater blessing can one conceive than, once divested of our garment of flesh and thus free from these chains, reaching the day . . . when we, having overcome death, put on immortality, thereby restoring indissolubly and reforming the rotten garment of our flesh half eaten by worms and altogether rotten?" Petrarch claimed that he himself "now confidently and full of hope" awaited "that day of death so dreaded by the human race." In a letter to Pellegrino da Messina, Petrarch commented on the death of their mutual friend Tommaso: "I confess that I wanted to die but could not; I hoped for it but I was denied . . . when I was finally repelled [from death] I suddenly returned to this life and now live so that anyone can see that I am living most unwillingly. However I do live hoping only for what others fear, and I cultivate my grief with the idea of the brevity of life." To the archdeacon of Genoa, he lamented his present condition, wrapped in "the mire" of the transitory present:

> Human distress holds me thus far either sitting or lying in the mire of the flesh and in the chains of my mortality. . . . Empires, kingdoms, wealth, honors, and other such things are hers [fate's] and let her keep them. . . . Let it not be said that because of the love of my body or the desire of this life I fear the day of death, for I have appropriated this other saying of a very deep truth for myself, namely, that what is called this life of ours is really a death.[49]

During the plague of 1348 Petrarch wrote three letters to his friend Socrates. His subject concerned "a tearful plaint concerning that unequaled plague which befell in their time."

> I believe that it was God's purpose to strip us of the sweet charms and impediments of this life so that we might now more freely desire the next life.

> Man is too frail and proud an animal, he builds too securely on fragile foundations.
> Go forth now, you mortals, rage, pant, toil, circle the earth and the seas to accumulate endless wealth and temporary glory. The life we live is but a sleep, and whatever occurs in it is very similar to a dream. Death alone breaks up the sleep and disperses the dreams.
> . . . this kind of life is for me no more pleasant than death, and I long for its end with my prayers and I detest any delay.[50]

Despite the magnitude of horror evoked by this "unequaled" demographic catastrophe, Petrarch's recoil did not in 1348 fundamentally break from the mold cast by the earlier letters. Though couched in a wholly different rhetoric, we find in these letters echoes of Saint Catherine—joy in death, the fragility of this world, our lives as only a pilgrimage—as well as the exemplification of the patterns of piety plotted for the integral population of Siena. The year 1348 did not prove to be the crucial divide in the psychology of death. From the heights of culture to the illiterate peasant testator, the horrific mortality of 1348 could be rationalized within the world view of mendicant piety.

These sentiments, moreover, remained in place during the intervening years between the catastrophe of 1348 and the recurrence of pestilence in 1361. Again, Petrarch stressed "the true" relation between life and death in a letter of condolence to Luca da Piacenza, whose loved one

> has died, leaving behind us who are continually dying, and now he is the first to live; he has been buried, but indeed delivered of his heavy chains. . . . Freed of its fleshy prison, however, his spirit, more joyful now, more beautiful than before and more vigorous, has ascended to the stars . . . I thus consider what happened to him so fortunate that to weep for his sake may seem like envy rather than sympathy.[51]

Then, several letters before we learn from Petrarch's own hand that the plague of 1361 was at the doorsteps of Milan—"the plague, which has thus far terrified rather than invaded this city"—a distinct change shadowed Petrarch's obsession with death.[52] Life in the temporal world, "the garments of flesh" and mortality, no longer cast the mendicant and stoic pall which, throughout his previous letters of consolation, was the antechamber to the true "life" and joy of spiritual immortality. Instead of the dreaded wait for deliverance from earthly toil and misfortune, Petrarch made an aboutface: "mortal cares" instead of the spiritual joys of death took center stage in his preoccupations. In the letters of 1361 he clung hungrily to his last waking hours of temporal life, now coveting his fleshly garments and earthly chains as a far different sense of the worth of labor and earthly accomplishment entered for the first time his epistolary advice:

> Thus by night and by day I read and write, finding relief in alternating my work so that one labor serves as repose and solace for another. I find no other source of pleasure, no other joy in living; this one occupation so absorbs and immerses me that, were it removed, I would scarcely know where to seek work or repose.

> My labor is certain; the results uncertain.... My remaining days flow on, and I am carried along with them toward my end; thus I, a mortal, am closely pursued by immortal cares.
>
> My bed never sees me well and awake, but only when ill or when tossing in my sleep; as sleep leaves me, I leave my bed, for I consider sleep a kind of death and the bed a tomb.[53]

In a letter immediately following that containing the news of renewed pestilence, Petrarch harped on these same themes of earthly accomplishment and, here, temporal glory and earthly remembrance. "Do you not sense the passage of time and the swift flight of life? Do you not realize the necessity to devote your time to the pursuit of virtue and to your conscience, and then to your glory and to the judgment of posterity?" Invoking ancient authorities, he waxed on: "Do you not hear Virgil.... 'Every man's hour is appointed: brief and unalterable for all is life's duration; but to prolong fame with deeds, this is the work of valor'? ... Do you not hear Statius, 'Use your life to acquire eternal glory'"[54] In a letter dated 11 December 1361, Petrarch addressed a final exhortation to Charles IV of Bohemia "to seize this opportunity" to enter and bring order to Italy, otherwise

> Who among your contemporaries or posterity will ever be able to excuse you? ... You are no less mortal than I or anyone else among your subjects: time is fleeing never to return, fortune is unstable, life is brief, the hour of death is uncertain; there is but one remedy: economize with time, do not have faith in fortune, prolong life with good works, and have the body and mind ever ready for death, an impossible task for one who has not completed his primary duty. Though the end of life is uncertain, it is certain that it cannot be too distant; when it does come, nothing will remain of all your wealth and empire except what you have earned through a good life for the eternal life of your soul and the immortal glory of your name.[55]

Again, Petrarch's outlook on terrestrial time, on life, and on death had turned 180 degrees. Instead of longing for the end of the dreaded prison of flesh and the chains of mortality, he urged Charles to "economize time," to prolong life with good works. From a garment "half eaten by worms and altogether rotten," the precious moments of earthly activity had suddenly become the chief means for immortality. Earthly glory and remembrance, which before 1361 had been matters of utter contempt, suddenly had become founts for inspirations—the crowning achievements for the eternal life.

In the opening letter in the last book of letters on familiar matters, he reversed even more forcefully his previous disgust with life, craving for its continuation:

> Faithfully, carefully, prudently care for it [life] and offer it all that is in you; drive away recurring diseases; postpone old age, which is subject only to death's power; resist death, which will come soon enough ... we are all dying, we are always dying; we

never live except when doing something virtuous to pave our path to the true life, where in contrast no one dies, everyone lives and lives forever.[56]

The year 1361 was important for Petrarch for other reasons. The plague of that year took the lives of his son Giovanni and that of his friend Socrates, to whom he dedicated the first twenty-four books. Thus 1361 was also the crucial break in Petrarch's epistolary enterprise. In that year he began his second collection of letters called *Rerum senilium,* on matters regarding old age. These books open with Petrarch doing what he had earlier deplored in others: we find him weeping over the death of his dear friend Socrates. The pestilence of 1361, moreover, resurrected the memory of 1348, but 1348 came back in 1361 with an altogether different ring:

> While one day writing to my friend Socrates, I was saddened by the death of so many friends who had passed away in the year 1348. It robbed from me almost all the reasons for living. How well I remember my sorrows and tears! Now, in this year of '61, how must I bear being stripped, not only of every other treasure, but of the one which has been the most valuable and dear, my Socrates.[57]

This letter completely removed the meaning of life from what had been a "fleshy prison" to a source of "treasures." A "this-worldly" stoicism elevated the realm of human action. "I do not know truly if little or much is left for me to do or to live, but what little or much there may be, I must bear it well because all of it will be for you," he wrote to Simonides, the friend to whom he dedicated the *lettere senili*.[58] Petrarch developed the same outlook on life in another letter written in 1361. He chided his friend the poet Giovanni Boccaccio on the very stance that he himself had taken throughout all but the last letters of the *Rerum familiarum*. "It is most useless to hold on to death; rather we must learn to improve life. . . . Think rather about doing that work which is always good, which is seen as noble and beautiful at any age, but which in old age is necessary." In this letter, Petrarch pleaded further that Boccaccio would not suddenly, in preparation for death, abandon and obliterate the material side of his scholarly life. Petrarch beseeched Boccaccio not to disperse his library but to grant it as a single "treasure" to be perpetually preserved for the memory of their work and achievement:

> I do not have the heart to see the books of such a man dispersed or landing in the hands of uncouth men. Rather than seeing this collection divided among various persons . . . I wish that this treasure which was the resource and the guide to our studies . . . should pass to some religious institution, which would preserve in perpetuity our memory.[59]

Here, we come to matters closer to the concerns of the individual testators of Siena, who after the recurrence of plague in 1363, began to consolidate their pious bequests into significant units dispersed among only a few religious institutions. By the early sixteenth century, unrenowned merchants, such as Alfons de Petronibus, left libraries to religious institutions with specifications that matched Petrarch's advice to Boccaccio. The Sienese patrician left 300 florins to the monastery of Santa Maria dei Servi to build a library in the sacristy of this church so that "all of his books, *vulgares et latinos*," might always remain on deposit there.[60]

Finally, in a letter to Francesco Bruni, Petrarch again ridiculed his earlier passion rampant through the letters on familiar matters—the desire for death: "Your attachment and desire for death is so foolish. Your impatience is cowardly—that vanity of fear, the inutility of this desire."[61]

Petrarch's aboutface on life, death, earthly work, and terrestrial glory was, however, in one important respect, unlike the transformation of the general patterns of piety found for the population of Sienese testators after the recurrence of plague. In Siena, 1363 was the decisive watershed. From the late thirteenth century through the period of the early plagues, ordinary testators, often at the end of lives made profitable through the "ill-gotten gains" of commercial activity, sought in their final acts to break "the earthly cell."[62] Their patterns of piety before 1363 marked an extraordinary distance between worldly accumulation and the spirituality of the life of the soul. Far from an attachment to worldly goods or a cult of remembrance, they sought to decimate their patrimonies by dispersing the fruits of their labors as hard-headed artisans, shopkeepers, and merchants into negligible monetary sums. Our statistics demonstrate that, after the recurrence of plague in Siena, this "mendicant" pattern of piety never again characterized testamentary bequests in Siena.

For Petrarch, and indeed humanist culture in general, the chronology was not the same. By 1368, it was clear that Petrarch's 1361 reversal had not been just a matter of approaching old age. His desire for death and disgust with the drudgery of worldly matters had returned:

> Since you would certainly not ask what is the more damaging to others: on the one hand, vain wealth, the frailty of copious worldly accumulation, the futility of honors, the wretchedness of power, [and] on the other, the mercy of God and the salvation of the soul. If you should achieve the latter, you would be richer than any king on earth in the midst of all courtly splendor, which foolishly lords over these poor blind men, oblivious to the fact that such matters are worth no more than a fistful of ashes.[63]

Again the passion for death adorned his epistolary enterprise:

> I beseech you when you pray with saintly sighs and pious tears . . . that you beg in my behalf for what I desire most of all, the saintly comfort of the grace of death: since this would be, as best one knows, my ultimate and only desire.[64]

Similar sentiments abound throughout the remaining letters of the *lettere senili*. In his last years, he turned increasingly toward a Platonic Christian asceticism.[65] The drift of high culture, moreover, was in the same direction. Petrarch's most promising students, such as Lombardo della Seta, who flourished during the last decades of the Trecento, continued to renounce life, worldly goods, and earthly glory. They adhered vehemently to values "in which the authority of St. Francis reigned supreme in the hearts of men."66

What can we make of this journey through Petrarch's life and massive epistolary production? First, the letters provide texture and flesh, albeit from another intellectual stratum, for what emerged from our statistics as mostly changes in ratios and interpretations of their meaning. To be sure, Petrarch was armed with a classical and intellectual apparatus that set him above his peers and worlds apart from the contemporary peasants, artisans, and merchants of the territory of Siena. Yet his psychological reaction to the period of early plagues coincides with the general reactions of ordinary testators. The enormity of the catastrophic and incomprehensible events of 1348 reached far beyond the collective memories of men and women of the mid-Trecento, and failed to register significant changes in attitudes or piety. To make sense of this sudden calamitous event, Petrarch, like the peasant exposed to the periodic preaching of itinerant friars, used fully "the mental equipment" at hand—the sermons and philosophy of mendicant piety. Ideologically, little changed in 1348. The unfathomable events of the summer months were too horrific to be assimilated the first time around. Rather, the trauma was relived when the plague returned (for Tuscany, fifteen years later, for Milan, only thirteen) and became comprehensible for new directions of thought and action.67 Epidemiologically and demographically the world had changed, and it cried out for a change in ideology—one that would lend greater psychological resolve to those who survived. These lesser plagues then penetrated and transformed fundamentally the emotions of men and women across social class, geography, and intellectual strata. It changed their attitudes toward life and death and spawned new relations between the efficacy of earthly deeds and eternal glory. Petrarch's epistles provide a detailed intellectual biography illustrating one man's journey over the troubled terrain of the experiences of plague and, to date, Western civilization's most monumental mortality.

Second, the social statistics compiled from the last wills and testaments of those living in the territory of Siena offer a new documentary context for examining the life and letters of Francesco Petrarch. Scholarship on Petrarch's Latin and Italian works has usually interpreted 1348—the year of the plague and the death of Laura (the guiding figure in Petrarch's sonnets)—as the critical turning point in his life as well as the pivotal date for understanding "the irreconcilability of Petrarch's haunting polarities" of life and death, classical glory, and Christian spirituality.68 The direction of change, moreover, is usually the opposite to that found in our analysis. From the more corporeal interests of his youth, the long line of development leads straight to Petrarch's dotage—his return to Augustine and Platonic asceticism. No one has given any significance to 1361. In the most recent biographies of Petrarch, it receives at most a few paragraphs.69

The question of 1348 or 1361 is not simply one of dating. It suggests another way of looking at Renaissance culture and its relation to the catastrophic period of European pestilence. Previously, intellectual historians have seen the plague as setting back the development of humanist values a full half-century. Artists and intellectuals returned to the mendicant values of the previous century and only by the beginning of the Quattrocento did painters, sculptors, and humanists emerge from the pessimism and renunciation of worldly and civic values.[70]

The general patterns of piety in Siena, as well as the epistles of Petrarch, plot a different trajectory. The year 1348, far from being the turning point that induced the renunciation of the world, fits perfectly well the cultural and psychological milieu formed in the Duecento. Mendicant values—the passion for Christ and poverty and the rejection of worldly things—were already well ensconced, dominating the hearts and minds of ordinary testators at least when it came to making their final decisions over property and for salvation. The recurrence of the pestilence in 1363, on the other hand, proved just as traumatic for ordinary testators as it had for Petrarch in 1361. Suddenly, petty merchants, artisans, and peasants, known only through the random survival of their wills, ceased to fragment their patrimonies into negligible sums of money scattered to numerous beneficiaries and instead placed few but sizable gifts in churches to recall their memory. Social charity changed from indiscriminate, one-shot handouts of bread or pennies to the "poor of Christ" to dowry funds which made possible the creation of new and ongoing families. More and more, testators were not happy to sever their ties with the earthly world once they had passed to "the other side of death." They imposed their wills over generations of heirs, attempting to preserve their landed properties for their remembrance. Just as acts in the concrete world of quotidian behavior had become for Petrarch by 1361 the hallmark for salvation, the quantitative survey of testaments shows a similar reaction taking hold of ordinary men and women in Siena. Just as Petrarch had spilled as much ink over 1348 in 1361 as earlier, the Sienese relived their Black Death trauma fifteen years later. The second time around, however, they took pyschological control and abandoned the century-old program for salvation structured by now-dated economic, social, and demographic realities. From the late Trecento through the Quattrocento, our samples of testaments show a humanist subculture deeply entrenched in the social psychology of an integral population.

II

The High Renaissance

❧ 6 The Great Age of Selfishness

> *How many great masters and gentlemen are in Hell even though they left beautifully adorned tombs behind them! These rich men desired and loved riches in life and in death, possessing them in life and wanting to be buried in rich tombs in death. They did not even want to rot unless in a luxurious place. . . . Oh rich gentlemen and lords of the world who have wanted so much pomp and luxury in this world, the saints and servants of Christ did not want your riches and your vanities. Where are the trials and poverty and martyrdom and the grievances and the passions of the saints? All of these have passed and they enjoy for eternity the greatest peace and glory; while you are perpetually damned and in the flames of hell.*
> —Girolamo Savonarola, *Prediche Italiane ai florentini*

Over the 300 years crossed in the first part of this book one divide appeared—the watershed marked by the return of pestilence in 1363. To demonstrate that the changes of the late Trecento were not temporary deviations, our analysis pushed beyond this divide and continued through the fifteenth century. Indeed, several changes—dowry funds as the predominant form of social charity, the complete disappearance of gifts wrenched through the guilt of ill-gotten gains, clauses restricting the alienation of real property—did not occur all at once. Rather, the psychological trauma wrought by the second coming of pestilence created the broad structures of a new culture which grew through the fifteenth century.

The reader may well wonder just how long this pattern of piety lasted. As early as chapter 2 on pious choices, signs of change may have been evident. For instance, the category of miscellaneous choices, which was only a thin sliver for the earliest documents through the Trecento, grew to slightly over one-fifth of all pious bequests in the years 1451–75, and during the last quarter of the century it became the major category of charitable giving. What were the new forms of charity hidden by this residual category?

Second, the late Trecento and early Quattrocento do not present a single unitary picture in terms of the values of charitable and ecclesiastical donations. The reduction in the number of gifts after 1363 by no means signaled a decline in pious giving. In the period of Bernardino's preaching in the Piazza del Campo (circa 1427) the value of pious gifts rose sharply. By constant florins, the estimates from the early Quattrocento reached even above those years of the early Trecento, when testators gave on average more than twelve pious gifts apiece. Our sources may well understate the extent of this rise. The earlier period, drawn largely from the *Diplomatico,* most likely represented a more elitist sample than the testaments from the early Quattrocento, which derived largely from the chance survival of records in the notarial records. But was this outpouring of charity and piety to continue unabated?

Calculations of Piety

Did the testators give less in the High Renaissance (roughly, the later half of the Quattrocento and the first half of the Cinquecento) than their ancestors of the previous two generations? Given the problems of averages and indices for the cost of living, the most direct indication of changes in piety might be simply the number of pious gifts per testator. After 1363, the most the Sienese gave to pious causes in terms of the number of gifts came in the first quarter of the fifteenth century (4.4 gifts per capita). Afterward, the rate declined steadily, reaching 1.3 gifts or less than one-third of the early Quattrocento figure by the first decades of the Cinquecento (see Tables 2.1 and 6.1, and Graph 6.1). Pious

Table 6.1. Value of Pious Bequests, 1401–1800

Period	Testators	Number of Pious Bequests	% Monetized	Average Value/ Testator	Constant Florins	Average Constant Florins
1401–25	45	196	70.41	106.45	1.64	64.91
1426–51	56	141	54.61	44.89	1.48	30.33
1451–75	59	129	48.84	21.25	1.58	13.45
1476–1500	99	176	49.43	50.34	2.24	22.47
1501–25	92	123	51.22	44.19	2.56	17.26
1526–50	63	103	43.69	101.11	4.26	23.74
1551–75	126	164	45.73	93.63	5.29	17.70
1576–1600	122	190	43.68	84.03	6.77	12.41
1601–25	82	253	51.38	310.86	7.22	43.05
1626–50	113	273	29.67	324.18	7.51	43.17
1651–75	91	201	25.87	320.47	5.67	56.52
1676–1700	102	237	19.83	348.65	5.17	67.44
1701–25	103	313	32.27	516.33	5.02	102.85
1726–50	73	208	28.37	524.88	5.23	100.36
1751–75	88	154	21.43	142.80	6.11	23.37
1776–1800	63	146	40.41	111.12	8.82	12.60

Graph 6.1. Value of Bequests, 1501–1800

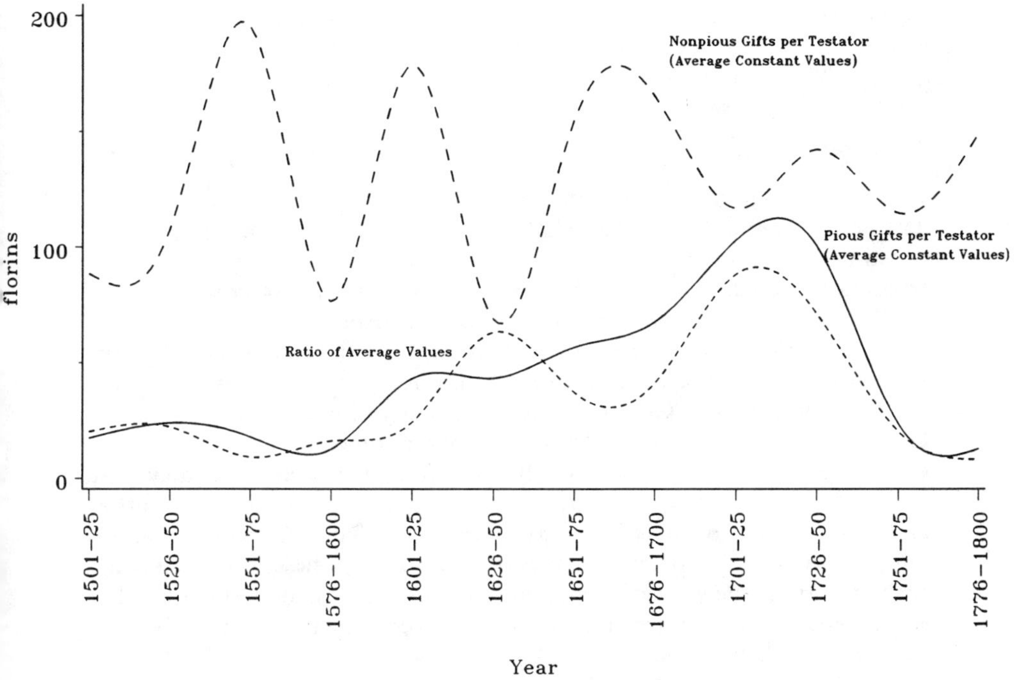

giving rested at a low ebb through the sixteenth century, bottoming out between 1.6 and 1.3 gifts per testator.

This measure of piety, however, might reflect the problems uncovered earlier. Perhaps the changes in intellectual perspectives—the pooling of resources for earthly posterity—had increased through the High Renaissance. Changes in monetization of pious gifts might indeed suggest that the earlier Renaissance tendency to cling to the physical goods of one's past might have intensified over the Cinquecento. To control for changes in the structure of piety, we need to examine the values of testators' pious contributions.

The High Renaissance does not present the surprises that the earlier figures initially hid from us. Here, the values reflect quite consistently the trend cast by the number of gifts per testator (see Table 6.1). Pious bequests per testator in the days of San Bernardino's preaching averaged just under 65 (constant) florins. The amount declined steadily through the century, reaching its nadir at the end of the sixteenth century, 12.41 florins per capita. Thus, until the seventeenth-century Catholic revival, the number of pious gifts per testator and their values declined in tandem. Why did the Sienese of the High Renaissance turn away from the needs of the poor and the demands of ecclesiastical institutions? (Once qualified in time and by degree) does this arithmetic of piety give credence to the most disputed of Jacob Burckhardt's theses—Renaissance amortality and religious indifference?[1] Or did the decline result merely from changes in the wealth of those writing testaments? Before recalculating piety, let us look more specifically at the pious choices of the High Renaissance.

Miscellaneous Gifts

First that opaque category of gifts—miscellaneous—needs to be opened (see Table 6.2). Chapter 3 examined what had been up to 1363 the most important constituent of this residual category: the donations of pennies to hermits, the restitution of credits because of the sins of usury, and gifts left indiscriminately to all pious places. From 79 percent of all "miscellaneous" bequests for 1205–50, these gifts declined to one-third by 1363, and then continued to fall through the late fourteenth and fifteenth centuries. Of the three, gifts to hermits was the first to disappear. A widow Giovanna from the parish of Mansione in 1376 was the last to make such a bequest.[2] Gifts atoning for the crimes of usury and extortion continued to appear in testaments through the Quattrocento. Yet they were extremely rare after 1363, and after 1400, all remaining cases came from foreigners (one from Todi in 1416, two from Castro Vecchio Fabriano in 1423 and in 1485, and two from a painter from Ferrara, 1456).[3] Of these forms of giving, characteristic of the years of mendicant piety, only the vague bequest to all or some "pious places" survived into the sixteenth century although it had become negligible by then.

In addition to these "styles" of giving, several others colored the earliest testaments. Gifts directed to the "Crusades" experienced only a brief moment. The first appeared in 1279, the last in 1301.[4] In all cases, the donors possessed substantial estates, giving large monetary sums or generous amounts of grain "for the passage beyond the sea to subsidize [the mission] to the Holy Land (*pro passagio de ultra mare in subsidium terre sante*)." At the beginning of 1279, Rinuccius Benincase from the village of Montechiello made five separate bequests (one for as much as 25 lire) for the Crusades. In 1298 Conte Nepoleonis Caponis made two substantial bequests to sponsor troops to reconquer the Holy Lands. In the same year, Rustichinus olim Azzolini from Lucignano in Asso gave 20 lire to finance the holy war "when it should happen." Finally, a widow in 1301 made the last bequest for these purposes.[5] From this evidence and similar trends from neighboring Florence, the propaganda campaigns of Pope Gregory X (1271–76) appear to have been more influential than historians of the Crusades have generally assumed.[6] As far as the testamentary evidence goes, only during the last years of the thirteenth century did papal efforts to encourage the financing of the Crusades actually penetrate the neighborhoods and villages of small merchants and middling landowners.

Another type of pious giving that appeared predominantly in the early documents smacks of a secular flavor: gifts to rural communes, presumably for funds

Table 6.2. Miscellaneous Pious Bequests, 1205–1800

Period	Hermits, Restitutions, etc.	Archbishop	Altars	Chapels	Tertiaries	Adopted + Foster Children	Rural Communes	Crusades	Contrada Churches	No Ecclesiastical Institution Specified
1205-50	11	1									2
1251-75	22	6	4	1			1	9			1
1276-1300	41	9	6			2	2	1			8
1301-25	40	12	3	5			6				13
1326-47	37	19	1	6			4				14
1348	20	5		3			2				6
1349-62	8	2		1			1				5
1363	2			1							3
1364-75	2	5	1								2
1376-1400	5	2	2								5
1401-25	4			6		4	1				6
1426-50	3	3	1	2		1	1				1
1451-75	7	1	2	4			1				4
1476-1500	3	3	4	20							15
1501-25		1	2	3	2	2					14
1526-50			1	17							14
1551-75		2		6		10	1				12
1576-1600	1	5	8	8	1	8					29
1601-25	3	5	5	5							41
1626-50		3	4	8		2					48
1651-75	3	3		11		2				1	71
1676-1700		2	6	7						8	59
1701-25	2	6	6	10		2				3	60
1726-50	1	4	3	6							64
1751-75	1			2							105
1776-1800	3	1				1					51

to buy land for peasants living within the villages of the communes' jurisdictions.[7] Perhaps surprisingly, nearly 70 percent of the donors to the rural communes were not rural residents, nor were they identified as former residents of the Sienese *contado*. In no period did these gifts constitute a major form of this miscellaneous giving; the most came in early years of the fourteenth century. And after 1363, only four examples survive in these documents. Finally, donations to the cathedral, the *opera* of the cathedral, and the archbishop of Siena grew in relative importance during the early Trecento, only to decline in the second half of the Quattrocento from half of all miscellaneous gifts in 1364–75 to a negligible 5 percent by 1451–75.[8] When broken down into their constituent parts, those gifts made personally to the archbishop disappear altogether after 1374.[9]

What then were the forms of giving (in this residual category of pious donations) which took up the slack left by the decline and disappearance of those gifts that prevailed during the age of mendicant piety? First, contributions to altars form a curious pattern. They were popular at the end of the thirteenth century, then dwindled to negligible percentages during the early fourteenth century, when the fragmentation and proliferation of estates peaked in Siena. From the Black Death of 1348 until the recurrence of pestilence, moreover, they disappeared entirely from our records. But in the latter part of the Trecento, testators once again revived their interests in decorating individual altars. A qualitative change, moreover, characterized the revival. The earlier, pre–Black Death contributions to altars are difficult to interpret. Unlike such gifts after 1363, which specified a particular altar within a parish church, monastery, or the cathedral, by name and often by location, the earlier bequests always were directed toward the major altar of a church. After the phrase *supra altare,* the donor did not name the saint or saints of the altar or chapel within the church; instead, only the name of the church was recorded. Was this notation simply illustrative of the laconic style of late Duecento and early Trecento scribes? Or were the additional words *supra altare* merely a notarial phrase, which in no way distinguished the gift from a bequest to the particular ecclesiastical building where the altar was housed? At any rate, the more specific instructions for altarpieces and other gifts to individual altars named by particular patron saints assumed from 8 percent to over 10 percent of the miscellaneous category. These contributions to specific objects of devotion, accompanied by more detailed instructions for wax, decorations, and masses, once again corroborate the significance of the late Trecento watershed in the patterns of piety. But we have not yet found the slack taken in by this residual category of giving.

Chapels

One form of giving does stand out from these miscellaneous bequests and might give clues for the shifts in piety from Bernardino's preaching to the Machiavellian scandals surrounding the Petrucci of High Renaissance Siena. Chapel foundations and gifts to these places for private devotion were hardly constant over the long sweep of time. Their ebb and flow, moreover, can be correlated with other changes narrated by testaments from the demise of mendicant piety to the Counter-Reformation. By the end of the Quattrocento, gifts to chapels constituted nearly half of this residual category and comprised over 11 percent of all pious gifts (see Tables 6.2 and 6.3). In the earliest records for the thirteenth century, testators bestowed only one gift to a chapel (0.3 percent of all pious gifts). For the Trecento the number increased to eighteen (1.01 percent), then to twenty-six in the Quattrocento (4.05 percent), and peaked in the Cinquecento with forty-two gifts (7.24 percent)—more than seven times the frequency found for the numerous itemized bequests of the Trecento. Afterward, with the Counter-Reformation, the figure declined to thirty-one (3.22 percent) for the Seicento, sliding further in the last century of analysis to eighteen (2.19 percent).

These increases understate the growth in importance of the chapel in the late Renaissance. First, throughout the duration of this study, gifts to chapels were simply more weighty and costly than other religious bequests. Before 1500, foundations and donations to private chapels were three-and-a-half times more valuable than other pious contributions—13.13 florins compared to 47.70 florins—and the divergence in values grew during the Cinquecento: chapels eclipsed other pious donations by six times. In the quarter preceding the papal visitations (1575) this gap reached its pinnacle: average bequests to chapels topped 500 florins, more than seven times that of other religious legacies.[10] These monetary values still do not do justice to the weight of these gifts. Over time 73.5 percent of all pious gifts were in coin and another 6.7 percent were given monetary equivalents. Before 1500, gifts of landed property to pious corporations were rare, 128 (4.4 percent). The lion's share went in fact to chapel foundations, whereas chapels received only 6 gifts in cash (11.3 percent) and only another 17 percent estimated monetarily.[11]

Gifts to chapels in our sample date back only to the beginning of the fourteenth century.[12] We know, however, that in Western Christendom, foundations and subsequent gifts to family chapels and altars hailed from late antiquity. In the late fourth and fifth centuries, the old Roman aristocratic families struggled against the church to establish their familial burial grounds near the important relics in monasteries and cathedrals to gain political and social prestige in the changing hierarchies of Christian civilization.[13] This struggle, however, did not end with those tumultuous years of late antique interregnum.

The desire of families to establish a concrete architectural grip on the sacred spaces of ecclesiastical foundations in late medieval and early modern Siena traces an intriguing pattern. To reconstruct this historical pattern, we need to delve into the notarial descriptions of the major chapel foundations and endowments found in our samples with some narrative detail. The testaments provide more than a quantitative picture composed by the numbers of chapel founda-

Table 6.3. Percentage of all Miscellaneous Pious Bequests, 1205–1800

Period	Hermits, Restitutions, etc.	Archbishop	Altars	Chapels	Tertiaries	Adopted + Foster Children	Rural Communes	Crusades	Contrada Churches	No Institution	Total Misc.
1205-50	15.49%	1.41%	0.00%	0.00%	0.00%	0.00%	0.00%	0.00%	0.00%	2.82%	19.72%
1251-75	11.06%	3.02%	2.01%	0.50%	0.00%	0.00%	0.50%	0.00%	0.00%	0.50%	17.59%
1276-1300	10.30%	2.26%	1.51%	0.00%	0.00%	0.50%	0.50%	2.26%	0.00%	2.01%	19.35%
1301-25	6.51%	1.95%	0.49%	0.81%	0.00%	0.00%	0.98%	0.16%	0.00%	2.12%	13.03%
1326-47	5.89%	3.03%	0.16%	0.96%	0.00%	0.00%	0.64%	0.00%	0.00%	2.23%	12.90%
1348	5.46%	1.37%	0.00%	0.82%	0.00%	0.00%	0.55%	0.00%	0.00%	1.64%	9.84%
1349-62	3.19%	0.80%	0.00%	0.40%	0.00%	0.00%	0.40%	0.00%	0.00%	1.99%	6.77%
1363	2.60%	0.00%	0.00%	1.30%	0.00%	0.00%	0.00%	0.00%	0.00%	3.90%	7.79%
1364-75	1.92%	4.81%	0.96%	0.00%	0.00%	0.00%	0.00%	0.00%	0.00%	1.92%	9.62%
1376-1400	2.72%	1.09%	1.09%	0.00%	0.00%	0.00%	0.00%	0.00%	0.00%	2.72%	7.61%
1401-25	2.04%	0.00%	0.00%	3.06%	0.00%	2.04%	0.51%	0.00%	0.00%	3.06%	10.71%
1426-50	2.13%	2.13%	0.71%	1.42%	0.00%	0.71%	0.71%	0.00%	0.00%	0.71%	8.51%
1451-75	5.43%	0.78%	1.55%	3.10%	0.00%	0.00%	0.78%	0.00%	0.00%	3.10%	14.73%
1476-1500	1.70%	1.70%	2.27%	11.36%	0.00%	0.00%	0.00%	0.00%	0.00%	8.52%	25.57%
1501-25	0.00%	0.81%	1.63%	2.44%	1.63%	1.63%	0.00%	0.00%	0.00%	11.38%	19.51%
1526-50	0.00%	0.00%	0.97%	16.50%	0.00%	0.00%	0.00%	0.00%	0.00%	12.62%	30.10%
1551-75	0.00%	1.22%	0.00%	3.66%	0.00%	6.10%	0.61%	0.00%	0.00%	7.32%	18.90%
1576-1600	0.53%	2.63%	4.21%	4.21%	0.53%	4.21%	0.00%	0.00%	0.00%	15.26%	31.58%
1601-25	1.19%	1.98%	1.98%	1.98%	0.00%	0.00%	0.00%	0.00%	0.00%	16.21%	23.32%
1626-50	0.00%	1.10%	1.47%	2.93%	0.00%	0.73%	0.00%	0.00%	0.00%	17.58%	23.81%
1651-75	1.49%	1.49%	0.00%	5.47%	0.00%	1.00%	0.00%	0.00%	0.50%	35.32%	45.27%
1676-1700	0.00%	0.84%	2.53%	2.95%	0.00%	0.00%	0.00%	0.00%	3.38%	24.89%	34.60%
1701-25	0.64%	1.92%	1.92%	3.19%	0.00%	0.64%	0.00%	0.00%	0.96%	19.17%	28.43%
1726-50	0.48%	1.92%	1.44%	2.88%	0.00%	0.00%	0.00%	0.00%	0.00%	30.77%	37.50%
1751-75	0.65%	0.00%	0.00%	1.30%	0.00%	0.00%	0.00%	0.00%	0.00%	68.18%	70.13%
1776-1800	2.05%	0.68%	0.00%	0.00%	0.00%	0.68%	0.00%	0.00%	0.00%	34.93%	38.36%

tions and the competition for sacred space over time. Qualitatively the foundation charters show a progression toward the privatization of sacred space and the usurpation of ecclesiastical prerogatives.

For the whole of the thirteenth century, not a single pious bequest was directed toward a private chapel, a burial place, or to any edifice specifically called a *cappella*. The first mention of a chapel comes in a testament of 1305. Domina Sanese, the daughter of the former Filippo and the widow of Buonfiglius Dietavive, from the parish San Vincenti, gave a mere 20 soldi to the *cappelle et opere* of Sant'Ambrogio.[14] The beneficiary of this gift clearly was not a private chapel belonging to domina Sanese or to her husband's lineage, however. The first donation to a private chapel comes instead in the next decade. In 1318 Nicholaus olim Vannuccij of Torrita in the Sienese Crete, ordered a chapel to be built in the parish church of Saint Constantine of Torrita. To this end, he bequeathed five strips of plough land of 20 staii. He further directed that a chaplain stay in this chapel to celebrate offices perpetually. The testator nominated the priest Agnolus from Rome as chaplain for life. The office would be passed on "perpetually" to the priest's successors. The testator entrusted his heirs with the responsibilities and privileges of selecting Agnolus's successors. If the *plebe* of Torrita did not wish to assume these responsibilities, the property and obligations would devolve to the parish to Santa Margherita. To oversee the construction of this chapel, the testator appointed three *fideicommissari* and demanded that construction begin within the year of his death.[15]

During the Trecento three other foundations of private burial chapels appear. Yet none were as far-reaching in their control over chapel appointments as this one from the country parish of Torrita. In 1340, Vannes q. domini Tofi called Forgia from the powerful Salimbene family designated his son as universal heir. Should his son die without male heirs, the inheritance would pass to the hospital of Santa Maria della Scala. In return, the brothers of the hospital were to build in the cathedral of Siena "del Duomo" a "most beautiful chapel, skillfully painted and ornamented." A chaplain from the cathedral was to reside "stet et moratur" many days (during the year) to sing masses in perpetuity. If not in the cathedral, the chapel should be built in the hospital with masses sung for the souls of the testator and his son. The testator would provide an annual income in perpetuity to the chapel of double candles (*doppieri*), candles, torches, bread, and wine.[16]

Evidently the first choice of heir did not last long. On the very same day, 1 June 1340, the son died and was buried in the church of the minor friars. On that same day, the scion of the Salimbene fortunes drew up another testament. It was not a codicil or appendix to the earlier one; in fact no reference was made to the first. The testator, moreover, went from the *domus* of the minor friars, the first place of redaction, to the hospital of the Misericordia. Oddly, he changed his mind after the death of his son. He first directed that his son's body be exhumed from a grave (*mortuario*) in the church of the minor friars and buried afresh in a new one (*mortuario novo*) still within the church of Saint Francis but beneath the vaults of the former place and in the testator's chapel (*in cappella mea*). Then, in the very next item in his will, he bequeathed the income from his farm in San Piero Chiusdino to the monks of the wealthy Cisterian church of San Galgano located below the village. He ordered the abbot and monks of San Galgano to build adjacent to their church "a most beautiful chapel of stone, lavishly ornamented, with vaulting and skillfully painted ("una pulchierima capella de lapidibus bene concis et cum voltis et bene picta"). He held that the abbot and monks should delegate to one monk ("teneantur et debeant in dicta capella deputare unum ex monacis") the tasks of priesthood for this chapel to "sing and say masses and divine offices on certain days in perpetuity" "commending" the souls of the testator and his son to "the omnipotent God, the blessed Virgin Mary, the blessed Galgano and the entire celestial court."[17]

Similarly, in 1351 the "religious knight" (*venerabilis et religiosus miles*) dominus Minus q. Cini Ugonis "recthor laudabilis" of Santa Maria della Scala neither retained nor stipulated the nomination and election procedures for the clerics, who were to hold masses in his chapel. The dying rector donated a chapel, which he had already built in Belriguarda, just outside Siena. For the chapel's maintenance, he provided 90 lire.[18] Few of these early chapels were clearly designated as burial grounds for a family; none was associated with a family name or emblazoned with familial coats of arms. Only the earliest of these foundations, from the rural district of Torrita and perhaps a throwback to an earlier aristocratic past, retained the rights to elect the chapel's cleric and his successors. Those foundations of the mid-Trecento, instead, left substantial sums for the beautification of church buildings, but placed no conditions on the church's use of the properties. Nor did the benefactors reserve any privileges regarding the future governance of these sacred places; they only requisitioned the services of clerics for the benefit of their souls. Families had not yet made significant inroads into ecclesiastical topography qualitatively or quantitatively: the number of foundations in comparison to the multitude of pious gifts bestowed during the age of mendicant piety was negligible.

By the beginning of the fifteenth century chapel foundations had penetrated social classes beneath the old magnate families. In 1403 Marianus f. q. Sozini ser Mini ordered his belongings to be spent for the construction of "our chapel" on a new site in the church of the preaching friars (the Dominicans).[19] From the proceeds, his *fideicommissarii* were to give the Dominican brothers 100 florins. He gave these properties for the salvation of the soul of his deceased brother, the former Francischinus. Marianus, the grandson of a ser (probably a notary), clearly did not come from the social class of those magnates who founded chapels during the previous century, the scion of the illustrious Salimbene family, and the "religious knight" who had been rector of the wealthiest hospital in southern Tuscany. Moreover, Marianus's foundation most likely was a burial chapel. The opening clauses of his testament expressed his desire to be buried in the Dominican church. Finally, the identification of *nostre cappelle* is both ambiguous and suggestive. The possessive pronoun "our" probably refers to himself and to his brother. The donor clearly intended the sacred property to be cordoned off in the church of the preaching friars as his own, but it is not clear if the foundation was associated with family in the sense of lineage both past and future or with an individual's family name.

The sense of the privatization of ecclesiastical space is again suggestive in a testament of 1423. The first woman donor found in these documents, the "Magnificha domina" Bartolommea, daughter of a "magnificent man" from Monte Lupo, widow of another "magnificent" one from Fabriano (Marche) and later wife of a man from Castro Durante, made several bequests to a chapel in the church of Saint Francis located in the village of her birthplace, Monte Lupo. The notary identified it as "the chapel or altar belonging to this testator."[20] For ornamentation she bequeathed 25 florins and ordered that the friars delegate a *cappellanus* to sing masses and divine offices every day. She gave the "rights" to this chapel, which carried subsidies for food, clothing, and other necessities, to the friars' designated chaplain, who could "take and possess" all the fruits from a strip of plough land, 18 modii in size, located in the curia of Monte Lupo. Further, she bequeathed to her chapel another strip of plough land of 7 modii on condition that the friars never alienate the property. Thus for the first time a testator sought to restrict a religious corporation's use of the temporalities that it had been granted. The noble Bartolommea threatened the monastery with the complete loss of all these legacies should the friars sell or in any way alienate the last-mentioned property provided for the chapel's maintenance.

The foundations from the latter part of the Quattrocento asserted more strenuously the privatization of chapels and family possession over church property. In 1477, the "Egregius Vir" Johannes olim Raynaldi from the important political family, the Petrucci, left the relatively small sum of 20 florins to the Dominicans in Siena "to spend in ornamentation and to build *de novo*" a chapel in their church. This laconic foundation was the first to associate sacred space with the honor and prestige of an individual's family. The chapel was to be constructed "for those of the house of Petrucci, "faciende in dicte ecclesia pro illos de domo de Petruccijs."[21] The 1477 testament of a linen manufacturer Francescus f. q. Nanninis Nerii del Garga left substantial funds for building a chapel in the newly established church of San Bernardino, the house of the Observant faction of the Franciscans. Here, the testament leaves no question that the chapel was built to house and commemorate the testator's bones. Francesco gave the order 200 florins "to establish and construct" a chapel with an altar and another 40 florins for a "honorable painting" to be placed within this building.[22] In 1497, donna Cristophana f. olim Michaelis Ambroxii, from "la Palaza" but living in the village of Barontola and the widow of a man from Belforte, desired to be buried in the grave of her husband in the church of Santa Croce in Belforte. In a short will that comprised only three itemized gifts, she left "all her belongings" to "the confines" of a place called "the Chapel of the Nativity," constructed by her deceased husband Domenicus. In this foundation, however, the property rights and prerogatives of election were not privatized.

The woman from "la Palaza" nominated the church of Santa Croce, "its present priest," and "the future successors" as her universal heirs.[23]

At the turn of the century, yet another twist appears in these foundations. Here, the impetus comes first from the clergy itself. On 16 January 1500, ser Petrus f. olim Danielis Petri, venerable sacerdotos and "perpetual chaplain" (*Capellanus perpetuus*) of the chapel of San Vittore in the cathedral of Siena, "elected" to have his body placed in a sepulcher located at the altar called San Iacomo Interciso. (Later in this lengthy testament ser Petrus specified more concretely that his body was to lie under "his" chapel, "under the step and altar of the chapel.") He then ordered his heirs to construct "de novo" a chapel in the cathedral on the site of the same chapel of San Iacomo Interciso.[24] He stipulated, moreover, that the name of the chapel was to be changed to "the chapel of the Conception of the Virgin Mary." Once the title had been changed the chapel would be endowed with all rights to an extensive "possessionem" with houses, vineyards, plough land, olive groves, pastures, uncultivated lands, and woods, located in the village of Santa Petronille in the Masse at a place called "Chiarena." The venerable priest then levied various conditions on his generous bequest. The properties were to provide in perpetuity for "a good and capable" chaplain. Next, the testator appropriated the discretionary powers of the canons and clerics of the cathedral and stipulated the rules for selecting the chapel's chaplain. The first chaplain was to be elected by the testator himself, "and he thereupon elected his nephew, Cristofanus Franceschi Danielis" (who may not even have been ordained at the time of the testament's redaction; he does not bear the customary title of "ser"). After his nephew, the rights of the office of chaplain would descend through the male line of his nephew. Here, for the first time, a testator bound ecclesiastical space (in this case, space within the most venerable of ecclesiastical buildings, the cathedral of the Virgin Mary) by entail to his family's lineage. The cathedral would regain its discretionary prerogatives over election only after the extinction of the male line of ser Petrus's nephews. But even with this eventuality, the dying sacerdotos determined the procedures. Two voices (*duas voces*) would decide who was to succeed: the college of the canons of the cathedral and the members of the Opera del Duomo.

Ser Petrus next imposed certain tasks and obligations, not only on the chaplains who were to inherit the *usufructus* of his extensive possessions, but also on the sacristans of the cathedral. After the death of the testator, the chaplain was to celebrate three masses each week, and for each month masses should be celebrated on Sunday. These masses were to be performed by the sacristans of the cathedral, according to their written schedules. Further, on the eighth day of the festival of the Conception a pound of wax was to be burnt on the altar of his chapel, a mass called "demane tempestina" was to be sung, and another mass said elsewhere in the cathedral.[25] On the following day, yet another mass was to be celebrated in the chapel and another pound of wax consumed on the altar.

Ser Petrus made other provisions for his chapel: a weekly supply of candles weighing 2 pounds and valued at 4 lire and a silver chalice with a silver plate. Finally, he stated that all of his possessions in the community of Santa Petronille (itemized previously in the testament) should become the property of the chapel and its chaplain. Ser Petrus nominated his grandnephew Daniele, the son of Cristofanus, as universal heir to his estate. He added, however, that his heir might "in no way" sell, lease, or alienate any of the real properties of the estate. Clearly, the ultimate heir to the estate was of the tonsured ser Petrus's own siring, the chapel of the Conception in the Duomo, whose properties and rights were to flow through the male line of his secular family. Thus the priest at the beginning of the Cinquecento claimed, renamed, and then separated sacred space in the most sacred of Sienese buildings from its spiritual moorings within the college of the canons. Through the elaborate legalistic mechanisms of the will, he invested his family and lineage with the material and spiritual benefits of sacred space.

In 1529 another priest, ser Ansanus Cristofori Bartolommei Andree from Asciano, required his heirs to bury him in the sepulcher that he had constructed during his lifetime. The tomb was located in front of the altar of Saint Sebastian in the *plebis* church of Asciano, Sant'Agata. All but one of this lengthy testament's itemized bequests—a 10-florin gift to his sister—pertained to the endowment of his chapel. He elected as its *clericum* the possibly untonsured Angelus Francischi de Boschiis, his nephew (who appears without the customary priestly title of ser). Angelus was to enjoy the *usufructus* of the chapel's properties during his lifetime; afterward, they would pass to the chapel. The chaplains were obligated to say "commemorative" masses at the altar of San Sebastian and to celebrate the festival of the Conception with a mass in commemoration of "the most holy Trinity" and Saint Sebastian. Angelus, however, was not required "to officiate in this chapel" during the lifetime of the testator.

Ser Ansanus did not forget altogether certain obligations to the church where the chapel was to be constructed. Each year, 50 soldi were to be given to the parish priest of Sant'Agata for 2 pounds of wax to celebrate the "solemn vigil of the Corpus Christi" in his chapel and for 10 pounds of wax to perform the "sacred eucharist." Yet ser Ansanus, like his colleague in the cloth ser Petrus, reserved for himself the rights of election and of succession of future chaplains. After his nephew's death, the holy property would go to his other nephew, Franciscus Johannis de Boschiis, then to Franciscus's sons. Then the sacred property and the rights of clerical election would descend "always through the male line of his nephews, first to the nearest consanguineal male relative, then to the nearest male affine [related through marriage]"; if both failed, the office would devolve to a male of the nearest female line of descent. Ser Ansanus left his other sister, donna Evangelista, as his universal heir with the obligations first of burying the testator "honorably," then of saying masses in the church of Sant'Agata. If she proved delinquent in these obligations, his chapel and its chaplain would become the universal heir.[26] Again, a testator of the early Cinquecento separated sacred space and the prerogatives of clerical election from the corporate and ecclesiastical moorings and made them a part of the testator's family possessions to flow through the male blood of his lineage.

The testament of "Magnificus ac Generosus Eques Dominus" Bartolommeus olim Laurentii de Griffolis, redacted four years later, shows further uses to be made from chapel foundations for family honor and the prestige of lineage. In this case, the testator had already "designed" the construction of his burial chambers, named after the saint of his forename. If the testator himself was not able to complete the construction of the chapel, his heirs were to build it in the church of Saint Francis. He endowed the chapel with 200 florins to be kept on deposit ("qui deponantur et deponi debeant supra bancho Chisiorum de Senis"). His heirs were to draw on this money once a year to pay the friars 10 florins (the *usufructus* from the deposit). For this income the prior and friars of Saint Francis were obliged to celebrate the festival of San Bartolomeo in the month of August with a solemn mass and to sing "what was commonly called the di, with candles and other sumptuous lights." On the following day the monks were to say an office for the dead with solemn masses for the souls of his deceased wife Catherina and his son Pius. Two candles and four torches were to be burnt for the *corpus christi* and placed over his sepulcher while the monks were performing the holy office. If performed defectively, the donation would pass to the hospital of Santa Maria della Scala.

Dominus Bartolommeus further bequeathed a landed property worth 475 florins "to be converted" for the ornamentation of the chapel with marble and paintings and for other necessities. His brother dominus Victorius could decide "in eius arbitrio" the program for this ornamentation. Then, the testator in his final stipulation sewed new stitches into these chapel donations: he obliged his heirs to make a fabric of crimson velvet bearing his coats of arms and other customary honors (*et aliis consuetis*). For the memory and honor of the family, the garment was always to stand in the church of Saint Francis.[27]

In 1535 the "spectabilis vir" Celidonius olim ser Michelangeli Johannis de Marchobindis elected to be interred in the sepulcher of his ancestors, whose bodies lay in the chapel of San Lodovico housed in the church of Saint Francis. He donated 100 florins for two weekly masses and a solemn mass with vespers to be celebrated in his chapel on the festival of San Lodovico. His heirs were to provide 10 pounds of wax a year for these celebrations plus yearly provisions of 2 starii of bread, 2 starii of wine, and 20 pounds of meat. If these brothers failed to fulfill their spiritual obligations, the gift would pass to their rivals, the Observants of La Capriola.

The "worthy man" Celidonius further required his heirs to make major improvements and alterations. First, they were to commission a painting "with the figure of the Virgin Mary *in assunta* and with the figure of San Lodovico on one side and San Michelangelo on the other." Second, the coats of arms of the testator's house "were to be painted and placed in the customary place" in this chapel "with painted ornaments and well furnished with gold for which 150 florins should be spent." Third, his heirs should build a *predella* for the chapel's altar "where the sacerdotos was to place his feet." Fourth, the heirs were to purchase two altar cloths for the chapel, one of crimson satin, the other of white damask with painted flowers. On these cloths were to be emblazoned the arms of the testator's house along with his family's emblem, "cum firgo." His last demand suggests that, by the third decade of the Cinquecento, chapel space in Siena's churches and monasteries was now in short supply. The testator required his heirs to whitewash the chapel entirely, to erase all signs of the present possessors of this sacred space—their paintings and their familial ornamentation. This cove in the church of Saint Francis had been the property of the prominent Sienese family the Bandinelli.[28]

In 1546 the "Honestissima ac Nobilis" domina Mariana olim Iacobi q. Christofori de Francesconibus, the widow of Hieronimi de Orlandinis, bequeathed 200 florins "to subsidize" a small chapel ("capellaniae") named for Saint Thomas Aquinas. The chapel was located in the cathedral of Siena on the left-hand side of the main altar and beginning with the "enumerated chapels." The donation was made with the understanding that she would possess the *ius patronatus* or "voice in electing the chaplains."[29] In this case, the testator was not the only donor involved in what appears to have been a crowding by patrons of limited chapel space by mid-century. She recognized that her *vocem* was to be taken together with the other "fundatoribus et dotatoribus sive dictatoribus" of this chapel, whether their votes "be one or many." Domina Mariana used her testament as her ballot by "electing" the "Magnificent Lord Rector," the present governor of the Opera del Duomo. Then the office should pass to the children and descendants of domina Barbara, the wife of Bendecti Gregorii Crochi from Asinalonga. If none wished to become "religious" or if more than one chose to compete for the office, the descendants of Barbara together with the present rector of the Opera del Duomo would have the rights of "presenting and electing" the new chaplain. The testator donated another 100 florins to the chapel on behalf of the children of Barbara.[30]

In 1552, the Magnificus dominus Thomasius f. q. Hyeronomi de Palmeriis, "citizen and patrician of Siena and presently *gonfaloniere* of the 'third' of San Martino," appended a short codicil to his testament, which he claimed to have redacted "many years ago." Its purpose was to convey 100 florins to his chapel in the monastery of San Francesco. The patrician insisted that these additional sums "be reinvested in stable properties." In return, the brothers were to perform every year in perpetuity a "grand mass" (*missam magnam*). Accompanying this spiritual demand, the language of the scion of the Palmeriis family exemplifies well the extent of privatization by mid-century and the importance of these sacred niches for the glorification and memory of family and lineage. The mass was to be performed "in the said chapel of his house and his lineage (*in dicta cappella sue domus et Casatus*) for his soul and the souls of his house and for the bloodline (*pro anima sua et suorum de domo et casatu Consanguineorum*)."[31]

The foundation of chapels and the encroachment by testators and their families over sacred space was not restricted to the old lineages and the patriciate elite. In 1552, a silk manufacturer without a family name, Petrus f. q. Dominici Blasii, bequeathed his newly acquired properties called "la ceppa," purchased only two years before the redaction of his will, to the brothers of the monastery of Santo Spirito. These properties, which had fetched 2,300 florins, constitute the largest single monetized pious bequest found in these samples. The crowding and competition for chapel space is once again evident. Few chapel foundations *de novo* appear after the end of the Quattrocento. Again a burial chapel already existed in the alcove—"just within the entrance to the church on the right hand side"—where the silk merchant wished to place the bones and honors of his lineage. He prohibited alienation of the chapel's properties which were "to serve in perpetuity the aforementioned chapel."[32]

By the mid-Cinquecento the term *ius patronatus* appeared more regularly in these foundations and legacies to chapels. These testators made absolutely explicit that they possessed and could convey the rights over the election of the priests, who were to preside in these sacred spaces, founded for the souls and memory of a family. By the sixteenth century, these rights had become valued family possessions, whose prerogatives descended through the succession of male heirs. In a will of 1590 another priest, the Reverend Accarius f. q. Lodovichi de Petrangelis from Siena, made only one pious bequest: a house in the parish of San Giovanni and half of the house which lay under it for the construction of a chapel "ad altare Sancti Ansami" under "the title of the Annunciation when God appeared to the Virgin Mary."[33] He made this foundation in conjunction with the desires expressed in the will of his brother Hieronimus. Accarius bequeathed an additional 100 florins to the new rector of this chapel to perform the "honors and duties specified in his brother's testament" including the celebration every Monday in perpetuity of masses "commemorating the deaths of the testator and his brother." Accarius bestowed the *ius patronatus* over these soon-to-become-sacred grounds to his brother Hieronimus. If his brother should die before him, these rights would pass to his nephews.

Although the priest channeled the rights of election through the lineage of his brother and his nephews, his encroachments seem moderate in comparison with earlier Cinquecento foundations. This chapel does not appear as the receptacle of family coats of arms and other mundane displays to honor a lineage. At the same time, the number of private foundations began to wane in the last decades of the century, this being the only foundation found in our samples for the last quarter of the Cinquecento.[34] The last session of the Council of Trent in 1563, which controlled the alienation of church properties into the private hands, by now had made an impact at the local level.[35]

These examples of the foundations of chapels show a clear progression in the assertion of secular rights over sacred space from the age of mendicant piety through the Cinquecento. Despite the large numbers of bequests to multifarious pious causes, negligible numbers of foundations appear before the second decade of the Trecento, and the few that did were mostly from the old aristocracy. At the beginning of the Quattrocento, subtle changes appear. Not only did foundations begin to become more common; testators began to associate their chapels with their "house" or family.

The sixteenth century, however, saw the most significant familial incursions, both quantitatively and qualitatively, into the topography of Siena's churches. Foundations spread through the social hierarchy to manufacturers without family names and show the crowding of the available spiritual space.36 New chapels were founded on top of old ones as donors ordered their heirs to whitewash the walls which had borne the honors and arms of their previous occupants. Other testators had to divide the rights over certain spaces with the spiritual and electoral claims of other families. Testators restricted the churches' use of their chapels' dowries, and they themselves appointed the clerics responsible to officiate within these sacred niches. For successive generations these Cinquecento donors mapped out in legalistic detail the rights of election, the perpetual chain of succession. These rights, like the souls to be commemorated in their family chambers, were to flow through the male line of the testator's blood. Bishops, canons, priests, friars, and deacons no longer controlled their own appointments within the confines of their own buildings. Instead, testators could ensure generations of future sinecures to family members, who might not even have been ordained. By mid-century, the *ius patronatus* had become the valued private properties of families and lineages. Finally, these Cinquecento donors determined the chapel's artistic programs, which for the most part painted these sacred receptacles with the secular regalia of family and lineage.37 Such secular hubris may have reached its zenith when the Sienese patrician Alberto Arringhieri commissioned Pintoricchio to paint the altarpieces for the Arringhieri family chapel of San Giovanni in the Duomo. Instead of the usual Virgin with saints or portrait of the chapel's patron saint, Pintoricchio graced the walls of the private chapel with portraits of Alberto himself—one as a young man, clad in knightly armor, the other as an older man. Nor is Alberto found at the feet of a much larger saint. No spiritual figures entered the decorative schemes of this enclave dedicated to family pride and to the glory of its donor. But quantitatively and qualitatively, the steady progression of the privatization of the church's hold over its own edifices slowed with the approach of the Seicento.38

Burials

According to Peter Brown, "burial customs are among the most notoriously stable aspects of most cultures."39 Yet these documents from Siena carve out several decisive changes over the centuries. Through the testators' burial choices, the analysis of chapel foundations can be placed in a larger statistical and social context. The elites of Siena, whether of the old aristocratic families or of new mercantile wealth, were not alone in their passion to incorporate sacred space for family remembrance. The transition marked by the growth in chapel foundations rode the crest of a broader transformation in the general burial practices of late Renaissance Siena. As we have already observed, testators before the Trecento rarely indicated their choice of burial. Only two testators specified their final resting places. During the Trecento, testators began to pay closer attention to the future destinations for their corporeal remains: 16 percent (53 of 322 testators) specified their burial places. Yet, of these, not a single testator chose a familial tomb or specified to be buried in the place of a parent or a spouse. Instead they all freely "elected" to "give" (relinquere) their bodies to a particular religious institution—the parish church, the local monastery, or, in special instances, the cathedral. Then, for the first half of the fifteenth century, the proportion of those specifying their burial places more than doubled to 37 percent.[40] Although the vast majority (83 percent) continued to elect places under the floors or in the yards of churches, for the first time three testators elected to be buried in the tombs of their fathers, and two selected those of their ancestors.

The impact of lineage intensified during the second half of the century.[41] Of those who "elected" their graves, 40 percent chose places where their parents, husbands, or ancestors had been buried. For the first half of the sixteenth century the proportion choosing the previously established sepulchers of fathers, husbands, and ancestors remained at the same level as those choices of the previous fifty years (38 percent, or 38 out of 98 testators). Within these statistics, the importance of the graves of the ancestors, however, increased from half to more than three-fourths of these previously established graves. By the early sixteenth century, the obsession with lineage touched all levels of Sienese society. The ancestors loomed even in the testaments of peasants.[42]

The pull of the ancestors continued to draw on the burial decisions of the living through the sixteenth century. Some 42 percent chose familial graves, and of these two-thirds were the tombs of the lineage. Then, during the seventeenth century, for reasons to be discussed, the proportion of familial graves fell precipitously to 28 percent of all choices.[43] Further, the ancestors' hold over the living constituted the major portion of this decline; of familial graves, those belonging to the lineage fell to 59 percent.

We need now return to the original problem: if a new pattern of piety and a new vision of the afterlife did arise during the later part of the fifteenth century, how is it to be described? We have examined the peripheral or miscellaneous pious choices of Sienese testators and have found a significant change, both quantitatively and qualitatively. The foundation and contribution to family chapels hardly existed in Siena before the Quattrocento, whereas by the second half of the fifteenth century it had become a major contribution of testators pondering the finite arrangements of their property while calculating the infinite prospects for the next world. How then did the major bulk of pious decisions change over the course of "the long sixteenth century" (circa 1470–1590)?[44]

Pious Choices: The Bulk of Giving

As the size of the pious pie declined, did new patterns of choices emerge? The most striking and consistent change over this period concerned donations to parish churches (see Tables 6.4 and 6.5, and Graph 6.2). The number of pious bequests to these corporations of neighborhood religiosity declined steadily from their pinnacle in 1451–75, when the parishes attracted one-third of all pious gifts, to 6.1 percent on the eve of the Counter-Reformation.[45] Indeed, the anxieties expressed at the Council of Trent over the decay of parochial institutions appear to have been well founded in Siena. The number of gifts had fallen steadily over the long sixteenth-century from more than two gifts for every three testators to less than one gift for every ten. In constant florins, the decline was even more precipitous. From an expenditure of 3.67 florins per testator in 1451–75, the Sienese, by the third quarter of the sixteenth century, funded their parishes at a rate of 0.13 florins per capita—twenty-eight times less than in the mid-Quattrocento (see Table 6.6).

Other donations do not show consistent trends over the late Renaissance (see Table 6.4 and 6.5). Contributions to monasteries fluctuated between 40 percent of all pious gifts in 1501–25 to 11 percent at the end of the century. Gifts to hospitals at the mid-Quattrocento constituted 5.43 percent of pious gifts; they doubled over the next fifty years, then fell during the first half of the Cinquecento, and bequests to religious confraternities did not shift substantially through the period, resting at a little under 8 percent of all pious gifts. On the other hand, a more fundamental shift arose in social charity. Although contributions to hospitals as a proportion of total pious gifts show no radical fluctuations over the sixteenth century, the number of pious bequests per testator outlines another story. At the beginning of the fifteenth century, one-third of the testators gave gifts to hospitals, then to one-fourth at mid-century. After a slight reprieve, the rate then sank drastically to one gift for every twenty-five testators at the beginning of the sixteenth century. The rush of gifts to hospitals, and to Santa Maria della Scala in particular, never recovered.[46] The values of gifts to hospitals, calculated in constant florins, convey a similar message (see Table 6.7). At the beginning of the Quattrocento, Sienese gave on average 14.45 florins to hospitals. This figure dropped percipitously through the Quattrocento to as little as 0.38 florins. Unfortunately, we have no estimates for the first half of the sixteenth century, but by the period of Counter-Reform, the value of these gifts was only about one-third of what it had been in the days of San Bernardino.

The two categories that most closely approximate social charity—indiscriminate gifts to the poor and dowries for poor, deserving girls—followed roughly in tandem the changes in charity traced by the pious bequests to hospitals. The change, this time, was not structural. Dowry funds continued to predominate as the major form of poor relief. Even during the period of dire material constraints and social dislocation created by the war with Florence in 1552–55 and its aftermath, the Sienese did not return to the mendicant practices that had been

Table 6.4. Pious Choices, 1501–1800

Period	Testators	Frequencies	Miscellaneous Gifts	Parishes	Monasteries	Hospitals	Confraternities	The Poor	Servants	Welfare Congregations	Burial Societies	Dowries
1501–25	92	123	24	16	49	4	9	6	6	0	0	9
1526–50	63	103	31	10	17	8	8	6	12	0	2	9
1551–75	126	164	31	10	50	20	13	4	17	1	0	18
1576–1600	122	190	53	17	21	2	48	11	7	18	2	11
1601–25	82	253	59	17	43	6	48	8	16	14	31	11
1626–50	113	273	65	25	48	3	51	16	12	8	36	9
1651–75	91	201	91	11	25	3	26	14	10	5	14	2
1676–1700	102	237	82	33	44	5	24	6	20	1	16	6
1701–25	103	313	89	65	68	9	14	16	27	4	10	11
1726–50	73	208	78	33	32	5	13	9	19	0	10	9
1751–75	88	154	108	14	9	2	0	8	9	0	1	3
1776–1800	63	146	56	25	19	2	1	9	31	0	0	3
Total	1118	2365	767	276	425	69	255	113	186	51	122	101

Table 6.5. Percentages of all Pious Choices, 1501–1800

Period	Number of Pious Gifts/ Testator	Miscellaneous Gifts	Parishes	Monasteries	Hospitals	Confraternities	The Poor	Servants	Welfare Congregations	Burial Societies	Dowries
1501–25	1.34	19.51%	13.01%	39.84%	3.25%	7.32%	4.88%	4.88%	0.00%	0.00%	7.32%
1526–50	1.63	30.10%	9.71%	16.50%	7.77%	7.77%	5.83%	11.65%	0.00%	1.94%	8.74%
1551–75	1.30	18.90%	6.10%	30.49%	12.20%	7.93%	2.44%	10.37%	0.61%	0.00%	10.98%
1576–1600	1.56	27.89%	8.95%	11.05%	1.05%	25.26%	5.79%	3.68%	9.47%	1.05%	5.79%
1601–25	3.09	23.32%	6.72%	17.00%	2.37%	18.97%	3.16%	6.32%	5.53%	12.25%	4.35%
1626–50	2.42	23.81%	9.16%	17.58%	1.10%	18.68%	5.86%	4.40%	2.93%	13.19%	3.30%
1651–75	2.21	45.27%	5.47%	12.44%	1.49%	12.94%	6.97%	4.98%	2.49%	6.97%	1.00%
1676–1700	2.32	34.60%	13.92%	18.57%	2.11%	10.13%	2.53%	8.44%	0.42%	6.75%	2.53%
1701–25	3.04	28.43%	20.77%	21.73%	2.88%	4.47%	5.11%	8.63%	1.28%	3.19%	3.51%
1726–50	2.85	37.50%	15.87%	15.38%	2.40%	6.25%	4.33%	9.13%	0.00%	4.81%	4.33%
1751–75	1.75	70.13%	9.09%	5.84%	1.30%	0.00%	5.19%	5.84%	0.00%	0.65%	1.95%
1776–1800	2.32	38.36%	17.12%	13.01%	1.37%	0.68%	6.16%	21.23%	0.00%	0.00%	2.05%

Graph 6.2. Composition of Pious Bequests, 1501–1800

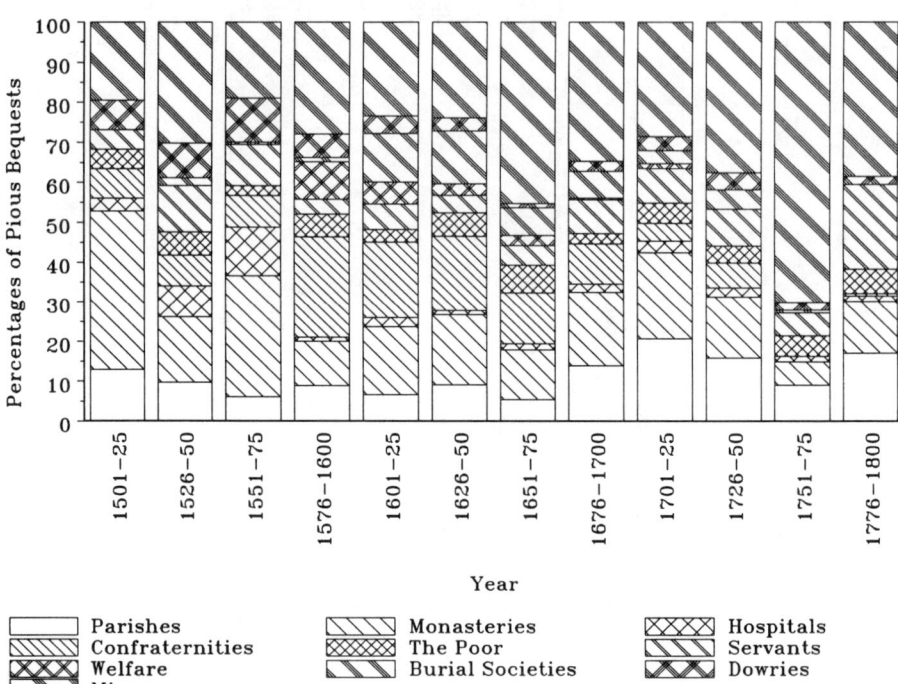

common in earlier periods of crisis. But were the patterns of social charity entirely unrelated to fluctuations in economic and social conditions in the sixteenth century?

It is notable that the high point of giving to the poor—the years of San Bernardino's preaching and several decades thereafter—coincided with "a golden age" for artisans, salaried workers, and peasants over most of Western Europe.[47] In Siena, peasants possessed the wherewithal to buy back landed properties and to reverse the flow of land into the hands of urban investors, which had steadily burgeoned over the previous two centuries.[48] During this period of relative prosperity, especially for the lower segments of society, testators conveyed nearly one-sixth of their pious gifts to the poor, either as indiscriminate gifts to the poor or as dowries.[49] For the subsequent half-century, the proportion fell by half to 8.5 percent and 9.6 percent (see 2.1). Then, when matters worsened, those with last wills responded more generously (see Table 6.5). Their proportions to the poor increased in the opening years of the sixteenth century to 12.2 percent and continued to rise during the years of the war and its ravaging aftermath, approaching early Quattrocento levels.

Table 6.6. Gifts to the Parish, 1451–1800

Period	Testators	Bequests	Bequests/ Testator	Average Value/ Testator	Average in Constant Florins
1451–75	59	43	0.73	7.96	3.67
1476–1500	99	37	0.37	13.98	2.33
1501–25	92	16	0.17	6.50	0.44
1526–50	63	10	0.16	9.30	0.35
1551–75	126	10	0.08	8.50	0.13
1576–1600	122	17	0.14	7.19	0.15
1601–25	82	17	0.21	8.67	0.25
1626–50	113	25	0.22	178.85	5.27
1651–75	91	11	0.12	70.30	1.50
1676–1700	102	33	0.32	11.38	0.71
1701–25	103	65	0.63	130.67	16.43
1726–50	73	33	0.45	78.93	6.82
1751–75	88	14	0.16	69.25	1.80
1776–1800	63	25	0.40	105.00	4.72

The Arithmetic of Piety

Yet these foregoing figures need qualification. As we have seen, the general level of pious giving *in toto* declined over the long sixteenth century. Therefore changes in just how the pie was to be sliced might be misleading in comparison with other periods. First, the number of donations to the poor per testator does not follow the same pattern as the distribution of testators' pious votes over this period. The number of gifts per testator to the poor instead registers a substantial fall from the first half of the fifteenth century to the second (see Table 6.8). From slightly more than one gift per testator in 1401–50, fewer than one in four gave to the poor in the second half of the century; nor did the pattern change for the Cinquecento.

The values of these gifts in terms of constant florins relay a similar message. In the days of San Bernardino's preaching and relative prosperity, testators contributed an average of 18.40 florins per capita in poor-relief (see Table 6.8). The amount fell to 10.85 florins during the next quarter. Then, in the second half of the Quattrocento, testators reduced their contributions to less than one-fifth of the early Renaissance level. The rate, moreover, remained remarkably stable, at the rock bottom, between 2.03 and 2.87 florins over both the good times and the hard times of the sixteenth century. Accordingly, the disastrous period of warfare and Sienese patriotism did not jolt the Sienese into renewed concern over the indigent at least in their wills.[50] These patterns of charity appear to have been resistant to fundamental changes in economy and demography.[51] Their later transformation depended instead on the spread of a new Catholic culture.

Table 6.7. Gifts to Hospitals, 1401–1800

Period	Testators	Bequests	Bequests/ Testator	Average Value/ Testator	Average in Constant Florins
1401–25	45	15	0.33	71.09	14.45
1426–50	56	14	0.25	32.50	5.49
1451–75	59	7	0.12	5.00	0.38
1476–1500	99	19	0.19	18.93	1.62
1501–25	92	4	0.04		0.00
1526–50	63	8	0.13		0.00
1551–75	126	20	0.16	184.60	5.54
1576–1600	122	2	0.02	5.00	0.01
1601–25	82	6	0.07	36.67	0.37
1626–50	113	3	0.03	1049.13	3.71
1651–75	91	3	0.03		0.00
1676–1700	102	5	0.05	175	1.66
1701–25	103	9	0.09	556.79	9.69
1726–50	73	5	0.07	109.38	1.43
1751–75	88	2	0.02	2.75	0.01
1776–1800	63	2	0.03		0.00

Table 6.8. Gifts to the Poor, 1401–1800

Period	Testators	Bequests	Bequests/ Testator	Average Value/ Testator	Average in Constant Florins
1401–25	45	32	0.71	42.44	18.40
1426–50	56	22	0.39	40.88	10.85
1451–75	59	11	0.19	19.13	2.26
1476–1500	99	17	0.17	26.48	2.03
1501–25	92	15	0.16	45.13	2.87
1526–50	63	15	0.24	39.45	2.20
1551–75	126	22	0.17	190.83	6.30
1576–1600	122	22	0.18	116.25	3.10
1601–25	82	19	0.23	162.12	5.20
1626–50	113	25	0.22	70.87	2.09
1651–75	91	16	0.18	25.48	0.79
1676–1700	102	12	0.12	78.75	1.79
1701–25	103	27	0.26	248.50	12.98
1726–50	73	18	0.25	373.63	17.62
1751–75	88	11	0.13	159.07	3.25
1776–1800	63	12	0.19	115.17	2.49

The Economic Straits of Those Who Gave

Before condemning the Sienese for selfishness, we need to consider their economic straits during the long sixteenth century. Testators just may not have had the resources of their ancestors. If we consider their nonpious gifts, both in terms of their numbers and values, a decline emerges not very different from that traced by the pious gifts. At the beginning of the Quattrocento they averaged almost five gifts apiece to nonpious beneficiaries (see Table 6.9). The number slid gradually to 3.3 gifts per capita by the end of the century, then collapsed to less than 2 at the beginning of the sixteenth, hovering there for the remainder of the century.

Similarly, in constant florins, the Sienese gave on average 657.03 florins to friends, relatives, and neighbors at the beginning of the Quattrocento. These amounts then fell steadily. At the beginning of the sixteenth century they were less than one-seventh their figure in the days of San Bernardino (88.31 florins). By the end of the century they slipped even further, arriving at 76.37 florins. By the ratios of pious to nonpious gifts, the trend in piety for the long sixteenth century appears now nearly the opposite of what the previous statistics showed. Instead of reaching a high point at the beginning of the Quattrocento and then falling steadily, relative expenditure for pious causes lagged for the first seventy-five years of the Quattrocento, and then began to rise in 1476–1525.

Table 6.9. Value of Nonpious Bequests, 1401–1800

Period	Testators	Number of Nonpious Bequests	Nonpious Bequests/ Testator	Average Value/ Testator	Nonpious in Constant Florins	Ratio Pious to Nonpious
1401–25	45	215	4.78	1077.53	657.03	0.06
1426–50	56	249	4.45	703.02	475.02	0.04
1451–75	59	240	4.07	349.92	221.47	0.06
1476–1500	99	324	3.27	344.21	153.66	0.14
1501–25	92	174	1.89	226.07	88.31	0.20
1526–50	63	171	2.71	457.51	107.40	0.22
1551–75	126	353	2.80	1031.77	195.04	0.09
1576–1600	122	314	2.57	517.02	76.37	0.16
1601–25	82	221	2.70	1289.38	178.59	0.24
1626–50	113	233	2.06	515.28	68.61	0.63
1651–75	91	201	2.21	876.33	154.55	0.37
1676–1700	102	239	2.34	853.71	165.13	0.41
1701–25	103	272	2.64	584.73	116.48	0.88
1726–50	73	200	2.74	742.26	141.92	0.71
1751–75	88	262	2.98	699.74	114.52	0.20
1776–1800	63	226	3.59	1313.43	148.92	0.08

Should we conclude that testators of the High Renaissance were less charitable only because they had less to spare? After all, Siena had become a backwater in the regional economy of central Italy. Once a center of international banking and trade, Siena had lost her economic hegemony in commerce to Florence and was reduced largely to an agrarian center. This transformation, however, was not a fact of the mid-Quattrocento. The critical divide in the Sienese urban economy relative to the fortunes of central Italy and to Florence is better placed nearly 200 years earlier.[52] A recent analysis of the tax records of 1453 (the *denunzie*), however, shows a more vibrant Siena than historians heretofore have seen in this medieval center after the fall of the Nine.[53] Siena had not slipped entirely to the status of a sleepy agrarian village center bereft of a significant commercial and manufacturing infrastructure. Although Sienese elites hardly equaled the Florentine *ottimati,* Siena was still the second city in Tuscany; her occupational structure, the distribution of wealth, and the investment portfolios of the merchant class reflected a dynamic and bustling economy in comparison with the other provincial centers in Tuscany—Pisa, Arezzo, Cortona, and Pistoia.[54] Evidence of early Cinquecento prosperity and economic growth in Siena seeps through the lines of that account which, to date, most closely approximates a general economic history of Siena.[55] For the early sixteenth century, Mengozzi momentarily interrupts his story of a Siena in steady and irrevocable moral, political, and economic decline from the halcyon days of the late Duecento. Despite the moral decadence of the Machiavellian Petrucci, Mengozzi claims that the silk industry of Siena "attained its perfection" in the sixteenth century and describes the general flourishing of industry and commerce.[56] Unfortunately, no detailed statistical studies of economic, demographic, or social change yet exists for early modern Siena. Nonetheless, for the broad outlines of economic changes and how they affected various social classes over the long haul, we might rely on other local and regional studies as well as general economic histories and price-series analyses for Italy and Western Europe.[57] Though crucial structural differences developed in Europe during the early modern period, remarkable consistencies appear in the general chronologies of prices, wages, and standards of living from local study to local study. Conditions for artisans and wage-earners improved through the fifteenth century. Demographic pressures resumed by the end of the century and stimulated inflation and the cost of living, particularly for fuel and foodstuffs. As a result, the wages and income for artisans and peasants began to decline in real terms and may have even reached crisis proportions in some areas by the first decades of the sixteenth century.[58]

On the other hand, it would be wrong to identify the early sixteenth century with economic depression. Economic historians associate the "phase A" of price increase ("the sixteenth-century price revolution") with economic growth.[59] Landlords as well as artisans, shopkeepers, and merchants, who derived the bulk of their income from market transactions (the majority of those writing testaments in Siena), as opposed to wage-earners, stood to gain from the price and market mechanisms of the sixteenth century. The demographic history of Siena suggests a similar pattern. From 1460 to 1552 she experienced "notable" demographic growth.[60] The international war with Florence of 1552–57 devastated the population of Siena both in the city and the countryside and as a result population sank below even its Black Death level (13,679 for the city). Yet, even this Sienese holocaust did not mark the end of her long-term trend in economic growth. In the war's aftermath, Cosimo I took special pains to repopulate southern Tuscany and to restore the city's prosperity, and despite these devastating years, Siena's economic curve followed a general Mediterranean pattern.[61] The years 1556–95 were years of repopulation; only by the end of the century did economic depression and the collapse of Siena's silk and wool industries cause the population to enter a downturn.[62]

Indeed, captions from the Sienese wills themselves suggest artisan prosperity and economic growth over the sixteenth century. For instance, in 1508 a lowly artisan, the tanner (*cerbolattarius*) Gelius Petri possessed the wherewithal to make several large pious bequests, such as a dowry fund of 300 florins to marry off twelve poor girls. He gave his shop to his partner with whom he had been in business for "many years." The shop possessed large sums (*plures summas*) of money belonging to the testator.[63] In addition, the most valuable single pious gift expressed in coin for all these documents comes from the mid-Cinquecento: 2,300 florins for the foundation of a chapel. Its benefactor, moreover, was not the scion of one of Siena's ancient lineages, but rather a manufacturer in one of Siena's newest and fastest growing sectors, silk production.[64]

In 1554 another artisan merchant, master oven builder Magister Albertus f. q. Stephani Stampinelli from Sala in Lombardy but living in Siena, left a considerable estate with several large pious bequests. He left 250 florins to Santa Maria della Scala and bequeathed 300 florins to marry fifteen poor girls; 570 florins in credits were left for his funeral and sepulcher. What was left over would go to dower other "honest" poor girls at 25 florins apiece. This master artisan, in addition, left vast stores of building materials: 10,000 bricks to the monastery of San Niccolò; another 10,000 were to be distributed for the health of his soul "in the necessities of the poor and indigent."[65] The monetary values of this artisan, in short, may have equaled the wealth of many members of the patriciate.

The Cinquecento testaments show signs of mercantile vigor in measures other than money. In 1551, the master barber Magister Gregorius sive Gorus q. Domenici left a long and complex will that conveyed more than straightforward gifts of property. He named his only son Deiphebus as universal heir with conditions regarding behavior which Max Weber might have seen as more appropriate to seventheenth-century England. The barber commanded his son "to lead an honest life and act on those motives that are becoming to the good man." He should, moreover, "obey his mother and practice one of the liberal arts or become engaged in another productive trade" and, in whatever profession he should choose, his father exhorted him "always to be busy, never lax or lazy" and to behave "always with decorum."[66]

In the same year, the spice merchant "Sapiens Vir" Hieronimus olim Andree de Lunadoriis left messages of moral suasion to his sons which again recall Weber's "Protestant ethic": "Since Oratio, the first child among the male children, has begun to practice the spice trade in the testator's shop, the testator desiring that he continue in this trade leaves his son the custody and management of this shop along with all its goods and accouterments."[67] In a testament found thirty years later, redacted by another notary, the final business and property relations which his father left Oratio appear to have worsened. Despite the intervening years of Oratio's faithful "toil and obedience" (for which the spice merchant does not mince praise), the father in this later will (redacted in the early years of the Counter-Reformation in Siena) hammered out a more egalitarian settlement between the testator's wife, his oldest son, and his other children. Hieronimus begins by praising his oldest son for his "many years of practice in the trade," his "administration and what he had acquired with his own hands," and "his industry and diligence," which had "considerably swelled" the testator's patrimony. Yet Hieronimus desired that Oratio "appreciate more the benevolence of his brothers." His brothers, in turn, ought to appreciate the share remitted by their elder brother and "use it lovingly."[68] In the earlier testament, the spice merchant left other arrangements more favorable to the independence and authority of the oldest son. After the death of the testator, his first son "ought to appoint a partner who could practice the trade to the benefit and utility of his sons and who would keep the accounts and the administration of the shop in good order.[69] In addition, Hieronomus desired "somamente" that his other sons would follow in his own and his eldest son's footsteps in the trade of spice selling, in which case the goods and properties of the shop should be divided and disposed in such a way as to maximize the trade.[70]

In the last "item" of a testament drafted in 1581 the sausage maker Lucus f. q. Giliani turned his final thoughts not to God or the soul, but to matters of the shop. Again, the desire that a son follow in his father's profession was his overwhelming preoccupation. Lucas attested that his nephew Marsilio had been engaged in the trade of selling pork sausages. In the future he should form a company with the testator's son and heir in which Marsilio should "participate" in one-fourth of the profits, unless "it should be pleasing to God that the shop would incur a loss." In that case, the nephew would shoulder a larger portion of the debts; "he should share in one-half of the company." In closing, the pork butcher pleaded that "his dear, delightful and loving son . . . be a *buon figliolo,* attend faithfully to the shop, and stay lovingly with his cousin as they had done over the past year."[71]

Finally, in 1594, the "Spectabilis vir" Marcus f. q. Bartolommei Bindi from the mountain village of Radicondoli paused in the itemized lists of property conveyances to compliment two of his three sons, Scipione and the deceased Giulio, for their "efforts, skill, and industry in their work and trades which created great profit and many acquisitions." The father claimed that his sons' "industry" never took sums away from the business or cost their father expenses. In contradistinction to his eldest son, the "Reverendo et Eccellente" Messer Cosimo, who had squandered the father's patrimony through his education in Siena, Pisa, San Gimignano, and Rome, the other sons had stayed at home in the less-cosmopolitan rural confines of Radicondoli and through their industry had accumulated 3,000 scudi—an extraordinary patrimony for a shopkeeper-merchant even in a provincial town during the late sixteenth century, and all the more so for a rural village. Such a sum would not have been beneath that expected for a noble dowry.[72]

These examples are few and scattered. Yet they signal a certain chronology. Before the Cinquecento, such phraseology about *industria*, diligence, acquisition, and profit, mixed with pleas by fathers that their sons follow honestly and diligently in their trades, were altogether absent from Sienese testaments and then disappeared by the Seicento. In the testaments of hard-headed cobblers, druggists, sausage makers, oven builders, and other artisans, the "Protestant ethic" thrived in the Cinquecento without the Reformation. Their praise and exhortations cut against the grain usually imagined for the economy of southern Tuscany in the late Renaissance. Only during the war years (1552–55) did any testaments evoke pictures of misery.[73] But even for these years, no examples of testators proclaiming the paucity of their estates, no appeals to the goodwill of patrons and friends to give them a decent burial or to say masses or prayers, appear. These "moral wills," which conveyed little if any property, sprout up only once prices began to fall, after the crucial divide of the seventeenth century, when the Sienese economy entered its economic downturn in absolute terms, its "phase B."[74]

Social Class

If the Sienese had not fallen on hard times (again, in absolute terms), could the general decline in values of the itemized bequests (both pious and nonpious) be explained by a change in the testament-writing population—a democratization of the testaments? Because of the infrequency of occupational designations at the lower end of the social ladder, especially for rural inhabitants, difficulties arise in judging to what extent testament writing penetrated the lower orders. We only know that these samples contain the testaments of share croppers (*mezzadri*) and salaried artisans from the late Trecento. On the upper end of the social scale, occupational identification and the presence of family names provide possibilities for comparison over time. If we consider as the elite those who bore noble titles (*messer, comes, patricius, equus, nobilius*) or possessed family names, we may note the following changes in the will-writing population. For the first fifty years of the Quattrocento 19 percent of the testators (20 of 105, including those who drafted codicils) were of elite status; in the second half of the century the social character of the wills remained roughly the same (32 of 162 testators). In the first half of the sixteenth century, the social status of those writing wills rose to nearly one-third of the testators (29 percent; or 47 of 163) and remained at this level (76 of 262) through the century. These indices of status, however, raise questions. The nobility in Siena became a juridical class by the early Cinquecento; it became synonymous with membership in one of Siena's political factions (*monti*) and was a prerequisite for office holding.[75] Since ancestry in any of Siena's five historic *monti*—whether of the gentilhuomini or the others (the Nine, the Twelve, the Riformatori, and the *popolo minuto*)—had become a pedigree for noble status, the ranks of the patriciate most likely widened in the Cinquecento. Notaries, moreover, certainly would have indicated the noble status of their clients more consistently after this date. Second, family names penetrated more deeply the social hierarchy of Siena, although not to the same extent as in Florence and Bologna.[76] By the sixteenth century even peasants became graced for the first time with a family name. Nonetheless, despite these changes in the indication of status, the data do not show any pause by the elites in drafting notarized testaments.

Dowries, *bene* which in and of themselves were expressions of honor and status, provide a more telling index.[77] The wills of both husbands and wives often mentioned the wife's dowry. Before allocating other gifts or reimbursing other creditors, the husband first had to assure his wife of her rights to her dowry. She was the first creditor to his estate.[78] The dowries in nominal terms increased over the fifteenth and sixteenth centuries from 370.13 to 633.11 florins (see Table 6.10). The real values (at least in terms of grain prices) trace another trajectory, however: they declined steadily over these centuries to less than one-half what they had been in the days of San Bernardino. How can we now evaluate the piety of late Quattrocento and Cinquecento Sienese? First, from these data alone we cannot factor out two possible tendencies: a decline in the well-being of the Sienese, on the one hand, and the democratization of testament writing, on the other. Given the tendency, in these data, of the dowries to decline over the first 400 years of our study, even over the years of Sienese commercial expansion and governmental stability, dowry prices might indicate more the social "opening" of testament writing than a decline in the well-being of the Sienese. Both trends, however, may have been happening simultaneously. Second, we might question whether these "real values" based on

Table 6.10. Dowry Prices for Wives

Period	Number of Dowries	Average Dowry	Index	Real Values
1400–50	8	370.13	1.56	237.27
1451–1500	9	376.44	1.91	197.09
1501–50	15	395.73	3.41	116.05
1551–1600	37	633.11	6.03	104.99

grain prices overstate the decline in wealth of the Sienese who wrote testaments over this period. We know from other studies of prices that fuel and grain prices were the "leaders" in commodity inflation during the price revolution of the sixteenth century.[79] As the dowry usually corresponded with the gift of a house for the new couple, particularly in the cases of well-to-do peasants, artisans, and shopkeepers, housing values would prove a better basis than grain, but as mentioned earlier such indices are not yet available. At any rate, the wealth of those writing testaments in constant florins may have declined over the fifteenth and sixteenth centuries by as much as 50 percent.[80] Yet the decline in the amounts these same testators spent on charitable and pious causes diminished much more drastically, by well over 500 percent, and gifts to the poor fared even worse, declining by 836 percent from the beginning of the Quattrocento to the mid-Cinquecento.

A Recalculation of Piety

Despite these precipitous declines, the figures still understate the magnitude of the Cinquecento collapse in piety and charity. We have already seen that one form of pious giving—gifts to private chapels—in contradistinction to the other trends in charity and contributions to ecclesiastical corporations, increased over the long sixteenth century. Unlike the foundations of chapels in the Trecento or after the Council of Trent, we have seen that these contributions did not necessarily flow into church coffers. Rather, these "sacred" incomes often supported family sinecures for generations of male heirs. The testator, rather than giving, circumscribed to himself and to his lineage prerogatives over ecclesiastical property, which in the earlier chapel foundations had been in the hands of the canons, abbots, friars, and parish priests. Thus the values of these "gifts" are better placed apart from the previous averages of pious giving. As a result, the general fall in piety over the long sixteenth century becomes as sharp as that found for social charity, pious expenditures in the days of Bernardino's preaching being eight times what they were by the mid-Cinquecento.

Still, how can we solve the enigma posed by the ratios of pious to nonpious gifts? Even if patrimonies on average declined by as much as 50 percent over the long sixteenth century, some arithmetic remains to be explained. Not only itemized pious bequests but nonpious ones as well declined at far steeper rates than possible declines in the average levels of Cinquecento patrimonies suggest, by as much as five to eight times. Where, then, did the bulk of these patrimonies go? The answer lies in that residual category impenetrable to quantification: the universal heirs.

~~ 7   Property

> *Oh someone may say: surely it would be better now that we are preparing the comedy to say Pater Nostra and Salve Reginas, as though our souls while dressed in their earthly garb, could, like the angels, contemplate continually, without refreshing the spirits which sustain our daily lives. Since such recreation as the performance of comedies is worthy, I cannot see why these pious humbugs should censor it, ah, ah.*
> —Alessandro Piccolomini (1508–79)

A casual reader of the testaments without computer assistance can detect changes in the flavor and form of these documents at the end of the Quattrocento. Previously, the bulk of them started with simple preambles and went on to itemize bequests, usually expressed in single-line entries. If the bequest was destined for a pious institution, the customary phrases—for the "love of God," the "remission of sins," or the "health of the soul"—introduced it. If to a friend or relative, usually the notary mentioned no more than a description of the properties or the amount of money. Finally, these documents ended with the testator's "nomination" of the universal heirs to the estate. After the formulaic phrase *in omnibus rebus,* the testaments through the first half of the Quattrocento rarely attempted to regulate the future flow of patrimonies through contingency clauses or to place conditions on their heirs.

In the Cinquecento, this final section of the will grew in length and importance. Testators were no longer content to leave the lion's share of their estates (usually the landed wealth) to heirs unconditionally. Besides restricting the alienation of their landed properties, increasingly they plotted contingencies to govern and control the future devolutions of their patrimonies beyond the first generation. More, as the center of gravity in these wills crept ahead from the lists of itemized bequests to where testators in complex and legalistic language spelled out the details governing their universal heirs, other aspects of the sixteenth-century will changed as well. Before turning to the universal heirs, let us first consider those other sections, which shed light on the preoccupations of Cinquecento testators.

Calculations in the previous chapter might, on first impression, suggest that the testators of the Cinquecento were less well off than previously, but their wills certainly did not decline in complexity or length. On the contrary, a new array of literary matter entered the documents. In addition to property and instructions for matters regarding the soul, testators of the Cinquecento began to leave exhortations and expressions of gratitude to their children and wives. In the preceding chapter we saw examples of fathers commending their sons for their obedience, "industry," and diligence and advising them to continue their fathers' acquisitive efforts in the shop, to follow their footsteps, or to pursue one of the "liberal arts." Similarly, husbands began to preface their final arrangements with their wives with expressions such as "eius dilecta uxor," "dilecta consorta," "in bona consideratione," "volendo ricognoscere l'affectione et benemeriti . . . sua dilecttissima consorte," "attenta bonitate et obbedientia et benemeretis."[1]

The major reason these documents increase in length pertains to obsessions central to the mentality of sixteenth-century Siena. These concerned property and lineage. In this new litigious culture of the Cinquecento, testators attempted more carefully than before or afterward to foresee and forestall future lawsuits.[2] They sought to avert possibilities for ambiguity and addressed all possible claimants to their property. Hence these testaments flesh out the reasons for certain bequests to a much greater extent than those of previous periods. These explanations went beyond the old formulaic religious phrases; the new reasons put forth not only were often unformulaic, but they pertained mostly to the nonpious bequests. Yet in some cases, their justifications did express charity—a charity, however, particular to the Cinquecento and removed from the older ecclesiastical channels and rationales for giving.

A Charity of Familiarity

By the mid-Quattrocento, testators increasingly "recognized" with phrases of affection and, on occasion, with substantial properties the services of those who had assisted them during periods of illness or while they lay on their deathbeds. For instance, in 1446 donna Magia f. q. Andree de Tolomeis, widow of a man from Verona, left to a barber, Bastiano, all the expenses he incurred for food and medicine while attending to her present illness ("quam spenderet ipse Bastianus in et pro vittu et gubernatione infirmitatis in qua ad presens est").[3] In a brief testament of 1487, a woman "between 14 and 25" from Chiusi nominated her blood relation "suum consanguineum" Carlumantonium ser Tederici de Clusio as her universal heir. Whether she had closer living relatives is not clear. At any rate, she justified her decision: ". . . since from him she had received many benefits and maximum care while in her present infirmity."[4] In 1501 a victim of the plague, domina Ginevera f. olim Ciambordi from Corsica (but then living in Siena) gave a small gift and 20 soldi to a woman who was at present caring for her.[5] In 1551 a nun of San Prosperi, the daughter of a Lombard linen weaver, named as her universal heir and *fideicommissaria* a nonrelative, the daughter of a *mezzadro* and the wife of a baker. The notary then felt inclined to justify this decision: "and the testator did this since her heir handled her affairs well and cared for her diligently during the testator's present state of illness." The nun "affirmed" that this daughter of a sharecropper "had thus always treated her well."[6] In a will of 1553 a donna Domenica f. q. Domenici del forte from San Promiano, the widow of a man from the same place, gave the *usufructus* to a vineyard in the rural commune of Roccastrada to a nonrelative, the widow Sandra f. q. Mariotti from Casale "to attest" the "many, many times" she had been welcomed into Sandra's home in the city of Siena and there cared for when she had been "ill and in need," which had caused her friend "to incur and suffer many expenses and inconveniences." The gift was meant to compensate Sandra "for her labors and expenses." Domenica appointed Sandra as her heir "because of the merits and the love which she had shown," even though she was survived by a nephew.[7] She granted this nephew, her nearest of kin, several farm animals, grain, and coins, but added that he could not expect to inherit any more from her estate.[8] In 1568, Agnolus f. q. Parris Cinelli from Rapale near the° boundary between Florence and Siena in the *podesteria* of Bucine granted his wife the right to choose any goods she wished to constitute her modest dowry of 50 florins. He justified this grant because of "the love and affection which she had always brought him and the trouble and toil she had endured during his illness."[9] Finally, in 1580, a monna Margherita di fu Niccolò de Fraticelli from Radicondoli, wife of a mason from Siena, began the one and only itemized bequest in her will with the words, "now bedridden for many months with illness and at present found in these same straits, and having received and at present still receiving many and infinite benefits from the said Alisandro, her husband, who has treated and continues to treat her well. . . ." She bequeathed him her dowry of 200 florins plus 25 florins earned from the principal. Monna Margherita, who was survived by a brother (with legal claims to a portion of her dowry), had to justify her decision, "desiring to acknowledge in some measure all the benefits she had received and was receiving daily by way of a bequest and for the best intentions."[10]

Illegitimate Heirs

Other grants of the High Renaissance show the same need to justify allocations and give further evidence of a charity of familiarity. First, the number of testators who recognized illegitimate sons and daughters in their wills multiplied sharply during the Cinquecento. Curiously, no gifts or, for that matter, mention of illegitimate children appeared until the Quattrocento, the earliest coming in 1418. This bequest, although to a blood relation, takes the flavor of a pious donation. The testator, Andreas q. Cini Andree from the parish of Sancti Petri Castri Veteris, declared that the illegitimate son of his deceased son Niccolaus was a "pauper and beggar." "Moved by pious love and the contemplation of the omnipotent God," the testator bequeathed to his illegitimate grandchild 100 florins "so that the "spureus" Laurentius could feed and nourish himself and would grow up to act properly."[11] In addition, Andreas "pro amore dei" gave his illegitimate grandchild the *usufructus* to a house in the Chiasso Porcinese in his parish. In 1450, a testator granted his daughter, "formerly spurious but now legitimate," "'her dowry" of 300 florins. Here the father made no pretense of charity. He gave his heirs six years to make the payment during which time they should not bother their half-sister. Afterward, she could ask no more from the estate, but ought to remain content with the stated dowry."[12]

Not until the sixteenth century, however, did gifts to one's own illegitimate children become common. In 1502 a wax merchant gave a small dowry of property valued at 28 florins to an illegitimate daughter. In this case the gift carried spiritual pretensions: it was granted for the "love of God and the remission of his sins."[13] In 1519 an *honesta mulier,* "older than 12," bequeathed to her illegitimate brother 100 florins, insisting that he ask for no more.[14] In 1535 the "spectabilis vir" Celidonius de Marchobindis, the pious donor we encountered earlier as the benefactor of the chapel of San Lodovico, unabashedly made provisions for the possible birth of his children in the future. He declared that his heir, the hospital of Santa Maria della Scala, bore the responsibility of feeding these children whether they happened to be "natural" or "spurious," "whether they were kept in the hospital or outside of it."[15] Similarly, the nobleman Maximianus f. q. Alessandri de Turannis declared forthrightly at the beginning of his testament of 1546 that he had many children from his wife Elizabeth, two of whom were illegitimate, Marcantonius and Cassandra. The major portion of this will was then devoted to the arrangements his heirs should make in regard to their illegitimate brother and sister. First, Maximianus granted Marcantonius the rights of food and clothing. Second, Marcantonius might remain in his father's house as long as he desired, and the heirs to the estate "might not molest [him] in any way." Third, the testator clarified Marcantonio's material (or at least sartorial) rights. The legitimate sons were to provide him with one pair of boots and two shirts every year and twice a year with a doublet and a cloak, *ala spagnola,* shoes, a hat, and other clothing of "honorable quality according to the status and grade of clothing that the heirs could provide." Fourth, the testator provided his illegitimate daughter with a dowry of 300 florins. "Until she found a husband," she could remain in the household of her father, where his heirs were obliged to feed and clothe her. If she did not marry she would lose her rights to the dowry but could remain under her father's roof for as long as she lived. Fifth, Maximianus added, perhaps as an afterthought, that Marcantonio would have to behave himself (*se gerat*) as long as he lived in the house of his heirs.[16]

The next appearances of illegitimate children come after the Council of Trent. In 1583, the citizen Silvio di Bernardo de Capacci used his testament as a confessional: "Being of this world . . . I hold and believe that Portia, born from monna Calidonia, the daughter of the late Guiliano di Bernardo, is indeed my child. And although I did not mention it, I treated her as such and by such treatment I raised her and still do so. Thus I do not want there to be any doubt that she is my daughter; not because of any reason, but rather because I wish to do and say this in my testament so that it might have an effect for her benefit." "For the love of God," Silvio, then, insisted that his heirs provide her "with food and use of all the furnishings in the house until she married." "Under the obligation of blood relation," his heirs were obliged to dower her. Although his final testamentary act treated his illegitimate child generously, Silvio expressed a tension and a sense of guilt not found earlier in the century. His confession suggests that previously he had covered up his paternity and only in facing death was he moved to make a declaration for her material welfare.[17]

Another testament redacted the same year conveys a similar impression: testators of the Counter-Reformation might no longer be so matter-of-fact about their illegitimate children.[18] The nobleman Christofanus q. Iacobi de Bilanchis bequeathed to a Lorenzo euphemistically called "dello spedale," *supposedly* the son of a former servant of the household, "all that he could demand" in compensation for his mother's salary.[19] By the Seicento, references to spurious offspring faded away. In the three remaining references to those born out of wedlock, testators, like the nobleman Cristofanus in 1583, used euphemisms, here "della scala." In one case the illegitimate child received a ring and several cooking utensils; in another, alimentation for one year; in the third, food until the child entered a monastic order.[20]

What do these cases prove? First, the Cinquecento stands out numerically: the vast majority of gifts to illegitimate children appeared in the years 1500–83. Second, the Cinquecento took a different stance on illegitimacy. Except for the single case following on the heels of Bossi's Counter-Reform visitations of 1575–76 (see chapter 10), these testators did not attempt to hide their illegitimate births with euphemisms and expressed little sense of shame. Third, the gifts and property settlements bequeathed to "spurious" children were more generous in the Cinquecento than before or afterward. Do we then find support here for another Burckhardtian generalization about the Renaissance, or at least the High Renaissance—public indifference to illegitimate birth?[21] Perhaps. On the other hand, these examples may fit a larger puzzle, whose pieces we are now assembling. First, they show a sense of charity that circumvented the church. It was a charity of familiarity, which, in the case of illegitimate children, followed bloodlines even if not sanctioned through marriage. Second, these examples illustrate the obsessions and anxieties of sixteenth-century testators in mapping out precisely the property relations between all future claimants to their estates. To avoid future litigation that might fragment the material bases of their lineage, they desperately sought to impose their wills over their temporalities long after they had departed them.

Adoption

The sharp rise and decline of foster and adopted children (*allevati, alumni*) draws another band in this sixteenth-century charity of familiarity. The importance of these surrogate members of the family and the relations they bore to their resident families differed from testament to testament. Some were identified as nephews; others were clearly servants. But over the long duration of these documents, qualitative and quantitative changes arise. The earliest donations to adopted or foster children appear at the end of the thirteenth century (see Table 6.2).[22] Then, despite the large numbers of bequests for the fourteenth century (2,224), not a single mention of an *alevati* or *alumni* occurs. In the age of mendicant piety, did the Sienese simply not raise nonrelatives in their households? If they did, their charitable concerns, at least while on their deathbeds, turned to the myriad of other pious needs and outlets. They might help indiscriminately the unidentified *pauperes cristi*, before recognizing the needs of those closer to home, nonrelatives or even nieces or nephews raised in their households. Again, the complaints of Siena's Cecco Angiolieri might be imagined.

The Quattrocento, on the other hand, found a sprinkling of *allevati* among its beneficiaries, but their number was negligible: 5 out of 642 bequests. Only during the second half of the Cinquecento did the frequency of donations to adopted and foster children soar in importance. In these years, the testators granted eighteen separate bequests to such members of the household. Could the social dislocations, resulting from the brutal war with Florence (1552–55), which pushed large numbers of starving refugees and war victims into the city, have been the cause? If so, the documents, which in several testaments did refer to the disastrous economic and social consequences created by this war, might have said so. Only one document, however, alluded to the circumstances that led to the adoption or rearing of one of these children. In a will of 1566, the knight Eques dominus Hieronimus f. q. Johannis Beringuccis, rector of Santa Maria della Scala, maintained that he had found the "poverina orfana" Agnesa di Tonino from Modena "in the street" and "because of charity" had reared her in his household.[23]

The appearance of these surrogate children in the mid-Cinquecento went beyond a mere increase in numbers. Their gifts were substantially larger than previous such contributions. Before the sixteenth century all these gifts were single allocations of cash and the amounts were hardly enough to tide the child over once the benefactor died: they ranged from 30 soldi in a testament of 1290 to 10 florins in wills redacted in 1424 and 1430.[24] In the sixteenth century, testators' universal heirs were not able to dispense with their surrogate brothers and sisters so easily. The allocations were rarely single-shot, cash awards. When they were, the gift was often a dowry, which would support the adopted or fostered girl for life.[25] More often, the obligation was placed on the heirs "to administer and concede food and clothing for as long as the *alumnus* lived." The noble testator Paulus olim Bernardini alterius Pauli de Credis even added "in perpetuum."[26]

In contradistinction to the earlier settlements, testators of the Cinquecento left their surrogate children substantial real properties. In 1510 the priest ser Laurentius, a sacristan of Santa Maria della Scala, left his *nutrito*, who was a priest from the rural hamlet of Serre, the *usufructus* to a house in the *contrada* of Santa Maria delle Gratie, "where he might live for the rest of his life."²⁷ In 1554 "the Excellent and Reverend" dominus Minus f. q. Magnifici Johanbaptiste de Inciriculis, a doctor of jurisprudence and a cleric, devoted his entire codicil to providing for the children of his *alumnus*. Among other things, he bestowed on them his farm called "il Palazzo."²⁸ The Magnificus dominus Augustinus f. q. Franceschi de Bardis bequeathed to his *educatam* Maddalena a house with a garden in the Terzo of Camillia in the *contrada* of Borgo Franco. She further received "authority" over all of this property's rental income.²⁹ In 1569, the "honorable noble" lady Camilla f. q. Thomasi de Burgensibus, widow of a scion from the Saraceni family, left her *alumnus* Guilellmus from the village of Monte Orsaio two vineyards plus a small house (*domuculium*) with a hut (*casalino*) and a stable in the curia of his birthplace. She, moreover, prevented her heirs from expelling Guilellmus from the testator's house for at least two years after her death.³⁰

The most extraordinary gift to an adopted family member came not from the *Eques ac Generosi* of Sienese patriciate society, nor did it consist of extensive landed estates. In 1581, monna Caterina di fu Pasquino Neroni, widow of Girolamo di Lenzino, nominated the daughters of her *allevata* as her universal heirs. If they died in infancy, the estate would then pass to the parents, the testator's *allevata* monna Pasquina and her husband, a slipper maker.³¹ Not only did adopted children become a means of charity that circumvented the church: they also could provide a conduit for channeling the majority of the patrimony of those without offspring to secular hands instead of the church.³²

The few bequests made to those "raised in the house" during the seventeenth and eighteenth centuries (only 6 out of 1,785 pious bequests) returned to the forms preceding the sixteenth century.³³ They tended to be single-occasion cash payments without any assurance of support for a lifetime. In 1611 a testator from the village of Vescovado granted his *allevato* 50 scudi "for the love of God."³⁴ In 1632 Giovanbaptista, a nurse at Santa Maria della Scala and of illegitimate birth (*scala*), gave 20 scudi to each of two boys, both identified as *scali*, who were the *allevati* of the testator.³⁵ A widow in 1659 bequeathed a "furnished" bed to Giusta, the girl she "kept in her house."³⁶ Another widow, donna Ursola from Siena, granted the boy (*fanciuletto*) raised in her household a pair of sheets, a mattress, other articles of household linen, and 10 scudi "for charity and for the affection she brought him."³⁷ Finally, in the eighteenth century a surgeon bequeathed 100 scudi to a boy "whom he had raised from the sacred font."³⁸

The only striking exception to this post-Cinquecento pattern came from an outsider to the grand *stirpe* of Siena. In 1633, Maestro Giovanni, a *scala* and presently the manager (*granciere*) of Santa Maria della Scala's largest estate (Cuna), granted to his *allevato* Scipione, also a *scala* and at present a *granciere* at the hospital at Castelluccio, considerable properties and rights of possession: the *podere* called "Cartaio" with all its properties plus the rights of habitation in the testator's home. This *scala* and estate agent further entrusted his *allevato* with the responsibilities and obligations for restoring the dowry to Maestro Giovanni's wife and for determining the dowries to his two sisters.[39]

Disinheritance

While sixteenth-century testators were careful to explain why certain individuals were included in their wills, a new narrative elaboration accompanied their decisions to exclude family members and other possible claimants to their patrimonies. Earlier, the Sienese bequeathed small sums to the family members they felt were undeserving of major bequests. Grants of 5 soldi to 5 lire were often followed by the phrase "and he should ask for no more but be quiet and content." Table 7.1 tallies the frequency of these *non-petere* phrases over time for all nonpious gifts and for those pertaining only to family members.[40]

The frequency of such phrases warning friends and family to be content with what they received found its high point in the Trecento, perhaps showing once again the efficacy of mendicant preaching and ideology. As in the letters of Giovanni Colombini, Saint Catherine, and others, the ascetic appeals of the late Duecento and Trecento extended beyond the attachment to worldly goods; such preachers coaxed laypeople to cut their ties to kin as well. On the other

Table 7.1. The Frequency of the *Non-Petere* Clause

Period	Number of Nonpious Gifts	Number of Clauses	Number of Nonpious Gifts to Family	Number of Clauses
1205–1347	1340	85 6.3%	628	70 11.1%
1348–1400	916	70 7.6%	498	62 12.4%
1401–50	464	22 4.7%	294	18 6.1%
1451–1500	564	32 5.7%	392	29 7.4%
1501–50	345	25 7.2%	242	22 9.1%
1551–1600	667	35 5.2%	517	28 5.4%
1601–50	454	11 2.4%	348	10 2.9%

hand, testators of the late Duecento and Trecento made bequests to a wider range of relatives and nonrelatives than in the periods that followed. Custom may have encouraged more expectations for testamentary gifts, and testators may have needed to rebuke their claimants more often.

The frequency of these cautionary clauses fell in the early Renaissance, but then rose again through the first half of the sixteenth century. For the late Renaissance, the reasons for the rise were entirely different from those of the earlier period. Certainly, the figures were not related to a revival of ascetic and other-worldly principles or to an increase in the expectations of distant kin and nonrelatives. By the period of the Counter-Reformation, the percentages once again fell, at the moment when testators began to pour substantial portions of their worldly accumulations into church coffers. Hence, the ebb and flow of these figures does not correspond closely with a single underlying phenomenon, such as religious piety and asceticism. It would be misleading to interpret these figures strictly as evidence of waves in the importance of disinheritance. The exact reasons why a testator or the notary would attach such a clause to a bequest are not always clear. These commands and wishes on occasion accompanied sizable gifts or even a series of important bequests.

In fact, clear and direct cases of disinheritance are completely absent from this documentation until the beginning of the sixteenth century. Again, the more litigious-minded testators of Cinquecento were not content to let matters stand by simply granting a nominal sum followed with the formulaic "be content." Only by the sixteenth century did testators actually explain their reasons for granting a close relative less than one could assume by custom and law. Only then did they explicitly "disinherit" their spouses and offspring.

In 1544 Angelus olim Johannis de Cristofanis from the *pieve* of Sant'Anocrazio declared that his daughter Arminia had lived an unchaste life (*inoneste vixit*) "and now for a long time had withdrawn from the testator's authority, advice, and encouragement." He thus did not name his only child universal heir but "disinherited her" with a parting gift of 40 soldi to avoid a statutory infraction and "wished her to have no more from his goods."[41] The master tanner Magister Iacobus Iacobini Tabarini from Navarra in the territory of Milan, who lived in the city of Siena, declared in his testament of 1552 that Antonio, his son by his deceased first wife, had behaved badly (*male se gessit*)—that "this son had always treated and still treats his father badly and with dishonesty. He always borrowed in excess from the testator without repayment, and before leaving the house of his father, he stole and carried off almost entirely all the furnishings from the household: linen and wool cloth, clothing and other utensils and household goods, invidiously and against the wishes of the testator." The father calculated that his son's booty was valued at greater than 250 florins—which (conveniently) equaled his portion of the dowry left to him by his deceased mother Niccola. The tanner concluded by demanding that his son be entitled to no more of his property, except a nominal sum of 10 soldi "and no more."[42]

In 1552 a silk manufacturer, Petrus Mariani de Macanis, "attested" in his will to the "evil ways" and the "low life" of his son Ascanius. His son

> had committed many grave and dishonest deeds against the testator. Item. In the present year he had stolen from the cantina of the testator's house in Castro Vetero 4 salmas of wine and four years ago took an immense wine-cask from his wife which he pawned to a Jew for two gold scudi. Item. During the past year the aforesaid, to use common parlance, "conterfeited" the keys to the testator's shop located in the Chiasso Largo. On many different occasions he had run off with great sums of silk and money. Item. Many days have elapsed since this son accepted in marriage a poor and unchaste woman against the will of his father. Item. During the past year, the testator once wanted to get into his house, located beyond the gate of Ovile in a place called "l'arbolo." The house was locked and this son had the keys. And when the testator wanted to enter his house, the son refused to let his father in. Thus while this one stayed in the house, his father, against his will, was forced to remain and sleep for the entire night in a cellar. Item. Daily this son perpetrates new injuries against his father. For these reasons, the testator personally and expressly has disinherited his son and has deprived him of all of his property and desires that this son neither have nor partake of any of his goods or property.[43]

He appointed his other son Bernardino as universal heir. For the first time in this documentation, a father "expressly" disinherited a son without even bothering with the formulaic 5 soldi.

Later in the same year another silk manufacturer possessing a loftier title and grander estate than Petrus had troubles with his wife and sought to disinherit her. The "Spectabilis vir" Petrus f. q. Domenici Blasii, whose chapel foundation we have already examined, used his testament to make lengthy complaints against his wife. He began by damning his bad luck and misfortune that he chanced to marry domina Laura Iacobi de Landis, "who," he complained, "has always lived badly and behaved just as she pleased."

> She refused to listen to the admonishments which the testator made on many occasions and in diverse ways. She refused to be persuaded by the good and honest life and instead has always been evil and unchaste. On many occasions she has withdrawn from the testator, and because of her evil disposition and lack of self-respect has not slept or lived with the testator now for thirty months or longer. Nonetheless, the testator did not suspect that there was anything so serious and questioned her often during the past year and always believed everything she said to him. But domina Elizabetha, the widow of Niccolai de Cerchinis, and friar Hieronimus Minigainotti from Pistoia, and a monk of the order of Santo Spirito, and others . . . have said and have affirmed certain things over the present year after his wife had withdrawn from him and had left his house. The testator several days ago heard that his wife had given birth to a . . . child. Concerning this, the testator knows for certain that it was given birth outside of wedlock and is the product of adultery. He affirms and asserts that he

wishes to expel this child born of his wife, whether male or female, entirely from the succession to his estate and to exclude [him or her] completely from all of his property.[44]

In a long-winded and complicated legal restatement of his present marital circumstances and his charges against his wife, the silk manufacturer repeated several times the crux of his anxieties, that "a creature" not of his siring, "female or male, or any other issue," might later lay claims on a share of the patrimony.

In 1554, the *honesta mulier* Caterina f. q. Bernardini Antonii Nuti, after specifying the details of her burial, devoted the entirety of her will to explaining her reasons for treating unequally her two daughters. She first attested that her married daughter Virginia, who lived in Massa Marittima, had already received her dowry of 50 florins "and this was all she could ask." Unlike earlier testators, however, she did not end her comments here. She went on to claim that "this donna Virginia had many times and on many occasions, in one way or another, received her share and quota and even beyond her portion of the estate. She thus wished this daughter to remain quiet and content with the bequest of 50 florins and not to ask for any more." Caterina, then, left her other daughter Hortensia as the sole universal heir. Furthermore, she expressed her reasons. This daughter had welcomed her mother into her home, where "for a long time" the mother "has been able to stay and reside with her daughter and her son-in-law Bernardino Maestruccis. The mother attested that her daughter Hortensia "has provided for her at her own expense, has labored in her behalf and continues to care for her mother in her current state of illness."[45]

Finally, the "Spectabilis vir" Marcus f. q. Bartolommei Bindi from Radicondoli (encountered earlier) left his sons disproportionate shares to his estate. He spent the major portion of his 1594 testament explaining his reasons: "For a long time he has supported and kept his other son, the Reverend and Excellent Messer Cosimo, while he pursued his studies in the cities of Siena and Pisa and even in San Gimignano, where he was under the discipline of . . . Maestro Agostino of Montalcino of . . . the Dominican preachers. During this time the testator provided his son with clothing and books and with other expenses beyond food and the usual necessities. The testator has supported him through the degrees of the doctorate and that of priesthood and has paid all the expenses which these degrees have incurred." And "he is still ministering this son's expenses in Rome . . . where Messer Cosimo has spent the sum of 2,000 scudi and more. And this Messer Cosimo has never given his father the slightest benefit or profit, rather only expenses and damages."[46]

This testator then compared his son the doctor-priest with his other two sons, who had stayed behind tending to the mundane affairs of the shop in Radicondoli: "His other sons, Scipione and the former Giulio, now deceased, always had been diligent, skilled, and industrious. In their work and their trade, they have made great profit and have gained many acquisitions without ever taking sums of money or incurring expenses or damages from their father." He then asserted that "Messer Cosimo had already acquired more than his share" of the testator's properties. Nonetheless, "for reasons of a bequest" he bestowed on Messer Cosimo 50 scudi but left one-half of the estate to Scipione and the other half to the sons of his deceased son Giulio. The spendthrift, professional student and priest Messer Cosimo, was not mentioned at all in this portion of the will.

In the seventeenth century, these elaborate explanations for depriving family members from "participating" in the estate disappeared. In our samples only one case is found. In 1617 the master artisan Giovanbapttista di Pietro Pettorali began "with great sadness and afflication of spirit." He asserted that his daughter Fortuna, the wife of a linen maker, "had not accepted his admonitions and paternal corrections. Many times he had besought her to live honorably and to return to live with her husband. Instead, she had offended God with the public sins of sensuality, carnality, and wantonness. Therefore, the testator disinherited and excluded this daughter from his estate and property."[47] Here, the tone was different from the mid-Cinquecento disinheritances. The obsessions over property and with ensuring through legalistic provisos that the estate would be channeled exactly through the bloodlines a testator intended are not apparent in Maestro Giovanbaptista's decision to disinherit his daughter. Rather, religious outrage and moral indignation lay behind his embarrassed declarations in the new milieu of the early Counter-Reformation. Fortuna had sinned and had offended God. To be sure, the silk manufacturer Petrus in 1552 was none too happy with the sexual adventures of his wife. But his anxieties were not provoked by "public sins" or "offenses against God" but with the concrete matters of property—the possibility that other children neither of his making nor by his decisions might later, after his death, lay claims on his estate.

Conditional Gifts

Other sections of the sixteenth-century will point to other secular and material obsessions. Testators rarely imposed restrictions on the alienation of property on itemized gifts to friends and relatives. Such restrictions were generally reserved for the largest and most prized landed possessions, which testators channeled to universal heirs and, in the sixteenth century, through successive generations of male heirs. Nonetheless, the percentage of these restrictions, which crept into the body of nonpious bequests, mark a trend. In the earliest documents, when vestiges of a seigneurial patriciate still lingered on in Siena, 5 percent (4 bequests from 79 testators) of the testators restricted the alienation of properties found in the itemized lists. In the period of mendicant piety the percentage reached its lowest point, 1.5 percent of testators (5 bequests from 322 testators) and fluctuated only slightly higher in the Quattrocento (between 2 and 3 percent).[48] Then, in the second half of the sixteenth century, it reached the highest point found over the six centuries of this study (5.24 percent, 13 bequests from 248 testators).

Quantification alone, however, does not capture the character of these Cinquecento itemized bequests. Previously, clauses prohibiting the alienation of landed property were the only conditions testators attached. In the sixteenth century, a new internal complexity began to shape the body of these testaments. Space, previously reserved for the simple enumeration of itemized gifts—a succinct description of the property plus the name of the beneficiary—now included multifarious stipulations regarding property divisions or use rights and threats to ensure that a testator's designs would be enacted after his or her departure from the temporal realm. For instance, the principal function of the 1551 will of a doctor, "Excellent Lord" Hieronimus degli Albertis, was to specify in exacting detail the property rights, possessions, and privileges between his two sons. Lord Hieronimus was less content than testators in earlier periods to allow his beneficiaries to iron out among themselves conflicts that might ensue after his earthly departure. Twenty-seven of twenty-nine itemized commands and allocations of property stipulated the exact property relations among his heirs—two sons, two daughters, and his *dilecte uxor*.

The doctor began with Annibale, giving him an estate (*predium*) in the commune of Asciano; in another item, he bequeathed him half of a field (*agri*) in the same rural district; and in another, a house in this district. Then, the son received certain rights in the house where the doctor and presumably his family currently resided, a house in the parish of San Pietro alla Scala. Here, he made his son's territorial rights clear with the painstaking care of an architectural blueprint: "And that in facing the house from the right hand side he does not have rights from the head [of the house] to the main entrance, but has the right of entry of 2 bracchie in width." The doctor also granted this son a well in the courtyard of his urban residence. He then turned to his other son, Ventura, who was given an estate in the commune of Rosia, a house in the commune of Asciano, a half-field in the same district, and another estate in the district of Vignani. Similarly, the testator granted Ventura his urban palazzo in the parish of San Pietro alla Scala "except for those portions" already granted to his brother and the specified rights of passage. He further bequeathed to this son the right to build a shop or study "from which he can enter from this floor which leads into the courtyard where the well is located." The father granted him further permission to "descend the stairs to the rooms" and the rights to "all of the apartments located on the floor beneath the previous level." Next, the father commanded Ventura to agree that his brother Annibale was to have the rights of possession to all the clothing and jewelry the testator had given to Annibale's wife. For this agreement, Annibale was to pay Ventura 250 scudi. "For the benefit of his study," dominus Ventura was given all the books that the testator had previously designated. On the other side of the balance, the doctor commanded that neither Annibale nor Ventura disturb one another's "dowries" or their assigned landed estates. All the jewelry and furnishings in the house were to be divided equally between the two brothers. The itemized bequests continued in a similar vein, listing ad nauseam the detailed arrangements over the estate's division.⁴⁹

Domenico di Silvio Piccolomini spent the major portion of his rather lengthy testament of 1556 on the initial "item." Discontent that his mother and his widow would be left with the responsibilities of raising the children, he prevented them from selling off the clothing and furnishings of the household and insisted that they share the household goods and responsibilities. He desired that they agree to stay together "through thick and thin (*agli bene e male gli porgiora lo omnipotente iddio*)." He conceded to his wife her dowry but maintained that its "fruits" should support his mother and concluded that he would be "very content" only if his mother and wife "would remain content living together for their own welfare and utility."⁵⁰

Madonna Catherina, daughter of a dealer of linen cloth, who had succeeded in marrying the nobleman Messer Anibale Ugurgieri, left in 1566 one of the richest legacies to churches and for charitable causes found in the Cinquecento testaments. Fifteen bequests were directed to pious beneficiaries, conveying money and debts and property valued at least 2,115 florins. In her largest legacy, she directed her heirs to choose five nubile women from the nobility (*cicole nobili*) and to donate 250 florins to support three of the women who would enter nunneries and the two who wished to marry. She gave 500 florins to the monastery of Santo Spirito with the proviso that the monks say a mass for her soul every day *in perpetuo* and three offices every year for the first seven years after her death. The linen salesman's daughter further demanded that her heirs invest this money in real property (*beni stabili*) which could never be alienated. The heirs were to withdraw the "fruits" at a rate of 3 percent per annum to pay for the monks' services. She directed them to grant the *poveri vergognosi* 2 moggi of grain a year in perpetuity—1 moggio for the health of her soul, the other for the soul of her deceased husband, the "most delectable" Messer Anibale. Again, monna Catherina was not content to let her pious decisions stand as such. She interjected her intentions into the future after her death. In order "to satisfy these *poveri* in perpetuity," she required her heirs to purchase *beni stabili*. The most intriguing bequest in this testament, however, regarded a nonpious legacy. To a man with no apparent kinship to her she gave a "palazzo" called "i Grotti" with all its furnishings and a farm adjacent to it, in addition to her residence in Siena and all its furnishings. She demanded that he could never sell, rent, or any way alienate any of this property. If he did or died without heirs, the estate would pass on to her universal heirs. The shopkeeper's daughter further stipulated that neither this man nor any future recipients of her property might use "for their own benefit" any of the money, "whether of great or little quantity," found in the houses of her estate. Rather, this money should pay for 300 masses and the remainder, if any, was to be distributed to noble girls for dowries, for the *poveri vergognosi*, and for *luoghi pii*, "not including the legacies listed above." Then monna Catherina introduced a clause truly unprecedented in these documents: if her beneficiaries used these monies "for their own benefit" she threatened them with the "pain of papal excommunication."⁵¹

In 1568 the Magnificus dominus Antonius f. q. Alexandri domini Antonii de Niccoluccis drew up a will without a single pious bequest and only five itemized nonpious legacies. Nonetheless, the testament is lengthy and complex. First, he stipulated the rights of his widow, domina Caterina filia Camilli de Ugurgeriis, as "patron" (*patronam, usuariam et usufructariam*) of his household. He specified that his *dilectissimam uxorem* should possess the use of all his movables found in his residence at the time of his death: this pertained "equally" to all the money, silver, and jewelry. He freed her from rendering any accounting of these properties and bequeathed to her the "full and free" administration of the home so long as she lived a widow's life and stayed with his children. Otherwise, she would receive only her dowry, 200 scudi. The second "item" was a bequest to his son dominus Rutilius of "the office (*officium*)" of cavalier of San Pietro in Urbino. He was given the right to alienate or dispose of this office, to provide himself as he saw fit with the "necessities" and books for his education. The proceeds from its sale were to be invested in real estate (*in bonis stabilis*), according to the advice of the testator's *fideicommissarii*, or used to dower his daughters. Should dominus Rutilius be unable to sell the office, he might keep it but would then be held to compensate the other heirs. Antonio provided for his three daughters, too—and a fourth if the child with whom his wife was presently pregnant happened to be a girl. His wife, along with the executors of the estate, should decide on the "sum and quantity" of these dowries. They should, furthermore, call on the advice of a certain dominus Robertus de Sergardis. The amounts of the dowries should reflect "the capacities" of the family and "be congruent" with its "decency." The fifth item was short and direct. He gave his *alumna* 10 scudi for her salary to be paid within two years.⁵²

In a will of 1569, "the noble and honest" domina Camilla f. q. Thommasii de Burgensibus, widow of a man from the Saraceni family, provided her great-granddaughter Comitissa a dowry of 3,000 florins with the stipulation that Comitissa would not ask for anything else from either her father's or mother's inheritances. Further, the interest that had accrued from her part of the maternal and paternal inheritances ought to go to Comitissa's brothers. The testator then tried to control other eventualities through legal contingencies. She "declared that if for some unforeseen reason or need this Comitissa, by some impediment of nature, brought on by God, should be incapable of marriage, or if she should not marry because of the decisions of those left with the paternal power and authority to approve her marriage, or if she should lose the suit she presently was bringing against the testator in the orphan's court (Curia Placiti)," then the two sisters of the testator should inherit the 3,000 florins.⁵³

Similarly, by the mid-sixteenth century, the settlements that husbands left their widows became more intricate than previously. Traditionally, widows were entitled to the *usufructus* of the testators' possessions as long as they "remained chaste and lived the widowly life." By mid-century, husbands were not always content to leave the final arrangements between their offspring or other heirs and their wives to the vagaries of customary formulas. Again, these Cinquecento testators became obsessed with mapping out with precision the final arrangements for their worldly possessions. As a result, new clauses and property conditions crop up in these wills.

In 1568, the "Magnificent" Giulio di Girolamo Bargagli left his widow the rights of patronage and the usufruct to only one-half of his possessions. "Because he wanted the other half to be at the disposition of his sons, the income (*ragione*) from this half was reserved for them." Thus these sons "should remain free from any demands" that their mother might make on this other half of the possessions. As for the first half, however, the wife was to enjoy its use in full. He emphasized that these rights included not only income for food and dress, but (he repeated) "the full and entire use," the "holding and corporale possession" of these properties. The testator made further contingency plans. If his widow could not or wished not to stay with his children, she would then be entitled to the usufruct of all the properties in the region of the Creta in the commune of San Martino in Grania and in the Comune de la Ripa. Or she might elect in exchange to have the usufruct of a *podere* called "Novelleto" in Monteriggioni. She might have, moreover, two rooms of her choosing in their house of residence in Siena. The "Magnificent" Giulio then proceeded to undermine the traditional social security for widows and orphans in late medieval and early modern Europe—the widow's right to her dowry. He maintained that the legacy of this usufruct meant that his widow might not ask for her dowry; if she did so, she would then lose the income from all of the gifts mentioned. He further asserted that if any of his sons could not get along with one another or obey one another or stay with their mother, then they were to have 500 scudi of the testator's possessions. These properties, the testator clarified, would be their share from both the paternal as well as the maternal side of their inheritance.[54]

On first examination these examples might only elaborate the earlier distinction: testators after the plague of 1363 and the erosion of Trecento mendicant culture turned their attention to more worldly matters. They could no longer be content to leave matters of the terrestrial realm to chance with pat formulaic phrases or to the whims of their heirs and beneficiaries. But by the mid-Cinquecento these documents had changed qualitatively from the records of the Quattrocento. The degree to which testators were obsessed with manipulating and controlling future relations between heirs, kin, and other beneficiaries had changed overwhelmingly. In the Quattrocento, itemized nonpious bequests continued to be straightforward, simple legacies. Rarely were restrictions placed on these bequests; rarely did contingency clauses seek to regulate the future of terrestrial holdings—precise divisions of property or alienability over the course of generations—or to control the future behavior of beneficiaries. By the mid-Cinquecento, testators, such as Lord Hieronimus, Domenico Piccolomini, monna Catherina (the daughter of the linen salesman), and others went much further than their Quattrocento ancestors ever imagined in mapping out future relationships between spouses, siblings, and other heirs, imposing plans for the future long after departing the temporal realm. As we have seen, they decided minute details for successive generations, such as which heirs should possess which rights of passage in the testator's domicile. Husbands were no longer content to let matters stand with the traditional notarial formulas regarding their wives' *usufructus* to their estates. For the first time new and specific provisions appeared which gave both widows and children other property options if they found they could not cohabit. In short, those on their deathbeds in the Cinquecento, while not abandoning completely matters of the soul, pushed them to the background to concentrate on the future of their properties and blood relations after they had departed the earthly scene.

In the itemized bequests, before the testator turned to his or her universal heirs, two obsessions emerge from the Cinquecento wills. The first concerned the future transmissions of property. The second regarded that other transitory "loan from God" against which ascetics from Francis to Carlo Borromeo railed—family and lineage. A new ideology of family emerged in these Cinquecento documents. Although most forcefully reflected in provisions pertaining to the universal heirs, this obsession also colored the itemized bequests. "Nobilissimus Iuvenis" dominus Laurentius olim Magnifici domini Bartolommei de Griffolis, "citizen and patrician of Siena," faced in his testament of 1551 the prospects of the extinction of his particular branch within his noble lineage. Most of this long and elaborate will confronted this demographic hazard and attempted to surmount it through nonbiological means. In one itemized bequest, the nobleman created a new twist on a charitable annuity as God and family for one moment were melded together. "For the love of God and the heart of his family," he donated rights of habitation in his residential palace and an annual income for seven years of 10 salma of grain, 8 salma of wine, 2 staii of oil, and 50 florins to two "honest and single-born sons, who were noblemen of the Griffoli family, twenty years or older, and who were not vile but of good morals and virtue." If one of those chosen was found to be "defective," then these rights and goods would pass on to his relatives along either the agnatic or consanguineous lines. The testator then obliged these noblemen of the Griffoli family to repeat "the Penitential Psalms of David" for the soul of the testator every day for as long as they enjoyed the legacy. They were "expressly prohibited," moreover, from wearing any article made of silk during these seven years of service to the Griffoli family name.[55]

These examples of intricate nonpious gifts, which grew in importance and complexity in the sixteenth century, illustrate that more was happening than simply a decline in piety and charity. As we have argued, the radical decline in both pious and nonpious bequests suggests that the opaque residual category— the lion's share of the estate which descended to the universal heirs—must not have been constant over time. As we have seen, the sixteenth-century tightening of both pious gifts and legacies to friends and distant kin freed more property to be channeled down lines of universal heirs, who (as we will see in the next chapter) became, as the century progressed, more consistently the nearest related males along consanguineal, that is blood, lines.

~~ 8   Universal Heirs

> *La terra manda l'abbondanza e voi mettete la fame, omini avarii alla terra tornate.*
> —Brandano da Petroio

A casual and nonquantitative reading of the wills shows a change in testament writing by the sixteenth century. The notary's attention had drifted from the itemized legacies to the final settlements involving the testator's heirs. Unfortunately, these final sections rarely described or indicated the values of these residual possessions. Thus the quantitative historian is disarmed to a far greater degree when approaching these portions of the testament. Nonetheless, quantification of these final decisions in the will does chart certain trends.

Table 8.1 gives a sense of the growing complexities embodied in testators' final decisions in their wills regarding their universal heirs. In the table, UH1 indicates the number of testaments in which testators specifically designated their heirs; UH2, testaments with one set of contingent heirs; UH3, a third tier of contingency; and UH4, four or more generations of contingencies and substitutions. For those testaments categorized UH2 through UH4, the testator looked into the future beyond his or her death and one generation or more beyond those alive at the time of redaction and chose an heir or a group of heirs to inherit the patrimony. Usually, these contingencies regarded matters of survival and the procreation of future heirs. The testators did not leave it to the decisions of their heirs, or, if they happened to die without a will, to the statutes regarding intestate inheritance. Rather, testators made clear in their wills to whom the property should flow if their sons, daughters, nephews, and so on died without heirs or died in childhood (*in pupillari*). Regarding successive transitions of property to other heirs, these contingencies based on failures of the original heirs to produce subsequent heirs accounted for the majority of alternate heirs.

Second, testators placed conditions on their heirs and stipulated another tier of heirs who would assume the rights and responsibilities of the inheritance if the initial ones failed to follow the dictates in the testament, such as distributing the itemized bequests, saying masses, or performing other charitable and pious acts. Third, testators in the Cinquecento hoped to rule over their heirs from the

Table 8.1. Contingent Heirs, 1205–1800

Period	Testator	UH1	UH2	UH3	UH4
1205–1300	79	67 84.8%	10 12.7%	5 6.3%	2 2.5%
1301–1400	322	313 97.2%	57 17.7%	21 6.5%	6 1.9%
1401–1500	259	250 96.5%	42 16.2%	16 6.2%	1 0.4%
1501–50	155	155 100	41 26.5%	13 8.3%	7 4.5%
1551–1600	248	248 100%	78 31.3%	18 7.2%	7 2.8%
1601–50	197	191 97%	43 21.8%	16 8.1%	4 2.0%
1651–1700	195	189 96.9%	48 24.6%	14 7.2%	3 1.5%
1701–50	179	171 95.5%	32 17.9%	20 11.2%	7 3.9%
1750–1800	157	150 95.5%	9 5.7%	3 1.9%	0 0.0%

grave. If these heirs violated those stipulations imposed on them by the will, then the contingent heir who stood next in line in the will could assume possession over the testator's patrimony. Often, as in several testaments we examined earlier, these regulations regarded the alienation of real property. But by the middle of the sixteenth century testators pried further into the future business of their heirs. For instance, to protect their properties from state confiscation, they asserted that the heir would lose all claims to the property if convicted of a criminal offense or if banished from the territory of Siena. In these cases, the dead testator, through the legal devices of the will, could indicate to whom the inheritance should fall.

Although the death of an heir or his failure to produce a successor was the most common contingency for which testators specified substitute heirs, the proportion of these contingencies was not constant throughout these documents. Instead, other conditions, to fulfill certain obligations or not to alienate property, became more common. During the Trecento, testators placed such threats and obligatory clauses in only 16.7 percent of all conditions. By the second half of the sixteenth century, their demands had nearly trebled in relation to the survival clauses, accounting for 44.6 percent of the conditions. With these qualitative changes in mind, let us return to the statistics in Table 8.1. From the Quattrocento to the end of the sixteenth century, the percentage of those testators who made contingencies for the transition of their patrimonies for at least one generation beyond the initial choice of heirs nearly doubled from one-sixth to one-third of all wills.

Yet these statistics fail to do justice to the massive transformation in the structure and content of testament writing of the sixteenth century. Again, the narrative materials found in these wills can flesh out the skeletal outlines of our statistics. Most often testators' demands continued to restrict the alienation of real property. In the sixteenth century, however, these clauses became more common than before and began to include the testaments of those beneath the merchant elite. For instance, in 1553, the "honest woman" donna Magdelena f. q. Sanctis Blasii, the daughter of a stonecutter from Siena, left her estate to a linen manufacturer, the husband of her niece on her father's side. She nominated this *linaiolus* on condition that "he never sell, rent, or in any way alienate" any of the patrimony. If he should do so, then the estate would pass to another niece.[1] In a testament of 1554, Magister Albertus, an oven maker from Sala, saddled his universal heir, the nephew of his deceased wife, with a complex set of obligations. For each of ten years following the testator's death, his heir was obliged to donate to the Cappuccin friars and the friars of Santa Maria de Albigorio in Lombardy 2 scudi as well as bread, wine, and oil. For these gifts, the friars were to say Gregorian masses for Master Albert's soul. He, moreover, prevented his heir from alienating any of the patrimony. If he violated these stipulations the estate would pass into the hands of the "men and commune" of the testator's birthplace, Sala.[2]

These alienation clauses became ever more complex and variable. In addition to the general clause prohibiting heirs from alienating a testator's "goods" (*bona*), testators by the mid-sixteenth century increasingly made distinctions among their real properties and entailed certain treasured estates never to be sold, mortgaged, donated, or alienated. On occasion they assigned to their estates advisors, from whom the heirs had to receive "the consent and the express permission" before selling off any of their inheritances.[3] In other instances, the ambit of alienation was specifically restricted in such a way as to reflect a new sense of family consciousness and of lineage. Thus the "honorable and most noble" domina Camilla f. olim Magnifici Raynaldi de Tolomeis, widow of Niccolai de Petruccis, prohibited her heirs from alienating their portions of the patrimony *extra cippum,* outside the family stock.[4] Or again, in 1553 the "Spectabilis" Marcus Antonius alterius olim Marci Antonii Domini Raynaldi de Fungariis in naming his two brothers as universal heirs prohibited them from alienating a certain familial estate without the approval of the most closely related "agnates" and the other male descendants of the family.[5]

The obligations and threats grew in complexity by the middle of the Cinquecento. For instance, the "provident man" Magister Johannes Pierus olim Magistri Bartolommeo de Odorinis, a blacksmith from Cuna and "at present" residing in Siena, left his son as universal heir on condition that he never sell, donate, trade, rent, or lease out *in emphiteusia* any of his properties. If he did so, the properties along with the same obligations would pass to the hospital of Santa Maria della Scala. If the hospital failed to execute the will within one month or prosecuted against it, the patrimony would pass to the Franciscans. If they did not meet the same restrictions, then it would devolve to the confraternity of San Bernardino. If they failed in these obligations they were held to celebrate "an office for the dead with masses sung." The blacksmith did not end his restrictions here. He heaped yet another restriction on his original heir: "Wishing to provide the best for this testator and that the aforesaid heir not dissipate his properties but conserve them, the testator wished, disposed, ordered and demanded that . . . his heir might not promise or be obligated to any person for any amount exceeding 2 lire." If he should become so indebted, he was to pay a penalty of 500 florins to Santa Maria della Scala. Further, should this contingency arise, the hospital would be required to use these funds to marry off poor girls of the hospital at 25 florins per dowry.[6]

In a testament of 1547, the "prudent man" Guidonis f. q. Francischi de Marris, a peasant (*laborator terrarum*) from Abadia a Isola, named his son Marianus as universal heir on condition that he reinstate his brothers as coheirs only if the commune of Siena would lift its sentence of exile against them.[7] By the latter part of the century, testators regularly attached clauses to protect their estates from confiscation by disinheriting prospective heirs who were prosecuted in civil or criminal courts.[8]

Testators of the Cinquecento pried into other affairs of their heirs. The testament of the "Magnificent and Noble" Lord Count Achille q. Comitis Alexandri of the Counts of Ilcio prevented his heirs from dividing their vast estates and from "any act of property transaction" until the youngest son had reached age twenty-five on pain of losing their inheritance.[9] The testament of "the Noble and Chaste" Madonna Pantasilea f. gia Bartolommei Donati, widow of the "Magnificent" Pio Onofrii, placed no property prohibitions on her non-related universal heir Achille. Instead, she required him to marry her sister Atalanta within a year following her death—or, should Atalanta no longer be available, to marry someone else from his neighborhood (*di suo paraggio*) within the same period; otherwise the inheritance would pass to his brother Anibale, who was likewise required to marry someone from the neighborhood within one year or else the inheritance would devolve to another brother, Ardnibale, who was subjected to the same conditions in turn.

The testator, obsessed with the continuation of offspring and lineage to accompany her worldly possessions, did not stop with these contingencies. If Achille should marry and his wife die before bearing legitimate heirs, he was to remarry another from the neighborhood, again within a year; otherwise, the inheritance would pass to Anibale and then to Ardnibale with the same conditions. If all three failed to marry, or if they married and produced no heirs, or if their wives died and they failed to remarry within one year, the patrimony would pass to another lineage of another nonrelative, Marcellus Niccoli Donati. The honest Pantasilea placed on this possible heir (six possibilities removed from the original choice of heir) the same set of obligations: to marry within the neighborhood and within one year. Finally, if this Marcellus did not succeed in finding such a woman, the properties would then pass to the poor tertiaries of the Convent of Paradiso in the section of Siena called Poggio Malavolti, who would be required to pray for the soul of Madonna Pantasilea.[10]

In 1596, domina Maddalena f. q. Bartolommei from Castro Florentino but living in Siena, the widow of a wholesaler of footwear (*emporii calceolarii*), set similar restrictions on her universal heir, her nephew on her sister's side. The youth was required to "take a wife (*pigliar moglie*)" within eighteen months following his inheritance; otherwise the properties would pass to the testatrix's brother under the same conditions. By the close of the century—after the Council of Trent and the Counter-Reformation visitations of Bossi—new demands began to influence the testaments: Lady Maddalena also required her heirs "to live like Christians (*e viver Christianamente*)."[11]

In contrast, the demands of the "Magnificent and Generous" knight Dominus Hieronymus q. Johannis de Beringuccis, citizen and "dignissimus" rector of Santa Maria della Scala, were more in keeping with the spirit of Cinquecento property transmission. His will of 1566 commanded his heirs "to live always as laymen." "If any of them became monks, sacerdotes, or priests," their portion of the patrimony would be divided among the others who continued "to live the life of laymen (*che vivino secolari et in vita laicale*)."[12]

Whereas portions of the will previously reserved for the universal heirs had by the sixteenth century spilled into the body of itemized legacies, other wills of the period dismissed entirely the itemization of individual gifts and jumped directly to the clauses governing their universal heirs. The testament had become an elaborate gloss on the rights, conditions, obligations, and contingencies pertaining to universal heirs and the veins of property descent through the bloodlines of future generations. The first itemized bequest in the 1543 testament of Johannes olim ser Johannis ser Dominici de Fidelibus from Piano Servi concerned the devolution of all his properties to his universal heirs. He thus nominated the "*creaturam seu creaturas, masculum seu feminam, masculos sive feminas* conceived in the uterus of his most honest wife who was at present pregnant." The remainder of this testament, eleven items and clauses, plotted out the possible contingencies in case the posthumous child or children died *in pupillari etate*. First, the monastery of Santa Maria dei Servi would receive an estate (*predium*) in Maggiano, being required in return to spend 10 lire a year for the perpetual celebration of two holy offices a year. Then a contingency was placed on this contingency: if the monastery should cease for any reason to celebrate these offices, the rural estate would pass to the hospital of Santa Maria della Scala. Second, if his posthumous children should not survive childhood, the testator would donate his house of residence in the village of Piano Servi to the monastery of Santo Spirito, which would be obliged to celebrate two offices a year in perpetuity or else these possessions would pass to Santa Maria della Scala. Third, if these potential heirs did not survive, all the household furnishings (*massaritias*) would go to a donna Caterina, the daughter of a cobbler. Fourth, an estate in the commune of Ravicciano would descend on "the heirs in the first degree" of Johanbaptista f. q. Torinis de Mannellis, who would be required to celebrate divine offices in the church of the Servites and spend 10 lire a year for as long as Johanbaptista lived. The document continues thus plotting out contingencies and, on occasion, contingencies on the already contingent legacies.[13] Others, for example Margherita f. q. Gabrielis Hyeronimi de Ghinis, the wife of Hannibale de Albertis and who received the perplexing title "chaste virgin (*honesta virgo*)," similarly, without any itemized bequests, dove straight into the future contingencies of possible lines of universal heirs.[14] The servant Lucrezia Marcii from the village of Ilcinea began her will directly by "instituting" her three sons and her employer, Augustinus Verdiani, a pork butcher, as universal heirs. She instructed her sons that their inheritance was in the hands of her boss and that they must litigate for the properties against the pork butcher, his wife, and his successors. She declared that her inheritance was "namely" her salary and other merchandise, which Augustinus and his wife owed her for her services as maid and wetnurse (*balia*) in their home over the past twenty years. Thus the sole purpose of her will was in this case not to avoid future litigation over her inheritance but to establish the legal grounds by which her sons could initiate proceedings against her employer as soon as she died. Through the instrument of the will she claimed to be her employer's creditor.[15]

In a less complex will of 1553, Susinus q. Francisci Corsus de Loreto, presently a soldier (*miles*) under the command of Captain Bernardini Corsi, launched directly into the substance and qualifications regarding his heirs. No long preambles invoking the health of his soul or itemized bequests to pious institutions, friends, or relatives fill the spaces between the opening notarial formula and the clauses concerning his major heirs. He nominated his nephew from Loreto, a Corsican, as his heir, but again not unconditionally, for the testator held his heir to the condition that "if ever his brother Giannus . . . , who had been captured by pirates and Turks, nine or ten years ago while serving his country, should return, then all the testator's property should pass to this brother and this Giannus would be instituted as the universal heir."[16]

Family and Lineage—the Male Line

The most common reason for testators and their notaries to expand and concentrate on these final portions of a will concerned family and lineage. In 1549 "lo spectabile homo" Girolamo gia di Mariano Cerchii, a linen or used cloth dealer, left his son Thommasso (who followed his father's business) as universal heir along with Thommasso's legitimate sons. If his son "should die or live without sons," the linen dealer stipulated that the properties would pass to his brother Giovanni who also practiced the trade and to Giovanni's sons and grandsons. If Giovanni died without sons, then the properties should pass to Mariano and to Marcantigone, also *righittieri*, who were his nephews and the sons of his deceased brother Achille. Girolamo further specified that one of his prized *podere*, Argiano, located in the Masse of Siena, should pass to all the male offspring of these nephews according to the branch of the family (*stirpe*) and not according to the individual (*a capite*). If this *podere*, moreover, should come into the hands of these two nephews, the testator "demanded that the farm should never be sold, exchanged, donated, or in any way alienated, *except* within the family of the Cerchii, and that it should remain always in the house (*casa*) of the family of the Cerchii." Here, the Latin patronymic, Cerchii, is for the first time prefaced by the preposition "de," and the successful used-clothes salesman appears to have employed his testament to create a family name, to be associated and honored perpetually by its connection with inalienable property, the *podere* of Argiano. In addition, if anyone of these successors should want to alienate this estate, he would be obliged to offer the property to someone from "the Cerchii" at a price determined by officers of the commune of Siena. In regard to another estate, the *podere* of "Galinaio" in the curia of Monteriggioni, the testator's restrictions were slightly different. If the sons or heirs of a certain Cristofano Santi should wish to repurchase the property or if the testator or his son Thommasso should wish to sell this land, then their heirs were obliged to reinvest the monies in other real estate (*beni stabili*). The testator, however, did not extend the same options to the secondary tier of property devolution, the brothers Mariano and Marcantogno and their male heirs. Finally, in contradistinction to property restrictions of the eighteenth century, which focused on the actual estate management and profits to be accrued from the land, the testator gave his son Thommasso a carte blanche to the use of these real properties: "he could use, hold, and enjoy these farms and the animals on them in any way he pleased; like the testator himself, he could cut down trees, plant vines, or do whatever he wanted and his heirs would have to accept these properties however they may find them on the death of his son Thommasso, for better or for worse."[17] The testament of the used-cloth dealer Girolamo spelled out clearly the symbolic power of real property as opposed to its economic value: its identification with family name and the prestige and duration of the male line.

In addition, this testament along with others employed a new vocabulary that began to infiltrate testaments by the mid-Cinquecento: words such as *casa* (to denote lineage and family), *stirpe, fameglia* or *familia*. As in the document just discussed, the early appearances of these new words do not show a clear sequence of devolution from the ranks of the aristocracy to the plebeians. The term *cippum*, for example, appears for the first time in this documentation in the 1551 testament of a domina Baptista, the daughter of the tanner or cobbler (*aluttarius*). She does not even bear a family name and her only possession, apparent in this testament, is her house in the *contrada* of Salicotti and its furnishings (*massaritia*). Domina Baptista bequeathed this property to her mother. She then entailed the property through the lines of her "family stock and to the nearest kinsmen of the house (*ad cippum et proximiores domus*)."[18]

The first appearance of the term *primus genitor* also originated in the mid-Cinquecento. The "Magnificus ac Generosus Eques" dominus Scipio olim Magnifici Mariani de Ventinis, who at present was the *mentissimus Vicarius* of Santa Maria della Scala, in 1554 left his two brothers as universal heirs. "For love and esteem and in compensation," he demanded that they recognize the rights of his wife to all the fruits and to reside in a part of his urban residence with her family, the Serafini. After her death, he left all the rights of this house to the *primo genito* from the sons of one of his brothers, whom he had designated as a universal heir. The "Magnificent and Generous" Scipio emphasized that this child must be male and "might not mortgage or in any way alienate the house." If the primogenitor should violate this stipulation, his wife's portion of the residence would then pass to Santa Maria della Scala.[19] The testator, however, did not entail this property beyond his brother's offspring.[20]

One of the earliest examples in which a testator entailed his inheritance specifically through the lineage of the first-born son comes, surprisingly, not from a scion of one of the ancient and noble families, but instead from a churchman who did not bear a family name. In a codicil of 1562, the "Venerable friar" Joannes q. Laurentii, treasurer of Santa Maria della Scala, named his brother Alessandro as his heir, the *primogenito* of the family. He left him his house in the *terzo* of San Martino, in the *contrada* of Salicotti. The monk next declared that the property should, from then on, descend *de primogenito in primum genitum*. The venerable friar specified that if the said Alessandro or *li detti primogeniti* alienated this house, then they "were required to buy another piece of real estate (*cosa stabile*) equivalent to and of the same value as" the house in Salicotti. The friar emphasized that this demand applied whether "Alessandro, the primogenitor of Alessandro, or any future primogenitor down the line (et di poi di primogenito in primogenito) should ever sell the property."[21]

In a testament redacted a year and three months later by a different notary and for another client who, again, did not bear a family name, another technical term for the specification of lineage and family—*agnatio*—first appears. Three daughters survived Matthias called Maffio olim Pieri Domenici from the rural village of Boscona in the territory of Colle Val d'Elsa. The testator dowered his daughters and named them as the universal heirs. He then specified if any of these daughters died, their share of the patrimony should descend to the "nearest agnate of the testator's family stock." The testator further emphasized that the "substitutes" were to be of "masculine birth" and that women, even if agnates, "should not be called and for no reason should they succeed, since the succession was intended for the nearest male relation."[22]

Knight Hieronymus, rector of Santa Maria della Scala, in 1566 made use of another technical term in the growing vocabulary defining the new ideology of family and lineage. The transmission of his estate was to descend *in ordine successive* "to those males of the family stock who at that time would be the closest living relative," by "substitution commonly called '*fideicommissum* [entail].'"23

By the 1560s property descent through the male line had become standard, at least among the nobility of Siena. At the same time, testators heaped other demands, qualifications, and restrictions on their heirs. Giovanbattista di Messer Deifebo Brogioni, for instance, named his three brothers as his heirs. First, he prohibited them from becoming involved in any dispute, whether before a judiciary or "outside the law," which would in any way challenge the property rights of his *alevato,* the mother of this child, or their descendants. If they violated these stipulations, his inheritance would pass to the hospital of Santa Maria della Scala.24 He next asserted that a kinsman, Magnificus Niccolò Brogioni, "could in no way participate in the inheritance or have any of his properties" and finally specified that if any of his heirs should die without sons, the property would descend to the other two brothers and then to their male heirs, *in stirpe e non in capite*. If they produced no male offspring, the properties would go to the female children, again *in stirpe,* and afterward to their male children.

The testament of the "Magnificient and Noble" Count of Ilcio also defined family according to the male line. He prohibited "his sons and heirs and their descendants, who would succeed forever through the male line (*ipsis descendentibus per lineam masculinam in perpetuum et in infinitum*)," from all acts of alienation, all contracts and transfers of the testator's "dominion" found in the *curie* of Monte alle Gengnoli and Ilci. The count emphasized further that these properties could never be alienated "for reasons of granting dowries, for pious causes, or for the constitution or foundation of churches or for any other cause, no matter how important or privileged its expression." Rather, they "were to remain in perpetuity as the properties of the Count and should stay *in familia.*"25

Not all testators of the late sixteenth century were as self-assured about the continuation of their progeny and their male line *in infinitum.* In 1594 a Messer Franciscus q. Thommassij de Boscarellis from the village of Montichiello and at the time residing in the country (*terre*) of Civitella of the Maremma left his small estate to his sons and "all other masculine children" whom he might father as universal heirs. They were "to conserve the real properties through the male line and in the family (*in agnatione et familia*)" and were not to alienate them "until the last family member died and the male line had become extinct." He then planned for this final eventuality: "For the exoneration of his conscience and that of his son Giulius" the properties of the lineage would pass to the plebis church called Santa Maria in Montibus. The church would be held to celebrate every year offices for the dead for the souls of all of those bearing his family name, the Boscarelli. If the church reneged, the ancestral properties would pass to the congregation of the clergy of Saint Peter in the cathedral of Siena with the obligation of "erecting and founding" a chapel in a place of poverty and greatest spiritual need. The rural artisan then would grant the *ius patronatus* "to the nearest male relative by blood or through marriage." These rights, moreover, would descend, in perpetuity, to the nearest "existing" kin of the testator. Similarly, the congregation of San Pietro was required to celebrate each month of every year one mass "in commemoration of the dead of the Boscarelli family."[26]

Conclusion

Initially our statistics suggested that one of the least-accepted conclusions of that standard-bearer of the Renaissance, Jacob Burckhardt, might, with qualifications, deserve some reconsideration. "Renaissance" men and women were never atheistic or freethinking and the new attitudes to the church charted by our statistics bracket a "Renaissance" which begins only by the latter half of the Quattrocento. Nonetheless, in "the great age of selfishness" of the late fifteenth and sixteenth centuries, testators cut back sharply their contributions to the church and even more drastically their support of charitable causes. Their most spectacular donations went to foundations of private chapels. But these "pious bequests," instead of channeling property and monies into church coffers, increasingly usurped sacred space for the power and glory of family and lineage.

This chapter described a fundamental change in the form and structure of Cinquecento testaments. The attention of notaries and their clients had moved from the itemized bequests to long and complicated contingency clauses, to demands and threats placed on their universal heirs to control the succession of their properties. In the sixteenth century, a new strategy for the afterlife emerged. The Sienese departed from the charitable instincts of their forefathers—whether expressed through the allocation of numerous gifts of minuscule value or through the donations of a few but substantial properties to pious institutions. Although anxiety over the future of the soul certainly had not disappeared, their hopes for immortality no longer concentrated either on the "good works" of charity or through sacramental avenues. Their predominant obsessions with the afterlife focused instead on their material attachments to property and family—the survival of the family name and the flow of real properties through the male bloodline. By the middle of the Cinquecento, a new vocabulary, reflecting a new consciousness and ideology of family, entered the documents—*familia, stirpe, cippus, agnatio, primogenitum*—providing the legal mechanisms for entailing prized familial properties through the male line in perpetuity. The concluding testamentary clauses drew a maze of contingencies to circumvent demographic failures, even the extinctions of lineages, as well as to control the conduct of future heirs. Our examples have shown that these obsessions with the flow of blood and property were certainly not confined to the nobility alone. Blacksmiths, cobblers, friars without family names, small

Figure 5. Pinturicchio, fresco of Alberto Arringhieri, in the Arringhieri chapel of San Giovanni, the cathedral of Siena, 1502

landowners from the villages of Siena's periphery, and used-clothes salesmen were among the first to employ the new terminologies and legal structures to perpetuate family honor.

The statistics show that a new secularism, if not the Machiavellian hedonism of Burckhardt's *Civilization of the Renaissance,* did define the testaments from the late fifteenth through much of the sixteenth century. The flush of literary production staged for the new Sienese academies founded in the early Cinquecento corroborates the transition traced by the wills. Instead of the hackneyed themes of both late medieval and Renaissance *exempla*—matters of the mundane world versus ethereal concerns of the soul—Sienese comedies of the Cinquecento acted out new secular repertoires of the virtues and vices.[27] For example, the central dilemma facing the protagonist of *Alessandro* by Alessandro Piccolomini (Siena's most prominent literary figure of this century) skirts altogether spiritual issues. The character Alessandro accuses his friend Cornelius of "shrugging off *(che hai posto dietro a le spalle)* kin, friends, study [of the law, as it happened], honor, property, life, and every good." "And what for?" Alessandro asks and then answers himself: "For a woman who even if she were the most beautiful and intelligent girl in the world, would not merit all of this."[28] Similarly, in his manners book for women, Piccolomini, later the archbishop of Patrasso and assistant (*coadiutore*) to the archbishop of Siena, laughs out of court the old values of chastity imposed on women from the mendicant misogynists to "Renaissance men."[29] The wise old matron Raffaella gives the young and beautiful noble lady Margarita, the spouse of a traveling patrician, instructions on how best to select the perfect paramour. Here, family honor, not faith, is the final arbiter on questions of sexual license as well as general comportment.[30]

The secularism of the sixteenth century, however, had little to do with those parallel developments that Burckhardt found central to the civilization of the Italian Renaissance—individualism and modernity. As we have seen, the new ideology of family and lineage created a complex of new and intricate restrictions by which the ancestors sought to bind and control the future uses of property and the conduct of their heirs—as testators put it, "in infinitum." As a result, individual choices in regard to decisions over the final resting places for their bodies, over the uses of property, and over the ultimate allocation of inheritance had become more constrained by the middle of the sixteenth century than at any other time over the six centuries covered in this book. Instead of "modernity," the century for Siena, like other areas in central and northern Italy, is better placed within the context of those changes in property law, government, and the ethos of family, honor, and nobility, often labeled "the re-feudalization" of Italy.[31]

The dynamic of social and intellectual change during the long sixteenth century was different from the changes in the strategies of the afterlife found for the late Trecento. Unlike the earlier period, no convenient event "on the surface of history" appears to have sparked the changes for this "great age of selfishness." The period of "tyranny" first of Pandolfo Petrucci (1497–1512), followed by the misrule of his son Borghese and nephew Raffaello (who died in 1522) contributed to a general atmosphere of corruption and the usurpation of church property.[32] Pandolfo attempted to block legally the accumulation of real property in the hands of ecclesiastical corporations.[33] When these measures failed, he turned to illegal devices. In 1504 he forced the still-wealthy Santa Maria della Scala to sell off several of its largest estates to members of the Petrucci family at extremely low prices. A year later they forced the hospital to buy them back at market value, thereby realizing large profits.[34]

Scandals and family feuds over church properties and prerogatives, moreover, flared during the opening decades of the century. In 1500 Pandolfo's thugs fatally wounded his archrival and father-in-law Niccolò Borghesi while he was returning from prayer in the cathedral.[35] In 1514, the most sacred of church grounds, the cathedral of Siena, became the scene of armed struggle between the ruling clans of Siena—the Piccolomini and the Petrucci.[36] The dispute opened over questions of *ius patronatus* and the rights of a certain canon (appointed and protected by Borghese Petrucci) to perform masses in the cathedral. To oust the appointee of the Petrucci, the Piccolomini staged a *tumulto* while the disputed cleric was in fact celebrating the holy mass. The canons, disgusted with the violent tactics of the ruling elites, protested by leaving temporarily their posts in the cathedral.[37] In 1516 Rafaello Petrucci freely confiscated the properties of Santo Stefano in Siena and San Giovanni in the village of Lornano to create prizes for political patronage. Later in the year, in his struggles against the papacy and the appointment of Cardinal Alfonso to the bishopric of neighboring Sovona, Rafaello confiscated the income from the vast properties held by the archbishop of Siena in Vescovado as well as vast landed estates belonging to the wealthy monastery of San Galgano.[38]

The Petrucci were not the only ones guilty of the confiscation and even destruction of church property during the early Cinquecento. In 1525, after the Petrucci had been ousted from power, the senate of Siena passed a decree to demolish the nunnery of Santa Maria Maddalena, near the Porta Tufi, "in order to destroy the memory of Pandolfo Petrucci, who had built the monastery in honor of his patron saint whose day of solemnity was the day when the Nine returned to power."[39] Although these events and others, such as the papal interdict of the city in 1504 or, still earlier, modified mortmain legislation of the mid-Quattrocento, may well have contributed to the general religious malaise, none of these events correlates clearly and decisively with the changes in charity and piety charted by our statistics.[40] Indeed, extensive abuses of the church were not peculiar to Siena. Paolo Prodi has shown that the practices of the accumulation of multiple benefices and the "mondanizzazione" of church office had become so extensive that they had become accepted as "normal church practice" during the Cinquecento. More particularly, he describes for the diocese of Bologna "the systematic pillage" of church property on the eve of the Council of Trent, the "pauperization" of church revenues through nepotism, and the alienation of church lands through falsified long-term rents (*locazioni ad longum tempus*).[41]

The demarcation between the piety of the early Renaissance and the "secularism" of the Cinquecento is more difficult to pinpoint than the change sparked by the return of pestilence in 1363. Certainly the strategies for the afterlife embodied in the testaments of their early Quattrocento forefathers—their attempts to leave behind a visible sign for their remembrance—anticipated the broad tendencies of sixteenth-century testators. Yet the statistics on giving and the obsessions made explicit in the texts of testaments display a new testator by the last decades of the Quattrocento who would have been unrecognizable to the contemporaries of San Bernardino. When did this Cinquecento testamentary stamp begin to collapse? Already, we have mentioned signs of change that emerged in the last years of the century. To understand these transformations we must return again to the realm of events.

III

Counter-Reformation Piety and the State

9 The Counter-Reformation

> *Considering that the city of Siena fell day by day into greater poverty and that unfortunately it was already full of many pious places and convents, living on charity, it was doubtful that the city could fulfill the needs of so many. Thus she [Passitea Crogi] wished not to go to them, since she judged that it would not be helpful to increase the number of these mendicants while their means of subsistence was lacking.*
> —F. Venturi

When did one pattern of thought and behavior cease to predominate and another begin to take its place? Our statistics for late Renaissance suggest that the convenience of rounded centuries might not be far from the mark. Both in terms of nominal payments and in constant florins, the sums expended on pious causes declined steadily from 1525 to the end of the century. In the last quarter of the sixteenth century these statistics reflected the depths of that "great age of selfishness"; the average in constant florins descended to its lowest point thus far encountered in these series.

Then, in the first quarter of the Seicento, despite the persistence of high levels of inflation, and the ensuing economic malaise,[1] the average sums to pious causes increased by well over three times (347 percent), to 43.05 florins. This amount outstripped every quarterly average since the days of Bernardino. Nor was the figure a statistical aberration created by the chance appearance of several extraordinary testators leaving hefty sums.[2] Instead, the turn of the century initiated a new trend, which continued unabated through the first half of the eighteenth century. By the quarter 1726–50 the value of pious gifts had increased 8.3 times over the donations of the late Cinquecento.

The ratios of pious to nonpious bequests tell a similar story (Table 6.9). From a low-water mark in 1551–75, when the sums of monetarized pious gifts were a mere fraction of the nonpious gifts (0.09%), the ratios mounted steadily through the next one hundred years. By the middle of the Seicento, the portion of gifts marked for pious causes stood at a ratio as high as at any time since the Black Death, having risen by a factor of seven over the ratios for the third quarter of the Cinquecento. These ratios, moreover, dampen the real difference between these periods. As discussed previously, testators of the Cinquecento cut not only their share to pious institutions but also their itemized gifts to friends and kin in order to funnel greater proportions of their estates to their lineages of universal heirs. As we will soon discuss, these family strategies of the Cinquecento did not altogether disappear in the seventeenth century. The nobility continued to entail prized properties, certain *poderi,* or their urban palaces through their male lines. The Counter-Reformation, however, made significant inroads into the Cinquecento strategies of lineage. By about 1600 these practices had become the sole obsessions of the nobility. In their place, the Counter-Reformation brought new anxieties to the deathbed.

The Pattern of Piety

Before the Seicento, testamentary demands give glimpses of change. Even with the Cinquecento strategies for the afterlife, certain signs of change emerged by the last decades of the century. Remember the widow of the shoe salesman, who in 1596 ordered her heir not only to take a wife within eighteen months, but "to live like a Christian"; or the villager who in 1594, proud of his family name, sought to preserve the remembrance of his lineage as a last resort by placing his properties in the hands of churchmen; or the 1583 gift to an illegitimate daughter brought on by religious guilt.

In addition, new pious choices may have been harbingers of change before the bellwether shift marked by the values of pious donations. The change in beneficiaries was no return to the old medieval patterns of piety. Contributions to monasteries and parish churches, previously the giants of Sienese charity, declined sharply during the last quarter of the Cinquecento from 36.6 percent to 20 percent of all pious bequests (Table 6.5). Nor was the slide simply further proof of "the great age of selfishness." During the seventeenth-century "age of faith," these corporations, so central to the religious fabric of the medieval and Renaissance city, fell on even harder times, relative to total spiritual expenditure.[3] Collectively, their shares stabilized at the lowest levels yet found in these documents. For 1576–1675, it hovered between 17.9 percent and 26.7 percent of all gifts. At the end of the century, parishes and monasteries recovered somewhat their pull on the pious; yet the rates never returned to their late medieval levels of as much as two-thirds (1349–62) and consistently over one-half of all pious contributions.

That other great religious corporation from the central Middle Ages—the hospital—fared even worse. Again, the significant signs of change came before the Seicento. In the last quarter of the Cinquecento, hospitals' proportion of gifts (primarily Santa Maria della Scala) collapsed from 12.2 percent to less than 1.1 percent. The Seicento "age of faith" here registered no turnabout. The new waves of spiritual investment, instead, must have cut other paths. Hospitals had earlier attracted as much as 17 percent of all pious gifts; with the Counter-Reformation they would never garner more than 3 percent. The most important source for social charity since the early Renaissance, dowry funds for poor girls, also registered a critical change in the last years of the Cinquecento. Their share fell nearly in half from the previous quarter, from 11 percent to less than 6 percent. Again, the drop was not of the short term. Gifts to dower poor girls of *buon costume* continued to fall through the century, until it bottomed out at 1 percent in 1651–75. Nor do these statistics show a converse rise in the earlier forms of social charity prevalent in the age of mendicant piety—small handouts to the "poor of Christ." For the first time since the mid-Trecento these charities *did* momentarily (1626–75) outstrip the dowry funds; their proportion of all pious bequests, however, fluctuated only between 3 and 7 percent.

With the collapse of the traditional forms of late medieval and Renaissance piety, what organizations and charitable causes began to fill the vacuum and then lead toward the spiritual revival of the following century? Most spectacularly, religious confraternities, by the late Cinquecento organized most often around the parish church whether in the city or the countryside, took hold of the Sienese with an unprecedented vigor. In the past, these lay brother- and sisterhoods had only once attracted more than 10 percent of pious donations. At the end of the Cinquecento, their share more than trebled, soaring from 7.9 percent to over one-fourth of all pious gifts. This dramatic surge appears on first impression to have been short-lived as their share obtained at the end of the Cinquecento declined gradually over the Seicento.

Yet at the beginning of the century a new lay organization—the burial societies—burst onto the religious scene. If these societies are lumped with the confraternities, the attractiveness of the lay religious associations shows no loss of charitable enthusiasm. Instead, the percentages jumped even higher to nearly one-third of all pious gifts during the first half of the seventeenth century. Some of these groups, such as the Congregazione di San Pietro, which possessed communal burial vaults in the cathedral of Siena, were not entirely new to post-Tridentine Siena. Yet the Counter-Reformation spirit of the late Cinquecento had transformed fundamentally the character and constituency of this society. Previously, it had not been a lay association, but an organization for priests and the canons of the cathedral. By the close of the century, this society had widened its vaults. From the priestly privileged, the mass of new contributors seeking spiritual deliverance came from the bottom classes of testament writers. Artisans, peasants, and poor widows had joined this now trans-social and co-sexual organization for the laity and in their wills demanded to be buried by their religious brethren and sisters. San Pietro was not the only new burial society to sprout on the new ecclesiastical landscape of Counter-Reformation Siena. The congregations of the Centurate located in the monastery of San Martino of the Conception in San Francesco and of the Rosary in Santo Spirito cordoned off sacred space in Siena's most venerable buildings to make room for new communal burial grounds. For several scudi (ranging in value between 7 and 7.5 lire) artisans and peasants could now buy their way into places under the prestigious *pavimenti* of the cathedral and the great monasteries of

Siena.⁴ By democratizing sacred space, the Counter-Reformation undercut the prerogatives of patrician families which over the past 150 years had converted the chapels and burial grounds of the most venerable religious foundations into their own private preserves for family honor.

The changes in piety may have been even more striking than our percentages suggest. Extant membership rolls, preserved mostly in the Biblioteca Comunale of Siena, show a dramatic resurgence in membership in the last decades of the sixteenth century for the old religious confraternities such as the company of Santa Trinità, whose members gathered in the church of the Servites, the *disciplinati* of San Domenico, the most ancient of the Sienese societies, or again the venerable society of the Virgin Mary, which met "under the vaults" in the hospital of Santa Maria della Scala.⁵ Yet the more dramatic increase came from the blossoming of new companies and congregations, whose organizational basis was the parish church of the artisan neighborhood and the village of the rural commune.⁶

Other sections of the will leave further traces of the popularity of confraternities. Most important, the lay societies became the centerpieces of the Counter-Reformation funeral. With increasing regularity, testators by the early Seicento no longer left their last rites exclusively to the discretion of heirs, spouses, and executors. Now they devoted large chunks of notarial space to orchestrating the precise movements of their last rites, from their homes to the parish church to their graves. Counter-Reformation testators of all social classes now demanded to be paraded in the biers of their companies, their bodies dressed with the caps or robes of their brotherhoods and carried to new confraternal graves by the assembled force of their surrogate brethren.

By 1600, artisans, peasants, and poor widows generally belonged to at least one society and many to more than one. The Counter-Reformation testator Vettorio di gia Girolamo Franceschini, a sausage maker, for instance, had affiliations with at least three confraternities. In 1610 he first ordered his body to be buried in the cathedral of Siena in the vault (*avello*) of the congregation of Saint Peter, where twelve priests of the congregation, twelve men from his parish, six friars from San Francesco, six from the Servites, and several from the congregation of beggars were to "intervene" with torches and candles of various weights "according to their rank and order." The brothers from his "esteemed" confraternity of the Sacred Trinity and ten brothers from another lay society, the Company of San Rocco, were to carry the casket holding "his dead body." His body was to be decked out in the vestments of San Rocco. Torches and crosses each holding various amounts of wax would decorate the coffin on its final journey from the parish to the communal tomb in the cathedral of Siena.⁷

In addition to the new lay societies, the Counter-Reformation left other marks on the testaments. The spread of Tridentine religious enthusiasm restructured the welfare system of the early modern city. Again, the impact of the Counter-Reformation first appeared in the final decades of the Cinquecento and beneath the steady decline in the values accruing to pious causes. Burial congregations were not the only *congregazioni* to alter the spiritual landscape of the late Cinquecento city. Contributions to new clusters of the poor and the disadvantaged suddenly took over as the principal form of social charity. Immediately following the visitations of Bossi (1575–76), gifts to congregations called the *convertite, derelitte, abbandonate, mendici,* and *orfanelli* outflanked the old forms of charitable distribution.[8] In 1576–1600 9.5 percent of all pious donations went to these new groups, while neither the indiscriminate contributions to the poor nor the foundation of dowry funds could attract over 6 percent.

The earliest appearances of the congregations suggest that they had a prehistory before becoming formally constituted as enclosed, organized places governed by statutes and presided over by a priestly hierarchy. The notaries and their clients, in fact, do not use the term *congregazione* with any regularity until 1600. Instead, these individuals appear to have been part of inchoate groups associated by streets and *piazze* and identified by their proximity to certain ecclesiatical landmarks. The first donation to one of these groups of reformed piety occurs in the will of the wife of a barber. In 1572 she bequeathed, "for charity and the health of her soul," property from her household furnishings and goods valued at 25 florins to be distributed to "the girls who were called the derelicts in the Piazza Mantellini (*Puellis que dicuntur le Derelitte in Platea mantellinorum*)."[9] In 1580 a tanner of deerskins (*cerbolattaio*) donated annual provisions of grain to the *convertite* (the converted and reformed prostitutes), the *orfanelli* and the *mendici*, here not called *congregazioni* but instead simply *detti luoghi pii*.[10] In 1591 the wife of a linen salesman left as her universal heirs "the virgin girls commonly called the *l'Abbandonate* who stayed in front of the Convent of All Saints (*puellas Virgines vulgo nuncupatas l'Abbondonatc que morantur a' fronte conventus Monialium omnium sanctorum in Palatio Sancti Galgani*)."[11] The testament of a musician, from the city of Nodis but who resided in Siena, identified that group of derelict girls who hung out in the Piazza Mantellini for the first time as a congregation, but still felt the necessity to identify them by locale: "Congregationem pauperarum Derelictarum in planicie Mantellinorum." He ordered his wife to distribute 50 florins apiece to four of the other new associations which the notary identified only by the places where these disadvantaged ones gathered. The *abbandonate* were specified as those "near the Monastery of the nuns of All Saints" (later they would become the Congregazione della Virgine del Soccorso).[12] Another group of women called the *Pauperarum ad Deum* he described "as those who walk up and down (*conversarum*) the via Santa Maria alla Grazia"; the orphans (*orfanelli*) were called those "who stayed near the Porta San Viene"; and the beggars (*mendici*) as those "in via Camillie ad Sanctum Onofrium."[13] Later, other groups, such as the "dispersed little girls" (*fanciulle sperse*), who appeared without domestic moorings or strict organizational structure, became the recipients of Counter-Reform charitable outpouring.[14]

As early as 1572 at least one of these groups had its own church. In designing his funeral processions, "the noble and patrician" Magnificus dominus Capitanus Anibales f. q. Magnifici Girmani de Bichis ordered his confraternity, the Company of the Dead, to carry his coffin for one stage of the funeral, from the company's church to the church "called that of the little orphans (*alla detta Chiesa delli orfanelli*)."[15] By 1583, others appear to have gained some semblance of internal organization along with their own oratories. The "provident man" Johannesbattista f. q. Angeli de Vanninis left instructions to his widow to endow the "poor beggars" and the "poor orphans" with his *podere* called "Il Penaro" which lay in the Masse commune of Maggiano. He granted this estate under the condition that these *congregazioni* (used here for the first time in these documents) not sell or rent the farm "except among themselves." In addition, he burdened both congregations with the obligation to say five masses and one office for the dead in the rural church of San Mamiliano. The beggars were to say them eight days before Easter, the orphans eight days after Easter. Finally, he required the beneficiaries to say a *corona* (crown) of the seven penitential psalms with the litanies and, following these, prayers (*orationi*) for the health of the souls of the testator and his ancestors.[16]

To return to the statistics: a curious inconsistency emerges from the two sets of data—the values and the choices of pious bequests. The declining values show that piety continued to slide after the final acts of the Council of Trent (1563) and after the papal visitations of Bishop Bossi (1575–76) perhaps until the turn of the century. Yet beneath these averages, the patterns of piety reveal the beginnings of new religious sentiments as early as the 1570s. While contributions to the venerable medieval institutions—parish churches, monasteries, and hospitals—declined, confraternities, both old and new, burial societies, and new welfare *congregazioni* staked their claims over a new religious landscape.

The Grip of Purgatory

The last years of the Cinquecento not only marked a change in pious choices, they also initiated a trend in the form of giving that would endure for the next century and a half. Increasingly, testators required something in exchange for their donations. Tridentine culture fueled the fires of purgatory, and at the same time offered the faithful an assemblage of alternatives from their own "works" to the actions of clerics on their behalf once they had passed from the temporal sphere. The testaments embodied the penetration of new fears and anxieties about purgatory in the consciousness of ordinary citizens and villagers. In the mid-Cinquecento when the bishops of Europe were still deliberating at Trent and for the years immediately thereafter, the number of masses per testator sank to a secular low-water mark. Requests for masses had declined in 1551–75 to one for every three testators (see Table 9.1). In the years immediately following the papal visitations the ratio almost doubled. Then, at the beginning of the Seicento the numbers increased even more dramatically to a ratio of more than two bequests for masses per testator. The numbers fluctuated over the next century at roughly this high level, reaching their pinnacle around the middle of the

Table 9.1. Masses, 1501–1800

Period	Testators	Number of Bequests with Masses	Average Value of Masses	% of Pious Bequests w/Masses	Average Number of Specified Masses	Perpetual Prayers	Number of Prayers	% of Masses with Prayers
1501–25	92	50	42.90	40.65	5	9	0	0.00
1526–50	63	34	18.02	33.01	4	12	0	0.00
1551–75	126	48	158.95	29.27	39	17	7	14.58
1576–1600	122	85	14.76	44.74	8	37	20	23.53
1601–25	82	170	115.33	67.19	31	58	29	17.06
1626–50	113	181	143.69	66.30	46	65	23	12.71
1651–75	91	149	231.63	74.13	30	40	28	18.79
1676–1700	102	165	97.50	69.62	122	27	8	4.85
1701–25	103	205	171.64	65.50	124	40	18	8.78
1726–50	73	153	186.94	73.56	51	17	26	16.99
1751–75	88	127	80.99	82.47	59	7	16	12.60
1776–1800	63	93	41.73	63.70	52	0	12	12.90

Settecento, just before another fault line in consciousness abruptly transformed the patterns of piety and belief in Siena. The proportion of masses to all pious bequests shows a similar trend, and the foundation of masses to be sung in perpetuity, whether daily or yearly, increased significantly.[17] Again, 1575–1601 constituted the critical years.[18]

Not only did masses increase quantitatively; a new specificity structured the instructions of the pious. Instead of vague requests for masses or offices for the dead, testators by the last decades of the Cinquecento stated with much greater frequency the exact number of masses from 12 to over 1,000. They distinguished more carefully between offices for the dead and separate Gregorian masses. The term "the thirty" (the masses of Saint Gregory) entered for the first time the vocabulary of the testaments.[19] Another popular number for masses was "the twelve" in reverence for the twelve Apostles.[20] Testators distinguished between masses to be sung and low masses (*messe basse*) and between requiem masses and masses without requiems (*messe private di requie*).[21] New names of masses specified the time of day they were to be performed. At the beginning of the Seicento, "mattins" became popular, first at the graveside, then for masses in general. The sausage maker Vittorio Francheschini specified time even further, ordering his heirs to have a mass called *la prima mattina* celebrated at the high altar in the cathedral of Siena.[22]

By the first decade of the Seicento, testators placed on their orders for masses special "applications" for indulgences. Donna Caterina f. gia di Gianni Rasoi, the wife of a villager from Toiano, in 1610 left the congregation of Saint Peter in the Duomo as her universal heir. In return they were obliged to celebrate four masses for the health of her soul "with the application of the Indulgences conceded to the medallions blessed by Our Lord Pope Paul V."[23] In the same year, the wife of a slipper maker bequeathed to the "reverend fathers" of the monastery of Santo Spirito 5 florins for "the thirty" requiem masses "with the application of the Indulgences conceded by our Lord to the Medallions blessed in the canonization of Saint Carlo Boromeo [sic]."[24] A servant in the Communal Palace of Siena, Maestro Vincenti, "otherwise called" Centi di Santi Signorini, ordered his universal heirs to have "the thirty" performed every year with the same application of the indulgences conceded in the canonization of Carlo Borromeo.[25] Still later in the century, other "applications" placed on masses gained currency in sacramental practices. The gardener of the monastery of Ognissanti, Annibale di fu Giulio, who lived just beyond the Porta Nuova, gave his confraternity, the Company of Saint Stephen, 4 lire to chant six masses on the morning of their feast day. For the salvation of his soul, they should apply to these masses "the most sacred and ever august sacrifice (*applicando il sanctissimo e Sempre Augustissimo Sacrificio*)."[26]

Just as testators had begun to orchestrate Counter-Reform funerals, they took similar pains in arranging the details of their masses, such as the number and weight of the candles. For instance, the nobleman Horatius olim Magnifici Antoniimarie de Ninis gave to the Opera del Duomo of Siena an annuity, called a *censo*, of 15 scudi a year from his landed estate. For this donation, he placed the "weight" on the "church of the Duomo" to perform in perpetuity three offices for the dead each year. Each office was to include a mass to be sung plus twenty "low masses." In each office 8 pounds of "worked" wax (*di cera lavorata*) were to be consumed and distributed in the following sizes: one torch (*falcole*) weighing 2 pounds, forty candles collectively weighing 1 pound, and 2 pounds making forty-eight candles to be distributed to the canons and priests of the cathedral. (The testator did not specify the composition of the candles for the other 3 pounds of wax).[27]

Testators also became more particular about just who was to perform the sacraments in behalf of their souls; they began to specify by name the clerics who ought to officiate. The pious demands of a widow of a trombone player at the court of Siena who came from the Florentine village of Dicomano reveal possibly closer and more personal ties between the laity and the cloistered in the early Counter-Reformation. The Augustinian friary at Lecceto was designated as her universal heir; however, the income from her estate was to be given in part to support a certain father and preacher for as long as he stayed in the monastery. Another 200 florins were to go for masses for her soul and that of her deceased husband. She then insisted that the prior of the abbey, Angelico Vecchi, whom she called her spiritual father ("suo padre spirituale") and to whom she had earlier entrusted the matters of her burial and funeral, chant these offices.[28]

In addition, a new array of masses, sacraments, prayers, and penitentials entered the language of testaments following the papal visitations of 1575. For instance, the recitation of "the crown" appears for the first time in a testament of 1583. The "Provident man" Johanbaptista f. q. Angeli de Vanninis demanded a *corona* for the health of his soul and those of his ancestors. He left 50 florins to dower two girls. Unlike the majority of dowry funds in previous centuries, his gift came with obligations. For 30 days after receiving their dowries the girls were obliged to go every day to a "pious place" and before the image of the Virgin Mary say a *corona* for the health of the testator and his ancestors' souls. In subsequent spiritual demands placed on the congregations of orphans and beggars, he defined the new spiritual exercise: the seven penitential psalms and their litanies. This pious testator introduced other rituals. He required "the whole body of his confraternity," the Company of the Madonna, "on every first Monday of the month, during the time of prayer" to say "five Pater Nostri and five Ave Marie" for the health of his soul and those of his ancestors.[29]

Just as the pious Johanbaptista placed new spiritual demands on his beneficiaries, other spiritual requests cropped up where previously there had been none. In the first decade of the Seicento the "most dignified governor of the Terzo, la relatives and loved ones to pray for their souls, in return for property and money. The "honest woman" Elisabetta di fu Domenico gave her two daughters and her niece various articles of bedding and clothing, beseeching them to pray (*a pregarne orationi*) to God for the benefit of her soul.[30] Similarly, the nobleman Pietro del gia Magnifico Federigo Santi requested from his daughters already born as well as those still to come, "to have consideration for the status of this testator and in their prayers to remember to pray to God for the soul of the testator."[31]

In addition, testators at the turn of the Seicento instructed the new cloistered groups of the welfare *congregazioni* to say new sets of formalized prayers. The patrician Magnificus Hieronomus f. q. Magnifici Camilli de Bandinelli, presently the *dignissimus Vexillifer* or ward officier of the third of the city called "The City," demanded that the *povere convertite, derelitte,* and *abbandonate,* in return for *censi* placed on his landed estates, each say "prayers commonly called 'the forty hours' in their churches on all the saints' days every year in perpetuity."[32]

Other testators sought formal prayers from new groups of the holy such as those who venerated the recently nourished vision of the miracle of the Madonna of Provenzano.[33] The noblewoman Livia f. q. Magnifici Hortii de Ranconibus donated 100 piastre (scudi) to these new devotees for ten masses a year over a fifteen-year period. She called these "the masses of the Madonna"; they were to be followed with "orations of the commemoration of the dead."[34] Still other testators asked to be remembered "in the spiritual exercises" of confraternities or in the prayers of these fellow brothers and sisters.[35]

Mary

In the last years of the Cinquecento, testators began to pay greater attention to the altars where their masses were to be performed. They often instructed the clerics to chant them at the "major" or "privileged" altars of the church or monastery. A special cult of the Madonna, as witnessed earlier in Lady Livia's "masses of the Madonna," contributed to the further differentiation of time and space in testators' final arrangements for those future acts for the deliverance of their souls.[36] The importance of Mary arose first in the testamentary preambles, where the spiritual intercession of the Virgin took on a new role as their own "advocate" or the "advocate and protectrix" of the city of Siena. We have already seen that the Sienese established a special congregation in the name of the Madonna of Provenzano. The wealthy church of this congregation stands today as one of the architectural jewels of the Baroque period in Siena. In the last decade of the sixteenth and early years of the seventeenth century, it attracted large sums of money and property, particularly from the nobility of Siena. In 1628 the nobleman Giulio del gia Francesco Piccolomini claimed "this most sacred Virgin" as his personal advocate. If his heirs failed to pay "to the devotion" of the Madonna di Provenzano 100 scudi within six months after his death, he ordered them to sell off all his property, both real and movables. They were to be "invested for honest profit" (*si mettino ad honesto quadagno*) in either *censi* or shares in the Monte dei Paschi of Siena. With "the fruits" of this investment, the rector of "the Devotion" was to keep two lamps of wax burning forever. His heirs were to place these torches between the two angels in front of the Virgin. Second, they were to construct "in a prominent position" a carving out of olive wood (*faccino di legname intagliato di ulievo*) of the testator's family arms and underneath add the words of individual praise: "Julius Francisci de Piccolomineis a' Modanella devotionis" (the model of devotion). Finally, this madonna had her own special feast day. Signor Giulio provided funds from his estate to dower five poor girls a year. They had to be of good parentage and from the parish of San Pietro d'Ovile, one of the poor neighborhoods of Siena. The rector of the devotion was to grant these dowries of 10 scudi at the portal to the church "in tante Gratie" to one or two poor girls on the festival of the Madonna di Provenzano.[37]

The Madonna of Provenzano was not the only madonna to receive special masses. In 1653 a donna Lucrezia, the wife of a cobbler, obliged each of her universal heirs (two religious confraternities) to celebrate fifteen masses for the health of her soul, which were to be offered to the Madonna of San Maurizio.[38] For the artisan Maestro Giovanbaptista del gia Agnolo Rossi, the "Madonna del Verde" commanded a special veneration. He bequeathed 40 pounds of white wax to the Servite fathers at the monastery of Santa Maria to burn forty candles on two occasions in the year following the testator's death. While the candles were lit, the monks were "to expose the most holy sacrament for the 40 hours" to the altar of "the most sacred Madonna del Verde." In another bequest, the artisan requested the fathers to celebrate five masses at the same altar of this madonna.[39] A corporal of the cavalry sharp-shooters (*corporale dell'Archibusieri a Cavallo*), Magnifico Domenico di fu Tastone Tassoni from the village of Monte Rotondi, ordered his wife to have masses chanted "for the love of God and in honor of the most holy Virign." He prayed that she act "propitiously and promptly" in this *suffraggio* for the soul and that she celebrate it at the altar of "the Santissima Vergine del Choro." His wife was to order the mass to be sung on this madonna's feast day, whether "high (*grande*) or low, one or many" together with other masses at this madonna's altar on all the other feast days of this church.[40]

Time

A Counter-Reformation calendar emerges in the testaments from the last decades of the sixteenth century. For the first time, Easter became a critical landmark in the yearly course of events, signaling the performance of legacies to endure *in perpetuo*. We have already seen that in 1583 the "Provident" Johanbaptista de Vanninis ordered the welfare congregation of the *poveri mendici* to celebrate five masses and one office for the dead eight days before Easter (Pasqua di Resurrectione) and the *poveri orfani* to do the same eight days after Easter.[41] In the first decade of the Seicento the "most dignified governor of the Terzo, la Citta," donated a *censo* "imposed on" his *podere* in Lucignano Val d'Asso to the Company of the Dead. From the income, the brothers were required once a year, on Easter Day, to give to each of the poor prisoners of the Stinche two loaves of bread (weighing a pound a piece), two eggs, and a decanter (*boccale*) of wine. In addition, they were to select on this day one poor person from the prison to whom they were to grant at least 4 piastre.[42] The testaments give indirect evidence of a new consciousness of and reverence for the religious calendar. Post-Tridentine testators judiciously instructed their heirs and other beneficiaries to avoid those days when "such masses" were prohibited. They then provided for such contingencies, commanding their beneficiaries to celebrate the masses on days immediately before or after. If those days were encumbered by restrictions, they specified still other days to ensure that their pious monies would indeed be cashed in.[43]

The Cult of the Saints

Saints were even more important than Mary or Easter in the differentiation of pious acts in time and over space. In earlier periods, gifts to special altars venerating individual saints had, as discussed earlier, become common. By the Seicento, however, the veneration of saints went beyond the topography of giving in individual churches. Saints' days, feasts, and festivals introduced a new sense of time to these documents. Only then did testators begin to punctuate the performance of their masses according to a calendar rigorously fixed on the veneration of these "special advocates." In 1594 a musician from Nodis donated 100 florins to the rector of the urban parish church of San Giovanni to chant in perpetuity one mass a month and one mass every year on the festival of Santa Cecilia (the patron saint of music).[44] In 1627 Giovanbattista di Frosino Chiantini gave his confraternity, the Company of Santo Stefano, extensive properties: three houses and a warehouse in the *contrada* of Salicotto. With the rents from these properties, the confraternity was to dower "a number" (*tante*) of nubile girls (*citole*) who had to reside in Siena and whose parents were "honorable and respectable (*di padre e madre honorati e da bene*)." The names of the contestants were to be submitted in the month before the festival of Santo Stefano, and the company was to make its selections ("confare li scontrini") on the feast day of their patron, Saint Stephen.45 The gardener for the monastery of Ognissanti, "the provident" Annibale, requested masses from his confraternity of Santo Stefano on the morning of their feast day, again the day of special veneration for Saint Stephen.46 The corporal of the calvary sharp-shooters from Monte Rotondi commanded his wife every year for as long as she lived to have "the most sacred sacrifice" celebrated on the festival of Santissima Annunciata "in reverence and to honor the most holy Virgin" and another sacrifice in honor and reverence to Santa Mattia on her feast day. These were to be celebrated by all the priests "who are and will be in Monte Rotondi." In addition, other masses were to be performed on the days immediately following these holy days.47 The "noble and honorable" Signora Juditta di fu Signor Giovanni Billo and widow of Signor Scipione Gabrielli venerated the "most Glorious Patriarch" San Giuseppe and Santa Maria Maddalena. She bequeathed to the fathers of Santo Spirito 100 scudi to celebrate fifteen masses every year for seventy years. One of these masses was to be performed "on the day of the most glorious Santa Maria Maddalena" and six masses on the day afterward. Another mass was to be performed on the day and festival of San Giuseppe and another six on the day after. The final mass was to be held on the day of Sant'Anna.48 The "Illustrious" Rubertus f. q. Curtio Francisci de Cenninis, who was identified as a patrician of twelve cities in Lazio, Umbria, the Marche, Tuscany (including Siena), and Emilia, ordered the priests of San Francesco in Siena to celebrate three "sacrifices for the dead" in perpetuity on the feast days of the Corpus Christi, the Annunciation of the Virgin, and of Saint Catherine of Siena, for the souls of his father, mother, wife, children, and himself.49

Saints served to punctuate perpetual masses and other pious acts; their importance, like Mary's, arose in the testamentary preambles of the last years of the Cinquecento. Through the first half of the Seicento, testators with increasing regularity called upon their special advocates by name. Often, as we have mentioned, this was the patroness and protectrix of Siena, the Virgin Mary. But as the century progressed, the Sienese went beyond Mary in their "humble, devout, and Christian" pleas for their souls and in their desires, as the Counter-Reform formula put it, "to be liberated from the universal enemy and gathered among the elect."50

Of course, testators going back as early as the beginning of the Trecento "commended" their souls to special saints. But pleas for special intercession remained extraordinarily rare until the seventeenth century. Only three cases appear from the fourteenth, five from the fifteenth, and six from the sixteenth century. By the first half of the seventeenth century alone, the number of cases jumped to thirty-one. Before the Seicento only two testators identified more than a single saint to intervene in their behalf. Both were from the Trecento, and both invoked the pair of apostles Peter and Paul. In contrast, for the first fifty years of the Seicento at least nine testators specified two or more saints. In 1604 the eighty-year-old carpenter Maestro Benedetto prayed for assistance at the time of death to fortify him in "the faith of Roman Catholicism" and "to defend him against all the temptations of the enemy of mankind." To this end, he invoked the Virgin Mary, San Giuseppe, San Niccolò, Santa Lucia, and his guardian angel (*et l'Angelo Suo custode*).[51] After claiming to be a "faithful Christian" and beseeching the "Passion and Misery of the omnipotent Lord," Giovanni called Pinaccha, from Castro Fiorentino but living in Siena for over twenty years, prayed for the "intercessione" of the Virgin Mary, San Francesco, San Domenico, San Rocco, Santa Caterina of Siena, and Sant'Antonio of Padua in his 1604 will.[52] The "Illustrious" Rubertus, the patrician of twelve cities who bore five family names, appealed first to the "Passion and for the Mercy of the Savior Jesus Christ" and to the Virgin Mary "Advocata mea." He then called upon the spiritual aid of the saints Joseph, John, Stephen, Francis, Catherine of Siena, Bridget, "and my other patrons."[53]

In the few examples of the invocation of individual saints before the Council of Trent, Peter and Francis each appeared twice. Two invocations of saints came from monks about to enter monasteries; both called upon their monastic namesakes. In two other cases, testators invoked the patron saints of their parish churches. For the fifteenth century, no distinctive pattern emerges from the meager set of examples.[54] One example, however, typifies the stamp of spirituality we discovered earlier for the late Quattrocento and Cinquecento, when matters of blood took prominence over the ethereal anxieties of the soul. "The Excellent" doctor and citizen of Siena dominus Hieronimus of the de Albertis family began his testament by recommending his soul to Saint Albert, whom he identified as "eius familiae advocato." For all the invocations of individual saints (which by the second half of the Seicento ran well into the hundreds), this is the only one to invoke otherworldly intercession from a "family saint."[55]

In the early seventeenth century, not only did the invocations increase exponentially, but the patterns changed as well. First, the late medieval pattern disappeared almost completely: no monks invoked the patrons of their monasteries, and only one testator sought the assistance of the patron of his parish. This case, moreover, came from a small village in the countryside. Instead (as our earlier statistics might have forecasted) patron saints of religious confraternities accounted for at least six of these individual advocates. Most important, and more perplexing, was the sudden prominence of Siena's own, Catherine and Bernardino. Before the seventeenth century, both had appeared in these documents only in single incidents: San Bernardino in 1455 and Saint Catherine in 1526.[56] For the first half of the seventeenth century, 150 years after their canonizations, the two became suddenly the most popular among the testators.

Catherine was called on in eleven preambles and Bernardino in six (out of a total of fifty-one individuated saints, 1601–50). Next in importance came Saint Francis; then San Giuseppe, who became popular toward the end of this period, and finally Saint Stephen (because of his association with the confraternity of his namesake).[57]

How can we explain the rise in fame of the two Sienese patrons? We might speculate that they fit well with the enthusiasm at the turn of the century for the Virgin Mary. Testators began to invoke her assistance not only in her religious role as the Mother of Christ, but also in her political role.[58] Early seventeenth-century testators prayed for her spiritual intervention as the "patron saint of all Senesi," the "protectrix of our city," and the "special advocate of this city." Local pride might have similarly been behind the rationale for turning to Catherine and Bernardino. The two were often called upon side by side. In the preamble to a testament of 1616 the nobleman Fabio Salvetti besought "most particularly" San Bernardino to intercede with "His Divine Majesty" for the salvation of his soul. In the body of his will, his devotion to San Bernardino was expressed further, this time, however, in connection with Siena's other saint of late medieval vintage. The *gentilhuomo* Fabio donated 20 scudi to the congregation of the Conception in the church of Saint Francis to construct the pilasters for two statues to be placed at the altar of the Madonna della Conceptione; one was to be San Bernardino, the other Saint Catherine.[59]

In other words, the spiritual conduit of saints and concerns for the soul gave rise to a sense of local pride and chauvinism at the very moment when Grand Duke Cosimo I of Tuscany had severed administrative and political avenues for such expression. This spirit certainly would have run against the grain of both secular and ecclesiastical designs of the early Counter-Reformation. After the war with Florence and Siena's loss of independence, the Medici in the early days of the formation of the new Duchy of Tuscany struggled to crush old medieval city-state sentiments of Sienese patriotism. According to the early twentieth-century historian William Heywood, and more recently, Sydel Silverman, the Medici in fact curried the neighborhood localism of the *contrada* and the competition of the famous horse race, the Palio, to dampen citywide attachments— the allegiance of the Sienese to their old city-state.[60] The Counter-Reformation, on its part, sponsored parochial association by reforming parish administration, by rigorous enforcement of the residency of local priests, and by encouraging the spread of new parish confraternities.[61] The early enthusiasts for the cult of the Sienese saints were in fact Sienese patricians—the *gentilhuomo* Fabio Salvetti, the nobleman Francesco del gia Messer Giulio Piccolomini, and the historian, cavalier, and doctor Giugurta Tommasi.[62] These noblemen, proud of their ancient Sienese lineages, had for generations held the reins of power in southern Tuscany; with the defeat of 1555, they were the ones who had in fact lost the most. Symbolic and religious patriotism was their last frontier.

In the second half of the Seicento, the number of testators who invoked the intercession of their patron saints increased still further, soaring to 97 or nearly one-half of all the testaments in our sample. On first impression the panoply of new saints seems to evince a more imaginative selection and veneration of saints as Counter-Reformation culture progressed. A second glance suggests that the selection of individual saints may have become less inspired. More than half of the saints were the namesakes of the testator. By the later part of the century, notaries perhaps began to ask their clients automatically for the names of individual spiritual helpers, and one's namesake probably came to mind first. As with the new array of special masses and prayers, the new possibilities for burial, the new groups of devotion, and the new forms of welfare, the Counter-Reformation in its initial phases gave vent to multifarious forms of imagination and spirituality. But by the second half of the century expressions of piety may have become more routinized, more controlled, and more wooden. Generalizations about the Counter-Reformation must be modulated historically; a single set of descriptions will not do justice to its historical complexity. We will return to this theme in chapter 11.

Objects and Icons

The evidence of a new Counter-Reformation culture spilled beyond the pious portions of these documents. For the first time testators in Siena passed down through generations and across to friends and neighbors the objects of religious devotion. The short will of the widow Clementa del gia Niccolò Prolissi, a woman of modest means, itemized only three bequests. One was a debt to her two sisters, who were also her landladies: it was payment for her rent, which amounted to a meager 4 giuli. She also owed a woman baker in the market area of "Postierla" (in the parish of the Baptistry) 3 lire, 10 soldi for bread.[63] Yet "in recognition of their benefits" she bequeathed to her sister-landladies "Saint Francis's crown of wood (*una corona del legno di S. Francesco*)" for which "they should pray to God for the health of her soul."[64] The noblewoman Virginia f. q. Bendetti de Ceccarinis from Florence, the widow of a Sienese nobleman, gave a certain "Mother" donna Inditta Spagnuola, who was a converted prostitute, her bench (*scannello*) "for genuflecting."[65]

For the first time in these sources we find the exchange and circulation of religious art works.[66] Gifts of and commissions for paintings for church altars, as we have seen, had appeared much earlier. The evidence for the seventeenth century, however, was new. Here, the domestic cultivation of religious works of art found in the homes of ordinary citizens and villagers penetrated beneath the ambit of important patrons and commissions usually studied by art historians. Instead of masterpieces or even altarpieces for rural churches, these works were the objects of mass religious devotion, now inventoried as *masseritia* or common household goods. For instance, "the most chaste and noble" Signorina Caterina del gia Signor Giovanbattista Zondedari, a young girl (*fanciulla*), left her cousin "alcune robbe" consisting of a cotton blanket, a small painting portraying the Madonna with the baby Jesus in her arms ("un quadretto con un' pocha di tavoletta a piedi di pentorci la Madonna con Giesù Bambino in braccio"), another painting of the baby Jesus with the cross and a small basket ("un'altro quadretto di pentorci Giesù bambino con la Croce et un panerino"), a small painting of San Bastiano. On a higher social scale, "the doctor and philosopher" Hieronimus de Casularis left the usufruct to all his farm animals and "those other things usually left to widows . . . to live honorably." Included in these "usual things" were four paintings. But he held back on a fifth, "the *Quadro grande* of the birth of our Saviour," which he reserved for his heirs.[67]

The circulation of religious works of art and devotion even touched the laboring classes of Seicento Siena. In 1660 a widow of a wall builder (*murarius*) redacted a modest will consisting of only three itemized bequests. The first conveyed gifts to an unrelated woman friend, which included certain pieces of jewelry, her bed, and two paintings (*quadri*): one was "with" Santa Magdalena, the other portrayed the flight into Egypt of Joseph and Mary.[68] At the beginning of the Settecento, testamentary evidence of the number of works of art in circulation between friends and kin and down through generations increased substantially. Although the first signs of the circulation of these religious icons antedated the Counter-Reformation, their mass circulation arrived only during the latter stages of the new Catholic culture.

Preambles

The appearances of new confraternities, new welfare congregations, larger numbers of masses, and the new terms of devotion show Counter-Reformation culture taking root in the last decades of the Cinquecento and deepening through the first half of the Seicento. The stamp of a new Counter-Reform will, however, can be seen even at the outset of the testament. From the late sixteenth through the first decades of the eighteenth century, the attention of the notary moved away from the complex, legalistic clauses involving restrictions and contingencies on properties funneled to the universal heirs. Before delving into the itemized list of individual gifts, Counter-Reform notaries and their clients penned the weight of their prose in long preambles, which lifted their glances from the temporalities of property allocation to matters of salvation. The new prefatory elaboration, however, sprouted from notarial soil well seeded by the last decades of the Trecento. Testaments continued to start "with the nobler part," the soul, then passed to the disposition of the body and finally to the allocation of property. By the early 1580s, the introductory phrases to this "nobler part" became more complex and literally more sanguine. Instead of the simple one-line phrase commending the soul sometimes to God, sometimes to Mary, and sometimes to the whole celestial court, the postvisitation testaments now were prefaced with ornate variations. The Roman Iacobus olim Laurentii Tabernanis, then living in Siena, began his will of 1583: "Having received atonement from the most precious blood of the only son of God, he [Iacobus] relinquished his soul to God his creator and redeemer, and devoutly and humbly commended [his soul] to God as well as to the Virgin and the entire celestial court."[69]

Christ, who hardly had made an appearance in the pre-Tridentine testaments, had become the central figure in preambles of the Counter-Reformation. Along with the stress on his grace and "the blood he shed on the cross," testators and their notaries nailed down the Tridentine doctrine—the separate but indivisible identity of the Holy Trinity. The noble lady Lucia f. q. Magnifici Christofani de Santis, widow "in the last instance" of the Magnate Ghinus de Azzonis, began her treatment of 1582 "praying with all her heart that she would deserve from this present life to be held in His most sacred grace and then received in the other life in the most holy paradise and to enjoy together with the Blessed His divine essence, not for her own merits, but only because of His infinite Mercy. And equally she prays to the most holy and Immaculate Virgin Mary and to the entire court of the Heavens that they intercede for this grace to the most sacred Trinity, the Father, the Son and the Holy Ghost, Three (*Trino*) and one, now and forever."[70] The testament of a kinsman, redacted by a different notary, similarly stressed the importance of the Trinity (never once mentioned in these documents before 1580) and the significance of the Lord's grace for salvation. But the testament of this nobleman dressed these themes in different robes:

> Praying with the greatest affection of his heart that through the compassion of His infinite Mercy [the Lord] might erase his sins, and that when it pleases the Lord for his soul to depart the body, He may wish by the merits of His most sacred passion and of the ever glorious Virgin Mary to gather it among the Blessed spirits. He beseeches the most glorious mother of Jesus Christ that she may wish to receive it into her most sacred hands and to present it with her patronage of the Almighty Tribunal of the most Holy Trinity and implore its Holy Benediction.[71]

Certainly these formulations of church doctrine cannot be attributed to the religious stance or understanding of the testator alone. At the same time it would be wrong to assume that the testator had no role in the selection or variation of these passages. Some testators continued to rely on rather pithy preambles, whereas considerable variation in formulas characterized the preambles of testators within the books of a single notary.[72] Even if the notary was alone responsible for the selection and drafting of these Counter-Reformation formulations, the changes mapped by this evidence would still prove to be valuable and a new source for the historian of ideas—at the level of the local intelligensia, beneath the canons and decrees of church councils and published religious discourse.

Another formulaic phrase appearing at the end of the Cinquecento registers another new perception after the Council of Trent, at least at this middling level of religious and intellectual activity. Testators and their notaries began to recognize that two types of Christian might exist. This change in formula springs forth not with the threat of Lutheranism in the 1520s, nor with the waves of heresy that ensued by mid-century, nor immediately after the Council of Trent, but instead after the papal visitations and during the last years of the sixteenth century.[73] Testators began their wills with the declaration "ut fidelis et catholica (-us), come fedele e cattolica (o)," as faithful and Catholic Christians.[74] This need to distinguish Roman Catholics from all others went beyond the opening lines of testaments. A deerskinner (*cerbolattarius*) pleaded for the grace of the Lord "in the war waged between Christians and their adversaries" and "desired to be buried according to the customs of a true Christian."[75] By the end of the first decade of the Seicento such phrases had become standard.

The preambles were not the only places where testators asserted their Counter-Reform faith. Their sentiments on occasion introduced their pious bequests. Purgatory, for instance—not as an implied concept (earlier apparent in the mere phraseology "pro anima mea"), but the actual word itself—appears for the first time in the testament of Luca olim Juliani, a sausage maker. Before "burdening" the consciences of his heirs for a series of different masses to be chanted for his soul, he explained his reasons: "To placate the majesty of God, if this testator has transgressed in anything or should be retained, like other sinners, for the punishments of Purgatory."[76] Indeed, the preambles in certain testaments clearly went beyond the choices offered by the notarial forms. After customary introductory phrases and the arrangements for burial, the major part of the 1590 testament of Magnificus Dominus Niccolaus f. q. Magnifici Domini Giorgii Berlingherij from Florence, then living in Siena, professed in concrete terms his philosophy of charity. These proclamations clearly set this late Cinquecento testament apart from the earlier preoccupations of that century. The testator had

> considered for a long time the four things for which each Christian man is obliged when making his will. First, he must recognize that the property he owns and possesses all comes to him from God. Second, he must consequently render gratitude for these things with complete humility by sharing them and leaving them for the love of his Divine Majesty to honest families or to places for the poor and needy. These matters have been preached warmly by Christ our Lord and are recommended . . . in the gospels. Third, the commandments of sacred Christian gratitude often forces us to look at families and places of need, to select that man or woman most deserving of these services. Fourth . . . one must tend to the matters of kin individually, giving enough comforts and riches but without entailing the property through generations of kin from the side of the Mother. All these considerations are judged for the most important resolution, the health of the soul, which must be placed before every consideration, in every respect. So that the Lord our God may have mercy with this work for the ends of charity. And for the love of His Lord, that the Divine Majesty may cancel his sins, having resolved to dispose of his things and to select as heir an honorable family from whom the testator has already in former times received help and various forms of accommodation, but which, at present, as befits the things of this World, which never stay the same, has been reduced to dire straits.[77]

This testator's principles for charity stood the hierarchy of charity practiced since the late Quattrocento on its head. Last in line came the recipients for whom the Cinquecento had placed its bets for immortality—the survival of the lineage.

Funerals

Although anxieties about the soul may have turned the final glances of testators away from obsessions with property and blood, they did not turn the testator's mind away from matters of the body and its final journey to the grave. Before listing the concrete allocations of property, notaries and their clients enlarged another section of the will to elaborate with new degrees of precision the final rites for the body—the funeral bier, the procession, the dressing of the body, the grave, and the masses and candles to accompany every movement of the last journey. From the chronicle sources we know of large and elaborate funerals reaching back to the late Middle Ages.[78] These funerals, however, were affairs of state planned for the most part by the commune of Siena. They involved the death, praise, and burial of important military leaders, governors, statesmen, and occasionally men of culture.[79]

In the testaments that extend over the first four centuries of this book, there is surprisingly little mention of the precise arrangements for funerals.[80] As we have seen, the earliest documents from the thirteenth century often left even the choice of burial ground unstated. When testators mentioned the amounts their executors should spend on their final rites of passage, the values were meager indeed, falling as low as 10 soldi.[81] Quite apart from the massive displays and expenditures that can be found in the chroniclers' descriptions of the public funerals of heroes, the highest expenditure for funerals in these samples was 50 florins, which in a testament from Asciano of 1348, went to clad the poor in *tunicas*.[82] The average cost of funerals and burials (where stated) before the sixteenth century amounted to a mere 6.63 florins.

By the mid-Cinquecento, concern for funeral rites had grown. But more often than not, the testator who mentioned these rites sloughed it off to the heirs, such as the nobleman Alexandus f. q. Magnifici domini Sigismundi de Chiseis, who in 1546 directed his heir to bury his body in their ancestral tomb "with those ceremonies and funerary display which his heir might find suitable."[83] Others, such as the rector of Santa Maria della Scala, "Magnifus ac generosus eques" Scipio f. q. Magnifici Mariani de Ventinis, simply left the arrangements to the customs of the religious house where the body was to be buried.[84] Still others, like the "Magnificent" Giulio di Geronimo Bargagli, were more forceful. He commanded his heirs to bury him "sensa pompa funebre," desiring only to be dressed in the vestments of his flagellant brethren (*veste da Battitori*). Unlike testators in the Seicento, who expressed such designs for simplicity but then proceeded to arrange processions enlisting large numbers of friars, priests, and lay brethren, this noble testator of the mid-Cinquecento may have been sincere. He ordered that his heirs spend no more than 20 florins on his funeral expenses.[85]

Before the papal visitations of 1575, specific instructions concerning funeral processions are extremely rare. Where they do occur, little more is listed than the name of the religious confraternity entrusted with the duties of carrying the corpse to the grave. Unlike those in the next generation on their deathbeds, these testators did not order specific numbers of their surrogate brethren to fill the processions or allocate exact quantities of wax and candles. The most they wished for at the grave was in keeping with the spirit of family and lineage. In 1572 the patrician Capitanus Anibalis f. q. Magnifici Girmani de Bichis ordered that his coffin be draped with two tapestries (*drappellori*), each bearing the arms of the "Bichi."[86]

In contrast, noblemen of the Seicento never called for the presentation of their family coats of arms on their litters or coffins; nor were these familial honors to be paraded in their processions. On occasion, they even asked explicitly that their heirs strip from their funerary robes the old familial regalia of their lineages. In 1612, the Magnifico Curtio gia del Magnifico Messer Marcantonio Marretti ordered that his corpse be carried to the church of the Servites by his lay brethren in a "naked" bier "without any worldly (*mondano*) ornamentation and in particular without the brocaded cloth (*panno di broccato*) that exists in this church." In place of the old family coat of arms, he ordered new religious symbols. His heirs were to drape his bodily remains with four newly manufactured flags (*drappelloni*): "one with the insignia of the Holy Cross, another with the Sacred Mother of God, another with Saint Catherine of Siena, and the fourth painted with the figure of Saint Ann, the advocate of the testator's house."[87]

To be sure, we cannot conclude from silence that earlier funerals and burials were always without pomp, without trains of terrestrial intercessors from the ranks of the clergy or the poor, and without large expenditures of wax and money. Nevertheless, the absence of such instructions does suggest that these arrangements were not foremost in the minds of testators whether on their deathbeds or in the best of health. Once again, the years immediately following the visitations of 1575 form the critical divide. A new type of Counter-Reformation funeral and burial plotted the precise steps of the corporeal transition from deathbed to parish church to grave and on to "the life on the other side of death." One of the earliest testaments to arrange a funeral in detail came not from the ranks of the patriciate but from a pork dealer. The "spectabilis" Andreas Laurentii, in fact, devoted his testament entirely to the details of his last rites of passage. He ordered his body to be buried in the church of the artisan parish of San Pietro d'Ovile in the sepulcher "made by himself and his descendants." He then planned the details of his last journey: "and in my sepulcher there is no need to make other expenses, except [to purchase] 12 pounds of worked wax (di cera lavorata); in addition, four priests should serve at the graveside. They should be given the customary charity (*elemosine*) of 1 carlino apiece. The wax should be distributed among the priests and to honor the cross and [given] to the brothers of his [the testator's] company, who are to carry and accompany him to the grave." Should his heirs fail to observe these instructions "they are to be penalized 10 scudi, which ought to be donated to the poor derelict girls."[88] After these instructions and the customary gifts of 5 soldi to the archbishop, the cathedral, and the hospital of Santa Maria della Scala, the testator concluded by naming his son as universal heir.

By the last decades of the century, testators, even when they professed a desire for "a modest burial," enumerated the funerary details. The Magnate Orlandus-Malavolta f. q. Magnifici et Excellenti Bernardi de Malavoltis expressed in 1581 his wishes to be buried "without pomp and ceremony." He nevertheless added that the funeral was to take place "only with the friars of San Domenico, the Father of his parish, plus eleven other priests, thus twelve in all, together with twelve brothers from the company of Sant'Ambrogio." In exchange for the office of the dead, he wished them to say twelve masses at the "privileged altar in San Domenico."[89] Silvius Bernardi de Capaccis also wished "to flee from all pomp." Yet nearly half of his testament dealt with the details of his "modest" funeral: "And when it might be pleasing to the Divine Majesty," Silvius planned for his body to be buried in the church of the Dominicans "in our customary sepulcher." He ordered his devout brothers of the Company of San Hieronimo to carry him to his grave. "Fourteen brothers and no more should carry me in the old litter (*cataletto*) without the velvet drapery." He was to be dressed with the cap of the flagellants (*cappa da battente*), and the brothers were to be given fourteen torches weighing 4 ounces apiece, which were to be lit and placed around his bier when the body was brought to the grave. "The brothers, in addition, were to be given one torch of yellow wax weighing 6 pounds, which was not to be lit for the procession but to serve the brothers and their confraternity in their other services." Silvius continued:

> And at my grave I wish that the reverend fathers of the order of San Domenico to intervene and, in their company, I wish for another eight reverend sacerdotal fathers. And they should receive their accustomed charity (*solita elemosina*), and on the following day or the day afterward, these or other fathers should say eight masses for the dead in my parish for the salvation of my soul, and they should be given the usual payment. And at the cross, instead of the candles (*staggiuoli*) or other wax, I wish them to carry two lighted torches, weighing 5 pounds apiece. And if the Company of San Hieronimo will give the cap for my body, I wish my heirs to make them a new one within fifteen days. And this should be all that is done in order to flee from pomp and for the best effect (*si faccia per fuggire la Pompa, et ad ogni buono effetto*).[90]

Other testators of the Seicento made no pretense of modesty and asked unabashedly for grand processions. For instance, the Magnate Celio f. q. Magnifici Adriani de Pieris planned his obsequies to involve the intervention of all the fathers of the Servite order, all the friars of San Martino, together with twenty priests and twenty-four flagellants from his company of Santa Trinità.

Each was to receive one-half pound of yellow wax to carry in the procession. Two torches were to be placed on the crosses carried by the Servite fathers and by the friars of San Martino and another two were to go around the litter. He was to be dressed with the cap of his flagellant brethren.[91]

The sausage maker Vittorius de Franceschinis, mentioned earlier, ordered twelve priests from the congregation of Saint Peter, twelve priests from his parish, six Franciscan friars, six friars from the Servites, and six mendicants to assist in his burial. In addition, ten brothers from his confraternity of Santa Trinità with another ten brothers from the Company of San Rocco were to carry his body to the communal grave of the congregation of Saint Peter. The sausage maker, like others who orchestrated their last rites, calculated the weights of wax, candles, and torches to be distributed to each participant and to be placed on crosses and around his bier.[92]

A simple estate agent or clerk (*fattore*) for the Florentine company of Dell'Antella, who came from a *podere* in the state of Florence but resided in Siena, was even more ambitious. For his graveside, he called on the "intervention" of twenty men from his Company of San Giovanni Baptista, all the friars from Santa Maria dei Servi, four monks from each monastery in Siena, twenty orphans, twenty beggars, and finally all the priests of the congregation of Saint Peter in the cathedral. Again, this testator arranged in a long and drawn-out fashion the intricacies concerning the distributions and placements of wax, candles, and torches—when, where, and by whom they were to be placed, lit, and carried.[93]

By the middle of the Seicento, the complexity of funerals, at least in one respect, mounted further. Testators added to their lists of arrangements numbers of masses, often to be sung at different churches and at different times in the transition of the body and soul from the deathbed to the afterlife. The "illustrious" nobleman Alessandro del gia Signor Celso Sozzini asked for "at least" 200 masses to be chanted in his parish while he lay in his litter. The *gentilhuomo* Scipione del gia Illustrissimo Guido Savini called on thirteen brothers from his confraternity, forty priests, all the friars of Sant'Agostino, and four friars each from the monasteries of San Domenico, San Francesco, Santa Maria dei Servi, San Girolamo, San Martino, and Santa Maria del Carmine. After specifying the expenditures for wax, he requested 1,000 masses to be sung for his soul "as soon and as expeditiously as can be done." At the same time, however, increasing numbers of testators professed to "reprove, in all and for all, every mundane display of pomp and appearance."[94] The numbers to file in the ranks of funeral processions shrunk as the emphasis turned more to matters of the soul—to the numbers of burial masses to be said at different moments and in different churches, from the home to the parish to the grave. Again, the styles of post-Tridentine Catholicism had evolved from the spontaneous inventiveness of its initial phases to the solemnity of order and control.

Conclusion

This chapter ends with an unresolved paradox. Although the values of the pious gifts continued to decline through the last quarter of the sixteenth century, the testaments during these years give evidence of changes in charity and the strategies for the afterlife. First, contributions to the late medieval corporations—the parish church, the monasteries of the mendicant orders, the hospitals—continued their long secular decline. For the same years, however, new sources of piety sprouted up in the testamentary bequests: gifts to the new welfare congregations, to new burial congregations, to both old and new lay religious confraternities. The sources of piety and religious participation during the first generation of the Counter-Reformation give an impression of the diffusion of this new religiosity which deviates from the usual view. Although the Catholic reformers certainly stressed doctrines of obedience and hierarchy, their methods of organization were populist. The success of reform was not a "one-way" street as one historian has recently concluded. From rural villages and artisan neighborhoods, the testaments offer glimpses of a populace yearning to participate directly in religious life. Widespread participation in the new confraternities, membership in the new burial societies, and the organization and popular support of new welfare congregations appear at the heart of this revival of religious and cultural propaganda.

Second, the form of giving changed fundamentally during the last decades of Cinquecento. Not only did the percentage and number of masses increase significantly, their vocabulary changed as well. Specificity in the kind, place, and timing of masses entered the documents: the thirty, *mattins,* high and low masses, the *corona,* the devotion of forty hours; prayers from family members; the application of special indulgences; masses at high altars and nonprivileged altars, and masses in veneration of specific madonnas (Provenzano, del Verde, del Choro, and so on); the veneration of saints; the importance of Easter in the yearly calendar; and the significance of saints' days.

Third, the testament as a literary document changed. The notaries' central point of emphasis moved to the openings of these documents—the religious preambles—and away from those clauses that stipulated the flow of the lion's share of properties down generations of universal heirs. Here, Purgatory can be sensed looming over the lives and deaths of the Sienese. Fear, however, came with consolation through long passages describing the "passion of Christ and the gift of his blood shed on the cross." The notaries and their clients proclaimed their faith as "true Christians" and "Roman Catholics" and professed the Counter-Reform doctrine, which hammered down with a new rigor the indivisibility of the Holy Trinity. Their concerns over the soul "once it had migrated from the body" grew in words. Testators prayed in their preambles to be received "in the lap of paradise" and to gain the comforts of the elect; for this election, they increasingly enumerated by name and placed faith in special advocates and patron saints. Yet the ephemeral matters of the soul did not deter them from attending to the exact movements of the body from deathbed to the grave. Even artisans and peasants calculated in their wills the expenses and precise movements of their last rites, calling on the intercession of monks, priests, their lay brothers, and often the ranks from the new welfare congregations. They weighed and counted the amount of wax, torches, and candles to be placed in the sacred places or to be distributed by the each of the various "terrestrial intercessors" assigned to the various stages of their last earthly drama.[95] By the seventeenth century these funeral plots thickened; requests for different graveside and postmortem masses at precise moments in different churches accompanied the testator's funeral plans. Thus, beneath the raw averages in the values of gifts, the buds of the Counter-Reformation had already begun to blossom. How do we explain the paradox? When and from where did Trent arrive in Siena?

❧ 10 The Differentiated Consequences of Trent

> *Thus Passitea Crogi came to discover either by human assistance or divine revelation the illegitimate births of those who threatened to hide their crimes by killing them. With manly acuity she succeeded in saving these innocent ones, nurturing them miraculously and bringing them at night to the holy font of the Hospital of the Scala.*
> —F. Venturi

By the beginning of the Seicento, the Cinquecento strategy for the afterlife had been broken as interest turned from universal heirs and the channeling of ancestral properties down the male line to justification by works—through the new charities and through elaborate sacraments for the benefit of the soul.[1] By the last decades of the Cinquecento, while signs of the Counter-Reformation became well imprinted in wills, the flow of contributions to pious causes slowed to a trickle. When did the Counter-Reformation arrive in Siena? Historians of the Reformation have proposed various turning points. Some have seen an independent movement for Catholic reform in full bloom before Luther posted his Ninety-Five Theses (1517).[2] The Catholic reform, in other words, was little different from earlier periods of renewal and reform. It needed no external threat; it grew from the church's own internal evaluations and criticism. Other historians have located the critical divide with Luther or immediately after the sack of Rome in 1530.[3] The split in the Catholic West stimulated a response. Reformist bishops and cardinals and, more broadly, new movements such as the Oratory of Divine Love tended promptly to the problems in their own backyards, the age-old abuses of corrupt clergymen.

Still others date the shift at various stages in the long history of the Council of Trent. The evangelism of this initial phase of "popular Catholic reform" was grouped around the Venetian cardinal and diplomat Gasparo Contarini—Cardinal Reginald Pole, Gian Matteo Giberti, Bishop of Verona, Cardinal Iacopo Sadoleto, Cardinal Gerolamo Seripando, Cardinal Giovanni Morone, the Sienese-born Bernardino Ochino—and spread more widely through the Camaldolese and Cappuccin monastic movements.[4] Until the Colloquy of Regensburg (1541), the hope for reunification dominated the approach to reform set by humanist clerics. But by mid-century compromise on issues such as "double justification" had failed; Luther had disowned his humanist successor, Philip Melanchthon (1497–1560) and the faction led by Gian Pietro Carafa had mobilized its forces in Rome.[5] In 1542 the new pope, Paul IV, issued the Bull *Liceat ab initio*, which established the "Holy Office" of the Roman Inquisition. From evangelism Catholic reform turned to heretic hunts. Lucca and Siena, in fact, became the first grounds for this shift in the spirit of reform.[6] In 1545 new intellectual figures in Rome, accompanied in many cases by turncoat reformers of the previous generation—Pole, Seripando, and Morone—opened at Trent the longest church council in the history of Christianity. The Council of Trent, with several interruptions and convening in several places, lasted from 1545 to 1563.[7] Its longevity in the determination of church law and liturgy is even more impressive. The Canons and Decrees of Trent continued as the cornerstone of Roman Catholicism through the end of the 1950s.[8] Trent broke decisively with the previous period's attempt of reform by conciliation. By 1563 the battle lines between Protestant and Catholic Europe had been drawn. The Council of Trent defined matters of doctrine and liturgy with an unprecedented rigor and thoroughness.[9] Thus in the period of Trent at least two other chronological breaks can be argued. The first emphasizes the radical change of the 1540s in leadership on the eve of this council; the second finds the divide with its final dictates promulgated in regional synods through Western Christendom in the early 1560s but not taking hold until the seventeenth century—Voltaire's "Age of Faith."[10]

The testaments from Siena, redacted by those whose intellectual horizons lay beneath the great reformers, provide a seismograph for registering the tremors of reform for an integral population. From this evidence, the early sixteenth-century reform movements made little impact. Nor did the building of the new militant church of the 1540s through the 1560s affect piety on the local level. Testators from the late Quattrocento through the mid-Cinquecento instead erected counterecclesiastical forms of charity, and their obsessions with the afterlife successfully circumvented church coffers. In 1564, the year after the conclusion of the Western church's longest council, the synods of Siena promulgated the Canons and Decrees of Trent.[11] Yet again little changed, both from the perspective of the church hierarchy in Siena and from the wills of ordinary citizens and villagers.

The Papal Visitations

The decisive break instead came later. The new charities, new forms of devotion, and new obsessions with the journey of the soul emerged in the testaments during the late 1570s and 1580s. As for many city-states in Italy, the jubilee year 1575 must have been critical for subsequent religious and social history.[12] The thoroughgoing papal visitation which continued into the early months of 1576 corresponds closely with the appearance of these earmarks of a new religious consciousness in Siena. Francesco Bossi, bishop of Perugia, appointed Episcopus Visitator Apostolicus by Gregory XII, immediately erected an inquisitional court under the aegis of his troop of papal investigators at the monastery of San Francesco.[13] He began systematically to scrutinize the behavior of clerics and parishioners from the Piccolomini to peasants. The bishop and his officials traveled through city and territory examining the state of church buildings, the upkeep of graveyards, the presentation of the host, the character of religious paintings, and the Latin of parish priests; they interrogated parishioners and priests to ferret out salacious details of moral scandals, principally ones involving sex.[14] Behind this papal visitation, moreover, unlike the earlier ones (which in Siena were little more than inventories of liturgical possessions) lurked mechanisms for persuasion and enforcement.[15] Bossi's court stripped clerics of their vestments and sent lay sinners into exile.

The historian can even gauge the effectiveness of Bossi's work. On 25 January 1598, the reformer and later the archbishop of Siena, Cardinal Francesco Maria Tarugi, conducted another detailed and lengthy visitation. Against the stark inquisitional tones of a generation earlier, Tarugi's investigation evokes a festive and joyous affair. In nearly every parish, whether urban or rural, the parishioners, both men and women, came to the borders of their parish carrying the host. Their processions "with all those of the *populo*" (parish community) escorted the cardinal from the borders of their parish to the parish church. There, the grand visitor "absolved the dead and after the celebration of mass delivered an Evangelical sermon to those present." Finally, before embarking on the chores of inspection, the cardinal gave the holy communion, blessing "as many women as men *tam viros quam mulieres.*"[16]

Beyond these impressions a systematic comparison might be drawn between these two points in time. Such a study would be too extensive to undertake here, but a cursory reading of these lengthy visitations reveals a radical change in behavior, architecture, and spiritual life during the intervening twenty-three years. Confession booths, which in 1575 were altogether missing or inappropriately constructed (even in the cathedral of Siena), were in place in the smallest rural churches; graveyards, formerly the feeding grounds for stray dogs, were now enclosed according to the prescriptions of Carlo Borromeo; paintings that Bossi had considered either lascivious or ugly (often the comment was simply "too dark") had been replaced with new altarpieces; church roofs in need of repair had been repaired (except for those rural churches most badly battered by the war with Florence); the host, often left on window sills, unprotected and unadorned, had been appropriately enclosed in tabernacles with appropriate baldachins.[17] The interrogations of parishioners and priests in 1598 are less scintillating than earlier ones. In Tarugi's ledgers, sexual scandals were few; clerics resided in their rural parishes, and most could pass the rudimentary requirements of their Latin examinations.[18]

Rich as the evidence is from these visitations, space allows for only two observations. Bossi's instructions and condemnations proved to be effective not simply from force or authority.[19] In the visitations of 1575, artisans and peasants expressed resentment from parish to parish against absentee priests who siphoned off their tithes but were unavailable to perform the last rites when neighbors and relatives lay dying. Bossi and his troop listened sympathetically to the complaints of parishioners. Absenteeism led the list. Accordingly, the act most often read to the annually congregated clergy of Siena was the Tridentine Decree regarding the residence of parish priests, and perhaps the most effective reform achieved in these years was the residency of parish clerics, who would regularly sing masses, hear confessions, and visit the ill. The enforcers of Trent tapped popular appeal.[20]

Second, Bossi recommended but did not demand the formation of parish lay confraternities and said nothing at all about women's confraternities. The synods of the archdiocese of Siena from 1575 through the early seventeenth century neither required nor urged women parishioners to form or join such companies to praise the holy host. During the intervening quarter century a major transformation had nonetheless taken place beyond the dictates of Counter-Reform enforcement. Parish confraternities, which had been rare in 1575, were almost nonexistent for women. By the beginning of the Seicento nearly every parish had at least one lay society; many had two, and women were participating in these new forms of spiritual life in numbers equal to men. In the 1575 records, women were almost totally absent from the spiritual life of the parish. In the visitations of Tarugi, on the other hand, enthusiastic women swelled the ranks of those parish processions, greeting the cardinal with praises and prayers. These observations provide clues for solving our paradox—the continued decline in gifts to pious causes while the forms of a new Counter-Reformation culture emerged. Tridentine culture, unlike the effects of pestilence on consciousness, had sharp cleavages across class, geography, and gender.

The Nobility

From the information that notaries normally provided to identify their clients, the nobility is the easiest group to isolate. From the early sixteenth century, the nobility was no longer merely a class de facto; it had become a class de jure with distinct privileges and the right to "reside" in the highest council of government, the Concistoro.[21] From the sixteenth century on, notaries thus were careful in noting the status of noblemen in public documents; not only do they appear with the grandiloquent combinations of prefixes *magnificus, illustrissimus, miles, capitaneus, dominus, excellentius,* and so on, the notaries did not fail to add at the end of their names *nobile de Senensis* or *patriticus Senensis*.

The trend in both the number of pious bequests and their values sets the nobility apart, not as the forerunners of the Counter-Reformation but as the stalwarts of the Cinquecento. In the pivotal generation (1576–1600) following the reforms of Bossi, the number and value of their contributions collapsed even more drastically than that for the population as a whole (see Table 10.1). For this quarter pious bequests per testator dropped by 20 percent. The nobility had

Table 10.1. Pious Bequests of the Nobility

Period	Noble Testators	% of Noblemen	Average of Pious Bequests	Pious Value/ Nobleman	Ratio of Bequests/ Nobleman	Ratio of Noble Gifts to Population	Ratio in Value
1501–50	11	7.10	18	247.50	1.64	1.12	3.68
1551–75	24	19.05	48	172.90	2.00	1.54	1.85
1576–1600	22	18.03	35	45.72	1.59	1.02	0.54
1601–25	20	24.39	80	672.60	4.00	1.30	2.16
1626–50	15	13.27	57	181.56	3.80	1.57	0.56
1651–75	15	16.48	55	658.68	3.67	1.66	2.06
1676–1700	13	12.75	58	1301.16	4.46	1.92	3.73
1701–25	25	24.27	122	1015.97	4.88	1.61	1.97
1726–50	7	9.59	51	1947.40	7.29	2.56	3.71
1751–75	6	6.82	15	329.60	2.50	1.43	2.31
1776–1800	4	6.35	8	147.00	2.00	0.86	1.32

bequeathed one-and-a-half times as many pious legacies as the population as a whole before the visitations; afterward their share only reached the general level. Not until the middle of the Seicento (1626–50) did higher rates for this wealthier and more powerful class return to its previsitation levels.

The late Cinquecento decline in the piety of the nobility is even more pronounced in terms of the values of pious bequests. Earlier in the century, the patriciate spent almost four times more than others on pious causes. This figure, however, is inflated by the peak in private chapels founded largely by the nobility in these years. In the subsequent quarter, 1551–75, when few foundations enter these calculations, the value of their piety nonetheless nearly doubled pious gifts in general. Then in the critical years of reform (1576–1600), their contributions sank to little more than one-half the donations of ordinary shopkeepers, artisans, and peasants.

Again, economic realities may have determined their giving. In addition to the loss of political independence, the nobility may have paid especially dearly in material terms during Siena's war for independence. Yet, even if this had been the case, their fall in pious giving outstripped any possible change in economic standing. The ratio of their pious to nonpious gifts follows closely the trend traced by their frequencies of pious gifts (see Table 10.2). In the first half of the Cinquecento their pious gifts were one-eighth the values of those to friends and kin; in the next quarter the ratio fell to one-twentieth; then in 1575–1600 their relative value of piety tumbled to its lowest point, one-fiftieth of the values.

Although pious contributions generally declined through the last decades of the sixteenth century, the charitable patterns of the elites accounted disproportionately for this decline. Our earlier narrative reading of the testaments would lead to similar conclusions. Whether we consider the first to contribute to the new welfare congregations or the first to stage the elaborate "baroque funerals,"

Table 10.2. Nonpious Bequests of the Nobility

Period	Number of Nonpious Bequests	Average Value/ Nobleman	Nonpious Bequests/ Nobleman	Ratio of Gifts Pb:Npb	Ratio of Values Pb:Npb
1501–50	65	2026.46	2.65	0.28	0.12
1551–75	118	3718.72	1.75	0.41	0.05
1576–1600	52	2199.58	0.92	0.67	0.02
1601–25	64	3343.46	1.19	1.25	0.20
1626–50	54	1437.59	1.75	1.06	0.13
1651–75	37	2778.95	1.12	1.49	0.24
1676–1700	41	2788.60	1.35	1.41	0.47
1701–25	89	1203.00	1.35	1.37	0.84
1726–50	30	892.50	1.56	1.70	2.18
1751–75	17	4698.04	0.95	0.88	0.07
1776–1800	34	3928.79	2.37	0.24	0.04

the innovators of Counter-Reform culture came not from the highest echelons of society but rather from middling or even the lower orders, such as Merediana, a wife of a barber; the deerskinner Michele Franceschi; Virginia, the wife of a linen dealer; the musician Simone; the sausage maker Vittorius; Catherine, a villager from Toiano; the wife of a slipper maker; the wife of trombone player; the "provident man" Giovanbaptista; the carpenter Benedetto; Lucas the sausage maker; Andreas the pork dealer.[22]

At the beginning of the Seicento, matters changed and the nobility suddenly resumed their traditional role as the most lavish donors to the church (Table 10.1). In the first quarter, while pious gifts in general doubled, the nobility's piety in terms of the number of gifts per testator jumped from 1.59 to 4. The change in the values of their pious gifts followed, increasing by more than four times in this second generation after Bossi's reforms. Again, economic changes cannot explain their delayed reaction. The ratios of pious to nonpious bequests (see Table 10.2) shows an even more meteoric rise: their relative expenditure on piety jumped by a factor of 40.

Bringing the nobility into the fold of Counter-Reform Catholicism was protracted in time; moreover, it took place under conditions that suggest a compromise. First, the visitations of 1575 did attack the nobility's grip over the ecclesiastical hierarchy of Siena, both on an individual level and in general in its condemnations of multiple benefices and the nonresidence of clerics. Nonetheless, after the dust had settled the nobility remained well entrenched in the hierarchy through the seventeenth and eighteenth centuries.[23] Second, the testaments themselves reveal the compromise—an intermingling of strategies of lineage with new emphases on charity and the soul. For instance, the historian of Siena called "Cavalier and Doctor" Giugurta gia di Francesco Tommasi still fits well into the mold of mid-Cinquecento testators.[24] A considerable portion of his 1605 will stipulated the conditions guiding the descent of his property. He designated his only surviving child, a daughter, as his universal heir. She was to inherit his estate, however, only for her lifetime. He explicitly demanded that children born "from her present marriage or any other marriage" not inherit his real properties. "And this I have thus ordered for the purposes of the maintenance and benefit of my lineage, that of Tommasi, which descends directly from Bandino di Cecco, and I wish this benefit not to extend to other lines of our Family."[25]

The doctor then established the rights of inheritance through primogeniture of his lineage. As in noble testaments from the Cinquecento, Giugurta burdened his line with elaborate property restrictions and made provisions for lifting the patrimony out of the hands of any *primogenito* who after his inheritance might become criminally convicted, a stipulation provoked not by questions of morality but by fears of losing ancestral properties through state confiscation. The demands of this early Seicento nobleman did not end here; new wrinkles entered his final blood and property arrangements. These went beyond the materialistic and familial strategies typical of earlier Cinquecento wills. He insisted that this *primogenito* "remain faithful to the holy Roman church and to its Pontiffs." He further required him "to have the festival of the birth of the Glorious Virgin, the Mother of God, celebrated every year in perpetuity on September 8 or on the Sunday before in 'our church' of Montaperti as has been the custom of our ancestors, with such number of priests as he [his heir] should find fitting." His first itemized bequest shows further transformations in the ideology of lineage wrought by the new Counter-Reform culture. He commanded his heirs to place in the Opera del Duomo (where he had been rector for the past fifteen years) a drapery brocaded in gold and of crimson velvet (*un' Panno di broccato d'oro, conformato di velluto cremusi*). On this richly embroidered cloth were to be woven (much in keeping the Cinquecento) the two arms *nel Fregio* of the family of Tommasi. But with this banner, the cavalier amalgamated the competing cultures, sewing them together with a religious twist never before interlaced in the brocades of the Cinquecento: "at its head," his heirs were to embroider the crucifix and "at the feet," the inscription "MARIAE SENENSIUM TUTRICI JUGURTHA AEDITUUS D." (To Mary, protector of the Sienese, Giurgurta, sacristan of the Duomo). The will's conclusion welded the spirit of this historic compromise. Giurgurta exhorted his line of future heirs to read carefully his will and "to enforce it for the honor of God and for the maintenance of our lineage, the family of the Tommasi, which comes from Bandino di Cecco."[26]

The testaments provide further evidence of the nobility's compromise. During the opening years of the Seicento they began to curry fervently the special veneration of the Madonna of Provenzano. One such devotee, Giulio del gia Francesco Piccolomini, in 1628, mixed the competing ideologies of reformed Catholicism with what had become by the early Seicento the exclusive preserve of the nobility, the ideology of lineage. Beneath his contribution of carved angels "for the ornamentation" of the new church, he ordered his heirs to have carved in olive wood and to place in "an eminent place" his family coats of arms. Beneath this regalia of Cinquecento pride in lineage was to be inscribed "Julius Francisci de Piccolomineis a' Modanella devotionis" (Julius Francis Piccolomini, the model of piety).[27]

The lengthy testament of the patrician of twelve cities who carried three family names, "the Illustrious" Rubertus, shows another way in which these competing cultures might become amalgamated. A considerable portion of his will concerned the inalienability of certain properties and the legal intricacies of devolution through the male line of a single son. Since the *primogenitor* had chosen a career in the church as an abbot and had "followed" the service of Cardinal Francesco in the Roman curia, the noble testator begged his first-born "for brotherly love" to transfer the rights of *primogeranza* and the subsequent lines of lineage to the second-born, Curtius. From this son the property would then descend in the next generations once again by *primogeranza*.[28] At the same time, the stamp of the Counter-Reform piety was boldly embossed on this testament. Unlike noblemen of the Cinquecento, this patrician began by beseeching the intercession of his special advocates. He entreated spiritual favors from five individual saints. Then with Counter-Reform ritualism, Rubertus turned to the funeral. His body was to be laid out and dressed according to the customs of his religious confraternity. After an elaborate procession, 1,000 masses were to be chanted for his soul. For these, he orchestrated the gathering of the minor friars and the brothers of his religious company, carefully prescribing the precise weights of the wax each was to burn. Again, like his noble predecessors of the previous century, Rubertus left extensive properties and orders to his *primogenito* to construct a chapel (*sacellum seu capellam*). To upgrade the burial grounds, he even ordered his heir "to transport" and to inter the body of the hermit Friar Bonventure in this chapel behind the high altar of the parish of Castro Leoncello. Similar to the demands of his Cinquecento predecessors, his family and lineage were to retain the *ius patronatus* over these sacred grounds. Yet preoccupations of the new religious movement shine through the old prerogatives. Rubertus ordered numerous weekly masses to be sung in perpetuity and stipulated exacting instructions regarding their timing. Here again were the earmarks of the Counter-Reformation: details of high and low masses, various sacramental celebrations, all timed according to the Counter-Reform calendar of religious festivals and saints' days.

Most fundamentally, the cultural compromise between the Counter-Reformation and the ideology of lineage altered property arrangements in the Seicento. How did families support numerous and expensive masses for their souls and at the same time retain within the lineage their old ancestral properties, the near-sacred *beni stabili*? The answer was the revival of a feudal property arrangement called the *cens* or *censo*—an annuity derived from or "imposed on" real property. Their values varied between 7 and 10 percent of the purchase price of the real estate and thus probably reflected the total expected "fruits" of the property. By the first decades of the Seicento, the *censi* begin to appear with mounting regularity in the testaments. Although bequeathed on occasion to their heirs, most often these feudal annuities became the pious gifts to churches with demands for perpetual masses. For example, the nobleman Hortio f. q. Magnifici Antonmariae de Ninis, "for the remission of his sins and the health of his soul," bequeathed to the Opera del Duomo "un'censo" of 15 scudi a year on a *podere* in Maggiano, which he had purchased in 1604 for 200 scudi. In return, the Opera was to celebrate every year *in perpetuo* three offices including a mass that was sung (*messa cantata*) and twenty low masses. These sacred performances should consume 8 pounds of wax in various forms of torches and candles.[29] The *censo* made possible the mutual existence of what had previously been in tension, two distinct strategies for the afterlife—one which looked down the male-dominated lineage and the other which looked above to the future journey of the soul. The lineage could retain everlasting the *ius dominii* over their real properties, while siphoning off the fruits for perpetual masses chanted with a new "baroque" elaboration. For instance, the corporal of the cavalry sharp-shooters, Messer Domenico, accomplished both goals in a bequest of 1636. "For the love of God and for pious reasons" annual bequests of grain were to be distributed to his religious Company of the Rosary and to the church of Santissima Maria called del Frassino. The corporal added, however, that the mill in Monte Rotondi, from where these rents in kind derived, was always to be "conserved" through the male line.[30]

In other cases, the blend of Counter-Reform ritual and familial ideology appears to have become quite natural by the mid-Seicento. Reverend Adrianus of the Panducci family and the curate of the parish of Sant'Antonio, in the style of Counter-Reform piety, invoked "with humble devotion and all the affection of his heart" the intercession of "his particular (*eius peculiares*) advocates and protectors," the martyrs Fabian and Sebastian, Adrian and Anselm, and Saint Antony. The reverend, however, began his pleas by addressing his preeminent advocate (*suum precipuum advocatum*) Saint Andrew the Apostle, the patron saint of his relatives and of all of the Panducci family (*suorum parentum ac totius Panduncciorum familiae*).[31] The "honestissima" Madonna Caterina, a resident of Radicondoli and wife of a notary, named her husband as her universal heir with the rights to the fruits of half her dowry. She set aside 600 of the 700 scudi her husband was entitled "to use" to be passed on, after his death, to "the Holy Temple of the Most Sacred Madonna of Provenzano." These sums were given for the spiritual health of her husband, her father-in-law, her ancestors, and others according to the intentions of her husband. The priests of this "temple" were to recite every month in perpetuity fifteen masses for the souls of her family. For the honor and salvation of the ancestors she ordered the canons of Provenzano "to preserve [these instructions] for everlasting memory in a *tavola* placed in the sacristy or another place where they could always be seen."[32]

Piety in the Countryside

Of those social groups which can readily be distinguished through the notarial conventions of identification, the nobility was not alone in resisting initially Counter-Reform culture. The values of pious gifts from the countryside reached their nadir in the critical years of Bossi's reforms (see Table 10.3).[33] Then, like the nobility, residents of the countryside began at the beginning of the Seicento to enter the Counter-Reformation fold. In nominal terms, their pious gifts soared by more than eight times. Compared to the population as a whole, their gifts increased in value from one-ninth to one-quarter of the overall averages. Yet the increases in pious spending from the villages of Siena's dominion were even more staggering during the next twenty-five years, the full impact of the new religious movement taking even longer to penetrate the countryside than to spread upward through the recalcitrant ranks of the nobility.[34] But, once infected, those from the countryside became Trent's most zealous followers. In these years their per capita pious contributions for the first time outstripped those of their urban cousins both in number and in value, exceeding even those of the much wealthier nobility.

To explain this meteoric rise, certainly more than piety could have been at question. Since the war with Florence (1552–55), a geographic involution began to reverse the centrifugal tendency which had endured probably since the year 1000—the concentration of power and property in the hands of an urban elite.[35] Documents of land transactions as well as the testaments reveal increasingly through the seventeenth century the appearance in small towns and villages of wealthy magnates as well as nouveaux riches, such as the notary and citizen of Siena residing in the village of Radicondoli who left a business valued

Table 10.3. Pious Bequests from the Country

Period	Number of Nonpious Bequests	Average Value/ Countryman	Nonpious Bequests/ Countryman	Ratio of Gifts Pb:Npb	Ratio of Values Pb:Npb
1501–50	345	89.88	1.71	0.71	0.27
1551–75	353	105.06	2.07	0.34	0.11
1576–1600	314	147.02	2.76	0.34	0.06
1601–25	221	127.70	2.30	0.87	0.60
1626–50	233	301.43	2.06	1.19	1.60
1651–75	201	106.92	2.40	0.75	4.71
1676–1700	239	445.08	1.69	0.93	0.52
1701–25	272	189.24	2.00	0.69	0.54
1726–50	200	147.87	2.25	0.56	0.81
1751–75	262	372.67	3.04	0.65	0.46
1776–1800	226	956.66	5.23	0.63	0.06

over 3,000 scudi (see chapter 6). The reversal of economic and demographic patterns during the war-stricken years deserves a separate study. For our purposes, it is safe to conclude, however, that the postwar reversal cannot possibly explain the dramatic changes mapped by these statistics. Once again, the ratios of pious to nonpious bequests might serve to control for shifts in the economic fortunes of testators. The average value of gifts to friends and kin soared three-and-a-half-fold from the last years of the Cinquecento to the early Seicento (see Table 10.4).[36] Yet, despite these dramatic increases in nonpious gifts, the ratios of values follows the line drawn by the numbers and values of pious gifts confirming our conclusion: country dwellers, although the last to arrive, had become (at least for the groups thus far examined) the Counter-Reformation's most ardent supporters. By 1651–75 their pious gifts had climbed to over five times the values of their gifts to friends and kin.

Case studies embedded in the testaments tell a similar story. Before the Seicento, no outstanding donors of the Counter-Reform stamp (qualitatively or quantitatively) sprang from the countryside. By the early years of the Seicento, individual cases can illustrate their aboutface in piety. For example, the sharecropper (*mezzadro*) Antonio di Filippo di Rede, who worked the *podere* of Messer Magnifico et Eccelente Filippo Buoninsegni in the village of Costalpino, several kilometers southeast of Siena, ordered in 1610 the brothers of his religious Company of the Centurati to "accompany" his body to its grave in the parish of Sant'Andrea a Montecchio. "To honor these brothers" he contributed 25 lire alone for the wax to be consumed in his funeral procession. "For the love of God and the remission of his sins" he bequeathed 6 piastre (scudi) to the rector of the parish to celebrate five masses a year for as long as the money lasted. He also donated 8 piastre to the church of Maria della Grotta to recite an office of

Table 10.4. Nonpious Bequests from the Country

Period	Countrymen	% from Country	Number of Pious Bequests	Average Value/ Countryman	Pious Bequests/ Countryman	Ratio of Countryman to Population	Ratio of Values
1501–50	49	31.61	60	23.94	1.22	0.84	0.36
1551–75	14	11.11	10	11.51	0.71	0.55	0.12
1576–1600	21	17.21	20	8.98	0.95	0.61	0.11
1601–25	10	12.20	20	76.50	2.00	0.65	0.25
1626–50	18	15.93	44	481.14	2.44	1.01	1.48
1651–75	10	10.99	18	504.00	1.80	0.81	1.57
1676–1700	16	15.69	25	230.59	1.56	0.67	0.66
1701–25	18	17.48	25	102.86	1.39	0.46	0.20
1726–50	8	10.96	10	119.76	1.25	0.44	0.23
1751–75	26	29.55	51	172.67	1.96	1.12	1.21
1776–1800	13	20.63	43	61.39	3.31	1.43	0.55

five requiem masses once a year. The full weight of Trent struck hardest, however, in his final testamentary act. Although his wife, a nephew, and a niece were alive at the time of redaction, the *mezzadro* skipped over these loved ones when it came time to select those with ultimate authority and responsibility over his estate; he passed the lion's share of his property to that hallmark of Counter-Reform spirituality, the lay confraternity. He required his Company of the Centurati (called the Laici alla Maria della Grotta) to invest his worldly wealth in "an honest form of profit" or to buy a *censo*, the "fruits" from which were "to serve in the utility, comfort, and improvement of the brotherhood," to support the perpetual recitation of an office with ten requiem masses for his soul once a year in the company's church, and finally to "serve the divine cult" by sponsoring those "they judged to be meritorious and needy."[37]

The stamp of the Counter-Reformation was again forged in the testament of the widow Laura di Pasquino from the village of Brenna, who lived in Vescovado in a place called Tinoni. In 1623 she bequeathed 300 florins to two confraternities, the Company of the Holy Rosary and the Company of Maria della Neve in the neighboring village of Murlo for two masses a month for her own and her parents' souls every year in perpetuity, "without termination, even after 100 years." She further required her heirs to have an office celebrated in the *pieve* of Murlo with ten low masses and one mass to be sung, plus another four masses wherever her heirs might choose.[38]

The final dispositions of Pietro del gia Francesco Provedi, whom the notary labeled a peasant (*contadino*), bears this same imprint. He elected to be buried in the cathedral of Siena in the vault of the Counter-Reform congregation of Saint Peter "del Duomo." He was to be carried there by his religious Company of San Bernardino dell'Osservanza. He left several gifts to individuals *per elemosina*. Finally, he "instituted" a priest, the "molto Reverendo Signor" Francesco Lotti, as his universal heir, burdening him "with the weight" of paying off his debts and "consuming" the remainder of his possessions in "numerous works of piety" and "suffrages" for his ancestors' and his own souls according to the wishes of his heir. The *contadino* wished for no one to check on the priest, "because he believes that the latter as a cleric and from knowing him well could be counted on to dispose of his possessions punctually, celebrating even more acts of piety than those imposed."[39]

The Urbanites: Artisans and Petty Merchants

If neither the rustics nor the social elites were at the vanguard of cultural change, then who were the first to be enraptured by Tridentine fervor? As the notaries identified testators by profession or title in far less than half the testaments, we have isolated the urban artisans and shopkeepers more by default than by designation. Table 10.5 shows the statistics of pious giving by those who resided in the city and were not nobles of Siena. By the Seicento, magnates were not the only ones who derived the mass of their income from landed property; nor were the

Table 10.5. Pious Bequests of Urbanites

Period	Urbanites	% of Testators	Number of Pious Bequests	Average Value/ Urbanite	Pious Bequests/ Urbanite	Ratio of Urbanites to Population	Ratio of Values
1501–50	94	60.65	146	66.38	1.55	1.07	0.99
1551–75	82	65.08	102	166.94	1.24	0.96	1.78
1576–1600	74	60.66	134	119.79	1.81	1.16	1.43
1601–25	52	63.41	153	218.44	2.94	0.95	0.70
1626–50	79	69.91	46	83.80	0.58	0.24	0.26
1651–75	65	71.43	18	27.42	0.28	0.13	0.09
1676–1700	73	71.57	25	18.04	0.34	0.15	0.05
1701–25	60	58.25	25	52.91	0.42	0.14	0.10
1726–50	58	79.45	10	26.44	0.17	0.06	0.05
1751–75	55	62.50	52	56.81	0.95	0.54	0.40
1776–1800	46	73.02	43	49.82	0.93	0.40	0.45

old aristocratic lineages the only ones graced with the grandiloquent titles of noble status. Doctors and lawyers as well as important and wealthy merchants comprised a substantial segment of this new juridical elite. Even shopkeepers or artisans theoretically could have been noblemen. Noble qualification simply depended on whether a resident of Siena was the descendant of someone who had been a member of one of the old *monti* of the city.[40]

Piety as measured by numbers and values of pious gifts ran a different course for urban artisans and shopkeepers than for the nobility and the rural population. Not only was the timing of their "conversion" different, these middling sorts from the city failed to experience the same radical jolt into the Counter-Reformation as did their superiors and rural inferiors. Unlike the others, the urbanites, in the critical quarter (1576–1600), gave slightly more than before to pious causes. Through the first decades of the Seicento their pious generosity increased from less than two gifts per testator to nearly three. Yet this increase relative to the nobility and their rural cousins, who suddenly became infected with Counter-Reform spirituality, was modest. In contrast to the late Cinquecento, the urbanites now trailed the general population in piety. Then for the next 150 years, while the numbers of others' devout giving continued to climb, that of the modest urban dweller diminished. The trends in the values of pious gifts sketch a similar picture. In the critical years following Bossi's reforms, their pious donations were almost two-and-a-half times more than that of the more wealthy nobility. But by the opening of the Seicento, these urbanites had been left behind, now giving only 70 percent of that contributed by the general population. For the remaining years of the century, years of Counter-Reformation zeal, the pious values contributed by urban artisans and shopkeepers declined even in absolute terms and, by the second half of the century, had dropped below its Cinquecento level. In relative terms, their collapse in pious spending was dramatic. By mid-century their pious gifts sank to one-quarter the general rate, by the next twenty-five years to one-tenth, and by the end of the century to one-twentieth.

Did the weight of the seventeenth century crisis fall disproportionately on the shoulders of these urban artisans and petty merchants? Indeed, their ratio of pious to nonpious bequests suggests that this may have been the case.[41] Yet despite possible impoverishment in absolute or relative terms, the ratios show that the worsening of their economic conditions cannot account for their drastic decline in piety (Table 10.6). While the Counter-Reformation spread with robust zeal through the countryside and upward into the echelons of the nobility, those groups which had been more prompt to espouse the new forms of devotion were also the first to slip from its grip. Still, our analysis of pious giving by class and over geography has not yet entirely resolved the riddle of the continuing decline in the gifts to the church that accompanied the signs of devotional revival in the critical last years of the Cinquecento.

Counter-Reformation Women

Beyond social status and geography, the division of the population by gender does most to delineate the early adherents of the new Counter-Reformation.[42] The rise in religious enthusiasm of women was both more startling and more enduring than it had been for urban artisans and petty merchants or compared with any other group that the notarial conventions allow us to distinguish. When we think of the rigorous ascetic regulations and the special discipline that Counter-Reformation fathers such as Carlo Borromeo imposed on women, this

Table 10.6. Nonpious Bequests of Urbanites

Period	Number of Nonpious Bequests	Average Value/ City	Nonpious Bequests/ City	Ratio of Gifts Pb:Npb	Ratio of Values Pb:Npb
1501–50	345	264.38	2.00	0.78	0.25
1551–75	353	466.76	2.37	0.53	0.36
1576–1600	314	325.84	2.68	0.68	0.37
1601–25	221	935.19	2.58	1.14	0.23
1626–50	233	95.86	0.47	1.24	0.87
1651–75	201	132.20	0.43	0.64	0.21
1676–1700	239	97.71	0.37	0.93	0.18
1701–25	272	110.76	0.60	0.69	0.48
1726–50	200	96.26	0.31	0.56	0.27
1751–75	262	227.78	1.58	0.60	0.25
1776–1800	226	620.78	1.48	0.63	0.08

claim appears even more surprising.[43] At this critical juncture, women deserve especially close attention.

What did the Counter-Reformation offer women?[44] First, the numbers and percentages of women who redacted wills suggest that conditions may have begun to change for them immediately after Bossi's reforms. From the mid-fifteenth through the sixteenth century less than one-third of the testators were women. By the first quarter of the Seicento, as the repercussions of Tridentine reforms were felt, women nearly reached parity with men. This increase was not simply the result of a long linear progression.[45] By the beginning of the eighteenth century, when the indices of reform vigor had peaked, the sex ratio of testators declined once again to the levels of the late Renaissance.

While the numbers of women redacting wills increased, the number and range of their charitable bequests expanded dramatically. From the mid-Quattrocento until the reforms of Bossi, women on average had rarely given more than a single gift to pious causes. The same held for their itemized gifts to friends and relatives; never had these bequests exceeded an average of two gifts per testator, whereas men's gifts to friends and kin in 1551–75 were more than three times that of women (3.55 gifts per testator, see Table 10.7).

With the first signs of the penetration of the Council of Trent on the local scene (after the visitations of 1575–76), matters began to change for women. The widening of the range of choices presented in their testaments reflects these changes. In the critical years, the number of nonpious gifts bequeathed by women increased by nearly 40 percent and pious ones by 70 percent. Their trend, moreover, unlike that of artisans and shopkeepers, did not diminish soon after its initial enthusiasm; in the Seicento, the pious bequests of women trebled their pre-Tridentine numbers. In terms of value, the increase was staggering. By the mid-century, the average value of those gifts had soared thirty-five-fold since its low-water mark in the mid-Cinquecento. Even in terms of constant prices the change remains impressive; these donations increased in value by a factor of more than 16.[46]

With Trent in motion, the pious bequests of women, despite their financial inferiority, exceeded those of men for the first time. These statistics show women clearly at the vanguard of the Counter-Reformation. In the critical years following Bossi's reforms, women were fully engaged in the new devotional practices, while men (who controlled by far the greater resources) stuck fervently to their old ways. Their pious bequests (regardless of class or residency) continued to slide both in number and value.[47] The "conversion" of men came at least a generation later.

Why were women the first ones drawn to the Counter-Reformation? Not only did the Counter-Reformation provide new outlets for women to dispose of their wordly goods; a considerable proportion of the new institutions of reformed devotion directly concerned both the spiritual well-being and the social welfare of women. Women's religious confraternities and women's participation in parish societies devoted to the Holy Sacrament grew by leaps and bounds.[48]

Table 10.7. Piety by Gender, 1451–1800

		MEN				
Period	Testators	% of Testators	Number of Pious Bequests	% Monetized	Average Value/ Testator	Ratio of Values m:f
1451–75	40	100.00	96	50.00	26.20	3.25
1476–1500	65	65.35	114	50.88	60.07	2.53
1501–25	65	71.58	92	53.26	50.04	1.74
1526–50	40	66.18	69	43.48	103.10	1.06
1551–75	78	63.36	111	43.24	151.51	13.00
1576–1600	80	67.18	110	41.82	93.33	1.34
1601–25	48	59.52	143	48.95	322.65	1.08
1626–50	62	54.87	168	30.36	260.24	0.64
1651–75	53	58.24	99	28.28	321.55	1.06
1676–1700	59	58.65	153	25.49	312.78	0.55
1701–25	70	67.62	225	31.56	561.69	1.33
1726–50	46	62.16	143	27.97	636.54	1.88
1751–75	59	64.52	99	21.21	155.65	1.32
1776–1800	42	67.19	116	43.97	133.68	2.08
		WOMEN				
Period	Testators	% of Testators	Number of Pious Bequests	% Monetized	Average Value/ Testator	Ratio of Values m:f
1451–75	19	34.43	26	57.69	8.06	0.31
1476–1500	34	34.65	49	59.18	23.71	0.39
1501–25	27	28.42	31	45.16	28.72	0.57
1526–50	23	33.82	34	44.12	97.57	0.95
1551–75	48	36.64	53	50.94	11.66	0.08
1576–1600	42	32.82	80	46.25	69.80	0.75
1601–25	34	40.48	110	54.55	297.46	0.92
1626–50	51	45.13	105	28.57	409.77	1.57
1651–75	38	41.76	102	23.53	304.71	0.95
1676–1700	43	41.35	84	9.52	573.47	1.83
1701–25	33	32.38	88	34.09	422.56	0.75
1726–50	27	37.84	65	29.23	339.32	0.53
1751–75	29	35.48	55	21.82	117.71	0.76
1776–1800	21	32.81	30	26.67	64.38	0.48

The new congregations for the poor mainly ministered to the problems of needy women: the *congregazione delle derelitte,* the *abbandonate,* the *convertite,* the *fanciulle sperse,* the *mulieres de deo.*[49] Perhaps the presence of these new institutions reflects new levels of social need on the part of women during the late sixteenth century. With the emergence of the European marriage pattern, greater numbers of women remained celibate at the very moment when nunneries were either becoming aristocratic in membership or "dilapidated repositories for famine."[50] Thus, growing numbers of women were left without the financial support and protection of those individuals more favored monetarily by the inheritance patterns of the sixteenth century—in other words, men. From the evidence at our disposal, it cannot be determined whether the social and economic conditions of poorer women suddenly worsened precisely when these new institutions for the care and support of impoverished and usually unwed women began to flourish. But it is clear that the founders of these Counter-Reformation institutions were more sensitive to the problems of distressed women.[51] Most likely these problems were not new but had been on the social horizons since the reemergence of demographic pressures toward the end of the fifteenth century.[52] One may question whether these new institutions which confined the poor ultimately benefited them.[53] But at the very least they provided new charitable choices to propertied women. These choices, moreover, possessed feminine interest and feminine identification.

Women's Bodies

The Counter-Reformation affected the choices women made with their bodies, at least in the last resort: the choice of their graves. In the late Middle Ages and early Renaissance, women freely chose their place of burial as the parish and the local monastery competed for the proceeds.[54] Where it is possible to reconstruct the burial choices of both husbands and wives, women often selected places other than the vaults or ditches of their spouses. During the first fifty years of the Quattrocento, five of every six women (based on thirty-six women's wills) who specified their place of burial freely chose places separate from husbands, fathers, or of their male lineages ("in solito tumulo suorum antecessorum sive precessorum"). In only six cases did women explicitly "elect" the resting grounds of husbands or male ancestors. During the second half of the century the proportion of new graves that women selected independently of husbands and lineage fell by over half (based on forty women's wills), declining still further during the first half of the Cinquecento (based on thirty-eight women's testaments). For the first time since the earliest notarized wills, the dictates of husbands or of the male line predominated over the individual choices of those women powerful or independent enough to redact their own wills—a group which, as we have seen, had been shrinking over the course of the late Renaissance. Then with the beginnings of the Counter-Reformation the trend reversed: the proportion of women's burial choices apart from husbands and lineage increased to half in the second part of the Cinquecento, then to nearly two-thirds during the first half of the Seicento; and finally to almost three-quarters for the last fifty years of that century of faith.55

Nor was this return to independent choice simply a return to the late medieval period, where the choice had been between the parish and the local monastery. To break the hold of the family vaults, the Counter-Reformation created entirely new categories of choice, which proved to be of particular significance for women.56 By the late Cinquecento women could choose among a growing number of places reserved exclusively for them—the burial vaults of women's confraternities and, more important, the new congregations for women such as the *congregazione delle centurate* in the parish church of San Martino, the congregation of the Rosary in the monastery of Santo Spirito, or the congregation of the Conception in San Francesco. In return for dues of only a few lire to the congregation of Saint Peter, women from all social classes might leave their bodily remains under the *pavimento* of the Duomo, once the exclusive burial place of the lay elites and clerics. This congregation, similar to other Counter-Reform institutions, segregated its vaults by sex. Formerly the privilege of monastic orders alone, these sex-segregated tombs provided an alternative to the decisions of male executors, universal heirs, husbands, and fathers as well as the past decisions of the male line. In the first fifty years of the Quattrocento, only two women, both nuns, were buried in communal vaults with other women; by the first half of the seventeenth century nearly two-thirds of women chose such places against the grain of husbands' choices and the traditions of lineage.57

The Gratitude of Husbands

The testaments permit us once again to go beyond quantification. The language of these generally laconic contracts was not always formulaic. In addition to property, obligations, and conditions, men and women often left brief personal expressions of gratitude and trust to servants, children, friends, masters, and, most often, spouses.58 These phrases, in aggregate, suggest possible changes in marital relationships. Phrases, such as the one that prefaced the grant of *usufructus ex patrona* to the wife of the butcher Quiricus olim Pasquini, in 1551, were not untypical of the mid-Cinquecento: "In consideration of the goodness, obedience, and deserving worthiness of this domina Batista, should it be acceptable to her, he leaves her the *usufructus ex patrona* of all of his goods."59 In other words, for all his attention to her "bonitate et obbedientie et benemeritis," she received only a widow's expected inheritance—the use of her husband's property.

In January 1576, Andrea di Giovanni from Ancaiano expressed gratitude to his wife, which suggests a new spirit behind the living matrimonial relationship: "cognizant of the love and benevolence which his most esteemed consort, donna Margherita, had brought him and her toil through her continuous assistance . . . in managing his properties, causing them to increase in value and to expand in size, desiring to acknowledge and to remunerate her for so many labors and to insure that after his death she should not be dispossessed by the heirs . . . and so as never to suffer from need or through any contingencies . . . he left her as *patrona* and *usufructaria* of all of his possessions in the hope . . . that she would maintain the honest and widowly life."[60] Although the actual legal conditions do not vary between these two documents, the shift from an appreciation of obedience to gratitude for her labors in matrimony and wifely efforts to increase the wealth of the household betrays sentiments not so far removed from what Lawrence Stone has called the transition from the "patriarchal" toward the "companionate" marriage.[61]

During the Seicento, beneath statutory law, the testaments in aggregate reflect concrete changes in the prerogatives and property rights that husbands transmitted to their wives.[62] Husbands' wills over the long haul defined with varying degrees of specificity the rights and the divisions of property between widows and surviving children. In some cases, husbands redacted detailed inventories of the property rights of each of these parties. On occasion they specified with architectural rigor precisely the rights of occupancy in the home; the rights of passage to various chambers and the use of wells and stairways were carefully separated for the use of their widows and their progeny (see chapter 6). More generally, from the earliest notarized wills through the late sixteenth century, the most common settlement was one in which the husband left his wife her dowry and the *usufructus toto tempore vite* to the residual properties of the estate, usually the bulk of real property marked ultimately for their universal heirs, who in most cases were the surviving sons. The *usufructus* to these properties, however, was rarely given unconditionally. If the widow decided to remarry or was found to be unchaste, she would lose all claims to those properties beyond her dowry, including her right to continue living in the household with her children.[63] Sons, as the universal heirs, were generally also the executors. In addition to receiving most of the property, usually all the landed properties, they assumed the responsibilities for enforcing the wills' instructions. Thus they were entrusted with observing and patrolling their mothers' future behavior and in particular their mothers' chastity. More, these sons stood to benefit most directly and immediately from a mother's sexual infraction. Hence they could curtail the widow's enjoyment of the ancestral properties or prevent her from squandering its future resources, thereby assuming all the earlier their inheritance.

In post-Tridentine Siena, the power and property relations of widows at least within the ambit of the family improved. Although husbands certainly did not suddenly depart from the formulaic grants to wives, curious wrinkles begin to appear for the first time in the *usufructus* clauses. In 1590 a man from the region of Pisa, then living in Siena, nominated his wife as universal heir on the condition that "she remain chaste and serve the widowed life"—not, however, indefinitely, but for only one year following her husband's death.[64] Three days later, the testator redacted a codicil to elaborate further his wife's freedom. He repeated that she was to be his universal heir and made explicit that she might remarry, "liberating her totally" from any obligations made in his present testament, "except the prohibition that she should serve the honest and widowed life for one year following the death of the testator."[65]

Husbands, at least by the second half of the Seicento, more often left their wives as their universal heirs with the ultimate rights of controlling the descent of property. Along with these rights often came other prerogatives and responsibilities, such as determining the amounts of the dowries for their daughters and selecting the recipients of certain pious bequests, from the selection of those entrusted with singing masses for the husbands' souls to the election of those poor girls of *buon costume* to receive dowries. During the Cinquecento husbands left their wives as universal heirs between 37 and 31 percent of the cases in which their wives survived them. The figures did not then change significantly until the second half of the Seicento, when wives as husbands' universal heirs soared to nearly 60 percent.[66]

Once the actual conditions and clauses regarding wives as universal heirs are scrutinized, the changes become more striking. Earlier, when husbands "nominated" their wives they often persisted in attaching the usual conditions found in the other formulaic marital settlements: if the widow remarried or was unchaste she lost the patrimony. Thus, as the universal heir in the Cinquecento, the widow found herself in the same position she would occupy had her husband left her with only the widow's customary rights; she could not exercise any discretionary powers over the direction of her husband's estate. During the late sixteenth a qualitative change occurred; the formulaic conditions placed on widows disappeared altogether when they succeeded as their husbands' universal heirs.

The wills reveal other changes that undercut the prescriptions of statutory law. The number of mutual and reciprocal wills made by husbands and wives together, usually while both enjoyed good health, was negligible before 1575.[67] Only one of these partnerships appears during the Cinquecento, but for the second half of the seventeenth century alone, our sample contains nine. Of those identified by profession, all were from humble backgrounds: a cobbler, a barrel maker, a mason, a silk weaver, three *maestri,* and a sharecropper. In these wills each spouse entreated the surviving spouse to say prayers or have masses sung for the other. Each became the executor of the other's will, and each proclaimed the full faith and confidence in the other's devotion which "so many years of marriage and companionship would have led each to expect." Further, the widow was more than the *usufructaria* of her husband's estate; no conditions were attached to her enjoyment of the patrimonies in these mutual testimonies. Instead, their property rights were exactly identical. For instance, the "Provido huomo" Cristofano, from the village near Monteriggioni of Abbadia Isola presently residing in Siena, and his wife Madonna Maria drew up a will together in 1642. Cristofano named Maria, Maria named Cristofano as universal heirs to their mutual estates, and then appended the following: "They wish not to impose any weight or aggravation on one another, because each of them confides in the good conscience of the other, that the one who survives will have performed as many suffrages as possible for the health of their souls."[68] But even before the diffusion of these practices in the second half of the Seicento, testators expressed similar sentiments in other wills. In 1611, for example, a baker for hostels in the rural villages of Pontremoli explained why he chose his wife as universal heir: "for her infinite loving deeds" and the services she rendered him while he was ill. He began his praise by claiming that "there has always been between them a reciprocal love and benevolence."[69]

Finally, the appearance of new hortatory phrases reveal other changes in property rights between widows and sons. By the mid-Seicento, husbands reflecting explicitly on the doctrines of Trent, on the importance of hierarchy and obedience, placed their wives at the apex of the family and urged them to assume the responsibilities as surrogate fathers to continue the education of their children in "the holy fear of God." In 1663 the sharecropper (*mezzaiolo*) Austino del gia Francesco Marianini, who worked the *podere* of San Maffei owned by the Dominican order, named his wife along with his daughter and son as universal heirs to the estate.[70] Quite out of line with Cinquecento property arrangements for widows—the grant of the *usufructus*—Austino gave his wife the explicit rights of selling property and using the house according to her judgment. Instead of *patrona usufructaria*, the sharecropper left his wife as the *padrona assoluta*, which meant that "she might do whatever she pleased" with his property, since "he was certain that she would be accountable for her children as indeed she had been in the past." He did, however, burden her with the "weight" of "educating" the children "in the holy fear of God." But the nature of the obligation was again quite unlike those conditions men placed on their wives during the Cinquecento. Instead of instituting watchdogs, either *fidecommissarii*, other relatives or, as was most often previously the case, the sons themselves to oversee the behavior of the mother, the Seicento notary for the peasant merely added, "and all of this because he places faith in her goodness and integrity." In closing, the peasant besought his spouse "for the love of God" to dower "according to her capabilities" their daughter when she attained marital age.[71]

Other cases of husbands' mutual respect and affection rather than discipline and control over the future behavior of their widows come from the second half of the Seicento. In August 1678, Iacomo di Antonio Benvenuti from Florence, who "had lived for many years" in Siena as a commissioner in the office of the tobacco tax collection, left expectations and instructions in addition to property to his nearest kin—his wife and a fraternal niece who had lived in the household "for many, many years" and now "merited to be considered as his own daughter." He named his wife universal heir and "appealed to her charity and love . . . that she educate and rear his niece in the service of God and for the health of her soul and that she feed her as best she could." Iacomo was quick to add that he was not, "however, placing any obligations on his heir, but only appealing to what could be expected from her will and desire." He made it clear to his niece that she might not pretend to any gifts other than the ones previously enumerated in the will; she was expected to live together with his wife "with the obedience and love toward his heir that should be expected from a daughter, serving and assisting her in all her needs."[72]

In another seventeenth century will, the nobleman Tullio del gia Nobile Fausto Ugurgieri began the sections pertaining to his wife: "Having known through practical experience the cordial love which his most loving consort, domina Giulia, had always brought him, and confident that she would continue that same love and affection which she bore him toward their dearest children." He left her the rights and responsibilities as *curatrice et amministratrice* over the children and the household and then added: "because he trusts in an especial way that his wife will carry out the responsibilities for their dearest children, and since he hopes that she will always retain with maternal affection the responsibilities of educating their children, he beseeches her in the love of God to stay with the children, to educate, feed and clothe them . . . and to govern the household through divine and human laws." The noble testator next appealed "with paternal love" to his eldest son, Signor Francesco, "to assist lovingly" the needs of his other brothers and wished his son to show his mother "the eminent deference (*la grande obbedienza*)" which hitherto he had accorded his father. The father, moreover—in striking contrast to Cinquecento formulas that granted the sons ultimate rights in the house of residence—obliged his son to leave to his mother the house *in promiscuo uso*. The son was not to make any demands on his mother's dowry or its fruits. If the testator's wife did not wish to remain with her children, then the children were to provide her with an annual income of 30 scudi.[73] In the sixteenth century by way of contrast, when an annual income was to be provided for the widow, it always had been the sons' prerogative whether to live with their mother or to expel her from the household with some compensation.

After the spread of Tridentine culture through the local parishes, husbands entrusted their widows more often than surviving sons with the ultimate rights of overseeing the moral order of the household. Here, concerns for religious education "in the holy fear of God" outweighed the old preoccupations with the widow's remarriage or chastity. Earlier matters of remarriage and chastity, after all, had not been simply concerns of morality; they threatened the flow of properties to the husband's progeny and the splintering of patrimonies. To understand further what Trent offered to women, the historian must understand the world of property relations and the role of women in property descent on the eve of the Counter-Reformation. In the Cinquecento, women were little more than cogs in a mechanism bent on directing property through the male line. Even powerful aristocrats, such as the "Honesta ac nobilissima" domina Camilla, the daughter of the deceased magnate Raynaldi de Tolommeis and the widow of Niccolai de Petruccijs (1560), had made few individual decisions in their testaments.[74] Beyond the long and complex clauses regarding the channeling of her patrimony through the future of male heirs and the preservation of the lineage, this extraordinarily wealthy woman, related to two of the most powerful of sixteenth-century Sienese families, left only four separate bequests, and one was the repayment of a debt. As we have seen, these patterns of property descent and the ideology of lineage went beyond the social ambit of the aristocracy.[75] They permeated Sienese society, reaching even peasants proud of their recently minted family names and possessing the wherewithal to leave notarized testaments.

By the early Seicento noble women were the first to break ranks with their class in regard to the property strategies of the male line. Thus "la nobile et honestissima" Signora Erminia Bellanti, the wife of Bernardo Francesconi, named all eight of her children as the universal heirs, "the daughters as much as the sons." Again, against the grain of Cinquecento family and property strategies, the noble Erminia maintained that her inheritance was given "as much for their [her children's] possession as for their alienation of the properties." She further prohibited her husband from "acquiring any of the *usufructus*" to this inheritance. Rather, she wished her children to enjoy "its income, returns, and fruits" "freely, fully, and immediately," and "especially her daughters, since they have the greater needs and the less security." Signora Erminia's final comment appended to her final disposition gave a new twist to the meaning of family—one that went to the immediate concerns and well-being of the then-living children as opposed to the Cinquecento ideology of lineage, the generational flow of property through the male blood. She asserted "that her husband should be the first to approve" these special provisions because they were made "for the benefit of the family."[76]

Other noble ladies, such as "the most chaste" Elisabetta q. Domini Michaelis Angeli de Ferrandinis, gave preferential treatment to nieces over nephews. She left her married niece, "the most chaste" Lisabetta, as universal heir, while her nephews were left holding the household linen (*la biancheria*).[77] The humble tertiary of the Dominican order, monna Cassandra del gia Francesco Bianchi went the furthest in her Counter Reform policy of affirmative action. In reaction to the Cinquecento ideology of blood and descent through the male line, her testament of 1691 left as universal heirs "all the legitimate and natural female children born or to be born of the said Chiara Papari [the testator's niece]." She further clarified her decision over the future devolution of her property "excluding always and in whatever case or time, with the greatest of precautions, all males so long as there are female children."[78]

Changing notions about the family were not all that was here at stake. Our statistics show that the growth of the Cinquecento strategy of the afterlife of lineage robbed the church of sacred space and cut deeply into its revenues. Again, harking back to the years of Catherine and the reformers of the late Trecento, ideologues of the Counter-Reformed church sharply contrasted attachment to family and worldly goods with the grander sanctity of the spiritual life achieved through ascetic ideals and, at least in part, by the loosening of transient familial affections.[79] The militant church's attack on the interests of lineage had an unintended ally. Women had also suffered from the practices of late Renaissance property transmission.[80] Unlike the mechanisms of inheritance through the male line, Trent (again, without any premeditation) opened new possibilities for women: participation in the spiritual life of the parish, new women's confraternities, new organizations that assisted impoverished women, new burial societies where women could make decisions independently of their husbands and fathers, and a new authority in the household once their husbands had died. As the life of Siena's Passitea Crogi illustrates, these new opportunities were not simply matters offered on a platter by the church fathers at Trent; rather they were opportunities taken through women's initiatives during the crisis of ideologies at the end of the Cinquecento.[81] Indeed, the testaments reveal ordinary women, a full generation before their brothers and husbands, as the vanguard of the Counter-Reformation.

One question, however, remains unanswered. Why did husbands change their minds? Why did they reduce the previous restrictions on the properties they granted to their wives? Certainly the Counter-Reformation had not transformed men into paragons of feminism, always attentive to their wives' rights and needs.[82] Perhaps because women enjoyed a relatively stronger position in Sienese society and were better protected by church courts which were more sensitive to the routine violence against women, testaments after the papal visitations of Bossi in fact give more evidence of women's complaints with married life and with their husbands' behavior.[83] In a testament of 1580 a man bequeathed the *usufructus* to his small shop (*botiguccia*) in the "Third" of Camollia near the Fonte d'Ovile to assist his daughter Laura, who was married to a tanner. He granted her this "subvention for her needs" because, "he attested," she "is poor and has been abandoned by her husband and does not possess the means to live except from her own toil."[84] In a will of 1602 monna Silvia gia di Pierantonio Ciappettini, the wife of Savino Locci, thanked her brother for all she had received from him "in her adversities." "Among many other courtesies and loving gestures" she had been able "to stay in his house and at his table for a long time. He had fed her and had seen to her every need, not only in health but also in her troubles, especially in her long litigations with her husband, Savino." Because of this and "moved by other reasons of conscience," she bequeathed to her brother and his heirs one-fourth of her dowry and property, "praying that he would with charity make the necessary arrangements for her body and soul, once she had passed to the other life."[85]

Nor had the Counter-Reformation altered fundamentally the parameters of welfare and financial security for the majority of women—namely, the dowry. This long-entrenched custom could prove precarious even for those women most favorably situated in early modern society. The "nobile and honestissima" Signora Camilla alias Caterina, daughter of the nobleman Cesare Bianchi and widow of a nobleman from Florence, named her son universal heir. If he should die before the testator, she "substituted" her brother, the nobleman Signor Alcide. She was greatly obliged to him "for his trouble and for the expenses he incurred during her previous adversities," particularly in the litigation for recovering her dowry in Florence. For five years he had assumed her financial burdens and those of her children when they were young and most in need of assistance.[86]

The Counter-Reformation had not produced a new feminist man. Nor had it overturned the most fundamental material bridge between the sexes, the dowry. Nonetheless, attitudes as well as property, social, and legal relations did not remain hardened in some ideal-typical premodern mold. As we have seen, husbands' attitudes toward their wives moved from suspicion requiring legal force and outside agencies of surveillance to appeals to conscience, mutual respect, and a new confidence, which they claimed was rooted in lives of affection.

How do we explain these changes? Again, the testaments provide clues. The culture of the Counter-Reformation changed the ways in which both men and women imagined the afterlife and lived in the present. During the late fifteenth and sixteenth centuries, while the number and value of pious bequests declined, testators were preoccupied less with their souls and more with the survival of their family names. In less than a quarter of a century, the reforms instituted at Trent transformed first for women but finally for both sexes that investment in lineage and the materialist hope for the afterlife. After the reforms, testators once again filled the treasuries of religious corporations and even alienated ancestral properties for the sake of the soul. In the charged atmosphere of seventeenth-century spiritual fears, obsessions, and expectations, men such as the "Illustrious" Annibale Piccolomini relied much more heavily than during the sixteenth century on the terrestrial intercession of their wives to say prayers and masses, to organize their funeral processions, to select the most deserving persons and charities. In the new spiritual ambience of the Counter-Reformation, the wife had become, a generation ahead of the men, the spiritual smiths of the household. Husbands preparing for death, now pondering their soul's passage more than the devolution of their properties, found their wives' assistance of more use than trust mapped through the notaries' legalistic contingencies on property.

❧ 11   Late Counter-Reformation Piety

> *Thus the Grand Duke elected the Holy martyrs as his special protectors and every year on the occasion of their feast days, which fell during the summer, would formally go into the Mugello on a sacred pilgrimage and there practice these pious days with acts of devotion and piety. Such being the character of Cosimo III, it is no wonder that while foreigners laughed at him, his subjects hated him.*
> —Riguccio Galluzzi

The strengthening of Counter-Reformation culture from the second half of the Seicento through the first decades of the Settecento presents new enigmas in the statistics of pious giving and the variety of pious choices. The number of pious gifts per testator shows no clear trend over this hundred-year period (see Table 6.1). In the opening years of the Seicento testators on average gave slightly more than three pious gifts. For the next seventy-five years, the number fluctuated between two-and-a-quarter and two-and-a-half. Then, at the beginning of the eighteenth century, testators returned to the high point of a hundred years earlier, giving on average slightly more than 3 pious grants apiece.

Despite continued inflation through the first half of the Seicento, the values of pious gifts expressed in constant florins tell a slightly different story: they more than trebled in the first years of the century and sustained these high rates through 1650. The economy of Siena (along with large regions of southern Europe) entered the deepest throes of malaise during the second half of the century.[1] Almost precisely at mid-century the secular rise of grain prices ended and Siena entered the deflationary "phase B." Yet the slump did not undercut investments in piety. The real values of pious gifts continued to climb by 31 percent in 1651–75 and by another 19 percent in 1676–1700 (Table 6.1). At the opening of the eighteenth century, despite the deepening of economic malaise, the pull of Purgatory redoubled its impact on the lives of the Sienese. The values of pious gifts reached their high point, 102.85 constant florins per testator, representing a 53 percent increase over the last quarter of the seventeenth century, 8.3 times the values of these gifts for the last quarter of the sixteenth century and more than double the figure for the first years of the Seicento, when the Counter-Reformation in its initial stages fanned across Siena geographically and socially. In the next twenty-five years these values leveled off. Then, at mid-century, piety in Siena (at least as expressed in monetary value) plummeted. In 1751–75, at the very moment when grain prices marked the end of "phase B" and possibly renewed agricultural growth, the values of pious gifts declined to one-fourth of what they had been in the previous twenty-five years.[2] Their decline continued through the end of the century.

Do these values reflect the economic fortunes of those who actually wrote testaments in our samples or the progressive encroachment of the Counter-Reformation? Generally, the economic depression or "phase B" of the sixteenth and early seventeenth centuries may have in fact benefited (especially relative to landlords and the nobility) those who worked for wages and who purchased their foodstuffs in the market place.[3] In our segmentation of pious contributors, however, we have seen that those who might have profited most from the deflationary economy—city wage-earners, artisans, and petty shopkeepers—were not the ones riding the crest of mounting pious gifts of the latter half of the Seicento and early Settecento. Their pious contributions, instead, were on the decline.

The ratios of pious bequests to nonpious gifts for the population as a whole, moreover, lends further substantiation to the religious side of the argument (see Table 6.9). These ratios do not reflect a correlation between changes in economic fortunes and piety during the period of declining prices. In the economically dark years approaching the crisis of the mid-seventeenth century (1626–50), this ratio jumped to a secular high of 0.63. During the next twenty-five years, it declined, but to a level still higher than the period of sharply rising prices of the late Cinquecento and the first quarter of the Seicento. Then, in 1676–1750, the remaining years of "phase B," relative piety again marched forward. The first half of the Settecento was a period of redoubled religious zeal: these ratios—0.88 in 1701–25 and 0.71 in 1726–50—soared beyond the high point in piety during the last years of increasing grain prices (1626–50). In fact, relative piety reached the highest level found in these documents, exceeding even that of 0.69 at the peak of mendicant piety (1326–47).

Pious Choices

During these changes in pious expenditures did the Sienese alter the composition of their charitable and holy choices? To whom were the new revenues flowing? In general, the second half of the Seicento marked the decline of those organizations that gave the Counter-Reformation in Siena its distinctive character. The share of pious votes cast for the religious company fell from almost 19 percent of pious gifts in 1626–50, to less than 13 percent and then to 10 percent for the last half of the century (Table 6.5). Finally, in the first half of the eighteenth century, when piety in the reified terms of scudi and florins reached its apogee, the attraction of the lay confraternities collapsed to 4 percent of all holy donations.

The appeal of the new Counter-Reform *congregazioni* fared no better. First, burial societies—the congregations of Saint Peter at the Duomo, the Rosary at Santo Spirito, the Conception at the church of the minor friars—reached their apex by the middle of the Seicento, when they attracted over 13 percent of all pious gifts. During the second half of the century, their share was cut to almost one-half their levels attained at the outset of Counter-Reform zeal. Attempts to revive them may not have been lacking; at least one new burial congregation emerges in the testamentary records of the early eighteenth century, the congregation of the Sisters of the Crown of Our Savior Jesus Christ.[4] Just the same, contributions to and decisions to be buried by *congregazioni* continued to decline.

The draw of the pious welfare congregations—the *convertite,* the *abbandonate,* the *orfanelli,* the *derelitte,* and so on—collapsed even earlier, beginning almost as soon as they appeared on the religious horizons in the critical years 1576–1600. During the late seventeenth and early eighteenth centuries, new congregations for the disadvantaged appeared—the *fanciulle sperse* (the dispersed little girls), the *fanciulle sperse alle prigioni* (the little girls dispersed in prisons, perhaps the same group), a group of *fanciulle* called *delle ravolae,* the "venerable" *conservatorio delle povere fanciulle,* the *congregazione della carità,* the *venerabile congregazione detto "i vergognosi,"* and the *poveri della pietà,* also called *dello Spirito della Pietà.*[5] Like the societies that had appeared in the initial stages of the Counter-Reformation, the majority of the later associations assisted women. Yet these new groups did not succeed in exerting the same pull as the earlier welfare congregations. In the mid-Seicento all of them together gathered only 2.5 percent of all pious donations. In the last quarter of the century, their share had become negligible, and in the Settecento, before the dramatic collapse in pious giving, these communities disappeared completely from the testaments.

Had social and economic changes assuaged the problems confronting the poor, particularly women living on the margins of society, outside the protection of fathers, husbands, and male kin? The general patterns of the crisis of the seventeenth century suggest that matters, particularly for women, instead may have worsened at the very moment when the enthusiasm for these feminine welfare congregations flagged. Dowry prices, at least for the elites, continued to climb in the second half of the seventeenth century after other prices had begun their deflationary spiral.[6] More women probably would have been outside the protection of the family; celibacy and ages at marriage rose throughout Western Europe, while the decline in total agricultural production led to increasing waves of famine and misery.[7] Thus, the price-scissors of the mid- and late-Seicento would have cut through the economic fortunes of women even more severely than of men.

Indeed, by the late Seicento, the appeal of the Counter-Reformation began to differ from its initial years of expansion. Enthusiasm over one side of the doctrine of justification, that is, the efficacy of works—active social charity—

dampened. While gifts to the poor fluctuated between 3 and 7 percent, dowry funds decreased in importance as a source of poor-relief. In 1651–75, their share of pious expenditures dwindled to one percent. A closer scrutiny of these funds suggests at the same time a qualitative shift in their social character. Increasingly, testators tightened eligibility for funding. Previously, those left to distribute dowries were asked to judge only the merits of the nubile girls themselves. In the Seicento the criteria included the character of the girls' parents, sometimes coupled with geographical restrictions. Later, the testators drew class barriers for qualification. In 1616 the daughter of a cobbler and widow of a sausage maker left her confraternity of San Michelangelo 40 florins to marry four *fanciulle citole e virgini*. They were to be, moreover, of "a good father and a mother of chaste behavior (*d'honesto costume*)." The girls also had to be natives of the city of Siena.[8] In 1681 a wax manufacturer left property to dower five girls a year either for marriage or *la vita spirituale*. He also required the girls to be of Sienese birth.[9] The "Magnifico" Luigi del gia Magnifico Simone Malagrida left funds in 1707 for dowering three "poor and honest girls" from the city and the Masse of Siena.[10] The "illustrious signor and count" Ercole-Dorino del gia Illustrissimo Signor Conte Don Iacomo Dorini, a Sienese resident from Milan, left a massive dowry fund to marry twenty girls at the general level of 50 scudi apiece. In this instance, however, all but one of these poor girls had to be natives of the city of Milan.[11] Earlier, we saw the elaborate application procedures for the dowry competitions designed in the 1691 will of the "Illustrissimo Signor" Bernardino Bandinelli. The girls had to be from the district (*corte*) of Contignano, between the ages of eighteen and twenty-five, and of *buona vita, fama e costumi*. In addition, the local parish priest was to submit a form including the name of each contestant, her father's family name, her address, her precise age, the quality of her life, her behavior (*costumi*), her profession, the extent of her poverty, and the number and "quality" of her family.[12]

Some testators restricted the pool of contestants even further geographically. The nobleman Signor Giulio del gia Francesco Piccolomini left property to dower five poor girls each year in perpetuity. They were to be the children of "good fathers and mothers" and from the artisan parish of San Pietro d'Ovile.[13] The priest Il molto reverendo Signor Camillo Conelli in 1683 left "a charitable dowry (*un elemosina dotale*)" to marry a girl "of good and honorable kin (*di buoni et honorabile parenti*)" presumably from the urban neighborhood of the *contrada* of Chiocciola. At any rate, the priest left the selection to the inhabitants of this *contrada* along with another dowry fund entrusted to the discretion of the cobblers' guild (Arte delli Calzolari).[14] In 1735 Pietro-Paolo di Girolamo Vieri bequeathed dowries for poor girls born in the parish of San Giovanni Baptista. Still later, the Jew Gisseffo del gia Rubino Gallichi left funds to be distributed to the poor Jews of the ghetto of Siena.[15] These geographic restrictions carried implicit class restrictions. The provisions in effect excluded the vagabonds, immigrants, and servant girls, who floated from parish to parish in search of employment.[16] Those dowries that restricted the applicant pool to those born in a particular locale went to girls with a certain stake in that locale—who possessed (or whose fathers possessed) stable employment and, most probably, held property there.17

Beyond these implicit qualifications of class, testators of the late Seicento for the first time designated charitable bequests explicitly according to social class. The "molto illustre et honestissima" Signora Fausta del gia Signor Giovanbattista Luti, widow of the nobleman Signor Alessandro Vecchi, left a substantial portion of her estate to the confraternity of Santa Caterina da Siena della natione Senese in Rome. She instructed the lay society to provide a dowry of 100 scudi every two years in perpetuity with the following priorities. The lay sisters were to give first consideration to a female descendant of the noble Luti family who was at least twelve years old. If no one qualified within two years, then the funds would devolve to a descendant of the Mazzoni family. If no one was available from this family, then the confraternity was to choose "other noble girls who were Sienese, that is, who could trace their ancestry as Sienese natives for at least three generations and had been *riseduti* or members of the Sienese nobility for at least two generations."18

Class distinctions became a factor even in selecting "the poor" of the Seicento. The earliest example of a gift granted to the *poveri vergognosi,* or the shamefaced poor, reaches back to the early Trecento.19 However, gifts to these fallen individuals remained extremely rare through the first 400 years of this documentation. During the later part of the seventeenth century, economic and demographic crises narrowed radically the ranks of the Sienese nobility.20 As a corollary, those who had fallen from a higher station in life, particularly from the nobility, increased in number.21 By the early eighteenth century, a congregation devoted exclusively to the needs of this special class appeared for the first time in the testaments. Again, like the earlier congregations of the first generation of Counter-Reform charity and spirituality, this one may have comprised principally fallen women. The noble lady Maria-Francesca, the daughter of a Belgian officer and nobleman, gave 25 scudi to dress *povere donne vergognose.*22 But the *vergognosi* were certainly not all from the nobility. In 1683, for instance, the widowed noblewoman Signoria Ortentia Cerretani left "for the love of God" all her clothing to "persone povere vergognoise [sic]." For this bequest she then specified *particolarmente* Lucia Mezzetti, who "had been her servant for many years."23

Testators of the late Counter-Reformation tuned their class distinctions more finely than previously. As with the dowry funds, increasingly they aimed their pious sums at the middling level of the poor, the respectable poor—those with a means of livelihood, those known to the testators, those with fixed residences. These beneficiaries were distinguished from the *poveri* or the old *pauperes cristi* by a new category of status, the *ignobile.* In his testament of 1628 the nobleman Giulio del gia Francesco Piccolomini "for the love of God" canceled all the debts, both "in goods and in cash," owed to him by those he identified as the *gente Ignobile.* He then defined this middling class of the poor as "poor shopkeepers (poveri buttighai) and peasants and similar people." In 1691 the "Gentildonna" Camilla del gia Nobil Signor Pompeo Cacciaquerra left all her clothing in part as a "pious legacy" to individuals she knew personally—as "*Poverelli* and particularly those persons whom the testator had previously mentioned *in voce*." In 1711 Andrea del gia Francesco Vitali named his confraternity of the Sacri Chiodi (the sacred nails) as his substitute universal heir if the children his wife was presently carrying died before they reached their twentieth birthday—in which case "his charitable brothers" were required to dispense the fruits of his estate "to poor artisans of the city for assistance in their old age or for other needs should they become disabled."[24]

Later, persons from yet another stratum of society were carefully selected for charity. The notary and citizen Giuseppe-Antonio del gia Francesco Maria Tambruini, and his wife Alessandra del gia Signor Camillo Usinini, left a house valued at 2,500 scudi to the congregation of San Pietro. From this property the congregation was to grant a dowry of 250 scudi every year for five years to a girl between the ages of eighteen and twenty-four. This couple of the upper echelons of non-noble Siena required their applicants to be "the daughters of honorable and civil persons of the second class." They then defined precisely what they meant: "for example, of lawyers, doctors, or citizens of Siena." Moreover, neither the father nor the grandfather should have ever practiced any vile trades, such as "cobbler, wine dealer, ironmonger, butcher, blacksmith, or the like." They added that these qualifications were not meant to exclude the daughters of "those who practiced the noble and liberal arts of painting, sculpture, pharmacy, and similar professions."[25]

Testators of the late Seicento began to attach conditions and obligations to what previously had been pure and simple acts of charity. For instance, Niccolò di fu Giulio Falcieri left his confraternity of San Sebastiano as his universal heir with the "burden" of providing doweries for thirty-three girls of *buoni et honesti costumi*. To receive dowries of a mere 5 scudi, these girls were to go to the church of this company "dressed in white and there confess and take communion." Afterward, they were to go to the church of Provenzano "dressed in white and there confess, take communion, and pray for the soul of the testator." Luigi del gia Magnifico Simone Malagrida required the same from three girls awarded from his dowry funds.[26]

Through the first decades of the Settecento the levying of spiritual returns from the beneficiaries of testamentary poor-relief grew in importance.[27] The requirements imposed in the 1743 testament of the notary Giuseppe-Antonio and his wife Alessandra on the recipients of their poor-relief were even more complex and rigorous. Their heirs were to dower *fanciulle* "of the second class" with grants not for civil marriage but for financial support to enter the monastic life. In return, these girls, every first Sunday of the month "unless there were legitimate impediments," were held "throughout their natural lives" to take holy communion and "to recite the third part of the Rosary in suffrance of the souls of the testators as well as for the soul of Giuseppe-Antonio's brother, Bernardino." The testators appealed to the conscience of their beneficiaries, but at the same time exhorted the mother superior of their nunnery to "remind" these girls of their spiritual duties and to perform them "whenever they pleased or together with the rest of the monastic congregation."28

Testators in the earlier phases of the Counter-Reformation had called on members of the welfare congregations, particularly the orphans, to participate in funerals. Funerals, however, had not been traditionally the scene in Siena for the dispersal of alms in return for joining the ranks of mourners. Only by the beginning of the Settecento did testators initiate this form of funerary charity which had long been customary in other parts of Europe.29 For instance, in 1700 Reverend Hieronomo del gia Celio Calderini, the rector of San Pietro d'Ovile, dispersed small sums of money to thirty-three poor girls, seventy paupers, and the *vergognosi* who lived within the *contrada* of his parish. In addition, he granted 24 *sextaria* of flour to twenty-four poor families who lived within the limits of his parish. Unlike past dispensers of handouts, however, he required something in return: these indigents were to fill the ranks of his funeral procession.30 In 1705 the count-patrician Pietrus Capitani Carolis de Beringucci provided for one hundred *homines pauperi* to march in his funeral procession, receiving torches and charity of 13 soldi apiece.31

Another change in the pious choices of the late Counter-Reformation parallels the drift toward more restrictive charity. The first wave of Counter-Reformation enthusiasm had dampened the old Cinquecento forms of "familiar charity." In the opening decades of the Seicento, the relative share of gifts to servants, whether they were domestics or *mezzadri*, fell to almost one-third of what they had been in the mid-Cinquecento. By the mid-Seicento, however, such *legati pii* to one's servants began to climb once again in number and in value (Tables 6.4 and 11.1). By the middle of the Settecento, they had overtaken all other charitable gifts to the poor, whether in the form of handouts, dowry funds, or endowments of Counter-Reform welfare congregations, more than doubling their share of bequests in the critical years 1576–1600. Again, these "pious legacies" served a category of the "poor" quite different from the amorphous "poor of Christ" or unknown girls of good morals. Servants were in a sense the most respectable of all the poor; their very occupations were expressions of deference to their benefactors. Similar to their Protestant contenders to the north, ardent believers of the Counter-Reform mold sought earnestly to distinguish between the "deserving" and the "undeserving" poor; unemployment was identified with sloth, and vagrancy and begging were associated with impiety and ill will.32

Yet the increase in gifts to servants, from 3.7 percent to 9.1 percent of all pious bequests, hardly balances the collapse in the number of donations, which had previously gone to the confraternities, the burial congregations, and the new welfare groups in the opening phases of Counter-Reformation spirituality. What then were the growth sectors of the mature Counter-Reformation? First, gifts to monasteries, after falling in 1651–75, rebounded between 1676 and 1725,

Table 11.1. Gifts to Servants, 1401–1800

Period	Testators	Bequests	Bequests/ Testator	Average Value/ Testator	Average in Constant Florins
1401–25	45	5	0.11	8.00	0.54
1426–50	56	4	0.07	60.33	2.91
1451–75	59	7	0.12	10.00	0.75
1476–1500	99	9	0.09	26.57	1.08
1501–25	92	6	0.07	10.63	0.27
1526–50	63	12	0.19	17.14	0.77
1551–75	126	17	0.13	37.06	0.95
1576–1600	122	7	0.06	24.17	0.20
1601–25	82	16	0.20	23.40	0.63
1626–50	113	12	0.11	14.79	0.21
1651–75	91	10	0.11	10.25	0.20
1676–1700	102	20	0.20	20.63	0.78
1701–25	103	27	0.26	27.30	1.43
1726–50	73	19	0.26	27.73	1.38
1751–75	88	9	0.10	7.88	0.13
1776–1800	63	31	0.49	56.24	3.14

increasing slightly above the levels of the first half of the Seicento. This increase in part reflects the enthusiasm for new or reformed orders during the latter part of the Seicento. The Cappuccini and their sisters the Cappuccine, and the reformed Carmelites, "the Scalzi" (after persisting zealously for governmental permission to found their order in Siena), drew greater numbers of donations and requests for masses.[33] The increase in bequests to monasteries, however, was not massive; at its late Counter-Reformation peak in 1701–25 monasteries accounted for less than a quarter (nearly 22 percent) of all pious bequests, a far cry from the proportions drawn by convents and monasteries during the late Middle Ages or even in the first decades of the Cinquecento.

Instead, that other medieval corporation, the parish church, reformed thoroughly by the Decrees and Canons of Trent, showed a more substantial revival. From about 5 percent of all spiritual gifts, its pull over these investments for the soul increased almost fourfold from the mid-Seicento to the opening years of the Settecento (Table 6.5). This increase is even greater if the contributions to a new kind of neighborhood church are added to the parish. For the first time, donations to churches of the *contrada* appear in these documents. In 1659 Angelus q. Dominici de Vangiolittis left as his universal heir the monastery of Santo Spirito with the obligation of celebrating thirty masses a year in perpetuity for his spiritual health. If the monks were negligent in performing these spiritual services, the estate would pass to "the Madonna of the Chapel of San

Salvatore, where the *contrada* of Onda gathers." In the final quarter of the Seicento the neighborhood churches of the *contrade* Onda, Oca, and Chiocciola reached the height of their popularity, receiving 3.4 percent of all pious gifts.[34] Then, in the opening years of the Settecento, mysteriously they fade from the documents, by 1725 disappearing altogether.

Along with the rise in contributions to the parish church, the figure of the curate emerges more prominently in testators' lives and in their preparations for death. He appears more often as the executor of wills and by the second half of the century became the principal religious recipient as universal heir. In these capacities the curate was entrusted with the responsibilities of selling off testators' property, organizing the expenditures for the funeral, and arranging masses at the graveside and afterward. By early Settecento, some testators wished no longer to reveal all of their final plans for the disposition of their estates to the notary and instead turned to their neighborhood priests. For instance, "Gentildonna Baronesa" Caterina del gia Baron Giovanni Cerbone declared that she "had the intention of making other legacies but at present had not made them definitively." Instead, she listed these on a separate sheet of paper closed "with her seal" and consigned it to "her *sacredotos*."[35]

In addition to the curate, others in the parish hierarchy held prominent places in the hearts and plans of testators. Donna Cecilia left all the arrangements regarding her funeral, burial, and the masses for her soul to the "Molto reverendo" Domenico Frei, the vice-curate of her parish. The confessor, moreover, begins to loom more prominently as the beneficiary of important gifts and spiritual responsibilities. The artisan Bartolommeo del gia Maestro Bartalino from Fuligno, who had resided in Siena for fifty years, left in 1739 his estate's *usufructus* to his wife. She was not to sell anything and was to remain a widow. Bartolommeo "confided" in his confessor to oversee her behavior. If she violated the stipulations, his estate would pass to the parish priest and his universal heir would thereby become "pious causes."[36]

These ties of affection were not one-sided from parishioner to *pievano*. In late Counter-Reformation Siena the testaments of clerics show a sense of responsibility and noblesse oblige for their communities not found earlier. The noblecanon of the Collegiate church of Provenzano, Reverend Lorenzo del gia Nobile Leonetto Griffoli, left 200 scudi to Reverend Carlo Bocci: 40 were to be distributed to the poor of Christ and the other 160 donated "to those particular persons whom the testator had confessed."[37] In a later document the *pievano* of the village church of San Giovanni Baptista a Corsano left 12 scudi to buy grain, which was to be distributed to all the heads of household "who found themselves in need." Second, he provided the incentive of 5 scudi each to all 400 of his parishioners, "grandi, piccoli, maschi, femine," who would come forward to say the service of the holy rosary and make the sign of the cross "for the happy repose of the testator's soul."[38]

The rise in contributions to parish churches and to their curates roughly parallels the decline of that other institution connected with parish piety which rose meteorically in the opening phases of the Tridentine culture: the religious lay confraternity. This switch in allegiance and enthusiasm in the last decades of the Seicento suggests a change in character of Counter-Reformation culture. In its years of maturity, the locus of spirituality had moved from the populism of the community as a whole to the lines of obedience and authority between the curate and his flock. This later, more authoritarian Counter-Reformation should not overshadow the spontaneity and popular exuberance of its initial phases.

Piety into Coin

The testaments provide other clues about changes in the culture of the Counter-Reformation. The great variety of new forms of expression the testaments introduced at the end of the Cinquecento—new liturgies, new masses, new congregations and confraternities, new ways to stage funerals—were losing their dynamism and becoming routinized by the second half of the Seicento. Spirituality became more mechanical, more easily calculated, quantified, and controlled. First, the proportion of those who requested masses did not increase substantially through the second half of the century. But the average number of masses actually specified in wills increased by four times from the beginning of the century to 1676–1725. For these two quarters 1676–1700 and 1701–25 the Sienese ordered on average 122 and 124 masses, respectively, for the health of their souls. This growth in the number of masses roughly paralleled the decline in requests for perpetual masses (see Table 9.1). In effect, testators of the late Counter-Reformation had reduced the indefinite notion—masses in perpetuity—to large, finite, concrete numbers of masses to be sung either immediately after the testator's burial or over the course of a long but well-delineated period. In the second half of the Seicento, moreover, the staging of masses across the spiritual landscape of Siena grew in complexity. For instance, the "noble and honorable" Arla del gia Nobile Signor Alcavio Bulgarini, widow of the noble Count Bargagli, gave 4 dopplieri valued at 40 lire each to her vice-curate of the parish of San Cristofano. He was to celebrate eight sets of 30 masses each at the churches of San Domenico and Sant'Antonio, at those of the Conventual and Observant Franciscans, Cappuccin fathers and mothers, and at two other churches wherever the vice-curate wished. The noble and reverend Alberto del gia Domenico degli Alberti, curate of the parish of Basciano in the Masse, required his heirs to celebrate within ten months after his death 120 masses—10 in his parish, 10 in the church of Santo Stefano (which had been annexed by his curate), 20 in the church of the Provenzano, 20 in the Duomo, 20 in the Dominican chapel of the Holy Rosary, and 20 at the church of the Cappuccin fathers. The noblewoman Ortensia Cerretani granted one of her sons 250 scudi and required him in return to have 1,000 masses celebrated at the high altars of four churches in the city within a period of six months following her death.[39]

Requests for 1,000 or more masses were not a rarity by the second half of the century. The Illustrissimo Bernardino del gia Cavalier del Sacro Ordine di Santo Stefano . . . del Giulio Bandinelli, the Illustrissimo Antonmaria del gia Giovanbaptista Tommasi, the noble "Capitano" Giovanbaptista del gia Nobil Pompilio della Ciaia, the Nobil Scipione del gia Moro Bargagli, the "Nobile et Onesta" Caterina-Gaetana-Maria del gia Nobil Lelio Griffoli, and others demanded large numbers of masses to be performed as soon as possible after their deaths.[40] By the last decade of the Seicento such masses had become the crowning events of their orchestrated funerals. On occasion, noble testators demanded even more than 1,000 masses to be said for their souls immediately after their deaths. Antonio del gia Alessandro Ugolini, a cavalier of the Sacred Military Order of Santo Stefano and rector of Santa Maria della Scala, demanded that 1,400 masses be said at high altars in the various churches on the day of his funeral. The Illustrissima domina Maria-Francesca f.q. Nobili Capitani Henrici Loos from Belgium, wife of Count Marius Nerucci of Siena, required her heirs to celebrate 2,000 masses at high altars in at least six different churches within two months of her death.[41]

When testators demanded perpetual masses for their souls, they often prescribed the timing at specific moments in the church calendar even more meticulously than in the past. The nobleman Iofrancescus f. Nobilis et Excellesimi del Domini Iacobi Ugurgerii, a canon of the cathedral, left property to his sister and, after her death, to his brother. In return, they were to pay the nuns of Ognissanti to perform perpetual masses at the church's high altar, "where the Miraculous Virgin under the title of the Holy Manger appears."[42] The masses "with the application of the Holy Sacrifice" were to be sung on the days dedicated to the Blessed Virgin Mary: five masses with two torches of white wax on 6 February plus one each on the days of the Nativity, the Holy Name of Mary, the Presentation, the Immaculate Conception, the Purification, the Sponsalitium, the Annunciation, the Seven Sorrows, the Visitation, of Santa Maria della Neve, and the Assumption. We have already argued that the devotion to Mary and to patron saints had punctuated and crowded the religious calendar in the everyday lives of Senesi during the initial phases of the Counter-Reformation. The earlier demands found in these series of testaments do not, however, even approximate the proliferation of holidays and special moments found later.

Beyond the reduction of "perpetual" to large finite numbers, the late Counter-Reformation reified piety with exact price equivalencies for masses. The wide discrepancies between the numbers of masses requested and the price paid suggest that pious donors of earlier periods did not actually pay for masses per se; rather, they made contributions to ecclesiatical corporations and in return asked for masses to be said for their souls. The request for masses was a reciprocal relation between the testator and the church and not a cash nexus. Only toward the end of the century did a consistent and exact relationship between the number of masses and their pricetags emerge. Testators such as the Dominican tertiary monna Cassandra del gia Francesco Bianchi ordered the Dominican fathers to say up to one hundred masses on the day of her funeral at the altar of the holy rosary. For these, she left "the customary charity" (1 lire) for each mass.[43] This rate of exchange between Gregorian masses at high altars and soldi became standardized across the ecclesiastical landscape of Siena from the 1690s through the first half of the Settecento. The monks and curates apparently did not grant discount rates for large numbers of masses nor did they calculate for changes in the value of money. Yet this was a period of general deflation; thus the church gained from fixed prices. Still, in 1722, the cavalier of the Order of Santo Stefano, Signor Antonio degli Ugolini, purchased 1,400 masses for his soul at various high altars through the city at the same rate as in the past century, "a charity" of 1 lire per mass.[44]

Alongside the monetization of charity, testators exerted stricter control and cost-accounting mechanisms to guarantee the enactment of spiritual services. By the last decades of the Seicento, testators such as Signor Cesare del gia Girolo from Rigomagno asked that the enactment of masses be shown (*con adempirsi*). The Nobile Verginia del nobil gia Girolamo Accarigi, in ordering her heirs to have 500 scudi worth of masses celebrated for her soul within five years of her death, obliged them "to keep a book where the masses should be marked down . . . and reported annually to the Curia." Indeed, for the late Seicento these special record books of celebrated masses begin to fill monastic archives and can still be found in the collections of the *Conventi Soppressi*.[45]

In 1741, the "Illustrissimo Signor" patrician cavalier Leonido dell'Illustrissimo Signor Francesco Landucci carried the demands for the performances of his masses a step further. For perpetual masses to be celebrated on seventeen specified feast days, he first required the Cappuccin mothers "to notify the archbishop of Siena immediately after celebrating each mass"; second, he obliged them "immediately to carve in stone 'a memorial' to be placed in the sacristy of their church with an exact description of all these obligations and their days" of celebration.[46] If they failed to make this plaque, they would be fined 50 scudi to be paid to Santa Maria della Scala.

The wooden quality of religious sentiment, which began to harden in the last decades of the seventeenth century, draws parallels to the world of religious thought that Johan Huizinga depicted for the French aristocracy in his book *The Waning of the Middle Ages*. For Siena, the vitality of religious devotion during that period following the Black Death appears far removed from Huizinga's subjects. For this earlier period, references to saints' days, the invocation of special advocates, the "crystallization of religious thought" into complex, mechanistic acts, are absent. The piety purchased by testators of the late Seicento— the precise counting of masses, the reification of "perpetual" to large numbers of masses and cost-accounting for "holy sacrifices"—on the other hand, evokes the spirituality of Huizinga's fifteenth-century Counter-Renaissance. The proliferation of saints, which multiplied through the testamentary preambles, strikes further parallels. At the beginning of the sixteenth century barely 1 percent of the Sienese testators invoked special advocates or patron saints to assist their souls' journeys to the "lap of Paradise." By mid-Seicento, nearly one-fifth of the testators invoked these special intercessions. In the last quarter of the century, the proportion climbed to 45 percent. And in the first twenty-five years of the Settecento, one-half of all testators called on their spiritual patrons for especial treatment in the affairs of the afterlife. Some, such as the greengrocer Maestro Buonventura del gia Maestro Giuseppe Mori, after beseeching spiritual aid from Christ and the Virgin Mary, invoked the spiritual intercession from as many as seven individual saints; these "particular advocates" were Saint Joseph, Saint Anthony of Padua, Saint Catherine of Siena, Saint Bonaventure, Saint Louis, Saint Guy (Gaetano) as well as the holy souls of Purgatory.[47] Yet the particular saints chosen by the majority in the closing years of the Seicento suggest again a dampening of devotional imagination. The Sienese occasionally invoked new Counter-Reformation saints: Teresa, Francis Xavier, San Pietro del Cantara, Filippo Neri, and Francis of Sales.[48] But these choices were rare. The vast majority of the specially chosen and enumerated saints of the late Counter-Reformation were simply the testators' namesakes.

The Bifurcation of Piety

It would be misleading to characterize the period of spirituality in Siena between 1650 and 1750 as "the waning of the Counter-Reformation." Instead, these were the years when the values of pious giving peaked. Another side to this late Counter-Reformation emerges on occasion even in the very same testaments that demanded specific and large numbers of masses controlled by strict cost-accounting. These controls grew at the very moment when husbands and wives began to rely more and more on their own ties of affection and the dictates of conscience for the performance of postmortem prayers and services. In addition the bulge in the number of "miscellaneous" pious gifts during the late Counter-Reformation now needs explanation. In the middle of the Seicento the percentage of pious donations which fall into this category nearly doubled, from 24 percent to 45 percent of all pious gifts. Furthermore, 78 percent of these gifts were bequests in which the testator did not explicitly name any ecclesiastical corporation or cleric as the beneficiary. From less than 18 percent, this category of unmentioned beneficiaries doubled to 35 percent.

These pious bequests were in fact the flip-side of piety characterized by the mechanistic demands and controls imposed on the church. At the very time that testators desired greater guarantees and more control over clerics' performances of their masses, they turned increasingly to their heirs, relatives, and spouses to pray for their souls and bear responsibility for suffrages. These requests were different from the demands made on monks, canons, and priests. Here no numbers, timetables, controls, or need for spiritual inventories of performances find mention; testators instead appealed to the love and the conscience of their beneficiaries. Often, as we saw in the preceding chapter, the appeals were reciprocal ones between husbands and wives. In 1667, for instance, the "Provident

Figure 6. Giuseppe Nicola Nasini, *Immaculate Conception*, in the sacristy of Sant'Andrea (Siena) circa 1730

man" Francesco del gia Oratio Mandotti left his wife as universal heir with the following message: "Leaving all to her, believing in her conscience and that she not be held accountable for anything, he beseeched her to desire to remember him by making some suffrages for the health of his soul. In this, however, he wished not to burden her, hoping in this way that she might do more than he could reasonably impose on her." Similarly, he prayed that his *confratelli* would do good deeds for his soul as best they saw fit, believing in their munificence (*gran carità*). The water-worker (*acquavitaio*) Maestro Giovanbattista Perfetti nominated his wife as universal heir. He "left all to her conscience, wishing not to penalize her in any way . . . he prayed that she might wish to remember the testator in every way she could."[49]

Such appeals to simplicity and conscience were not the exclusive preserve of a special affection that may have grown up between husbands and wives. Consider the "Molto Reverendo Signor" Michelangelo del gia Messer Domencio Santi, a *sacerdote* of Siena, who opened his itemized gifts by enjoining the Cappuccin fathers and the Observant friars to celebrate 200 masses "for the poor abandoned souls of Purgatory," "as soon as possible," and "to demonstrate their enactment by noting them down as soon as they were celebrated" so that "one might see that they had been fulfilled according to the will of the testator." Several "items" later the cleric expressed another side of his devotion far removed from monetized masses and cost-accounting spirituality. The will reads:

> This cleric realizes and confesses to be gracious to God and the work of Charity to be able to avoid that crime and odious sin of Ingratitude. He never knew any parent but only the love and esteem of his poor nursemaid, who is named Margherita Comellini. Thus he wishes to nominate and elect her as his universal heir. He does so all the more because she nursed him and fed him in the city of Florence with every kindness and act of charity and at her own expense. He wishes that she should be able to take possession of his property and do with it whatever she pleases. He desires this since the poor little woman would remain naked without the assistance of her adopted child. He prays that she will want to remember her adopted child in her prayers, hoping that she will do more than he could impose on her, since he has already experienced the charity which she has always brought him.[50]

Matters of the heart as opposed to cold calculation and regulation often governed, moreover, the exchange of gifts and services between friends. In 1679 "the Illustrious Reverend" Giovanni di Magnifico Gugliellmo Buzzi from Campagnatico, who lived in Siena, charged his "esteemed friend, the very illustrious" Antonio Beccabelli with having as many suffrages and masses at the testator's funeral as his friend saw fit. He also enjoined his "most cordial friend" to sell off all his household furnishings and with the proceeds "to do as much good" for the testator's soul as he saw fit. He chose this friend as his executor "with all the inherent powers," adding that no one should check up on him, "rather in everything and for everything he submitted to his integrity and goodness." Similarly, Eufrasia del gia Carlo Tossi left a friend, Pietro Marchetti, a book dealer, as her universal heir. "She prayed that he would do some good for her soul, the celebration of masses, and other suffrages. In this, she entrusted all to him and for everything according to his conscience." And the sand-digger (*renaiolo*) Matteo appealed to the conscience of "his dear friend" and universal heir, Maestro Giovancarlo, a furnace-builder, for terrestrial intercession, trusting his "affection and charity."[51]

These appeals to loved ones abounded in the language of bequests to kin beyond the nuclear family. For instance, the blacksmith Maestro Annibale del gia Iacomo Fieravanti, "in part to show his affection," named as universal heirs his two nephews, whom he had kept in his home when they were young, and "prayed with all his heart that they should wish to remember him with suffrages and pious works for the sake of his soul and not be ingracious, but do what they found fitting and what they pleased, especially in their prayers."[52]

These examples suggest that the bifurcation of piety (although sometimes mixed in the same testaments) may have cut roughly along class lines. We have already seen that urban artisans and shopkeepers, after having been among the first to adopt the new forms of Counter-Reformation piety, were the first to drift away from lavish expenditures on charity and devotion. In the late Counter-Reformation those who demanded hundreds of masses from heirs and monasteries and who instituted rigid controls for demonstrating the performances of spiritual services came almost exclusively from the nobility, whereas those who turned away from the religious corporations but relied on the consciences of spouses, friends, and kin, did not bear those inflated titles "the most excellent," "illustrious," or "Magnificent." Instead, those making simple appeals to the heart for unspecified charity and religious service were mere "provident men": water-workers, sand-diggers, and blacksmiths. They all, moreover, came from the city of Siena—and were the ones who first eased from the vise of Counter-Reformation expenditures.

Funerals

The devotional practices of the late Counter-Reformation showed other strains and tensions. Interestingly, the fault lines do not here corroborate the class alignments seen earlier. Extravagant and complex funeral arrangements and requiem masses entailing intricate instructions continued into the second half of the Seicento. The wax maker Il Magnifico Domenico del gia Giovanbattista Parrini in 1680 staged one of the most elaborate expressions of "baroque piety" found in these documents. First, his body was to be transported in the bier of his religious company of San Giovanni Baptista in Pantaneto and interred in the communal vault of this confraternity. He assigned fifteen lay brothers of this company; fifteen brothers from the Company of San Ansano; thirty "pious ones," all orphans; and ten fathers of the Observant order to escort his corpse to the grave. His heirs were to distribute wax, in amounts left to his wife's discretion, to all of the participants in his cortège. "For the health of his soul" his wife and heirs were to arrange the celebration of thirty requiem masses "while his cadaver lay exposed" in his parish church. Thirty more masses were to follow, celebrated by his Company of San Giovanni Baptista, and then sixty were to be performed by the Observant fathers within two months. In addition, he left these fathers "the customary alms" to celebrate thirty masses a year for ten years following his death.

But the wax dealer's posthumous plans did not terminate with his funeral. "For the health of his soul," he obliged his heirs to give the brothers of his company forty handmade torches, some white and some yellow, for ten years following his death to be distributed once a year when the "Holy Arm of the Glorious Saint John the Baptist" was exposed in the Duomo of Siena. The brothers were to march under the pulpit where the Holy Arm was on display and to keep their torches lit for as long as the relic was exposed. Afterward, they were to return the torches to the testator's heirs.[53]

Domenico also prescribed other light-shows at other times and places to take place after his earthly departure. He ordered his heirs to give to his Company of San Giovanni Baptista funds for six masses every year on the Monday of their carnival—or on the following Tuesday if that Monday was prohibited. On the following morning the Observant fathers were to say one mass and sing another for the soul of the testator and celebrate a holy office. In the middle of the church, on the spot of his funeral canopy (*catafalco*), his heirs were to place six large candles (*falcole*) of yellow wax weighing 1 ounce apiece; two other candles weighing 1 pound each were to be placed on the high altar; the heirs were to fill with 2 ounces of wax each of ten torch stands (*torcieri*) placed on the reading desks (*leggii*) of this church plus 3 ounces of wax on the altar of the Madonna della Pace and 2 ounces on the altar of San Giuseppe located in the chapel of his confraternity. While these torches were burning, the fathers were to sing ten masses. His heirs were to distribute another 2 pounds of yellow wax in small candles (*moccoli*) to the fathers' assistants. Finally, the wax dealer planned another torch-show of similar grandeur with masses for his soul for ten years on the festival of San Giovanni.

The drift in funeral plans and the celebration of masses in the late Counter-Reformation, however, did not follow the waxman's example. (After all, he may have had economic interests in such lavish consumption of wax and candles.) But of those who did continue to sponsor elaborate funeral processions, Domenico was not exceptional in class terms. The majority of these ornate and intricate funerals of the late Counter-Reformation were the plans of wealthy shopkeepers from Siena.[54] The nobility, on the other hand, who led late Counter-Reformation society in their charity and lavish expenditures for sacramental assistance, here turned away from the baroque displays and requested modesty and prudence. The wealthy noblewoman Ortensia Cerretani, who left sums for the celebration of thousands of masses, instructed her heirs to bury her in the tomb of her husband's family, the house of Beninsegni, in the church of Saint Francis, "with the greatest modesty for the funeral." "In the place of funeral pomp, she desired as many masses as possible to be said for her soul. The nobleman and cavalier Bartolomeo del Nobile gia Signore Lonetto Griffoli was even more stern. He asked to be interred "with the body" of his deceased mother in the sepulcher of his "house" in the church of Saint Francis, "without pomp and without any expense." Rather, "as soon as possible" 500 masses (plus an office with 12 masses) were to be said for his soul in the village church of Poggio di Santa Cecilia. He further "exhorted" his heirs to perform as many services as they could for the souls of their ancestors. The "illustrious" patrician Bernardino, son of the cavalier of the order of San Stefano, Giulio Bandinelli, ordered his body to be buried in the sepulcher of his religious company "and with that pomp fitting to the prudence and charity of his heirs." He then ordered "as soon as possible" 1,000 requiem masses to be celebrated at high altars for the health of his soul. Others, among them "Onestissima fanciulla" Eleonara del gia Domenico Fornari, left the matters of the funeral pomp to "the discretion, charity, and prudence" of respected individuals. In her case, she turned to the rector of Santa Maria della Scala and to the "Molto Reverendo" Signor Don Giovanni Donzellini, to whom "she declared she had been much obliged for his civil and charitable assistance." She "besought him to wish to procure as many masses as possible" to be recited in the morning while her body lay open to view in her parish church.[55]

Pleas for modesty and "decency" in the arrangement of last rites were not solely the predilections of the wellborn, however. Madonna Maddalena del gia Messer Iacomo, the wife of a peddler, elected to be buried in the "church of the honorable *contrada* of Oca." She declared that her funeral expenses should reflect "her condition and the force of her inheritance." She left the determination of these matters to the "Holy Officials of the said *contrada*," who should decide "with moderation and discretion." Maestro Francesco del gia Mariotto Francioni asked to be carried from his house to his parish church in the bier of his confraternity and only that the "necessary" amount of wax be distributed. Instead of then enlisting the ranks of numerous lay brothers, friars, fathers, and other "pious ones," he ordered that "all be done by his parish priest, with the approval and consent of his wife . . . using parsimony and discretion in these expenses, since he coveted good acts rather than pomp."[56] Many others from the city and through the countryside simply left these matters to the discretion of their spouses or heirs. The waxman's torches had become the exceptions by the latter decades of the Seicento.

How can one explain this discretion on the part of the Sienese and especially the nobility during the late Counter-Reformation? "Giansenismo" (Jansenism) may have penetrated Siena; it was, however, a later development.[57] The very testaments that appealed most explicitly to modesty and parsimony in matters of funeral cortèges were at the same time the ones that demanded the greatest number of masses—a practice that would not have pleased the revolt by the Jansenists against useless ornamentation.[58] The bifurcation of funeral practices in late Counter-Reformation Siena instead reveals tensions inherent within the liturgy and piety of post-Tridentine Catholicism. It was mixed in terms of class and even on occasion within individual testaments. These contradictions or poles of piety can indeed be seen in Counter-Reform piety from its outset. From the reforms of Carlo Borromeo, the zeal for asceticism, and the assault on earthly goods and family pride had at the same time been overlaid with new and formalistic baroque devotional practices.[59] The overwhelming economic success of the Counter-Reformation, which the testamentary outpouring of pious gifts well attests, exacerbated these internal contradictions buried within the practices and intentions of Counter-Reformation culture. Toward the end of the Seicento, while preambles continued to extol the grandeur and majesty of the kingdom of the Lord, an underlining of asceticism began to slip into these formulas. The simple and unwrought testament of the "Honorable Virgin" Lucia del gia Magnifico Signor Giuseppe Martini, for instance, was explicit. She proclaimed the virtue of "distancing oneself totally from the world, away from its pomp and falsehoods, and away from earthly property."[60]

In the interstices of these tensions, new elements seeped into the late Counter-Reformation testaments of the early eighteenth century. In 1726 the surgeon Giulio del gia Francesco Francesevoli added a new clause to the formulaic exhortation of Counter-Reform "education." He insisted that his sons and heirs "live with the fear of God and of the civil laws."[61] The melding of religion and the state, on occasion, entered even the bequests of the most pious. In 1722 "Illustrissima et Onestissima" Caterina-Gaetana-Maria del gia Nobile Signor Lelio Griffoli, widow of a nobleman from the Piccolomini family, left a substantial fund for the dissemination of Jesuit devotion and learning. The piety of this noble testator was not restricted to the religious institution of "the holy ones of Jesus Christ." Her legacy began with a lengthy assertion that she was "quite aware through trustworthy persons of the faith that 'the spiritual exercises' have brought great profit to this city [Siena], which have been recently introduced with the help of the Royal Clemency of our most devout Sovereign. The city, moreover, has until now experienced very visibly the effects of these exercises." She noted that "these cannot be sustained for long without a financial corps and fund. Since she desires to promote and bring such great relief to her beloved Country . . . she donates to the divine [society] of Jesus Christ 2,000 scudi so that the seed of this Evangelical work should not be lost."[62]

The circulation of paintings through bequests in early eighteenth-century wills also hints at the rise of a new cult of the state. Alongside *quadri* and *quadretti*, which for the last century had circulated in the wills of artisans and merchants, paintings with secular subjects appear for the first time in testaments around 1720. The nobleman Scipione del gia Mario Bargagli, a grain inspector for the state of Siena, left his brother thirteen paintings (*pezzi di quadri*). The first four portrayed the usual subjects of such exchanges: a madonna with the baby Jesus, Saint Ann and Saint John, Saint Jerome, and a Maestà. The next five, on the other hand, cultivated an entirely different icon. These included the portraits (all in ornamented frames) of the "Grand Duke" (who was not named), the "Most Supreme" Cardinal Medici, the "Most Supreme" Prince Ferdinando, the "Principessa Governatrice," and finally the last of the Medici line, the "Most Supreme" Prince Giovanni Gastone. In addition, he bequeathed two portraits of the Sienese nobleman Pietro Bandini. After describing three other religious subjects, he finished without revealing the contents of his other household paintings, declaring only that "all the other paintings must remain as the property of his heirs." In the same year, the noblewoman Dorotea Piccolomini, widow of a nobleman from the Bellanti family, left her son "the effigies and portraits of members of the House of the Bellanti and of other persons."[63] Even in the "great age of selfishness" no such icons of a political and secular nature surfaced in the quotidian evidence of ordinary testaments. Thus, forces gnawing from outside the framework of the church and its own sets of contradictions complicated still further the mesh of mentalities of early eighteenth-century Siena.

Yet this melding of cultures and ideologies—the state, family, and religion—did not dampen the vigor of the Counter-Reformation at least in financial terms. While new icons crept into the testaments, the art world bristled with the circulation (and presumably the production) of religious art. Pious gifts continued to fill church coffers through the 1740s. The ideologues and enthusiasts of the Counter-Reformation in fact reached the pinnacle of their success by the 1720s, when yet another innovation entered our gallery of documents. Increasing numbers of testators, in every case from beneath the ranks of the nobility, began to disinherit wholesale all kin who in the past might have laid claims on their patrimonies by giving their entire estates to the church. Testators such as Caterina del gia Filippo Mercanti, the wife of a notary (who was in fact living at the time of this will's redaction), "nominated her own soul (*l'anima sua propria*)" as the universal heir to her estate. The "benefit" of the estate was to flow to "the souls of Purgatory."[64] In other cases, the testator, after leaving the estate to his or her "own soul," clarified matters by appointing a priest, monk, or confessor as the executor with precise instructions to sell off the testator's worldly goods and convert the cash immediately into as many masses and "as many suffrages as possible" for the salvation of the testator's soul. Those middle-class zealots who left everything to their own salvation (at least in these samples) were childless at the time of the drafting. They were not, however, without close kin—husbands, wives, brothers, and nephews—relatives who in previous times would have been the likely heirs to such patrimonies.

After mounting in importance for three decades, these paragons of spiritual egoism and the dismissal of kin suddenly around 1750 disappeared. At the same time, the number and value of pious bequests plunged. Spirituality in Siena crashed. The Counter-Reformation, which so effectively broke the strategies of lineage prevalent in the late Renaissance and which then structured notions of the afterlife for the subsequent century and a half ended, abruptly. Our tables chart its crisis and its steady precipitous demise. In the latter part of the eighteenth century, the church showed no visible hints of recovery. Why did this sudden abandonment of the church occur? Was the Counter-Reformation simply destroyed from its own internal tensions and contradictions, which the testaments show sharpening through the late Counter-Reformation? Or did its fatal virus come from beyond the religious horizons of Siena and outside testamentary practices, which thus far has been the center of our inquiry?

12 Enlightened Despotism

> *Among the objects, which are of our Paternal care and constant watch, for the well-being and for the advantage of Our most loving Subjects and which we have especially before our eyes, concerns the growth and propagation of Commerce, and wishing to facilitate its practice for those most capable . . . we have sought to extend the law prohibiting the passage of stable Property into Dead Hands.*
> —Preamble to the 1751 Mortmain law

> *Le désir de faire passer son nom à la posterité est général en Toscanne, et mesme dans la plus vile populace, par cette raison tous faisoient de fideicomis perpétuels qui alloient finir dans les gens de main morte.*
> —Count Richecourt

By mid-Settecento, Purgatory had lost its grip over the hearts and plans of the Sienese. The number of pious gifts per testator between 1750 and 1776 dropped by a third and their values tumbled more dramatically by over four times.[1] In the final years of the century, these values continued to fall. The figures understate the actual decline in the traditional religious forms of piety. By the last decades, gifts to servants constituted fully one-fifth of all pious bequests, double the number attained during the high-point of Cinquecento secularism and more than five times the number when Counter-Reform devotion was in its prime, 1626–50 (see Table 6.4). In terms of values, these donations were even more important (see Table 11.1). More than half the value of pious gifts in the last quarter of the eighteenth century went to servants (56.24 florins of a total of 111.12 florins).

By the latter half of the Settecento, the organization of the grand households of the nobility had changed. Previously, gifts to servants consisted of small amounts of money, clothing, or the residues of their salaries. Almost always these *servi* were women. By the mid-Settecento new and more specialized servants of the household, officers, and estate managers—*fattori, fattoresse, computisti, economi*—entered the legacies. In contrast, those in these new service professions were men. Moreover, the staffs of these new familial proto-bureaucracies commanded substantially larger gifts than their female counterparts in domestic service. In 1741 the patrician-cavalier Leonido di Cavalier Francesco Landucci left 100 scudi "to *tutta fameglia*, which included cooks, male servants, estate agents (*fattori*), chambermaids, and servant girls."[2] In 1780, the noble marchese Alessandro del gia Nobile and Marchese Flavio Chigi left 30 scudi each to his *maestro di casa*, to his accountant (*computista*), and to the accountant's assistant. On the other hand, he left "his serving girl and chambermaid" only clothing valued at 10 scudi.[3] In the following year the "Excellent Cavalier" Priore di Francesco Siminetti, a counselor to the Grand Duke and "lieutenant general of Siena," left gifts to twelve individually named *domestici in Servizio*. All were men, and all received gifts ranging from 20 to 100 scudi, except one servant, singled out for "his long and faithful service," who received a lifetime annuity of 36 scudi a year.[4]

If grants to servants are subtracted from the sums of "pious bequests," then the drastic decline in pious gifts becomes even more catastrophic for the church. Were these sharp reversals in piety determined by changes in the fortunes of testators, either through economic depression or a radical change in the constituency of those writing testaments? Although grain prices began after a century of deflation to turn upward, "phase C" may not have been a blessing to all sectors of the population. Initially, price inflation stimulated by demographic growth resulted in the pan-Italian famines of 1764 through 1766. These proved even more disastrous at least to peasant economies than had the "seventeenth-century crisis."[5] For those possessing the wherewithal to draft last wills, the story appears to have been different (see Table 6.9). During the last quarter of the century the average values of nonpious gifts more than doubled, from 699.74 florins to 1,313.43 florins, attaining the highest figure for these gifts over the long course of this analysis and despite an unquestionable extension of will writing through Sienese society.[6] Thus the decline in the values of pious gifts relative to nonpious ones was even more precipitous than that traced by the earlier statistics. In 1750–75 pious gifts went from near parity with nonpious ones to only one-fifth of that expended on friends and kin; for the final years of the century the downward spiral depressed them to 8 percent of the nonpious values (or 4 percent if gifts to servants are struck from the sums of pious charity).

An analysis of pious bequests by decade demonstrates that the collapse occurred at mid-century (see Table 12.1). In the 1740s the values of these gifts soared to 1,081.50 florins for every testator sampled. In the next decade they collapsed to barely more than one-tenth of this amount. What explains this swift reversal in the power of purgatory and the efficacy of hell (which only entered the preambles in the 1730s)?[7] We have already examined the tensions and contradictions in Counter-Reform devotion which began to encumber simple belief by the last decades of the seventeenth century. We have seen that the Counter-Reformation had reached its logical absurdity in the 1720s through the 1740s, at least for the middling ranks of society, who increasingly disinherited their kin by leaving their own souls as the universal heirs, thus disproving the cliché: they

Table 12.1. Pious Gifts by Decade, 1701–1770

Period	Testators	Number of Pious Bequests	Average Value/ Testator
1701–10	28	78	339.80
1711–20	46	92	484.46
1721–30	28	152	747.57
1731–40	46	129	346.93
1741–50	26	65	1081.50
1751–60	26	38	115.32
1761–70	38	63	116.43

could take it with them. By 1750, this practice suddenly and mysteriously disappeared. And demands for large numbers of masses, though they do not vanish entirely, suddenly became extraordinarily rare. Why the abrupt change—the most rapid transformation yet uncovered in our journey through the last thoughts of ordinary citizens and villagers from Siena?

Mortmain

Here, the chronological coincidence with matters of state is clear. On 11 February 1751 the new Grand Duke of Tuscany, Francesco Stefano from Lorrain, passed legislation, designed by Count Emmanuele de Richecourt, "prohibiting the passage of the properties of the laity (*dei secolari*) into the 'dead hands' (*mani morte*) of the church."[8] The law limited the total value of such gifts to 100 zecchini (or scudi). This law restricted the flow of gifts to the church more than any such legislation heretofore promulgated in Europe (or so clerics in Rome argued).[9] Its effects on testament writing and the disposition of property was immediate and explicit. In the 1750s, notarial acknowledgment of the law prefaced gifts to ecclesiastical organizations and to clerics, even to those who happened to be members of the testator's family. For instance, the widow donna Girolama del gia Francesco Oliva from the rural town of Asciano left her stepchild and "legitimate heir," the *sacerdote* and prior of Sant'Ansano in Dofano, 25 scudi and another 15 scudi from a *censo* which had become extinct. She then confirmed that she "was well informed regarding the law prohibiting the passage of the property of the laity into the dead hands of the Church and that with this she was not transgressing that law for the reasons expressed above."[10]

After the passage of mortmain legislation, how accurate a lens were testaments for interpreting changes in morality, devotion, and belief? Did the "enlightened despotism" of the Lorrainian Hapsburgs simply remove the will as the principal conduit for channeling property from the laity to the church?[11] Certainly this legislation did not go down easily with the Sienese. Evidence of their distaste, subterfuge, and resistance can be detected even in these often clinical documents of property transferals. First, certain individuals simply refused to make their testaments public. Notices of *schedole* sealed with wax are found throughout the notarial books of the 1750s and 1760s. Often these were the testaments of priests. Thus Reverend Giorgio Francheli registered in a notarial protocol of 1756 that he had consigned his will, first drafted in 1744, to two priests, an artisan, and a nurse at Santa Maria della Scala.[12] In 1765, the same reverend (now "Don") Giorgio registered that he had retrieved his *schedola* from the individuals to whom it had been consigned. Yet he continued to keep secret the final decisions over the disposition of his properties.[13]

On occasion notaries "published" in their protocols these "secret" sealed packets. Once the wax was broken, the contents revealed that not all Senesi willingly accepted the new commandments from Florence. One such packet was opened and entered as a part of the public record in a protocol of 3 October 1795. Giovanfilippo del gia Antonio Rognoni, who had "passed to the better life that morning," had sealed his testament on 13 March 1777. He began by invoking the intercession of God and his protector the Virgin Mary and then declared, "in the second place," his intention to comply with the laws of Tuscany, "even if he had never been content with them to even the slightest degree." He asserted that "they were contrary to natural law and that nothing in any part of them was of value." Nonetheless, he would grudgingly "comply with these same laws."[14] Curiously, he left nothing to the church in his secret packet, not even an amount within the legal limits.

By the late 1760s and 1770s the *schedole* appear less often in the protocols; moreover, in these years, admissions to being *ben informato* or notices that the testator had not exceeded "the limits permitted under the new law prohibiting the amortization of property" cease to preface every pious bequest.[15] The authorities of the Hapsburg state seem to have slackened their vigilance. In fact, almost from the outset, Francesco Stefano's advisors softened the law. At the end of 1752 the Consiglio di Reggenze recommended a more liberal interpretation of the law. In 1759 the magistracy of the Nine proposed that pious places (*i Luoghi Pii*) and lay confraternities would be excluded from the 100-zecchini ceiling; only donations of landed property to them were to be prohibited. In 1760 gifts of annuities (*contrattazioni censuarie*) were to be allowed. Finally, in 1763 the Grand Duke issued a *motuproprio* (his personal decree) which legalized donations to lay societies (*Luoghi Pii laicali*) without the permission (*grazia*) of the sovereign.[16]

Yet even in the first decade after its promulgation, at least one violation appears in these samples of notarized testaments. In 1753 the widow Anna del gia Antonio Borghi, then eighty-four years old, instructed her executor to sell off her goods (*robbe*) at a public auction to finance the singing of 1,050 masses at 1 pavolo or 1 lire each. This expenditure alone (140 zecchini) exceeded the legal limits. The widow then ordered the Augustinians at San Martino to celebrate another 100 masses within six months of her death.[17] This widow's notary had rigorously stated the law after the pious bequests of his other clients.[18] In this case, he allowed the aged lady's final preoccupations with her soul to pass without drawing attention to them.

By the 1770s, circumventions of the law became more frequent. The noble cavalier Marco del gia Nobil Domenico-Antonio Bianchi, who "today" had assumed the family name of Bandinelli-Paparoni, exceeded his pious rations with alacrity and without pleas to the Grand Duke for special dispensation. His first legacy ordered the 100-scudi maximum for his funeral masses alone. Then he instructed his executor to spend another 200 scudi for the distribution of bread to "the poor of Siena," to "those persons truly poor and needy." The cavalier donated another 100 scudi from his mother's inheritance to "his *Casa di Carità*" in Pisa (probably permissible according to the *motuproprio* of 1763). In yet another legacy he restituted one-half of the debts of all those *contadini* who would be on his property at the time of his death. Although this charitable allocation may not have counted as a pious gift, a fourth one, boldly labeled *legato pio,* furthered his charitable contributions through the 1763 loophole. He left to his wife's discretion donations to "all the persons who will be at service" at what appears in these documents to have been a new charitable institution, the "Casa di Siena."[19] Such circumventions were not limited to cavaliers and noble ladies. An artisan, Maestro Giuseppe del gia Giovantonio Palazzi from Asciano, first ordered that 50 scudi be consigned to the treasurer of the Cappuccin mothers to say as many masses as possible while they gathered in front of the "Sacred Image of the Holy Virgin." A second bequest of another 50 scudi went to these same mothers to celebrate masses and for their needs in the sacristy, the church, and the convent. He further requested that he be "in their holy prayers." Although Maestro Giuseppe now had reached his pious quota, he also gave his daughter, a nun in the convent of Campanzi, an annual income of 3 scudi a year to be doubled if his heirs were not punctual in payment. The artisan added, however, the subtle distinction that he intended this income not for the assistance of the convent but rather for "the small needs" of his daughter.[20] Perhaps by the 1770s this distinction would have swayed the local authorities. Yet the Lorrainian laws did not make for such allowances.[21] Subterfuge can be detected in the 1780 testament of the noble and reverend canon Giovanni-Francesco del Nobile gia Signore Iaccinto Nini. Like the cavalier Domenico-Antonio, he consumed his quota in his initial legacy with 100 zecchini to be spent on his funeral. Next, the canon left a further 300 scudi to a parish priest to pay a nun in the convent of Santa Marta. The canon claimed that the monies constituted a repayment on a loan.[22] Perhaps they did. But they could easily have been a ruse for circumventing the new laws of the sovereign.

Donna la Signora Teresa Orsi in 1781 was more blatant. The entirety of her estate went to pious causes. She gave a chamber closet to an oblate in the Conservatory of the Derelitte; she requested sixty masses for the health of her soul from her parish church; and she then split the residue of her estate between her parish priest and the sisters of a religious order called the Certi. Of course, this "donna la Signora," who happened to be a domestic servant, may not have had an estate valued at 100 zecchini. Of her worldly possessions, however, she mentions a farm, the Podere dei due Ponti, from which the cost for singing the masses and her funeral were to be subtracted. With this gift, her infraction was in fact twofold: it is difficult to imagine a *podere* in the late eighteenth century valued at less than 100 zecchini, and the laws emphatically prohibited the transferal of real property, no matter its value, from *secolari* to the "dead hand" of the church.[23]

By 1790 notaries regularly made the sealed *schedole* part of the public record once their clients had died. In 1795 the previously secret testament of the nobleman Giulio-Lorenzo Petrucci was opened. He asserted "with caution" that his "*schedola* contained nothing against the prevailing laws especially not to those concerning *fideicommission* [or entailing properties for more than a generation] and mortmain." Yet the itemized bequests make us pause. He left orders for his wife and executor to celebrate 200 requiem masses; he left his curate 100 lire to distribute to the poor of the parish, additional sums to recite 12 masses a year on his death anniversary, and an annuity of 8 scudi a year to his sister, a nun in the Monasterio della Maria, who was to remember him in her prayers. He left no specific instructions in regard to funeral procedures and expenses; rather these matters were all left "to the charity and love of his wife and executors."[24] Of these five pious bequests one alone would have outstripped his quota. At the going rate of "charity" per mass, the 100-zecchini limit would have been easily exceeded in eight years.

Finally, other sources evince resistance by the faithful against the new incursions of the state. The bishop of Pienza, Monsignore Francesco Piccolomini, was for years in conflict with the Lorrainians. He continued "obstinately" to refuse to turn over to the regime the customary monetary gift on the occasion of the marriage of Joseph II, insisted on maintaining control over pious places within the diocese, refused to turn over the registers of these institutions to the secular administrators, and excommunicated the Grand Duke. In 1764 the Grand Duke (Francesco Stefano) retaliated by banishing Francesco Piccolomini forever from Tuscany.[25] After the Jansenist Synod of Pistoia in 1786 (discussed later) popular revolts fueled by anti-Semitism and traditional Catholic sentiments spread through Prato, the villages of the Val di Nievole, and the working-class districts of Livorno.[26] Later, similar revolts erupted in Florence, leading to the siege of the Fortress of Belvedere.[27] Stuart Woolf has argued that the reforms of Leopoldo ultimately failed: "His departure in 1790 . . . was marked by an immediate wave of discontent and reaction."[28]

Since the studies of Vovelle, Chaunu, Chiffoleau, Lebrun, and others, historians have stressed the slow-moving character, imperceptible to contemporaries, of changes in devotion and religious belief; these mentalities cut beneath matters of legislation, such as the de-Christianization policies of Robespierre, and even beneath political history in general.[29] Did mortmain laws simply push piety underground, at least in regard to the last decisions notarized in wills? In the first place, as we have seen, the reformers modified the original laws and eased their vigilance over the testaments. For instance, by 1763 testators could give gifts freely to the religious lay societies without incurring the acrimony of the state. But contributions to the lay companies did not revive; instead they all but disappear from our records (see Table 6.4), well before Pietro Leopoldo abolished most of the confraternities and confiscated their properties in 1784.[30] More generally, the statistics on pious giving show no corresponding backlash by believers zealously attached to the old Counter-Reformation forms of devotion. Indeed, once gifts to servants and *mezzadri* are struck from the pious sums, the per capita amounts tumbled in the final quarter of the century even more drastically than they had immediately following promulgation of the mortmain laws.

In the second place, testaments of the latter Settecento illustrate the possibilities of drafting wills within the boundaries of the law which still carried the earmarks of the Counter-Reformation. Several testators, for instance, besought their wives to "educate their heirs in the Holy Fear of God" or as good Christians. Overwhelmingly, however, such pious phrases, which enlightened despots did not suppress, nearly disappear by the last decades of the century.[31] When they did arise, in a manner similar to the pious hopes of their ancestors in the late Counter-Reformation, these sentiments were mixed with appeals of a secular character. In 1752, the greengrocer Magnifico Buonaventura del gia Giuseppe Mori, after requesting his heirs "to live with the fear of God" and "to pray to the Most High for the salvation of his soul," further enjoined them to "apply themselves to their respective trades and abstain from vices as the testator had done."[32] Such fatherly appeals to the industriousness and prudence of sons had not appeared in these samples since the last years of the Cinquecento. Nor was the greengrocer's appeal to a renewed secular morality an isolated instance. The wax worker Angelo del gia Marc'Antonio Bartoliai "prayed" that his son "would wish to continue to practice honorably the business in the wax shop and to treat with the greatest comfort and love Signora Maria, his sister, as well as the testator's wife, Signora Caterina." He further desired that, when the time came to marry, his son would choose an "honorable person of his class and condition." In parting, the waxman commanded his heir to "keep himself far away from lending security to anybody."[33]

The new laws in no way prohibited testators from soliciting the spiritual assistance of their patron saints and special advocates. In fact, through the 1790s (and most likely in the years after) testators continued to make special pleas for their souls' journey to everlasting peace and comfort by calling on individual saints of the Counter-Reformation—Xavier and Francis de Sales—besides the old standbys, Peter the Apostle, Joseph, and Siena's own Bernardino and Catherine. Those making such special solicitations were, however, either priests or people from rural villages. And again, their percentage fell precipitously.

Within the boundaries of the new legislation, room still remained for the orchestration of elaborate funerals: trains of religious companies, friars, priests, and the holy from the ranks of the orphans and of the poor.³⁴ In 1752 the greengrocer Magnifico Buonventura, after invoking the intervention of his *santi particolari* San Gaetano and Sant'Antonio of Padua, asked that his body be exposed in the bier of his confraternity. Ten priests in addition to his *parocco* were to accompany the casket in the procession to the parish church. Afterward, his lay brothers, eight priests, and eight Servite fathers were to transport his remains to the burial site in the communal vaults of the congregation of the Holy Crucifix in the monastery of Santa Maria dei Servi. He ordered his company to distribute 1 pound of white wax and small candles (*maccoli*) to their members, the friars, and the priests. Each candle was to weigh 3 ounces. Similarly, his parish priest was to distribute fourteen torches, six to be placed on the high altars of the parish church and six on low altars, while the body remained on view in his parish and while masses were being sung and ten nocturns recited.³⁵ The honorable Caterina degli Usinini in 1772, and Angelo del gia Marcantonio Bartolai, the waxman, in 1781, organized a partnership will with similar funerary displays. She revived the Cinquecento practice of having her casket draped with the cloth of the noble house of the Usinini. Angelo requisitioned twenty priests, twenty friars from the minor orders, and four monks and four nuns from each of the religious orders in the city of Siena to fill the procession led by his religious company from his parish to his family burial site.³⁶ These, however, were the exceptions. As a rule, testators of the later Settecento left these matters to their wives or heirs and pleaded for modesty.

Testators during the latter Settecento could legally request large numbers of masses of the old Counter-Reform stamp if only their cost did not exceed 100 zecchini. We have seen that the eighty-four-year-old widow Anna demanded 1,150 masses in 1753. Although this pious demand did in fact break the bounds of the Lorrainian law, other requests for large numbers of masses did not. In 1763 the artisan, Maestro Lorenzo del gia Domenico Tosi, after laying plans for an elaborate funeral calling on the intercession of thirty-four clerics, gave equally elaborate instructions for masses at his funeral and shortly thereafter. First, 58 lire were to be spent on 58 masses for the funeral. In addition, two sets of 30 masses were to be celebrated by the Dominicans, another 60 in the church of San Donato, 30 in San Francesco, 30 in the Collegiate church of the Madonna of Provenzano, and 30 by the Carmelites.³⁷ In 1770 the curate of the village church of San Martino in the Val d'Ambra, after requesting masses at his funeral, ordered his heir to celebrate 500 masses for his soul within three years.³⁸ Furthermore, the *onesta* widow Teresa del fu Giovanbattista Cinotti in 1774, the servant girl of Gaetano Fabbroni from the Val d'Arno in 1781, the *pievano* of the village of Corsano in 1783, and the innkeeper from Isola in the Masse in 1790 left detailed instructions for numerous masses to be celebrated by various religious groups at different places and times.³⁹ Again, nearly all of these examples bearing the imprint of the Counter-Reformation came from the countryside. And again, those testators who persisted in expending their pious allowances for their souls figured as the distinct minority after 1750.

Although simple requests for funerary masses did not vanish altogether from the records, testators did abandon the elaborate instructions on precise numbers, places, and times which had been common in the previous century (see Table 9.1). In contrast, testators of the late Settecento simply left their funerary masses to the discretion of their executors; in 1751–75 pious bequests where the testator failed to mention the cleric or the ecclesiastical institution more than doubled, and in the second half of the century nearly 70 percent of all pious bequests reflected such indifference. Finally, unlike the abolition of the chantries in England, the mortmain legislation of the Lorrainian Hapsburgs did not censure funds for perpetual masses.[40] Yet anniversary masses in perpetuity or even ones over extended periods all but disappeared. In 1751–75 only seven such requests surface in these documents, and in the final quarter they vanish entirely.

The testaments show, moreover, that the 100-zecchini limit was not an ironclad law. The testator could apply within the will for special dispensations. First, the Grand Dukes published numerous *rescritti* in the decades following the mortmain laws, which reviewed testamentary gifts and often granted the benefactors their wishes.[41] Trust in the benevolent discretion of the Grand Dukes can be found on the local level. In 1753 the itemized pious bequests of Domenico del fu Pietro Oliva from the countryside (*terra*) of Asciano, exceeded the 100-zecchini limit. He left an annuity from landed property (*censo*) of 100 scudi to the Collegiate church of San Asciano for the celebration in perpetuity of twelve yearly masses for his soul and the souls of his brother, sister, and other dead relatives. From what remained of the revenues, he instructed his executors to distribute grain to "the poor and destitute of Asciano" every year on 2 November "in commemoration of the dead." At the end of his will Domenico requested the sovereign of Tuscany's permission to spend 200 zecchini in total to meet the pious obligations specified in his brother's will, which had been redacted in 1734. He argued that the new legislation should not affect his brother's testament, as it was drafted before 1751. In addition, the small-town notable tried another line of argument. He petitioned that his will should be considered not as one will but as "two testaments" since he was required by his brother's will to meet those previous charitable obligations; therefore, the ceiling on pious expenditures should be raised to 200 zecchini.[42]

In 1770 the "miniature" artist (capo maestro minatore) Filippo del gia Magnifico Giovanni Francini petitioned for special dispensation for other reasons. His will, from its opening formula regarding the body and the soul, has the tone of the previous century. It began by beseeching the special intercession of his four personal protectors, Joseph, Francis of Assisi, Antony of Padua, and Catherine of Siena. He directed his body to be exposed in the bier of his confraternity, then buried in the communal vaults of the congregation of Saint Antony of Padua in the monastery of Saint Francis. His very first itemized bequest exhausted his pious quota. He further left 100 zecchini to the minor friars. He then proceeded to violate the mortmain legislation on two counts. Not only did this third pious bequest exceed the monetary limits (in fact, by leaps and bounds); in addition, it turned over landed property to the "dead hand" of the church. He left the Company of Piety the task of administering the income from two wealthy *poderi* for the "poor of Jesus Christ" at the Hospice of Piety, Pio Ospizio. Beyond caring for the poor, the proceeds from these properties would go to a chapel in the hospice "under the title of the Sacred Family" for the perpetual celebration of three low masses a year.[43]

The remainder and more detailed portion of the painter's instructions, however, did not concern religious obligations or specific performances of pious duties. Rather, his thoughts turned to a matter not present in the pious bequests of the previous century: the actual estate management of his real properties. He instructed the company to hire at a salary of 10 scudi a year "a faithful and practical member of the confraternity who would serve as the overseer (*fattore*) and who would inspect the operation of the estates frequently." He specified that this secular brother of the company should be an *economo*, that is, one experienced in estate management. The professional's term of office should not exceed nine years; rather, the testator insisted that the administration should carry short terms of service so that the *economo* might not "take an affection to the properties."[44]

For the implementation of this pious foundation valued at well over 1,000 scudi, far beyond the limits of the law and grounded in real property, the painter entreated "the Divine Providence of the Almighty" and pleaded for "the protection of the Most Merciful, our Sovereign," for the "direction of his inheritance to the benefit of the poor." The *minatore* maintained that the sovereign had more than once demonstrated "his Paternal Piety toward this Pious place especially with the privilege of exemption from the laws of Mortmain."[45]

In the same year (1770) the Reverend Signor Giuseppe del gia Signor Domencio Zampi, the curate of the parish of San Martino in the Val d'Ambra (near the Florentine border), left property for a charitable cause that again far exceeded the regulations of the mortmain laws. Yet this contribution, similar to the detailed instructions on property management found in the pious donation of the miniature painter, bears the stamp of new era. Because the curate "desired that the young of his village have the benefit of reading and writing," he would leave his *podere* of "Gavignano" in the district of Ambra to provide the salary in perpetuity for a village schoolmaster. He further stipulated that the community of Ambra should have the right to elect "in the usual way and for valid reasons" the *maestro di scuola*. The "teacher should be capable and suitable and should teach with love and attention the young of this place and neighboring places, all who have the capacity to learn."[46] This legacy is the first in our samples to endow a secular educational institution.[47] This transformation in charity, which W. K. Jordan charts for England during the first decades of the seventeenth century, showed signs of arising in Siena only toward the end of the Settecento.[48]

The *rescritti* and the testaments of the painter of miniatures *maestro* Filippo and of the Reverend Giuseppe show that enlightened despotism did not present the barriers of an absolute law without chances for appeals, arbitration, and exceptions. Yet the great majority of testators, as witnessed by the statistical trends over the last decades of the century, neither tried to circumvent the law, nor appealed for special dispensation, nor even met the limits of their pious rations. The law of 1751 punctured decisively that model of piety that had endured since the Papal Visitations of 1575.

Indeed, the two pious donors, who on first impression appear as throwbacks to the old style of Counter-Reform piety, reveal signs of a new era. The painter was concerned with his real properties, not in the Cinquecento sense of their symbolic importance to an afterlife grounded on lineage and the flow of the male bloodline, but in a new physiocratic sense, oriented to the actual use and estate-management of the properties for their maximum profitability—in this case for the benefit of the poor.[49] The country curate Giuseppe appealed for special dispensation from the laws for a charitable purpose that appears for the first time in this documentation. His landed property would establish a public grammar school in his village. The charity of these testators was aimed solidly at improving matters in the present temporal realm as opposed to a poor-relief or education "in the Holy Fear of God" which would better prepare the testator's soul for its migration to what the testators used to call "the better life."

The cataclysmic drop in the number and value of pious bequests hinged on the Hapsburgian legislation of mortmain. Despite signs of disenchantment, resistance, and subterfuge, the vast majority of testators abruptly redirected their strategies for the afterlife. Not only did these testators give less; the majority abandoned entirely the old Counter-Reform stamp of piety, including matters not touched or only slightly modified by the new laws—funerals, specific sets of masses, and spiritual and terrestrial intercessors. In these practices testators of the second half of the Settecento might have persisted along many of the old tracks of the Counter-Reformation without violating the new law. Certain testators—particularly from the priesthood and from the villages and small towns of Siena's *contado*—in fact did persist in those tracks; yet overwhelmingly they were the exceptions.

Perhaps the decline of piety and the passage of mortmain legislation were merely coincidental. Historians have generalized that the decline in masses and donations to the church were endemic to Europe in Voltaire's "Age of Reason."[50] Unfortunately, precious few studies of wills or other sources that tap changes in religiosity beneath the literate elites are now available for comparative purposes. However, when this literature is compared, a universally uniform picture does not emerge. In England, the change harks back to the Reformation.[51] For Paris the turning point was as early as 1690; for Marseilles, around 1750; and for Nice, the demand for masses and "baroque ostentation" continued to mount throughout the century.[52] Nor should we conclude that the mortmain legislation of 1751 was simply part and parcel of a general sweep of such legislation throughout Europe. Earlier mortmain legislation existed. The Venetian state passed laws limiting the clergy's use of property and gifts given to the "dead hand" of the church in 1472, 1536, 1605, and 1607; mortmain laws date from 1489 in Montemerano and from 1593 in Pistoia. In England these laws were on the books as early as the reign of Edward I; England's eighteenth-century laws were promulgated in 1736.[53] As we have already mentioned, mortmain legislation in Siena stretched back to the Renaissance. But no place in Europe had heretofore passed as stringent and all-encompassing legislation as those laws designed by Count Richecourt and promulgated by Francesco Stefano in 1751. The Tuscan laws became a model for the rest of Italy.[54] Yet even the enlightened despot par excellence, the Hapsburg emperor and brother of Pietro Leopoldo, Joseph II, was still unable by the end of the eighteenth century to legislate mortmain in the capital of Italian enlightenment culture, Milan.[55]

The laws of the Lorrainians certainly were not manufactured in a vacuum. According to the biographer of Pietro Leopoldo, in Tuscany "better than any other place in Eighteenth-century Italy, a true harmony between intellectuals and power made possible the 'economic, social and administrative revolution.'"[56] Nor should we point exclusively to the mortmain legislation of 1751. Though Pietro Leopoldo eased the harshness of these laws in 1769, he continued through the 1790s to use the arm of the state against militant Catholicism and its political counterclaims.[57] In 1769 he legislated against religious houses as places of asylum for criminals.[58] In 1782, he abolished definitively the Inquisition in Tuscany. In 1784 he confiscated the patrimonies of numerous monasteries, oratories, religious confraternities, and chapels, and in 1786 sponsored Scipio Ricci's Jansenist Synod of Pistoia.[59]

Could Jansenism have been the hidden hand behind our statistical series? Evidence of this reformed circumspect Catholicism reached back in Tuscany as early as the turn of the century. Testamentary clauses from the late Counter-Reformation, moreover, specified "modesty" and attempted to restrict lavish funerals. Yet we found these same testators indulging in practices antithetical to Jansenism—elaborate designs for numerous masses. In fact, explicit examples of Jansenism before the period of Pietro Leopoldo come exclusively from the educated elites of Tuscany and appear to have flourished only within restricted intellectual circles such as those at the University of Pisa and perhaps at the University of Siena.[60] Jansenism in Tuscany was hardly a grass-roots popular movement.

More important to the ordinary testator in Siena was the character of the late Counter-Reformation itself. Despite the mounting of testamentary gifts into ecclesiastical coffers, piety by the second half of the Seicento had become routinized, regimented, and wooden. At the same time, new icons and impulses weeded their way into the documents—respect for modesty in the outward expressions of belief and a new secular reverence for the state. But the quantitative side of piety—the redoubling of its successes in the early Settecento—suggest that these forces alone would not have brought the Counter-Reformation to its knees in less than a decade. Our statistics draw a model of religious change far closer to the realities of "cuius regio, eius religio" or to the political facts of Reformation in England than to the slow-moving history of religious change recently stressed in Vovelle's Provence, Chaunu's Paris, Croix's Brittany, and Hoffman's Lyon.⁶¹ In Settecento Siena, the raw facts of political power were absolutely pivotal. Similar to Henry VIII's Reformation, the laws of the Lorrainians quickly and decisively ruptured a strategy for the afterlife centered on Purgatory and the efficacy of pious acts, which had endured over the past 150 years and without state intervention might well have continued growing for many more years, sucking up the deathbed gifts of the religious.

Fidecommission

Did Siena then return in proper cyclical fashion to the "great age of selfishness"? To return to the sealed *schedola* of the nobleman from the Petrucci family, we saw that the testator expressed "caution" not only in regard to mortmain legislation but equally toward other new laws governing fidecommission.⁶² These laws actually antedated those of mortmain. The Grand Duchy passed legislation on 22 June 1747 which limited entail to one generation and prohibited primogeniture for all classes except the nobility.⁶³ Although this legislation on first impression appears to shore up the privileges of the old elites, the laws also constricted the previous rights of the *riseduti* to plot the future of their properties. Under these laws, they could not predetermine the flow of properties beyond four degrees of relatives ("*gradi*" or "*vincoli*"), including their first nomination of the universal heir. The law limited these contingencies or degrees of nomination, moreover, "by head and not by stock," and permitted only "stable" properties and "credits in the state debt (*Luoghi di Monte de'Nostri Stati*), to be entailed. "All other rents, annuities, credits, money, furniture, and other movables had to be left without the encumbrances of *fidecommission*.⁶⁴ According to the historian Giuseppe Conti, the law of 1747 spelled the demise of the Tuscan nobility; the nobles "despised these laws more than any others promulgated by the Lorrainians."⁶⁵

Even if Conti's observations or the contemporary remarks of Richecourt (in the Epigraph) are overstated, preoccupations during the first half of the Settecento with primogeniture, the male line, family name, and the preservation of inalienable properties were not yet dead issues. In 1741 the Magnifico Domenico Barni, a merchant of leather goods (and not a nobleman), lay on his deathbed as the last male heir of his family and lineage. He first requested burial in his family vault in the monastery of the Servites and then provided for the succession of his sizable patrimony along with his family name. He left one Giovanni-Domencio Mezzani (who bore no apparent kinship to the testator) 4,000 scudi provided the heir would assume the name and the family coats of arms of "the house of Barni." Moreover, this Mezzani was required "to conserve" these properties and to pass them on *infinito* to his descendants, "to advance the house of Barni (*tirare avanti la Casetta de Barni*)" and to entail the properties (*fare fideiussioni*).⁶⁶ Similarly, when the patrician and cavalier Leonido di Cavalier

Francesco Landucci drafted his will in 1741, he had no offspring. The survival of family name was his central obsession. He left his estate to his nephew Febro, the son of his sister, and entailed the properties through the male line of his nephew "for all time." If the male line became extinct, then the properties were to descend through the female line. "In the absence of both of these lines . . . the properties would revert to his niece, Virginia Bandini, and then flow through the male line of her offspring. The cavalier further prohibited the alienation of any of his properties, and conviction for any crime would carry the additional penalty of immediate disinheritance. Finally, his nephew Febro "ought to add the family name and the Arms of Landucci to his own *Casato* so that they would be one family and so as to propagate at the same time his own Family, the Bandini." The last lines of his testament, perhaps an afterthought, provided for the possibility of the extinction of all the lines of succession mentioned in the will. In such a case, the archbishop of Siena, his rector, and his wife should elect a successor "whose father and mother were *riseduti* and who would always assume the *Cognome* of Landucci."[67]

Our samples suggest, however, that the laws limiting fidecommission proved in fact to be more decisive than those regarding mortmain. Despite these attachments to the Cinquecento notions of lineage and blood, which lingered on through the 1730s and 1740s, the legislation of 1747 appears to have been accepted without great protest in Siena. Unlike the subterfuge and even blatant violations of mortmain legislation, no obvious infractions of fidecommission appear in our samples; nor did testators beseech the *grazia* of the Grand Dukes to grant them special consideration. The only exceptions arise from wills such as those of the artist Filippo and the country priest Giuseppe. These pious testators of an Enlightenment stamp, however, sought special dispensation to bind perpetually their real holdings, not for the symbolic powers of family and lineage, but for the benefit of their charitable organizations. Oddly enough, the elaborate maze of contingency clauses of fidecommission disappeared after 1747, not only for those without noble distinction, but for the *riseduti* as well. The transformation of will writing for the Sienese nobility did not even have to await the equalizing legislation of Pietro Leopoldo of 23 February 1789, which extended the prohibitions of 1747 to the entire population of Tuscany.[68]

One of the few testators in the second half of the century to continue to use fidecommission terms and to tie perpetually his properties through his male line was the cavalier Marco del gia Nobil Domenico-Antonio Bianchi ("today de Bandinelli-Paparoni"): the notary's addition of this double-butted family name attached to the earlier family name suggests that this "Noble Cavalier" had been himself the beneficiary of a complex will that had provided against a noble family's extinction. Cavalier Marco "was moved to entail his real properties and his shares in the funded debt" for motives earlier shared by other testators. In this case, the testator was explicit: "for the conservation and decorum of his noble lineage (*casata*) and the maintenance of his secular heirs." Yet the cavalier Marco, who earlier in his will ignored the regulations regarding expenditures on the "dead hand" of piety, was much more circumspect about that other set of legislation regarding fidecommission. More than once in this testament he profusely claimed "to desire to adhere to, respect, and execute these laws as a most faithful subject."[69] Indeed, his testament closely heeded the letter of the new laws of the sovereign. He judiciously funneled through the *vincolo* of this fidecommission only his "stable" properties and his holdings in the various funded debts of Tuscany. The cavalier did not even make full use of his prerogatives as a nobleman. Primogeniture was not established, and if more than one grandson survived, the estate in the second generation would then be divided. Second, the law of 1747 permitted noblemen to plot contingencies governing the possible transition of their real properties to the fourth degree. This nobleman, who bore the inherited responsibilities of three family names, did not bother even to map his way beyond his grandchildren, who were alive at the time of the redaction.

In the second half of the Settecento the new legislation discouraged testators from considering their patrimonies in terms of family blood, honor, and lineage, and instead forced them to focus their last dispositions of property concretely and immediately on those members of the family who were alive and present. Increasingly their thoughts turned from the two abstractions that had governed testamentary transactions since the invention of the will in the late eleventh century—concerns over the soul and over future generations of familial blood. In their place the Settecento testators turned to the mundane matters of household management, which their testaments coined "domestic economy." To a certain degree, these concerns did lead testators back to the secularism found earlier in the wills of hardheaded and practical shopkeepers and petty merchants of the Cinquecento. The greengrocer Buonventura wanted his heirs to "apply themselves in their respective trades."[70] The entire will of Vincenzio Giardi had a single "object": "to maintain and conserve as long as possible a perfect union and agreement within his family." The cavalier Marco besought the executor of his estate, "for the love of God, the duty as a subject to the royal supreme Sovereigns, their laws, and the affection for Country to oversee the sustenance of the House, the noble education of the family, and the domestic economy of the household." Antonio del gia Francesco Pozzetti from Pontremoli, who had been living in Siena for many years and at the time was the estate agent (*fattore*) of the nunnery of San Sebastiano, advised his wife "to bring up their children in the Holy fear of God and to instill in them a good regimentation not only for the Christian life but for civic life as well . . . and that they should endeavor to advance the affairs of this inheritance." The wax merchant Angelo Bartolai urged his wife to continue "to attend with her customary vigilance the domestic affairs of the household." The "Illustrious" nobleman Mario Serguidi exhorted his wife to administer the estate "according to the laws, prudence, and the demands of economy."[71]

Preoccupations with the "good regimentation" of sons or an eye to potential family squabbles were not new. Earlier, the Sienese, however, had placed these concrete fears of conflict and hopes for harmony within the grander scheme of lineage—the preservation of the family name, coats of arms, and inalienable properties. These Settecento exhortations emphasized, by contrast, a new sense of family cut loose from its earlier teleology, and its faith in a materialistic afterlife sustained by the flow of property through the male line. The testators' hopes by mid-Settecento had turned to the immediate and practical consequences for their then-living family members, moving the meaning of family from lineage to "domestic economy."

13 Conclusion

Two literatures now dominate the systematic study of last wills and testaments in past times: one uses wills to trace property transmission, the other to view changes in piety. This book has studied the will both as a conduit for inheritance and as an expression of collective religious attitudes. Not only were these two functions embodied in every will individually; the strategies for the afterlife structured a long history of the conflict between them. The 600-year history of piety charted by this book, however, does not draw simple dialectics or a cyclical history with Kondratieff predictability. Nor does it portray the logic of the hidden hand of structure, imperceptible to ordinary citizens and villagers; rather events supposedly "on the surface of history" in at least three of the four crucial junctures over this long haul cut rapidly and decisively through one strategy for the afterlife, clearing the way for the growth of another.

From the earliest documents until the second onslaught of pestilence (1363), hard-headed merchants, shopkeepers, and peasants from the halcyon years of Sienese polity and economy regularly fragmented their patrimonies into numerous but negligible sums to pious causes through the city and countryside. With less poetic verve than Siena's Saint Catherine and less heroic pains than generations of little-remembered blessed ones seeking martyrdom through self-humiliation, ordinary testators practiced, at least in their final arbitrations over property, what the mendicants preached; they endeavored to "break the earthly cell" in preparation for their joyous entry to "that side of death where life began." Rarely did their gifts come with any strings attached as they demanded from their heirs only the immediate liquidation of their estates.

The catastrophic mortality of 1348 did not crack this strategy for the afterlife. As the letters of Petrarch and our statistics on pious bequests well attest, the "mental equipment" of the previous century's mendicant spiritualists was able to absorb felicitiously the shocks of the Black Death's unfathomable assault on humanity. They read the unprecedented mortality as an exodus from "the fetters of this gloomy dwelling," rather than as the scourge of God. With the second coming of plague, the Sienese relived the traumas of 1348, but this time they abandoned their mendicant lessons, stockpiling, instead of scattering, their pious donations. They changed their charity from single-time, indiscriminate handouts for hundreds of the "poor of Christ" to dowry funds to support for a lifetime carefully choosen poor girls. After the second pestilence, the directions regarding nonpious bequests changed as well. Instead of the formulaic demands to sell off estates, testators began to heap demands and contingencies on their heirs to preserve prized landed possessions. The change of the late Trecento, however, recorded no simple swing of the pendulum from ascetic piety and distrust in kin to a this-worldly interest in family with spiritual indifference. Instead, testators of the early Renaissance poured even more money into church coffers. When San Bernardino was preaching in Siena's Piazza del Campo, piety peaked, even if not always in the directions he urged.

The late Renaissance (the last decades of the Quattrocento through the Cinquecento) assumed, however, an entirely different posture on ecclesiastical charities. Out of the early Renaissance cult of memory grew a new cult of lineage, with testators resting their futures less with the soul and more with the preservation of landed estates and family names through the succession of their male heirs. In this legalistic culture, testators used the wills to manipulate from the grave the eternal flow of their properties as well as the behavior of heirs. From a new and enlarged social base, these testaments give credence to some of the most discredited of Burckhardt's conclusions. The flow of properties into church coffers slowed to a trickle as testators turned their backs on pious causes and invented new charities of familiarity—gifts to foster children, to domestic servants, and to their own illegitimate children (only in these years were the latter mentioned unabashedly and treated generously). Despite these resonances of Renaissance secularism, Cinquecento Siena hardly affirmed Burckhardt's broader messages. Instead of modernity and individualism, the late Renaissance strategies for the afterlife encumbered property and limited individual choices more than ever before or after.

The Canons and Decrees of Trent brought to Siena in 1575 by the papal visitations of Bossi broke the hold of the ancestors over their legalistic schemes for immortality. Unlike the change of 1363, this change was not all of one social piece. Women were the vanguard of the Counter-Reformation, whereas individuals from the country and the nobility held on longest to the ties of lineage. Again, the swing of the pendulum back to the church was no simple "repeat performance." Rather, the Counter-Reformation invented a new panoply of ritual, devotion, and charity. Women, both as beneficiaries and practitioners, were central to the new lay congregations, burial societies, and welfare congregations. By the second half of the Seicento, the exuberance of the initial phases of Counter-Reformation began to wane, becoming more regimented and routinized, exposing its contradictions between ascetic ideals and the invention of baroque liturgies. Yet, despite these internal conflicts and the wooden character of late Counter-Reform devotion, pious sums continued to fill church treasuries—and in the opening years of the Settecento with renewed fervor. In these years, Purgatory obtained its ultimate success; testators disinherited their kin wholesale by leaving as their universal heirs their own souls.

But by mid-century yet another strategy for the afterlife came crashing down. Its swift fall coincided again with an event—this time, the passage of

Richecourt's mortmain law (1751). Again, there was no simple return of the pendulum; no revival of Cinquecento ideologies of lineage to substitute for Purgatory. The laws of fidecommission had four years before jettisoned that eventuality. In the name of a new idol—Commerce—the enlightened despots constrained investments in the two tracks of immortality, which had mapped the mental contexts of wills since the very inception of testament writing in the central Middle Ages. Boxed in on both sides by the new laws, the will no longer served as the conduit for that intellectual history we have traced from the Duecento. From peasants to patricians, the Sienese ceased here to ponder the infinite—how best to dispose of property for the survival of one's blood or for the salvation of the soul.

~~ Appendix: Selecting the Samples, 1205–1800

Housed in the State Archives of Siena are numerous collections of last wills and testaments. They survive for almost every monastery and religious confraternity now found in the archives of the *Conventi Soppressi* and the *Patrimonio resti*. Religious institutions kept copies of the testaments (the notary's parchment or *pergamena* copy) and often, at some later date, would make more copies (usually partial ones) of those bequests that benefited the religious groups for their inventories and to defend against future claimants of the property. By far the largest collection of these wills belong to the largest property holder in the territory of Siena from the thirteenth century until the modern period, the hospital of Santa Maria della Scala.[1] I have not incorporated these wills in this book for two reasons. First, legislation promulgated by Pietro Leopoldo in 1784 confiscated all the original *pergamene* from ecclesiastical hands to form new archives of parchments known as the *Diplomatico*, to be considered shortly.[2] As a result, what remains in the archives of these religious houses are not the notarial original copies but later ones, sometimes made centuries after the testator's death. The impressive collection of testaments found in the ledgers of Santa Maria della Scala, for instance, is largely the work of eighteenth-century hands. The copyists did not usually bother transcribing the documents in their entirety; rather they mostly supplied only those portions of the original which directly concerned their religious house. Nor have I utilized the collections of *pergamene* now preserved in the *Diplomatico* archives for individual religious houses. A sampling from these might still misrepresent bequests to religious institutions.

Instead, I relied on two other archival collections which contain only testamentary originals and copies made at the time of redaction. The first is the *Notarile*, comprising the notaries' protocols which they tri-monthly submitted to the offices of the *gabelles* and from 1389 on deposited within the communal archives.[3] Because of changes in the survival rates of these notarial protocols, I have compiled various samples according to different criteria. From their earliest appearance in 1223 to 1300, extant notarial protocols were selected and perused for wills. From 1300 to 1480, because the number of surviving books increased, I selected at least one notarial book for each notary cataloged as working within the city of Siena. After 1480, archival practices must have changed for the commune, because a much greater percentage of notarial books survive.[4] To further restrict the number of records, I selected all the testaments found for any four different notaries (again, those cataloged as working in Siena), per decade for the period between 1480 and the reforms of Francesco I in 1585. For the last period, 1585–1800, I selected roughly thirty testaments from the books of at least three different notaries per decade. Thus these samples concentrate on urban Siena but do not disregard residents of the rural suburbs (the Masse) or of other villages and towns within the district of Siena, from Sinalunga to Montalcino to Grosseto. (See map for the geographical distribution found for my samples.) Often these "Sienese" notaries sought business in the countryside or migrated temporarily to work in the villages of the Sienese territory. Conversely, residents from the rural districts and towns sought out Sienese notaries or found themselves on their deathbeds while in the city.

The second source for this study is the *Diplomatico* of the Archivio Generale. These presented fewer problems for selection. The eighteenth-century summaries of 10,000 separate scrolls of parchment extant for Siena and her territory in the Archivio Generale list fewer than 600 testaments (including *causae mortis* and codicils)—few enough for all to be scrutinized, regardless of the provenance of the notary or the testator.[5] All have been included in the present sample except the incomplete *causae mortis* and codicils. As mentioned, Pietro Leopoldo legislated the compilation of this valuable fund of ancient scrolls. However, the particular sources from which this archive was created remain shrouded in mystery. Clearly, the hospital of Santa Maria della Scala and the principal monasteries of the city had been the most important documentary repositories. But the proportions of these documents previously preserved by religious houses or by private family archives cannot be reconstructed. Some testaments in this collection betray no links to any Sienese institution or family, whether by their place of redaction or their lists of pious bequests.

Comparison of the Two Archival Sources

Before comparing the two sets of data, the rules for distinguishing the pious from the nonpious bequests must be elaborated. Notaries and their clients often prefaced the itemized gifts with spiritual and charitable language such as "pro remedio peccatorum suorum," "pro amore dei," "pro salute anime sue." The inclusion of such phraseology did not, however, follow any consistent pattern from notary to notary or over time. Before the Black Death, these phrases did not always occur even in bequests that were in fact pious gifts, such as donations to the "poor of Christ," to monasteries, parish churches, and hospitals. After the Black Death and more markedly during the fifteenth century, these phrases proliferated even in gifts left only to kin and friends and without spiritual demands.

I have drawn certain distinctions to be upheld throughout my analysis of the sources. Pious bequests are defined as (1) bequests made to ecclesiastical institutions—hospitals, parish churches, chapels, monasteries, cathedrals—except when they were repayments of salaries, loans, or tithes; (2) gifts to religious confraternities; (3) gifts to servants beyond salaries or debts; (4) gifts to the poor (*pauperes cristi*), poor prisoners, recluses or hermits; (5) dowry funds for poor girls; (6) gifts to individual men and women specified as poor or indigent (*miserabiles*); and (7) gifts to individual monks, friars, nuns, and hermits unrelated to the testator. If the bequest did not meet one of these criteria, I then classified it as nonpious.[6]

The calculations of the values of gifts, both pious and nonpious, and the ratios of these values present other problems. These go beyond the standard historical problems in price-series analysis; that is, the conversion of rates of exchange among different currencies and evaluating changes in the cost of living and thus the inflation of monies. For the purposes of the present comparison of sources, I have standardized the currencies into florins. On the other hand, the question of the "real" value of money and its fluctuations over time does not seriously hamper our comparisons, at least within specific periods. (These problems are confronted in the text.) The question of the total resources of the testator at the time of redaction presents the more formidable problem. After the formulaic preamble, the notaries listed the individual bequests, both pious and nonpious. In the final section of the will, the testator "instituted" his or her "universal heirs." These residual legatees, most often the testator's sons, inherited all that had not been itemized in the will, and inventories of these properties were seldom included. Thus the historian is left with an unspecified, nonmonetized residual category. We know, moreover, from the inventories which do survive and when the sum of these properties was specified, that this residual category often comprised the lion's share of the inheritance.

If it can be assumed that this residual category was roughly constant over time, then the ratios of pious to nonpious gifts would chart changes in the relative generosity to charitable causes of testators from various social classes. As we have argued in the text, this assumption, however, would not always be safe, at least not for the last decades of the fifteenth and the early sixteenth centuries. This aberration, on the other hand, arises after the notarial records have become almost the exclusive source for our samples.

In the first fifty years of this book, the sample sizes from both sources are small (eight testaments from the Archivio Generale, *Diplomatico* (hereafter called *Diplomatico*) and only four full testaments from the *Notarile*). The chronologies of these two sets in those earliest years, moreover, are somewhat at variance. The earliest document from the *Diplomatico* comes on 29 March 1205; the earliest document from the notarial archives is dated 27 Feburary 1222 (by the Sienese calendar, 27 February 1223). The origins of these sources might suggest that surviving testaments of the *Notarile* included the contracts of the notaries' more elite customers. The *Diplomatico*'s earliest testator, Arrichenus Ganni, was probably a peasant. He resided in the village of Uopini, just off the via Cassia, several kilometers beyond the city walls in the district known as the Masse. At the time of redaction, probably near the end of his life, he did not even possess landed property (his universal heirs collected a paltry 9 lire). The *Notarile*'s

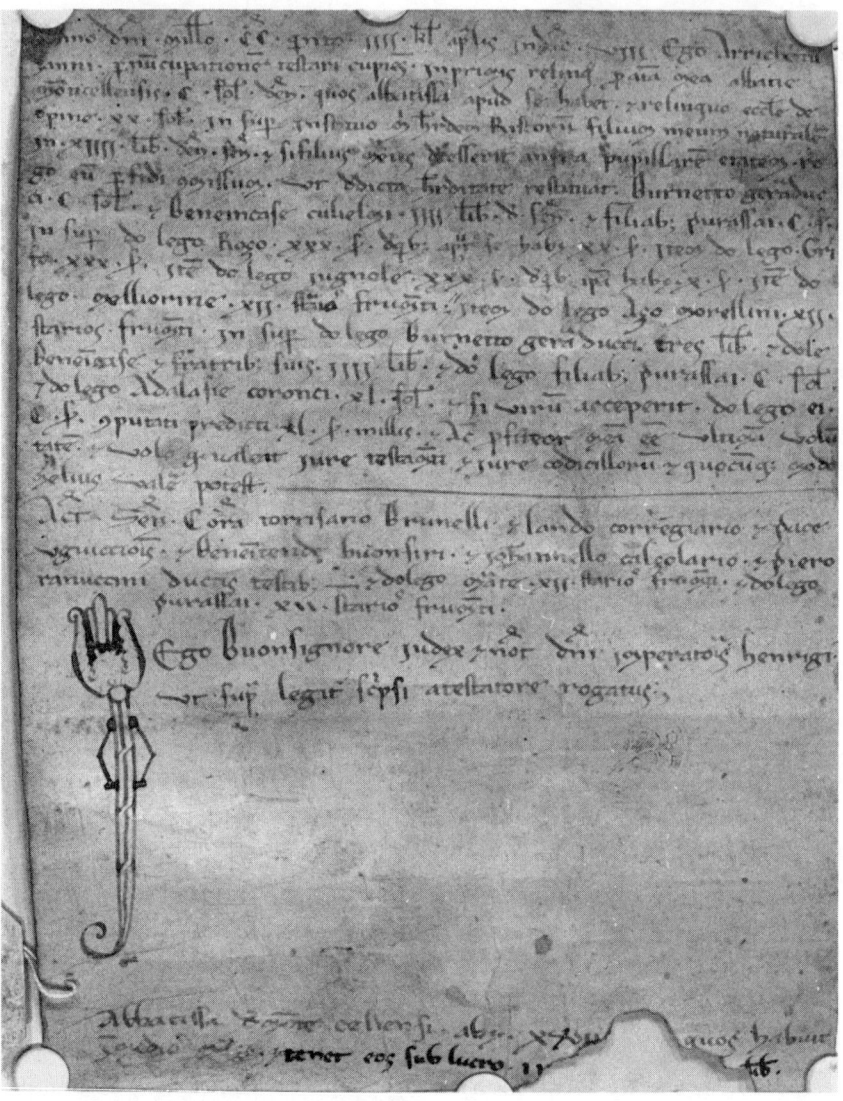

Figure 7. The 1205 testament of Arrichenus

earliest testator, Crescenbene Gerrardi of Arezzo, then residing in the Sienese parish of San Donato, gave several pious bequests to hospitals and to the poor. Yet over the course of the thirteenth and fourteenth centuries those clients whose testaments were preserved in the *Diplomatico* proved to be more wealthy than their compatriots whom we now know through the notarial protocols. Although testators in both sources bequeathed roughly the same number of gifts (both pious and nonpious), the monetary values of those gifts were considerably greater in the *Diplomatico*. Their average size nearly doubled the value of those found in the notarial books during these first fifty years. In the case of pious bequests, the average value of gifts was 1.85 times greater in the *Diplomatico* than in the *Notarile;* nonpious bequests were 1.67 times greater. The percentage of gifts found in these two sources which were monetized was roughly the same for both categories of bequests. The discrepancies between the testaments found in these two archives, moreover, increase in the ensuing years before the Black Death. The most striking difference concerns the rates of survival, the numbers rising sharply for the *Diplomatico*. Consequently, the *Diplomatico* overwhelmingly provides the documentary basis from the late thirteenth century through the early fourteenth century, the halcyon years of the Sienese artists Duccio and Simone Martini and the governmental stability of the Nine.

Where enough testaments from the *Notarile* once again survive for comparison, a divergence in the structure of giving appears between the two sets. First, testators of the *Notarile* made considerably fewer bequests to pious institutions. In 1301–25, when the pious bequests reached their peak in the *Diplomatico* (just over thirteen gifts per testator), the Sienese of the notarial archives contributed on average between four and five gifts to pious causes. Curiously, the unit value of those gifts was almost exactly equal between the two sets of data; both averaged 3.3 florins. As a result, the total value of the *Diplomatico* pious gifts for the first twenty-five years of the fourteenth century amounted to nearly four times that of the notarial protocols, and in 1326–50 they were five times higher.

Did the parchments consigned to monasteries, hospitals, and religious confraternities represent the more generous, the more charitable, and the more religious-minded among the Sienese? Or were those whose records are preserved in the *Diplomatico* simply wealthier than their compatriots in the notarial records? A consideration of the nonpious bequests shows again that testators with surviving parchments had longer and more involved testaments and conveyed more gifts. For the nonpious gifts, however, a second difference appears. The average size of those gifts to friends and kin in the *Diplomatico* more than doubled those in the *Notarile* for the first half of the fourteenth century. Consequently, the ratios of the values of pious to nonpious gifts cut against our earlier expectations. The less wealthy of the *Notarile* gave a larger share of their wealth to ecclesiastical and charitable institutions than did the better-off citizens and villagers whose records now survive in parchment. In 1301–25, when testators of the *Diplomatico* made the most numerous contributions to pious causes, these same Sienese contributed less than 15 percent of their goods expressed in coin to the poor or to ecclesiastical institutions, while those in the notaries' books left nearly 60 percent of their itemized wealth to pious causes. During the next quarter, through the horrific mortality of 1348, these ratios remained almost identical. Those documents preserved by the church, therefore, did not comprise the more generous testators (at least relative to their own wealth). They were simply wealthier and relative to their financial standings actually less pious than their counterparts in the *Notarile*.

After the onslaught of plague in 1348, testaments preserved as individual scrolls declined sharply; in 1351–75 they fell by half, and in the last quarter of the century by 60 percent—from fifty-nine to thirty-five—and stabilized at this level through the fifteenth century. On the other hand, those records surviving in the *Notarile* gradually increased through the Trecento from a low starting point of fifteen testaments to twenty-nine for the third quarter of the century. Then, in the last quarter of the Quattrocento, the numbers jumped significantly to sixty-two records, surpassing for the first time the number of testaments in the *Diplomatico*. Indeed, after 1475 the historian of Siena is no longer confronted with a scarcity of materials from the notarial books. Instead the problem becomes just the opposite: how to sample the wills. Fortunately, this change in the preservation of notarial books occurred almost at the very moment when the survival of testaments on loose scrolls was fast disappearing: only thirty-two testamentary parchments survive after the turn of the sixteenth century; then they disappear entirely (one last codicil exists for 1551 in the *Diplomatico*).

The systematic comparison of these two sources shows that the testators of the *Diplomatico* were wealthier than those whose records survive through the notarial books. Those whose posterity runs through the loose sheets of parchments could bequeath more pious "items" and more money to charitable causes and churches than their compatriots. This differential might be explained simply by common sense: monasteries, hospitals, and confraternities would have been more apt to requisition and preserve the testaments of their wealthier benefactors.

This may have been the case, but other structural matters in the samples also may help account for these differences in wealth. First, the comparison of these two sets of data presents at least one unexpected result. The samples drawn from the *Notarile* were taken from the protocols of notaries who worked primarily in the city of Siena, whereas every full testament preserved in the *Diplomatico*, no matter what its provenance, was included for this study. Yet a greater percentage of testators from the territory are found in the notarial protocols than in the *Diplomatico*. This difference was particularly pronounced for the earliest documents. Before 1300, 60 percent of the testators from the *Notarile* resided in the countryside, whereas only one-fifth of those in the *Diplomatico* lived beyond the city walls. During the fourteenth and fifteenth centuries, when the differential in wealth between the two samples became less accentuated, the difference in the places of origin of the notaries' clients in the two lessened correspondingly.

Finally, during the sixteenth century, when those testators of the *Diplomatico* were less wealthy than those from the *Notarile,* the percentage of country testators from the *Diplomatico* outstripped, for the first time, those found in the *Notarile.*

Indeed, testators from the city were considerably wealthier than those from the countryside. In the *Notarile,* (1223–1550) pious gifts from residents of Siena were four times more valuable on average (29.92 florins) than those of villagers (7.44 florins). The average value of gifts per testator accentuates further the city-country difference. Testators from the city gave nearly six times as much to pious causes as those from the countryside (34.86 and 6.03 florins, respectively). This geographical differential holds for nonpious bequests as well: those made by city folk were nearly six times the size of those from the country (53.99 compared with 9.33 florins), and each testator from Siena proper gave on average almost five times as much as the testator from the territory (28.3 versus 132.29 florins). For the *Diplomatico* the differences were not so extreme: pious gifts from the city came to over three times those from country dwellers (78.83 versus 23.58 florins on average), while legacies to kin and friends from the city totaled slightly more than twice those from villagers (175.99 and 79.93 florins, respectively). Thus the overrepresentation of poorer testators from the country in the *Notarile* accounts for part of the differential in the values of bequests comprised by these two sources.

The greater percentage of women in the *Notarile* also accounts for some of the differences. In the notarial books, pious gifts by men averaged nearly twice those by women (28.46 as opposed to 16.52 florins.) The value per testator of these pious gifts marks a similar differential (31.50 compared with 15.75 florins). When bequests to friends and family are considered, the gap in their values widens even more. Those by men were over three times the size of those of women (50.10 to 15.51 florins), and totaled five times as much on average (147.07 as opposed to 30.14 florins). The differences in the values of pious donations by men and women is even greater in the records of the *Diplomatico:* those by men were around two and a half times greater. As for last gifts to family and friends, men's exceeded women's by nearly seven times. Both sources show that women gave more to pious causes than men, relative to the properties at their disposal. But men controlled more property than women. Thus, despite women's more pious proclivities, the preponderance of their testaments in the notarial protocols, particularly in the earliest ones, helps to explain again the lower values of gifts recorded there.

Surprisingly, differences in social class explain little of the difference between the two sources, at least as far as the upper echelons were concerned—those whom the notaries labeled as nobles (*messer, miles, comes,* and so on) or who bore ancient family names such as Piccolomini, Tolomei, Saraceni, and later Petrucci, Borghesi, and so on. Curiously, a greater proportion of these notables crop up in the notarial records. On the other hand, the *Diplomatico* house the truly remarkable wills to be found in these samples before the sixteenth century—such as the one redacted by the nobleman and knight *Nobilis et sapiens Vir miles dominus Blasius quondam domini Tolomei de Tolomeis*, who on 22 January 1299 left his massive landed estates for the construction of four hospitals "for the maintenance of paupers, the sick, pilgrims, and other miserable persons"; or those redacted by wealthy merchants who did not always bear prominent Sienese names but who in some cases left more than fifty separate bequests. The *Diplomatico* holds ten commissions for the foundation and construction of family chapels dating before the fifteenth century, whereas none appear in the records of the *Notarile* until 1477. Similarly, the *Diplomatico* contains per capita three times as many transferals of landed property—houses, *poderi*, and often sizable landed possessions—to pious institutions, as do the notarial books. And the notarial collection includes only five testaments before 1550 which drafted more than ten separate bequests to pious institutions, whereas the *Diplomatico* includes more than forty. In one of these, a widow listed sixty separate bequests to holy causes. Yet, despite these richer patrons and the fact that religious houses had for centuries been the repositories of the parchments which later came to comprise the *Diplomatico*, the comparative statistics show no bias in the *Diplomatico* toward the more devout, as might be expected. The ratios of pious to nonpious gifts, both in numbers and in value, demonstrate that the relatively poorer testators of the *Notarile* displayed stronger interest in charitable and ecclesiastical causes than their wealthier countrymen from the *Diplomatico*. We have demonstrated (chapter 3), however, that these differences in the sources have not biased our interpretations of the transformations in piety over the first 300 years of this analysis.

✣ Notes

Chapter 1. Introduction

Epigraph: Le Roy Ladurie, *The Territory of the Historian,* 1:284. Unless otherwise noted, all translations are my own.

1. For an illustration of the importance of the local priest at the bedside of the dying testator, see *Gli "Assempri,"* by the late fourteenth–early fifteenth century moralist Fra Filippo degli Agazzari, Prior of the Augustinian monastery of Lecceto on the outskirts of Siena, "XLV. D'un mercatante mal'uomo che dette falsamente un testamento." According to Zdekauer, *Il mercante senese nel dugento,* 8, when called to redact a testament, the notary's "first word was dedicated to reminding the testator of his *male acquisti* and other usurious extortions." For the conflict between the bishop and the commune of Florence on the presence of curates at testators' bedsides, see Trexler, "Death and Testament," 40–42. Regarding laws against confessors influencing testators' deathbed decisions, see Ascheri, *Diritto e Peste,* 106. Later, the Grand Duke Cosimo III (1702) required notaries to solicit from testators gifts for hospitals or monasteries for the benefit of the poor. See Scaduto, *Stato e chiesa,* 170. On the difficulties in evaluating testamentary formulas, see Petrucci, "Note su il testamento," 11–15.

2. The notarial charges for redacting testaments were regressive. For wills conveying property valued at less than 50 lire, the charge was 20 soldi or at least 2 percent of the estate's value; for estates between 50 and 100 lire, the fee was 30 soldi; then 12 soldi for every 100 lire until 1,000 lire; 10 soldi per 100 lire for estates between 1,000 and 2,000 lire; 8 soldi per 100 lire between 2,000 and 4,000 lire and 6 soldi per 100 lire beyond 4,000 lire; *Statuti senesi dell'arte dei giudici e notai* 12. Nonetheless, of those classes which possessed property, even if only "movables," the aristocracy, those bearing the prestigious and ancient lineages of the political faction (or *monte*) of the *gentilhuomini* appear the most underrepresented in our samples.

3. The testament of the seventeenth-century historian Giugurta Tommasi (*Historie di Siena*) is included in these samples; Archivio di Stato Siena (ASS), *Notarile postcosimiano* (hereafter *Not. post-cos.*) n. 423, no. 134, 1605.iv.4. On Tommasi, see Ugurgieri-Azzolini, *Le Pompe Sanesi,* 1:636.

4. See, for instance, *Not. post-cos.,* n. 423, no. 134.

5. See, for instance, Braudel, *The Mediterranean and the Mediterranean World,* 1: 17–22; Braudel, "History and the Social Sciences, the Long Term," 11–40; and Le Roy Ladurie, "L'histoire immobile," 673–92. Within the vast ecumenical borders of *Les Annales,* I know of only one clear exception to this historical perspective, Paul Bois, *Les paysans d'Ouest.*

6. More recently, Vovelle, in *La mort et l'occident de 1300 à nos jours,* has stretched the history of death over a larger canvas in time and space. He stresses the general evolutions of these *"représentations collectives"* as changing "aux longues plages d'évolution lente" (p. 24). See also p. 23.

7. Chaunu, *La mort à Paris*.
8. Chiffoleau, *La comptabilité de l'au-delà*. Chiffoleau, "Perche cambia la morte nella regione di Avignon."
9. Chiffoleau, *La comptabilité de l'au-delà*. p. 201.
10. Ariès, *The Hour of Our Death*, and *Western Attitudes toward Death*. See also Brentano, "Death in Gualdo Tadino," 79–100.
11. Lebrun, *Les hommes et la mort en Anjou aux 17e et 18e siècles*, Ariès, *Western Attitudes toward Death*, and *The Hour of Our Death*. Lorcin, "Les Clauses religieuses dans les testaments du plat pays lyonnais aux XIVe et XVe siècles"; and Croix, *La Bretagne aux 16e et 17e siècles*.
12. For Italy, see for instance Brandileone, *I Lasciti per l'anima e la loro trasformazione;* Ascheri, *Diritto e peste.*, 106ff; and Gatti, "Antonomia privata e voiontà di testare," 17–26. For France, see Auffroy, *Evolution du testament en France des origines au XIIIe siècle*. The most exhaustive of these studies in the cartography of inheritance is Yver, *Essai de géographie coutumière*. For an earlier study, see Homans, *English Villagers of the Thirteenth Century*.
13. Goody, Thirsk, and Thompson, *Family and Inheritance;* Stone and Stone, *An Open Elite?*
14. Recent works on French social history have analyzed large numbers of wills to address problems beyond religious belief and practice. Hoffman, *Church and Community in the Diocese of Lyon*, and Norberg, *Rich and Poor*, have studied wills to educe changes in the clergy and poor relief in the *ancien régime*.
15. Bakhtin, *Rabelais and His World*, 5–10, distinguishes "official" culture from "folk" culture. The pioneering work of Jordan, *Philanthropy in England*, does not altogether fit the generalization just given. Nor do other works that have examined the differences between the wills of Anglicans and dissenters; see for instance Dickens, *Lollards and Protestants in the Diocese of York*, 214–35. These works, however, have not systematically considered questions beyond charity and religious dissent or, like the French works on mentality, the full range of choices over property in both the pious and nonpious bequests.
16. For populations, see Bowsky, "The Impact of the Black Death," 6, 9. On the territory of Siena, see Repetti, *Dizionario geografico fiscio e storico della Toscana*, 5:295–396; for the earlier period, see Redon, *Uomini e communità del contado senese nel Duecento*, and Bowsky, *A Medieval Italian Commune*, chap. 1, 1–22.
17. Unlike in Florence, the old noble (*magnati*) families continued to play a crucial role in communal politics after the coming of power of the merchant Noveschi, or the Nine. According to Bowsky, *A Medieval Italian Commune*, 293–310, this fact lent Siena its distinctive political and cultural physiognomy during the latter medieval period.
18. Douglas, *A History of Siena*, 72–131.
19. Principally, Mengozzi, *Il monte dei Paschi*, vol. 1; and Bowsky, *The Finance of the Commune of Siena* and *A Medieval Italian Commune*.
20. Bowsky, "The Buon Governo of Siena," 368.
21. Wainwright, "Conflict and Popular Government in Fourteenth Century Siena"; and Douglas, *A History of Siena*, 153–63.
22. Isaacs, "Popoli e monti nella Siena del primo cinquecento."
23. Pecci, *Memorie storico-critiche della città di Siena;* and Mondolfo, *Pandolfo Petrucci*.
24. On the war and loss of independence, see Cantagalli, *La Guerra di Siena;* and D'Addario, *Il problema Senese nella storia italiana della prima metà del cinquecento*.
25. Malavolti, *Dell'Historia di Siena*.
26. For the political economy of Siena during the period of the Nine, see Bowsky, *Finance of the Commune of Siena* and *A Medieval Italian Commune*, chap. 6.

27. Chiaudano, "I Rothschild del Duecento," 103–42.
28. Bowsky, *A Medieval Italian Commune*, 230, "Siena of the Nine, however, was not the Siena of pre-Montaperti years. . . . It had fallen behind in the struggle for the hegemony of Tuscany, and Florence far outstripped it in international commerce and banking." Baker, *Sallustio Bandini*.
29. Hicks, "Sources of Wealth in Renaissance Siena."
30. Pardi, "La popolazione," 1–48; and Ottolenghi, "Studi demografici sulla popolazione di Sienna dal secolo XVI al XIX." Parenti, *Prezzi e mercato del grano a Siena*.
31. For Europe in general, see Simiand, *Recherches anciennes et nouvelles;* Vilar, *Or et monnaie dans l'histoire*, 51–53; de Vries, *The Economy of Europe in an Age of Crisis;* Wallerstein, *The Modern World-System I* and *II*.
32. Pardi, "La popolazione," 31–37.
33. Misciatelli, *Studi senesi* and *Misticismo senese*.
34. For this literature, see chapter 2. Bowsky, *A Medieval Italian Commune*, 293, has argued that Siena in contrast to Florence had "a greater tradition of cultural investment through government and civic rather than private display." I have just embarked on a comparative study of reactions to the Trecento plagues in Florence, Arezzo, Pisa, Siena, Perugia, and Assisi.
35. Goubert, "Local History," 120: "The word 'crisis' is itself unsuitable; *crise* in French means a violent but brief phenomenon; the use of the term in this sense seems to be disappearing. In my own study of Beauvaisis, I found no justification for the idea that there was a severe crisis in the period previous to the Fronde except for the incidence of epidemics and high mortality."
36. See Febvre's resounding condemnation "Specificity, dating and nationality" at the end of "The Origins of the French Reformation," 88.
37. Ariès, *The Hour of Our Death*, xii.

Chapter 2. Pious Choices

Epigraph: Cited in Origo, *The World of San Bernardino*, 116.
1. Le Roy Ladurie, *The Territory of the Historian*, 1: 277.
2. Of the published guild statutes for Siena only the 1298 statutes of the wool guild made specific provisions for charitable expenditures, *Statuto dell'università ed arte della lana di Siena* in *Statuti senesi*, 1: 191–92, rubr. lxxxiv–lxxxvi. The governors of the guild were to take 4 soldi each month from the common fund for allocations "for the love of God." In addition, on the feasts of San Domenico, Sant'Ambrogio, and Sant'Agostino, the governors and treasurer accompanied by the underlings (*sottoposti*) of the guild were to give wax (*uno cero*) to each of these respective churches in Siena, as well as wax once a year to the Opera del Duomo. On confraternities, see Weissman, *Ritual Brotherhood*. The commune regularly made allocations to churches and for the support of orphans, pilgrims, and the poor. The entire first quarter (*distinctio I*) of the 1262 Constitution of Siena (*Il constituto del comune di Siena dell'anno 1262*) gave assurances and property to numerous ecclesiastical institutions through the city, from 25,000 bricks to the minor friars (rubr. li) to 12 denarii (pennies) a day to be disbursed by the hospital of Santa Maria della Scala (rubr. xxxvii). The constitutions of 1309–10 made similar provisions; *Il costituto del comune di Siena*, I, dist. vi–xxxvi. According to Bowsky, *A Medieval Italian Commune*, 264, "Throughout the history of the regime [the Nine], the subvention of hundreds of holy men and women was a fixed item in the semiannual communal budgets, and annually thousands of lire were expended in statutorily decreed alms in cash and building materials for numerous churches, monasteries and nunneries."
3. In 1205–1348, 220 testators indicated their health at the time of redaction; in 1349–

1500, 375; and afterward, 1028. See the results of the regression analyses, chapter 3, note 20.

4. From a systematic sample of 5,000 records from the *gabellae dei contratti* (ASS), *donazioni intervivos* represented only 0.8 percent of the taxed contracts, 1296–1647, while testaments appeared nearly three times more frequently, 2.3 percent. The donations, moreover, usually conveyed only a single gift, while testaments could convey more than fifty separate bequests.

5. Norberg, *Rich and Poor*, 115.

6. Trexler, "The Bishop's Portion," 408.

7. Herlihy, *Medieval and Renaissance Pistoia*, 240–58; Becker, "Aspects of Lay Piety," 177–200.

8. Brucker, *Renaissance Florence;* Herlihy, *Medieval and Renaissance Pistoia*. In *Medieval Italy*, 99, Becker demarcates earlier than in previous studies the reorientation of devotion and charity. In contradistinction to his essay "Aspects of Lay Piety," Becker sees here in the eleventh century "a charitable revolution"—the foundation of institutions "ministering to the weary traveler, the poor, the aged, the sick and the infirm."

9. Herlihy, *Medieval and Renaissance Pistoia*, p. 258.

10. By a standard error of a proportion test, this change is significant at the critical level .05; $z = 2.80$, $hp = .1221$, $p = .0929$, $n = 994$; where z = the z-score, hp = the hypothesized proportion, p = the observed proportion, and n = the number of cases. The hp was calculated by adding the two observed proportions and dividing by two.

11. Significant at 0.05 by a standard error of proportion; $z = 2.20$, $p = .1688$, $hp = .1282$, $n = 328$.

12. Epstein, "Dall'espansione alla gestione della crisi," 111; for the earlier history of the hospital, see Redon, "Autour de l'Hôpital Santa Maria della Scala," 17–34.

13. Catoni, ed., *Le pergamene dell'università di Siena*, 27–35.

14. *Diplomatico*, Archivio Generale (hereafter *Dipl.*) 1296.viii.8 (see Appendix). The Sienese calendar before 1750 began each year on 25 March. In the text I have rendered the dates according to our calendar; in the Notes they appear as given in the documents.

15. The testators of our samples gave gifts to the hospital of Santa Croce in the *terzo* of Camillia, the hospital of the *purgi* at San Marco (*Dipl.*, 1323. ix. 1 and 1297.viii.21), that of the minor friars, to the hermits of Sant'Agostino (*Dipl.*, 1298,i.22), to the hospital attached to the monastery of Santo Spirito (*Dipl.*, 1305.ix.3), to the hospital of the Abbadia Nove di San Iacobo (*Dipl.*, 1325.ii.19), and to the hospital of San Lorenzo (*Dipl.*, 1335.iii.13).

16. The hospitals of San Luca called the *purgi* (also called San Luca of San Marco, *Dipl.*, 1340.ix.13), Sant'Andrea, San Donato, San Salvatore post San Cristofano, Beato Niccolò located behind the Mansione in Camillia (*Dipl.*, 1325.vi.5, called in other testaments simply the hospital of the Mansione, *Dipl.*, 1340.vii.10), San Niccolò de Camporeggio, San Vincenti, San Piero, Sant'Angelo Montone (*Dipl.*, 1340.vii.10), and Santa Maria "imbellecorum" (*Dipl.*, 1323.ix.1). There was a hospital named after the Salimbene family (*Dipl.* 1323.ix.1) and one named after a man called Spinellus possibly from the Spinelli family (*Dipl.*, 1325.vi.5).

17. The hospitals of the *Donne fantuccie* in Maciareto, of Lappeto in the commune of Monteriggioni (*Dipl.*, 1325.vi.5), of Sciano (*Dipl.* 1290.iv.8), of Sant'Andrea Renario in the curia of Petriccio (*Dipl.*, 1330.iii.26), of Santa Maddalena at the monastery of San Galgano (*Dipl.*, 1325.vi.5), of Orsaria (*Dipl.*, 1329.x.19), of Santa Maria at San Gimignano (*Dipl.*, 1339.i.21), of Carmignano (*Dipl.*, 1334.v.20), of Pacina (*Dipl.*, 1342.x.23), the Misericordia of Montechiello (*Dipl.*, 1314.i.16).

18. The figures are as follows: before 1348 Santa Maria della Scala received 84 of 268 bequests to hospitals; in 1348–1399, 47 of 99; for the fifteenth century, 41 of 61.

19. To resolve this problem, the number of gifts for any time-frame was multipled by the average value of those gifts which were monetized. This sum was then divided by the number of testators for that time-frame.

20. *Dipl.*, 1298.i.22. Unless otherwise specified, all individuals cited in this book were from the city of Siena. Similarly, all places are within the territory of Siena unless otherwise indicated.

21. *Dipl.*, 1383.vii.23.

22. See Henderson, "The Flagellant Movement and Flagellant Confraternities in Central Italy"; Weissman, *Ritual Brotherhood;* de la Roncière, "Mélanges de l'école française de Rome," 31–77; for Siena, Bowsky, *A Medieval Italian Commune*, 264–66.

23. See Edgerton, *Pictures and Punishment;* Paglia, *"La pietà dei carcerati" confraternite e società a Roma*, and *La morte confrontata riti della paura e mentalità religiosa*.

24. See Schneider, "Mortification on Parade."

25. Monti, *Le confraternite;* Meersseman, *Ordo Fraternitatis*.

26. *Dipl.*, 1300.vii.18; according to Monti *Le confraternite*, 1: 228–29, this company was the oldest of the flagellant companies in Siena, dating before 1260; in addition see Prunai, "I capitoli della compagnia di S. Domenico in Campo Regio."

27. *Dipl.*, 1301.vi.13. From the simple listing, it is not certain whether this company was the *disciplinati* society of Santa Maria della Scala whose legendary origins go back to A.D. 898 or the *laudesi* company which congregated in the Carmelite church of San Niccolò and whose 1345 statutes are among the most ancient extant for Siena, see Monti, *Le confraternite*, 1: 26ff and 233. *Dipl.*, 1322.vi.4; 1321.xii.28; 1305.ix.3; 1318.xi.7.

28. *Dipl.*, 1313.vi.5.

29. Michel Mollat, ed., *Etudes sur l'histoire de la Pauvretè (Moyen Age-XVIe siècle)* (Paris, 1974); Trexler, "Charity and the Defense of Urban Elites," 64–109; and Lesnick, *Preaching in Medieval Florence*.

30. *Dipl.*, 1314.i.16.

31. See Cherubini, "Proprietari, contadini, e campagne senesi all'inizio del Trecento."

32. The Constitution of 1262 provided 25 libris for these poor called *fraternite pauperum vergognosurum;* Zdekauer, *Il constituto del comune di Siena dell'anno 1262*, rubr. LXXX, 44. On the "shamed-faced poor" in Florence, see Trexler, "Charity and the Defense of the Urban Elites."

33. *Dipl.*, 1323.ix.1: Iacobus Guilillemi, a citizen of Siena (*civis senensis*), in a long list comprising seventy separate bequests, left 40 soldi for a Francesco, identified as a *rigattierius* or a retailer of used clothing (a guild profession of a certain middling respectability which should not conjure up the nineteenth-century images of the destitute ragman). He was to distribute these funds among *pauperibus vergnognosis*. It is not clear whether this Francesco was among their ranks. *Dipl.*, 1495.iii.22: Alfonso di Ser Lorenzo, called Giusa, a cloth dealer, made an unspecified gift to the *poveri vergognosi*. None, unfortunately, were identified.

34. See Trexler, "The Bishop's Portion," 433–36.

35. For this negative picture of the economy and well-being of laborers and the poor during the late Duecento and Trecento, see Herlihy, *Medieval and Renaissance Pistoia;* Pinto, "Aspetti dell'indebitamento e della crisi della proprietà contadina."

36. To chart the shifts in social charity and the concern for the Sienese for "the poor," I have grouped under this rubric several subcategories: those gifts made (1) to *pauperes, pauperes cristi, miserabili*, indiscriminately; (2) to individual poor men or women; (3) to poor or indebted prisoners; (4) to orphans (a rare stipulation before the end of the sixteenth century); and (5) to the sick and indigent. I have classified dowry funds and dowries for poor girls (*paupere puelle*) separately and will consider them shortly.

37. All but one testator for the plague years 1348 and 1363 redacted their wills when the plague was rampant, the late spring and summer months, and only 10 out of eighty-three testators claimed at the time to be in good health. Biraben, *Les hommes et la peste*, 2: 150–58, gives illustrations of notaries jotting down the legacies of plague victims.

38. *Dipl.*, 1318.xi.7, He alloted funds to marry four *femine;* he designated only a certain Margarita Ghezi to receive 6 florins. Since Nicholaus did not specify any institution or person to select these *femine*, and no executors were named, the universal heir, his sister, domina Francesca, most likely assumed the responsibility of selecting the others.

39. The first dowry fund from the *Notarile* (see Appendix) does not appear until much later; *Notarile antecosimiano* (hereafter *Not.*) n. 228, 128r–129r, 22.ix. 1387, when the nobleman Loisius olim domini Loisis de Galleranis ordered his executors to distribute 200 lire to *puellas pauperas* for the health of his soul.

40. Since dowry gifts did not require masses from their recipients until the late sixteenth century, I have calculated these percentages solely from pious bequests that did not demand masses. The trends, however, are no different if both pious gifts and masses are considered.

41. Henderson, "Charity and the Poor," 16ff. Similar regulations appeared immediately after the Black Death in the Sienese records of the Concistoro. (I wish to thank Peter Denley for this notice.)

42. For Europe generally, see Genicot, "Crisis: From the Middle Ages to Modern Times," 660–742; for England, Postan, "Medieval Agrarian Society in its Prime," 557–59; for Florence, Goldthwaite, "I prezzi."

43. For land distribution in France, see Le Roy Ladurie, *Les paysans de Languedoc*, and Bois, *Crise du féodalisme;* for Siena, Cohn, "The Relationship between City and Countryside." For wages, see Bois, *Crise du féodalisme*, and Goldthwaite, "I prezzi." For caloric intake see Phelps-Brown and Hopkins, "Seven Centuries of Building Wages." This is Le Roy Ladurie's phrase in *Les Paysans de Languedoc*.

44. Historians have yet to explain fully why pious institutions, which assisted the sick and indigent, should have increased in wealth and importance during the early Quattrocento when the material conditions of the poor were improving. Becker suggests, in passing, a political explanation—the revolt of the Ciompi and the merchant class's (*popolani grassi*'s) fear of its recurrence. This explanation might work for Florence, but would require far more elaboration to explain a transformation in piety which Becker and others argue characterized much of central and northern Italy. Becker, "Aspects of Lay Piety," 190.

45. *I, Catherine: Selected Writing*, 82, 103.

46. *Bibliotheca Sanctorum*, 5: 1186–88. Pardi, "Il Beato Giovanni Colombini de Siena."

47. *The Dialogue* of Catherine, moreover, is filled with the metaphors of matrimony and family for spiritual matters and relations.

48. See de Capua, *S. Caterina da Siena*. The following quotes are cited in the text by page numbers from *I, Catherine: Selected Writing*.

49. See Origo, *The World of San Bernardino*, 58, and the *Prediche scuopra-magagne*.

50. On the composition of Bernardino's listeners, see Origo, *The World of San Bernardino*, 44. Page numbers for the following quotes are given in the text.

51. See for instance Brucker, *Renaissance Florence*, 190–91.

52. These statistics give credence to Trexler's impression ("The Bishop's Portion," 406) that "the income of seculars was in rapid decline" in the early Trecento. Moreover, the counteroffensive of the bishops in southern Tuscany during the early Renaissance must have been successful.

53. Did this change result simply from a shift in the sources, from the predominance of *Diplomatico* records to a dependence on equal numbers of testaments from both these *pergamene* and the *Notarile?* One might expect an overrepresentation of gifts to monasteries from the *Diplomatico*, since monasteries had been the principal collectors of these records. An investigation of these trends solely from the *Diplomatico* does not, however, belie the expected; instead, the differences over time are even more accentuated toward the parishes. Before the Black Death only 7 percent of pious bequests in the *Diplomatico* went to parishes and 42 percent to monasteries (out of 1,838 pious bequests). In the period 1348–1400, parishes received 21 percent of 758 gifts and monasteries 40 percent. For the Quattrocento, similar to the results derived from both sources, parishes became for the first time the more important beneficiary of pious wealth: the Sienese directed 26 percent of their gifts to parishes as opposed to 21 percent to members of the cloistered orders (of 345 gifts). See Appendix.

54. Cohn, *The Laboring Classes in Renaissance Florence*, 65–90.

55. An investigation of the networks of association would be more difficult than for Florence (if not impossible), since the Sienese notaries after the Trecento rarely specified the parishes of parties to contracts. The social history of the Sienese *popolo minuto* (disenfranchised artisans); akin to its political history, most likely differed greatly from that in Florence. In Siena, artisans managed to retain more power and influence in the commune than their confrères on the Arno; see Wainwright, "Conflict and Popular Government in Fourteenth-Century Siena."

56. Of the mendicants, the Franciscans attracted the largest number of gifts over this period (101 if only the original house in the neighborhood of Ovile is considered; 121 including the Quattrocento gifts to the Observants' house at La Capriola, and 197 when gifts to rural communities are included). The Augustinians followed in importance with 98 bequests to those in the city and another 24 to the hermitage at Lecceto. Then came the Dominicans with 91 bequests and the Servites with 65 gifts.

57. Little, *Religious Poverty and Profit Economy in Medieval Europe;* Baron, "Franciscan Poverty and Civic Wealth"; Moorman, *The History of the Franciscan Order.*

58. Herlihy, *Medieval and Renaissance Pistoia*, 155–79, discusses the rationalization of services, banking, and manufacturing for Tuscany. For these endeavors, the crucial changes resulted after the demographic collapse of the late Trecento.

59. See the inventories for the *Conventi Soppressi*, ASS. In Florence the number of nunneries instead increased from the fourteenth through the sixteenth centuries; see Trexler, "Le célibat," 1333.

60. Schevill, *Siena: The Story of a Mediaeval Commune* 327; see also Misciatelli, *The Mystics of Siena*, 77.

61. Edgell, *A History of Sienese Painting*, 184. Pope-Hennessy, *Sienese Quattrocento Painting*, 8.

Chapter 3. The Structure of Pious Giving

Epigraph: Mommsen, ed., *Petrarch's Testament*, 75.

1. Huizinga, *The Waning of the Middle Ages.*
2. Becker, "Aspects of Lay Piety," 177, 185.
3. Bowsky, "The Impact of the Black Death," 1–34, discusses the political significance of the plague—the beginnings of the demise of the long period of political stability under the auspices of the government of the Nine.
4. Brucker, *Renaissance Florence*, 207, and Herlihy, *Medieval and Renaissance Pistoia*, date the religious and charitable changes later, toward 1400. For the consequences of the

plague of 1348 on the subsequent character of the medical profession, see Park, *Doctors and Medicine*. For changes in health policy, see Carmichael, *Plague and the Poor*.

5. Huizinga, *The Waning of the Middle Ages;* Delumeau, *La peur en Occident;* and *Le pèché et la peur*.

6. McNeil, *Plagues and Peoples*.

7. *Dipl.,* 1271.xii.1. Before 1275 long lists of itemized gifts to numerous pious parties were rare; only two testators bequeathed more than twenty-five itemized bequests to charitable causes: the first from 1251 (*Dipl.,* 1251.xii.4), a man from Poggibonsi made thirty-three pious donations.

8. *Dipl.,* 1290.iv.8; 1297.viii.21; 1298.ix.27.

9. *Dipl.,* 1301.vi.13; 1312.ix.12; 1314.xii.1; 1316.iii.27; 1318.x.29; 1323.ix.1; 1325.vi.5.

10. The difference between the means in the periods, 1301–25 and 1326–47, is highly insignificant by a T-test: n = 129, t = .74. On bequests to "pious places" see Trexler, "Death and Testament," 62–63.

11. For 1300–27 the mean number of bequests per testator was 10.67 (sixty-one cases). In the famines years, 1328–30, the number dropped insignificantly to 8.5 (twelve cases). Nor did these years initiate a new trend in the structure of giving. For the years following the famines until the Black Death, 1330 to 1347, the mean was 8.73 (fifty-six cases). By a T-test, the difference before (1301–27) and after the famines is highly insignigicant: T = 0.74, a probability of only 0.461. *Dipl.,* 1325.iii.5; 1335.ix.15; 1340.vii.10; 1344.vi.13.

12. Recently, Bonanno, Bonanno, and Pellegrini, "I legati 'pro anima,'" have concluded that neither the Black Death of 1348 nor subsequent strikes of pestilence fundamentally altered mentalities in Florence in the expected directions towards greater piety and increased donations to the church and the poor.

13. According to the most recent and thorough history of the plague in Western Europe, Biraben, *Les hommes et la peste,* the "pestilence" of 1340 was not the bubonic plague. The bubonic plague was exogenous to the European disease pool. It came from the Middle East and only made its first appearance in 1347. See del Panta, *Le epidemie nella storia demografica italiana,* 106. In addition, Epstein, "Dall'espansione alla gestione della crisi," 115, lists 1360 as a plague year. This possible outbreak of plague, however, made no impression either on contemporary chroniclers or on our samples of wills.

14. Origo, *The World of San Bernardino,* 18.

15. Five testaments are found for this year, but only one was redacted during the summer and only one by a testator in ill health; *Dipl.,* 1400.viii.19. the will of a tanner of skins (*cerdobolarius*) from the parish of San Egidio.

16. See Corradi, *Annali delle epidemie*.

17. *Cronaca Senese di Donato di Neri e di suo figlio Neri,* in *Cronache senesi,* t. xv, pt. 6, pp. 599–605. Malavolti, *Dell'Historie di Siena,* pt. 1, 124r–v, reports that this plague (*peggior natura*) struck the Palazzo pubblico with particular violence and killed off a number of bureaucrats (*persone pubbliche*); in addition the deacon of the Augustinian house of San Leonardo on the outskirts of Siena, Fra Filippo degli Agazzari, *Gli "Assempri,"* 41(VII), 57 (XII), 135 (XXXVII), 220 (LVII), mentions the plague of 1363 in his moral examples. He reports that in that year the monastery buried sixty-three people, forty-four in two months alone.

18. See Genicot, "Crisis," 660–741.

19. Meiss, *Painting in Florence and Siena,* 87, comments that "when the plague appeared for the second time, however, in 1363, so many Sienese interpreted it as a sign of God's displeasure with the ban [of the Fraticelli] that it was hastily lifted." The change from both the Black Death, 1348, and the interval, 1349–62, to the year of pestilence's reappearance in 1363 is highly significant: t = 2.06 and 2.28, respectively.

20. Petrarca, *Rerum Familiarum, Libri I-VIII,* fam. VIII, pp. 146 and 419.

21. To estimate the relative wealth of each testator, the values of pious and nonpious gifts were added. For occupational status, first the forty-six different occupations found in these testaments were divided into five groups: clergy, nobility, merchants, shopkeeper-artisans, and peasants. Higher results were obtained when the categories were reduced to simply the elites (those with family names, noble titles, or merchant professions) and others. Beta = .143, T = +3.71 and is significant at .0002.

22. The R square of the multiple regression increases from 0.026 to .162.

23. Beta = .0934, T = +2.57 and is significant at .01.

24. Beta = .163 and T = 2.23, significant at .03.

25. Beta = −.228, T = −2.99 and is significant at .0029.

26. Beta = −.073, T = −1.66 and is significant at .0965; however, our hypothesis was that 1363 marked a significant decline in the median number of gifts and not a just a change in any direction. Therefore, the test for significance should be a one-tail instead of a two-tail (or dual directional) test. By this criterion, 1363 is significant at .0483, despite the small sample size.

27. Beta = .016, T = .307, which is insignificant at .758.

28. To improve the model, wealth was multiplied by the period variables to control for possible shifts over time in the direction and impact of wealth on the mean number of pious gifts. These "interactive variables," however, were all highly insignificant and created a weaker overall model, R square = .157.

29. See discussion of hospitals and nunneries in chapter 2. *Dipl.,* 1348.vii.27, and vi.30.

30. Meiss, *Painting in Florence and Siena.* For a criticism of Meiss and his dating of paintings, see Smart, *The Dawn of Italian Painting,* 108–25; Meiss himself, "Notable Disturbances in the Classification of Tuscan Paintings"; Hank vos Os, "The Black Death and Sienese Painting," 237–49; and Bruce Cole, "Old and New in the Early Trecento," 229–48.

31. Coulton, *The Black Death* (London, 1929), 66–67, quoted in Meiss, *Painting in Florence and Siena,* 67.

32. *Cronaca Senesi,* 556, 560.

33. See de la Roncière, *Florence;* Goldthwaite, "I prezzi"; and Epstein, "Dall'espansione alla gestione della crisi."

34. Parenti, *Prezzi,* Tabella 1, 27–28. ASS, Archivio della Gabella Generale e dei Contratti (Mercuriali), no. 1289. Until 1783 a Sienese staio of grain was 15/16 of a Florentine staio; Archivio della Gabella Reg. n. 1290, 1767–1801, 96v. See Parenti, *Prezzi,* 30.

35. See Cohn, "Florentine Insurrections," 149–50. According to Litchfield, *Emergence of a Bureaucracy,* 257, the regional character of grain prices, because of the mercantilist policies of the Medici, began to splinter into separate subregions by the 1590s.

36. *Cronache senesi,* 645, 717.

37. Ibid., 788, 793, 794.

38. Bois, *Crise du féodalisme;* Le Roy Ladurie, *Les paysans de Languedoc;* Herlihy, *Medieval and Renaissance Pistoia.*

39. The year 1437 was possibly the only exception in this period of good health and economic tranquility; the chronicler Donato di Neri mentions *grande moria* in Siena, but does not indicate its cause. Some have assumed that this mortality was the recurrence of the bubonic plague; see Lisini, *Le tavolette,* tav. 29.

40. Becker, "Aspects of Lay Piety," 179.

41. See Epstein, "Dall'espansione alla gestione della crisi," and Bowsky, *A Medieval Italian Commune,* 273–74.

42. *Statuti senesi,* III, *Statuto dello Spedale di Siena,* xvi.

43. *Le pergamene dell'università di Siena*, ed. by Catoni. As early as the 1262 Constitution, the Potestas of Siena held the right to oversee (*retinere*) those "*procuratores et administratores*" called the friars of the Misericordia, "who served orphans and other poor and destitute persons of the city of Siena," *Il constituto*, rubr. lxxx, 44.
44. *Dipl.*, 1296.iii.26.
45. *Dipl.*, 1325.vi.5.
46. *Dipl.*, 1318.x.29.
47. *Dipl.*, 1321.xii.28.
48. *Dipl.*, 1301.vi.13.
49. In 1349, a testator granted 40 soldi to each of the hermits of his hometown of Poggibonsi. But by then 40 soldi would have purchased actually less than the 30 soldi of a half-century earlier. *Dipl.*, 1349.vi.20.
50. *Dipl.*, 1348.vii.8.
51. In the short period 1349–62, nine testators bequeathed such handouts of small sums of pennies to hermits residing in and around Siena. *Dipl.*, 1376.viii.27.
52. *Dipl.*, 1416.xii.2.
53. See Origo, *The World of San Bernardino*, p. 111.
54. *Dipl.*, 1430.vii.26; *Not.*, n. 435, no. 73 (1449.ix.27).
55. See Origo, *The World of San Bernardino*, 80. Bernardino's contemporary Fra Filippo degli Agazzari, *Gli "Assempri*," railed against usurors with threats of eternal damnation, V, IX, XI, XII, XLVI.
56. For the economy of Duecento and early Trecento Siena, see Mengozzi, *Il monte dei Paschi*, 1:9–28; Chiaudano, "I Rothschild," 103–42; Douglas, *A History of Siena*, 28–41; and Bowsky, *A Medieval Italian Commune*, 184–259; Zdekauer, *Il mercante senese*. Douglas, *A History of Siena*, 9–10. For Florence, see Trexler, "The Bishop's Portion," 397–450; and "Death and Testament," 48–50.
57. Zdekauer, *Il mercante senese*, 89, "When the notary was called to draw up a testament, his first word was dedicated to recalling *mali acquisti* and usurious extortions."
58. For Agazzari's threats against gamblers, see *Gli "Assempri*," examples XIII, LX, and LXI. For examples of prominent patricians gripped with guilt over ill-gotten gains and usury who left significant bequests to hospitals and for other charitable causes, see Chiaudano, "I Rothschild," 104–5; Sanesi, "Il testamento di un prestatore Senese," 115; Zdekauer, *Il mercante senese*, 8.
59. *Dipl.*, 1298.i.22.
60. *Dipl.*, 1285.xii.2. Noblemen made only 12 out of 165 such bequests.
61. *Dipl.*, 1242.iv.2.
62. The constitutions of the bishops during the early Trecento placed pressure on merchants and shopkeepers under the threat of refusal of a Christian burial to restitute in their wills usurious profits. The bishops, moreover, stood to gain one-third of the returns from these acts of contrition; see Trexler, "Death and Testament," 48–50, 64; and "The Bishop's Portion," 430ff.
63. See Mengozzi, *Il monte dei Paschi*, 1:33.
64. Herlihy, *Medieval and Renaissance Pistoia*, 155; Mengozzi, *Il monte dei Paschi*, 1:60–61, 90.
65. This early Trecento increase probably resulted from the counteroffensive of the pope and the seculars to gain income from testamentary bequests; see Ronzani, "Gli ordini mendicanti," 126ff and Trexler, "Death and Testament" and "The Bishop's Portion" on Boniface VIII's *Super Cathedram* (1300) and the episcopal constitutions of Florence.
66. Trexler has commented that the "recurrence of testamentary restitution for usury was in slow decline" in Florence, but he offers no explanation.

67. Two came from residents of Fabriano in the district of Viterbo, *Dipl.*, 1416.xii.2 and 1484.iii.22; a painter from Ferrara, discretus vir magister Angelus, made three such bequests, *Dipl.* 1456.vii.5; the others came from testators residing in Monte Lupo in the district of Florence, *Dipl.*, 1423.vi.5, in Linari, *Dipl.*, 1395.vii.26, and in Chiusi, which straddled the boundary of the Siena territory, *Dipl.*, 1432.iii.25. After 1363, only eight (2 percent) of all testaments found in these samples came from foreign places.

68. *Dipl.*, 1247.xii.26.

69. *Dipl.*, 1285.xii.2.

70. The bishops may have influenced the popularity of these gifts left *indistincte ad pias causas seu pro anima*. In the early Trecento constitutions, the bishops had the prerogatives of distributing one-third of these revenues; another third went to the parish rector, and the last third was to be distributed by the testator's executors.

71. *Dipl.*, 1322.ix.12.

72. *Dipl.*, 1346.x.5.

73. *Dipl.*, 1305.ix.3, "Item de dictis bonis suis iussit fieri duo alia bona cerea seu dupplerea de cera bona pulcra et decentia ponderis competentis videlicet sex librarum cere que cerea seu dupplerea portari debeant accensa ad funeram pauperarum qui ea habere non possunt vel emere et debeant ista cerea semper remanere penes dictam dominam Minam eius uxorem et istud observetur toto tempore vite sue vixerit."

74. *Not.*, n. 243, 79r–81r, 1390.xi.7.

75. *Not. post-cos.*, n. 3110, no. 148, 4v–6v, 1689.i.15.

Chapter 4. Souls and Bodies: The Subsoil of Humanism

Epigraph: Catherine of Siena, *The Dialogue*, 43.

1. Historians of ideas have defined "humanism" in various ways. Kristeller, *Renaissance Thought*, 3–23, restricts the definition to the *studia humanitatis*, or the educational curriculum introduced by scholars during the Renaissance. Other historians and philosophers insist on the broader definition of an intellectual and cultural movement that "confirmed the value of man and of earthly life." See Garin, "Problemi di religione e filosofia nella cultura fiorentina del quattrocento," 78; and Ullmann, "The Medieval Origins of the Renaissance." Here, the broader definition will be assumed.

2. For a corrective, see Bossy, *Christianity in the West*.

3. Historians have questioned the simplicity of the frequency of masses as an index of "Christianization" for the eighteenth century; see Delumeau, *Le Christianisme va-t-il mourir?* and *Le pèché et la peur*, 627; and McManners, *Death and the Enlightenment*, 441: "'Déchristianization' with its revolutionary overtones, is, surely, too sweeping a term to sum up these tendencies of the *ancien régime* 'laicization.'" As far as I know, historians have yet to challenge the utility of the term regarding the earlier process of late medieval "Christianization."

4. Le Goff, *La naissance du Purgatoire*, finds Purgatory transformed from an adjectival clause to a substantive place as early as the late twelfth century. He places the high point in the evolution of purgatory's geography in early Trecento Tuscany (the appearance of *The Divine Comedy*), that is, at the moment when the majority of our testators were making pious bequests rarely with any explicit commands or expectations.

5. Bernstein, "Esoteric Theology." Until 1363, 525 bequests out of 2,522; afterward, 400 out of 944 bequests. On these testamentary formulas, see Bonanno, Bonanno, and Pellegrini, "I legati 'pro anima.'"

6. *Not.*, n. 1, n. 393, published by Dina Bizzarri, ed., *Imbreviaturarum Appulliensis notarii senarum*, 159.

7. *Not.*, n. 39, 52v.

8. *Not.*, n. 2, no. 177; published by M. Chiaudano, *Liber imbreviaturarum Ildibrandini notarii*. 100, "the testator desires not to die intestate and to avoid future litigation; he orders his testament to be made through an oral oath."

9. Similar clichés can be found throughout Western Europe, see Croix, *La Bretagne*, t. II, 899, Chiffoleau, *La comptabilité*, 116.

10. *Not.*, n. 89, 26r.

11. *Not.*, no. 153, 9r.

12. *Not.*, n. 3, p. 15r, 1252.v.27.

13. See, for instance, *Not.*, n. 293, 126r.

14. *Dipl.*, 1311.x.4.

15. *Dipl.*, 1348.vi.26.

16. *Dipl.*, 1454.iii.12.

17. *Dipl.* 1490.iii.10; *Not.* n. 333, 56r.

18. See, for instance, *Dipl.*, 1447.iii.21 and *Not. antecos.* n. 484, no. 51.

19. By a standard error of a proportion the difference is highly significant: $p = .7000$, $hp = .7650$, $n = 694$, and $z = 4.03$. By the beginning of the fourteenth century Pope Boniface VIII and the bishops went on the offensive against the rising tide of mendicant popularity both for burials and for testamentary bequests. The Bull of 1300, *Super Cathedram*, required the mendicant orders to return to the parishes one-fourth of all the bequests they received from those testators who elected to be buried in their cemeteries; see Trexler, "Death and Testament," 34.

20. In contrast, testators from neighboring Florence already by the early Trecento requested that their bodies be donned in monastic habits; see for instance, Archivio di Stato, Firenze, Archivio Diplomatico Domenicani, 1310.vii.16.

21. See *Not.* n. 266, 29r–v, 1396.xi.31; n. 291, 11r; *Not.*, n. 435, 2d busta, no. 23; n. 704, n.p., and n. 770, n.p.

22. The commune promulgated special legislation on mourning and funeral feasts during the late Trecento and early Quattrocento, see "Il pranzo de' morti," 28–29 and "Funerali," 185–86. *Dipl.*, 1426.x.16, "Quod post decessum dicti testatoris per tempus unius annj statim post mortem et prius dicta domina Dominica induatur et induta vadat de panno coloris azzurini. Et quod bene videatur et appareat coloris Azzurini et non alterius coloris. Et si secus facere auderet vel presummeret, voluit dictus testator quod ipsa cadat a dicta hereditate. Et voluit quod dicta hereditas eo casu adveniente deveniat ad hospitalem Sancte Marie dela Scala de Senis et non aliter vel alio modo." In the early fourteenth century the mendicant orders prohibited the erection of prominent tombs in their churches and even exhumed the ones already placed there; see Julian Gardner, "Arnolfo di Cambio and Roman Tomb Design," 434. *Not.*, 518, n.p., 1457.x.26.

23. *Not.*, n. 958, n.p. 1484.iv.21.

24. *Not.*, n. 795, 117r, and n. 1145, n. 86, 1499.vi.19.

25. *Dipl.*, 1268.iii.5.

26. For 1364–75: 16 of 104 (15.4 percent); 1376–1400: 23 of 184 (12.5 percent); 1401–25: 26 of 196 (13.3 percent); 1426–50: 21 of 141 (14.9 percent).

27. This percentage was significantly higher than the high-water mark of the Trecento (1326–47); $z = 6.73$, $hp = .275$, $p = .169$, $n = 804$.

28. Petrarch, *Rerum familiarum, Libri I–VIII*, fam. II, 5, 87.

29. *Dipl.*, 1313.vi.5; in addition, see: *Dipl.* 1290.ix.16; *Dipl.* 1296.viii.8; *Dipl.*, 1340.vi.18; *Dipl.*, 1348.i.13.

30. *Dipl.*, 1330.iv.2, Nerius olim Gregorij, *cives senis*, from the parish of San Martino gave 12 lire, 10 soldi, to priests for 1,000 or more masses.

31. The change is highly significant: hp = .1618, p. = .23, n = 493, z = 9.66.
32. *Dipl.*, 1305.ix.3; 1325.xi.23; *Dipl.*, 1334.v.20.
33. Of those masses between 1363 and 1500, stipulated for precise moments, one testator ordered masses for the eighth and thirtieth days following his burial (*Not.*, n. 484, n. 13, 1458.xi.30); another ordered his sons to celebrate an office within fifteen days of his death (*Not.*, n. 484, 1477.xii.7); another gave his heirs a year and three months to perform four offices for his soul; if not celebrated within ten years following his death, the heirs were to double these expenditures (*Not.* n. 652, n.p., 1479.v.12). In two cases, masses were to be sung one year following the testator's burial (*Not.*, n. 518, 1459.xii.24 and n. 698, 1477.i.19). In three cases, the masses were to be performed over a two-year period (*Dipl.*, 1451.ix.22; 1479.iv.30; and *Not.*, n. 435, 2d busta, no. 65, 1449.v.6). Two were for three years (*Dipl.*, 1482.iv.11 and *Not.*, n. 357, 4v–5v, 1428.viii.15); one was for five years (*Not.*, n. 243, 37v–38v, 1390.xii.15). Three were for six years (*Dipl.*, 1489.ix.21; 1482.vii.12; and *Not.*, n. 765, 2d busta, 1487.x.6). The most common period was for ten years—five testaments—(*Dipl.*, 1383. ind. vi; 1446.vii.21; 1484.iii.27; *Not.*, 795, 4v, 1477.iv.13; and *Not.*, n. 291, 11r–12v, 1410.vii.17). One was to last for fifteen years (*Not.*, n. 909, 65v–68r, 1484.vi.28); and finally two were specified for a twenty-year period (*Dipl.*, 1411. ind. iv, and 1446.vii.6). *Dipl.*, 1383.ind. vi.
34. *Not.*, n. 795, 4v.
35. *Not.*, n. 484, no. 1, 1443.iii.12.
36. *Not.*, n. 435, 2d busta, no. 65, 1449.v.6.
37. *Not.*, n. 518, n.p., 1452.iii.26.
38. *Dipl.*, 1470.ix.11; *Not.*, n. 484, 1477.xii.7; *Not.*, n. 652, n.p., 1479.iv.19; *Dipl.*, 1484.iii.27.
39. Delumeau, *La peur en Occident*, 507.
40. This theme resonates through both of Delumeau's most recent books, *La peur en Occident* and *Le pèché et la peur*. See especially pp. 40 and 147, respectively.
41. Delumeau, *La peur en Occident*, 287.
42. Delumeau, *La pèché et la peur*, 295, 277. In the conclusion to *La peur en Occident*, 508, Delumeau draws the geographic distinction that in Renaissance Europe, two countries, Italy and Poland, escaped the fears that tortured men of power: This distinction, one of the few drawn over his vast range of time and space does not follow from his evidence. A large part of his documentation (as indicated earlier) in fact concerns Italy.
43. *Dipl.*, 1284.i.3, "In omnibus . . . Riccium Boncompagni nepotem meum carnalem michi heredem instituo sub conditionibus . . . videlicet quod bona mea immobilia seu aliquam partem eorum vendere vel donare vel alienare aliquo iure vel modo non possit. Et si aliquam venditionem pignorationem donationem vel alienationem faceret de ipsius bonis meis immobilibus vel aliqua parte eorum non valeat neque teneat. . . . Iubeo quod in bonis meis et rebus thomasina uxor Ricij dicti nullum jus possit acquirere vel habere aliquo iure vel causa et ex nunc volo et iubeo quod hereditate mea et omnibus bonis meis ipsa thomasina omnimode privetur."
44. *Dipl.*, 1290.iv.8; 1300.x.10.
45. White, *Custom, Kinship, and Gifts,* and Duby, *Hommes et structures*.
46. *Dipl.*, 1373.vii.25; 1390.vii.10; and 1425.iii.6, "Ita tamen quod de bonis suis non possit vendere alienare sive suppigniorare dum dictus Antonius vir dicte domine Andree et pater ipsius Guasparis vixerint et in humanis steterint. Et si ipsi sui heredes vel aliquis eorum venderent sive venderet de dictis suis bonis aut alienarent sive suppigniorarent ipsas priventur a dicta hereditate et substuatur eis et cuilibet eorum supradictam societatem."
47. *Dipl.*, 1446.vii.6.

48. *Dipl.*, 1467.vi.12.

49. *Dipl.*, 1478.ix.16. "Cum condictione quod dictus Minus non possit aliquo modo vendere vel aliquo modo donare vel alienare aliqua bona inmobilia de bonis ipsius testatoris, detractis dotibus et antifatio donne Agnetis uxoris sue."

50. *Not.*, n. 698, n.p., 1479.iv.19, "In omnibus ... suos heredes universales instituit .... fratres capituli et conventus Sancti benedicti ordinis montis oliveri extra et prope portam tufi de senis, cum hac conditione, quod possessio ipsius testatoris sita infra massam Tertii Civitatis et comuni Sancti Maffei ... non possit predictos fratres ... vendi aut alienari, sed voluit quod in perpetuum sit conventus predicti et quatenus dicta possessio possit remanere libera et exempta ab omni honenere [sic] hereditati et aliquod de bonis suis supra sit ultra dictam possessionem saltus legatis predictis, voluit de eo pluri quod supra fuerit posset disponere ad libertum ipsius testatoris cum hoc, quod dicti fratres capitulum et conventus dent sibi testatori et ad ipsius usum unum breviarium et unum monachinum."

51. *Dipl.*, 1482.iv.11. "Volens et mandans quod dicte sue heredes non possint ullo tempore unam ipsius testatoris et hereditatis domum sitam in comitatu Sancte Columbe prefate in ville que dicitur Montebuono ... de dicto loco et, si qui sint, confines et possessiones eiusdem vendere alicui persone, comuni, collegio et universitati sine licentia et consensu trium suorum proximorum consanguineorum, et si contra predictam facerent, tunc dictam domum reliquit suis proximis consanguineis."

52. Tenenti, *Il Senso della morte*, 165; for a favorable assessment of Tenenti's seminal work, see Olivieri, "Spazi mentali ed urbani della morte"; for a critical review, see Camporeale, "Senso della morte e amore della vita nel Rinascimento."

Chapter 5. High Culture

Epigraph: Catherine of Siena, *The Dialogue*, 40.

1. See Bowsky, *A Medieval Italian Commune*, 262; Misciatelli, *Misticismo senese*, ed. Aldo Lusini (Florence, 1966), chap. 3; Pardi, "La rappresentazione del Beato Giovanni Colombini" and "Il Beato Giovanni Colombini," 305.

2. On the cultural importance of "the model" of Francis, see Holmes, *Florence, Rome and the Origins of the Renaissance*, 45–69.

3. Colombini, *Le lettere*, 54.

4. Daniel Lesnick in *Preaching in Medieval Florence*, 42ff, argues that the Dominican and Franciscan preachers of early Trecento Florence were not concerned with the actual social conditions of poverty or our modern notion of poverty.

5. Colombini's gutter style goes so far as to compare Christ's fidelity to that of a dog (*Le lettere*, 138): "Puri dall'altra parte a uno suo figliuolo leale, più leale che mille morti, più fedele ch'l cane."

6. Catherine of Siena, *I, Catherine: Selected Writing*, 62.

7. Ibid., 83, a letter to Berengario, abbot of San Pietro, Lézat (after 17 May 1375).

8. Ibid., 86, 134. Similar metaphors abound in *The Dialogue*: such as p. 45, "the spouse of the soul"; and p. 50, "the marvelous milk and blood of this bride."

9. For the mendicant attack on familial attachment in Florence see the sermons of Giordano da Pisa: "At the moment of death the family, like money, comes to nothing, and its loss causes unwarranted suffering" (cited in Lesnick, *Preaching in Medieval Florence*, 240); for further references to Giordano's conclusion, that "reliance on family is a form of idolatry," see Lesnick, "Religion and Social Transformation."

10. Agazzari, *Gli "Assempri,"* 181. For other examples of the conflict between piety and

family in the late Duecento and Trecento, see Bynum, *Holy Feast and Holy Fast,* 147, 223–24. In particular, Bynum stresses women's food practices as a rejection of family.

11. We know of these preachers best from saints' lives and the compilations of short biographies, the *Fasti senenses,* by members of the Academy of the Intronati (Intronatorum Academiae) (Siena, 1669); Razzi, *Vite di Santi;* and Ugurgieri-Azzolini, *Le Pompe Sanesi.* The most prolific preacher for this period was the Florentine Giordano da Pisa.

12. Holmes, *Florence, Rome and the Origins of the Renaissance,* 67.

13. See Douglas, *A History of Siena.* 464–68; Zdekauer, *La vita privata,* 56; and Bowsky, *A Medieval Italian Commune,* 279. Angiolieri, *Il canzoniere,* 129, Sonnet 99: "S'i' fossi."

14. Nietzsche, Burckhardt, and others found in that ascetic ideal the very *specificum* of Christianity. I wish to thank my colleague Rudolph Binion for this observation. In addition, their asceticism differed from that of Saint Francis or the brothers who wrote the "Little Flowers" in the subsequent generations. The near pantheistic love for nature does not pervade the Sienese mystics.

15. By 1316 Latin Christendom counted 1,400 Franciscan houses and over 500 Dominican convents (Little, *Religious Poverty,* 152 and 158); but already by 1282, there had been 1,200 Franciscan houses; see Cresi, "Statistica dell'ordine minoritico dell'anno 1282."

16. Székely, "Le movement des flagellants au 14e siècle"; Holmes, *Florence, Rome and the Origins of the Renaissance,* 61; Papi, "Confraternite ed ordini mendicanti a Firenze," 724. According to Bowsky, *A Medieval Italian Commune,* 266, and Monti, *Le confraternite,* 1:228, "Siena was the Tuscan home par excellence of the disciplinant confraternities" which "spring forth with particular vigor in the late thirteenth and early fourteenth centuries."

17. In addition, see Bowsky, *A Medieval Italian Commune,* 261, "Long before the appearance of either Catherine or Bernardino, Siena had more than its share of *beati,* saints, and disciplinants—and of heretics."

18. The image taken from these laconic jottings differs from that romanticized by Sienese populists from Gigli, *Diario Sanese,* to Misciatelli, *Misticismo senese.*

19. *Cronache Senesi,* 307.

20. Brucker, *Renaissance Florence,* 172–212.

21. Trexler's term, in *Public Life in Renaissance Florence,* 217.

22. The only exception comes in 1329: Agnolo di Tura, *Cronache Senesi,* 490; For Florence, see Trexler, *Public Life in Renaissance Florence,* 217–18.

23. *Cronache Senesi,* 308; Witness the report for 1310: "E poi quasi per tutta Italia con molta gente minuta: omini e donne e fanciulli sanza numaro lassavano i loro mestieri e co' le croci i' mano s'andavano battendo di luogo in luogo predicando la pace e gridando misericordia e facendo fare all'uno all'altro molte paci, tornando più gente a penitentia. . . . E molti miracoli Dio mostrava per lui (uno romito chiamato frate Cristofano)."

24. Ibid., 382–83.

25. *Cronaca Senese conosciuta sotto il nome di Paolo di Tommaso Montauri (continuazione—Anni 1381–1431)* in *Cronache Senesi,* 689.

26. Ibid., 697, "Una indulgenza vene in Siena dal papa Urbano, la quale era a tutta la città di Siena, recolla publicata . . . e pagò al Comuno di Siena in Roma per la detta bolla e sugelli fiorini 60 d'oro, e fecesi onore in tutto el chericato."

27. Ibid., 711.

28. Ibid., 711, "La festa si fe' grande, che facevano le brigate per Siena vestite per le giostre come gente d'arme robe, e fare disinari e cene e balli di donne e omini, ardere cera e

dare confetti con solenni vini e fare ogni di falò, e furno tanti e tali, infino e' preti e frati e monache per tutta la città e in tutto el contado, che non sarebe possibile a dire."

29. See Brucker, *Renaissance Florence*, 199, 207–8.

30. Razzi, *Vite de Santi; Fasti Senenses;* and *Bibliotheca Sanctorum*, 5:1186–88; 1:375–81; on Agnese, also see Holmes, *Florence, Rome and the Origins of the Renaissance*, 67.

31. In addition to the saints' lives, see Bowksy, *A Medieval Italian Commune*, 261–64, and "Il contesto religioso precedente a S. Caterina"; Misciatelli, *Mistici Senesi*, chap. 1, 3–66; and Vauchez, "La Commune de Sienne, les ordres mendicants et le culte des saints," 757–67.

32. Razzi, *Vite de Santi*, and *Fasti Senenses*. Donald Weinstein and Rudolph Bell, *Saints and Society: The Two Worlds of Western Christendom, 1000–1700* (Chicago, 1982), have not found a critical line separating styles of sainthood during this period; instead they argue that "with respect to virtually every aspect of sainthood . . . from conversion to the differentiation of sex and class—the years from about 1200 to about 1540 . . . emerge as a coherent period in the history of Catholic piety."

33. For instance, the *beati* Franciscus of Montichiello (ca. 1400) and Franciscus de Vincentibus (died 1367) had been part of Colombini's *brigata;* another Catherine of Siena was the cousin of Giovanni and the founder of the female order of the Jesuati.

34. *Bibliotheca sanctorum*, 2:153, 1259.

35. Origo, *The World of San Bernardino*, 205–28; and Moorman, *The History of the Franciscan Order*, 441–56.

36. Herlihy, "Santa Caterina and San Bernardino," 929; in addition, see Moorman, *The History of the Franciscan Order*, 456–66; and Mesini, "La sociologia di S. Bernardino."

37. Herlihy, "Santa Caterina and San Bernardino," 930.

38. See for instance de Roover, *San Bernardino of Siena and Saint'Antonio of Florence*, 13, Bernardino "is unusually realistic; he fully realized that managerial ability, far from being common, is a rare quality. . . . The rational and orderly conduct of business, according to San Bernardino, was a virtue."

39. Herlihy, "Santa Caterina and San Bernardino," 930.

40. See Garin, "Problemi di religione," 76.

41. For a conflicting view of Saint Catherine, see Scott, "'This is why I have put you among your neighbors.'"

42. Friedman, "The Burial Chapel of Filippo Strozzi"; Clearfield, "The Tomb of Cosimo de' Medici in San Lorenzo"; and Panofsky, "Mors vitae testimonium." 221–37. Camporeale, "Senso della Morte," 440, describes the *Commentaries* as "that corporeal sense of duration that now sustains and orients human energies toward earthly activity."

43. Enea Silvio Piccolomini, *The Commentaries of Pius II*, 8–9. The critical edition is *I commentari*, ed. by Luigi Totaro, 2 vols. (Milan, 1984). For a recent assessment of this work, see Mario Ascheri in *BSSP* 93 (1986): 549–54.

44. *Continazione della cronaca di Paolo di Tommaso Montauri, che rimane interrota a metà dell'anno 1431 . . . che va sotto il nome di Tommaso Fecini dal 1431 al 1479*, in *Cronache Senesi*, 869.

45. I wish to thank Salvatore Camporeale for suggesting that I read the letters of Petrarch. Against the current of the history of philosophy and the history of ideas, Camporeale, "Senso della Morte," 449, has argued forcefully that Petrarch's work cannot be read as "solely or narrowly elitist"; rather his thoughts and impulses "partook" of the "collective feeling . . . diffused through various social strata and across various levels of consciousness."

46. Kenelm Foster, *Petrarch: Poet and Humanist* (Edinburgh, 1984), 2.

47. The earliest letters were written in 1325 but collected and revised in 1345, when

Petrarch was forty-one years old. He concludes the first and largest collection of letters, *On Familiar Matters:* "I have arranged this work not according to subjects but chronologically, with the exception of the last letters addressed to illustrious ancients, which I consciously brought together . . . because of their unity of character, and with the exception of the first letter, which, though written later, preceded . . . as a preface; nearly all the others are arranged chronologically. Thus, the reader may, if he wishes, follow my progress and the course of my life." *Rerum Familiarium, Libri XVII–XXIV,* fam. XXIV, 13, 351.

48. Ibid., Libri I–VIII, fam. II, i, 57–64.
49. Ibid., fam. II, 3, 70; 5, 87; fam. III, 10, 139; 12, 147; fam. IV, 3, 185–87; 10, 200; fam. V, 18, 276–77.
50. Ibid., fam. VIII, 7, 416–20; 8, 421; 9, 427.
51. Ibid., *Libri IX–XVI,* fam. XIV, 3, 229–30. For expressions of similar sentiments during this intervening period, see the letters to Socrates, fam. IX, 2; and to Giovanni Boccaccio, fam., XI, 1; and the condolences to the bishop of Torto, fam. XIII, 1. See also *Libri XVII–XXIV),* fam. XVII, 3, 17, another letter to the archdeacon of Genoa, "Foolish is man to hope for anything eternal on earth, when we see that kingdoms are mortal." To a Francesco of the Church of the Apostles, fam. XIX, 14, 104, Petrarch concludes: "The more I travel throughout the world, the less I like it."
52. *Libri XVII–XXIV,* fam. XXII, 12, 237.
53. Ibid., fam. XIX, 16, 106–9.
54. Ibid., fam. XXIII, 2, 258–59.
55. Ibid., fam. XXIII, 21, 306.
56. Ibid., fam. XXIV, 1, 310–12.
57. Petrarca, *Lettere senili* (hereafter *Sen.*), vol. 1, *Sen.* I, 1, 11. In a letter to Boccaccio in 1363, Petrarch laments the disaster of 1361, which transformed Milan, known for its "healthy skies, sweet climate and the multitude of cheerful and famous citizens," into "a squalid and deserted place." Once again, 1361 brings back to mind the "unheard of violence of the morbidity" of 1348. (*Sen.* III, 1, 140–41.)
58. Ibid., 12.
59. Ibid., *Sen.* I, v, 40, 43; 48.
60. *Not.,* 1457, 1512.xi.30.
61. *Sen.* I, 7, 60 (dated 1362).
62. Catherine of Siena, *I, Catherine: Selected Writing,* 51–52.
63. *Sen.,* vol. 2, *Sen.* X, 1, 81.
64. Ibid., 84.
65. See Bernardo, *Petrarch, Laura, and the 'Triumphs,'* 193.
66. Baron, "Franciscan Poverty and Civic Wealth," 11.
67. For the varieties of relived trauma and their consequences in different historical contexts, see the work of Binion, *Hitler among the Germans; Soundings: Psychohistorical and Pyscholiterary,* chap. 2, 15–61, and chap. 3, 62–96; *Introduction à la psychohistoire* 25–42; and "Corrigenda." In the 1984 preface to the second edition of *Hitler among the Germans,* xv–xvii, Binion defines the traumatic unconscious determination behind certain historical events:

> A traumatic experience is one too painful to be assimilated. It engages the mind at first in a full-time, futile struggle to accommodate or ignore it. . . . An exact, continual, unbearable remembering is, at the other extreme, the traumatic neurosis. This neurosis is like a first approximation to the normal mode of coming to terms with a traumatic experience . . . which is to relive it. . . . Every emotionally charged component of the old experience enters

into the new one vicariously—starkly overdrawn as a rule, and with key relational elements reversed, such as east and west, or before and after. The point of reliving a traumatic experience seems to be to will, to control, to master it after having been overcome by it the first time, and to inure oneself to it so that it will "pass" after all. . . . This traumatic mechanism will be seen to have operated not only with Hitler individually but with Germans collectively.

68. Bernardo, *Petrarch, Laura, and the 'Triumphs,'* 201 and 30, "That the awesome power of the Great Reaper was truly impressed upon the poet during that terrible year and contributed greatly to his sense of the transitoriness and instability of all things human can hardly be disputed." The additions to the fifth edition of the *Canzoniere* (1359–62) are strikingly corporal in contrast to both earlier and later editions: no. 300 expresses "the poet's envy of the earth for possessing Laura's body." In no. 301 "the poet sees '*l'usate forme*' [Laura] in the various aspects of the landscape around Vaucluse . . . 'la sua bella spoglia' lies buried in that earth from which 'al ciel nuda è gita.'" No. 302 is a vision of Laura in "the heaven of Venus" (p. 30). Yet Bernardo pays no heed to the aberrations of the fifth edition. Recent debate has turned on the dating of Petrarch's confessions, the *Secretum*; whether it was composed in the early 1340s, the late 1340s or the early 1350s; see Rico, *Vida y obra de Petrarca*, and Baron, *Petrarch's Secretum*. In these discussions the plague does not figure at all. René Watkins, "The Uses of Adversity," pays more attention to 1361; nonetheless her emphasis falls on the outbreak of plague in 1348 for explaining Petrarch's psychology.

69. Foster, *Petrarch*, 18. Dotti, *Vita di Petrarca*, 341 and 343; Trinkaus, *The Poet as Philosopher*; and Mann, *Petrarch*, do not even mention the plague of 1361.

70. Baron, "Franciscan Poverty and Civic Wealth," 12; and Baron, *The Crisis of the Early Italian Renaissance*; 102–4; and Meiss, *Painting in Florence and Siena*, 164–65; More globally, see McNeil, *Plagues and Peoples*, 182–85.

Chapter 6. The Great Age of Selfishness

Epigraph: Sermon on Sunday, 2 November 1494, edited by F. Cognasso (Perugia/Venice, 1930), I, 32; quoted in Friedman, "The Burial Chapel of Filippo Strozzi," 123.

1. For recent commentary on and criticism of Burckhardt's classical interpretation, particularly regarding religion, see Brucker, *Renaissance Florence*, 172–81; Herlihy, *Medieval and Renaissance Pistoia*, 240–58; Trexler, "Ritual in Florence."

2. *Dipl.,* 1376.viii.27. As mentioned earlier, the last example of a bequest to hermits comes in 1416 from a widow from Todi with no connections to Siena.

3. The last Sienese to restore money in a will because of guilt over extortion or usury appears in the testament of a tanner (*cerbolatarius*) from the parish of San Egidio, *Dipl.,* 1400.viii.19. *Dipl.,* 1416.xii.2; 1423.vi.5; 1456.vii.5; 1484.iii.22.

4. The response in wills to assist the Crusades' "passage to the Holy Lands" was equally short-lived in the testaments of Florence; see Pirillo, "La terrasanta nei testamenti fiorentini del Dugento."

5. *Dipl.,* 1278.i.14; 1298.viii.25; 1298.ix.3; 1301.vi.13.

6. According to Mayer, *The Crusades,* 270, Gregory X "made tremendous efforts to organize a crusade but met with nothing except disappointments. From 1272 to 1274 he called for reports and plans for a new crusade. . . . In them we have clear evidence for contemporary criticism of the crusading movement, criticism which was directed chiefly at the trade in indulgences."

7. The *Gabelle dei Contratti* of the thirteenth and fourteenth centuries contain numer-

ous instances of rural communes buying land to distribute in small plots, either by gift or sale, to residents of the commune.

8. These statistics do not include the mandatory gifts of the canonical portions (in most cases 5 to 10 soldi, regardless of the wealth of the testator) to the archbishop of Siena, the *opera* of the cathedral, and the hospital of Santa Maria della Scala. These gifts became part of statutory law in 1388 but began to appear regularly in testaments as early as the end of the Duecento (Ubaldo Morandi, *Cattedrale di Siena*, 27). The early Trecento increase again reflects the success of the counteroffensive of Boniface VIII (*Super Cathedram*) and the bishops against the depletion of incomes of the Duecento. In addition, the bishops devised other indirect ways of gaining revenues from testamentary bequests—through burials among the mendicant orders, unspecified gifts to "pious places," and the restitution of usurious gains; see Trexler, "Death and Testament," 29–74; and "The Bishop's Portion," 397–450. These excellent studies, however, do not discuss the reasons for a decline in revenues accruing to bishops and seculars from testaments in the later part of the Trecento through the Quattrocento.

9. *Dipl.*, 1374.vii.1.

10. Gifts to chapels averaged 504.50 florins; pious donations in general were 71.94 florins.

11. Before 1500, fifty-three gifts to chapels appear in these samples.

12. *Dipl.*, 1269.viii.2. In the first "item" of his testament, Maffeus q. Guiderii from the village of Castro Piano gave the church of San Quirico 40 soldi to be placed on the altar of this church where he "elected" to be buried ("iudico et lego -XL- solidos denariorum senis ecclesie Sancti Quirici ponendos supra altare dicte ecclesie ad quam ecclesiam mihi eligo sepulturam").

13. See Brown, *The Cult of the Saints*.

14. *Dipl.*, 1304.ii.19, "Item iudico et relinquo capelle et operi Sancti ambrogij de bonis meis .xx. solidos denariorum Senis."

15. *Dipl.*, 1318.xi.7.

Item reliquid et judicavit quod de bonis suis fiat et fieri debeat unam capellam in plebe Sancti constati de Torrita et in ipsa facienda et ornanda expendantur de bonis suis .xx. florenos auri. In qua cappella sit et maneat perpetualiter unus cappellanus sacerdos ad divina offitia celebranda. Quam capellam predictam dictus testator dotavit et dedit et donavit sibi inter vivos pro vita cappellani predicti .xx. stariora terre laborate. . . . Item alia petia terre est in loco dicto Rapaio . . . de qua quidem predicte capelle dictus testator fecit nunc ad presbiterum suum heredem et eius capellam perpetualiter in vita sua presbiterum Angelum olim Ser Clari de Roma . . . quod post mortem dicti presbiteri heres seu heredes dicti testatoris et eorum subcessores possint et debeant perpetualiter mantenere et ponere cappellanum in dicta capella ad eorum voluntatem et petitionem sine aliqua contradictione. . . . Item quod supradictus cappellanus possit intrare et accipere tenutam et corporalem possessionem de petijs terre predictis dicte cappelle post mortem dicti testatoris ad suum beneplacitum.

16. On double candles, see Strocchia, *Burials in Renaissance Florence*, 81; these large candles contained between 5 and 10 pounds of wax. *Dipl.*, 1340.vi.1.

17. *Dipl.*, 1340.vi.1.

18. *Dipl.*, 1351.viii.3: "Quod in donatione bonorum quam fecit fratri Jacobo Ghini futuro Sindico dicti hospitalis pro dicto hospitali reciperit cum honeribus . . . quod dictum hospitalem teneatur et debeat in cappela beati Iacobi iam constructa per dictum Minum prefatum in loco de Belriguardo prope Senas in perpetuum retinere unum bonum honestum et sufficientem presbiterum ad officiandum pro anima dicti domini Mini Cini. Dicto hospitale debeat annualiter perpetuum dare Nonaginta libras de-

nariorum senis. . . . In super si contingent eum de presenti egritudine animam et spiritum suum reddere domino yhu xpo et de presenti vita migrare in capella dicti hospitalis voluit sepelliri suumque corpus tumulari debere ubi ex nunc elegit sui corporis sepulturam." In contrast to Rome, Borsook, *Mural Painters of Tuscany*, 39, comments that few painted burial niches survive even for Florence before the second half of the Trecento.

19. *Dipl.*, 1402.ii.5.
20. *Dipl.*, 1423.vi.5.
21. *Dipl.*, 1477.v.5. For examples of the use of chapel space for the exhaltation of patrician families and lineages in Quattrocento Florence, see Strocchia, "Burials in Renaissance Florence," 236ff, 260.
22. *Not.*, n. 484. n.p. 1477.ix.25.
23. *Not.*, n. 1145, n.p. 1497.xi.3.
24. *Not.*, n. 800, n.p. 1499.i.16.

Item supradictus Ser Petrus testator voluit et sic ordinavit et fecit de novo unam Cappellam in dicta Cathedrali et Maiori ecclesia, videlicet in eadem Cappella predicta Sancti Jacobi In Tercisi que eius Cappella voluit intitulari et vocari 'La Cappella della Conciptione della Vergine Maria' et sic ipsam ex nunc intitulavit. Cui quidem Cappelle reliquit et legavit unam ipsam possessionem cum domibus super eam cum terris . . . in Massa Camillie populi Sancte Petronille. . . . Cum infrascriptis tamen oneribus . . . videlicet: In primis voluit quod in ipsa Cappella perpetuo sit et esse debeat unus bonus et sufficiens Cappellanus ad servitium ipsius Cappelle Ecclesie et Cori. Qui Cappellanus eligatur et eligi debeat hoc modo, videlicet: Primus Cappellanus eligatur per eundem Testatorem. Et deinde et de cetero alii Cappellani ipsius Cappelle eligantur et eligi debeant per Cristoforum Francisci Danielis eius nepotem et per eius descendentes per lineam Masculinam et legitimam et non aliter nec alio modo. Et extincta dicta Masculina linea dicti Cristophori voluit quod dictus Cappellanus eligatur in dicta Cappella hoc modo, videlicet predicte voces, quarum vocum prima sit Capituli et Collegia Canonicorum predicti Cathedralis Ecclesie. Seconda vox sit in dicta electione et esse debeat Operarii ipsius ecclesie Cathedralis qui pro tempore erit et quod sit perpetuo, fiat et fieri debeat electio ipsius Cappellani. . . . Cum infrascriptis tamen modis oneribus et gravedinibus, videlicet: In primis quod dictus Cappellanus . . . obligatus sit post mortem ipsius testatoris pro quibuslibet ebdomada.

25. Ibid.

Qui quidem Cappellanus sic eligendus ipsius Cappelle teneatur . . . [et] post mortem ipsius testatoris dicere et celebrare in dicta Cathedrali ecclesia pro singulibus ebdomadis tres missas . . . includantur duo dies dominice sive due Domenice. Et dictas missas celebrare teneatur in illis diebus et eo modo et forma et prout erit ordinatum per sacristanos et per tabulam ordinabitur in dicta sacristia. Item quod dictus Cappellanus teneatur et obligatus sit in die octavo festivitatis conceptionis virginis Marie emere et accendi facere suis sumptibus et expensis ad ipsam Cappellam et altare unam libram candelarum cerearum et cantari facere unam missam, videlicet de mane tempestive, videlicet secundam misam que dicitur in dicta ecclesie ad quam intervenerint . . . solum Cappellani dicte ecclesie et cappellani opere videlicet illi qui in dicta die servire teneantur dicte ecclesie.

26. *Not.*, n. 1773, n.p., no. 153, 1529.viii.11.

Item voluit et mandavit quod dictus Cappellanus vel alius eligendus et presentandus durante vita dicti testatoris non teneatur officiare dicte cappelle nec aliquid predictorum facere. Item voluit et mandavit dictus testator quod post mortem supradicti Angeli rectoris ut supra electi dicte cappelle, electio et presentatio ipsius rectoris sive cappellani pro una voce tantum sit et pertineat ad Franciscum Johannis Boschi si vivet tunc temporis, sin autem ad eius filios et defectu filiorum ad nepotem, semper lineam masculinam intelligendo et ultra dictam electionem et presentationem ut supra faciendam. Electio et presentatio dicti rectoris et cappellani pertineat spectet pleno iure ad proximiorem consanguineum ipsius testatoris per lineam masculinam, qua deficiente eadem electio et presentatio pertineat et spectet ad ipsius proximiorem affinem ad quos consangiuneos [sunt]. . . . Electio et presentatio modis et formis predictis pertineat pro duobus vocibus et pro alia voce plebano plebis Sancte agate et pro alia quarta voce comuni et universitati hominum terre Asciani, qui omnes superdicti eligere debeant in Cappellanum ipsius cappelle presbiterum seu clericum proximiorem per lineam masculinam dicti testatoris. Et in defectu dicte linee masculine proximiorem per lineam femminam, et iustaque linea deficiente debeant eligere quempiam presbiterum seu clericum de asciano ad predictam idoneum. Et hoc voluit mandavit perpetuo iure patronatus inviolabiliter observatij.

27. *Not.*, n. 1773, no. 283, 1532.iii.12.

28. *Not.*, n. 2207, no. 178, 1534.ii.5, "Item gravit infrascriptos eius heredes quod in dicta capella fiat una tabula dipinta cum figura virginis marie asunte et ab uno latere sit figura sancti Ludovici et ab alio latere figura sancti Michelangeli et similiter apponantur et depingantur arma domus dicti testatoris in loco consueto cum ornamentis picturis et aura bene fornita in qua expendantur florini centum quinquaginta, cum alio onere quod fiat predella altaris ubi firmantur predictis sacerdotis. . . . Item gravavit dictos eius heredes quod teneantur dealbare dictam cappellam et depinger lavinar[e] et totam capellam deducere depictam et ornatam eo modo et forma prout ad presens est capella famillie de' Bandinellis."

29. On *ius patronatus*, see *Dictionnaire de droit cannonique*, 2:691–706; and Landau, *Ius Patronatus*. See also Gaetano Greco, "I giuspatronati laicali nell'età moderna," 531–72. For Tuscany, Liebowitz, "The Medici and the Sienese Church." 10, 37, claims that the Cathedral of Siena became during the sixteenth century "a stronghold of the local [Sienese] aristocracy." More generally, see Bizzocchi, "Chiesa e aristocrazia nella Firenze del Quattrocento," and "Patronato politico," 95–106.

30. *Not.*, n. 2528, no. 67, 1546.vii.22.

31. *Not.*, n. 2863, Fasc. 1, no. 80, 1552.x.23.

32. *Not.*, n. 2657, no. 183, 1552.iv.30.

33. *Not.post-cos.*, n. 590, no. 17, 7v, 1590.viii.8.

34. On the effects of the Council of Trent in regulating *ius patronatus* and the proliferation of private chapels, see Liebowitz, "The Medici and the Sienese Church," 198, 207–8, 213; and Greco, "I giuspatronati," 558.

35. See Hallman, *Italian Cardinals, Reform, and the Church as Property*, 127.

36. The transformation of church space did not go unnoticed, at least not in Florence. Savonarola, *Prediche Italiane*, III, 1, 391–92 (cited by Friedman, "The Burial Chapel of Filippo Strozzi", 131) was outraged with these forms of familial idolatry: "Guardi per tutti li luoghi de' conventi: tutti gli troverai pieni d'arme di chi gli ha murati. Io alzo el capo là sopra quello uscio; io credo che vi sia un crucifisso ed el v'è una arme; va più là, alza el capo: el v'è un'altra arme. Ogni cosa è piena d'arme. Io mi metto un pazamento; io credo ch'egli sia un crucifisso dipinto; ella è un'arme, e sia che egli hanno poste l'arme dietro a' paramenti, perche quando el prete sta allo altare si vegga bene l'arme da tutto il popolo. Questi sono adunque li idolo vostri, a' quali voi destinate questi vostri sacrifici."

37. These examples do not illustrate completely the exaltation of the mortal life of a particular individual, such as Bernini's tomb of Urban VIII (see Panofsky, "Mors vitae testimonium," 221–37), or the chapel of Filippo Strozzi, where "for the first time the

special functions of a place of burial—the commemoration of the life of the deceased and the celebration of his salvation—are given priority over the expression of the spirit of devotion." (Friedman, "The Burial Chapel of Filippo Strozzi," 109.) Instead "death the guarantor of immortality" here worked through the channels of blood and the survival of heirs.

38. Similarly, Hallman, *Italian Cardinals, Reform, and the Church as Property*, 66, argues that the church property and incomes of Italian cardinals fell steadily into the hands of laymen in 1520–63, despite the reformers.

39. Brown, *The Cult of the Saints*, 24.

40. This was 37 out of 101 testators; the change from the previous period is significant: $p = .3663$, $hp = .2655$, $n = 423$, $z = 4.70$.

41. During the second half of the Quattrocento the proportion of those selecting their graves in testaments increased to 44 percent, 70 of 158 testaments.

42. *Not.*, n. 793, np., 1525.vii.20, for instance, Olivierus olim Johannis, a sharecropper (*laborator terrarum*), elected his sepulcher in the monastery of the Carmelites "in the tomb of his ancestors (*in tumulo suorum anticessorum*)."

43. In the seventeenth century 67 percent (265 of 392) testators specified their places of burial.

44. Braudel and Spooner, "Prices in Europe," 401–7; Wallerstein, *The Modern World-System I*, 67–68.

45. For a discussion of the chronology of the Counter-Reformation and its impact on Sienese society and religious behavior, see chapter 7.

46. Di Simplicio, "Due secoli di produzione agraria," argues that this massive charitable and ecclesiastical corporation not only held its own through the sixteenth and seventeenth centuries but increased its property holdings. If indeed it did, its means must have been ones other than through the attraction of numerous small and middle-sized gifts from ordinary citizens and villagers. The older work of Mengozzi, *Il monte dei Paschi*, 2:244, instead, stresses the decline and financial crisis of della Scala by the early seventeenth century.

47. Bois, *Crise du féodalisme;* Le Roy Ladurie, *Les paysans de Languedoc*, 1:135–85; Goldthwaite, "I prezzi," 5–36.

48. Samuel Cohn, Jr., "The Relationship between City and Countryside."

49. For 1401–25, 16.32 percent of pious bequests went to the poor; in the following quarter the indigent received 15.60 percent of these gifts.

50. On the effects of warfare on the economy of the territory, see Di Simplicio, "Due secoli di produzione agraria," 787–88.

51. These findings differ from those of Brian Pullan for Venice, *Rich and Poor in Renaissance Venice*, 216: "About 1500, a combination of economic, non-economic and intellectual forces highlighted the existing awareness of the problem of poverty."

52. Douglas, *A History of Siena*, 68ff.

53. Hicks, "Sources of Wealth," 9–42; in addition, for the vitality of certain commercial institutions, such as the Mercanzia (merchant court) through the early Quattrocento, see Ascheri, *Siena nel Rinascimento*, 107–35.

54. Siena remained the second city in Tuscany until overtaken by Livorno in the 1670s. Hicks, "Sources of Wealth," 9–42.

55. Mengozzi, *Il monte dei Paschi*, 1:214, 215, 233.

56. Ibid., 1:233. 1:254, "E malgrado tutte queste difficoltà di indole politica, e nonostante l'alto prezzo del denaro, tuttavia le industrie ed i commerci fiorivano insieme con gli studi, e con le arti geniali, e la fibra economica dello stato."

57. Herlihy, *Medieval and Renaissance Pistoia*, 180–92; Herlihy, "The Distribution of

Wealth in a Renaissance Community"; Herlihy and Klapisch-Zuber, *Les Toscans,* 241–300; Romano, "La storia economica dal secolo XIV al Settecento," argues that the old mercantile centers of the Middle Ages, such as Genoa, Lucca, Florence, and Siena, showed "an extraordinary vitality" through the sixteenth century. Particularly between 1560 and 1590 the old Italian cities "knew how to carry themselves to the highest levels in European trade especially in luxury goods and and money." Agricultural sectors may have begun to collapse by 1580, but the industrial and commercial sectors were more resilient and did not begin to falter until the 1620s. Similarly, Cipolla, "Four Centuries of Italian Demographic Development," 572 and 586, sees the 1620s as the beginning of economic decline and argues that from the mid-sixteenth to the mid-nineteenth century "a considerable similarity of structures and tendencies" characterized the various regions of the country." Other historians, however, stress variations across the Italian peninsula between sixteenth-century growth and seventeenth-century decline. For Tuscany, Fanfani, *Indagini sulla "rivoluzione dei prezzi,"* 167, marks the economic turning point around 1590. Similarly, for Del Panta, *Le epidemie nella storia demografica italiana,* 150, the typhoid epidemics of 1591–92 marked the beginnings of the "seventeenth-century crisis" for southern Tuscany. See Phelps-Brown and Hopkins, "Seven Centuries"; Le Roy Ladurie, *Les paysans de Lanquedoc,* 1:135–85; Bois, *Crise du féodalisme;* Hoskins, *The Midland Peasant;* de Vries, *Dutch Rural Economy in the Golden Age;* and more generally, de Vries, *The Economy of Europe in an Age of Crisis;* Wallerstein, *The Modern World-System, I,* and Simiand, *Recherches anciennes et nouvelles.*

58. See, for instance, Le Roy Ladurie, *Les paysans de Lanquedoc,* 1:187–259.

59. On "phase A," see Simiand, *Recherches anciennes et nouvelles,* 88ff; and Vilar, *Or et monnaie dans l'histoire,* 51–53.

60. Pardi, *La popolazione di Siena,* 26.

61. Ibid., 31–32.

62. Ibid., 38.

63. *Statuti senesi scritti in volgare,* 1:397, a *cerbolattaro* was a worker of deer and other animal skins. They were not members of the Arte de'Cuoiai e Calzolai della vacca, but instead were *sottoposti* of the wool guild. *Not.,* n. 1404, 12r, 1508.xi.1.

64. *Not.,* n. 2657, no. 183, 1552.iv.30.

65. *Not.,* n. 2657 no. 206, 1554.viii.14.

66. *Not.,* n. 2657, no. 152, 1551.vii.31. "Cum hoc tamen quod debeat viver[e] vita honesta et bonis moribus ut convenit bono viro, et dicte eius matri obedire et aliquam artem liberalem seu aliquod exercitium exercere, ad eumdem non sit otiosus et lucrosus et se bene gerat erga dictam eius matrem."

67. *Not.,* n. 2684 no. 160, 1554.x.20.

68. *Not.,* n. 3625, fasc. 1, no. 63, 1574.v.11.

Item perch' il detto Oratio in suo nome proprio ha fatto faccendo soto nella buttigna [sic] della spetiaria la quale per le sue mani per molti anni è stata amministrata quanto anchora fuore della Buttiga dichiarò et volse che tutto quello che cosi negotiando si é acquistato s'intendi essere et sia comune infra esso Oratio et li altri suoi figli, et cosi anchora li debiti, et crediti che vi fussero s'intendino essere, et sieno comuni, et del tutto ciascheduno ne decij [sic] participare per la rata sua. Item detto testatore asserisce et afferma che atteso che il detto Oratio ha per molti anni providata la buttiga della spetiaria sopra di se et in compagnia con altri et in detta buttiga, et per li nepotii della casa havendo assai sodisfato et essendosi mediate la sua industria et diligentia assai ampliato il suo patrimonio desiderava il detto oratio suo figlio, et cosi era sua intentione di ricognoscerlo del che non essendosene esso oratio suo figlio contentato mostrando et essendosi media(n)t la sua industria et diligentia assai ampliato il suo patrimonio desiderava che apprezzare più la benevolentia de i fratelli che la robba, et volendo esso testatore in questa parte sequire l'opinione del detto suo figlio confidando che devino li suoi fratelli ricognoscendo in parte sopra ciò si rimette alla discretione loro esortandoli a usarli amorevolezza, si come esso sia usata verso di loro.

69. *Not.*, n. 2684.

Et per fin tanto che pervenglii a detta eta dispone et vuole che a detto oratio li si dia uno idoneo et sufficiente compagno in detta buttiga dela spetiaria a electione et contento di detta sua consorte e delli detti suoi fratelli che sopraviveranno doppo la morte de detto testatore et quando occorrirà doversi eleggere detto compagno la quale buttiga si debba exercitar a benefitio et utilità come di detti suoi figli et in quella tenersi buon conto del administratione detta et delli utili occorrirà acquistarsi farsene alcune ragionevoli elemosine a electione delli governatori et ministri di quella secondo il solito.

70. Ibid., "Item perchè detto testatore sommamente desidera che li detti et infrascripti suoi figli masti si exercitino nella detta arte et exercitio della spetiaria et quello che tal arte exercitasse venendo infra di loro a divisione de beni comuni dispose et volse che di detta buttiga ne sia compiaciuto quello che tali exercitio et arte exercitasse."

71. *Not.*, n. 2265, 4r–6r, 1581.ix.16.

72. *Not. post-cos.*, n. 184, 8v–10r, no. 169, 1594.xi.11, "Et all'incontro affermò il medessimo testatore che il detto Scipione et il presentà gia Giulio prima defuncto finchè visse altri suoi figli, semper si sono affadigati, exercitati. et industriati, e' mediante l'opera loro, e della loro industria si sono fatti molti guadagni et acquisiti senza che mai si siano valsi d'alcuna somma di denari o, habbino dato alcuna spessa o, danno ad esso testator lor padre, di modo che valutando li beni e' faculta che detto testatore di presente disse ritrovarsi, assersi poter valere fino ala somma di scudi tremilia."

73. For instance *Not.*, n. 2863, Fasc. 1, n.p., no. 133, 1555.i.3, Domenico di Silvio, from the patrician family of the Piccolomini, begins his testament, written in his own hand: "Because we now find ourselves in the midst of these extreme afflictions and the greatest dangers against our lives. . . ."

74. For northern and central Italy, see Woolf, *A History of Italy 1700–1860*, 25, who argues that the later years of the sixteenth century saw the increasing pauperization of the peasantry.

75. See Isaacs, "Popoli e monti," 32–80; Marrara, *Riseduti e Nobilità*, 75ff; Mondolfo, *Pandolfo Petrucci*, 1–5.

76. Cohn, *The Laboring Classes*, 45–48.

77. See Kirshner and Molho, "The Dowry Fund and the Marriage Market"; and Cohn, *The Laboring Classes*, 49–51.

78. See Riener, "Women in the Medieval City," 40.

79. See Braudel and Spooner, "Prices in Europe," 378–486; and de Vries, *Dutch Rural Economy*.

80. In contrast, dowry prices soared for the kin of the Roman cardinals, from 1,500 to 3,500 ducats at the beginning of the Cinquecento to 40,000 to 50,000 by 1576, see Hallman, *Italian Cardinals, Reform, and the Church as Property*, 63.

Chapter 7. Property

Epigraph: L'Alessandro, ed. Florindo Cerreta (Siena, 1966), 112.

1. *Not.*, n. 2657, no. 152, 1551.vii.31; n. 3130, 21v–23r, 1563.ii.11; n. 2684, n.p., no. 64, 1551.viii.12.

2. In Ugurieri-Azzolini, *Le Pompe Sanesi*, 2:409ff, the lists of famous legists (*Titolo XVI: Sanesi famosi legisti*) bulge for the late fifteenth and sixteenth centuries, while famous preachers decline in number. For the legal culture of Renaissance Siena, see Nardi, *Mariano Sozzini;* and Elena Fasano Guarini, "I giuristi e lo stato nella Toscana Medicea cinque-seicentesca," in *Firenze e la Toscana dei Medici nell'Europa del '500 e '600* (Florence, 1983), 229–47.

3. *Not.*, n. 435, 2d busta, n.p., no. 23, 1446.ix.8.
4. *Dipl.*, 1487.v.18.
5. *Not.*, n. 1259, Fasc. 1a, n.p., no. 127, 1501.iii.31.
6. *Not.*, n. 2657, no. 153, 1551.viii.1.
7. *Not.*, n. 2657, no. 196, 1553.x.22.
8. Ibid.
9. *Not.*, n. 3368, n.p., n. 128, 1568.v.10.
10. *Not.*, n. 3631, 1r–1v, 1580.iv.13, "Item considerando detta testatrice essere stata già molti mesi ammalata et inferma in letto si come si trova al presente, et havere ricevuto et al presente ricevere da il detto Maestro Alisandro suo marito in detta sua malattia et infirmità molti et infiniti benefitii, et portatosi, et portarsi bene in verso di essa, desiderando in parte ricognoscerlo di tutti benefitti, che essa ha ricevuti, et giornalmente ricevere per ragione di legato et per ogni miglior modo al medessimo Maestro Alissandro suo marito lassò delle sue dote quali asseri essere in la somma di fiorini dugento."
11. *Dipl.*, 1418.ix.21, "Item cum Laurentius filius . . . spureus olim Niccholay olim filij suj dicti testatoris sit pauper et mendicus, dictus testator motus pietate amore et intuitu omnipotentis dey, ut ipse laurentius possit bene agere et se nuctrire et alimentare, reliquid et dari voluit atque iuxit de bonis suis dicti testatoris ipso Laurentio centum florenos auri. . . . Item legavit eidem Laurentio amore dey ut semper usum habitationis in domo sua et sua habitatione dicti testatoris toto tempore vite sue dicti laurentij sine conditione infrascriptorum heredum suorum vel alterius persone."
12. *Not.*, n. 518, n.p., 1450.vii.24.
13. *Dipl.*, 1502.viii.21.
14. *Not.*, n. 1465, n.p., 1519.vii.7.
15. *Not.*, n. 2207, no. 178, 1534.ii.5, "Item legavit quod si in futuri nascetur filius naturalis seu spureus [quod] infrascripti eius heredes teneantur eidem dare alimenta donec vixerit et de eo se servierint in domo vel prout placuerit dicto filio spureo stare. Si habitare noluerit et extra domum Hospitalis, quod eo casu dicti heredes teneantur dare alimenta donec vivat. Et si fuerit femina, eam nutrire et postea ipsam maritare cum dote florenorum centum . . . teneantur."
16. *Not.*, n. 2528, no. 104, 1546.xii.8.
17. *Not.*, n. 2742, no. 17, 1582.ii.27.
18. On the Counter-Reformation's decrees against illegitimacy, see Tamassia, *La famiglia italiana nei secoli decimoquinto e decimosesto*, 223–24.
19. *Not.*, n. 2265, 7v–8v, 1582.iii.6.
20. *Not. post-cos.*, n. 1786, no. 13, 25v–27v, 1643.i.22; n. 2761, no. 15, 35r–37r, 1674.ii.5; n. 3396. no. 82, 72r–74r, 1700.iv.26.
21. Burckhardt, *The Civilization of the Renaissance*, 38: "Closely connected with the political illegitimacy of the dynasties of the fifteenth century was the public indifference to illegitimate birth, which to foreigners—for example, to Comines—appeared so remarkable." (Comines wrote his memoirs toward the end of the fifteenth century.)
22. The earliest mention of a foster child appears in the testament of Ugolinus olim Bonaventure from the parish of San Vincentis, *Dipl.*, 1290.iv.8: "Item donne dignitose alumne cure filij mei .xxx. solidos denariorum."

23. *Not.*, n. 3368, no. 19.
24. *Dipl.*, 1424.vi.17. In the same year, the sister of the previous testator gave the same *allevato* 4 florins, *Dipl.*, 1424.viii.5. In another Quattrocento testament, a lawyer of both canon and civil law, Egregius Vir Magnificus Petrus f. q. Iachetti, claimed Iacobus Johannis Petri as his *figlianum*, whom "he raised from the sacred font," but left him only 10 florins, from which he was supposed to make one cloak, *Dipl.*, 1430.vii.6.
25. See *Not. post-cos.*, n. 3163, 189v–191v; *Not.*, n. 3261, no. 19, 1566.ix.28; n. 3625, no. 63, 1574.v.11; *Not. post-cos.*, n. 2742, no. 18, 1582.ii.27, and no. 19, 1582.iv.27; n. 509, no. 170, 1594.ix.17.
26. *Not.*, n. 2684, Fasc. 1, no. 129, 1553.xi.6. In addition, see n. 2720, no. 100, 1553.ix.14; n. 3368, no. 19, 1566.ix.28; n. 3578, 80r–v, 1577.viii.28; *Not. post-cos.*, n. 509, no. 170. 1594.ix.17.
27. *Not.*, n. 1404, 1509.iii.11.
28. *Not.*, n. 2863, 2d busta, no. 117, 1554.iv.16.
29. *Not.*, n. 3261, no. 8 1566.vii.24.
30. *Not.*, n. 3368, no. 104, 1568.i.23.
31. *Not. post-cos.*, n. 3631, no. 6, 11v–13r, 1581.vi.25.
32. For Christian antiquity, Goody, *The Development of the Family and Marriage in Europe*, argues that the church had successfully outlawed the practice by the early Middle Ages.
33. In addition, see the 1603 testament of the servant Laura, who worked in the household of the priest dominus Fausto. She nominated Sandrina "allevata in casa di decto dominus Fausto" as her universal heir. This case was not tallied in these statistics because Sandrina was not the *allevata* of the testator, but perhaps one of her co-workers. *Not. post-cos.*, n. 532, 20r, 1602.ii.27.
34. *Not. post-cos.*, n. 614, 26v, 1611.iv.
35. *Not. post-cos.*, n. 1284, no. 246, 18r–v, 1632.vi.16.
36. *Not. post-cos.*, n. 2397 no. 59, 63r–64v, 1658.i.10.
37. *Not. post-cos.*, n. 2397, no. 76, 75v–76r.
38. *Not. post-cos.*, n. 3815, no. 168, 15r–16v, 1725.iii.7.
39. *Not. post-cos.*, n. 1284, no. 254, 16r, 1632.iii.30.
40. Family member is here interpreted broadly—that is, whenever the notary specified a kin relation, including in-laws, or when the relationship could be discerned through the patronymics.
41. *Not.*, n. 2220, no. 223, 1543.iii.15, "Et alia filia eius que vocata Armina, eo quod inoneste vixit et iam pro pluri tempore effugit a potestate dicti testatoris presentatis, eam exheradat. Et quatenus exheradatio predicta non valeret de iure et suam formam statutorum, reliquit dicte Armine et eam instituit in solidos quadraginta denariorum, nec amplius de bonis eius voluit habere."
42. *Not.*, n. 2657, no. 143, 1551.ii.20.
43. *Not.*, n. 2657, no. 179, 1551.iii.22.

Item attentis malis moribus et pexima vita Ascanii eius filii et quod pluries causas ipsius graves et inhonestas iniurias fecit et commisit et presertim infrascriptas, videlicet: quia de anno proxime preterito furatus fuit sibi de eius cantina domus castri veteris salmas quatuor vini, et alias iam sunt anni quatuor furatus fuit eius testatoris uxori immanem vinarium quam pignoravit hebreo pro scutis duobus auri. Item quia de anno proxime preterito ut vulgo dicitur contrafecit *le chiavi de la buttiga* dicti testatoris sita senis in loco dicto *el chiasso largo* et de ea in pluribus et diversis vicibus abstulit plures summas sirici et denari. Item quia elapsis diebus accepit in uxorem quandam pauperculam et inhonestam personam contra eius voluntatem. Item quia de anno proxime preterito extra portam ovilis, in loco detto *l'arbolo* cum vellet dictus testator introire in eius domum que erat clausa et ipse nollet nec inde discederet iussu dicti testatoris, prefatus testator, ibidem astante dicto eius filio contra eius voluntatem ne simul cum ipso in dictam domum intraverit, fuit coactus per totam noctem dormire et permanere in quodam cellario. . . . Propterea prefatum Ascanium eius filium nominatim et expresse exheredavit et privavit omni eius substantia et noluit ipsum habere vel participare de bonis et substantiis suis. Et ita reliquit et mandavit infrascripto eius heredi, pro omnia et singula [ut] suprascriptis exequatur et observet.

44. *Not.*, n. 2657, no. 183, 1552.iv.30.

Item prefatus testator, prout ipse asseruit, attento quod mala eius sorte et fortuna accepit in uxorem dominam Lauram filiam Iacobi de Landis que semper male et eo modo quod sibi placuit vixit, et non obstantibus quam pluribus monitionibus sibi factis, quam pluribus et diversis modis ut seduceretur ad bonam et honestam vitam, nihilominus semper male et inhoneste vixit et pluries ab eo recessit, et ipse testator, tum propter eius malam dispositionem, tum etiam quia indignatus cum ea iam sunt menses triginta et ultra corrigere numquam cum ea iacuit nec rem secum habuit, et nichilominus dubitans ne esset gravida, pluries de anno preterito ipsam interrogavit an ita esset, que semper sibi dixit asseruit et affirmavit ac etiam sibi dici fecit per dictam Elisabettam relictam Niccoli de Cerchinis et fratrem Hieronimum giannotti de Pistorio ordinis Sancti Spiritus et per alias personas non fore nec esse gravidam. Et ita dicendo et affirmando de dicto anno recessit ab eo et aufugit de eius domo, et inde ad paucas dies prefatus testator, ut ipse asseruit, audivit dictam eius uxorem peperisse quamdam filiam seu filium, quem vel quam prefatus testator ex dictis Causis pro certo se scire dixit fore et esse quesitum ex adulterio et non ex se filium vel filiam. Et ita iure iurando manu tactis scripturis verum asseruit et affirmavit. Et propterea dictum partum ex dicta eius uxore sive masculum sive feminam voluit et mandavit tamquam talem penitus fore et esse exclusum a successione et bonis ipsius.

45. *Not.*, n. 2657, no. 209, 1554.xi.13.
46. *Not. post-cos.*, n. 184, no. 169, 8v–10r, 1594.xi.11.

Item disse dicto Testatore haver mantenuto e soggiornato per lungo tempo il Reverendo et Eccelente Messer Cosimo altro figlio nelle citta' di Siena e Pisa alli publici studii et ancora in San Gimignano, sotto la disiplina del Reverende et Eccelente Maestro Augustino da Montalcino dell'ordine de Predicatori di San Dominico e tenutolo perveduto di panni, e' libri opportuni oltre al vitto et altre spese, e di poi ancora haverlo condotto al grado del Dottorato e di Sacerdote et haver per ciò fatto le spese opportune et ancora di poi haverli suministrato e giornalmente sumministrarli nuove spese, e' souventioni mentre è trattenuto in Roma (dove di presente disse ritrovarsi) e per causa et occasione delle cose presente, et a servisio [sic] e commodo di detto Messer Cosimo havere speso la somma di scudi duemilia e piu, senza che mai il detto Messer Cosimo habbia dato a' esso testatore suo pardre alcuno minimo utile o guadagno, anzi sempre spesa e danno.

47. *Not. post-cos.*, n. 1164, no. 40, 48r–49r, 1617.xi.7.
48. From 1401 to 1450, 3 bequests from 101 testators; from 1451 to 1500, 3 bequests from 158 testators.
49. *Not.*, n. 2863, Fasc. 1, no. 30, 1551.viii.15.

Et sic de dicta domo totam dictus Anibal habeat ex parte de supra, intrando per portam de parte ante, et ascendendo schalas et eundo de supra in sala et sic totam salam, cum cameris et habitationibus omnibus de supra, excepta camera ad planum ad caput schalarum dictae aulae, in qua dormit prefatus Dominus Hyeronimus. [Et] eundo per cameras et in logiam versus sanctum Agustinum de supra totale, omnes Mansiones de supra et de subter in plano in Reducto habeat ius intrandi et ascendendi per scalam de supra. Et quod in reducto intrando a manu dextra dictus Anibal non habeat ius, a capite versus portam. Sed a pede fiat duo Bracchia latitudinis ubi possit habere introitum ad Cellarium cantinam et stabulum.

50. *Not.*, n. 2863, Fasc. 1, no. 133, 1555.i.3.
51. *Not.*, n. 3163, 50r–52r, 1565.ii.17.
52. *Not.*, n. 3163, 110v, 1568.x.20.
53. *Not.*, n. 3368. no. 104, 1568.i.23.
54. *Not.*, n. 3368, no. 225 1568.xii.26.
55. *Not.*, n. 2684, Fasc. 1, no. 54, 1550.i.12.

Chapter 8. Universal Heirs

Epigraph: Brandano da Petroio was a prophet of Siena at the time of the war with Florence. Cited in Tognetti, "Sul 'Romito' e profeta Brandano da Petroio," 35.

1. *Not.*, n. 2657, no. 194, 1553.vii.3.
2. *Not.*, n. 2657, no. 210, 1554.xi.13.
3. See, for instance, the testament of Scipio f. q. generosi ac Equitis domini Joannisbaptiste de Fantozziis, *Not.*, n. 3124, no. 29, 1562.x.12, "Cum hac tam conditione . . . quod dictus Bartolomeus [the universal heir] non possit dicta bona mobilia vel immobilia cuiuscumque generis dicti Testatoris nec aliquid ipsorum intotum vel pro parte quoquomodo vendere alienare distrahere pignorare nec aliquomodo de eis disponere neque aliquam obligationem facere absque consensu et expressa licentia Domine Virginie filie q. Laurentii de Burghesiis et relicte dicti Domini Joannesbaptiste de fantozziis matris dicti Testatori."
4. *Not.*, n. 3124, no. 3, 1560.viii.6, "Et mandans dicta testatrix quod dicti filii et heredes . . . non possint ratas et partes et pertienes bonorum quas unicuique pertenerit alienare neque vendere nisi hoc modo, videlicet quod unusquisque ipsorum altero fratri suam portionem concedere alienareque possit, ita quod bona predicta non transmictantur extra cippum; et preter eos vero alios transmicti non possint."
5. *Not.*, n. 2684, no. 127, 1553.x.25, "Cum hac declaratione quod quedam tenuta dicti testatoris nuncupata *lantone del Incosto* cum terrenis . . . vendi aut aliter alienari non possit nisi inter ipsos coheredes emere. . . , et casu quo aliquis ipsorum emere recuperet tunc liceat alteri ex prossimioribus uni vel pluribus agniatis et de familia fungariorum ordine successivo et gradatim intelligendo."
6. *Not.*, n. 2684, Fasc. 1, no. 53, 1550.xii.24, "Insupaer volens melius providere dictus testator ut eius bona predicta eius herede non dilapidentur sed magis et melius conserventur, voluit disposuit iussit et mandavit et expresse prohibuit supra dicto Johanni battiste eius filio et herede quod post mortem dicti testatoris non possit fideiussare promittere vel se pro aliqua persona obligare pro aliqua summa que transcendat summam librarum duarum denariorum. . . . Et casu quo contrafaceret voluit incurrere et incurrisse in penam florenorum quinquaginta . . . hospitali sancte Marie de Schala de Senis . . . . Teneatur nubere seu nuptui tradere duas filiarum Sancte Marie de Schala."
7. *Not.*, n. 2684, no. 28, 1547.x.4.
8. See *Not.*, n. 3261, no. 14, 1566.viii.27, and n. 2265, 4r–6r, 1581.ix.16.
9. *Not.*, n. 3368, no. 32, 1567.ii.8, "Item prohibuit infrascriptis suis filijs et heredibus divisionem inter eos . . . donec et quousque Amorattus ultimus filius eiusdem Domini Testatoris compleverit vigesimumquintum annum sue etatis. . . . Idem dictus Testator uetavit et prohibuit dictis suis filijs et heredibus omnem actum alienationis bonorum." Similarly, Domina Laura f. q. Filippi de Nutiis from Bologna but living in Siena, the widow of another Bolognese, named her *nutrito et allevato* "whom she held, treated, reputed, and loved as her own son" as universal heir. Like Count Achille, she prevented

her heir from initiating any act of alienation of her inheritance before he was twenty years old; *Not.*, n. 3368, no. 242, 1569.ii.4.
10. *Not.*, n. 3368, no. 154, 1568.vii.7.

In tutti . . . esser volse suo herede universale Messer Acchile di Gianni Donati si è caso che al tempo della morte d'essa Atalanta havera' moglie donna di paraggio, e non havendola se fra un anno di poichè sara' morta Atalanta la pigliara', e fin tanto che vive dicta madonna Atalanta se ben non havera' moglie sia herede con obligo di osservare il lassito fatto del usufrutto a essa madonna Atalante, la quale non possi in detto usufrutto molestare in alcun modo. E se dictus Messer Acchille al tempo della morte di dicta madonna Atalanta non havera' moglie o' non la pigliera' infra l'anno sussequente come di sopra e' detto, alhora et in tal caso institui' herede o'verso' sustitui . . . suo herede universale Anibale fratello d'esso Messer Acchille similmente se havera' moglie di suo paraggio o' almeno la pigliara' infra un anno finito il tempo dato al detto Messer Acchille. E se il detto Anibale non havera' o' non pigliera' moglie come di sopra all'hora et in tal caso institui. . . . Asdnibale suo fratello nel medesimo modo esatto la medesima conditione cioe'. . . . E se Messer Acchille pigliera' moglie come di sopra e di poi la si morisse sensa figli e infra un anno non pigliasse altra moglie di suo paraggio alhora sustitui Anibale. . . . E similmente se Anibale havesse moglie e si morisse sensa figli . . . sustitui Asdnibale nel medessimo modo, e se tutti li supradetti Messer Acchille Anibale e Asdnibale morisseno sensa figli legittimi e naturali sustitui. . . . l'uno al altro ordine successivo come di sopra. E se tutti e tre non pigliassero moglie e non osservassono come di sopra, o' osservando e tutti poi morisseno sensa figli legittimi e naturali, Alhora e in ogniuno di detti casi institui e sustitui vulgarmente e per fideicommissum e in ogni miglior modo Marcello di Niccolo Donati con il medessimo obligo e con la medesima conditione se havera' moglie di suo paraggio. . . . Al'hora et in ogniuno di detti casi sustitui . . . le povere o'vero mantellate del Monistero del Paradiso nel Poggio Malavolti obligate a' pregare per l'anima sua.

11. *Not. post-cos.*, n. 184, no. 175, 15r–16r. 1595.iii.31.
12. *Not.*, n. 3368, no. 19, 1566.ix.28.
13. *Not.*, n. 2220, no. 227 (bis), 1543.iv.3.
14. She first nominated her sons yet to be born (*nascituros*) from her husband Hannibale as the heirs. If these unborn sons should die before giving birth to sons, then "her most delectable" mother would succeed; after the death of her mother, the estate should pass to Antonius Geronomi de Monaldis, her uncle on her mother's side. *Not.*, n. 2657, no. 34, 1547.vii.17.
15. *Not.*, n. 2684, no. 1, 1545.ii.23.
16. *Not.*, n. 2657, no. 190, 1553.vii.16.
17. *Not.*, n. 2657, no. 54, 1548.iii.22.

Et caso che detto Thommasso morisse vivente detto Testatore o in qualunche tempo senza figlioli legiptimi et naturali alhora substitui a esso li infrascripti in questo modo, cioè, Giovanni di Mariano Cerchii suo fratello carnale già exercitante l'arte del righittiere et li suoi figlioli legiptimi et naturali et nepoti nati et da nascere maschi nel podere solo chiamato argiano posto fra le masse di Siena. . . . Et caso che esso Giovanni et suoi figli maschi morisseno senza figli maschi . . . substitui Mariano et Marcantogno righittieri suoi nepoti et figlioli gia' di Achille fratello carnale di esso testatore defuncto per equale portione et li loro figlioli nati et da nascere legittimi et naturali maschi et nepoti in stirpe. Et in caso che detto Poder pervenisse a Mariano e Marcantogno o loro figlioli o nepoti volse et cosi ordinò che mai detto Podere si possi alienare donare obligare vendere ne' impegnare per detti substituti se non in fameglia de cerchii acciò detto podere sempre rimanghi in casa et nela fameglia de Cerchii. Et caso che alcuno di loro volesse alienare in caso che possedesseno sempre sia obligato a darlo a uno de cerchii per prezzo da estimarsi per homini comuni et in caso di discordia per il terzo da eleggersi per li signori offitiali de la mercantia de la citta' di Siena. Et questo si fa per la affectione che detto testatore porta al detto podere et acciò detto podere semper rimanghi nela fameglia de cerchii.

Item substitui Mariano et Marcantogno suoi nepoti sopradetti . . . per equale portione et li loro figlioli legiptimi . . . et da nascere maschi et nepoti per ordine successive in stirpe . . . in detti modi nel podere chiamato el galinaio . . . nela corte di monteriggioni. . . . Et caso che accadesse che il detto podere del gallinaio si ricomprasse per li figli et heredi di Cristofano Santi o che per detto Girolamo testator o per detto Thommasso si vendesse in tal caso declara vuole dispose che il prezzo se ne trarra s'habbi a reinvestire tutto a beneplacito di detto Thommasso, et reinvestendosi . . . in beni stabili . . . cosi tali beni reinvestiti non si possino alienare donare obligare vendere ne' impegnare si non infra essi dela casa de cerchii. . . . Et caso che detti Mariano et Marcantogno et loro figli maschi et nepoti morisseno senza figli . . . substitui el prenominato Giovanni et suoi figli maschi . . . per ordine successive in stirpe. Et cosi esso Thommasso possi usare tenere e godere li detti poderi e bestiami nel modo gli piacerà e come esso testatore in potere tagliare arbori piantar vigne et fare come gli parrà et nel modo si trovaranno ala morte di esso Thommasso si habbino da acceptare da essi substituti ne si possi ricercare se stieno bene o male.

18. *Not.,* n. 2863, Fasc. 1, no. 14, 1551.iv.13.
19. *Not.,* n. 2684, no. 152, 1554.iv.23.
20. According to Goldthwaite, "The Medici Bank," 9, primogeniture and the tying of property through the male line did not become customary in Florence until the late sixteenth century.
21. *Not.,* n. 2684, no. 152, 1554.iv.23, "Cum expressa provisione quod transiret de primogenito in primumgenitum." This codicil moves back and forth from Italian to Latin. *Not.,* n. 3124, no. 45, 1562.xii.3, "Gravavit et ordinavit pro ut infra vulgari sermone videlicet: che detto Alexandro suo herede . . . sia obligato . . . al detto fra Giovanni et a me notario . . . per li detti primogeniti delli quali in detto testamento si dice comprare un altra cosa stabile equivalente et della medesima valuta che era detta casa di salicotto la quale in luogo di detta casa sia del primogenito del detto Alexandro et di poi di primogenito in primogenito come in detto testamento della detta casa."
22. *Not.,* n. 3130, no. 7, 10v–12r, 1562.ii.2, "Et si omnes decederent sine descendentibus leggittimis, tunc et eo casu substituit vulgariter pupillanter et per fideicommissum proximiorem de agnatione et cippo dicti Testatoris qui sit masculini generis, adeo que femine etiam agnationis non sint vocate et nullo modo possint succedere quia testator intendit de proximiore masculo."
23. *Not.,* n. 3368, no. 19, 1566.ix.28, "E morendi tutti sensa figli masti . . . sustitui vulgarmente et per fideicommissum et in ogni miglior modo quel mastio del ceppo che sara' in quel tempo il più prossimo vivente, e similmente se morisseno con figli masti legittimi et naturali e di poi essi e loro descendenti mancasseno substitui . . . il più prossimo mastio del Ceppo che sara' in quel tempo. E cosi de licentia a' tutti li sopra nominati instituti et substituti ordine successivo."
24. *Not.,* n. 3368, no. 19, 1566.ix.28.
25. *Not.,* n. 3368, no. 32, 1567.ii.8; for similar cases, see the testament of the "Noble and Honorable" Camilla f. q. Thomasi de Burgensibus, widow of Hieronomus Carli de Saracenis, *Not.,* n. 3368, no. 104, 1568.i.23; and that of the keysmith Magister Prosperus Bartolommeo from Pienza, who resided in Siena, *Not.,* n. 2265, 1r–2v.
26. *Not. post-cos.,* n. 509, no. 33, 16v–18r, 1594.x.26.
27. See Seragnoli, *Il Teatro a Siena nel Cinquecento.*

28. *L'Alessandro,* ed. Cerreta, 138.
29. Witness Leon Battista Alberti's *Libri della famiglia* in *Opere volgari*, I, ed. Cecil Grayson (Bari, 1960).
30. *La Raffaella ovver La Creanza delle Donne,* ed. Carlo Teoli (Milan, 1862).
31. For Florence, see Goldthwaite, *Private Wealth in Renaissance Florence,* 266–75; and "The Medici Bank," 9; and more generally, Quazza, *La decadenza italiana nella storia europea;* for the refeudalization of sixteenth-century Tuscany in the juridical and administrative sense, see Pansini, "Per una storia del feudalesimo nel Granducato di Toscana durante il periodo mediceo"; Elena Fasano Guarini, *Lo Stato mediceo di Cosimo I* (Florence, 1973); and Litchfield, *Emergence of a Bureaucracy.*
32. See Douglas, *A History of Siena,* 200–14; and Mondolfo, *Pandolfo Petrucci.*
33. Conenna, *Prata,* 8–9; see Mengozzi, *Il monte dei Paschi,* 1:256; the Balià (or ruling council) in 1507 and 1511 corroborated earlier legislation (2 November 1466) restricting the church's power to inherit real property.
34. Conenna, *Prata,* 10.
35. Mondolfo, *Pandolfo Petrucci,* 68.
36. On the Piccolomini family's control over the cathedral of Siena during the sixteenth century, see Liebowitz, "The Medici and the Sienese Church," 107–8; and Hay, *The Church in Italy in the FifteenthCentury,* 19.
37. Pecci, *Memorie Storico-critiche della città di Siena,* 21–22.
38. Ibid., 52–56.
39. Malavolti, *Dell'Historia di Siena,* pt. 3, 129r. According to Liberati, "Chiese, monasteri, oratori e spedali senesi," the nunnery was demolished in 1526.
40. Mengozzi, *Il monte dei Paschi,* 1:256.
41. Prodi, *Il Cardinale Gabriele Paleotti,* 2:323–24, 353.

Chapter 9. The Counter-Reformation

Epigraph: P. Venturi, *Vita della Venerabile Madre Passitea Crogi di Siena,* Biblioteca Comunale di Siena, MSS. K. VII, 43–49, 96r. Crogi founded the new Counter-Reformation monastery of the Cappuccin Mothers in Siena.

1. See Mengozzi, *Il monte dei Paschi,* 2:65, 69, 76, 78, 183; Rodolico, *Stato e chiesa in Toscana durante la Reggenza lorenese,* 68–69, from an analysis of the rates from *gabelles,* dates the secular decline of the economy of Tuscany to 1588. In addition, see chapter 6, note 57.
2. By multiple regression, the change from 1576–1600 to 1601–25 was highly significant (.0027): Beta = .2155, $T = 3.044$. With only 194 cases for this fifty-year period, R square = .12, $F = 4.26$ (which is highly significant). The independent variables for this model were sex, residence, health, wealth, occupation, and period. The only other significant variable was wealth, Beta = .2006, $T = 2.823$.
3. On the impoverished conditions of monasteries in the sixteenth and seventeenth centuries, see Catoni, "Interni di conventi senesi del Cinquecento"; Mengozzi, *Il monte dei Paschi,* 4:65; and E. Lazzareschi, "Una mistica senese," pt. 1, 425 and pt. 2, 15; according to the records of the papal visitations of 1575, those in monasteries were "abandoned indiscretely to misery and famine."
4. For instance, the painter Augustinus q. Anselmi de Carosis desired to be buried in the cathedral of Siena in the vaults of the congregation of San Pietro "Princeps Apostolorum." The total expenses for his burial and funeral were 12 scudi, which presumably included various sums for wax, candles, and possibly torches as well as the payment to his

confraternity of the Divi Antonii de Senis for their attendance and service in parading his litter to the Duomo. *Not. post-cos.,* n. 1122 no. 72, 13r–14v, 1627.iii.6.

5. See for instance the membership rolls for the confraternity of Santa Trinità, the Biblioteca Comunale, A.I.24 and A.II.1.

6. For evidence of these new societies, see the visitations of Tarugi, ASS, *Visite,* n. 23.

7. *Not. post-cos.,* n. 1164, no. 24, 29r–30r, 1610.x.4.

8. On the differences between these new congregations and the old convents and monasteries, see Pullan, "The Old Catholicism, the New Catholicism," 18ff. The earliest evidence regarding houses for the correction and worship of converted prostitutes (*convertite*) stretches back to 1338: Gigli, *Diario Sanese,* 2:35. Yet not a single bequest to this organization is found in our samples of over nearly 10,000 bequests until the 1580s. On the *convertite* more generally in Tuscany, see Cohen, "The Convertite and the Malmaritate." The *derelitte* were the second oldest of these groups, founded in 1554: see Gigli, *Diario Sanese,* 1:152, and Liberati, "Chiese, monasteri, oratori e spedali senesi." According to Liberati, "Chiese monasteri, oratori e spedali senesi," 11, (1940): 68, the *abbandonate* congregation was founded in 1580.

9. *Not.,* n. 3597, no. 21, 23r–24r, 1572.X.30.

10. *Not.,* n. 3631, no. 4, 5r–10v, 1580.ix.7.

11. *Not. post-cos.,* n. 509, no. 24, 11r–v, 1591.xi.28.

12. *Not. post-cos.,* n. 1284, no. 235, IV (bis). 1630.vii.5.

13. *Not. post-cos.,* n. 184, no. 170, 1594.ix.17.

14. *Not. post-cos.,* n. 2397, no. 59, 63r–64v, 1658.i.10. For the open and free-ranging character of these congregations during their initial years of operation, see Lazzareschi, "Una mistica senese," pt. 2, 13.

15. *Not.,* n. 3163, 189v–191v, 1572.x.1.

16. *Not.,* n. 3631, no. 14, 26v–29v, 1583.ix.12.

17. During the third quarter of the sixteenth century masses had descended to less than one-third of the pious donations. In the years following the visitations, the percentage climbed to 45 percent of the total; then, through the seventeenth and early eighteenth century, the clear majority of pious gifts demanded a return in terms of obligations on the part of the recipients to say masses for the souls of the dead. During the eighteenth century, the percentages fluctuated between two-thirds and three-fourths of all pious gifts.

18. In the third quarter of the Cinquecento, only 13 percent of testators requested perpetual masses; in the last quarter, the percentages more than doubled to 30 percent; then, in the first twenty-five years of the seventeenth century, they doubled again, reaching 71 percent of all these sacramental demands, before they leveled off.

19. See, for instance, *Not. post-cos.,* n. 184, no. 175, 15r–16r, 1595.iii.31; and no. 177, 17r, 1595.iv.27.

20. *Not. post-cos.,* n. 532, 66r–67r, 1612.i.29.

21. *Not. post-cos.,* n. 423, no. 137, 11r, 1607.vi.20; see also n. 614, 16v–20r, 1601.vi.7. *Not. post-cos.,* n. 1164, no. 48, 61v, 1610.xi.1.

22. *Not. post-cos.,* n. 1164, no. 24, 29r–30r, 1610.x.4; see, also, n. 2397, no. 72, 72v–73v, 1661.ix.13.

23. *Not. post-cos.,* n. 1051, no. 45, 59r–v, 1609.iii.11.

24. *Not. post-cos.,* n. 1051, no. 49, 62v–63v, 1610.xii.14.

25. *Not. post-cos.,* n. 1051, no. 50, 63v–64v, 1610.xii.20.

26. *Not. post-cos.,* n. 1568, no. 14, 18r–19v, 1633.xii.27. In addition, see, no. 50, 77r–78v, 1642.ix.21; n. 2397, no. 59, 63r–64v, 1658.i.10; n. 2466, no. 179, 18r–20r, 1660.iv.30.

27. *Not. post-cos.,* n. 423, no. 137, 11r, 1607.vi.20.

28. *Not. post-cos.*, n. 614, 24v–26v, 1606.vii.24; in addition, see n. 1122, no. 78, 21r–22v, 1627.vii.26; and n. 2479, no. 5, 7v–9r, 1664.x.4.
29. *Not.*, n. 3631, no. 14, 26v–29v, 1583.ix.12.
30. *Not. post-cos.*, n. 184, no. 168, 7r–8r, 1594.xi.5.
31. *Not. post-cos.*, n. 532, 14v, 1602.i.11; see also n. 1164, no. 20, 26r, 1610.iv.23; n. 1164, no. 38, 1617.iii.15, 46v.
32. On the "forty hours," see Gigli, *Diario Sanese*, 1:464; and Lazzareschi, "Una mistica senese," pt. 1, 422–23. The devotion originated in Milan and was instituted in Siena in 1567. According to Chabod, *Per la storia religiosa dello Stato di Milano*, 264, this liturgical practice originated as early as 1527. *Not. post-cos.*, n. 423, no. 138, 12r, 1607.vii.20; see, also, n. 1786, no. 11, 23r, 1642.ix.10.
33. See Franchina, "La chiesa della Madonna di Provenzano," 71–82.
34. *Not. post-cos.*, n. 423, no. 141, 15r, 1608.ix.2.
35. *Not. post-cos.*, n. 1164, no. 38, 46v, 1617.iii.15; and no. 44, 52r, 1619.ix.29.
36. On the cult of Mary in the Counter-Reformation, see Petrocchi, "La devozione alla Vergine," 281–87.
37. *Not. post-cos.*, n. 1122, no. 87, 33r–, 1628.ix.13.
38. *Not. post-cos.*, n. 2397, no. 50, 58r–v, 1653.vi.22.
39. *Not. post-cos.*, n. 1786, no. 11, 23r, 1642.ix.10.
40. *Not. post-cos.*, n. 1568, no. 24, 24r–39r, 1636.v.17.
41. *Not.*, n. 3631, no. 14, 26v–29v, 1583.ix.12.
42. *Not. post-cos.*, n. 423, no. 138, 12r-, 1607.vii.20.
43. See *Not. post-cos.*, n. 184, no. 178, 17v, 1595.v.7.
44. *Not. post-cos.*, n. 184, no. 170, 1594.ix.17.
45. *Not. post-cos.*, n. 1122, no. 76, 17v–19v, 1627.v.31.
46. *Not. post-cos.*, n. 1568. no. 14, 18r–19v, 1633.xii.27.
47. *Not. post-cos.*, n. 1568, no. 24, 34r–39r, 1636.v.17.
48. *Not. post-cos.*, n. 1762, no. 35, 69r–70v, 1641.vii.17.
49. *Not. post-cos.*, n. 2242, no. 28, 29v–35r, 1650.iii.27.
50. This formula becomes common by the beginning of the seventeenth century.

Sano per la Dio gratia di corpo, mente et intellecto, considerando, come disse, alla certezza della morte, et all'incertezza dell'ora di quella, volendo come a' huomo prudente, e descreto conviene, disporre per il presente nuncupativo testamento delle cose sue, e beni, et allo stato di quelli provedere, acciò libero da ogni pensiero et affetto terreno, e vanno, possa meglio nel punta della sua morte pensare alla salute dell'anima sua, di essi dispose, testò, et ordinò, nella forma, e modo, che seque, cioè, e per cominciar dalle cose più degne: Prima l'anima sua redenta con il pretiosissimo Sangue dell'Immaculato Agnello lassò al suo Creatore, et pregò con ogni humilità di cuore la Beatissima sempre Vergine sua Madre, e de Peccatori universale Avvocata, che si degni interceder per lui il desiderato perdono delli proprii errori, e che al tempo della sua morte voglia esserli in aiuto, e liberarla dall'insidie del comune Inimico, acciò avventurosamente venghi adcollocata fra il numero degl'eletti et darli luogo di salute.

See, for instance, *Not. post-cos.*, n. 1051, no. 57, 68v–69r, 1613.xi.8.
51. *Not. post-cos.*, n. 423, no. 131, 2v–3r, 1604.iv.18.
52. *Not. post-cos.*, n. 1568, no. 17, 21v–23r, 1634.x.31.
53. *Not. post-cos.*, n. 2242, no. 28, 29v–35r, 1650.iii.27.
54. From 1311 to 1455, the following saints appear in testators' invocations: Peter (twice), Paul, Dominick, Francis (twice), Andrew, Bernardino, Benedict, Leonard. The names of saints from the sixteenth century are Catherine, the Archangel Michael, Albert, Francis, and Lawrence.

55. *Not.*, n. 2863, 2d busta, no. 30. 1551.viii.15; n. 2265, 11r–12v, 1583.ix.13. *Dipl.*, 1454.iii.12.
56. *Not.*, n. 770, 2d busta, 1526.ix.29.
57. The frequency of saints over this half-century is as follows: Catherine of Siena (11), Bernardino (6), Francis (5), Joseph (4), Stephen (3) (in each case, the testator was a member of the Company of Santo Stefano), San Giovanbaptista (3), San Lorenzo (2), San Giosetto, San Niccolò, Santa Lucia, Sant'Andrea, San Domenico, San Rocco, Sant'Antonio da Padua, Santa Mattia, San Sebastiano, Santa Maria Magdallena, Sant'Orsola, Santa Brigetta (1 each), and one is illegible. In addition, several testators invoke their guardian angels, but did not name them.
58. The commune first invoked the Virgin as its special protectress on the eve of the battle of Montaperti (1260); see Bowsky, *A Medieval Italian Commune*, 274–75. She does not, however, figure explicitly in that capacity in the wills until the end of the Cinquecento.
59. *Not. post-cos.*, n. 1164, no. 36, 41r, 1616.iv.14.
60. Silverman, "Rituals of Inequality," 177–79; and "The Uses of History in Anthropology," 423–25; and Heywood. *Palio and Ponte* (London, 1904), 199, "In his [Cosimo I] policy of amusing the populace with spectacles and games, he found a convenient instrument in the *contrade,* which, in Siena, played very much the same part as the *Signorie* or *Potenze festeggianti* filled in Florence; and as, one by one, their old institutions were abolished, the passionate patriotism of the Sienese, deprived of every other outlet, narrowed and intensified into a spirit of parochial partisanship, which, even today, retains much of its ancient fervor."
61. For a discussion of the importance of parochial networks in the Counter-Reformation and their conflict with earlier republican, citywide social linkages, see Weissman, *Ritual Brotherhood in Renaissance Florence*.
62. *Not. post-cos.*, n. 1164, no. 31, 35v–, 1613.vii.17; n. 423, no. 134, 6r–, 1605.iv.4.
63. See Balestracci and Piccinni, *Siena nel Trecento*, 42 and 45.
64. *Not. post-cos.*, n. 1786, no. 19, 37r–38r, 1645.v.3.
65. *Not. post-cos.*, n. 2242, no. 29, 35r–36r, 1650.vi.17.
66. The first appearance of the circulation of art works to nonpious benefactors actually antedates the period of Counter-Reform culture. In 1548, the nobleman Giulius f. q. Ambruoghi de Britiis, in his first itemized bequest, gave to his niece a bed, linen, and several pieces of furniture including a painting (*unum quadrum*) "picturing the image of the divine virgin." *Not.*, n. 2657, no. 17, 1547.i.13.
67. *Not. post-cos.*, n. 1568, no. 15, 19v–21r, 1634.viii.24; n. 2319, no. 112, 4r–7v, 1661.v.11.
68. *Not. post-cos.*, n. 2397, no. 70, 72r–v, 1660.x.5.
69. *Not.*, n. 3648, 12r–14r, 1583.ix.5.
70. *Not.*, n. 2742, no. 19, 1582.iv.27, "Cominciando dalle cose di maggiore, ed più importanza, lassa et raccomanda l'anima sua a Dio omnipotente pregandolo con tutto il cuore che si degni in questa vita presente tenerla nella sua santissima gratia et da poi nella altra vita la ricetta, non per li meriti di essa, ma solo per sua infinita misericordia nel santissimo paradiso a godere con i beati insieme la sua divina essenza et parimente prega la santissima et immaculata vergine Maria e tutta la corte del Cielo che intercedino la detta gratia appresso la santissima Trinità Padre, figliuolo, et Spirito Santo Trino, et uno, hora e sempre."
71. *Not. post-cos.*, n. 532, no. 14, 1602.i.11, "In prima cominciando delle cose più nobili e lassò . . . e raccomandò alla di lei fattore e redentore pregandolo con quel maggiore affetto di quore che puo che per l'infinita misericordia sua si compiaccia perdonarli i peccati suoi, e che quando li piacerà che l'anima sua si separi dal corpo per li meriti della sua santissima passione e della sua sempre gloriosissima Vergine maria voglia collocarla

fra i beati spiriti, supplicando la madre gloriosissima di Giesù cristo che voglia la medissima ricevere nelle sue santissime mani et la medissima presentarla con il suo patricino all'omnipotente Tribunale della santissima Trinità, e dal medissimo impetrare la Santa Benedittione."

72. Norberg, *Rich and Poor,* 124, has found that the conventions of a particular notary in determining the character of a testator's will were an "insignificant variable."

73. For heresies, see Marchetti, *Gruppi ereticali senesi del Cinquecento;* Seragnoli. *Il Teatro a Siena nel Cinquecento,* 74ff; Liebowitz, "The Medici and the Sienese Church"; Cantimori, *Prospettive di storia ereticale italiana del Cinquecento.* For Lucca, see Berengo, *Nobili e mercanti nella Lucca del Cinquecento,* 435, 453.

74. This phrase first appears in the 1595 testament of the *honesta mulier* Joanna, the widow of Vittorius, an ironmonger *(fabri ferrarij)* from Ilcinea. Her modest testament specified only two itemized bequests: a repayment of a debt and 7 lire to her brother. Her universal heir was a canon of Elci, whom she burdened with the demands "to take care of her in her needs and to carry out her funeral." *Not. post-cos.,* n. 102, 9r–10r, 1594.ii.22.

75. *Not. post-cos.,* n. 509, no. 31, 16v–17r, 1594.vii.6.

76. *Not.,* n. 2265, 4r–6r, 1581.ix.16.

77. *Not. post-cos..* n. 509, no. 16. 7r–v, 1590.vi.1.

Item. havendo longamente considerato a quattro principali cose alle quali è, obligato, ciascuno huomo Christiano per la dispositione de la sua ultima volùntà delle quali la prima è il riconoscere a beni havuti et che li posseggano da Dio dat(o)re di tutti li beni, la seconda consequentemente rendere a lui gratie con ogni humilità compartergli et lasciargli per amor di sua Divina Maesta, a' fameglie honeste o luoghi poveri et bisognosi, li quali con tanta caldezza et cosi spesso da Christo Signore nostro nel vangelo ci sono raccomandati, la terza conforme a quanto comanda di una santa gratitudine christiana haver riguardo a dette famiglie e luoghi bisognosi et sceglirne quella o quello a cui più li deve per servigii ricevutine, la quarta et ultima il vedersi solo et senza successione comparenti solamente dal lato di Madre, et assai commodi et Ricchi, Havendo dico havute tutte queste considerationi guidicando questa resolutione sua essere importantissima alla salute dell'anima sua la quale deve ante forme ad ogni respetto. Acciòche il Signor Dio ne habbia misericordia et con quest'opera tale quale è fatta a fine di charità et per amor di Sua Divina Maestà si degni scancellare i suoi peccati ha risoluto disporre delle cose sue et farne herede una famiglia honorata et gia' commoda dalla quale in altri tempi ha' ricevuto aiuto et varii accommodamenti. Ma hora per la qualità delle cose del Mondo che mai stanno ferme redotta in grave bisogna.

78. For instance, Agnolo di Tura del Grasso in *Cronache Senesi,* 342, describes the 1314 funeral of the "savio e valentissimo omo e gran filosafo" El cardinale Ricciardo de' Petroni da Siena; 504, that of Messer Piero di Messer Curado de la Branca da Gobio (Gubbio) in 1331; 526, that of Messer Simone de' Gratiani del Borgo, Capitano del Popolo in 1341; 554, of Misser Luigi di Messer Fatio Gallerani de' nobili di Siena in 1347; and, 352, finally of the famous Messer Guido Riccio da Foligno, Capitano di Guerre in 1352. In the chronicles of Donato di Neri and his son Neri, and the continuation of Paolo di Tommaso Montauri, the lists of state expenditures on the public funerals of important statesmen of Siena increase greatly in number.

79. For the history of the elaborate funerals of military heroes, poets, and patrician magnates in late medieval and Renaissance Florence, see Strocchia, "Burials in Renaissance Florence."

80. Evidence from other sources suggests that funerals before the large-scale stately affairs arranged in late sixteenth-century testaments may have been more elaborate than

the silences in wills suggest. Zdekauer. *La vita privata*, 68–69. and appendix VII, has uncovered the funeral expenses arranged by the widow Madonna Becha f. del fu Diotaiuti for her husband in 1294. The funeral pomp included various expenses for curtains, cushions, double candles, official mourners, and a horse to transport the coffin. The funeral was followed by a large feast for relatives and strangers in which the minor friars consumed a hundred loaves of bread and a barrel of wine; moreover, the delicacy, eel, was served. The statutes of several guilds required their members to participate in the funeral processions of their colleagues. The druggists required the members of the guild to assemble for the funeral of any *sottoposto* of the guild or any father, mother, wife, or child of that subject-member (*Statuti volgarsi senesi*, 11). When a master locksmith or his father, mother, wife, children, brothers, or sisters died, the guild required all the masters and the rectors of the guild to congregate at the house of the deceased, go to the parish church, and stay there until the office for the dead had been recited (*Statuto dell'arte de'chiavari di Siena, 1323–1402*, in *Statuti senesi scritti in volgare*, 2:256). The guild of tanners and cobblers added to their 1329 statutes that the guild could demand only those subject to the guild to attend the funerals of its members and their families (*Statuto dell'università dell'arte de' Cuoiai e Calzolai . . . Siena 1329–1335*, in *Statuti senesi scritti in volgare*, 2:320.) The butchers commanded only their *sottoposti* to join the rector and treasurer of the guild to assemble at the grave of their dead members (*Statuto dell'università ed arte dei carnajuoli . . . Siena, 1288–1361*, in *Statuti senesi scritti in volgare*, 2:95). The notaries and judges were required to assemble at the homes of any dead members from the city and suburbs of Siena whenever any member requested their presence (*Statuti dei giudici e notai*, ibid., rubr. XXXI). On the other hand, the wool guild made no funerary demands on either its members or underlings (*Statuto dell'università ed arte della lana di Siena. 1298–1309* in ibid.). Finally, sumptuary legislation reaching back to the 1262 Constitution of Siena limited the mourning customs and funeral expenses from the number and weights of double candles, the mourning clothes of widows, the family members who might gather at the grave to those who could attend "the lunch of the dead," and the maximum allocation for its menu. See Zdekauer, *La vita privata*, 67–71; Liberati, "Un funerale a Siena nel XV secolo"; (the anonymous) "Il Pranzo de' morti," in *Miscellanea storica senese* 2 (1895): 28–29; and "Funerali," 185–86; Mazzi, "Alcuni leggi sumtuarie senesi del secolo XIII"; Hughes, "Sumptuary Laws and Social Relations in Renaissance Italy."

81. Before 1501, these amounts were stated in only seventy-five testaments (10 percent of the cases). *Dipl.*, 1305.vi.19; and *Dipl.*, 1330.iv.30.

82. *Not.*, n. 23, 1348.v.9.

83. *Not.*, n. 2528, Fasc. I, no. 78, 1546.ix.15. "Et quando de hac vita migrari contigerit si senis fuerit mandavit corpus suum sepelliri in ecclesia Sancti augustini in tumulo suorum antenatorum cum illis ceremoniis ac funeralium sumptibus prout videbitur infrascriptis suis heredibus respective"; for similar phrases, see n.p. 1553.x.22; n. 2684, no. 154, 1554.ix.29; n. 3124, no. 3, 1560.viii.6; n. 3163, 110v–, 1568.x.20; n. 2265, 1r–2v, 1579.iv.28; 3r–4r, 1579.iv.6.

84. *Not.*, n. 2684, no. 152, 1554.iv.23; for other testaments that left the expenses and decisions of "pomp and ceremony" in funeral to the "convenience" of the place, see no. 155, 1554.ix.19; n. 3163, 25r–v, 1563.vii.11; and 27r–28r, 1563.x.10.

85. *Not.*, n. 3368, no. 225, 1568.xii.26.

86. *Not.*, n. 2657, no. 209, 1554.xi.13; and n. 3163, 85r–v, 1567.ii.1. See *Not.*, n. 3163, 189v–191v, 1572.x.1.

87. *Not. post-cos.*, n. 1051, no. 57, 68v–69r, 1613.xi.8.

88. *Not.*, n. no. 10, 19v–21v, 1583.ii.11.

89. *Not.*, n. 2742, no. 15, 1581.x.6.

90. *Not.*, n. 2742, no. 17, 1582.ii.27.
91. *Not. post-cos.*, n. 184, no. 179, 19r, 1595.vi.4.
92. *Not. post-cos.*, n. 1164, no. 24, 29r–30r, 1610.x.4; for similar funerary arrangements, see the Piccolomini will, n. 1164, no. 31, 35v–, 1613.vii.17; and the testament from a widow whose father was a cobbler and whose present husband was a pork dealer, no. 35, 40r–41v, 1614.iii.7.
93. *Not. post-cos.*, n. 1164, no. 38, 46v–47v, 1616.iii.15.
94. *Not. post-cos.*, n. 1164, no. 54, 63v–64r., 1625.vii.19; and n. 2242, no. 31, 37v–40r, 1650.viii.20.
95. The term is Vovelle's, *Piété baroque*, 183.

Chapter 10. The Differentiated Consequences of Trent

Epigraph: Venturi, *Vita*, Biblioteca Comunale, MSS. K. VII, 48–50.

1. These findings conflict with recent literature on the Counter-Reformation. Authors such as Bossy, "The Counter-Reformation and the People of Catholic Europe," 68; and Wright, *The Counter Reformation*, have stressed the failure of Trent. According to Wright, 271, the triumphs of Trent "were on paper alone." Also see Liebowitz, "The Medici and the Sienese Church."
2. Daniel-Rops, *The Catholic Reformation*, 1–4, argues most vehemently for a "Christian Renaissance" whose "origins and initial achievements were much anterior to the fame of Wittenberg." Others, less adamant than Daniel-Rops, have pointed to the earlier spirit of sixteenth-century reform before 1517; see Dickens, *The Counter-Reformation*, 9–18; Evennett, "The New Orders" and *The Spirit of the Counter-Reformation*; Meersseman, "La riforma delle confraternite laicali in Italia prima del Concilio di Trento," 17–30; and Rosa, "Problemi di vita religiosa," 366; Petrocchi, *La Controriforma in Italia*, 17; Elton, *Reformation Europe*, 180; and most recently, Giorgio Chittolini, "Stati regionali e istituzioni ecclesiastiche," 152, 190.
3. See Contimori, "Italy and the Papacy," 255. Prosperi, *Tra Evangelismo e Controriforma*, xv–xxiv; and Alberigo, "Contributi alla storia delle confraternite," 202.
4. See Fenlon, *Heresy and Obedience in Tridentine Italy*. Prosperi, *Tra Evangelismo e Controriforma*.
5. For this periodization of the reform movement in Italy in two distinct phases—one of Catholic reform, the other of Counter-Reform—see Prodi, *La crisis religiosa del XVI Secolo;* Cantimori, "Italy and the Papacy," 257–59, and *Prospettive di storia ereticale, 10ff.;* Dickens, *The Counter-Reformation*, 91–106; and Elton, *Reformation Europe*, 180–86.
6. See Marchetti, *Gruppi ereticali senesi del Cinquecento;* Cantimori, "Italy and the Papacy," 263, and *Prospettive di storia ereticale*, 27–78; for Lucca, the critical year was 1542; see Berengo, *Nobili e mercanti nella Lucca del Cinquecento*, 400–54.
7. The definitive work on the Council of Trent is Jedin, *A History of the Council of Trent*.
8. Alberigo, "The Council of Trent," 86.
9. Jedin, *Riforma cattolica o controriforma?* challenges this periodization of the sixteenth-century reforms and argues for continuity. The period initiated by the Council of Trent continued its evangelical reform of the church's abuses from within; in addition, see Rosa, "Problemi di vita religiosa," 411–14.
10. Dickens, *The Counter-Reformation;* Grayson, "The Renaissance and the History of literature"; and Chastel, "The Arts during the Renaissance." For Italy see Rosa, "Problemi di vita religiosa," 412; Hall, "Problems of the Scientific Renaissance"; and Schmitt, "Philosophy and Science in Sixteenth-Century Italian Universities"; for France, Croix, *La Bretagne aux 16e et 17e siècles;* Delumeau, *Le catholicisme entre Luther et Voltaire*.

11. Archivio Arcivescovile di Siena (AAS), *Sinodi*, n. 3, 1r.
12. See for instance Turchini, *Clero e fedeli a Rimini in età post-Tridentina*.
13. See Prosperi, "Bossi" in *Dizionario Biografico degli Italiani* (Rome, 1971), 13, 303–5.
14. AAS, *Visite*, n. 26.
15. Johannes de Piccolominibus, archbishop of Siena, initiated in 1506 the most thoroughgoing visitation found in the surviving archepiscopal archives before the Counter-Reformation (AAS, *Visite*, n. 20, cc. 172). The evaluations and recommendations were laconic. In the rural parish of San Michele de Petroio, for instance, the visitors reported that a little girl of the parish, Bartolommea Montis, age eleven, died "without confession and the sacraments." The parish priest had failed to assist in her burial. Yet, beyond this report, the visitors made no recommendations and did not even reprimand the wayward priest (p. 26r). In their visit to the *pieve* of Sant'Agnetes, the visitors simply demanded (*mandavit*) that the church have a key made for securing the holy water (p. 5r).
16. On visitation processions in the Counter-Reformation, see Prosperi, "La figura del Vescovo," 260. See Castellini, "Il Cardinale Francesco Maria Tarugi"; and Nardi, "Aspetti della vita dei religiosi," 198–207. AAS, *Visite*, n. 27, and 79r. For instance, on 3 April, Cardinal Tarugi visited the urban parish of Saint John *Visite*, n. 27, 79r.

> Intendens visitare Curam Plebaniam nuncupatam S. Ioannesbaptiste de Senis, existentem in Domo sua Archepiscopali: Ad eam accesserunt multi nobiles dicte Cure qui associaverunt eum usque ad Portam Canonicorum Metropolitane ecclesie, ubi homines et mulieres eiusdem Curae cum clero expectantes ipsius Illustrissimum cum Baldacchino et Pontificaliter vestitus receptus fuit cum solitis Ceremonijs prout in Pontificali: Deinde procedens processionaliter cum toto dicto Populo circumferentes fines Parrocchie ad dictam ecclesiam pervenit, ubi absolutionem mortuorum de more fecit, prout in Pontificali. Qua finita Missam incohavit et (de) dicto Evangelio sermonem habuit ad populum de visitatione et muneribus eius. Missa finita communicavit multos de populo, tam viros, quam mulieres.

17. In parish after parish the visits of 1575 produced similar reports: "confessionale non adest." For the cathedral, Bossi's observations went further (ibid., *Visite*, n. 3, 39r–v): "Voluit visitare confessionalia, sed fuit sibi dictum a multum reverendo domino Scipione Bandineo vicario non adesse et non fuisse solitum in dicta ecclesia confessiones audiri, et non esse constitulos confessores, nec maiorem penitentiarum." His requirements, spelled out in detail the requirements instituted by Carlo Borromeo (53r): "Fiant confessionalia, saltem quatuor lignea ac decentia cum scanno, supra quo confessor sedeat, et cum scabello supra quo genuflectat confitens; et intra confessorem et confitentem tabula sit cum fenestrella parva in medio cooperta lamia ferrea vel alia tabella cum aliquibus foraminibus, nec extra dictum confessionale retineatur in sacristia, pro audiendis confessionibus celebrantium. In unoquoque confessionali sit affixa tabella casum reservatorum." In the parish of Saint John in Siena, the visitors demanded that a confessional be built, and so that women could confess at night and to "remove any suspicions" it ought to be placed "in an open place." See ibid., 59r. Within the period separating these two visitations, proper confessionals had been placed in all the parishes of urban Siena and in the great majority of churches in the countryside. Often the parishioners had constructed more than one confessional booth. For instance, in the parish of Saint John: "Confessionalia adsunt de satis decentia et honesta ad usum Confessarii" (*Visite*, n. 27, 82r). In almost every parish church in 1575 something was amiss with the tombs within churches or in their adjacent cemeteries. For instance, the cemetery at San Marco was exposed ("est apertum"). Bossi gave the parishioners one year to build a wall with a locked gate and to erect a cross in the yard ("et iussi in termino unius anni circumdetur muro et claudetur clave et erigatur crux"). Within the church, two tombs (*avella*) lay

open. Bossi demanded that the parishioners cover them decently with stones within three months (ibid., 71r). In churches such as San Donato in Siena, the conditions were so wretched that Bossi demanded that the parishioners "remove the bones from the unsanctified place and put them in tombs." He forbade them to continue burying their dead within the church unless they were placed within these tombs (ibid., 96r). See Alberigo, "Carlo Borromeo come Modello di Vescovo nella Chiesa post-Tridentina," 1031–52; Mols, "Saint Charles Borromée." Bendiscoli, *Dalla Riforma alla Controriforma,* 107–35; and Wright, *The Counter-Reformation,* 217–21. Other sources show that as late as 1580 that parishioners did not frequent the sacraments and that the 1580s saw the revitalization of that cult; see Nardi, "Aspetti della vita dei religiosi," 206.

18. This visitation did uncover violations, and the visitors made recommendations. The violations, however, are considerably fewer than those a generation earlier. Those at the end of the century occurred mostly within rural parishes, whose properties still suffered from the damages of the war of 1555. It would be misleading to assume that the more muted tones of the second visitation resulted from the disposition of a more lenient taskmaster. As the following years of his office of archbishop would demonstrate, the moralistic and inquisitional zeal for reform drove Tarugi as much as any of the early Tridentine episcopal reformers. The archbishop's court of the early Seicento prosecuted with increased fervor the misdeeds of parish priests and parishioners. Tarugi was particularly severe with regard to the reform of the clergy. They were to be "the mirrors of virtue" for the faithful—"santi vivi." In 1600 Tarugi established a special inquisition to scrutinize the behavior of clerics; indeed not all of them matched up to the suprahuman standards of this post-Tridentine zealot. Franco Nardi, "Aspetti della vita dei religiosi," has studied the episcopal court records through the first half of the Seicento, finding examples of sexual scandals involving the clergy. It is worth noting, however, that not a single example thus far provided by Nardi involved a parish priest from the city of Siena. Without a doubt, urban curates visited prostitutes and were involved in other scandals, as Oscar Di Simplicio's forthcoming work promises to demonstrate, but the major source of infractions still came from the poorer parishes of the countryside. Milan presents a comparable picture of the changes in piety wrought by the visitations of 1570. According to Wright, *The Counter-Reformation,* 218, the visitations of Carlo Borromeo's cousin Federigo show a laity from 1595 to 1631 "faithful to the sacraments, but not always fulfilling the terms of pious bequests of their ancestors; attentive to the catechetical Schools of Christian Doctrine, in the urban centres, but not always so in rural areas."

19. In his introduction, Obelkevich, *Religion and the People,* 8, expresses forcefully the common view of the Counter-Reformation as "essentially an elite pattern of religion, inaugurating an era of one-way religious pressure from the top down and equally an era of increasing resistance and partial conformity from below." For similar positions from historians of "the new social history," see the work of Delumeau, *La peur en Occident,* and *Le pèché et la peur;* Ginzburg, *I benandanti,* and *Il formaggio e i vermi.*

20. AAS, *Sinodi,* n. 3. Bossi's court prosecuted most severely those from the priesthood and the nobility. In sexual scandals the penalties were unequal; often peasants and artisans were slapped on the wrists, while noble men and women received stiffer sentences, even exile from the territory of Siena. For the populist appeal of Carlo Borromeo in the diocese of Milan, see Chabod, *Per la storia religiosa,* 272–77.

21. See Marrara, *Riseduti e Nobilità,* 59–60.

22. For Lyon, Hoffman, *Church and Community,* 41, finds a different social pattern in the acceptance of Counter-Reform piety. There the elites led the way, while "artisans and common people clearly did not follow the elites and rush to embrace Tridentine Catholicism."

23. The compromise depended on a three-way power play involving the Medici Grand Duke Cosimo I, the papacy, and the local aristocracy, primarily the Piccolomini, who maintained their power base within the cathedral of Siena.

24. See chapter 1, note 3.

25. *Not. post-cos.*, n. 423, no. 134, 6r–9v, 1605.iv.4, "E questo ho così ordenato perche miro al mantenimento et al commodo della linea mia de Tomasi, che viene per dritta descendenza di Bandino di Cecco, e non ad altre linee della Fameglia nostra alle quali non voglio che questo benefitio s'entenda."

26. Ibid., "Et a' mantenimento della nostra linea de Tommasi, che viene da' Bandino di Cecco."

27. *Not. post-cos.*, n. 1122, no. 87, 33r–38v, 1628.ix.13.

28. *Not. post-cos.*, n. 2242, no. 28, 29v–35r, 1650.iii.27.

29. *Not. post-cos.*, n. 423, no. 137, 11r–, 1607.vi.20.

30. *Not. post-cos.*, n. 1568, no. 24, 34r–39r, 1636.v.17.

31. *Not. post-cos.*, n. 1284, no. 240, 7v–13r, 1631.vi.4.

32. *Not. post-cos.*, n. 1568, no. 52, 79v–81r, 1642.i.13.

33. In Tables 10.3 and 10.4 "Country" includes all those testators in our sample who did not reside in the city of Siena and who were not noblemen.

34. For the sluggish penetration of the Counter-Reformation in the rural areas around Lyon, see Hoffman, *Church and Community*, 53.

35. These conclusions derive from my study of the land market from samples of thousands of land conveyances, which survive in abbreviated form in the *Gabellae dei contratti*. For the initial results, see Cohn, "The Relations between City and Countryside."

36. The jump in values might have reflected two simultaneous shifts: the appearance of more wealthy testators in the ranks of the *contado* as well as more gifts to those beyond the ambit of universal heirs as the Cinquecento obsession with passing the bulk of property through the male line began to wane.

37. *Not. post-cos.*, n. 1051, no. 44, 58r, 1609.i.6.

38. *Not. post-cos.*, n. 1164, no. 48, 56r–57v, 1623.xii.3.

39. *Not. post-cos.*, n. 2479, no. 5, 7v–9r, 1664.x.4.

40. At the end of the seventeenth century, those from the Monte of the *popolo minuto* were both the most numerous and the wealthiest among the Sienese nobility: Marrara, *Riseduti e Nobiltà*, 82; also see 63.

41. According to Litchfield, *Emergence of a Bureaucracy*, 205, the "middling class of traders and artisans" was hit hardest by the crisis of the seventeenth century.

42. For a similar trend in French history, see Hoffman, *Church and Community*, 126 and 145, and "Wills and Statistics."

43. See Bendiscoli, *Dalla Riforma alla Controriforma*, 128; Mols, "Saint Charles Borromée," 717; Zancan, "La donna," 811. Women and men were separated in church, and women were required to keep their heads veiled in church and in religious processions.

44. Historians have begun to look more favorably on the ambience of Counter-Reformation Catholicism for women. See, for instance, Davis, "City Women and Religious Change," 65–96; Hoffman, "Wills and Statistics," and *Church and Community*; Norberg, *Rich and Poor*; John Martin, "Out of the Shadow." These historians have compared the piety and devotion of Catholic women relative to men in the second half of the sixteenth and seventeenth centuries, or they have compared Catholic and Protestant women in this period, but they have yet to investigate changes in piety and women's rights, power, and property relations in Catholic societies before and after the Council of Trent.

45. The French historiography sees the percentage of women who redacted their own

wills as a progressive linear development paralleling the inexorable forces of modernity: see Vovelle, *Piété baroque,* 320. In Provence, before the eighteenth century, women redacted testaments only two-thirds as frequently as men.

46. Parenti, *Prezzi,* 27.

47. On the apathy of men in Lyon to the charitable causes of Trent, see Hoffman, "Wills and Statistics," 830.

48. See membership roles, such as those for the confraternity of Santa Trinità, Biblioteca Comunale, A.II.1; and the numerous new companies for women, which appear in the visitations of Tarugi, AAS, *Visite,* n. 27. Also see Rusconi, "Confraternite, compagnie e devozioni," 496–97.

49. For a discussion of Counter-Reformed congregations for women, see Cohen, "The Convertite and the Malmaritate."

50. For the condition of nunneries at the time of Bossi's visitation, see Catoni, "Interni di conventi senesi del Cinquecento," 187–94.

51. Nardi, "Matteo Guerra," pp. 36–37; and Cohen, "The Convertite and the Malmaritate."

52. In Siena, the war against Florence in 1552–55 compounded the economic and social crisis of the mid-Cinquecento. Although the disastrous consequences of this prolonged war and the Sienese patriotic zeal may have sparked charitable assistance (see Nardi, "Matteo Guerra," 17–18); new institutions to rehabilitate the poor did not receive significant funding and recognition until well after this military and demographic crisis.

53. For the repressive character of these institutions see Foucault, *Folie et Déraison,* 54–96; and Norberg, *Rich and Poor,* 297.

54. In addition to evidence in these testaments, see Trexler, "Death and Testament," 34ff.

55. Based on the following sample sizes for women's testaments: 30, 26, 61, and 50.

56. The struggle between the church and prestigious lineages over sacred space in churches is of long duration in Western civilization. See Brown, *The Cult of the Saints.* In the visitations of 1575–76, Bossi demanded that members of several of Siena's most prominent families exhume their ancestral bones from places that, according to new Tridentine specification, were too near high altars and other sacred places.

57. It might be argued that the statistical changes discussed thus far resulted from the demographic, social, and economic dislocations created by the war with Florence, 1552–55. The historian would then need to explain the reason for a time lag of twenty-five to fifty years. To borrow Robert Lopez's phrase, "I doubt the paternity of children who were born. . . . years after the death of their fathers" ("Hard Times and Investment in Culture," in *The Renaissance* [New York, 1962], 43). Second, though the occurrence of pestilence may have affected pious bequests and the differentials between men and women in charitable giving in the short term from one year to the next, they do not register in Siena as a force that fundamentally altered trends for the seventeenth century. For the short-term effect of plague on testament writing, see Pastore, "Testamenti in tempo di Peste."

58. No doubt the notary was in some measure responsible for the drafting of these personal expressions, but these remarks were not formulaic; they were not automatically replicated either from notary to notary or within the testaments drafted by a particular notary. In addition, these phrases often contain bits of variable information, such as the length of time the husband and wife "have lived together with sincere love," or more simply put in other wills, "per essere insieme habitati." See *Not. post-cos.,* n. 423, no. 134, 6r, 1605.iv.4; and n. 532, 91r–v, 1601.ix.7; n. 1786, no. 16, 31r–33r, 1644.vi.12; and no. 20, 38r–39v, 1645.viii.27.

59. *Not.*, n. 2684, no. 64, 1551.viii.12.

60. *Not.* n. 3625, Fasc. 1, no. 168, 1575.i.2, "Conoscendo l'amore et benevolentia inverso di essa portata da donna Margarita d'Andrea detto Bresia da Pretra arata sua dilettissima consorte et quanto si sia affadigata et si affadighi del continuo a servitio di detto Andrea et in mantenerli li suoi beni et essi accrescerli et augumentarli volendola riconoscere et rimeritarla di tante sue fadighe, et acciò che essa dopo la sua morte non sia scacciata dalli infrascripti suoi heredi, onde essa potesse per alcun' modo patire di farne la medissima donna Margarita per suo certo sper et non per forza o per inganno alcuno ma spontaneamente et in ogni miglior modo lassò donna madonna et usufruttuaria et libera et generale amministratrice di tutti li suoi beni." Similar statements of respect and affection or gratitude for a wife's *fadighe et industrie* are found in numerous documents from the late sixteenth and seventeenth centuries; for instance, *Not. antecos,* n. 3130, 21v–23r, 1563.ii.11; n. 2265, 11r–12v, 1583.ix.13; *Not. post-cos.,* n. 184, 4r, 1594.ix.24; 23r–25v, 1595.vi.21; n. 532, 9r–v, 1601.ix.7; n. 423, 6r, 1605.iv.4; n. 1164, no. 31, 35v, 1613.viii.17; n. 971, no. 50, 63v–64v, 1610.xii.20; no. 52, 65v–66r, 1611.x.24; n. 1762, no. 34, 68r–69r, 1641.vii.16; n. 2479, no. 6, 9r–10r, 1664.xii.13.

61. Stone, *The Family, Sex and Marriage in England,* 136–45 and 217–53. The hasty historian might suppose that the difference between these two documents reflects differences between artisan and peasant marriages. However, their dating is the essential difference. The testament of Andrea di Giovanni is the first in my sample to suggest the mutual affection and toil of years of matrimonial partnership. Later, particularly during the seventeenth century, such sentiments are found more often among the ranks of urban artisans.

62. During the period of the Grand Duchy, the only change in legislation that affected the property rights of women was promulgated in 1620. Cosimo II extended the rights of succession to parts of the inheritance to the female kin of those who died without a notarized testament. Cantini, *Legislazione Toscana,* t. 15, pp. 153–63, Riformatio rubr. 130, lib. II, Statuti Florentini de Mulierum Successione ab in testato.

63. On these practices, see Tamassia, *La famiglia italiana,* 325.

64. *Not. post-cos.,* n. 170, 34r, 1590.iii.7, "In omnibus . . . suam heredem universalem instituit . . . dominam Virginam . . . eius uxorem, cum hac tamen conditione . . . , quod teneatur ipsa domina Virginia per unum annum post hobitum dicti testatoris vitam vidualem et honestam servare."

65. *Not. post-cos.,* n. 170, 34v, 1590.iii.10.

66. In 1501–50, 10 of 27 cases; 1551–75, 9 of 29; 1576–1600, 9 of 27. For 1601–50, 12 of 37. In the second half of the Seicento, it was 19 of 33 cases, which constitutes a significant increase over the percentages of the Cinquecento; $p = .5758$; $hp = .4526$; $n = 118$; $z = 2.69$. Demographic factors may have conditioned these increases in the proportion of wives as universal heirs, particularly in consequence of the crisis of the seventeenth century. For the aristocracy in Siena, see Cohn and Di Simplicio "Alcuni aspetti," 313–30. From the wills it is possible to calculate the percentages of those men who left surviving wives but no sons to inherit the patrimony. These figures do not, however, correlate with changes in the percentages of widows as universal heirs. In 1401–1500, 43.5 percent of husbands left no surviving sons (wives were universal heirs in 12 percent of the relevant cases); 1501–50 the percentage of surviving sons increased to 54.3 percent, along with the increases cited above in wives as universal heirs. For 1551–75, the proportion of husbands without sons to survive them fell to 34.5 percent, but with no corresponding rise in wives as universal heirs; then in the last quarter of the Cinquecento, most likely as a consequence of the war, husbands without sons to succeed them jumped to its highest point, 73.1 percent, but again without any correspondence for wives as heirs. The percentage of

husbands without surviving sons declined slightly during the first half of the Seicento to 67.6 percent; then in the second half of the century, the rate returned to its late Renaissance level of 45.5 percent at the very time when the percentage of wives as the universal heirs to their husbands' estates almost doubled. Another demographic factor that might have conditioned these changes could have been the variance in the ages at marriage, particularly for women. According to Hajnal, "European Marriage Patterns," 101–43, the ages at marriage for women across Western Europe began to rise during the Seicento. It might be argued that women received more favorable settlements from their husbands because they had become husbands' equals in terms of age. Unfortunately, statistics on ages of men and women at marriage are not yet available for Siena. Herlihy and Klapisch-Zuber, *Les Toscans et leur familles*, show that for Florence already by the end of the fifteenth century the ages at marriage for women had begun to drift upward—that is, during the very period when property conditions for women in Siena were worsening.

67. Customarily, wives were to grant their husbands only a third of their dowries, if no children survived from the marriage, *Il constituto del Comune di Siena*, vol. 2, rubr. xxxiii, 214.

68. *Not. post-cos.*, n. 1762, no. 41, 75r–76r, 1642.vi.4.

69. *Not. post-cos.*, n. 1051, no. 52, 65v–66r, 1611.x.24, "E perchè fra di loro è stato sempre, et è reciproco amore, e benevolenza, et in oltre haver da lei ricevuto buona e fedel servitù, e governo nelli suoi bisogni di malattie, et altre infinite amorevolezze, e buona compagnia fattali." In addition, see the will of the saddle maker, *Not. post-cos.*, n. 184, no. 180, 23r–25v, 1595.vi.21.

70. *Not. post-cos.*, n. 2479, no. 1, 2r–3r, 1663.x.9.

71. Ibid.:

> In tutti . . . suoi heredi universali institutui . . . Francesco e Maria Anna suoi e di detta donna Maddalena figli, volendo anco che la medissima sia coherede delli medessima di dover tenere, e stare con detti suoi figli fino a' che essa viverà o viveranno respettivamente et educarli nel Santo timore di dio, e tutto perchè confida nella sua bontà, et integrità, e lassa la medissima donna e madonna e non solo usufruttaria, ma' volse ancora, che in caso di necessità per souvenire detti suoi figli, o' altra, possi vendere, o' impegnare di casa quello che gli piacerà, senza che da nessuno gli possi esser tenuto conto di quello, che essa facesse, che intende, e vuole fino che essa viverà che detti figli stieno appresso la medesima e sia padrona assoluta di fare quel tanto che gi piacerà essendo certo che essa terrà conto di detti suoi figli come ha' fatto per il passato però glieli raccomanda per l'Amor di Dio, e quando sarà in eta nubile detta Maria Anna sua figliola a' maritarla secondo le sue forse comporteranno.

For other examples of husbands' demanding their children's obedience and even "veneration" of their mothers, see n. 60, this chapter.

72. *Not. post-cos.*, n. 2730, no. 95, 1678.viii.26.

73. *Not. post-cos.*, 2730, no. 115, 56r–59r, 1680.iv.4.

74. *Not. antecos.* n. 3124, no. 3.

75. Cooper, "Patterns of Inheritance," 192–327, describes the inheritance only for the "great landowners" and does not concentrate on the possible transformations in these patterns over the long period of his study.

76. *Not. post-cos.*, n. 1164, no. 27, 31r–32r, 1612.ix.13.

> In tutti . . . esser volse suoi heredi universali l'infrascritti suoi figliuoli, tanto masti, quanto femine, per equal portione, cioè Filippo. Ferdinando. Petro. Portia. Verginia. Livia. Caterina. et Aurelia: con espressa proibitione e protestatione, ch'in tale sua heredità, al detto Signor Bernardo suo Consorte, e lor Padre non s'acquisti ragione alcuna d'usofrutto, o'

d'altro, che per ragione . . . ch'i suoi beni liberamente pienamente et immediatamente tanto per ragione di proprietà e quanto d'usofrutto, e di possesso appartenghino ad essi suoi figliuoli, di maniera che ne anco detto lor Padre n'habbia l'amministratione: e perciò dispose, e volse che l'attioni a lei competenti come sopra sieno a benefitio de medessimi esercitate et intentate dalla sopradetta Signora Margarita sua Madre, o da qualunque pure constituito da lei, facendola esecutrice della presente sua ultima voluntà, di maniera, che l'effetto sia, che i detti suoi figliuoli ne sentino l'utile, e commodo, et a lei appartenga il peso, e l'autorità di fare tutte le riscossioni, e mettere quanto prima insieme, et al netto tutte le sue facultà, acciò che quanto prima li detti suoi figliuoli possino a goderle e specialmente le femmine, che n'hanno maggior necessità; rendendosi sicura, che il detto suo Consorte sia per approvare questa sua dispositione e commendarla, conoscendo non esser fatta per far'a lui alcun torto, ma benefitio alla Fameglia, così richiendolo lo stato disagioso di lui.

Similar concern for the well-being of the family, meaning the immediate future of the testator's children as opposed to the lineage, is expressed in the will of the hat maker Julius f. q. Quirichi of Siena, *Not.*, n. 2265, 8v–9v, 1581.v.16.

77. *Not. post-cos.*, n. 2319, no. 114, 8v–10v, 1662.viii.25.

78. *Not. post-cos.*, n. 3110, no. 150, 7v–9r, 1690.iii.10, "Tutte le figlie femmine legittime e naturali, tanto nate quanto che avvienisse nascere della detta Chiara Papari . . . e ciascuna di esse figlie equalmente . . . esclusi sempre et in qualsi voglia caso e tempo per maggior cautela, . . . li figli maschi mentre però vi siano figlie femmine."

79. See, for instance, Carlo Borromeo, *Ammaestramenti*, 25, "Da loro avete la carne ed il sangue per cui siete loro parenti; questo li spinge, questo cercano e di qua proviene tutto il danno. Ma bisogna staccarsene, bisogna licenziarli. . . . Con questo divina risposta, dilettissime, dovete dar bando ai parenti, troncare le visite, chiudere i parlatorii, e allontanare da voi tutti questi impedimenti."

80. At the end of the sixteenth century, women were optimal targets for ecclesiatic designs and opportunities. Because of the lineage strategies of the Cinquecento, dowries, especially those of noble families, may have inflated more than any other commodity in early modern European economies. (See Cooper, "Patterns of Inheritance" and Cohn and Di Simplicio, "Alcuni aspetti"). This meant that women on their deathbeds often were left in control of patrimonies far grander than those of their mothers and grandmothers.

81. See Lazzareschi, "Una mistica senese," 22:419–33 and 23:3–46.

82. The forthcoming work of Oscar Di Simplicio will show through a detailed examination of ecclesiastical court records that wife-rape and wife-beating persisted through the early modern period.

83. Nardi, "Vita dei religiosi," 219, has argued that "manifestations of (sexual) violence tolerated in previous periods became entirely unacceptable" under the tighter and more severe scrutiny of ecclesiastical authority by the early Seicento.

84. *Not.*, n. 2742, no. 4, 1580.viii.30, "Et per la medissima ragione et legato lassò a Laura sua figlia et moglie di Pace Coiaio l'usufrutto d'una sua bottiguccia nel T. di Camollia presso alla fonte d'ovile sotto casa Paliti fincella . . . si possa aitare et sovvenire a suoi bisogni, atteso ch'essa è povara et abbandonata dal marito et non ha donde possa vivere se no con le sue fatighe."

85. *Not. post-cos.*, n. 532, 20v–21v, 1602.iv.27.

86. *Not. post-cos.*, n. 1568, n. 48, 73v–76r, 1642.vi.27, "Al quale disse havere molti obligati per la fadighe durante, e spese fatte nell'occasioni delle sue adversità passate, e nominatamente nell' occasione delle liti, e per recuperare le sue doti in fiorenza e fino che le recuperò, e così per lo spatio di cinque anni, e li vantaggi ha fatto le spese à essa, e suoi fighioli all'hora piccoli del proprio in numero di quattro figli e poi sempre trattatela bene."

Chapter 11. Late Counter-Reformation Piety

Epigraph: Galluzzi, *Istoria del Granducato di Toscana,* lib. 8, cap. 10, 400–401.
 1. See Mengozzi, *Il monte dei Paschi,* 3: cap. XXIII; Cohn and Di Simplicio, "Alcuni aspetti"; Parenti, *Prezzi.* For Europe, see Braudel and Spooner, "Prices in Europe," 374–486; Aston, *Crisis in Europe;* de Vries, *The Economy of Europe in an Age of Crisis;* Wallerstein, *The Modern World-System II.*
 2. The increase and consolidation of church property over the seventeenth century was universal throughout the Italian peninsula; see Stumpo, "Il consolidamento della grande proprietà," 287–88. On the economy of Tuscany, Rodolico, *Stato e chiesa,* 309, dates the turning point around 1751 with the passage of mortmain legislation. Anzilotti, "Piccola o grande proprietà nelle riforme di Pietro Leopoldo," 349, dates the change around 1767 with new legislation freeing the grain trade from the old monopolistic control of the Grand Dukes. On the other hand, from a microscopic study of the estates belonging to Santa Maria della Scala, Conenna, *Prata,* 35–36, finds signs of economic improvement as early as 1700. From analysis of other estates belonging to Santa Maria della Scala (Serre a Rapolano), Di Simplicio, "Due secoli," 812–13, speculates that the shift occurred later.
 3. See Wallerstein, *The Modern World-System II,* and Kula, *An Economic Theory of the Feudal System;* however, McArdle, *Altopascio,* has shown the continued impoverishment of *mezzadri* on the Medici estates through the seventeenth century. On the other hand, in Pisa, Prato, and Livorno the seventeenth-century decline of Florentine industry opened new avenues for industry and commerce; see Malanima, "Le attività industriali," 217–80. Fosi, "Lo stato e i poveri," 93–115, argues that poverty by the end of the seventeenth century had become endemic to Sienese society.
 4. On the changing character of religious confraternities during the seventeenth century, see Grendi, "Morfologia e dinamica della vita associative Urbana," 115–86. *Not. post-cos.,* n. 3815, no. 163, 11r–12r, 1723.x.25.
 5. The earliest appearance in these documents of the *fanciulle sperse* is 1679. See *Not. post-cos.,* n. 2730, no. 105, 27v–33v, 1679.vii.24; and n. 2945, no. 71, 3r–7v, 1683.iv.29. For little girls in prisons, see *Not. post-cos.,* n. 3855, no. 161, 73r–75r, 1722.iii.18. For *delle ravolae,* see *Not. post-cos.,* n. 2945, no. 70, 3r–7v, 1683.iv.29. For *delle povere fanciulle,* see *Not. post-cos.,* n. 3489, no. 69, 31v–34v, 1716.x.14. For *della carità,* see *Not. post-cos.,* n. 3855, no. 159, 69r–70v, 1721.iii.19. For "*i vergognosi,*" see *Not. post-cos.,* n. 3746, no. 15, 21v–24v, 1712.v.24; for *della Pietà,* see n. 3855, no. 160, 70v–73r, 1722.v.10.
 6. Cohn and Di Simplicio. "Alcuni aspetti," 321–24.
 7. Hajnal, "European Marriage Patterns," 101–43. On economic change, see Goubert, *Beauvais et le Beauvasis.* No comparable works exist for seventeenth-century Tuscany. Even for an exceptionally favored economy such as that of Pescia and its countryside, signs of economic decline were present by the 1620s. See Judith Brown, *In the Shadow of Florence,* 124–25. The economic fortunes for neighboring areas were more desperate, see McArdle, *Altopascio.* For Siena, see the descriptions and analysis of agricultural production in the period of falling prices by the contemporary physiocrat Sallustio Bandini, *Il Discorso sopra la Maremma di Siena,* edited by Baker in *Sallustio Bandini.*
 8. *Not. post-cos.,* n. 1164, no. 35, 40r–41v, 1615.iii.7; in a testament of 1627, a man from Siena left two dowry funds of considerable property, one with 1,000 scudi to marry each year five *fanciulle* and another to marry *tante citole* every year with the rents from three houses and a warehouse. The girls were to be born of worthy parents from the city of Siena, *Not. post-cos.,* n. 1122, no. 76, 17v, 1627.v.31.
 9. *Not. post-cos.,* n. 2730, 47r–52v, 1680.i.20.
 10. *Not. post-cos.,* n. 3476, 9r–v, 1706.iii.25.
 11. *Not. post-cos.,* n. 3663, no. 24, 35v–38r, 1709.ii.16.

12. *Not. post-cos.*, n. 3110, 4v–6v, 1690.i.20.
13. *Not. post-cos.*, n. 1122, no. 87, 33r–, 1628.ix.13.
14. *Not. post-cos.*, n. 2945, no. 71, 3r–7v, 1683.iv.29.
15. *Not. post-cos.*, n. 4027, no. 142, 3v–7r, 1735.x.4; n. 4486, no. 13, 18r–, 1759.viii.19.
16. On the 1671 ban on vagabonds in Siena, see Mengozzi, *Il monte dei Paschi*, 4:123. For a comparative perspective, see Norberg. *Rich and Poor*, 215ff.
17. In the late sixteenth and seventeenth centuries, Woolf, *A History of Italy*, 26, argues that "residence was a sign of respectability, vagrancy evidence of impiety and illwill."
18. *Not. post-cos.*, n. 2319, no. 110, 1r–3r, 1661.v.26.

Alla quale morendo avanti di maritarsi o monacarsi . . . sostitui la Venerabile Compagnia di Santa Caterina da Siena in Contrada di fonteblanda di questa citta' e la Venerabile Compagnia di Santa Caterina da Siena della Natione Senese nella Citta' di Roma. . . .
Che ogni due anni in perpetuo . . . devino dare una dote di scudi cento . . . quale dote si deva dare in parte alle femine descendenti del gia' Signor Piermaria Luti Nobile Senese mentre ve ne sieno e la domandino, purchè sieno d'eta' d'anni dodici, e maritandosi, o monacandosi e di poi alle figlie di Silvia di Crescentio Mazzoni di detta eta', benchè non sieno nate di Nobili e di poi altre fanciulle nobili Senesi, che di tre Generationi almeno, due siano di riseduti, e di detta eta', e maritandosi o' monacandosi da eleggersi da detta Compagnia di Santa Caterina da Siena come più informata.

19. *Dipl.*, 1323.ix.1.
20. For the crisis of the aristocracy in Siena, see Baker, "Nobilità in declino"; Cohn and Di Simplico, "Alcuni aspetti."
21. Di Simplicio, "La nobità 'povera' a Siena."
22. *Not. post-cos.*, n. 3746, no. 15, 21v–24v, 1712.v.24.
23. *Not. post-cos.*, n. 2294, no. 5, 5v–8v, 1682.ii.17.
24. *Not. post-cos.*, n. 1122, no. 87, 33r–, 1628.ix.13; n. 3110, no. 156, 16v–17v, 1691.iii.28.
25. *Not. post-cos.*, n. 4374, no. 26, 29v–37v, 1743.iv.9:

Successivamente poi debba continuarsi nel detto ordinato deposito per altri cinque anni, talmente che si faccia un cumulo di scudi dugento cinquanta i quali con titolo parimente di legato Pio, et in ogni altro lasciarono e legarono ad una altra Fanciulla, che voglia vestire l'abito religioso nel Convento predetto in qualita' di Servigiala, da eleggersi parimente nel modo che si dira' piu di sotto, e in tal forma deva proseguirsi in perpetuo, di modo che in ciascuno decennio debba esservi la dote per una monaca velata, et in ciascuno quinquennio sussequente la dote per una servigiata, perche cosi: Le fanciulle poi da monacarsi per velate vollero li detti Signori Testatori, che debbano avere l'infrascritti qualita' e condizioni, e non altrimenti, ne in altro modo. Primo che quando si purifichera' il tempo del sopradetto legato, e respettiva monacazione debbano avere compita l'eta' d'anni diciotto ne possano essere maggiori d'anni ventiquattro compiti. Secondo che le dette fanciulle siano di questa Citta' di Siena, e di Padre e Nonno nati in Siena, o' almeno domiciliati, escluse quelle dello scalo Sanese, e siano figlie di persone Civili et onorale della Seconda Classe, escluse quelle della prima, come a cagione di essempio di dottori di legge, o di medicina, o' di scolari Cittadini Sanesi, talmente che ne il Padre, ne il Nonno di queste tali Fanciulle abbia mai esercitata alcuna arte vile, come a cagione di esempio sarebbe quella del Calsolaro, del Pizzicaiolo, del Fornaio, Marcellaio, Fabro e simili, non intendendo per altro di escludere quelli che professasero, o' avessero professato le arti Nobili e Liberali della Pittura, Scultura, Farmeceutica e simili.

26. *Not. post-cos.*, n. 3476, no. 68, 4r–5v, 1704.viiiI; no. 73, 11r–13r, 1710; n. 3476, no. 70, 6v–8v, 1706.iii.19.

27. *Not. post-cos.*, n. 4027, no. 142, 3v–7r, 1735.x.4.
28. *Not. post-cos.*, n. 4374, no. 26, 29v–37v, 1743.iv.9.

Volsero di più et ordinarono che ciascuna di quelle Fanciulle, che sara' vestita in detto convento coll'assignamento come sopra lassatoli, ogni prima domenica del mese doppo fatta la Santa Comunione non essendo legittimante impedite, deva recitare devotamente sua vita naturale durante la terza parte del Rosario in suffragio dell'Anima di detti Signori Testatori di detto Signor Bernardino fratello, e Cognato respettivamente e di detta Signora Teresia Calecina loro dilettissima figlia gravandone sopra di ciò la loro coscienza, esortando la Madre Superiora a rammemorarli in tale obligo, o'pure quando le piaccia, fare recitare detta parte di Rosario doppo fatta la Comunione unitamente con tutte le religiose da applicarsi come sopra e non altrimenti.

29. See Chiffoleau, *La comptabilité de l'au-dela*.
30. *Not. post-cos.*, n. 3350, no. 61, 8r–12v, 1700.iv.1.
31. *Not. post-cos.*, n. 3350, no. 64, 16r–19v, 1705.xi.16.
32. On the similarities in the charitable attitudes between the Counter-Reformation and the Reformation, see Delumeau, *La peur en Occident*; for Italy, Woolf, *A History of Italy*, 26.
33. See Mengozzi, *Il monte dei Paschi*, 4:28; the Scalzi won permission on 17 December 1647 to establish a house in Siena. That other new order of the Counter-Reformation, the Society of Jesus, although without doubt important in the religious power structure, never successed in attracting pious legacies in large numbers.
34. *Not. post-cos.*, n. 2397, no. 60, 64v–65r, 1658.iii.4. The chapels of these three *contrade* are the only ones that appear in these documents, and Onda appears only once.
35. *Not. post-cos.*, n. 3815, 8r–9r, 1723.iv.15.
36. *Not. post-cos.*, n. 2945, no. 84, 27v–29r, 1691.x.2. See, for instance, *Not. post-cos.*, n. 2242, no. 29, 35r–36r, 1650.vi.17. *Not. post-cos.*, n. 4133, n. 164, 30r–31r, 1738.iii.24.
37. *Not. post-cos.*, n. 2730, no. 98, 11r–15r, 1678.ix.4.
38. *Not. post-cos.*, n. 5077, no. 105, 46r–, 1783.v.20.
39. *Not. post-cos.*, n. 2761, no. 6, 10r–11r, 1672.ii.4; no. 16, 37v–39v, 1674.iii.10; n. 2294, no. 5, 5v–8v, 1682.ii.17.
40. *Not. post-cos.*, n. 3110, 4v–6v, 1690.i.20; no. 154, 13v–16r, 1691.ii.16; n. 3396, no. 88, 92v–97v, 1705.vii.16; n. 3764, no. 204, 39v–46r, 1722.ii.20; no. 208, 49r–55v, 1722.iii.3.
41. *Not. post-cos.*, n. 3815, no. 158, 6r–8r, 1722.xi.2; n. 3746, no. 15, 21v–24v, 1712.v.24.
42. *Not. post-cos.*, n. 3350, 13r–14v, 1701.ii.5.
43. *Not. post-cos.*, n. 3110, no. 150, 7v–9v, 1690.iii.10.
44. *Not. post-cos.*, n. 3815, no. 158, 6r–8r, 1722.xi.2.
45. *Not. post-cos.*, n. 2730, no. 107, 35r–40r, 1679.viii.26; n. 3815, no. 169, 16v–17r, 1724.iii.17. See, for instance, ASS, *Conventi*, n. 1001, "Messe celebrate: Nomi dei celebranti e obligi perpetui," 1694–1704 (Sant'Abbondio); n. 1132, "Libro di messe," (1715–41 (S. Bernardino dei M.O.—Osservanza); n. 1261, "Obbighi di messe," 1674–88 (S. Caterina); n. 1268, "A Suor Cassandra Tondi. Note delle messe . . . all'altare di S. Tommaso d'Aquino nella chiesa di San Domenico . . . con i nomi dei sacredoti celebranti," 1719–86; n. 1999, "Messe per Inorato Tancredi. Date della celebratione e firma dei celebranti 1698–1781 (S. Girolamo di Campansi).
46. *Not. post-cos.*, n. 4440. no. 186, 25r, 1741.vi.22.

Et accio' detto legato pio sia precisamente adempiuto, subbito sequita la sua morte, obligo me Notario a' portarne subbito la notizia di esso a' detto Monsignore Arcivescovo, alla coscienza del quale rimesse il peso di far dare pronta esecuzione al medisimo pio legato e gravò detti suoi soprascritti Eredi, e sostituti, adempiuto che sara' a' tal augumento, di fare subito una memoria in pietra da apporsi nella Sagrestia di detta chiesa colla descrizzione esatta di tutti gli oblighi, e di quei giorni, che doveranno adempirsi, giacche' esso disse essere obligato a' fare tal memoria nell'infrascritto della Erezzione di detta Cappella . . . e mancando detti Signori Eredi e sostituti in fare detta memoria come sopra cadano in pena di scudi cinquanta da darsi allo spedale di S. Maria della Scala collo stesso obligo di fare detta memoria.

47. Huizinga, *The Waning of the Middle Ages*. *Not. post-cos.*, n. 4027, no. 150, 13r–15r, 1736.x.2.

48. *Not. post-cos.*, n. 2294, no. 6, 8v–10v, 1682.xii.16, and n. 4510, no. 26, 46r–47r, 1763.viii.21. *Not. post-cos.*, n. 2294, no. 6, 8v–10v, 1682.xii.16; n. 5114, no. 49, 43r–, 1791.ii.4.

49. *Not. post-cos.*, n. 2479, no. 12, 18v–19v, 1667.iv.26; no. 13, 1667.vi.11, 19v–21r.

50. *Not. post-cos.*, n. 2479, no. 20, 29r–31r, 1668.iv.28; no. 20, 29r–31r, 1668.iv.28.

51. *Not. post-cos.*, n. 2730, no. 110, 44r–45v, 1679.x.21; no. 111, 46r–47v, 1679.x.29; n. 3663, no. 27, 43r–44v, 1711.vii.13.

52. *Not. post-cos.*, n. 2761, no. 13, 33r–34r, 1673.x.22.

53. *Not. post-cos.*, n. 2730, no. 112, 47r–52v, 1679.i.20.

54. For other elaborate funeral arrangements during the late Counter-Reformation, see the wills of the artisan Domenico del gia Simone Centi of Siena, *Not. post-cos.*, n. 2730, no. 117, 61r–63v, 1680.v.3; the "Molto Reverendo" Giovanni-Domenico Romboli, a priest from Paganico, the curate at the parish of San Lorenzo a Terrensano (in the Masse), n. 3746, no. 12, 16r–18r; Magnifico Ansano-Bernardino del gia Raffaelo, an oven builder and merchant of Siena, n. 3855, no. 160, 70v–73r, 1721.v.10; Maestro Bonaventura del gia Maestro Giuseppe Mori, a greengrocer of Siena, n. 4027, no. 150, 13r–15r, 1736.x.2; a cavalier of the Order of Santo Stefano, Antonio del gia Alessandro Ugolini, patrician of Siena and rector of Santa Maria della Scala, n. 3815, no. 158, 6r–8r, 1722.xi.2.

55. *Not. post-cos.*, n. 2994, no. 5, 5v–8v, 1682.ii.17; and no. 6, 8v–10v, 1682.xii.16; n. 3110, 4v–6v, 1690.i.20; n. 3489, no. 60, 13r–15r, 1712.x.27.

56. *Not. post-cos.*, n. 3110, no. 167, 33r–35r, 1694.iv.13, "Con quella spesa funebre, che secondo la Conditione di detta testatrice e le forze della sua eredità parrà moderatamente e discretamente a' Signori Offiziali di detta Contrada con che permettendolo li beni ereditarii, chiamato al funerale, oltre à soliti Preti della Venerabile Congregatione di Santo Pietro in Duomo, due di S. Francesco, e nel resto a'sodisfazzione, e piacimento di detto Signori officiali della Contrada." *Not. post-cos.*, n. 4067, no. 58, 42r–45v, 1737.ii.21, "Il quale si faccia tutto dal Signor Curato coll' approvase e consenso di donna Agnesa sua consorte, usandosi pasimonia e discreterza nella spesa d'esso, mentre ambisce più al Bene che alla Pompa."

57. In examining the vanguard of intellectual activity in early Enlightenment Tuscany—the University of Pisa—Rodolico, *Stato e chiesa*, 45, concludes that before 1712 Italian Jansenism did not exist.

58. See Vovelle, *Piété baroque*, 459–62.

59. These tensions in fact might explain the contradictions in recent monographs on death and the rituals of post-Tridentine Catholicism in France. Vovelle distinguishes Counter-Reform piety by "baroque" funerals and elaborate liturgical display; Croix, *La Bretagne*, t. II, 1251, finds the opposite. The asceticism of Counter-Reformation in Brittany curbed earlier pomp and ceremony in church service.

60. *Not. post-cos.*, n. 3110, no. 160, 23r–24v, 1692.vi.21, "Staccarsi totalmente dal mondo e dalle sue pompe e fallacie e da beni mondani. . . ."

61. *Not. post-cos.*, n. 3815, no. 168, 15r–16v, 1725.iii.7; see also n. 4440, no. 186, 25r–, 1741.vi.22.

62. *Not. post-cos.*, n. 3764, no. 208, 49v–55v, 1721.iii.3.

Item disse, et asserì esser ben consapevole per mezzo di persone degne di fede dei gran profitti, che hanno portato e portano in questa città gl'esercizij spirituali, che modernamente vi sono stati introdotti coll'aiuto della Reale Clemenza dal zelantissimo nostro sovrano, e di' quali la città nostra fin'ora ne sperimenta molto plausibili gl'effetti, ma perché questi non posson lungamente sussistere per non aver corpo, ne Fondo, bramosa quanto in se di promuoverli e di portare così gran giovamento alla sua amata Patria, perciò in sodisfazione delle sue colpe et ad effetto, e dona con titolo, e causa di donazione irrevocabile, che non si perde la semenza di questo Evangelico lavoro, donò . . . e fra i divi a Giesù Christo Suo Redentore a la somma di scudi due milla.

63. *Not. post-cos.*, n. 3764, no. 204, 39v–46r, 1722.ii.20; no. 212, 59r–63v, 1722.ix.1.
64. *Not. post-cos.*, n. 3489, no. 69, 31v–34v, 1716.x.14.

Chapter 12. Enlightened Despotism

Epigraphs: The preamble to the 11 February 1751 mortmain law of Francesco Stephano is in Cantini, *Legislazione Toscana*, t. 26, 314. The second epigraph, from the count's letter to a friend in Rome, 21 April 1751, is found in Rodolico, *Stato e chiesa*, appendix, document 12, 445.

1. By a multiple regression, the change over time is highly significant (.0257): Beta = −0.097; T = −2.24. With the independent variables sex, health, occupation, residence, and wealth, the model is significant, R square = .27 and F = 23.66.
2. *Not. post-cos.*, n. 4440, no. 186, 25r–, 1741.vi.22.
3. *Not. post-cos.*, n. 4875, no. 139, 47r–, 1780.iii.31.
4. *Not. post-cos.*, n. 5071, no. 60, 5r–, 1781.x.10.
5. See chapter 11, n. 2. Woolf, *A History of Italy*, 25, maintains that when the population of Italy began to grow again in the eighteenth century "conditions immediately worsened." From maps charting population density, Alessandri, "La densità di popolazione," argues that the sharpest economic and demographic decline for southern Tuscany in the modern period occurred during the hundred years between 1645 and 1745. Pardi, *La popolazione di Siena*, 40, argues that the population of Siena began a period of "notable increase" in 1769. Others argue that conditions for the peasantry did not begin to ameliorate until after the famines of 1764–66 and Leopold's reforms of the grain trade. See Wandruszka, *Pietro Leopoldo*, 134, 169; Grab, "The Politics of Subsistence; Giusti, "Problemi di storia economica tra '500 e '600," 37. Still others do not find substantial changes in the condition of the peasantry in southern Tuscany until well into the nineteenth century; see Cecchini, "Le grance dell'ospedale di S. Maria della Scala di Siena."
6. The increase in the appearance of *mezzadri* and urban artisans in our samples constitutes one index of the democratization of testament writing over the seventeenth and eighteenth centuries.
7. See for instance *Not. post-cos.*, n. 4027, no. 175, 39r, 1730.vi.1; and n. 4067, no. 58, 42v, 1737.ii.21.
8. Lorenzo Cantini, ed., *Legislazione Toscana*, t. 26, 314–17. On mortmain legislation, see Anzilotti, "Piccola o grande proprietà," and *Pietro Leopoldo*, 241ff.
9. Rodolico, *Stato e chiesa*, 299.
10. *Not. post-cos.*, n. 4486, no. 7, 10v–11v, 1753.ix.13. "Ed essendo bene informata della legge proibente il passaggio dei Beni dei Secolari nelle mani morte non dimeno appunto perchè è la detta Testatrice sicurissima, che con ciò non trasgredisce alla medesima per il sopradetto motivo."
11. The law also applied to donations of pious gifts made during a Tuscan's lifetime, in

contracts called *inter vivos* as well as in other documents: codicils and *donazioni causa mortis;* see Cantini, *Legislazione toscana,* t. 26, 315.

12. *Not. post-cos.,* n. 4510, no. 23, 42v–43r, 1756.xii.28, "Costituito alla presenza delli Testimonj e di me Notaio infrascritto il Molto Reverendo Signor Don Giorgio Franchelli, quale ricordevole del Testamento, che fece fin del ventidue del Mese di Luglio 1744 per schedulam, cioè, nuncupativo nuncupatione implicita consegnato a Me notaio e avendo mutata la di la voluntà, perciò."

13. *Not. post-cos.,* n. 4510, no. 29, 58r–59v, 1765.iv.1.

14. *Not. post-cos.,* n. 5175, no. 195, 2r–5v, 1795.x.3.

15. See, for instance, *Not. post-cos.,* n. 4510, no. 20, 39v–, 1752.ix.30.

16. Ibid., 300–308.

17. *Not. post-cos.,* n. 4486, no. 8, 12r–14r, 1753.ix.28.

18. See, for instance, the testaments of domina Girolama del gia Francesco Oliva from Asciano, *Not. post-cos.,* 4486, no. 7, 1753.ix.13, and that of the nobleman Giovanfrancesco del gia Nobile Pandolfo Buoninsegni (who was eighty-six years old at the time of redaction), *Not. post-cos.,* n. 4486, no. 10, 15r–v, 1756.viii.22.

19. *Not. post-cos.,* n. 4833, no. 183, 38v–, 1772.vi.10.

20. *Not. post-cos.,* n. 4752, no. 231, 1774.i.24.

21. From other testaments, moreover, it is clear that gifts to sons and daughters in monasteries continued to be figured in the 100-zecchini allowance.

22. *Not. post-cos.,* n. 4875, no. 141, 52r–54r, 1780.vii.19.

23. *Not. post-cos.,* n. 5008, no. 15, 14v–15r, 1781.iii.29. Cantini, *Legislazione Toscana,* t. 26, 314.

24. *Not. post-cos.,* n. 5175, no. 196. 5v–15v, 1796.vii.26.

25. Scaduto, *Stato e chiesa,* 173–74; Wandruszka, *Pietro Leopoldo,* 250.

26. See Zobi, *Storia Civile della Toscana,* 2:422–23; and most recently, Mario Rosa, "La Chiesa e la città," 561–68.

27. Ibid., 516, 597.

28. Woolf, *A History of Italy,* 135. In 1790 Pietro Leopoldo left Florence for Vienna to become the Holy Roman Emperor until his death in 1792.

29. Most recently, see Hoffman, *Church and Community,* 5, "The transformation . . . was accomplished with excruciating slowness."

30. Regarding the law abolishing the "ancient" confraternities, companies, congregations, and tertiary orders, see Zobi, *Storia civile della Toscana,* 390–94.

31. In addition to the testament mentioned, only four other testators during the second half of the eighteenth century beseeched their heirs in this vein, which had been so common a half-century earlier, *Not. post-cos.,* n. 4497, no. 25, 6v–, 1758.x.30; n. 4557, no. 366, 4v–6v, 1764.iii.18; n. 4510, no. 27, 47r–, 1764.ix.10; n. 4842, no. 54, 16v–, 1772.xii.15; and n. 5071, no. 72, 22r–, 1791.viii.27.

32. *Not. post-cos.,* n. 4497, no. 23, 1r–, 1752.viii.7, "Vivere col Santo timore di Dio ed ad applicare alli loro respettivi mestieri et ad astenersi da vizi come ha fatto esso testator."

33. *Not. post-cos.,* n. 5077, no. 100, 41r–43r. 1781.v.26. "Pregandolo volere continuare a tirare avanti onoratamente il negozio di cereria come ha fatto detto Signore Testatore ed a trattare con la maggiore convenienza ed amore tanto la detta signora Maria, di lui sorella quanto la detta Signora Caterina di lui dilettissima consorte respectivamente pregandolo ancora se col tratto del tempo gli piaccesse collocarsi in matrimonio di prendere persona onorata e del suo grado e condizione e a tenersi lontano da far mallevadori per qualcunque persona."

34. Legislation promulgated on 10 October 1748 restricted mourning practices and funerals *(funerali e bruni)*. Floats and other funerary machines *(catafalchi o altre macchine*

funerarie) were prohibited. The nobility were limited to the burning of twelve candles at the high altar, citizens to six. All others were forbidden to carry out "any sort of funeral." In mourning the dead, these noncitizens were permitted to accompany "their corpses" from the house to the parish with only four large candles (*torce*). Those allowed to pay their respects had to be related to the dead within the fourth degree. (Curiously, this law does not appear in the collection of legislation edited by Cantini.) See Conti, *Firenze dopo i Medici*, 303–8; *Bandi e ordini*, vol. XIII, n. XLII; Marrara, *Riseduti e Nobiltà*, 5; Zobi, *Storia civile della Toscana*, 1:267–69. Further laws restricting funerary ostentation were passed in 1772 and 1789.

35. Most likely, the Magnifico Buonventura was a citizen. *Not. post-cos.*, n. 4497, no. 23, 1r–, 1752.viii.7.

36. *Not. post-cos.*, n. 4743, no. 29, 16v–, 1772.i.2; n. 5077, no. 100, 41r–, 1781.v.26.

37. *Not. post-cos.*, n. 4557, no. 364, 1r–, 1763.xii.30.

38. *Not. post-cos.*, n. 4752, no. 224, 1770.viii.22.

39. *Not. post-cos.*, n. 4833, no. 189, 1774.x.17; n. 5158, no. 70, 38r–, 1781.i.15; n. 5077, no. 105, 46r–, 1783.v.20; n. 5114, no. 48, 41v–, 1790.ix.25.

40. See J. J. Scarisbeck, *The Reformation and the English People* (Oxford, 1984), 20–45.

41. For instance, on 29 March 1753 the government gave its *grazia* to the Jewish woman Rachele d'Iacob Ergas di Livorno to grant in her testament 2,000 pezze to dower *povere Donzelle Ebree* and to distribute bread and clothing to "needy Jews." Further, she was given permission to grant 600 pezze to poor students in the schools of Livorno (Cantini, *Legislazione toscana*, t. 27, 14). On the other hand, the state on 30 September 1753 annulled retroactively the 1744 testament of Gio Batista Ricciardi because of violations of the 1751 mortmain laws (Ibid., 27, 7). For other *rescritti*, see ibid., t. 27, 17, 25, 160, 285; t. 29, 160.

42. *Not. post-cos.*, n. 4488, no. 27, 57r–, 1753.iv.28.

43. Archbishop Leonardo Marsili in collaboration with two Sienese noblemen founded the Company of Piety in 1698; see Fosi, "Pauperismo ed assistenza a Siena durante il Principato Mediceo," 160–64. *Not. post cos.*, n. 4752, no. 223, 47r–52r, 1770.vi.28.

In qualunque caso poi, che la presenta Signora Niccola non avesse figli maschi, in tutti i suoi Beni di qualunque genere presenti e futuri, e tanto li beni che amfiteoticci a forma dell'ultima Legge d'ammortizzazione, ragioni, ed azzioni, ecc. suoi eredi universali istituì fece ed essere volle, e respettivamente sostitui volgarmente e non mai per fidecommiso . . . i Poveri di Gesù Christo, e per essi il Pio Ospizio della Luarconia, con tanta lode, zelo, ed attenzione amministrato e governato della Venerabile Congregazione della Pietà . . . assendo sua unica mira . . . la sua Eredità serva d'un fondo, ed assegnamento perpetuo per benefizio dei Poveri, che sono il suo principale oggetto, la quale eredità doverà amministrarsi governarsi, conservarsi, ed erogarsene i frutti nella maniera che appresso: Ma perchè bisognasine da principio provedere di Persone e soggetti abili, che la rappresentino regolino ed amministrino fin' tanto che non sia depurata e sbrigata dalla predetta legittima e dalle differenze, che vi nascessaro affinché possa poi consegnarsi libara al predetto Pio Ospizio.

44. Ibid.

Ma perche i beni di Campagna non rendono il dovuto frutto e sono trascurati quando il Padrone, o altra diligente persona per esso non vi abbia tutto il riguardo e l'assisti a visiti frequentamente, perciò ordina e vuole che detti poderi siano dati in amministrazione ed un'Uomo di Campagna fedele e pratico, o vero ad un Fattore, che abbia qualche agenzia in quei contorni, il quale abbia tutte le facoltà solite aversi dai fattori, e dependa interamente e renda conto all'Economo infrascritto, al quale Fattore però per recognizione dei suoi incomodi il predetto Signor Testatore assegnò ed assegna l'annuo salario di scudi dieci. . . .

La generale amministrazione poi, e sopraintendenza non solo a detti Beni ma a tutta la sua Eredità . . . ordina, che sia presso un' Fratello secolare di detta Venerabile Congregatione col nome di Economo, che sia Persona sperimentata, ed intendente, per quanto sia pregiudiciale, che l'amministrazione di Beni di Communità stia per breve tempo presso una persona che sapendo essere il suo impiego di poca durata, non può prendere affetto ai Beni, e facilmente si Trascura. Deva per altro ogn'anno farseli un'esatta revisione come da basso, ed ogni tre anni mandarsi a partito per la conferma, e quando mancasse di diligenza, onestà, ecc. possa essere rimosso dal tale impiego dai Fratelli Segreti di detta Congregatione. . . .

E convientamente alle regole d'una buona amministrazione dei beni regolati Luoghi Pij e vuole che ogn'anno si faccia la revisione alli detti Agente ed Economo, al quale effetto l'onerendo Priore eleggerà due Fratelli . . . si possa pratichi di Campagna e di azzienda, col titolo di Revisori . . . doverà durare due anni variandone uno in ciascun'anno, acciò sempre vene sia uno inteso dallo stato precendente delle cose l'offizio di essi sarà non solo il fare la revisione una volta l'anno dell'amministrazione del detto Economo, e suo Agente, ma ancora di visitare due volte l'anno unitamente i detti Beni di Compagna in quei tempi, che parranno loro più propri, non solo quanto alle coltivazione e maniera di ritenerli, ma anco per riconoscere se si mantengano, ed esistono i Capitali di Bestiami, semi, paglie, tini, botti, ed ogn'altro mobile necessario, che averà in consegna l'Economo, ed Agente. Doveranno questi mandare la loro revisione dell'amministrazione alla Congregatione generale.

45. Ibid.

Raccomanda vivamente il buono incaminamento e direzzione di sua Eredità in benefizio dei Poveri in primo luogo alla Divina Providenza dell'Altissima, ed in secondo luogo alla protezzione del Clementissimo nostro Sovrano, che in più congiunture ha dimostrato le misere [sic] di sua Paterna Pietà verso questo Pio Luogo specialmente col Privilegiarlo dell'esenzione delle Leggi delle Mani Morte, e di poi alla vigilanza del Zelantissimo Monsignore Arcivescovo. . . .

Ma perchè è nella ferma persuasione che la detta Eredità sia per recare al detto Pio Luogo un' molto maggior' utile se non si alienaranno li Stabili di Campagna, e perche è costante, e fermo nella di sopra fattane proibizione, perciò in qualunque caso, e tempo che i detti e stabili vengano alienati per dato, e fatto, o per negligenza della detta Congregatione ordina e vuole che detto Ospizio della Luarconia immediatamente et ipso iure et facto decada dal godimento di tutta la sua Eredita.

46. *Not. post-cos.*, n. 4752, no. 224, 52r–53v, 1770.viii.22.

E perché esso sommamente desidera, e molto li è a cuore, che la Gioventù del suo Paese, e Luoghi circonvicini si possino impiegare e profittare nello Studio ordinò e volle (nel caso però e non alimenti, che mancasse senza figli maschi e femine l'infrascritto Signore Antonio Domenico suo dilettisimo Nipote erede istituto come da basso) che dalla detta Communità di Ambra, in perpetuo si deva eleggere nelle forme solite, e valide di ragione un' Maestro di Scuola capace, ed idoneo, il quale con attenzione e amore insegni ai Giovani di Detto Luogo, e Luoghi vicini quello, che saranno capaci d'imparare, al quale Maestro di Scuola lassò e legò il pieno uso ed usufrutto del Podere detto la Casa, ed il Podere detto Gavignano posto nella Cura d'Ambra, Potestaria del Bucine, assieme con la Casa paterna, e con altre terre spezzate quali stabili lassò e lassa per fondo perpetuo di detta scuola e perche l'usufrutto di detti stabili oltrepassa moto un' giusto onorario dovuto al Maestro di Scuola da eleggersi come sopra in perpetuo, ordina e vuole che dal Maestro di Scuola pro tempore si devino celebrare due Messe la Settimana per l'anima di esso Signore Testatore.

47. Although the will of the curate Zampi was the first to erect a foundation for

education in our samples, certainly it was not the first testament from Siena to establish an institution for education. Most spectacularly, Celso Tolomei in his testament of 8 September 1628 left one-half of his enormous estate (valued at 50,000 scudi) for the foundation of a seminary to be governed by the Jesuits. (See Pendola, *Il Collegio Tolomei di Siena*.) Yet the testament published in Mengozzi, *Il monte dei Paschi*, 3: appendix, does not appear in our samples and hardly was an institution for secular learning. It is a world apart from curate Zampi's simple appeal to improve the lot of his small rural community nestled in the foothills of the Chianti.

48. Jordan, *Philanthropy in England*.
49. On the physiocratic tradition in Siena, see Anzilotti, "Piccola o grande proprietà," 344f; Rodolico, *Stato e chiesa*, 95–99; Baker, *Sallustio Bandini*, 55ff.
50. Binion, *After Christianity*, 13–20; and Mat-Hasquin, "Aspects de la déchristianisation au XVIIIe siècle."
51. Jordan, *Philanthropy in England*, 16–20; and Scarisbrick, *The Reformation and the English People*, 162–70.
52. Chaunu, *La mort à Paris*, 434. Vovelle, *Piété baroque*, 318–33, and 128–33.
53. Scaduto, *Stato e chiesa*, 281. Pullan, *Rich and Poor in Renaissance Venice*, 112, 133–38, 140. Holdsworth, *A History of English Law*, 2:348–49; 11:591–92.
54. Venturi, "Church and Reform in Enlightenment Italy," 228, and *Settecento riformatori*, 2:68.
55. Grab, "The Politics of Subsistence," 209.
56. Wandruszka, *Pietro Leopoldo*, 285.
57. See Rosa, "Giurisdizionalismo e riforma," 259. See Scaduto, *Stato e chiesa in Toscana*.
58. Wandruszka, *Pietro Leopoldo*, 259.
59. Earlier in 1744 Richecourt had freed all the prisoners of the Inquisition and suppressed temporarily its operations, see Scaduto, *Stato e chiesa*, 177, 246. Rosa, "Giurisdizionalismo e riforma," 268, and 289–90; Wandruszka, *Pietro Leopoldo*, 421, 440ff.
60. On the spread of Jansenism in Tuscany, see Rodolico, *Stato e chiesa*, 19–51; Wandruszka, *Pietro Leopoldo*, 252ff, 425; Cannarozzi, "I collaboratori giansenisti di Pietro Leopoldo Granduca di Toscana," 33; Venturi, *Settecento riformatori*, 2:82–100; Ettore Passerin, "Giansenisti e illumininsti"; Jemolo, *Il Giansenismo in Italia prima della Rivoluzione*.
61. See Scarisbrick, *The Reformation and the English People*, 170ff.
62. *Not. post-cos.*, n. 5175, no. 196, 8r, 1796.vii.26, "Asserendo a cautela non contenessi in dicta schedola alcuna cosa contraria alle leggi veglianti e specialmente a quelle dei fidecommissi e mani morte."
63. Cantini, *Legislazione toscana*, t. 25, 362, "I. Avendo le Primogeniture, e li Fidecommissi per oggetto la conservazione, e sostegno delle principali Fameglie delli Stati, permettiamo a tutti quelli che godano della Nobiltà nel Nostro Granducato di Toscana di potere in avvenire instituire primogeniture, e Fidecommissi, o per atti fra' vivi, o di ultima volontà." On fidecommission, see Marrara, *Riseduti e Nobiltà:*, 5ff; Besta, *Le successioni nella storia del diritto italiano*, 159–64; and Zobi, *Storia civile della Toscana*, 1:259–65.
64. Cantini, *Legislazione toscana*, t. 25, 362–63, "IV. Le primogeniture, o Fidecommissi non potranno in avvenire fondarsi, se non sopra Luoghi di Monte de'Nostri Stati, senza che possino aver luogo sopra altre rendite censuarie, o redimibili, crediti, denaro, mobile, o altre effetti mobili."
65. Conti, *Firenze dopo i Medici*, 295–97.
66. *Not. post-cos.*, n. 4440, no. 180, 18r–, 1740.iii.8.
67. *Not. post-cos.*, n. 4440, no. 186, 29v–30r, 1741.vi.22.

68. On this law, see *Bandi e ordini*, 2:n. xlii, Zobi, *Storia civile della Toscana*, vol. 2; Wandruska, *Pietro Leopoldo*, lii; Marrara, *Riseduti e Nobiltà*, 185.
69. *Not. post-cos.*, n. 4833, no. 183, 38v–40v, 1772.vi.10.
70. *Not. post-cos.*, n. 4497, no. 23. 1r–, 1752.viii.7.
71. *Not. post-cos.*, n. 4691, no. 16, 1764.x.6; n. 4833, no. 183, 38v–40v, 1772.vi.10: "E finalmente diede e dà la paterna benedizzione a detto Signore Cavaliere Domenico-Antonio suo dilettissimo figlio, al quale inculca quanta tale e puole il timor di dio, la dovuta soggezzione alli serenissimi Reali sovrani, e alle loro leggi, l'affetto alla Patria, e il respetto ai maggiori la convienza alli Equali l'affabilità coli superiori, la christiana e nobile educazione della fameglia, e una onorata Economia domestica, assicurandolo, che mettendo in pratica questi paterni avvertimenti non solo ne riportare Lode presso le Persone senzate, ma anco premio Eterno da dio Benedetto conforme esso Signor Testator gli desidera." See n. 4842, no. 55, 17r–18r, 1773.iii.13; n. 5077, no. 100, 41r–43r, 1781.v.26; and n. 5225, no. 33, 50v, 1795.ix.21: "Colla dovuta regola, prudenza e ladevole economica che li conviene le cose loro, accade bene spesso che li lasciano sorprendere dilapidando senza considerazione il loro Patrimonio, di che poi inutilmente si pentono, volendo per tanto detto Signor testatore provvedere ad un tale incomenimente, e riparare ad tal preguidizio, che potrebbe accadere ai detti suoi signori figli ed eredi instituiti come sopra perciò come Padrone e libero disponi delle cose sue proibi e proibisce ai delli suoi signori figli Giovanni, e Luigi benchè maggiori d'età, equalmente che detto Signor Celso altro suo figlio ora per quando sia giunto all'età maggiore prescritta dagli statuti, la libera amministrazione della porzione della loro eredità come sopra, e volle e vuole che non abbiano la libera amministrazione predetta fino che non abbia ciascuno di essi compita l'età d'anni trenta."

Appendix

1. See Redon, "Autour de l'Hôpital Santa Maria della Scala à Sienne au XIIIe siècle." Founded as a hospice for pilgrims by the college of canons sometime before 1090, this hospital by the mid-Trecento had become the wealthiest ecclesiastical corporation in the territory of Siena.
2. Catoni and Fineschi, introduction to *L'Archivio Notarile (1221–1862)*; and Zobi, *Storia Civile della Toscana*, 2:328ff.
3. On the history of and legislation concerning the notarial archives, see Catoni and Fineschi, *L'Archivio Notarile*, 13–22; and *Statuti senese dell'arte dei giudici e notai*, 84–85.
4. No corresponding change, however, appears in the legislation regarding archival preservation of notarial documents.
5. See introduction to the inventories, *Inventario delle pergamene*.
6. On the distinction between pious and nonpious gifts, see Trexler, "The Bishop's Portion," 398. The distinction, however, was not always as simple as what meets the eye. As Trexler ("Charity and the Defense of Urban Elites," 74–77, and "Death and Testament," 51) has pointed out, executors of estates on occasion funneled pious funds specified for the "poor of Christ" back to the families. One reason Trexler gives for this obfuscation was to avoid payment of the *gabelles* on contracts; pious gifts were exempted.

Bibliography

Archives

Archivio di Stato, Siena
  Conventi Soppressi
  Diplomatico, Archivio Generale
  Gabelle dei Contratti
  Gabelle Generale (Mercuriali)
  Notarile antecosimiano
  Notarile postcosimiano
  Patrimonio resti
  Statuti

Archivio Arcivescovile, Siena
  Sinodi
  Visite
Biblioteca Comunale, Siena
Archivio di Stato, Firenze
  Notarile antecosimiano

Printed Sources

Academy of the Intronati (Intronatorum Academiae). *Fasti senenses*. 2 vols. Siena, 1669.
Aqazzari, Fra Filippo degli. *Gli "Assempri."* Edited by Piero Misciatelli. Siena, 1922.
Angiolieri, Cecco. *Il canzoniere*. Edited by Sebastione Blancato. Milan, 1946.
L'Archivio Notarile (1221–1862). Inventario. Edited by Giuliano Catoni and Sonia Fineschi. In *Ministero per i beni culturali e ambientali pubblicazioni degli Archivi di Stato.* 87. Rome, 1975.
Bandi e ordini da osservarsi nel granducato di Toscana. 17 vols. Florence, 1747–1800.
Bibliotheca Sanctorum. Istituto Giovanni XXIII. 12 vols. Rome, 1961.
Borromeo, Carlo. *Ammaestramenti.* Edited by P. Pio Mauri. 2d ed. Milan, 1902.
Cantini, Lorenzo. *Legislazione Toscana raccolta ed illustrata.* 30 vols. Florence, 1800–8.
Catherine of Siena. *The Dialogue.* Translated by Suzanne Noffke. New York, 1980.
———. *I, Catherine: Selected Writing of St. Catherine of Siena.* Edited and translated by Kenelm Foster and Mary J. Ronayne. London, 1980.
Colombini, B. Giovanni. *Le lettere.* Edited by Paolo Cherubini. Siena, 1957.
Il constituto del comune di Siena dell'anno 1262. Edited by Lodovico Zdekauer. Milan, 1897.
Il costituto del comune di Siena volgarizzato nel MCCCIX–MCCCX. 2 vols. Edited by Alessandro Lisini. Siena, 1903.
Cronache Senesi. Edited by Alessandro Lisini and Fabio Iacometti. In *Rerum Italicarum Scriptores,* n.s., 15, pt. 4. Bologna, 1931–37.
de Capua, Raimundus. *S. Caterina da Siena: Vita scritta dal B. Raimondo da Capua, confessore della Santa.* Translated by Giuseppe Tinagli. Siena, 1934.
Galluzzi, Riguccio. *Istoria del Granducato di Toscano sotto il governo della Casa Medici a sua altezza Reale il Serenissimo Pietro Leopoldo.* Florence, 1781.
Gigli, Girolamo. *Diario Sanese.* 3 vols. Lucca, 1723.

Imbreviaturarum Appulliensis notarii senarum (1221–23). Edited by Dina Bizzarri. Turin, 1934.
Inventario delle pergamene nel Diplomatico dall'anno 736 all'anno 1250. Edited by A. Lisini. Siena, 1908.
Liber imbreviaturarum Ildibrandi notarii (1227–1229). Edited by Mario Chiaudano. Turin, 1938.
Malavolti, Orlando. *Dell'Historie di Siena*. Venice, 1599.
Mommsen, Theodore, ed. *Petrarch's Testament*. Ithaca, N.Y., 1957.
Pecci, Giovanni, Antonio. *Memorie Storico-critiche della città di Siena*. Siena, 1755.
Petrarca, Francesco. *Lettere Senili*. 2 vols. Edited by Giuseppe Fracassetti. Florence, 1869.
———. *Rerum Familiarum*. Translated by Aldo S. Bernardo. 3 vols. Albany, N.Y., 1975–85.
Piccolomini, Alessandro. *L'Alessandro*. Edited by Florinda Carreta. Siena, 1966.
———. *La Raffaella ovver La Creanza delle Donne*. Edited by Carlo Teoli. Milan, 1862.
Piccolomini, Enea Silvio. *The Commentaries of Pius II, Books 1–9*. Translated by Florence Alden Gragg. *Smith College Studies in History* 22, nos. 1–2. Northampton, Mass., 1936–37.
Razzi, Don Silvano. *Vite di Santi e beati Toscani de' quali infino a hoggi*. Florence, 1627.
Statuti senesi dell'arte dei giudici e notai del secolo XIV. Fonti e studi del Corpus membranarum italicarum, VII. Edited by Giuliano Catoni. Rome, 1972.
Statuti senesi dell'arte dei giudici e notai dal XIV secolo. Edited by Giuliano Catoni. Rome, 1972.
Statuti Senesi scritti in volgare ne' secoli XIII e XIV. 3 vols. Edited by Filippo-Luigi Polidori and Luciano Banchi. Bologna, 1863–77.
Statuti volgari senesi. I: Breve degli speziali (1356–1542). Edited by Giovanni Cecchini and Giulio Prunai. Siena, 1942.
Tommasi, Giugurta. *Dell'historie di Siena*. 2 vols. Venice, 1625–26.
Ugurgieri-Azzolini, Fr. Isidoro. *La Pompe Sanesi*. 2 vols. Pistoia, 1649.

Secondary Works

Alberigo, Giuseppe. "Contributi alla storia della confraternità dei disciplinati e della spiritualità laicale nei secoli XV e XVI." In *Il Movimento dei Disciplinati nel Settimo Centenario dal suo inizio (Perugia—1260)*: 156–252. Spoleto, 1962.
———. "The Council of Trent: New Views on the Occasion of its Fourth Centenary." *Concilium* 7 (1965): 69–87.
———. "Carlo Borromeo come Modello di Vescovo nella chiesa post-Tridentina." *Rivista Storica Italiana* 79 (1967): 1031–52.
Alessandri, Maria Luisa. "La densità di popolazione nella Toscana meridionale negli ultimi secoli." *Rivista Geografica Italiana* 64 (1957): 224–243.
Anzilotti, Antonio. "Piccola o grande proprietà nelle riforme di Pietro Leopoldo e negli economisti del secolo XVIII." *Bullettino Senese di Storia Patria* (hereafter *BSSP*) 21 (1915): 339–69.
Ariès, Phillipe. *Western Attitudes toward Death: From the Middle Ages to the Present*. Translated by P. Ranum. Baltimore, 1974.
———. *The Hour of Our Death*. 1977. Translated by Helen Weaver. New York, 1981.
Ascheri, Mario. *Diritto e peste: Dalla crisi del Trecento all'età moderna*. Siena, 1974.
———. "I Commentari." *BSSP* 93 (1986): 549–54.
———. *Siena nel Rinascimento. Istituzioni e sistema politico*. Siena, 1985.

Ascheri and Ciampoli, Donatella. *Siena e il suo territorio nel Rinascimento. Documenti raccolti*. Siena, 1986.
Aston, Trevor, ed. *Crisis in Europe, 1560–1660. Essays from "Past and Present."* London, 1965.
Auffroy, Henri. *Evolution du testament en France des origines au XIIIe siècle*. Paris, 1899.
Baker, George R. F. "Nobiltà in declino: Il caso di Siena sotto i Medici e gli Asburgo-Lorena." *Rivista Storica Italiana* 84 (1972): 584–616.
———. *Sallustio Bandini*. Florence, 1978.
Bakhtin, Mikhail. *Rabelais and His World*. Translated by Helene Iswolsky. Cambridge, Mass., 1968.
Balestracci, Duccio, and Gabriella Piccinni. *Siena nel Trecento: Assetto urbano e strutture edilizie*. Florence, 1977.
Baron, Hans. "Franciscan Poverty and Civic Wealth as Factors in the Rise of Humanist Thought." *Speculum* 13 (1938): 1–38.
———. *The Crisis of the Early Italian Renaissance: Civic Humanism and Republican Liberty in an Age of Classicism and Tyranny*. Rev. ed. Princeton, 1966.
———. *Petrarch's* Secretum: *Its Making and Its Meaning* Cambridge, Mass., 1985.
Becker, Marvin. "Aspects of Lay Piety in Early Renaissance Florence." In *The Pursuit of Holiness in Late Medieval and Renaissance Religion: Papers from the University of Michigan Conference*, edited by Heiko Oberman and Charles Trinkaus: 177–200. Leiden, 1974.
———. *Medieval Italy: Constraints and Creativity*. Bloomington, Ind., 1981.
Bendiscoli, Mario. *Dalla Riforma alla Controriforma*. Bologna, 1974.
Berengo, Marino. *Nobili e mercanti nella Lucca del Cinquecento*. Turin, 1965.
Bernardo, Aldo S. *Petrarch, Laura, and the "Triumphs."* Albany, N.Y., 1974.
Bernstein, Allan. "Esoteric Theology: William of Auvergne on the Fires of Hell and Purgatory." *Speculum* 57 (1982): 509–31.
Besta, Enrico. *Le successioni nella storia del diritto italiano*. Milan, 1935.
Le Biccherne: Tavole dipinte delle Magistrature senesi (secoli XIII–XVIII). Edited by L. Borgia, E. Carli, M. A. Ceppari, U. Morandi, P. Sinibaldi, and C. Zarrilli. Rome, 1984.
Binion, Rudolph. *Hitler among the Germans*. New York, 1976.
———. *Soundings: Psychohistorical and Psycholiterary*. New York, 1981.
———. *Introduction à la psychohistoire*. Paris, 1982.
———. "Corrigenda." *Psychohistory Review* (1986): 69–79.
———. *After Christianity: Christian Survivals in Post-Christian Culture*. Durango, Colo., 1986.
Biraben, Jean-Noel. *Les hommes e la peste en France et dans les pays européens et méditerranéens*. 2 vols. Paris, 1975–76.
Bizzocchi, Roberto. "Chiesa e aristocrazia nella Firenze del Quattrocento." *Archivio Storico Italiano* 142 (1984): 191–282.
———. "Patronato politico e giuspatronati ecclesiastici: Il caso fiorentino." *Ricerche Storiche* 15 (1985): 95–106.
Bois, Guy. *Crise du féodalisme: Économie rurale et démographie en Normandie orientale du début du 14e siècle au milieu du 16e siècle*. Paris, 1976.
Bois, Paul. *Les paysans d'Ouest: Des structures économiques et sociales aux options politiques*. Paris, 1960.
Bonanno, Claudio, Metello Bonanno, and Luciana Pellegrini, "I legati 'pro anima' ed il problema della salvezza nei testamenti fiorentini della seconda metà del Trecento," *Ricerche storiche* 15 (1985): 183–220.
Borsook, Eve. *Mural Painters of Tuscany: From Cimabue to Andrea del Sarto*. 2d ed. Oxford, 1980.

Bossy, John. "The Counter-Reformation and the People of Catholic Europe." *Past and Present* 47 (1970): 51–70.
———. *Christianity in the West, 1400–1700*. Oxford, 1985.
Bowsky, William. "The Buon Governo of Siena (1287–1355): A Medieval Italian Oligarchy." *Speculum* 37 (1962): 368–81.
———. "The Impact of the Black Death upon Sienese Government and Society." *Speculum* 39 (1964): 1–34.
———. *The Finance of the Commune of Siena, 1287–1355*. Oxford, 1970.
———. *A Medieval Italian Commune: Siena under the Nine, 1287–1355*. Berkeley, Calif., 1981.
———. "Il contesto religioso precedente a S. Caterina: La chiese senese sotto i Nove." In *Atti del simposio internationale Cateriniano-Bernardiniano*, edited by Domenico Maffei and Paolo Nardi: 37–45. Siena, 1982.
Brandileone, Francesco. *I Lasciti per l'anima e la loro transformazione: Saggio di recerche storico-giuridiche*. In *Memorie del Reale Instituto Veneto di Scienze, Lettere ed Arti.*, vol. 28, no. 7. Venice, 1911.
Braudel, Fernand. "History and the Social Sciences, the Long Term." In *Economy and Society in Early Modern Europe. Essays from "Annales."* Edited by Peter Burke: 11–42. New York, 1972.
———. *The Mediterranean and the Mediterranean World in the Age of Philip II*. 2 vols. Paris, 1949. Translated by Siân Reynolds. New York, 1966.
Braudel, Fernand, and F. Spooner. "Prices in Europe from 1450 to 1750." In *The Cambridge Economic History of Europe, IV: The Economy of Expanding Europe in the Sixteenth and Seventeenth Centuries*: 378–486. Cambridge, 1967.
Brenner, Robert. "Agrarian Class Structure and Economic Development in Pre-industrial Europe." *Past and Present* 70 (1976): 30–75.
Brentano, Robert. "Death in Gualdo Tadino and in Rome." *Studia gratiana* 19 (1976): 79–100.
Brown, Judith. *In the Shadow of Florence: Provincial Society in Renaissance Pescia*. New York, 1982.
Brown, Peter. *The Cult of the Saints: Its Rise and Function in Latin Christianity*. Chicago, 1981.
Brucker, Gene. *Renaissance Florence*. 2d ed. Berkeley, Calif., 1983.
Burckhardt, Jacob. *The Civilization of the Renaissance in Italy*. Translated by S. G. C. Middlemore. New York, 1958.
Bynum, Caroline Walker. *Holy Feast and Holy Fast: The Religious Significance of Food to Medieval Women*. Berkeley, Calif., 1986.
Camporeale, Salvatore I. "Senso della morte e amore della vita nel Rinascimento: Susone, Valla, Erasmo, e il 'problema della salvezza.'" *Memorie Domenicane*, n.s. 8–9 (1977–78): 439–50.
Cannarozzi, P. Ciro. "I collaboratori giansenisti di Pietro Leopoldo Granduca di Toscana." *Rassegna Storica Toscana* 12 (1966): 5–59.
Cantagalli, R. *La Guerra di Siena*. Siena, 1962.
Cantimori, Delio. "Italy and the Papacy." In *The New Cambridge Modern History, II: The Reformation, 1520–1559*: 251–74. Cambridge, 1958.
———. *Prospettive di storia ereticale italiana del Cinquecento*. Bari, 1960.
Carmichael, Ann G. *Plague and the Poor in Renaissance Florence*. Cambridge, 1986.
Castellini, A. "Il Cardinale Francesco Maria Tarugi." *BSSP* 2–7 (1943–48): 88–109.
Catoni, Giuliano. "Interni di conventi senesi del Cinquecento," *Ricerche Storiche* 10 (1980): 171–203.

―――, ed. *Le pergamene dell'università di Siena e la "Domus Misericordiae": Seminario di Archivistia.* Siena, 1975–76.
Cecchini, Giovanni. "La grance dell'ospedale di S. Maria della Scala di Siena." *Economia e storia* 3 (1959): 405–22.
Chabod, Federico. *Per la storia religiosa dello Stato di Milano durante il dominio di Carlo V: Note e documenti.* 2d ed. Turin, 1971.
Chastel, André. "The Arts during the Renaissance." In *The Renaissance: Essays in Interpretation:* 227–71. London, 1982.
Chaunu, Pierre. *La mort à Paris: 16, 17 et 18e siècles.* Paris, 1978.
Cherubini, Giovanni. "Proprietari, contadini, e campagne senesi all'inizio del Trecento." In *Signori, Contadini, Borghesi: Ricerche sulla società italiana del basso medioevo:* 231–312. Florence, 1974.
Chiaudano, Mario. "I Rothschild del Duecento: La Gran Tavola di Orlando Bonsignori." *BSSP,* n.s., 6 (1935): 103–42.
Chiffoleau, Jacques. *La comptabilité de l'au-delà: Les hommes, la mort et la religion dans la région d'Avignon à la fin du Moyen Age, vers 1320–vers 1480.* Paris, 1980.
―――. "Perche cambia la morte nella regione di Avignon alla fine del Medioevo." *Quaderni Storici* 17 (1982): 449–65.
Chittolini, Giorgio. "Stati regionali e istituzioni ecclesiastiche nell'Italia centrosettentrionale del Quattrocento." In *Storia d'Italia: Annali 9: La chiesa e il potere politico del Medioevo all'età contemporanea,* edited by Giorgio Chittolini and Giovanni Miccoli: 147–93. Turin, 1986.
Cipolla, Carlo M. "Four Centuries of Italian Demographic Development." In *Population in History,* edited by D. V. Glass and D. E. C. Eversley: 570–87. Chicago, 1965.
―――. *Studi di storia della moneta. I. I movimenti dei cambi in Italia dal secolo XIII al XV.* In *Studi nelle scienze-giuridiche e sociali,* no. 101. Pavia, 1948.
Clearfield, Janis. "The Tomb of Cosimo de' Medici in San Lorenzo." *Rutgers Art Review* 2 (1981): 13–30.
Cochrane, Eric. *Florence in the Forgotten Centuries, 1527–1800: A History of Florence and the Florentines in the Age of the Grand Dukes.* Chicago, 1973.
Cohen, Sherrill. "The Convertite and the Malmaritate: Women's Institutions, Prostitution, and the Family in Counter Reformation Florence." Ph.D. dissertation, Princeton, 1985.
Cohn, Samuel Kline, Jr. *The Laboring Classes in Renaissance Florence.* New York, 1980.
―――. "Florentine Insurrections, 1342–1385." In *The English Uprising of 1381,* edited by R. H. Hilton and T. H. Aston: 143–64. Cambridge, 1984.
―――. "The Relationship between City and Countryside: Siena before and after the Black Death, 1300–1450." In *The Relationship between City and Countryside in the Later Middle Ages,* edited by Egmont Lee: Toronto, forthcoming.
Cohn, Samuel Kline, Jr., and O. Di Simplicio. "Alcuni aspetti della politica matrimoniale della nobilità senese, 1560–1700 circa." In *Forme e tecniche del potere nella città (secoli XIV–XVII),* edited by S. Bertelli: 313–30. Perugia, 1979–80.
Cole, Bruce. *Sienese Painting in the Age of the Renaissance.* Bloomington, Ind., 1985.
―――. "Old and New in the Early Trecento." In *Klara Steinweg in Memoriam. Mitteilungen des kunsthistorischen Instituts in Florenz* 12 (1973): 229–48.
Conenna, Lucia Bonelli. *Prata: Signoria rurale e communità contadina nella maremma senese. Quaderni di "Studi Senesi,"* no. 35. Milan, 1976.
Conti, Giuseppe. *Firenze dopo i Medici: Francesco di Lorena, Pietro Leopoldo, inizio del regno di Ferdinando III.* Florence, 1921.
Cooper, J. P. "Patterns of Inheritance and Settlement by Great Landowners from the

Fifteenth to the Eighteenth Centuries." In *Family and Inheritance: Rural Society in Western Europe 1200–1800,* edited by J. Goody, J. Thirsk, and E. P. Thompson: 192–327. Cambridge, 1976.
Corradi, A. *Annali delle epidemie occorse in Italia . . . fino al 1850.* 8 vols. Bologna, 1865–94.
Coulton, George Gordon. *The Black Death.* New York, 1930.
Cresi, D. "Statistica dell'ordine minoritico dell'anno 1282." *Archivium Franciscanum Historicum* 66 (1963).
Croix, Alain. *La Bretagne aux 16e et 17e siècles: La vie, la mort, la foi.* Paris, 1981.
D'Addario, Arnaldo. *Il problema Senese nella storia italiana della prima metà del cinquecento.* Florence, 1958.
Daniel-Rops, H. *The Catholic Reformation.* Paris, 1955. Translated by John Warrington. London, 1962.
Davis, Natalie Z. "City Women and Religious Change." In *Society and Culture in Early Modern France:* 65–95. Stanford, Calif., 1975.
de la Roncière, Charles. "La place des confréries dans l'encadrement religieux du Contado Florentin: L'example de la val d'elsa." *Mélanges de l'école française de Rome* 85 (1973): 31–77.
———. *Florence: Centre économique régional au XIVe siècle.* 5 vols. Aix-en-Provence, 1977.
Del Panta, Lorenzo. *Le epidemie nella storia demografica italiana (secoli XIV–XIX).* Turin, 1980.
Delumeau, Jean. *Le Christianisme va-t-il mourir?* Paris, 1978.
———. *Le catholicisme entre Luther et Voltaire.* Paris, 1971.
———. *La peur en Occident (XIVe–XVIIIe siècles): Une cité assiégée.* Paris, 1978.
———. *Le pèché et la peur: La culpabilisation en Occident (XIIIe–XVIIIe siècles).* Paris, 1983.
De Roover, Raymond. *San Bernardino of Siena and Saint'Antonio of Florence: Two Great Economic Thinkers of the Middle Ages.* Boston, 1967.
de Vries, Jan. *The Dutch Rural Economy in the Golden Age, 1500–1700.* New Haven, 1974.
———. *The Economy of Europe in an Age of Crisis, 1600–1750.* Cambridge, 1976.
Dickens, A. G. *Lollards and Protestants in the Diocese of York, 1509–1558.* Oxford, 1959.
———. *The Counter-Reformation.* New York, 1969.
Dictionnaire de droit canonique, 7 vols. Paris, 1935–.
Di Simplicio, Oscar. "Due secoli di produzione agraria in una fattoria del Senese, 1550–1751." *Quaderni Storici* 21 (1972): 781–826.
———. "La nobilità 'povera' a Siena, 1630–1680." *BSSP* 88 (1982): 71–94.
Douglas, Langton A. *A History of Siena.* London, 1902.
Duby, Georges. *Hommes et structures du moyen âge.* Paris, 1973.
Edgell, George H. *A History of Sienese Painting.* New York, 1932.
Edgerton, Samuel Y., Jr. *Pictures and Punishment: Art and Criminal Prosecution during the Florentine Renaissance.* Ithaca, N.Y., 1985.
Elton, G. R. *Reformation Europe, 1517–1559.* 2d ed. New York, 1966.
English, Edward. "Five Magnate Families of Siena, 1240–1350." Ph.D. dissertation, Centre for Medieval Studies, University of Toronto, 1981.
Epstein, Stephan. "Dall'espansione alla gestione della crisi: L'ospedale di Santa Maria della Scala di Siena e il suo patrimonio (1260–1450)." Tesi di laurea, Facoltà di Lettere, L'Università degli Studi di Siena (anno accademico, 1983/84).
Evennett, H. O. "The New Orders." In *The New Cambridge Modern History, II: The Reformation, 1520–1559:* 275–300. Cambridge, 1958.
———. *The Spirit of the Counter Reformation.* Cambridge, 1968.
Fanfani, Amintore. *Indagini sulla "rivoluzione dei prezzi."* Milan, 1940.
Fasano Guarini, Elena. *Lo Stato mediceo di Cosimo I.* Florence, 1973.

———. "I giuristi e lo stato nella Toscana Medicea cinque-seicentesca." In *Firenze e la Toscana dei Medici nell'Europa del '500,* vol. 1: 229–47. Florence, 1983.
Fenlon, Dermot. *Heresy and Obedience in Tridentine Italy. Cardinal Pole and the Counter Reformation.* Cambridge, 1972.
Fosi, Irene Polverini. "Lo stato e i poveri: l'esempio senese fra Seicento e Settecento." *Ricerche Storiche* 10 (1980): 93–115.
———. "Pauperismo ed assistenza a Siena durante il Principato Mediceo," in *Timore e carità i Poveri nell'Italia moderna. Atti del Convegno "La Pauperismo e assistenza negli antichi stati italiani (1980)."* In *Annali della Biblioteca Statale e Libreria civica di Cremona:* (1976–9): 27–30. 157–64.
Foster, Kenelm. *Petrarch. Poet and Humanist.* Edinburgh, 1984.
Febvre, Lucien. "The Origins of the French Reformation: A Badly-put Question?" In *A New Kind of History,* edited by Peter Burke: 44–107. New York, 1973.
Foucault, Michel. *Folie et déraison: Histoire de la folie à l'age classique.* Paris, 1961.
Franchina, L. "La chiesa della Madonna di Provenzano in Siena dalle origini alla traslazione dell'Immagine nel Tempio (1594–1611)." In *I Medici e lo Stato Senese 1555–1609.* Edited by L. Rombai: 71–82. Rome, 1980.
Friedman, David. "The Burial Chapel of Filippo Strozzi in Santa Maria Novella in Florence." *L'arte* 9 (1970): 109–32.
"Funerali." In *Miscellanea storica senese* 3 (1895): 185–86.
Gardner, Julian. "Arnolfo di Cambio and Roman Tomb Design." *Burlington Magazine* 115 (1973): 420–39.
Garin, Eugenio. "Problemi di religione e filosofia nella cultura fiorentina del quattrocento." *Bibliothèque d'humanisme* 14 (1952): 70–82.
Gatti, Gerardo. "Autonomia privata e volontà di testare nei secoli XIII e XIV." In *Nolens Intestatus Decedere:* 17–26. Perugia, 1985.
Genicot, Léopold. "Crisis: From the Middle Ages to Modern Times." In *The Cambridge Economic History of Europe, I.* 2d ed., edited by M. M. Postan: 660–742. Cambridge, 1966.
Ginzburg, Carlo. *I Benandanti: Stregoneria e culti agrari tra Cinquecento e Seicento.* Turin, 1966.
———. *Il formaggio e i vermi: il cosmo di un mugnaio del '500.* Turin, 1976.
Giusti, Renato. "Problemi di storia economica tra '500 e '600." *Archivio Storico Italiano* 138 (1980): 17–41.
Goldthwaite, Richard. *Private Wealth in Renaissance Florence.* Princeton, 1968.
———. "I prezzi del grano a Firenze dal XIV al XVI secolo." *Quaderni Storici* 28 (1975): 5–36.
———. *The Building of Renaissance Florence: An Economic and Social History.* Baltimore, 1980.
———. "The Medici Bank and the World of Florentine Capitalism." *Past and Present* 114 (1987): 3–31.
Goody, Jack. *The Development of the Family and Marriage in Europe.* Cambridge, 1983.
Goody, J., J. Thirsk, and E. P. Thompson. *Family and Inheritance: Rural Society in Western Europe, 1200–1800.* Cambridge, 1976.
Goubert, Pierre. *Beauvais et le Beauvaisis de 1600 à 1730: Contribution à l'histoire social de la France du XVIIe siècle.* Paris, 1960.
———. "Local History." *Daedalus* (Winter 1971): 113–27.
Grab, Alexander. "The Politics of Subsistence: The Liberalization of Austrian Lombardy under Enlightened Despotism." *Journal of Modern History* 57 (1985): 185–210.

Grayson, Cecil. "The Renaissance and the History of Literature." In *The Renaissance: Essays in Interpretation:* 201–26. London, 1982.
Greco, Gaetano. "I giuspatronati laicali nell'età moderna." In *Storia d'Italia. Annali 9. La Chiesa e il potere politico dal Medioevo all'età contemporanea.* Edited by Giorgio Chittolini and Giovanni Miccoli: 531–72. Turin, 1986.
Grendi, Edouardo. "Morfologia e dinamica della vita associativa urbana." In *Società, Chiesa e vita religiosa nell' "Ancien Régime."* Edited by Carla Russo: 115–86. Naples, 1976.
Hajnal, J. "European Marriage Patterns in Perspective." In *Population and History,* edited by D. V. Glass and D. E. C. Eversley: 147–58. London, 1965.
Hall, Marie Boas. "Problems of the Scientific Renaissance." In *The Renaissance: Essays in Interpretation:* 273–96. London, 1982.
Hallman, Barbara McClung. *Italian Cardinals, Reform, and the Church as Property, 1492–1563.* Berkeley, Calif., 1985.
Hay, Denys. *The Church in Italy in the Fifteenth Century.* Cambridge, 1977.
Henderson, John. "Charity and the Poor in Late-Medieval Florence." Unpublished essay.
———. "The Flagellant Movement and Flagellant Confraternities in Central Italy, 1260–1400." *Studies in Church History* 15 (1978): 147–60.
Herlihy, David. *Medieval and Renaissance Pistoia: The Social History of an Italian Town, 1200–1430.* New Haven, 1967.
———. "Santa Caterina and San Bernardino: Their Teachings on the Family." In *Atti del Simposio internazionale Cateriniano-Bernardiniano.* Edited by Domenico Maffei and Paolo Nardi: 917–33. Siena, 1982.
———. "The Distribution of Wealth in a Renaissance Community: Florence 1427." In *Towns in Societies,* edited by P. Abrams and E. Wrigley: 131–57. Cambridge, 1978.
Herlihy, David, and Christiane Klapisch-Zuber. *Les Toscans et leur familles: Une étude du catasto florentin de 1427.* Paris, 1978.
Heywood, William. *Palio and Ponte.* London, 1904.
Hicks, David L. "Sources of Wealth in Renaissance Siena: Businessmen and Landowners." *BSSP* 93 (1986): 9–42.
Hoffman, Philip T. *Church and Community in the Diocese of Lyon, 1500–1789.* New Haven, 1984.
———. "Wills and Statistics: Tobit Analysis and the Counter Reformation in Lyon." *Journal of Interdisciplinary History* 14 (1984): 813–34.
Holdsworth, William. *A History of English Law.* 2d ed. 14 vols. London, 1922–38.
Holmes, George. *Florence, Rome and the Origins of the Renaissance.* Oxford, 1986.
Homans, George C. *English Villagers of the Thirteenth Century.* Cambridge, Mass., 1941.
Hoskins, W. G. *The Midland Peasant: The Economic and Social History of a Leicestershire Village.* New York, 1957.
Hook, Judith. *Siena, a City and its History.* London, 1979.
Hughes, Diane O. "Sumptuary Laws and Social Relations in Renaissance Italy." In *Disputes and Settlements: Laws and Human Relations in the West,* edited by John Bossy: 69–99. Cambridge, 1983.
Huizinga, Johan. *The Waning of the Middle Ages: A Study of the Forms of Life, Thought, and Art in France and the Netherlands in the XIVth and XVth Centuries.* Translated by F. Hopman. London, 1924.
Isaacs, A. K. Chiancone. "Popoli e monti nella Siena del primo cinquecento." *Rivista Storica Italiana* 86 (1970): 32–80.
Jedin, Herbert. *A History of the Council of Trent.* 3 vols. Freiburg, 1949–75. London, 1957–61.
———. *Riforma cattolica o controriforma?* Translated by M. Guarducci. Brescia, 1957.

Jemolo, A. C. *Il Giansenismo in Italia prima della Rivoluzione*. Bari, 1928.
Jordan, W. K. *Philanthropy in England, 1480–1660: A Study of the Changing Patterns of English Social Aspirations*. London. 1958.
Kirshner, J., and A. Molho. "The Dowry Fund and the Marriage Market in Early Quattrocento Florence." *Journal of Modern History* 50 (1978): 403–38.
Kristeller, P. O. *Renaissance Thought: The Classic, Scholastic, and Humanist Strains*. New York. 1961.
Kula, Witold. *An Economic Theory of the Feudal System: Towards a Model of the Polish Economy, 1500–1800*. Paris, 1970. Translated by Lawrence Garner. London, 1976.
Landau, Peter. *Ius Patronatus. Studien zu Entwicklung des Patronats in Dekretalenrecht und der Kanonistik des 12. und 13. Jahrhunderts*. Cologne, 1975.
Lazzareschi, E. "Una mistica senese: Passitea Crogi, 1564–1615." *BSSP* 22 (1915): 419–433, and 23 (1916): 3–46.
Lebrun, François. *Les hommes et la mort en Anjou aux 17e et 18e siècles: Essai de démographie et de psychologie historiques*. Paris, 1971.
Le Goff, Jacques. *La naissance du Purgatoire*. Paris, 1981.
Le Roy Ladurie, Emmanuel. *Les paysans de Languedoc*. 2 vols. Paris, 1966.
———. "L'histoire immobile." *Annales: E.S.C.* 29 (1974): 673–92.
———. *The Territory of the Historian*. 2 vols. Translated by Ben Reynolds and Siân Reynolds. Chicago, 1979.
Lesnick, Daniel. "Religion and Social Transformation: Popular Preaching in Late Medieval Florence." *Europa* 3 (1979–80): 19–59.
———. *Preaching in Medieval Florence: Franciscans and Dominicans Compared*. New York, 1988.
Liberati, A. "Un funerale a Siena nel XV secolo." *BSSP*, 2d series, 10 (1939): 53–56.
———. "Chiese, monasteri, oratori e spedali senesi: Riccordi e notizie." *BSSP*, n.s. 10 (1939): 157–67, 261–68, 343–47; 11 (1940): 64–72, 159–66, 243–58, 332–38; 12 (1941): 66–80, 73–80, 247–55, 296–311; 3d series 1 (1942): 51–55, 117–26, 268–79; 2 (1943): 47–54, 110–15, 160–65; 3–6 (1944–47): 119–36; 7 (1948): 122–33; 8 (1949): 149–69; 9 (1950): 131–51; 12 (1953): 241–60; 13 (1954): 132–51; 14–15 (1955–56): 224–64; 16 (1957): 186–201; 17 (1958): 137–52; 18 (1959): 167–82.
Liebowitz, Ruth. "The Medici and the Sienese Church, 1557–1577." Ph.D. Dissertation, Harvard University, 1972.
Lisini, Alessandro. *Le Tavolette dipinte di Biccherna e di Gabella del R. Archivio di Stato in Siena*. Siena, 1904.
Litchfield, R. Burr. *Emergence of a Bureaucracy: The Florentine Patricians, 1530–1790*. Princeton, 1986.
Little, Lester. *Religious Poverty and Profit Economy in Medieval Europe*. Ithaca, N.Y., 1978.
Lorcin, Marie-Thérèse. "Les Clauses religieuses dans les testaments du plat pays lyonnais au XIVe et XVe siècles." *Moyen Age* 78 (1972): 287–323.
McArdle, Frank. *Altopascio: A Study in Tuscan Rural Society, 1587–1784*. Cambridge, 1978.
McManners, John. *Death and the Enlightenment: Changing Attitudes to Death among Christians and Unbelievers in Eighteenth-Century France*. Oxford, 1981.
McNeil, William H. *Plagues and Peoples*. New York, 1976.
Maffei, Domenico and Paolo Nardi, eds. *Atti del simposio internazionale Cateriniano-Bernardiniano*. Siena, 1982.
Mann, Nicholas. *Petrarch*. Oxford, 1984.
Malanima, Paolo. "Le attività industriali." In *Prato: Storia di una città*, vol. 2, edited by Elena Fasano Guarini: 217–80. Florence, 1986.
Marchetti, Valerio. *Gruppi ereticali senesi del Cinquecento*. Florence, 1975.

Marrara, Danilo. *Riseduti e Nobiltà: Profilo storico-instituzionale di un'oligarchia toscana nei secoli XVI-XVIII.* In *Biblioteca del "Bollettino Storico Pisano,"* no. 16. Pisa, 1976.
Martin, John. "Out of the Shadow: Heretical and Catholic Women in Renaissance Venice." *Journal of Family History* 5 (1985): 21–34.
Mat-Hasquin, M. "Aspects de la déchristianisation au XVIIIe siècle à propos d'un colloque récent." *Revue d'Institut de Sociologie* 52 (1979): 387–91.
Mayer, Hans Eberhard. *The Crusades.* Translated by J. Gillingham. Oxford, 1972.
Mazzi, Curzio. "Alcuni leggi sumtuarie senesi del secolo XIII." *Archivio Storico Italiano,* 4th series, 5 (1880): 133–44.
Meersseman, Giles. "La riforma delle confraternite laicali in Italia prima del Concilio di Trento." In *Problemi di vita religiosa in Italia nel Cinquecento: Atti del Convegno di storia della chiesa in Italia:* 17–30. Padua, 1960.
———. *Ordo Fraternitatis: Confraternite e pietà dei laici nel mondo medioevo.* 3 vols. Rome, 1977.
Meiss, Millard. *Painting in Florence and Siena after the Black Death: The Arts, Religion, and Society in the Mid-Fourteenth Century.* Princeton, 1951.
———. "Notable Disturbances in the Classification of Tuscan Paintings." *Burlington Magazine* 113 (1971): 178–88.
Mengozzi, Niccolò. *Il monte dei Paschi di Siena e le aziende in esso riunite: Note e storiche.* 6 vols. Siena, 1891–1902.
Mesini, C. "La sociologia di S. Bernardino da Siena." In *San Bernardino da Siena: Saggi e Ricerche:* 350–57. Milan, 1945.
Misciatelli, Piero. *Misticismo senese.* Edited by A. Lusini. Florence, 1966.
———. *Studi senesi.* Siena, 1931.
Mols, Roger. "Saint Charles Borromée, pionnier de la pastorale moderna." *Novelle revue théologique* 79 (1957): 600–621; 715–47.
Mondolfo, Ugo Guido. *Pandolfo Petrucci: Signore di Siena (14..–1512).* Siena, 1899.
Monti, Gennaro. *Le confraternite medievali dell'Alta e Media Italia.* 2 vols. Venice, 1927.
Moorman, John R. H. *The History of the Franciscan Order, from its Origin to the Year 1517.* Oxford, 1968.
Morandi, Ubaldo, *Cattedrale di Siena: Ottavo centenario della consacrazione 1179–1979.* Siena, 1979.
Nardi, Franco Daniele. "Aspetti della vita dei religiosi a Siena nell'età della Controriforma (1600–1650) (1ª parte)." *BSSP* 93 (1986): 194–240.
———. "Matteo Guerra e la Congregazione dei Sacri Chiodi (secc. XVI–XVII). Aspetti della religiosità senese nell'età della Controriforma," *BSSP,* 91 (1984): 12–148.
Nardi, Paolo. *Mariano Sozzini: Giureconsulto Senese del Quattrocento.* In *Quaderni di "Studi Senesi,"* no. 32. Milan, 1974.
Norberg, Kathryn. *Rich and Poor in Grenoble, 1600–1814.* Berkeley, Calif., 1985.
Oberman, Heiko. *The Harvest of Medieval Theology: Gabriel Biel and Late Medieval Nominalism.* Cambridge, Mass., 1963.
Obelkevich, James, ed. *Religion and the People, 800–1700.* Chapel Hill, N.C., 1979.
Olivieri, Achille. "Spazi mentali ed urbani della morte," *Ricerche di storia sociale e religiosa* 14 (1978): 119–34.
Origo, Iris. *The World of San Bernardino.* New York, 1962.
Ottolenghi, D. "Studi demografici sulla popolazione di Siena dal secolo XVI al XIX." *BSSP* 10 (1903): 297–358.
Paglia, Vicenzio. *"La pietà dei carcerati": Confraternite e società a Roma nei secoli XVI–XVIII.* Rome, 1980.

———. *La morte confrortata: Riti della paura e mentalità religiosa a Roma nell'età moderna*. Rome, 1982.
Panfosky, Erwin. "Mors vitae testimonium: The Positive Aspect of Death in Renaissance and Baroque Iconography." In *Studien zur toskanischen Kunst: Festschrift für Ludwig Henrich Heydenreich*: 221–237. Munich, 1964.
Pansini, Giuseppe. "Per una storia del feudalesimo nel Granducato di Toscano durante il periodo mediceo." *Quaderni Storici* 19 (1972): 131–86.
Papi, Massimo. "Confraternite ed ordine mendicanti a Firenze: Aspetti di una ricerca quantitativa." *Mélanges de l'école française de Rome* 89 (1977): 723–32.
Paravicini Bagliani, A. *I testamenti dei cardinali del Duecento*. Rome, 1980.
Pardi, Giuseppe. "La rappresentazione del Beato Giovanni Colombini." *BSSP* 4 (1897): 418–43.
———. "La popolazione di Siena e del Senese attraverso i secoli." *I: La città. Estratta dal BSSP* (1924): 1–48.
———. "Il Beato Giovanni Colombini da Siena." *Nuova Rivista Storica* 11 (1927): 286–336.
Parenti, Giuseppe. *Prezzi e mercato del grano a Siena (1546–1765)*. Florence, 1942.
Park, Katharine. *Doctors and Medicine in Early Renaissance Florence*. Princeton, 1985.
Passeri, Vincenzo. *Repertorio dei toponimi della provincia di Siena*. Siena, 1983.
Passerin, Ettore. "Giansenisti e illumininsti." In *La cultura illuministica in Italia*, edited by Mario Fabini: 189–207. Turin, 1957.
Pastore, Alessandro. "Testamenti in tempo di Peste: La pratica notarile a Bologna nel 1630." *Società e storia* 5, 16 (1982): 263–97.
Pendola, P. Tommaso. *Il Collegio Tolomei di Siena*. Siena, 1852.
Petrocchi, Massimo. *La Controriforma in Italia*. Rome, 1947.
———. "La devozione alla vergine negli scritti di pietà del Cinquecento italiano." In *Italia Sacra, 2: Problemi di vita religiosa in Italia nel Cinquecento*: 281–87. Padua, 1960.
Petrucci, Armando. "Note su il testamento come documento." In *Nolens Intestatus Decedere*: 11–16. Perugia, 1985.
Phelps-Brown, E. H., and S. V. Hopkins. "Seven Centuries of Building Wages." *Economica* 22 (1955): 195–206.
———. "Seven Centuries of the Prices of Consumables, Compared with Builders' Wage-Rates." *Economica* 23 (1956): 296–314.
Pinto, Giuliano. "Aspetti dell'indebitamento e della crisi della proprietà contadina." In *La toscana nel tardo medio evo: Ambiente, economia rurale, società*: 207–24. Florence, 1982.
Pirillo, Paolo. "La terrasanta nei testamenti fiorentini del Dugento." In *I. Italia, oriente, mediterraneo: Toscana e Terrasanta nel medioevo*, edited by Franco Cardini: 57–74. Florence, 1982.
Pope-Hennessy, John. *Sienese Quattrocento Painting*. Oxford, 1947.
Postan, M. M. "Medieval Agrarian Society in its Prime: England." In *The Cambridge Economic History of Europe, I*, 2d ed., edited by M. M. Postan: 549–632. Cambridge, 1966.
"Il pranzo dei morti." In *Miscellanea storica senese* 3 (1895): 28–29.
Prodi, Paolo. *Il Cardinale Gabriele Paleotti (1522–1597)*. 2 vols. Rome, 1959–67.
Prodi, Paolo. *La crisis religiosa del XVI secolo: Riforma cattolica e controriforma*. Bologna, 1964.
Prosperi, Adriano. *Tra Evangelismo e Controriforma: G. M. Giberti (1495–1543)*. Rome, 1969.
———. "La figura del Vescovo fra '400 e '500." In *La Chiesa e il potere politico*: 217–62.

———, ed. "I vivi e i morti." *Quaderni Storici* 17 (1982): 391–628.
Prunai, Giulio. "I capitoli della compagnia di S. Domenico in Campo Regio." *BSSP* 47 (1940): 117–46. *Bullettino Senese di Storia Patria*.
Pullan, Brian. *Rich and Poor in Renaissance Venice. The Social Institutions of a Catholic State, to 1620*. Cambridge, Mass., 1971.
———. "The Old Catholicism, the New Catholicism." In *Timore e carità: I poveri nell'Italia moderna*, edited by Giorgio Politi, Mario Rosa, Franco della Peruta: 14–24. Cremona, 1982.
Quazza, Guido. *La decadenza italiana nella storia europea: Saggi sul Sei-Settecento*. Turin, 1971.
Redon, Odile. *Uomini e comunità del contado senese nel Duecento*. Siena, 1982.
———. "Autour de l'Hôpital Santa Maria della Scala à Sienne au XIIIe siècle." *Ricerche Storiche* 15 (1985): 17–34.
Repetti, Emmanuel. *Dizionario geografico fiscio e storico della Toscana*. 6 vols. Florence, 1833–44.
Rico, Francisco. *Vida y obra de Petrarca*. Vol. I, *Lectura del "Secretum,"* Padua, 1974.
Riener, Eleanor Sabina. "Women in the Medieval City: Sources and Uses of Wealth by Sienese Women in the Thirteenth Century." Ph.D. dissertation, New York University, 1975.
Rodolico, Niccolò. *Stato e chiesa in Toscana durante la Reggenza lorenese (1737-1765)*. Florence, 1910.
Romano, Ruggiero. "La storia economica dal secolo xIV al Settecento." In *Storia d'Italia 2: Dalla caduta dell'Impero romano al secolo XVIII. 1813-1931*. Edited by R. Romano and C. Vivanti. Turin, 1974.
Ronzani, Mauro. "Gli ordini mendicanti e la cura animarum cittadina fino all'inizio del Trecento: due esempi." In *Nolens Intestatus Decedere:* 115–32. Perugia, 1985.
Rosa, Mario. "La Chiesa e la città, in *Prato*," II, 503–78.
———. "Problemi di vita religiosa in Italia nel Cinquecento (note e appunti)." *Bibliotèque d'humanisme et Renaissance* 23 (1961): 395–414.
———. "Giurisdizionalismo e riforma religiosa nella politica ecclesiastica leopoldine." *Rassegna Storica Toscana* 11 (1965): 257–300.
Rusconi, Roberto. "Confraternite, compagnie e devozioni," in *La Chiesa el il potere politico*, 467–506.
Sanesi, G. "Il testamento di un prestatore Senese . . . (1238)." *BSSP* 4 (1897): 115.
Scaduto, F. *Stato e chiesa in Toscana sotto Leopoldo I: 1765-1790*. Florence, 1910.
Scarisbrick, J. J. *The Reformation and the English People*. Oxford, 1984.
Schevill, Ferdinand. *Siena: The Story of a Mediaeval Commune*. New York, 1909.
Schmitt, Charles B. "Philosophy and Science in Sixteenth-Century Italian Universities." In *The Renaissance: Essays in Interpretation*: 297–336. London, 1982.
Schneider, Robert. "Mortification on Parade: Penitential Processions in Sixteenth- and Seventeenth-century France." *Renaissance and Reformation* 22 (1986): 123–46.
Scott, Karen. "'This is why I have put you among your neighbors': St. Bernardino's and St. Catherine's Understanding of the Love of God and Neighbor." In *Cateriniano-Bernardiniano:* 279–94.
Seidl, Max, and Peter Anselm Riedl. *Italienische Forschungen herausgegeben vom Kunsthistorischen Institut in Florenz Sonderreihe: Die Kirchen von Siena*, Band 1. Munich, 1985.
Seragnoli, Daniele. *Il Teatro a Siena nel Cinquecento: "Progetto" e "Modello" Drammaturgico nell'accademia degli intronati*. Rome, 1980.

Silverman, Sydel. "The Uses of History in Anthropology: The Palio of Siena." *American Ethnologist* 6 (1979): 413–36.
―――. "Rituals of Inequality: Stratification and Symbol in Central Italy." In *Social Inequality: Comparative and Developmental Approaches*, edited by Gerald D. Berreman: 163–80. New York, 1981.
Simiand, François. *Recherches anciennes et nouvelles sur le mouvement général des prix du 16e au 19e siècle*. Paris, 1932.
Smart, Alastair. *The Dawn of Italian Painting, 1250–1400*. Ithaca, N.Y., 1978.
Stone, Lawrence. *The Family, Sex and Marriage in England, 1500–1800*. Abridged ed. New York, 1979.
Stone, Lawrence, and Jeanne C. Fawtier Stone. *An Open Elite? England, 1540–1880*. Oxford, 1984.
Strocchia, Sharon. "Burials in Renaissance Florence, 1300–1500." Ph.D. dissertation, University of California, Berkeley, 1981.
Stumpo, Enrico. "Il consolidamento della grande proprietà ecclesiastica nell'età della Controriforma." In *La Chiesa e il potere politico*: 265–90.
Székely, G. "Le movement des flagellants au 14e siècle, son caractère et ses causes." In *Hérésies et société dans l'Europe préindustrielle, 11e–18e siècles*: 229–243. Edited by Jacques Le Goff. Paris, 1968.
Tamassia, Nino. *La famiglia italiana nei secoli decimoquinto e decimosesto*. Milan, 1910.
Tenenti, Alberto. *Il Senso della morte e l'amore della vita nel Rinascimento (Francia e Italia)*. 2d ed. Turin, 1977.
Tognetti, Giampaolo. "Sul 'Romito' e profeta Brandano da Petroio," *Rivista Storica Italiana* 22 (1960): 20–44.
Trexler, Richard. "Death and Testament in the Episcopal Constitutions of Florence (1327)." In *Renaissance Studies in Honor of Hans Baron*, edited by Anthony Molho and John Tedeschi: 29–74. Dekalb, Ill., 1971.
―――. "The Bishop's Portion: Generic Pious Legacies in the Late Middle Ages in Italy." *Traditio* 28 (1972): 397–450.
―――. "Le célibat à la fin du Moyen Age: Les religieuses de Florence. *Annals, E.S.C.*, 27 (1972): 1329–50.
―――. "Charity and the Defense of Urban Elites in the Italian Communes." In *The Rich, the Well Born, and the Powerful*, edited by F. C. Jaher: 64–109. Urbana, Ill., 1973.
―――. "Ritual in Florence: Adolescence and Salvation in the Renaissance." In *The Pursuit of Holiness*, edited by H. Oberman and C. Trinkaus: 200–264. Leiden. 1974.
―――. *Public Life in Renaissance Florence*. New York, 1980.
Trinkaus, Charles. *The Poet as Philosopher: Petrarch and the Formation of Renaissance Consciousness*. New Haven, 1979.
Turchini, Angelo. *Clero e fedeli a Rimini in età post-Tridentina*. Italia Sacra: Studi e documenti di storia ecclesiastica, no. 27. Rome, 1978.
Ullmann, Walter. "The Medieval Origins of the Renaissance." In *The Renaissance: Essays in Interpretation*: 33–82. London, 1982.
Van Os, Hank. "The Black Death and Sienese Painting: A Problem of Interpretation." *Art History* 4 (1981): 237–49.
Vauchez, André. "La Commune de Sienne, les ordres mendicants et le culte des saints: Histoire et enseignements d'une crise, novembre 1328–avril 1329." *Mélanges de l'école française de Rome* 89 (1977): 751–67.
Venturi, Franco. "Church and Reform in Enlightenment Italy: The Sixties of the Eighteenth Century." *Journal of Modern History* 48 (1976): 285–32.
―――. *Settecento riformatori II: La chiesa e la repubblica dentro l loro limiti*. Turin, 1976.

Vilar, Pierre. *Or et monnaie dans l'histoire, 1450–1920*. Paris, 1974.
Vovelle, Michel. *Piété baroque et déchristianisation en Provence au XVIIIe siècle: Les attitudes devant la mort d'après les clauses des testaments*. Paris, 1973.
———. *La mort et l'occident, de 1300 à nos jours*. Paris, 1983.
Wainwright, Valerie. "Conflict and Popular Government in Fourteenth-Century Siena: Il Monte dei Dodici." In *Atti del III Convegno di studi sulla storia dei ceti dirigenti in Toscana:* 57–80. Florence, 1981.
Wallerstein, Immanuel. *The Modern World-System I: Capitalist Agriculture and the Origins of the European World-Economy in the Sixteenth Century*. New York. 1974.
———. *The Modern World-System II: Mercantilism and the Consolidation of the European World-Economy, 1600–1750*. New York, 1980.
Wandruszka, Adam. *Pietro Leopoldo: Un grande riformatore*. Translated by Giuseppe Cosmelli. Florence, 1968.
Watkins, René. "The Uses of Adversity in Petrarch's Humanism." *Psychohistory Review* 2 (1982): 47–67.
Weissman, Ronald. *Ritual Brotherhood in Renaissance Florence*. New York, 1982.
White, Stephen D. *Custom, Kinship, and Gifts to Saints. An Essay on the* Laudatio Parentum *in Western France, c.1050–c.1150*. Chapel Hill, N.C., 1988.
Woolf, Stuart. *A History of Italy, 1700–1860: The Social Constraints of Political Change*. London, 1979.
Wright, A. D. *The Counter Reformation: Catholic Europe and the Non-Christian World*. New York, 1982.
Yver, Jean. *Essai de géographie coutumière*. Paris, 1966.
Zancan, Marina. "La donna." In *Letteratura italiana: Le questioni*, edited by R. Antonelli and A. Cicchetti: 765–811. Turin, 1986.
Zdekauer, Lodovico. *La vita privata dei senesi nel dugento*. Siena, 1899.
———. *Il mercante senese nel dugento*. Siena, 1925.
Zobi, Antonio. *Storia civile della Toscana dal 1737 al 1848*. 5 vols. Florence, 1850–55.

~ Index

Adoption, 132–35; testamentary bequests to adopted children, 133–34, 283n22
Agazzari, Fra Filippo degli, 76, 80
Agnese of Montepulciano, 77, 81
Altars, private, 102, 169–70
Angiolieri, Cecco, 77, 133
Annales: Economies, Sociétés, Civilisations, 2, 11, 259n5
Ariès, Philippe, 4, 11
Artisans: as adherents of Counter Reformation piety, 164–65, 184, 196–98, 225; testamentary bequests by, 35, 55, 56, 70, 122–25, 170, 184, 196–98, 218, 235
Asciano, 8, 109, 140, 179, 233, 235, 239
Avignon, 3–4

Becker, Marvin, 35, 37
Bernardino of Siena, Saint, 15, 29, 51, 56, 60, 83–85, 98–99, 102, 237, 248; attitude toward marriage, 30–31; attitude toward usury, 51; remarks on the plague of 1363, 40; veneration of, 173–74. *See also* Saints
Black Death, 3, 15, 25, 27, 37–40, 48, 51, 63, 86–87, 89, 93, 102, 247, 265n3; effect on testamentary bequests, 17, 38–40, 247, 266n12. *See also* Plagues
Boccaccio, Giovanni, 85, 91, 92
Borghesi, Niccolò, 157–58
Borromeo, Carlo, 144, 168, 187, 198, 228
Bossi, Francesco, Bishop of Perugia, visitations of, 132, 150, 165–66, 186–88, 190, 194, 197, 199, 208, 248, 296–97n17, 297n18, 299n56
Brown, Peter, 113
Brucker, Gene, 35
Bruni, Leonardo, 38
Burckhardt, Jacob, 57, 100, 132, 155–57, 248
Burial customs: during the Counter Reformation, 179–82, 192, 201–2, 216, 225–27, 293–94n80, 306n54; during the Enlightenment, 237–38, 308–9n34; during the Renaissance, 60–62, 113–14, 270n22, 293–94n80; of the nobility, 61, 113–15; of women, 201–2
Burial societies, 163–66, 195–96; membership in, 163–64, 208; testamentary bequests to, 212. *See also* Confraternities

Catherine of Siena, Saint, 58, 60, 66, 72, 78, 80–82, 85–86, 135, 222, 237, 239; asceticism of, 74–75; attitude toward marriage, 29–30, 74–76; veneration of, 173–74
Chapels, private, foundation of, 61–62, 102–13, 279n36, 279–80n37
Charitable bequests: during the Counter Reformation, 165–66, 188–201, 212–19; during the Enlightenment, 231–43; during the Renaissance, 16–32, 54–57, 94, 98–121; general pattern of, 247–49. *See also* Confraternities; Dowries; Hermits; Hospitals; Poor; Prisoners; Welfare Congregations
Chaunu, Pierre, 3–4, 16, 236, 242
Chiffoleau, Jacques, 3–4, 236; and "Christianization," 3–4, 37, 58, 269n3
Ciompi Revolution, 32
"Civic Christianity," 17, 23–29, 35, 49
Colombini, Giovanni, 30, 72–77, 80, 135
Conditional gifts, 139–45; to recipients of charitable bequests, 215–16; to universal heirs, 146–58; to widows, 142–44
Confraternities, 15–16, 24–25, 56, 149, 196, 234, 238, 240; during the Counter Reformation, 163–66, 169, 172, 211–13, 215; value of testamentary bequests to, 24–25. *See also* Burial societies; Penitent movements; Poor; Welfare congregations
Conti, Giuseppe, 243
Council of Trent, 11, 115, 127, 131, 150, 166, 177–78, 185–86, 199, 206, 208, 217, 248
Counter Reformation, 51, 132, 115, 139; chronology of, 166, 185–88; culture, 166–84, 191–93, 206–9, 218–19; effect on the nobility, 188–94; effect on rural testators,

327

Counter Reformation (*cont.*)
194–96; effect on urban testators, 196–98; effect on women, 198–209; pattern of charitable bequests, 165–66, 188–201, 212–19; pattern of religious bequests, 162–84, 188–201, 210–30; piety, 161–84, 185–209, 210–30, 248; reforms of, 174, 185–88
Croix, Alain, 4, 242
Crusades, testamentary bequests to, 100, 276n4, 276n6

Datini, Francesco, 16
"Dechristianization," 2–4, 236, 269n3
Delumeau, Jean, 38, 67–68
Diplomatico, 41, 98, 251–58
Disinheritance, 135–39
Dowries, 28–32, 55–56, 115–18, 126–27, 130, 131, 135, 142–43, 203–9, 212–14; decline in testamentary bequests to, 163, 213; funds established by testators, 28–32, 115, 123, 163, 169, 172, 213–14, 247; value of testamentary bequests to, 28. *See also* Charitable bequests; Women

Edgell, George H., 36
Education, testamentary bequests concerning, 228, 240, 310–11n47
Election of priests, testamentary bequests for, 108–13
Enlightened despotism, 231–49; legislation of, 233, 241–44, 249; pattern of charitable bequests, 231–43; pattern of religious bequests, 231–44; piety, 231–44; value of religious bequests, 231–33
Enlightenment, decline of piety during, 3–4, 232–33, 241–43, 248–49
Epstein, Stephan, 17, 47
Estate management, testamentary bequests concerning, 68–71, 240–41

Fidecommission, 236, 243–46; effect on testamentary bequests, 243–46; legislation concerning, 243, 249. *See also* Lineage; Nobility; Primogeniture; Real property
Flagellants. *See* Penitent Movements
Florence, 10, 16, 29, 32, 35, 36, 37, 46, 47, 75, 100, 115, 122–23, 174, 194, 234
Francesco Stefano, Grand Duke of Tuscany, 11, 236; legislation of, 11, 233–34, 242
Francis of Siena, Blessed, 30, 72, 76, 78, 81

Galluzzi, Riguccio, 210
Gioacchino of Siena, 76, 81
Goldthwaite, Richard, 47
Grasso, Agnolo di Tura del, 46, 78–80, 85
Guidini, Cristofano, 29–30, 75

Herlihy, David, 35
Hermits, testamentary bequests to, 50–51, 100. *See also* Charitable bequests
Heywood, William, 174
Hoffman, Philip, 243, 297n22
Hospitals, 16, 17–24; the Misericordia, 21, 49, 105; testamentary bequests to, 22–23, 115, 162; value of testamentary bequests to, 19–24. *See also* Charitable bequests; Santa Maria della Scala
Huizinga, Johan, 37, 38, 221

Illegitimate heirs, 130–32, 283n21

Jansenism, 227, 236, 242
Jesuati, 73
Jordan, W. K., 240, 260n15
Joseph II, Holy Roman Emperor, 236, 242

Lebrun, François, 4, 236
Le Roy Ladurie, Emmanuel, 1, 15
Lineage: impact of, on testamentary bequests, 108–14, 127–29, 144–45, 148–55, 206–7, 248; nobility's attitude toward, 155–58, 191–93, 243–46. *See also* Fidecommission; Nobility; Primogeniture; Real property
Lorcin, Marie-Thérèse, 4
Luther, Martin, 178, 185–86

McNeil, William, 38
Malavolti family, 39, 61, 181
"Malthusian Renaissance," 29, 31
Mary, 169–71; veneration of, 24, 56, 108, 172, 174, 176, 183, 191, 222, 234
Masses: perpetual, 66, 111, 112, 171, 193, 219–21, 238–39, 290n18; stipulations concerning bequests for, 5, 64–68, 167–68, 183, 220–21, 234, 271n33; testamentary bequests for, 62–65, 109, 166–71, 219, 225–27, 236, 238–39, 290n17. *See also* Religious bequests
Meiss, Millard, 45
Mendicants: Augustinians, 22, 33, 78–79, 83, 168, 234; Carmelites, 33, 217, 238; Conventuals, 33, 83, 219; culture of, 72–87, 272n9; Dominicans, 22, 33, 78, 106–7, 181, 205, 207, 219, 238; Franciscans, 22, 24, 33, 34, 60, 66, 78, 83, 105, 107, 149, 182, 219, 221; Observants, 33, 83, 107, 224, 226, piety of, 78–79; Servites, 33, 78, 151, 170, 182, 243; testamentary bequests to, 265n56. *See also* Monasteries; Monastic orders; Religious bequests
Mengozzi, Niccolò, 10, 122
Monasteries, 32–35, 187, 290n8; testamen-

tary bequests to, 22, 33–34, 70, 115, 150, 162, 216–17. *See also* Mendicants; Monastic orders; Religious Bequests
Monastic orders, 78–79, 182, 185, 202, 217; Benedictines, 16–17, 78. *See also* Mendicants; Monasteries; Religious bequests
Montalcino, 9, 69, 138, 252
Mortmain, 233–43; legislation concerning, 233, 239, 241–42, 248; effect on religious bequests, 234–43

Neri, Donato di, 40, 49
Nine, the, government of, 5, 40, 72, 79, 122, 126
Nobility, 125–26, 260*n*17; attitudes toward family and lineage, 108–13, 243–46; charitable bequests by, 189–90, 231–33, 235; effect of the Counter Reformation on, 188–94; foundation of private chapels, 102–12; funerals of, 113–14, 180–81, 226–27, 235, 293*n*78; religious bequests by, 44, 52, 56, 125–26, 188–93, 231–33, 235. *See also* Burial customs; Counter Reformation; Fidecommission; Lineage; Primogeniture; Real property; Religious bequests
Norberg, Kathryn, 15–16
Notarile, 41, 251–58
Nunneries, 33–35; demolition of Santa Maria Maddalena, 158. *See also* Religious bequests

Operai, 16–17; testamentary bequests to, 102. *See also* "Civic Christianity"; Religious bequests
Origo, Iris, 40

Papal visitations, 132, 180, 186–88, 241; effect on testamentary bequests, 168, 188–201, 248. *See also* Bossi, Francesco
Parenti, Giuseppe, 47
Parish churches, 32–35; testamentary bequests to, 59, 162, 217–18. *See also* Religious bequests
Parish clergy: testamentary bequests of, 108–9, 112, 227, 234; as universal heirs, 118–19. *See also* Religious bequests; Religious formulas; Universal heirs
Penitent movements, 24, 56, 78–80
Petrarch, Francesco, 37, 38, 42–44, 87–94, 247, 275*n*57, 276*n*68
Petroio, Brandano da, 146
Petrucci, Pandolfo, 5, 103, 122, 157–58
Petrucci family, 5, 107, 122, 157–58, 236, 257
Piccolomini, Alessandro, 128; *Alessandro*, 156–57

Piccolomini, Enea Silvio (Pope Pius II), 5, 72, 85–86, 157
Piccolomini, Francesco, bishop of Pienza, 236
Piccolomini family, 61, 69, 141, 144, 157–58, 170, 174, 191–92, 209, 213, 214–15, 228–29, 257
Pietro Leopoldo, Grand Duke of Tuscany, 10, 237, 242, 244, 251–52
Piety. *See* Counter Reformation; Enlightenment; Renaissance
Pious giving. *See* Religious bequests
Pious places, 39, 54, 100, 169, 234. *See also* Religious bequests
Pistoia, 16, 35, 122, 236
Plagues: of 1348, 3, 15–17, 25, 27, 37–40, 48, 51, 63, 86–87, 89, 93, 102, 247, 265*n*3; of 1363, 11, 17, 40–45, 53, 56–57, 65–68, 71, 92, 143–44; combined effect on the economy of Siena, 29, 48, 53; compared effect of the two plagues on testamentary bequests, 45–50, 93–94, 247–48, 266*n*19. *See also* "Malthusian Renaissance"
Poor: definitions of, 25–27, 214–16, 263–64*n*36; congregations for the relief of, 165–66, 169, 171, 201, 212–13; testamentary bequests to, 27–28, 54–57, 115–18. *See also* Charitable bequests; Confraternities; Welfare congregations
Pope-Hennessy, John, 36
Price-series analyses, 10, 122; to determine the value of testamentary bequests, 47–48
Primogeniture, 153–55, 191–92, 243–45. *See also* Fidecommission; Lineage; Nobility; Real property
Prisoners: testamentary bequests to, 51. *See also* Charitable bequests
Prodi, Paolo, 158
Provence, 2–3, 15, 243
Purgatory, 58–59, 183, 210, 231, 248, 269*n*4; reference to, in testamentary preambles, 178–79, 221–22, 224, 229. *See also* Religious formulas

Radicondoli, 9, 65, 124–25, 130, 138, 193, 194
Rapolano, 9, 62, 79
Raymond of Capua, 30, 74, 81, 82
Real property: entail of, 153–55, 243–46; income derived from, 192–93; restrictions placed on the alienation of, 68–71, 139–45, 148–51, 203–9, 243–46. *See also* Conditional gifts; Fidecommission; Lineage; Mortmain; Primogeniture; Universal heirs
Religious art, 110, 175–76, 228–29, 292*n*66

Religious bequests: by artisans and shopkeepers, 44, 196–98; during the Counter Reformation, 161–64, 188–201, 211–25; definition of, 252–53, 312n6; during the Enlightenment, 231–43; general pattern of, 247–49; by the nobility, 44, 52, 56, 125–26, 188–93, 231–33, 235; during the Renaissance, 17–25, 32–36, 37–54, 94, 98–121, 155–58; by rural residents, 44, 194–96; structure of, 37–57, 94; value of, 42–49, 97–100, 119, 120, 127, 161–62, 210–11; by women, 39, 107, 198–202. *See also* Charitable bequests; Confraternities; Masses; Monasteries; Nunneries; Parish churches; Pious places
Religious calendar, 171, 220
Religious formulas: of the Counter Reformation, 176–79; of the Enlightenment, 237; of the Renaissance, 58–60, 128–30, 146–48, 150–51, 155. *See also* Mary; Purgatory; Saints
Renaissance: culture, 72–94; pattern of charitable bequests, 16–32, 54–57, 94, 98–121, 155–58; pattern of religious bequests, 17–25, 32–36, 37–54, 94, 98–121, 155–58; piety, 15–36, 37–57, 94, 97–120, 127
Richecourt, Count Emmanuele de, 231, 233, 242, 243, 249
Roncière, Charles de la, 47

Saints, 78–83; cult of, 171–75; testamentary bequests in veneration of, 24, 109, 172–75, 183, 221–22, 236–37, 295n57. *See also* Benardino of Siena; Catherine of Siena; Religious bequests; Religious formulas
Salimbene family, 23, 66, 105–6
Santa Maria della Scala, 17–20, 49, 56, 105, 110, 133, 134, 150, 157, 220–21, 234; testamentary bequests to, 21, 22, 23, 47, 50, 69, 115, 131, 149, 153, 154, 157, 162, 221, 251–52. *See also* Charitable bequests; Hospitals; Religious bequests
Savonarola, Girolamo, 97
Secularism: Counter Reformation, 174–75; Enlightenment, 228–30; Renaissance, 49, 100–102, 157–58, 248–49
Servants, domestic, testamentary bequests to, 216–17, 231–32
Seventeenth-century crisis, 198, 212, 232, 280–81n57

Schevill, Ferdinand, 36
Siena: culture, 10, 36, 45–46, 80, 261n34; economy, 10, 53, 118, 121–25, 210–11, 280–81n57; political development, 5–10; population, 10, 31–32, 54, 122–23
Silverman, Sydel, 174
Society of Jesus Christ, 228
Sources, 41, 122, 251–58; comparison of *Diplomatico* and *Notarile*, 252–58. *See also* *Diplomatico*; *Notarile*
Stone, Lawrence, 203

Tarugi, Francesco Maria, 187–88, 297n18
Tenenti, Alberto, 70
Time, stipulations of, in testaments, 65–68, 171
Tolomei, Baldus, 52, 54
Tolomei, Blasius, 22, 27, 52–53, 258
Tolomei, Giovanni, 79
Tolomei family, 61, 63, 69, 129, 148, 206, 257
Trexler, Richard, 16
Twelve, the, government of, 5, 20, 126

Universal heirs, 127, 139–45, 202–9; conditional legacies to, 146–58; ecclesiastical institutions as, 22, 51, 69, 70, 108, 131, 149, 168, 196, 215, 217–18; testators' own souls as, 232–33, 248; *See also* Conditional gifts; Real property; Women
Usury, 51–54; influence on testamentary bequests, 51–54, 100, 268n62

Venturi, P., 161, 185
Villani, Matteo, 46, 85
Vovelle, Michel, 2–4, 15, 58, 236, 243, 259n6

Weber, Max, 123–24
Welfare congregations, 165–66, 169, 171, 201, 208, 212–13, 240. *See also* Confraternities; Poor
Women: as adherents of the Counter Reformation, 198–209, 248, 298n44; dowries of, 28–32, 55–56, 115–18, 126–27, 130, 131, 135, 142–43, 203–9, 212–14; expressions of gratitude to, in testamentary bequests, 202–9; pattern of religious bequests, 199–202; religious confraternities of, 188, 199–202, 208, 212; as universal heirs, 203–9, 224, 300–301n66
Woolf, Stuart, 236

About the author

Samuel K. Cohn, Jr., is associate professor of history at Brandeis University.

Death and Property in Siena, 1205–1800

Designed by Ann Walston.

Composed by The Composing Room of Michigan, Inc., in Galliard.

Printed by Thomson-Shore, Inc., on 50-lb. Glatfelter Offset and bound by John H. Dekker and Sons, Inc., in Holliston Roxite.